STUDY AND TEACHING GUIDE
FOR
THE HISTORY OF THE
ANCIENT WORLD

By Julia Kaziewicz

A curriculum guide to accompany

Susan Wise Bauer's

THE HISTORY OF THE ANCIENT WORLD:
FROM THE EARLIEST ACCOUNTS TO THE
FALL OF ROME

CHARLES CITY, VA

This study and teaching guide is designed to be used in conjunction with Susan Wise Bauer's *The History of the Ancient World*, ISBN 978-0-393-05974-8.

Photocopying and Distribution Policy
Families: you may make as many photocopies of these tests as you need for use WITHIN YOUR OWN FAMILY ONLY.
Schools and Co-ops MAY NOT PHOTOCOPY any portion of this book, without a written license from Well-Trained Mind Press.
Address requests for permissions to: support@welltrainedmind.com

welltrainedmind.com
1.877.322.3445

STUDY GUIDE for The History of the Ancient World

HOW TO USE THIS STUDY GUIDE

This Study Guide for *The History of the Ancient World: From the Earliest Accounts to the Fall of Rome* is designed to be used by tutors, parents, or teachers working with both individual students and groups.

For each chapter of *The History of the Ancient World,* four sets of exercises are given.

I. Who, What, Where

This section is designed to check the student's grasp of basic information presented in the chapter: prominent characters, important places, and foundational ideas. The student should explain the significance of each person, place or idea in one complete sentence.

II. Comprehension

This section forces the student to express, in his or her own words, the central concepts in each chapter. The student may use two to three complete sentences to answer each question.

III. Critical Thinking

This section requires the student to produce a brief written reflection on the ideas presented in the chapter. Some preliminary exercises are also provided.

IV. Map Work

This section uses a traditional method to improve the student's geography. In his *Complete Course in Geography* (1875), the geographer William Swinton observed:

> That form is easiest remembered which the hand is taught to trace. The exercise of the mind, needed to teach the hand to trace a form, impresses that form upon the mind. As the study of maps is a study of form, the manner of studying them should be by map-drawing.

Section IV asks the student to go through a carefully structured set of steps: tracing repeatedly, then copying while looking at the original, and finally, where appropriate, reproducing from memory. The student will be asked to use a black pencil (one that does not erase easily) as well as a regular pencil with an eraser, as well as colored pencils of various kinds. Large amounts of tracing paper are needed!

To avoid unnecessary repetition, not every chapter has a map exercise attached. You should also feel free to pick and choose among the map exercises rather than asking the student to complete every single one. **Section IV** should always be completed with the text on hand.

Instructors may decide whether or not to allow students to consult the text for the other assignments. Here are three possible ways of using the exercises in Sections I, II, and III.

1) Have students complete Section I while consulting the text, as a guide to careful reading. Use Section II as a quiz, after the student has carefully studied the material. Then, assign Section III as a writing exercise, allowing the student to use the text.

2) Ask students to complete Section I as a pop quiz to test reading comprehension. Assign Section II as a take-home writing assignment, done with text on hand. Every five chapters or so, ask the students to choose one of the Section III topics as a more extended essay project.

3) Allow students to complete Sections I and II while looking at the text. After study, assign Section III as an essay test and ask the student to write without consulting the book.

CHAPTER ONE: THE ORIGIN OF KINGSHIP

The student MAY USE his/her text when answering the questions in sections I and II.

Section I: Who, What, Where

Write a one or two-sentence answer explaining the significance of the items listed below.

11,000 BC – **pg. 4, ¶ 2 – Geologists tell us that, around 11,000 BC, ice spread down from the polar caps almost to the Mediterranean Sea. The melting of these ice caps, over the next few thousand years, changed the climate and topography of the Middle East.**

Alulim – **pg. 3, ¶ 1- According to the Sumerian king list, Alulim was the first Sumerian king. The Sumerians believed that he had ruled over Eridu for almost 30,000 years.**

Dumuzi – **pg. 8, ¶ 3 – Dumuzi was the fifth Sumerian king. According to Sumerian legends, he was a shepherd who wooed and married the goddess Inanna.**

Eridu - **pg. 3, ¶ 1 - Eridu was a walled city in Mesopotamia, which was ruled by the early Sumerian kings, according to Sumerian accounts of history.**

alternate answer:
pg. 8, ¶ 1 – Eridu was the Sumerian Eden.

Fertile Crescent – **pg. 7, ¶ 3 - The Fertile Crescent, in the Middle East, was where civilization began, when farmers had to cooperate with each other to collect and use scarce water.**

Sumerian king list – **pg. 3, ¶ 2 - The Sumerian king list is the oldest historical record in the world.**

Section II: Comprehension

Write a two or three-sentence answer to each of the following questions.

1. How did the Mesopotamian climate change as the earth warmed and the ice caps melted? What happened in the winter and the summer? What happened to the streams and fields?
A1. – pg. 4, ¶ 4 - The climate grew drier. In the winter, it rained infrequently. In the summer, winds blew across the plain. Each year, the streams overflowed and washed away fields.

2. What types of materials did the Sumerians use to build their homes, and where did the materials come from? What else did they make with the materials? Why were the Sumerians "people of the earth?"
A2. – pg. 4, ¶ 5 to pg. 5, ¶ 1 - Sumerians used mud and reeds from the plains close to the Gulf to build their homes. They also made city walls, pots, and dishes with the mud. The Sumerians were called "people of the earth" because they used the earth to build their cities, homes and goods.

3. Define the term "Semite-influenced Sumerians."

A3. - pg. 6, ¶ 2 - The Sumerians used Semitic words that came from people who lived south and west of the Mesopotamian plain. These people travelled up to Mesopotamia from the Arabian peninsula or over from northern Africa. They taught the Sumerians how to farm, and introduced them to the peaceful occupations that go along with farming.

If the student cannot come up with the answer, ask, "Where did the Semites come from?" In page 6 of the reading, the student finds that "The Semitic words belonged to a people whose homeland was south and west of the Mesopotamian plain. Mountains to the north and east of Mesopotamia discouraged wanderers, but travelling up from the Arabian peninsula, or over from northern Africa, was a much simpler proposition. The Semites did just this, settling in with the Sumerians and lending them words."

Then ask the student, "When the Semites moved up to the southern plain, did they interact with the Sumerians?" The text tells us that the Semites settled in with the Sumerians and lent them words; "And more than just words: the Semitic loanwords are almost all names for farming techniques (plow, furrow) and for the peaceful occupations that go along with farming (basketmaker, leatherworker, carpenter). The Semites, not the Sumerians, brought these skills to Mesopotamia." This passage shows us how the Semites influenced Sumerian life.

4. Explain how Sumerian hunters turned into farmers. In your answer, make sure to include how the changing climate influenced this transition.

A4. – pg. 6, ¶ 4 – The ice sheets retreated and the herds of meat-providing animals moved north and grew thinner. Sumerian hunters gave up the full-time pursuit of meat and instead harvested the wild grains that grew in the warmer plains, moving only when the weather changed. The hunters progressed from harvesting wild grain to planting and tending it.

5. Why did civilization begin in the Fertile Crescent? Explain what had to be done in order for the farmers and the non-farmers to survive, and how this led to the need for a king.

A5. - pg. 7, ¶ 3-4 - Civilization began in the Fertile Crescent because villages needed careful management to survive. Someone had to make sure that farmers worked together to construct canals and reservoirs that would capture floodwaters, and that the limited water supply was divided fairly. In addition, someone had to make sure the farmers sold grain to the non-farmers. A king made sure everyone fulfilled his or her duties.

6. Why did the goddess Inanna reject King Dumuzi's approaches? Use part of "The Wooing of Inanna" in your answer. How were shepherds perceived by Sumerian city dwellers?

A6. – pg. 8, ¶ 3 - Inanna rejects Dumuzi because he is a shepherd. She says, "The shepherd! I will not marry the shepherd! His clothes are coarse; his wool is rough." Sumerian city dwellers saw shepherds as uncivilized.

Section III: Critical Thinking

In this chapter we learned that Sumerians developed the first civilization. We also learned that even though all Sumerians needed to work together to survive, "mutual need didn't produce mutual respect." As the Sumerian civilization developed, so did inequality among men.

***

Farmer / Shepherd / King / Basketmaker

A. Order the occupations above from most civilized to least civilized:

King, Basketmaker, Farmer, Shepherd

B. Order the occupations above from most important to least important:

King, Farmer, Shepherd, Basketmaker

alternate answer:

King, Shepherd, Farmer, Basketmaker

C. Write a paragraph explaining how you ordered the occupations in part A. Then, write a paragraph explaining how you ordered the occupations in part B.

* The chapter spends quite a bit of time addressing the roles the king, farmer and shepherd played in early Sumerian society. The challenge for the student is to think about what role the basketmaker played. We know that basketmaking was introduced with farming, thus it is part of civilized society (pg 6, ¶ 2). However, the goods created by the basketmaker were not essential to the survival of the early Sumerian people.

The king should be first in both lists. He is the most civilized because he makes sure that every person does his job, and the king is the most important because he is a god and the ruler of civilization.

In list A, the basketmaker should follow the king. The basketmaker lives in the city and produces crafts that he sells to the farmers and herdsmen, which makes him the most civilized of the working people. The farmer follows the basketmaker because he is settled in the city. The shepherd is the least civilized because he still lives in the fields with the animals.

As long as the student explains the role of the farmer and the shepherd, either can follow the king in order of importance in list B. The farmer produces life-sustaining grain, and the shepherd provides essential meat, fresh milk and wool, all of which are essential for Sumerian survival. The basketmaker is the least important in society because his crafts are not necessary for survival.

Chapter Two: The Earliest Story

The student MAY USE her text when answering the questions in sections I and II.

Section I: Who, What, Where

Write a one or two-sentence answer explaining the significance of the items listed below.

Akkadian – **pg. 11, ¶ 2 - Akkadian is a Semitic language spoken in Mesopotamia. We have the story of Utnapishtim in Akkadian because it was eventually translated into that language.**

"Poem of Atrahasis" – **pg. 11, ¶ 3 – "Poem of Atrahasis" is the name of the Babylonian flood story. In it, a wise king is warned of a flood, and uses an ark to survive it.**

Enlil – **pg. 11, ¶ 2 – In the Sumerian flood story, Enlil is the king of the gods, who convinces the other gods to wipe out mankind because humanity's noise keeps him from sleeping.**

Ea – **pg. 11, ¶ 2 – In the Sumerian flood story, Ea is a god who has sworn to protect mankind. He warns Utnapishtim that a flood is coming, so that Utnapishtim can escape.**

Section II: Comprehension

Write a two or three-sentence answer to each of the following questions.

1. Why is the story of the Great Flood important to historians?

A1. – pg. 11 ¶ 1 - The story of the Great Flood is important to historians because it is the closest thing to a universal story that the human race possesses.

2. Briefly list all the Great Flood stories mentioned in the chapter. List where the story came from, the title (if listed in the text) and write a short summary of each story, making sure to name its key figures. Follow the format of the example provided.

Example:
1. Sumeria, no title. Enlil, the king of the gods, attempts to wipe out mankind, but the god Ea warns the wise man Utnapishtim of Enlil's plan. Utnapishtim escapes the flood in a boat with his family, a few animals and as many others as he can save.
A2-2. pg. 11, ¶ 3 - Babylon, "The Poem of Atrahasis." Atrahasis, the wisest king on earth, is warned of the coming flood and builds an ark. Knowing he can only spare a few people, he invites the rest of his subjects to a great banquet, so that they may have one last day of joy before the end. Knowing his people will die, Atrahasis does not enjoy the banquet because he is wracked with guilt.

A2-3. – pg. 12, ¶ 2 – Genesis, no title. God tells Noah to build an ark that will save him and his family from destruction, while the rest of the earth is swallowed in water.

A2-4. – pg. 14, ¶ 2 – Yang-shao and Longshan, no title. A warleader rips the sky open and water rushes through, covering the whole earth and drowning everyone; the only survivor is a noble queen who takes refuge on a mountaintop along with a small band of warriors.

A2-5. – pg.14, ¶ 2 – India, no title. A fish warns the wise king Manu that an enormous flood is coming, and that he should build a ship and climb into it as soon as the waters begin to rise. Manu alone survives the flood.

A2-6. – pg. 14, ¶ 3 – Mayans, no title. "Four hundred sons" survive the flood by turning into fish. They celebrate their survival by getting drunk, at which point they ascend into heaven and become the Pleiades.

A2-7. – pg. 14, ¶ 3 – Peru, no title. A llama refuses to eat; when its owner asks why, the llama warns him that in five days water will rise and overwhelm the earth. The owner of the llama climbs the highest mountain, survives, and repopulates the earth.

3. In the Akkadian creation story, why is half of the sea-being Tiamat's body tossed into the heavens?
A3. – pg. 15, ¶ 1 – Half of Tiamat's body is tossed into the heavens so that death-bringing salt water will not cover the newly dry land.

4. The Akkadian creation story, the Mixtec creation legend, the Indian Satapatha-Brahamana, the Bantu myth, and the beginning of Genesis are all related. What are these stories, and what narrative detail do they have in common?
A4. – pg. 15, ¶ 1-2 – These are creation stories. Each of these stores begins with chaotic waters that must recede so that man can begin his existence on dry land.

5. Describe the lost paradise that is the subject of the very ancient Sumerian poem "Enki and Ninhusag." Use at least two examples from the poem in your answer.
A5. – pg. 15, ¶ 3 – The lost paradise was a dream city filled with fruit trees and watered by fresh streams uncorrupted by salt. In this place, "the lion does not kill" and "the wolf does not seize the lamb."

The following excerpt from the poem "Enki and Ninhusag" is provided in the text on page 15:
the lion does not kill,
the wolf does not seize the lamb,
the wild dog, devourer of kids, is unknown,
he whose eyes hurt does not say: "My eyes hurt."
he whose head aches does not say, "My Head Aches."

Section III: Critical Thinking

Early in Chapter 2, the author writes, "The historian cannot ignore the Great Flood; it is the closest thing to a universal story that the human race possesses" (11). Write a paragraph in response to each of the following questions concerning the flood and its existence.

A. What can a historian learn from ancient stories about the flood? In your answer, explain this passage from the text, "Three cultures, three stories: too much coincidence of detail to be dismissed" (12).

B. What can a historian learn from physical evidence related to the flood? In your answer, explain this passage from the text, "If these American flood stories are related to the Mesopotamian tales, the flood could not have happened in 7000 BC; as the historian John Bright suggests, the shared disaster must have taken place before 10,000 BC, when hunters migrated across the Bering Strait" (14).

C. What conclusion can we come to about the Great Flood?

In response to prompt A, the student should focus on the consistent appearance of the flood in the stories of very different and remote cultures. If the student is having a hard time coming up with an answer, you might prompt her with something like, "If one big flood didn't happen, but all of these different cultures had stories about a flood, how do you think early cultures felt about floods and water?" This should get the student thinking about how scary large amounts of water were to early civilizations, and that even though there wasn't a universal flood, the fear of flooding was universal. The passage from the text highlights this same idea, that flood stories were a common theme in early oral traditions. Though a universal flood did not occur, the widespread rise of water levels resulted in flood stories in myriad cultures. Ultimately, the existence of the flood in the oral traditions of so many ancient cultures points us to the precarious relationship between early civilizations and water.

In response to prompt B, the student should focus on the scientific search for proof of a universal flood. Because the flood exists in so many oral traditions, it seems that evidence of a flood should exist. However, we see throughout the chapter that there is no perfect scientific answer as to when a Great Flood occurred. If the student is having a hard time grasping this concept, ask her to find evidence of a universal flood in the chapter. There is no evidence of a universal flood, only theories with evidence that falls short. This realization should help the student explain the quote from the chapter. The passage from the text attempts to set a date for a large-scale, global flood, however the date of this flood is far too early to line up with the dates of the Mesopotamian flood. Asking the student to think about questions one and two together, she should figure that localized floods, which there is evidence of, lead to local flood stories, which eventually turned into the mythic tales of a Great Flood.

The response to prompt C might only be a sentence or two. The most basic conclusion we can come to about the Great Flood is that it exists firmly in the oral traditions of many ancient cultures. There is no scientific evidence that a universal flood occurred, but there is enough evidence to support the theory that water slowly flooded man's world.

CHAPTER THREE: THE RISE OF ARISTOCRACY

The student MAY USE his text when answering the questions in sections I and II.

Section I: Who, What, Where

Write a one or two-sentence answer explaining the significance of the items listed below. For questions marked with *, use the map on page 19 to supplement your answer.

2700 BC – pg. 17, ¶ 1 – 2700 is the first date that can be assigned to a Sumerian King.

alternate answer:
pg. 17, ¶ 1 – 2700 is around the date that Enmebaraggesi ruled Kish.

Aristocracy – pg. 20, ¶ 5 – Aristocracy defines the class of people who are born to rule.

Etana – pg. 17, ¶ 3 to pg. 18, ¶ 1 and pg. 20, ¶ 6 – Etana was the thirteenth king of Kish after the Great Flood. Etana's struggle to produce an heir shows us that kingship had become hereditary.

Kish – pg. 17, ¶ 1 - Kish was a Mesopotamian city that became the new center of kingship after the Great Flood.

*Euphrates (Uruttu) – pg. 18, ¶ 2 & map on pg. 19 – The Euphrates is a large river that borders Mesopotamia to the west.

*Tigris (Idiglat) – pg.18, ¶ 2 & map on pg. 19 – The Tigris is a large river that borders Mesopotamia to the east.

"The First Dynasty of Kish" – pg. 17, ¶ 1 – "The First Dynasty of Kish" refers to the series of kings that ruled Kish after the Great Flood.

Section II: Comprehension

Write a two or three-sentence answer to each of the following questions.

1. Describe the ways that all of these cities were alike: Eridu, Ur, Uruk, Nippur, Adab, Lagash, and Kish.

A1. – pg. 18, ¶ 5-6 – Eridu, Ur, Uruk, Nippur, Adab, Lagash and Kish were walled cities, each circled by suburbs, that jostled each other for power. Each city was protected by a god whose temple drew pilgrims from the surrounding countryside. Each city sent tentacles of power out into the countryside, aspiring to rule more and more land.

2. Define "streaming-in" (make sure to include a date in your answer).
A2. – pg. 18, ¶ 3 - "Streaming-in" is the name of the phenomenon where large groups of

country-dwellers shifted their whole way of life and moved into walled cities. This was a common practice by the year 3200 BC.

3. How is Etana's entry on the king list different than those of his predecessors? What do we learn about Etana's reign and legacy from the entry?

A3. – pg. 17, ¶ 3 to pg. 18, ¶ 1 – Most of the kings on the king list are described with a single phrase: a name and a length of reign. Etana's entry is much longer. We learn that Etana ascended into heaven, made firm all the lands and reigned for 1,560 years. His son, Balih, reigned for 400 years.

4. What is the significance of Atab's succession by his son and grandson? How does this fundamentally change the way kings come to rule?

A4. – pg. 20, ¶ 3, ¶ 5 – Atab was the first king to have a dynasty; his was the earliest blood succession recorded in history. Because of Atab's dynasty, kingship becomes hereditary.

5. A later poem helps us understand the terms of Etana's rule. Summarize the later poem, and explain how it helps us understand the passage related to Etana on the king list.

A5. – pg. 20, ¶ 4-5 – The later poem tells us that Etana could not produce an heir, despite having honored the gods. This helps us understand that Etana "ascended into heaven" in order to have a son.

6. Explain how Mesopotamia shifted from an egalitarian society (a society that believes in the equality of all people) to an aristocracy. Make sure to incorporate what you learned from Chapter 1 into your answer.

A6. – pg. 20, ¶ 1-2 – In Chapter 1 we learned that as Mesopotamians settled down, farmers were considered to be more civilized than shepherds. As people continued to move from the country into the city, this division grew wider. The hierarchy took on a new form about ten generations after the flood, when men claimed the right to rule, for the first time, not by virtue of strength or wisdom, but by the right of blood.

7. Explain the organization of a typical Mesopotamian walled city, and what pilgrims, shepherds and herdsmen did in the city.

A7. – pg. 18, ¶ 6 to pg. 19, ¶ 1 – Each city was protected by a god whose temple drew pilgrims from the surrounding countryside. Shepherds and herdsmen came into the city to bring gifts to the gods, to sell and buy – and to pay the taxes demanded by kings and priests.

8. Why was the city of Kish so powerful around 2500 BC?

A8. – pg. 21, ¶ 1-2 – The city of Kish was between the Euphrates and Tigris rivers. Since most trading was done up and down the rivers, all goods had to pass through Kish. The king of Kish collected a percentage of the trade from the traffic passing by his city, and this made the city rich and powerful.

Section III: Critical Thinking

"The Rise of Aristocracy" ends with this thought, "The difficulty of moving armies up and down the length of the plain may have dissuaded the kings of Kish from actually conquering other cities; or perhaps they simply had, as yet, no thought of imperial leadership to complement the ideas of kingship and aristocracy" (21).

First, look up "empire" and write down its definition. Second, using what you know about "streaming-in," the beginning of aristocracy, and the power struggle between rising cities in Mesopotamia, write a paragraph explaining how creating empires is the next logical step in our history of the ancient world.

*The student can use a physical or online dictionary to find the definition of "empire." Empire is defined as a group of nations or peoples ruled over by an emperor, empress or other powerful sovereign or government.

Over the course of the past three chapters we have read about the slow development and hierarchical organization of ancient civilizations. First the nomads banded together to create small herding and farming communities, which developed into cities that needed rulers. Thus we see the development of ordered cities controlled by kings. **In Chapter 3 we read about the king of Kish "feather[ing] his own nest by plucking a few feathers from other princes" (21).** *The collection of taxes from country-dwellers combined with the exploitation of trade routes in Kish shows us that growing cities wanted more power. Once the land and water surrounding a walled city were conquered, the next logical step for a king would be to conquer other cities, thus building an empire.*

To guide a student to an appropriate answer to this question, first ask, "How did cities develop?" Once he recaps the transition from nomadic life to settled life, ask, "Who ruled the cities?" The student should recall the need for rule over developing cities and the rise of kings to power. Next, ask the student to revisit the relationship of cities in-between the Euphrates and Tigris. Use the bold sentence in the previous paragraph to spark the student's memory. Finally, ask the student how a king could gain more power if he already had control of the countryside around him and the rivers beside him.

CHAPTER FOUR: THE CREATION OF EMPIRE

The student MAY USE his text when answering the questions in sections I and II.

Section I: Who, What, Where

Write a one or two-sentence answer explaining the significance of the items listed below.

3200 BC – **pg. 22, ¶ 2 – 3200 BC is the year the Scorpion King made his effort to conquer the Egyptian world.**

alternate answer:

pg. 24, ¶ 2 – 3200 BC marks the year that Egyptian cities saw "streaming-in."

Dynasteia – **pg. 28, ¶ 2 – Dynasteia is a Greek term meaning "power of rule." Manetho organized the Egyptian rulers since 3100 into groups, beginning a new group each time a new family rose to power, or the kingship changed locations.**

Herodotus – **pg. 28, ¶ 3 – Herodotus was a Greek historian.**

Menes (Narmer) – **pg. 26, ¶ 3 to pg. 27, ¶ 1 and pg. 28, ¶ 3 – Menes appears in the Egyptian king lists as the first human king of Egypt. Menes first united Upper Egypt and Lower Egypt.**

Palette – **pg. 26, ¶ 1 – A palette is a flat piece of stone that served as a canvas.**

Turin Canon – **pg. 28, ¶2 – The Turin Canon is a papyrus that identifies Menes as the first king of Egypt.**

alternate answer:

pg. 28, ¶2 – The Turin Canon is a papyrus used by Manetho to reconcile different versions of the Egyptian king lists.

Section II: Comprehension

Write a two or three-sentence answer to each of the following questions.

1. What have archaeologists discovered beneath the sands of the Sahara? What do these findings suggest about the climate of the Sahara?
A1. – pg. 22, ¶ 3 – Archaeologists have discovered leaves, trees, and the remains of game animals under the sands of the Sahara. These findings suggest that the Sahara was once grassy and watered.

2. Which way did the Nile River flow? How did this affect the Egyptians' view of all other rivers?
A2. – pg. 23, ¶ 4 – The Nile flowed from south to north. Egyptians thought that every other river ran backwards.

3. How did the first Egyptians manage the overflow of water from the Nile?
A3. – pg. 22, ¶ 4 to pg. 23, ¶ 1 – The first Egyptians dug reservoirs to hold the Nile's flood waters, and built canals to irrigate their fields in the drier months.

4. Why did the Egyptians give their country two different names? In your answer make sure to identify the names of each land, the color associated with each land, and the significance of each color.
A4. – pg. 23, ¶ 5 to pg. 24, ¶ 1 – Egyptians had two different names for their land because the country was comprised of two very different climates. The land where the yearly flood laid down its silt was Kemet, the black land. Beyond the Black Land lay Deshret, the red land. Black was the color of life and resurrection, and red was the color of death, and sun-baked earth.

5. What kingdom were the cities of Nubt and Hierakonpolis a part of? How is the ruler of this kingdom identified?
A5. – pg. 24, ¶ 2 – Nubt and Hierakonpolis were part of the White Kingdom, or Upper Egypt. The king of Upper Egypt was identified by his cylindrical White Crown.

6. How does the construction of the oldest Egyptian king lists vary from the construction of the Sumerian king list?
A6. – pg. 24, ¶ 3 – Unlike the Sumerian king list, which chronicles kings from the beginning of time, the oldest Egyptian king lists do not go all the way back in time, so the names of some of the oldest kings are lost.

7. How do we know that the White King and the Scorpion King are the same person? In your answer, name and describe the object that links the two kings. Make sure to include where the object was found, and what markings on the object tell us that the two kings were the same person.
A7. – pg. 24, ¶ 3 - A macehead unearthed at the temple at Hierakonpolis depicts the White King, wearing the distinctive White Crown, as he celebrates victory over defeated soldiers of the Red Kingdom. To the right of the White King is a hieroglyph that tells us his name: Scorpion.

8. When did the first Egyptian dynasty begin according to Manetho's revised king list?
A8. – pg. 28, ¶ 3 – According to Manetho, the first dynasty began when the two parts of Egypt were united under the first king of all Egypt.

9. What did Narmer build to celebrate his victory over Lower Egypt? Why did he choose Memphis? What does "Memphis" mean?
A9. – pg. 28, ¶ 3 - Narmer built a brand new capital at Memphis. From Memphis, Narmer could control both the southern valley and the northern delta of Egypt. Memphis means "White Walls."

Section III: Critical Thinking

The student must use her text to answer this question.

Doubleness has deeply influenced the development of Egyptian culture. Find two passages in the text where doubleness appears and write them down, noting where a reader can find the passage by putting the page number after the quote. Then, write a few sentences for each example, explaining what each section means in the context of early Egyptian culture.

In this section, we want to familiarize the student with looking for and citing specific passages in a text. The student should write down the sentences that describe doubleness in Egyptian culture entirely. She should then put the page number that corresponds to the passage after the quoted text. In her explanation of the quote, the student should make sure to write how the quoted passage helps us to understand early Egypt's culture and history.

The following passages are acceptable quotations:
pg. 23, ¶ 5 to pg. 24, ¶ 1-2 – The Egyptians gave their country two different names. The land where the yearly flood laid down its silt was Kemet, the Black Land: black was the color of life and resurrection. But beyond the Black Land lay Deshret, the deathly Red Land. The line between life and death was so distinct that a man could bend over and place his hand in fertile black earth, the other on red, sunbaked desert. Pages 23-24.

In this passage, we learn that the difference in land and climate in Egypt was very distinct. The Black Land was fertile, and Egyptians were able to live off of that land. The Red Land was deadly; no life could survive in its dryness and heat. However different these climates, they both existed within Egypt. Very literally, Egypt was made of two lands.

pg. 24, ¶ 2 – Very early, these southern cities identified themselves not a separate and sovereign, but as part of a kingdom: the White Kingdom (also called "Upper Egypt," since it lay upstream from the Mediterranean), ruled by a king who wore the cylindrical White Crown. In the north of Egypt ("Lower Egypt"), cities banded together in an alliance called the Red Kingdom; the cities of Heliopolis and Buto grew to prominence. The king of Lower Egypt wore the Red Crown, with a cobra shape curing from its front (the earliest portrayal of the crown dates to around 4000 BC), and was protected by a cobra-goddess who spat venom at the king's enemies. The two kingdoms, White and Red, like the Red and Black Lands, mirrored that basic Egyptian reality: the world is made up of balanced and opposing forces. Page 24.

Egypt was divided into two kingdoms, the White Kingdom in southern, "Upper Egypt" and the Red Kingdom in northern, "Lower Egypt." The two kingdoms mirrored the essential nature of Egyptian culture – doubleness. Egypt is composed of two lands – the Black Land and the Red Land – and this duality is reflected in the division of Egypt into the White Kingdom and the Red Kingdom.

pg. 24, ¶ 4 – The Scorpion King himself may well have been a native of Hierakonpolis, which was itself a double city. Hierakonpolis was originally two cities divided by the Nile: Nehken on the west bank, was dedicated to the falcon-god, and Nekheb on the east was guarded by the vulture-goddess. Over time, the two separate cities grew into one, watched over by the vulture. Perhaps the Scorpion King, seeing the two halves united, first conceived his plan of drawing White and Red Kingdoms together under one king. Page 24.

The Scorpion King was king of the White Kingdom, and conquered the Red Kingdom around 3200 BC. The passage pairs the unification of Nehken and Nekheb into Hierakonpolis as the possible spark for the Scorpion King's military campaign to unite the White and Red Kingdom. The doubleness of Hierakonpolis reinforces the doubleness of all Egyptian life.

pg. 24, ¶ 5 – [The Scorpion King's] victory, which probably took place around 3200 BC, was temporary. Another carving records the reunion of the two kingdoms under another White King, perhaps a hundred years later. Like the Scorpion King macehead, the carving was found at the temple at Hierakonpolis. Done on a palette (a flat piece of stone that served as a "canvas"), the carving shows a king who wears the Red Crown on the front of the palette, and the White Crown on the back. A hieroglyph names the king: Narmer. Pages 24-26.

A note: This passage does not specifically use the word 'double,' however a student may consider the battle for the White/ Red Crown as a continuation of the doubleness related to Upper and Lower Egypt.

Narmer, also known as Menes, was the first human king of Egypt. The unification of the Red and White Kingdoms did not last long under the Scorpion king. Narmer, evidenced by the Narmer Palette, was able to bring the Red Kingdom under the White Kingdom, and Narmer became the first king of all Egypt.

pg. 28, ¶ 5 – For the rest of Egypt's history, the doubleness of its origin was enshrined in its king. He was called the Lord of Two Lands, and his Double Crown was made up of the Red Crown of Lower Egypt set on top of the White Crown of Upper Egypt. The southern vulture and the northern cobra, one crawling on the earth and the other inhabiting the sky, guarded the united kingdom. Two contrary powers had been brought together into a mighty and balanced whole.

The original doubleness of Egyptian life, that of the Red and Black Lands, paralleled the doubleness of Upper and Lower Egypt. The title "Lord of Two Lands" reflects this doubleness. The unification of the two parts of Egypt was so strong that the Egyptian priest Manetho starts his history of Egyptian Dynasties with the first king of all Egypt, Narmer. Narmer created the first empire, and one of the world's longest lived.

The Scorpion King attempted to unite the two lands, and Narmer did so successfully. Narmer's feat created the first empire. Once unified, the Egyptian priest Manetho recorded the First Dynasty of Egypt.

CHAPTER FIVE: THE AGE OF IRON

The student may use his text when answering the questions in sections I and II.

Section I: Who, What, Where

Write a one or two-sentence answer explaining the significance of each item listed below.

3102 BC – **pg. 30, ¶ 3 – In 3102 BC, Manu became the first historical king of India.**
alternate answer:
pg. 33, ¶ 2 – 3102 BC is the first credible date in India's history.
pg. 33, ¶ 2 – In 3102 BC, the villages in the Indus valley started to grow into towns.

NOTE TO INSTRUCTOR:
Though the text tells us that in 3102 BC the seven Rishis became the seven stars of the Big Dipper, this information is secondary to Manu's kingship and the growth of towns in the Indus valley. If the student includes information about the Rishis as part of the accepted answers above, full credit should be given. Answering that 3102 BC is important because of the Rishis alone is not acceptable.

Baluchistan – **pg. 32, ¶ 2 – Baluchistan is the name of the hilly land just west of the Indus River.**

Kali Yuga – **pg. 34, ¶ 3 – The Kali Yuga was the Age of Iron, and the age of towns.**

Khyber Pass – **pg. 30, ¶ 4 – The Khyber Pass is the name for the gap in the northern mountains of India.**

Manu– **pg. 32, ¶ 6 – Manu is the name-title of each of the six semidivine kings that had reigned in India.**

Manu Vaivaswata – **pg. 32, ¶ 7-8 to pg. 33, ¶ 1 – With the help of a tiny fish, Manu Vaivaswata survived the great flood and became the first king of historical India.**

Vindhya and Satpura – **pg. 32, ¶ 3 – The Vindhya and Satpura are the two mountain ranges that separate the north and south of India.**

Section II: Comprehension

Write a two or three-sentence answer to each of the following questions.

1. Why do we know so little about the first centuries of India? Why do we look at Indian epics written thousands of years after the first settlements for clues about ancient Indian civilizations?
A1. – pg. 30, ¶ 2-3 – The first people of India did not keep lists of their kings, nor did they carve images of their leaders on stone, and they did not set down their achievements on tablets. Though the epics we look at for clues about early Indian culture are far removed from these first settlements, the epics likely preserve a much older oral tradition.

2. Why is the upper end of the Indus River called the Punjab?
A2. – pg. 32, ¶ 2 – The upper end of the Indus River is called the Punjab because it breaks into five branches; Punjab means "Five Rivers."

3. Why did the people of south India, east India and northwest India live independent of each other?
A3. – pg. 32, ¶ 3 – The people of the south, east and northwest lived independent of each other because they were divided by enormous physical barriers.

4. Why did the settlers of the Indus valley bake their clay in kilns?
A4. – pg. 34, ¶ 1 – Oven-burned brick is more durable than brick dried in the sun, and less vulnerable to the swirling waters of floods.

5. How do we know the people of the Indus valley participated in trade outside of the valley?
A5. – pg. 34, ¶ 2 – Turquoise and lapis lazuli from the plains north of Mesopotamia were found in the ruins of the richest houses of the Indus settlers.

Section III: Critical Thinking

The people of ancient India have much in common with the early civilizations of Mesopotamia and Egypt. The following passages from the chapter connect in some way to your previous reading. Describe what each passage is about, and then explain how each passage about ancient Indian history relates to either Mesopotamia or Egypt.

In the INSTRUCTOR version, each passage is followed by information pulled directly from the text.
Use these examples to jog the student's memory of specifics related to Mesopotamia or Egypt.
"In the Iron Age, the sacred writings warned, leaders would commandeer the goods that belonged to their people, pleading financial need. The strong would take property from the vulnerable, and seize hard-won wealth for themselves. Rich men would abandon their fields and herds and spend their days protecting their money, becoming slaves of their earthly possessions rather than free men who knew how to use the earth" (34).

* *This passage is about the relationship between wealth and power.*
The student may connect this passage to any of the following examples from previous chapters:
* *pg. 18, ¶ 6 – As Sumerian cities grew, tentacles of power were sent out into the countryside, aspiring to rule more and more land. Shepherds and herdsmen came into the city to bring gifts to the gods, to sell and buy – and to pay the taxes demanded by priests and kings.*
* *pg. 21, ¶ 3 – The king of Kish, collecting some percentage from the traffic passing by his city, could feather his own nest by plucking a few feathers from other princes.*
* *pg. 24, ¶ 3 – A macehead depicts a White King celebrating his victory over defeated soldiers of the Red Kingdom.*
* *pg. 25, ¶ 2 – On the back of the Narmer Palette, Narmer, in his role as White King, holds a warrior of the Red Kingdom by the hair. On the front, Narmer – having doffed the White Crown and put on the Read Crown instead – parades in victory past the bodies of decapitated warriors. He has drawn the Red Kingdom under White Kingdom rule at last.*

Example of an appropriate answer:
This passage is a warning from the sacred writings of India about the dangerous relationship between wealth and power. As rulers of cities grow stronger and wealthier, they become greedy for more land, money and power. This connects to Mesopotamian culture and the history of the first kings of Kish. The king of Kish collected tribute from merchants passing through on the Euphrates or Tigris, exploiting the location of the city to increase his wealth and power.

"[Manu] was washing his hands one morning when a tiny fish came wriggling up to him, begging for protection from the stronger and larger fish who preyed on the weak, as was 'the custom of the river.' Manu had pity and saved the fish. Past danger of being eaten, the fish repaid his kindness by warning him of a coming flood that would sweep away the heavens and the earth. So Manu built a wooden ark and went on board with seven wise sages, known as the Rishis. When the flood subsided, Manu anchored his ship to a far northern mountain, disembarked, and became the first king of historical India" (33).

• *This passage tells us about the Indian flood story.*
• *pg. 11, ¶ 2 – The Sumerians have the story of Ea and Utnapishtim. Ea, a god who has sworn to protect mankind, warns Utnapishtim in a dream of the coming flood, and Utnapishtim is able to escape in a boat with his family and some animals.*
Example of an appropriate answer:
This is the story of the Indian flood. This connects to Mesopotamian culture and the story of Ea and Utnapishtim. Ea, the protector of mankind, warned Utnapishtim of the coming flood. Utnapishtim was able to escape the flood on a boat with his family, friends and animals.

"The earliest houses in the Indus river valley were built on the river plain, perhaps a mile away from the river, well above the line of the flood. Mud bricks would dissolve in river water, and crops would wash away" (32).

• *This passage is about the destructive powers of water.*
The student may connect this passage to any of the following examples from previous chapters:
• *pg. 13, ¶ 1 – In Mesopotamia, flooding from the Black Sea drowned villages on its edge.*
• *pg. 13, ¶ 2 – In Mesopotamia, there was a generalized anxiety about flooding from the braided streams that ran though the land.*
• *pg. 13, ¶ 2 – The slowly increasing Gulf swallowed villages in its rising tide as it crept northwards, reshaping the Sumerian homeland.*
• *pg. 22, ¶ 3 – Every year, when heavy rains poured down on the southern mountains, the gathered waters cascaded down the length of the Nile, northwards toward the Mediterranean, and rushed far out over the surrounding land. The flooding water was so violent that few groups of hunters and gatherers dared to linger.*
• *pg. 22, ¶ 4 – Thanks to decreasing rains, the Nile flood had become more moderate; the refugees found that they could manage the yearly inundation, digging reservoirs to hold the water at flood-time, and canals to irrigate their fields in the drier months. They built settlements on the banks [of the Nile].*

Example of an appropriate answer:
This passage is about the power of water to destroy the early settlements of ancient civilizations. In Egypt, early settlers of the Nile figured out how to manage the flood waters by digging reservoirs and canals.

CHAPTER SIX: THE PHILOSOPHER KING

The student may use her text when answering the questions in sections I and II.

Section I: Who, What, Where

Write a one or two-sentence answer explaining the significance of each item listed below.

2850 BC – **pg. 38, ¶ 4 – 2850 BC is the year Fu Xi began his rule.**

Eight Trigrams – **pg. 38, ¶ 4 – The Eight Trigrams were a pattern of straight and broken lines used for record-keeping, divination, and the interpretation of events.**

Fu Xi – **pg. 38, ¶ 3-5 – Fu Xi was the first king of China. He discovered the essential order of all things, and invented the Eight Trigrams for record-keeping, divination and the interpretation of events.**

Huangdi (The Yellow Emperor) – **pg. 39, ¶ 1 – Huangdi was the third great king of China. He fought his brother, the Flame King, and the southern warleader, Chi You, in order to spread and secure his rule over his brother's land.**

Shennong (The Farmer King) – **pg. 38, ¶ 6 – pg. 30, ¶ 1 – Shennong was the second great king of China. He taught his people to find the best soil, to sow and grow grain and how to choose good herbs over poisonous ones.**

Sima Qian (The Grand Historian) – **pg. 38, ¶ 4 – Sima Qian collected the traditional tales of China into an epic history.**

Yangtze River – **pg. 36, ¶ 2 – The Yangtze River, located farther south than the Yellow River, ran to the eastern coast of China.**

Yellow River – **pg. 36, ¶ 2 – The Yellow River ran east from Qing Zang Gaoyuan and ended in the Yellow Sea.**

alternate answer:
The Plateau of Tibet may be listed in addition to, or substituted for, Qing Zang Gaoyuan.

Section II: Comprehension

Write a two/three sentence answer to each of the following questions.

1. List the four early Chinese settlements, and where these settlements were located.

A1. – pg. 36, ¶ 36 to pg. 37, ¶ 1 – The four early Chinese settlements were the Yang-shao, the Dapenkeng, the Qinglian'gang and the Longshan. The Yang-shao were located near the Yellow River. The Dapenkeng were found on the southeast coast of China, near the East China Sea.

The Qinglian'gang settled near in the Yangtze River valley, and the Longshan were located beneath the great southern bend of the Yellow River.

2. How can we differentiate between the various early Chinese settlements?
A2. – pg. 38, ¶ 2 – **We can tell the difference between the various early Chinese settlements because they have different styles of pottery and different methods of farming and building.**

3. What is culture?
A3. – pg. 36, ¶ 5 – **Culture describes a group of people that live similarly; they have the same customs, the same methods of building houses, the same style of pottery and they speak the same language.**

4. The following passage is given to us on page 38 in Chapter Six. Explain what happens in the passage, and why it is significant to Fu Xi's historical legacy.

[Fu Xi] drew directly from his own person,
and indirectly he drew upon external objects.
And so it was that he created the Eight Trigrams
in order to communicate the virtue of divine intelligence
and to classify the phenomenon of all living things.

A4. – pg. 38, ¶ 4-5 – **In this passage, Fu Xi connects his world with the world of nature. He creates the Eight Trigrams as a way to communicate to man's world the virtue of divine intelligence and the order of all living things. Fu Xi found a way to link the patterns of nature and the impulse of the human mind to order everything around it.**

5. What did Shennong do to earn the label "The Farmer King?"
A5. – pg. 38, ¶ 6 to pg. 39, ¶ 1 – **Shennong first made a plow from wood and dug the earth. He taught people to find the best soil, to sow and grow the five grains that sustain life, to thresh them, and to eat good herbs and to avoid the poisonous ones.**

6. What two things did Huangdi do to secure his title as one of the great kings of China?
A6. – pg. 39, ¶ 2 – **Huangdi conquered his brother, the Flame King, and spread his rule over his brother's land. Also, Huangdi thwarted the rebellious attack of the southern warleader Chi You.**

7. Explain what qualified one to rule in China. What did <u>not</u> guarantee kingly power in ancient China?
A7. – pg. 40, ¶ 1 – **Wisdom qualified a man to rule in China. Being a blood heir to a king did not automatically gift a son with kingly power.**

Section III: Critical Thinking

We learn in this chapter that "excavations show Longshan ruins overtop of Yang-shao remains, suggesting that the Longshan may have peacefully overwhelmed at least part of the Yellow River culture" (38). This is not our first encounter with the Longshan and Yang-shao cultures, however. Look back over your notes and lessons and explain where you first heard about the Longshan and Yang-shao. Then write a few sentences explaining how this information supports the idea that the Longshan mingled with the Yang-shao culture.

The direct reference to the Yang-shao and Longshan cultures comes in Chapter Two, "The Earliest Story." In this chapter we learn that "In China, where two independent farming cultures – the Yang-shao and the Longshan – grew up during the centuries that the Sumerians were building their cities, a treacherous warleader tears a rent in the sky's canopy and water rushes through, covering the whole earth and drowning everyone; the only survivor is a noble queen who takes refuge on a mountaintop along with a small band of warriors" (14). The student should find reference to this story in his Chapter Two workbook questions, where he was asked to list all the flood stories in the chapter.

The idea that the Longshan overwhelmed the Yang-shao, as suggested by archaeological evidence, is supported by the shared flood story of the two cultures. The physical argument for the mixing of the two cultures is bolstered by the existence of a common oral history.

CHAPTER SEVEN: THE FIRST WRITTEN RECORDS

The student may use his text when answering the questions in sections I and II.

Section I: Who, What, Where

Write a one or two-sentence answer explaining the significance of each item listed below.

3000 BC – **pg. 43, ¶ 1 – 3000 BC was around the time written history began.**

alternate answer: **Pg. 49, ¶ 2 – 3000 BC was around the time an Egyptian scribe realized that papyrus could serve as a writing surface.**

Cuneiform – **Pg. 46, ¶ 1 – Cuneiform was the name given to Sumerian writing by Thomas Hyde.**

Determinant – **pg. 47, ¶ 1 – A determinant is a sign placed next to a hieroglyph to show whether it serves as a phonetic symbol or as a pictogram.**

Hieroglyph – **pg. 47, ¶ 1 – A hieroglyph is an Egyptian pictogram.**

Hieratic script – **Pg. 48, ¶ 2 – Hieratic script is a simplified version of hieroglyphic writing, with the pictorial signs reduced to a few quickly dashed lines.**

alternate answer: **Pg. 48, ¶ 2 – Hieratic script is the cursive version of hieroglyphic script. It was the preferred handwriting for Egyptian business matters, bureaucrats and administrators.**

Pictogram – **Pg. 44, ¶ 6-7 – A pictogram is a picture representation of something that can be counted, like a cow or grain.**

Protosinaitic script – **Pg. 49, ¶ 7 – Protosinaitic script is a type of writing that showed up in various places around the Sinai peninsula.**

alternate answer: **Pg. 49, ¶ 7 – Protosinaitic script is a type of writing that borrowed almost half of its signs from Egyptian hieroglyphs.**

Rosetta Stone – **pg. 48, ¶ 1 – The Rosetta Stone is a slab of stone with the same inscription written in hieroglyphs, in a later Egyptian script, and also in Greek. The three-way translation gave linguists the key they needed to break the code of Egyptian hieroglyphics.**

Thoth – **Pg. 47, ¶ 4 – Thoth is the Egyptian god of writing.**

NOTE TO INSTRUCTOR: The student must state that Thoth is the Egyptian god of writing, and then may include any of the facts below as additional information.

Pg. 47, ¶ 4 – Thoth, the divine scribe, created himself with the power of his own word.

Pg. 47, ¶ 4 – Thoth measured the earth, counted the stars, and recorded the deeds of every man brought to the Hall of the Dead for judgment.

Section II: Comprehension

Write a two or three sentence answer to each of the following questions.

1. Why did people start writing?
A1. – Pg. 43, ¶ 2 – People started writing in order to show ownership over goods.

2. How did pictograms develop?
A2. – Pg. 44, ¶ 6 – As Sumerian cities grew and ownership became more complex, more kinds of things could be owned and sold. Accountants needed a way to represent these various kinds of things, so they developed pictograms to represent individual types of items.

3. What is the difference between a mark and a seal? In ancient Sumer, how did a seal protect one's property?
A3. – Pg. 44, ¶ 1, Pg. 43, ¶ 4,– A mark could mean anything – a woman, or sheep, man or cow. A seal could represent only one person. A seal represented the owner's presence over his goods, and watched over the goods while he was absent.

4. Describe the transition from pictograms to a phonetic system.
A4. – Pg. 45, ¶ 4 – As the need for signs multiplied, pictograms began to represent sounds rather than individual words. In this way, any number of words could be built from a limited number of signs.

5. What happened to Sumerian cuneiform?
A5. – Pg. 47, ¶ 2-3 – Sumerian cuneiform never evolved into a fully phonetic form because it was replaced by Akkadian, the language of Sumer's conquerors, before its development was complete.

6. What power did the Egyptians believe writing had? How did this help to preserve the pictorial form of hieroglyphs?
A6. – Pg. 47, ¶ 3, 5 - Egyptians believed that writing brought immortality. The pictorial form of hieroglyphs was preserved because the hieroglyphs were thought to have immense power.

7. How did the defacement of the carved name of an Egyptian king kill the king eternally?
A7. – Pg. 47, ¶ 3 – Because the name of a king, carved in a hieroglyph on a monument or statue, gave him a presence that went on past his death, defacing the hieroglyph would kill him absolutely.

8. What were the benefits of using papyrus as a writing material?
A8. – Pg. 49, ¶ 4-5 – Papyrus was easy to carry, and could be stuffed under one's coat or in one's pocket. This made communication between far away places much simpler.

9. Why do we know so little about the daily life of pharaohs and their officials after the invention of papyrus?
A9. – Pg. 49, ¶ 5-6 – Papyrus dissolved when it got wet, cracked when it grew old, and eventually disintegrated into heaps of dust. Because Ancient Egyptians recorded their histories on papyrus, their stories had the same short lifespan as the material they were written on.

Section III: Critical Thinking

Explain how writing developed in Ancient Sumeria. In your answer, incorporate and explain the following four statements:
   * "From its earliest days, literature was tied to commerce."
   * "A step had been made towards triumphing over space."
   * "The relationship between *thing* and *mark* had begun to grow more abstract."
   * *"Ilshu, who was here, watched this transaction and can explain it, if you have any questions."*

* "From its earliest days, literature was tied to commerce."
The statement asserts that making marks has always been tied to ownership of goods, which is related to trade and commerce.

* "A step had been made towards triumphing over space."
Writing allowed a person to be near his goods even when he wasn't there physically, thus making man more in control of the space around him.

* "The relationship between *thing* and *mark* had begun to grow more abstract."
A tally on the outside of a clay envelope represented a counter, and that counter represented something like a cow, or a sack of grain. A mark was no longer a direct representation of the thing it stood for, making the relationship between <u>thing</u> and <u>mark</u> more abstract.

* *"Ilshu, who was here, watched this transaction and can explain it, if you have any questions."*
A seal on a Sumerian transaction represented a third party witness to the business deal. This seal told everyone that the owner of the seal could explain the transaction. This was more than just a mark that represented a cow, this was speech to the reader of the tablet.

Example answer:
Writing began when people had to claim goods as their own. Thus, "from its earliest days, literature was tied to commerce." Sumerians could make sure no one tampered with their goods by placing a seal on their things. The seal represented the owner's presence, so it was as if he was with his goods even when he was not there. This is how "a step had been made towards triumphing over space." A person no longer had to be present to claim his goods as his own. A man with many goods had to keep track of them all, so he used a system of marks and tallies to keep count, for example, of the number of cows he owned. The tallies that counted one's belongings were called counters. A Sumerian would lay his counters on a thin sheet of clay, fold the clay up like an envelope and seal his counters inside. A tally on the outside of a clay envelope represented each counter. These marks were no longer direct representations of the things they stood for, so "the relationship between <u>thing</u> and <u>mark</u> had begun to grow more abstract." Further, Sumerians had to find a way to show not only the things they owned, but they also had to create a record of their trading. When one man would trade with another, a witness would place his seal on a transaction record to prove the trade was valid. This was a sign that someone else had witnessed the trade and could explain it. The mark told a story, "<u>Ilshu, who was here, watched this transaction and can explain it, if you have any questions.</u>" Marks had moved from representing single things to telling stories to a reader. This is how writing developed in Ancient Sumeria.

Chapter Eight: The First War Chronicles

The student may use her text when answering the questions in sections I and II.

Section I: Who, What, Where

Write a one or two-sentence answer explaining the significance of each item listed below.

2800 BC – **Pg. 51, ¶ 4 – In 2800 BC, the Sumerian king Meskiaggasher ruled in the city of Uruk.**

Elamites – **Pg. 54, ¶ 7 – Elamites inhabited Aratta, and they spoke a language entirely unrelated to Sumerian.**

Enmebaraggesi – **Pg. 56, ¶ 7 – Enmebaraggesi was the king of Kish, and he was also the protector of sacred Nippur.**

Enmerkar – **Pg. 54, ¶ 5, Pg. 55, ¶ 5 – Enmerkar, the son of Meskiaggasher, tried to take over Aratta, but was defeated.**

Gilgamesh – **Pg. 55, ¶ 7 and Pg. 59, ¶ 4-5 – Gilgamesh was the king of Uruk, who conquered four Sumerian cities—more of Sumer than any previous king had ruled.**

Mesannepadda – **Pg. 58, ¶ 6 to Pg. 59, ¶ 2 – Mesannepadda was the king of Ur, who conquered Kish, brought the first dynasty of Kish to an end and took control of the sacred city of Nippur.**

Meskiaggasher – **Pg. 51, ¶ 4 and Pg. 52, ¶ 2-3 – Meskiaggasher was a Sumerian king who ruled in the city of Uruk. He was the first of many kings to attempt to take over Kish.**

Nippur – **Pg. 52, ¶ 2 – Nippur was a sacred city where the shrines of the chief god Enlil stood and where kings of every Sumerian city went to sacrifice and seek recognition.**

ADDITIONAL INFORMATION:

The student may include that at the time of Meskiaggasher's rule, Nippur was controlled and protected by Kish.

Section II: Comprehension

Write a two/three sentence answer to each of the following questions.

1. What is bronze?
A1. – Pg. 54, ¶ 3 – Bronze is a metal made from a combination of tin or arsenic and copper. It is stronger than copper, easier to shape, and takes a sharper edge than copper when ground.

2. Why is the period of Sumerian history between 4000 and 3200 BC called the Uruk period? (See footnote on page 51.)

A2. – Pg. 51, footnote – The period of Sumerian history which stretched from 4000 to 3200 BC is named the Uruk period, referred to a certain type of pottery characteristic of these years.

3. What piece of information is strong evidence that Meskiaggasher seized the throne of Uruk?
A3. – Pg. 52, ¶ 3 – Meskiaggasher is described as the son of the sun-god Utu in the Sumerian king list, which is the sort of lineage a usurper often used to legitimize his claim.

4. Explain why it was necessary for Uruk to find a southern trade route in order to declare war on Kish.
A4. – Pg. 52, ¶ 4 – Meskiaggasher needed swords, axes, helmets and shields in order to fight, but the plains between the rivers lacked metal. Kish already had control of the northern river route, so Uruk needed to find a southern trade route that would provide the raw materials with which to make weapons.

5. Describe a Sumerian reed boat and its purpose.
A5. – Pg. 54, ¶ 2 – Sumerian reed boats were caulked with bitumen and were capable of carrying twenty tons of metal. A Sumerian reed boat could trade grain, wool or oil for copper.

6. What made Aratta special, and why did Enmerkar want to conquer this city?
A6. – Pg. 55, ¶ 2 – Aratta was known for its riches, its metalworkers, and its skilled stonecutters. If Enmerkar could succeed in conquering Aratta, his fame would be assured.

7. How do we know that Enmerkar was unsuccessful in his attempt to conquer Aratta?
A7. – Pg. 54, ¶ 6, Pg. 55, ¶ 4 – At the end of the long epic "Enmerkar and the Lord of Aratta," the Elamites of Aratta are still free from Enmerkar's rule.

8. What was Gilgamesh's first step in preparing for war against his neighbors?
A8. – Pg. 56, ¶ 4 – Gilgamesh's first preparation in preparing for war against his neighbors was to fortify the walls of Uruk.

9. Describe the double parliamentary assembly of Sumerian city governments.
A9. – Pg. 58, ¶ 4 - The double parliamentary assembly was made of wise elders who were past fighting, and younger men who were able-bodied but hot-headed.

10. How did Gilgamesh finally conquer Kish?
A10. – Pg. 59, ¶ 4 – In his third attempt, Gilgamesh brought down Meskiagunna, and took over all of the territories he had won through war, including the city of Kish.

11. What four cities were in the four-cornered kingdom of Sumer?
A11. – Pg. 59, ¶ 4-5 – The four cities in the four-cornered kingdom of Sumer were Kish, Ur, Uruk and the sacred Nippur.

Section III: Critical Thinking

We can see ancient roots in the familiar saying "the pen is mightier than the sword." In this chapter, we find that epic tales "were written by scribes who were paid by the kings whose achievements they recorded, which naturally tends to tilt them in the king's favor." However, we can compare these fantastic stories to "accounts of battles won, trades negotiated, and temples built" to piece together what events actually occurred in the ancient world.

Explain how each passage below is related to the function of the written history of Ancient Sumer.

1. "At the tale's end ['Enmerkar and the Lord of Aratta'], the Elamites of Aratta are still free from Enmerkar's rule. Given that the story has come down to us from the Sumerians, not the Elamites, the ambiguous ending probably represents a shattering Sumerian defeat" (55).

This passage relates to Enmerkar's attempt to seize Aratta and bring it under the power of Uruk. Because the tale comes from the Sumerians, it is obvious that they would like to present Enmerkar in the best light possible. However, the story states that the Elamites of Aratta are still free, meaning that Enmerkar was defeated. The power of writing this history allows the Sumerians to hide Enmerkar's failure in an ambiguous ending.

2. "In an epic tale told not long after his reign, we find Gilgamesh claiming Lugulbanda, the warrior-companion of Enmerkar, as his father. On the face of it, this is silly; Lugulbanda had occupied the throne decades (at least) before Gilgamesh's birth. But from the view point of a man rewriting his personal history, Lugulbanda was a fine choice….By Gilgamesh's day, Lugulbanda – perhaps thirty years dead, or even more – was well on his way to achieving the status of a Sumerian hero. A hundred years later, he would be considered a god. He lent Gilgamesh a sheen of secular power" (55-56).

Gilgamesh was not a rightful heir to the throne of Uruk. Claiming Lugulbanda as his father gave Gilgamesh a fictional inheritance to power. This lineage added to Gilgamesh's stature. Because Gilgamesh was able to rewrite his personal history, he was able to claim the throne of Uruk and eventually rule over the four great cities of Sumer.

3. Gilgamesh's first attack on Kish was a failure. "We know this because the king lists record Enmebaraggesi's death from old age, and the peaceful succession of his son Agga to the throne of Kish" (57).

Gilgamesh was a brave warrior, and he is remember this way through stories. The king list, however, was an administrative document that gives us a pretty accurate record of the succession of Sumerian kings. Looking at the records, rather than the epic tales of the time, allows us to see what really happened in battles. If Gilgamesh had defeated Enmebaraggesi, it is Gilgamesh who would have succeeded Enmebaraggesi as the king of Kish. However, it is Agga who follows.

*If the student is confused, ask him how stories differ from administrative records. Point him back to the preface of this section. Ask him, "If you were a great king, would you want people to know that you were defeated?" The answer would be no. Records aren't as easily manipulated as epic tales,

so ask the student, "How would a king list give away your defeat?" This should drive home the power of administrative records in bringing to light the real ancient histories.

4. "Why did Gilgamesh retreat? In all the legends that accrue around Gilgamesh, the central figure remains vividly the same: a young, aggressive, impetuous man of almost superhuman vitality… In the story of Gilgamesh's expedition to the north, he has to seek the approval of a council of elders before he sets off…. They were not likely to suffer a king's encroachments for long without objecting, and in this case, they declined to go to war anymore" (57).

When answering this question, think about how this passage relates to the quotation in passage #3.

In this passage we find out that Gilgamesh was most likely defeated at Kish because he did not have the support of Uruk's council of elders. This gives us even more information than the king list. Agga's succession of Enmebaraggesi clues us in to Gilgamesh's defeat. Knowing that Gilgamesh was a virile and obstinate man, and that he had to have approval of Uruk's council of elders to go to war against Kish, helps us piece together that Gilgamesh was most likely defeated because he did not have the support of his city behind him.

CHAPTER NINE: THE FIRST CIVIL WAR

The student may use his text when answering the questions in sections I and II.

Section I: Who, What, Where

Write a one or two-sentence answer explaining the significance of each item listed below.

2890 BC – **Pg. 67, ¶ 5 – 2890 BC marks the beginning of the Second Dynasty of Egypt.**

Abydos – **Pg. 62, ¶ 4-5 – Abydos was in Upper Egypt, and it was where the First Dynasty rulers were buried.**

Djer – **Pg. 62, ¶ 2 – Djer was the third king of the first Egyptian dynasty. He sent Egyptian soldiers out on the first official expeditions past the borders of Narmer's kingdom.**

ADDITIONAL INFORMATION:
The student may include that an engraving of Djer and his army triumphing over captives of Lower Nubia was found 250 miles south of Hierakonpolis.

Horus – **Pg. 65, ¶ 3 – Horus, the son of gods Osiris and Isis, was associated with the sun, the stars, and the moon, "the permanent ruler of the sky." Pharaohs, while they were alive, were considered to be the earthly embodiments of Horus.**

Khasekhem – **Pg. 68, ¶ 4-5 – Khasekhem rallied the southern Egyptian army and conquered the north, ending Egypt's first civil war. Under Khasekhem, Egypt entered the Third Dynasty, a time of peace and prosperity.**

Osiris – **Pg. 65, ¶ 2-5 – Osiris was the king of the underworld, and the father of Horus.**

Saqqara – **Pg. 62, ¶ 5 – Saqqara, just west of Memphis, was where Egyptian noblemen were buried in a grand graveyard.**

Shabaka Stone – **Pg. 64, ¶ 7 – Pg. 65, ¶ 1 – The Shabaka Stone bears the "Memphite Theology," which lays out the underpinnings of the Egyptian king's powers.**

Section II: Comprehension

Write a two/three sentence answer to each of the following questions.

1. What brought an end to predynastic Egypt, and why?
A1. Pg. 61, ¶ 3 – The unification of Egypt under Narmer and his establishment of Memphis as a single Egyptian capital brought an end to predynastic Egypt. Narmer's son followed him to the throne, and was succeeded by six more kings. According to Manetho, this established the First Dynasty of Egypt, thus ending the predynastic period.

2. Why do we think that the kings of the First Dynasty of Egypt were going to join the sun in his passage across the sky?

A2. Pg. 64, ¶ 4 – First Dynasty engravings show the sun-god travelling across the sky in a boat. Because the kings of the First Dynasty were buried beside fleets of wooden boats, we can presume that the pharaoh would use the boats to accompany the sun-god in his journey.

3. Write a short summary of the "Memphite Theology."

A3. Pg. 65, ¶ 2 – The god Osiris is given the rule of the entire earth, but his brother Set, jealous of his power, plots Osiris' death. He drowns Osiris in the Nile. The wife (and sister) of Osiris, the goddess Isis, hunts for her missing husband-brother. When she finds his drowned body, she half-resurrects him. Osiris impregnates Isis, and then becomes king of the underworld. Horus, the son of Osiris and Isis, becomes king of the living realm.

4. What does it mean when we say the kings of the First Dynasty of Egypt were not simply individuals, they were the bearers of a Power?

A4. Pg. 65, ¶ 4 – The early pharaohs of Egypt claimed to be the earthly embodiment of Horus. When a pharaoh died, he became the embodiment of Osiris, who was both king of the underworld and the father of Horus, king of the living realm. The son of the dead pharaoh took on the role of Horus, meaning the new pharaoh was not just the son of the old pharaoh, but his father's reincarnation.

5. Adjib, the fourth king of the First Dynasty, added a new descriptive title to his royal appellations: the *nesu-bit* name. What does *nesu-bit* mean?

A5. Pg. 66, ¶ 2 – *Nesu-bit* refers to the realms above and below. The *nesu* is the divine power of government, the *above kingship* that passes from king to king; the *bit* is the mortal holder of this power, the *king below*.

6. How did Semerkhet attempt to rewrite Egypt's past?

A6. Pg. 66, ¶ 3-4 – To deface the written name of a pharaoh was to remove him from earthly memory. Semerkhet attempted to rewrite the past by chipping away Adjib's name from various monuments from where it was originally carved.

7. What do archaeological findings tell us about the annual Nile floods toward the beginning of the Second Dynasty? How did this change in the floods affect Semerkhet's power?

A7. Pg. 66, ¶ 6-7 & Pg. 67, ¶ 2 – By the Second Dynasty, the flooding of the Nile was, on average, three feet lower than it had been a hundred years before. Egypt relied for its very life on the regular return of the Nile flood. If the Nile flood began to drop during Semerkhet's rule, the power that the king was supposed to embody was unstable, meaning so was the king's hold on the throne.

8. Why did sacrificial burials stop in the Second Dynasty?

A8. Pg. 67, ¶ 4 – Sacrificial burials stopped in the Second Dynasty because the believability of the claim to the unquestioned power of Horus took a nosedive. The Second Dynasty king could no longer compel human sacrifice, perhaps because he could no longer guarantee that he and he alone held the position of nesubit.

9. What suggests that Sekemib, a southerner, might have been a northern sympathizer?

A9. Pg. 67, ¶ 6 – Pg. 68, ¶ 1 – Instead of writing his titles with the sign of the god Horus beside them, Sekemib wrote them next to the sign of the god Set. Set had always been more popular in the north.

10. How does the sibling rivalry between Set and Horus reflect the hostility between north and south Egypt?

A10. Pg. 68, ¶ 4 – The north and south continued to fight over who should control all of Egypt. The hatred between Set and Horus is a reflection of hostility between north and south because both brothers believed they had a right to the throne.

11. How did Khasekhem's name change to Khasekhemwy temporarily reconcile the Horus and Set problem?

A11. Pg. 69, ¶ 2 – Khasekhem's name change to Khasekhemwy reflected a middle ground between north and south. Khasekhemwy means "The Two Powerful Ones Appear" – a name which was written with both the Horus falcon and the Set animal above it.

Section III: Critical Thinking

In Chapter 7 we learned about the fragility of papyrus. Though papyrus enabled Egyptians to communicate quickly and effectively, the brittle paper on which Egyptians wrote their important records crumbled soon after they were created. Explain each passage below, and how the circumstances presented can be viewed as historical evidence in place of the written histories that long ago turned to dust.

1. What these eight kings were up to, in the six hundred years that they governed over unified Egypt, is more than a little obscure. But we can glimpse the growth of a centralized state: the establishment of a royal court, the collection of taxes, and an economy that allowed Egypt the luxury of supporting citizens who produced no food: full-time priests to sacrifice for the king, skilled metalworkers who provided jewelry for the court's noblemen and women, scribes who kept track of the growing bureaucracy (62).

Pg. 62, ¶ 1 – In this passage, we learn that during the First Dynasty, Egypt was unified, and there was some sort of central government. Although we do not know what the exact details were, we know that the establishment of a royal court and the collection of taxes meant that there were a set of rules that all Egyptians followed. Also, we know that Egypt had to have been somewhat prosperous at this time, because not everyone had to produce their own food, like priests and artisans. While there are no documents that tell us about this central government, or records of how non-essential labor was swapped for food, the circumstantial evidence tells us that Egyptian culture during the First Dynasty was growing and becoming more sophisticated.

2. Possibly, the pharaoh would continue his royal rule; we have no Egyptian proof for this, but Gilgamesh, once dead, joined the gods of the underworld to help run the place. If the early pharaohs were believed to continue their kingly functions in the afterworld, the sacrificial burials make a kind

of sense. After all, if a king's power only lasts until death, he must be obeyed during his life, but there is no good reason to follow him into death. If, on the other hand, he's still going to be waiting for you on the other side, his power becomes all-encompassing. The passage to the undiscovered country is simply a journey from one state of loyalty to the next (64).

Pg. 64, ¶ 4-5 – While there are no written documents explaining why hundreds of people sacrificed their lives when a First Dynasty Egyptian pharaoh died, the tale of Gilgamesh gives us a clue as to why these couriers and servants would die for their king. When Gilgamesh died he did not disappear. He lived on in the underworld, helping to govern this other realm. First Dynasty engravings show the sun-god travelling across the sky in a boat, and buried beside the kings at Abydos lie fleets of wooden boats. We know that Gilgamesh crossed over into eternal life, so it makes sense that First Dynasty Egyptian pharaohs believed that when they died, they would cross over and join the sun-god in his passage across the sky. If a pharaoh's subject believed this crossover would occur, then it makes sense to surmise that when a servant sacrificed his life to a king, the servant believed he was going to join the king in the next world. The servant's loyalty would be rewarded in the new phase of the kingdom's existence. Putting together Gilgamesh's story with the drawings of the sun-god and the human sacrifices at the tombs allows us to piece together the story of these early pharaohs and their burials without exact written records.

CHAPTER TEN: THE FIRST EPIC HERO

The student may use her text when answering the questions in sections I and II.

Section I: Who, What, Where

Write a one or two-sentence answer explaining the significance of each item listed below.

626 BC – **Pg. 72 ¶ 5 and Pg. 73, ¶ 1 – 626 BC is the date of the oldest surviving copy of the entire six-story Epic of Gilgamesh.**

Ashurbanipal – **Pg. 73, ¶ 1 – Ashurbanipal was an Assyrian king who had the world's first real library. The oldest surviving copy of the complete Epic of Gilgamesh is from his library.**

Enkidu – **Pg. 72, ¶ 1, Pg. 73, ¶ 4 – Enkidu was a creature the gods made from clay in order to tame Gilgamesh.**

Humbaba – **Pg. 75, ¶ 5 – Humbaba is another name for the Giant Hugeness, the monster that Gilgamesh slays in the forest.**

Shulgi – **Pg. 71, ¶ 3 – Shulgi was the King of Ur around 2100 BC. He assigned a scribe to write out the tales of Gilgamesh because he claimed Gilgamesh as his ancestor.**

Section II: Comprehension

Write a two/three sentence answer to each of the following questions.

1. List the 7 parts of the Epic of Gilgamesh, and write a short description of each section.

A1. – Pg. 72, ¶ 1 – Part 1 is "The Tale of Enkidu," in which Gilgamesh makes a friend of the monster sent by the gods to tame him.

Part 2 is "The Journey to the Cedar Forest," in which Gilgamesh defeats Humbaba.

Part 3 is "The Bull of Heaven," in which Gilgamesh irritates the goddess Inanna and Enkidu suffers for it.

Part 4 is "Gilgamesh's Journey," in which Gilgamesh reaches the land of the immortal Utnapishtim.

Part 5 is "The Story of the Flood," in which Gilgamesh listens to Utnapishtim tell him the story of the flood.

Part 6 is "Gilgamesh's Quest," in which Gilgamesh tries to find eternal life, but does not succeed.

Part 7 is the postscript that laments Gilgamesh's death.

2. What makes the clay tablets of the tales of Gilgamesh written by Shulgi's scribe different from the copy of the Epic found in the library of Ashurbanipal? How do the two copies differ in form, and in accuracy?

A2. – Pg. 72, ¶ 4 to Pg. 73, ¶ 1 & 2 – The copies of the Epic dating from the time of Shulgi's scribe only contain the first two parts of the tale and the ending lament. Ashurbanipal's copy contains all seven parts of the story. It is impossible to know whether the four additional stories in Ashurbanipal's copy of the Epic were part of the cycle early on and were lost, or whether they were added later. Therefore, the stories in Shulgi's copy are the only ones we can place within striking distance of Gilgamesh's life.

3. What were the two most important duties of a Sumerian king?

A3. – Pg. 74, ¶ 3 & 4 – A Sumerian king was supposed to bring justice to his people, and to protect the weak from being driven into poverty and starvation by the strong.

4. What two threats to Sumerian life were represented by the monster Enkidu?

A4. – Pg. 73, ¶ 4 & Pg. 74, ¶ 5 – Enkidu represented the nomads who roamed the plains, lived with animals and threatened the civilized life of Sumerian cities. Enkidu also represented a corrupt side of Gilgamesh, his uncivilized mirror image.

5. Why does Gilgamesh want to slay the Giant Hugeness? Cite a passage from the Epic of Gilgamesh that refers to Gilgamesh's battle in the cedar forest. Explain what the section of the poem you quoted means.

A5. – Pg. 75, ¶ 2 – A passage from the Epic of Gilgamesh that explains why Gilgamesh wants to fight the Giant Hugeness is "I will conquer the Giant Hugeness/I will establish my fame forever" (75). In this section of the poem, Gilgamesh states that killing the Giant Hugeness will give him everlasting fame. This is important because Gilgamesh is a man, and is not immortal. Gilgamesh thinks that by slaying the beast his name will live on forever.

ALTERNATE ANSWER: **Pg. 75, ¶ 5 – This quoted passage from the Epic is also correct: "Who can go up to heaven?/ Only the gods dwell forever./ Men number their days./ But even if I fall I will win fame,/ Fame will last forever." In this section of the poem, Gilgamesh admits that only gods live forever. Even if Gilgamesh dies in the forest, he knows the fame he will win by battling Humbaba will last forever.**

6. Use the footnote on page 76 to answer this question: Why was the world of the dead so horrifying for Sumerians?

A6. – Pg. 76, Footnote – The world of the Sumerian dead was neither light nor dark, neither warm nor cold, food was tasteless and drink was thin. Everyone wandered around naked. To get to this world, the dead had to cross a river that devoured flesh. No Sumerian wanted to spend an eternal existence in this gray and unattractive world.

NOTE TO INSTRUCTOR:

The student may not have read this footnote when they first went through the chapter. Make sure to emphasize that as she reads, she should be reading all footnotes.

7. The Epic of Gilgamesh ends with a lament. Gilgamesh is unsuccessful in his quest for immortality; "He has gone into the mountain; he will not come again" (77). How does this impact the idea of Sumerian kingship?

A7. – Pg. 77, ¶ 2 & 3 – Though Sumerian kings are given their power from god, they are not immortal. Even the strongest king of Sumer dies. A Sumerian king cannot rule forever, and his power, which works either for or against his people, will eventually come to an end.

Section III: Critical Thinking

Poems, epics, records and king lists give us great views into ancient cultures. To learn from these texts, we must be careful readers, piecing together significance from what we learned previously and what we are currently reading. The three questions below will test your skill as a reader, and historical sleuth.

1. Explain how the passage below asserts that the story of Agga and Gilgamesh was written within striking distance of Gilgamesh's life.

"Outside of the Epic, though, Gilgamesh's life is chronicled by a couple of inscriptions, the Sumerian king list, and a poem or two. The story of Agga's fruitless peace-mission to Gilgamesh… is one such poem; it is written in Sumerian, and was likely told orally for some decades (or centuries) before being written down on clay tablets" (71).

A1. We know that the Sumerian language disappeared and was replaced by Akkadian, the language spoken by the people who occupied the river plain as the Sumerian cities declined (Pg. 72, ¶ 4). Because there is a clay tablet with the story of Agga and Gilgamesh written in Sumerian, we know that this copy of the tale was written before the decline of Sumer. This places the written version of the story relatively close to the time of Gilgamesh's reign.

2. Using the passage below, explain why historians think "The Story of the Flood" was not originally included in the Epic of Gilgamesh.

"The story of the flood, which existed in a number of different versions well before 2000 BC, was likely shoehorned into Gilgamesh's story, as the fifth tale, at least a thousand years after Gilgamesh's death; it is clearly independent from the rest of the epic. ("Sit down and let me tell you a story," Utnapishtim orders Gilgamesh, and launches into the tale as though he's had little opportunity to tell it since getting off the boat.)" (72).

A2. The Epic of Gilgamesh follows the king as he battles Enkidu and Humbaba, as he searches for a way to live forever, and laments his death. The story of the flood is out of place because it has nothing to do with Gilgamesh's trials. In "The Story of the Flood," Gilgamesh is told by Utnapishtim, "Sit down and let me tell you a story." The fact that the story is told to Gilgamesh, and does not advance his cause to find immortality, or give him special direction on how to beat a foe, suggests to us that the story was added to the original Epic.

3. In this chapter, look up the term "droit de seigneur." How does "droit de seigneur" relate to the fine line between kingly privilege and kingly corruption, and the possible destruction of the king's realm?

A3. "Droit de seigneur" is a French term meaning "the right of the lord." It was the king's right to have intercourse with a subject's virgin bride on her wedding night, before she had intercourse with her new husband. A king's power can certainly go to his head, as exemplified by Gilgamesh's impetuous desires that are chronicled in Chapter 8. We know from our reading that "In Uruk, the king was the law, and if the king himself became corrupt, the nature of law itself had been distorted" (74). If a king took too much advantage of "droit de seigneur" he would be viewed as corrupt, and his realm would crumble.

Chapter Eleven: The First Victory over Death

The student may use his text when answering the questions in sections I and II.

Section I: Who, What, Where

Write a one or two-sentence answer explaining the significance of each item listed below.

Heb-sed – **Pg. 78, ¶ 3 – The heb-sed was a festival in which the king took a ceremonial run around a race course. Running, and winning, the heb-sed race reaffirmed the pharaoh's power to regulate the flood waters of the Nile, and to protect Egypt.**

Imhotep – **Pg. 79, ¶ 6, Pg. 80, ¶ 4 – Imhotep designed the Step Pyramid. He was honored as a great priest and wise man after his death, and was later deified as the god of medicine.**

Mastabas – **Pg. 80, ¶ 1 – Mastabas were stone-walled and square-topped covers, or buildings, that roofed over the graves at Abydos.**

Red Pyramid – **Pg. 83, ¶ 4 to Pg. 84, ¶ 1 – The Red Pyramid is another name for the Northern Pyramid. The Northern Pyramid got this nickname because its limestone facing began to flake off and left the red sandstone beneath to glow in the sun.**

Sadd al-Kafara – **Pg. 84, ¶ 6 to Pg. 85, ¶ 1 – The Sadd al-Kafara was the world's first dam, built by Khufu. Khufu built this dam in order to provide water to the thousands of workers who labored on the Great Pyramid.** *The student might also include that the Sadd al-Kafara created the world's first public reservoir.*

Serdab – **Pg. 79, ¶ 3 – A serdab was a small chamber found in a pharaoh's tomb, where a statue of the pharaoh sat facing east. The wall of the serdab had two drilled eye-holes, so that the statue could look out at the rising sun.** *The student might also include: Below the eye-holes was an altar where priests offered food so that the pharaoh could feast on the aromas.*

Step Pyramid – **Pg. 79, ¶ 5 – The Step Pyramid was the first Egyptian pyramid, built on top of Djoser's tomb.**

Ziggurats – **Pg. 80, ¶ 2 – Ziggurats were stair-step temples used by the Sumerians for their worship that may have inspired the shape of the Egyptian pyramids.**

Section II: Comprehension

Write a two/three sentence answer to each of the following questions.

1. What is another term for the beginning of the pyramid age in Egyptian history?

A1. – Pg. 81, ¶ 2 - The beginning of the pyramid age also marks a new era in Egyptian history called the "Old Kingdom of Egypt."

2. In what way did the construction of the Step Pyramid represent the beginning of a new, peaceful and united kingdom of Egypt?

A2. – Pg. 81, ¶ 1 – In order for the Step Pyramid to be built, there had to be an orderly bureaucracy in place in Egypt. Stone had to be quarried and brought from far away. The pyramid was built by an organized work force of strong men who could be spared from farming and fighting. Also, the funding of the pyramid came from tax dollars. Only in a kingdom that was prosperous, and at peace, could all of these components come together successfully.

3. How was Djoser's tomb different from the tombs of the pharaohs in the Second Egyptian Dynasty?

A3. – Pg. 79, ¶ 2, 5 – Djoser's tomb was built in the north, in Saqqara, far away from the royal graveyard at Abydos. Djoser did not use the traditional mud brick of the Second Dynasty to build his tomb; instead he used stone that would last forever. Djoser's tomb was not a place of departure for his spirit's journey into the next world, it was a place where the pharaoh would live for eternity. Finally, built overtop of the tomb itself stood the first Egyptian pyramid: the Step Pyramid.

4. Describe Sekhemkhet's vision for his pyramid. Why is Sekhemkhet's pyramid called the "Unfinished Pyramid"?

A4. – Pg. 81, ¶ 3 – Sekhemkhet planned his pyramid to rise seven steps, one step higher than Djoser's pyramid. Sekhemkhet died six years into his reign, and so the construction of his pyramid halted at the first layer. This is why the pyramid is called the "Unfinished Pyramid."

5. How can we distinguish the Fourth Dynasty of Egypt from the Third Dynasty of Egypt?

A5. – Pg. 81, ¶ 5 – In the Fourth Dynasty of Egypt, the kings were finally able to figure out how to build successful pyramids.

6. The Meydum Pyramid, started by Third Dynasty king, Huni, and finished by Fourth Dynasty king, Snefru, is surrounded by heaps of rubble. What does this rubble indicate about the intended construction of the Meydum Pyramid?

A6. – Pg. 82, ¶ 2 – The heaps of rubble around the Meydum Pyramid show us that workmen tried to cover the steps with a smooth layer of facing stones.

7. Describe the purpose of the causeway in the Meydum Pyramid, and the function of the mortuary temple.

A7. – Pg. 82, ¶ 1 – The causeway is a broad path leading down from the pyramid to a mortuary temple. The mortuary temple was a sacred building to the east, facing the rising sun, where offerings could be made.

8. What did Snefru figure out while building the Bent Pyramid that allowed him to construct the Northern Pyramid successfully? What is the Northern Pyramid like now, four thousand years later?
A8. Pg. 83, ¶ 1-3 – While working on the Bent Pyramid, Snefru figured out that the angles of a pyramid had to be less steep than 52 degrees in order for the building not to collapse. The Northern Pyramid was designed to have sides that sloped at 43 degrees. Even now, over four thousand years later, no cracks have appeared in the walls or ceilings of the chambers that lie beneath the Northern Pyramid.

9. Herodotus said that Khufu "was a very bad man" (83). Describe one story that illustrates Khufu's evil.
A9. – *The student may give one of the following answers:*
• Pg. 85, ¶ 1 – Herodotus tells us that in order to build the Great Pyramid, Khufu "reduced Egypt to a completely awful condition…and also commanded all the Egyptians to work for him."
• Pg. 85, ¶ 2 – To build the Great Pyramid, Khufu had to mobilize one of the largest work forces in the world. While these workers may not have been slaves, the king's ability to recruit such an enormous number of workers illustrated his ability to oppress his people.
• Pg. 85, ¶ 3 – Khufu was so busy building his Great Pyramid that he closed down the temples in Egypt and told the people to stop offering sacrifices.
• Pg. 85, ¶ 3 – Khufu prostituted his daughter in order to help fund the building of the Great Pyramid.

10. What is "monumental architecture?" Why is it said that monumental architecture is a universal sign for power?
A10. – Pg. 86, ¶ 1 – Monumental architecture is a term used to describe buildings which are much more elaborate in size or design than practicality requires. Monumental architecture is a universal sign for power because these creations are built at the expense of other people's labor.

11. How do we know that Erich Von Däniken's theory that "the pyramids suddenly appeared without any precedent, which meant that they had most likely been built by aliens," is not true?
A11. – Pg. 87, ¶ 2 – There is an easily traced line of development in design of the pyramids from Djoser's original step pyramid to Khufu's Great Pyramid. The progression of failed pyramids shows us that pyramid-building was an effort of trial and error.

Section III: Critical Thinking

In *Chapter 9: The First Civil War*, we read about the first two Egyptian dynasties and the evolution of pharaohs from men to gods. In the First Dynasty, a king's reign continued after death. The Second Dynasty held the same fortune for a king, but a pharaoh's power in the afterlife was questioned by Egyptians due to the lessening of the Nile floodwaters. In the Third and Fourth Dynasties, we see two more devolutions of divine power. However, an Egyptian king's earthly power was on the rise. Arrange the selected passages so that they reflect the correct transition of Egyptian beliefs about the afterlife and the king's power in the Third and Fourth Dynasties. When you are finished, write a short essay, in your own words, describing the changes from the First to

Fourth Dynasties in Egyptian thought and culture as related to the pharaoh and his power.

Part I:

A. By Khufu's day, the original purpose of that first necropolis built by Imhotep had been well obscured. The Great Pyramid and the monuments that came after are the oldest surviving example of what we call "monumental architecture"…The less necessary and useful the pyramids were, the more they testified to the power of their builders. The house of the spirit had become the glittering testament to power.

B. The Step Pyramid, the first of the great Egyptian pyramids, shows more than an effort to redefine death as the absence of the body and the presence of the spirit. It shows the beginning of a new kingdom of Egypt, a peaceful and unified one with an orderly bureaucracy…Pyramid building required prosperity, peace and tax money…Only a strong and well-to-do state could order workers to the quarries and afford to feed and clothe them.

C. [T]he tradition of Khufu's evil, which echoes down from more than one source, is an interesting one. To build his monument – a stone structure with something like two and a half million blocks of stone in it, each block an average weight of two and a half tons – Khufu mobilized one of the largest work forces in the world. Even if the laborers were not reduced to abject slavery, the king's ability to recruit such an enormous number of workers keenly illustrated his ability to oppress his people. The pyramids themselves stand as signposts to that power.

D. By Djoser's day, the pharaoh's rule as a buffer against change had solidified into ritual…Winning the *heb-sed* race reaffirmed the pharaoh's power to protect Egypt and to assure the continuing, regular rise and fall of the waters [of the Nile]…The fact that the Egyptians felt the need for a renewal festival at all suggests a certain fear that the pharaoh's power might fade if not ritually reinforced. The pharaoh was undoubtedly still credited with a kind of divinity, but the struggles of the first two dynasties had made his human side very obvious.

E. [The pyramids] stand as testaments, not to alien visits, but to the Egyptian reluctance to release power in the face of death. Gilgamesh had gone into the mountain and would not come again. But for the Egyptians, who could always see the house of the king's spirit looming in the distance, the might of the pharaoh was ever present.

F. Sekhemkhet's pyramid was planned to rise seven steps, not six as Djoser's had… The final pyramid of the Third Dynasty, the Meydum Pyramid, was also unfinished; it was built by the Third Dynasty's last king, Huni, and it would have had *eight* steps.

G. A pyramid and the complex underneath it "was a place where the pharaoh *still lived.*"

H. The fact that Snefru was able to complete one pyramid and build two more suggests that Egypt was now even richer, and more peaceful, and more subject to the authority of the pharaoh, than even before.

<u>**Part II:**</u>

Write two or three paragraphs, in your own words, describing the changes from the First to Fourth Dynasties in Egyptian thought and culture as related to the pharaoh and his power.

NOTE TO INSTRUCTOR: To help the student come up with an appropriate answer, guide him with these prompts:

- *What happened in the tombs of First Dynasty pharaohs? Did the pharaohs stay on earth or did they go to heaven? How did Egyptians see pharaohs, as gods or as men?*

- *Why did the Second Dynasty kings lose power? How was this loss of power reflected in the burials of the Second Dynasty kings?*

- *Why is the tomb of a Third Dynasty pharaoh equipped with a heb-sed course?*

- *What is the difference between the first pyramids and the monumental architecture of Khufu's pyramid? What was most important to Khufu while he was pharaoh?*

KEY TO PART I:

1. D – Pg. 78, ¶ 3-4 – By Djoser's day, the pharaoh's rule as a buffer against change had solidified into ritual…Winning the *heb-sed* race reaffirmed the pharaoh's power to protect Egypt and to assure the continuing, regular rise and fall of the waters [of the Nile]…The fact that the Egyptians felt the need for a renewal festival at all suggests a certain fear that the pharaoh's power might fade if not ritually reinforced. The pharaoh was undoubtedly still credited with a kind of divinity, but the struggles of the first two dynasties had made his human side very obvious.

2. G – Pg. 79. ¶ 2 – A pyramid and the complex underneath it "was a place where the pharaoh *still lived.*"

3. B – Pg. 80, ¶ 5 to Pg. 81, ¶ 1 & 2 – The Step Pyramid, the first of the great Egyptian pyramids, shows more than an effort to redefine death as the absence of the body and the presence of the spirit. It shows the beginning of a new kingdom of Egypt, a peaceful and unified one with an orderly bureaucracy…Pyramid building required prosperity, peace and tax money…Only a strong and well-to-do state could order workers to the quarries and afford to feed and clothe them.

4. F – Pg. 81, ¶ 3 & Pg. 81, ¶ 4 – Sekhemkhet's pyramid was planned to rise seven steps, not six as Djoser's had… The final pyramid of the Third Dynasty, the Meydum Pyramid, was also unfinished; it was built by the Third Dynasty's last king, Huni, and it would have had *eight* steps.

5. H – Pg 84, ¶ 3 - The fact that Snefru was able to complete one pyramid and build two more suggests that Egypt was now even richer, and more peaceful, and more subject to the authority of the pharaoh, than even before.

6. C – Pg. 85, ¶ 2 – [T]he tradition of Khufu's evil, which echoes down from more than one source, is an interesting one. To build his monument – a stone structure with something like two and a half million blocks of stone in it, each block an average weight of two and a half tons – Khufu mobilized one of the largest work forces in the world. Even if the laborers were not reduced to abject slavery, the king's ability to recruit such an enormous number of workers

keenly illustrated his ability to oppress his people. The pyramids themselves stand as signposts to that power.

7. A – Pg. 85, ¶ 4 to Pg. 86, ¶ 1 – By Khufu's day, the original purpose of that first necropolis built by Imhotep had been well obscured. The Great Pyramid and the monuments that came after are the oldest surviving example of what we call "monumental architecture"…The less necessary and useful the pyramids were, the more they testified to the power of their builders. The house of the spirit had become the glittering testament to power.

8. E – Pg. 87, ¶ 2 – [The pyramids] stand as testaments, not to alien visits, but to the Egyptian reluctance to release power in the face of death. Gilgamesh had gone into the mountain and would not come again. But for the Egyptians, who could always see the house of the king's spirit looming in the distance, the might of the pharaoh was ever present.

EXAMPLE ESSAY FOR PART II:

Early Egyptians believed that pharaohs were gods. These early kings were responsible, in the public's mind, for the continual rise of the Nile's waters. The Nile's controlled floodwaters nourished Egypt's fields. The regularity of the floods was credited to the king. During the First Dynasty, Egyptians were so sure that pharaohs were gods, loyal citizens would sacrifice themselves when a pharaoh died in order to live on with him eternally in the next realm. Towards the end of the First Dynasty, the Nile floods lessened dramatically, and with that decrease in Egypt's life source came the decrease in the power of the pharaoh. Egyptians were no longer sure if the pharaoh had control over life and death. In addition, civil war broke out between North and South Egypt. The struggle over the throne had shown that the pharaoh was not a god and that others could mount a claim to his power. Consequently, the pharaohs of the Second Dynasty were not considered absolutely divine.

In the Third Dynasty, the king's quest for eternal life manifested itself in the building of the pyramids. No longer guaranteed passage with the sun god across the sky, Third Dynasty pharaohs created earthly tombs, topped with pyramids, where their souls could live on forever. Though not all of the pyramids were built successfully, the point of the Third Dynasty pyramids was to create a place of worship and ritual, where Egyptians could pray to their deceased pharaohs for the renewal of the Nile floods.

By the time of the Fourth Dynasty, the original intention of the pyramid was obscured, and each newly crowned pharaoh was simply trying to outdo his predecessor in the architecture of his pyramid. The pyramids were no longer about the eternally living soul of the pharaoh, but about the earthly power of the Egyptian king. The best example of this change is the Great Pyramid. Khufu's pyramid showed not his religious devotion, but rather his ability to manipulate and oppress his subjects.

CHAPTER TWELVE: THE FIRST REFORMER

The student may use her text when answering the questions in sections I and II.

Section I: Who, What, Where

Write a one or two-sentence answer explaining the significance of each item listed below.

Amagi – **Pg. 92, ¶ 5 to Pg. 93, ¶ 1 – Amagi, the cuneiform sign that stands for freedom from fear, was the first appearance of "freedom" in human written language. Amagi means "return to the mother," and describes Urukagina's desire to return the city of Lagash to an earlier, purer state.**

Lugulannemundu – **Pg. 89, ¶ 3 – Lugulannemundu, the king of Adab around 2500 BC, drove a coalition of thirteen Elamite-dominated cities out of Sumer.**

Sataran – **Pg. 90, ¶ 3 – Sataran was the Sumerian judge-god. Mesilim claimed that Sataran showed him the proper border between Lagash and Umma.**

Stele – **Pg. 90, ¶ 3 – A stele is an inscribed stone that marks an important place or event.**

Susa and Awan – **Pg. 88, ¶ 3 – Susa and Awan were twinned cities that served as the center for the Elamite civilization. Awan was the more important of the two, and its king had jurisdiction over all of the Elamites.**

Urukagina – **Pg. 92, ¶ 2-4 – Urukagina, king of Lagash, inherited a corrupt city. He worked to return Lagash to the state of justice intended by the gods.**

Section II: Comprehension

Write a two/three sentence answer to each of the following questions.

1. Where were the cities of the ancient Elamite civilization located?
A1. – Pg. 88, ¶ 2 – Elamite cities grew up just south of the Caspian Sea and along the southern border of the large salt desert plateau that lay east of the Zagros Mountains.

2. After Uruk was conquered by Ur, Ur was then "defeated in battle, and its kingship was carried off to Awan." What evidence do we have from the historical record that indicates an Elamite invasion of Ur?
A2. – Pg. 89, ¶ 1 – After Ur's kingship was carried off to Awan, the kings of Kish's next dynasty have Elamite names. This suggests that the Elamites succeeded in conquering Ur, and taking its kingship.

3. How did Mesilim, the king of Kish, settle the dispute between Lagash and Umma concerning the proper boundary between the two cities?
A3. – Pg. 90, ¶ 3 –Mesilim intervened in the quarrel between Lagash and Umma and

announced that Sataran, the Sumerian judge-god, had shown him the proper border for both cities to observe. He put up a stele to mark the line, and both cities agreed to this judgment.

4. What is the Stele of Vultures – who created it, what does it depict, and what does it tell us about Sumerian warfare?
A4. – Pg. 90, ¶ 5-6 & Pg. 91, ¶ 1 – The Stele of Vultures was created by Eannatum, the king of Lagash. The carving shows Eannatum's victory over Umma. The stone has pictures of Eannatum's men marching, helmeted and armed with shields and spears, over the bodies of the dead. Vultures pick at the strewn corpses and fly off with their heads. Eannatum is shown riding in a war-chariot, pulled by a mule. The Stele of Vultures shows an advanced state of warfare. Eannatum's men are armed identically, showing that the concept of an organized army had gained ground.

5. What problems plagued Lagash during Urukagina's rule?
A5. – Pg. 92, ¶ 3 – When Urukagina came into power, Lagash was entirely run by corrupt priests and the rich, and the weak and poor lived in hunger and fear. Temple land, which was supposed to be used on behalf of Lagash's people, had been taken by temple personnel for their own use. Workmen had to beg for bread, and apprentices went unpaid and searched rubbish for scraps of food. Officials demanded fees for everything from the shearing of white sheep to the interment of dead bodies. The tax burden had become so unbearable that parents were forced to sell their children into slavery in order to pay their debts.

6. One of the actions Urukagina took to restore Lagash to a land of peace and justice was to take away authority from the priests by dividing religious and secular functions. How was this action partly responsible for the fall of Lagash to Lugalzaggesi's troops?
A6. – Pg. 93, ¶ 4 – When Lugalzaggesi attacked Lagash, there was little done by the priests and the rich men of the city to protect Urukagina's land; after Urukagina took away the elders' power, they did not fight vigorously on his behalf. In addition, the priests of Nippur, the sacred city of Enlil, were cooperating with Lugalzaggesi. The powerful priests of Nippur were not supportive of the curtailment of priestly power; it set a bad precedent.

Section III: Critical Thinking

Sumer's first epic hero was Gilgamesh. However, even though Gilgamesh was held to be a god, his godship was still limited by death. We learned, with relief, that "even the strongest king of Sumer dies." How did this time limit on the power of a king affect the way a Sumerian king ruled? In addition, how did the constant rivalry between Sumerian cities for dominance of the plain, as well as the constant threat of Elamite invasion, influence the way a king ruled over his Sumerian city? What connects the limited earthly power of a Sumerian king and the perpetual threat of invasion to Sumer's lack of an organized bureaucracy?

To help the student formulate a written response to these questions, start by talking about the previous chapter. We just finished reading about the great power of the Egyptian pharaohs, and how that power was very much tied up in ideas of immortality and eternal reign. The Egyptians were very organized, and had a strong bureaucracy in place. This allowed the pyramids to be built.

Part Two: Firsts

Sumerians did not have such a bureaucracy. What does the chapter say about how Sumerian kings ruled? We learn on page 90, ¶ 2 that "Sumerian kings ruled by force of arms and charisma. Their kingdoms had no settled bureaucracy to sustain them. When the crown passed from the dynamic warrior to the less talented son, the kingdom inevitably crumbled." The student's answer should start by explaining that a Sumerian king could not rely on a centralized system of government to ensure his throne; he kept his throne by force.

Later in the chapter we learn that "Inscriptions from the two centuries after Gilgamesh give us a glimpse of a churning mass of competition. The Elamites and the cities of the Sumerian plain – Uruk and Kish, but also the cities of Ur, Lagash, and Umma, now increasing in strength – fought an unending series of battles for primacy" (Pg. 88, ¶ 4). You might ask the student, if a Sumerian city was constantly working to keep invaders out, how could it find time to organize within itself a settled and fair bureaucracy? While villagers worked to protect their families and themselves, priests and lugals were taking advantage of loose laws and exploited the rest of the city. This was exemplified very clearly in the section of our chapter that described Urukagina's reformation of Lagash: "War with Umma was not the sole problem facing Lagash...It was entirely run by corrupt priests and the rich, and the weak and poor lived in hunger and fear. Temple land...had been taken by unscrupulous temple personnel for their own use...Workmen had to beg for bread, and apprentices went unpaid and scrabbled in the rubbish for scraps of food. Officials demanded fees for everything" (Pg. 92, ¶ 3). Lagash's officials and priests were not interested in creating a working bureaucracy for the good of their city – they wanted only more power for themselves.

To connect these two ideas, we can look to earlier in the chapter when we first learned about the boundary dispute between Umma and Lagash. When Mesilim, the king of Kish, marked the proper boundary between the two cities as told to him by the Sumerian judge-god Sataran, his ruling did not last long. Soon after Mesilim died, "the new king of Umma knocked the stele down and annexed the disputed land." A good question to ask the student would be, how could the king of Umma upset a decision made, for all intents and purposes, by the god Sataran? It seems that both Umma and Lagash agreed to the treaty because of Mesilim's earthly power, not because of his ability to channel the desires of the gods. The people were not listening to Sataran, they were afraid of what Mesilim might do if the new boundary was not accepted.

While the gods played an important role in Sumerian life, the earthly power of Sumerian kings was what really made Sumerian life tick. Since each king was fighting to keep his throne from possible invaders, he was also on the attack to seize weaker cities where he saw fit. There was no time to set up a working bureaucratic system when a king had to cement his power through earthly conquer. Rather than paying tribute to the gods, it seems that the sole want of a Sumerian king was to receive tribute himself from the four-quarters.

CHAPTER THIRTEEN: THE FIRST MILITARY DICTATOR

The student may use his text when answering the questions in sections I and II.

Section I: Who, What, Where

Write a one or two-sentence answer explaining the significance of each item listed below.

Agade – **Pg. 99, ¶ 4 – Agade was the new capital of Sumer that Sargon built in order to rule over his far-reaching empire. Agade was Sargon's eye over the southern part of his kingdom.**

Nineveh – **Pg. 101, ¶ 2 – Nineveh was Sargon's northern outpost where his sons watched out over Sargon's northern conquests.**

Rimush – **Pg. 102, ¶ 5 – Rimush was Sargon's son. Rimush inherited Sargon's kingdom, and was murdered by his servants less than ten years into his reign.**

Ur-Zababa – **Pg. 97, ¶ 1-5 – Ur-Zababa was the Sumerian king of Kish, and Sargon's master. Ur-Zababa was driven out of Kish by Lugalzaggesi.**

Section II: Comprehension

Write a two/three sentence answer to each of the following questions.

1. Part of the inscription that chronicles Sargon's birth reads:

> *[My mother] cast me into the river, but it did not rise over me,*
> *The water carried me to Akki, the drawer of water,*
> *He lifted me out as he dipped his jar into the river,*
> *He took me as his son, he raised me,*
> *He made me his gardener.*

Why was Sargon's trip down the river important to his new identity? How did it help him take on Akki's heritage?

A1. – Pg. 96, ¶ 5 – Sumerians thought that a river divided them from the afterlife, and that passing through the water brought an essential change of being. Sargon was one person before he was put in the water by his mother, and a different person when he was pulled out by Akki. The water washed away Sargon's past and allowed him to take on the persona of his adopted father.

2. What most clearly distinguished the Sumerians of the south from the Semites of the north?

A2. – Pg. 96, ¶ 3 – The Sumerians and the Semites spoke very different languages. In the south, Sumerians spoke and wrote Sumerian, a language unlike any other that we know. A Semitic language was spoken in the north.

3. Describe the duties of an ancient cupbearer. What was the significance of carrying the king's seal? Why did the cupbearer have to taste the king's food?

A3. – Pg. 97, ¶ 2 – Ancient cupbearers were butlers. They also controlled access to the king, carried the king's seal and tasted the king's food. Carrying the king's seal gave the cupbearer the right to bestow the king's approval. A cupbearer had to taste the king's food so that the cupbearer himself might not be tempted to increase his own power by poisoning his master.

4. As Lugalzaggesi approached Kish, Ur-Zababa sent the aggressor a message on a clay tablet asking him to kill Sargon. While this story may not be true, what evidence in the chapter suggests that Sargon was in fact not fully behind his king?

A4. – Pg. 97, ¶ 6 to Pg. 98, ¶ 1 – The fact that Lugalzaggesi was even able to attack Kish suggests that Sargon was not fully supportive of Ur-Zababa. When Lugalzaggezi marched into Kish, Ur-Zababa was forced to flee and Sargon was nowhere to be found.

5. What type of secret weapon did Sargon's army have that helped them conquer the entire Mesopotamian plain? How might Sargon have gotten this weaponry?

A5. – Pg. 98, ¶ 5 – Sargon's army was stronger than the Sumerian defenders, thanks to their heavy use of bows and arrows. A lack of wood in Sumer meant that bows were uncommon, so these were like a secret weapon for Sargon's army. Sargon must have had a source for yew, suggesting that he extended his reach over to the Zagros Mountains.

6. How did the abuses of the elite leaders in Sumerian cities, coupled with Sargon's commoner background, help Sargon's conquest of Sumer?

A6. – Pg. 98, ¶ 6 to Pg. 99, ¶ 1 – The elite leaders in Sumerian cities allied themselves with the priesthood and used their combined religious and secular power to claim as much as three-quarters of the land in any given city for themselves. This meant the poor laborers were abused and unhappy. Sargon, known for his non-aristocratic background, may have appealed to the downtrodden members of Sumerian society to come over to his side and help take down the corrupt leaders.

7. Why did Sumerians find themselves living as foreigners in their own cities after Sargon created his new kingdom?

A7. – Pg. 99 ¶ 5 – In Sargon's new kingdom, the Sumerians were surrounded by Semites from the northern plain. The Semites' dialect was known as Akkadian. Their customs and speech were different from those of the southern Sumerians. When Sargon took over a city, it became an Akkadian stronghold, staffed with Akkadian officials and garrisoned with Akkadian troops.

8. Why is Sargon's invasion of Purushkhanda questionable? Use a section of the surviving verses of Nur-daggal to explain why Sargon's attack on Purushkhanda seemed unlikely. What does the story of Sargon's invasion of the city tell us about Sargon's cultural importance?

A8. – Pg. 101, ¶ 3 – Purushkhanda was very far north of the Sumerian plain. Nur-daggal states: "He will not come this far. Riverbank and high water will prevent him. The massive

mountain will make a thicket and tangle in his way." Whether or not Sargon actually reached Purushkhanda, he must have seemed unstoppable, almost magically ever-present across the known world. His might seemed supernatural to the people of the ancient world.

NOTE TO THE INSTRUCTOR - This is the verse as it is presented in the chapter on page 101:

He will not come this far.
Riverbank and high water will prevent him.
The massive mountain will make a thicket and tangle in his way.

9. How did Sargon keep control of the vast expanse of land he had claimed as his own?
A9. – Pg. 102, ¶ 1 & 2 – Sargon had a standing army that helped him keep control over the land, and he also paid tribute to pretty much every important local god he ran across. Sargon also created a working bureaucratic system in Sumer. Sargon tried to standardize weights and measures. He also put into place an Egyptian-style tax system, run by state officials who managed the empire's finances. He also kept representatives of the old ruling families at his court.

Section III: Critical Thinking

Sargon was the first man to successfully turn Sumer into an empire. Sargon was able to build a strong enough bureaucracy that his descendants kept the throne of Agade for over a hundred years. Yet, as soon as Sargon died, internal fighting threatened his legacy. Write two or three paragraphs, using the questions below to structure your answer, explaining how Sargon's policies both strengthened and threatened his kingdom.

- How did the standardization of weights and measures, and the implementation of a tax system run by state officials who managed the empire's finances, help Sargon keep tabs on the cities under his control?
- How might Sargon's replacement of the Sumerian lugals with his own men help him build such a large empire so quickly? How did this policy cause unrest?
- Sargon kept representatives of old ruling families at his court in honor of their exalted lineage, however the chapter says "these representatives…were hostages for the good behavior of their cities" (102). How did this policy both help, and hurt, Sargon's kingdom?

These questions do not have to be answered directly. The student might want to use them to brainstorm, or to find passages in the text that will help him form his response. Below are three passages from the chapter that you can point the student to if he is stuck.

Pg. 102, ¶ 4 – The Sumerian king list credits Sargon with a reign of fifty-six years. Near its end, when he was most likely past seventy, a serious rebellion broke out. Old Babylonian inscriptions record that the "elders of the land," now deprived of their authority, gathered together and barricaded themselves into the Temple of Inanna, in Kish.
Pg. 102, ¶ 5 – It is beyond dispute that, almost as soon as Sargon died, his son Rimush had to mount an attack on a five-city coalition of rebels that included Ur, Lagash and Umma. Rimush reigned less than ten years and died suddenly. A later inscription says that his servants assassinated him.

Pg. 102, ¶ 6 - Despite this scuffle after Sargon's death, his descendants kept the throne of Agade for over a hundred years – far longer than any Sumerian dynasty. The Akkadian empire was held together by more than charisma. Sargon's bureaucracy and administration, like those of Egypt, had finally provided Mesopotamia with a structure that could hold an empire together even when the throne passed from great father to struggling son.

EXAMPLE RESPONSE:

   Sargon's stringent military actions and administrative policies made his conquest of Sumer swift and strong. Sargon did not leave any part of his takeover to chance. When Sargon took over a city, he replaced its leadership with his own men, ensuring the officials' allegiance to him. Once these officials were in place, Sargon was able to implement a set of standards that he could be sure would be administered correctly in all of his cities. He created a set of uniform weights and measures, and installed a tax system that was run by officials he trusted in each city. To ensure the old ruling families of Sumerian cities were appeased, Sargon kept representatives from these families at his court.

   While the system as a whole worked well when Sargon was in the height of power, some parts of his plan began to crumble towards the end of his reign. Serious rebellion broke out when Sargon was old in age. The elders of the land, who were deprived of their authority, revolted. When Sargon died and his throne was passed on to his son Rimush, five cities turned against the kingdom, and Rimush was forced to retaliate. Rimush died just shy of ten years into his reign, murdered by one of his servants. Despite these upsets, the bureaucracy and administrative structure that Sargon established held the empire together. While not everyone in the kingdom was happy, Sargon's work to build an empire based on more than just charisma kept his family in power for over a hundred years.

CHAPTER FOURTEEN: THE FIRST PLANNED CITIES

The student may use her text when answering the questions in sections I and II.

Section I: Who, What, Where

Write a one or two-sentence answer explaining the significance of each item listed below.

Citadel – **Pg. 106, ¶ 5 – A citadel, the most distinctive feature of a Harappan city, is a high section of a building surrounded by walls and watch towers. If the thick mud-brick wall of a Harappan city was breached, the population could retreat into the citadel.**

Harappa – **Pg. 104, ¶ 3 – Harappa is the namesake of the Harappan civilization. Harappa was one of the civilization's largest cities, and it was located on the northern branch of the Indus.**

Mohenjo-Daro – **Pg. 104, ¶ 3 – Mohenjo-Daro was one of the two largest cities in the Harappan civilization. It was located in the southern part of the civilization.**

Sutkagen Dor – **Pg. 106, ¶ 1 – Sutkagen Dor was the site of a Harappan trading post, just off of the Arabian Sea. Sutkagen Dor was almost within Elamite territory, suggesting the cultures had a working peace.**

Section II: Comprehension

Write a two/three sentence answer to each of the following questions.

1. What artifact leads us to believe that the Harappan cities had kings? How does the architecture of Mohenjo-Daro support the idea that there was indeed a king of the city?
A1. – Pg. 105, ¶ 1 – One of the only distinctive portraits found in the ruins of Mohenjo-Daro is the statue of a bearded man, wearing an ornate robe and a headpiece, his eyes half closed and his face expressionless. We can speculate that this was a portrait of a king of Mohenjo-Daro. The city has a series of buildings that appear to be barracks, or servants' quarters, suggesting there was a king to serve.

2. How do we know that Harappan merchants traded their goods with the people of Ur? How did Harappan merchants get to Ur?
A2. – Pg. 105, ¶ 2 to Pg. 106, ¶ 1 – We know that Harappan merchants traded in Ur because Harappan seals turned up in the ruins of Ur. Ur was close to the head of the Persian Gulf, on the southern end of the Euphrates. Indian merchants could sail out of the Indus into the Arabian Sea, up through the Gulf of Oman, north into the Persian Gulf, and from there into the Euphrates.

3. Describe the general architecture of a Harappan city, and the layout of a Harappan house. What about the planning of Harappan cities, and houses, suggests that this civilization put a high value on washing?

A3. – Pg. 106, ¶ 3 to Pg. 107, ¶ 1 – Harappan cities were low and wide, with well-planned streets, wide enough for two oxcarts to pass each other. The streets were equipped with elaborate gutters and drainage systems for waste water. Many of the larger cities had enormous swimming-pool-sized baths surrounded by smaller chambers. Storage buildings stand near the largest cities. Each city had a citadel, and was surrounded by a thick mud-brick wall. The houses, rarely more than two stories high, line the streets. The houses generally had bathrooms. The inclusion of public baths and private bathrooms suggests that the Harappans put a high value on washing and cleanliness.

ALTERNATE ANSWER: The student might have an alternate answer for the description of the general architecture of the Harappan city.
Pg. 107, ¶ 8 – The general plan of the cities was the same, with a citadel separate from the sprawl of houses and shops, and always to the west. The houses and shops, or "lower village," were organized around carefully planned streets.

4. Describe what archaeologists found as they excavated Kot Diji. What do these findings suggest about the history of the city?

A4. – Pg. 107, ¶ 4 – As archaeologists excavated Kot Diji, they found that, in the centuries before the Harappan cities grew to full size, Kot Diji's walls were reinforced against attack again and again. During the early years of Harappan dominance, theses walls were rebuilt yet again. Then a great fire swept over the city, destroying not only the walls but the city itself. A new city was built overtop of old Kot Diji. This city had wide streets, brick gutters, and houses with bathrooms. It was a Harappan city, its pattern unlike that of the town that had stood there before. This suggests that the citizens of Kot Diji were protecting themselves against Harappan attack, only to fail and have the city taken over by the Harappan people.

5. There were three kinds of roads in a typical Harappan city. What were they used for, how big were they, and how were they organized?

A5. – Pg. 108, ¶ 1 – The three types of roads in a typical Harappan city were used as main arteries, streets, and side lanes. The main arteries were twenty-four feet wide, the streets were eighteen feet wide, and the side lanes were twelve feet wide. The roads ran directly north-south or east-west, in a planned grid pattern.

6. What other relics from the Harappan excavations, beyond city planning and architecture, provide us with evidence that the Harappans were obsessed with uniformity?

A6. – Pg. 108, ¶ 1-2 – The Harappans used standardized weights, and mud bricks for building that conformed to exactly the same dimensions. Also, the building tools and artisans' utensils were organized into a standardized kit so recognizable they could be identified as Harappan from the shore of the Arabian Sea all the way north into the far Punjab.

Section III: Critical Thinking

We know very little about the Harappan people. However, archaeological clues give us some insight into the Harappan culture. While the people remain voiceless, piecing together these clues allows us to extrapolate characteristics of the Harappan civilization.

• What evidence from the chapter suggests that the Harappan cities had thriving trade?
There are three pieces of evidence from the chapter that suggest the Harappan cities had thriving trade. First, discovered in the ruins of the cities were "a whole assortment of seals used to identify goods for trading" (Pg. 104, ¶ 3). This suggests that the Harappans were active merchants. Second, Harappan seals were found at Ur, showing us that the various seals used to identify goods were in actual use. Third, the Harappans had a trading post at Sutkagen Dor, close to a water route to Mesopotamia, showing us that the Harappans had strategically placed posts that would facilitate trade. The student's answer does not need to include all three piece of evidence. Because seals are mentioned twice in the chapter, the student should include the existence of Harappan seals in her answer.

• What evidence from the chapter suggests that the Harappan cities had military might?
The strongest evidence in the chapter that suggests the military might of the Harappans is the spread of Harappan architecture. Even across half a million square miles of settlement, the Harappan cities are remarkably similar. This continuity gives us a picture of a very controlled, orderly and powerful people. Also, in the excavation at Kot Diji, the remains of walls that were reinforced again and again underneath the new Harappan city suggest that the citizens of Kot Diji were unsuccessful at keeping the Harappans out. In this answer, the student should refer directly to the spread of Harappan architecture, often over the remains of cities that were not previously Harappan.

• Using what you know from your reading, how might you explain this paragraph from the chapter:
        "What were the Harappans so afraid of that they needed two sets of walls? Neither the Sumerians nor the Elamites ever sent an army quite so far to the east. Nor is there much evidence of savage nomadic tribes in the area. Yet the double walls are high and thick, with ramparts and watchtowers: built to keep out enemies" (107).

This paragraph asks us, "What were Harappans afraid of?" This is what the student should be concerned with figuring out. From reading the 4-5 subsequent paragraphs, it seems that the Harappans, having taken over neighboring towns by force, thought that other people might try to do the same to them.

CHAPTER FIFTEEN: THE FIRST COLLAPSE OF EMPIRE

The student may use his text when answering the questions in sections I and II.

Section I: Who, What, Where

Write a one or two-sentence answer explaining the significance of each item listed below.

Khafre – Pg. 110, ¶ 2 – **Khafre was Khufu's second oldest son. Khafre took the throne of Egypt after his older brother, and then he kept the throne for over fifty years.**

NOTE TO THE INSTRUCTOR:

The text states specifically, "Khafre ruled for sixty-six years according to Manetho and fifty-six years by Herodotus's count." Since there is a discrepancy between these two histories, the answer of "over fifty years" covers both Manetho's and Herodotus's accounts.

Menkaure – **Pg. 112, ¶ 2 & Pg. 113, ¶ 2-3 – Menkaure was Khafre's son. He was a much more benevolent ruler than his father and grandfather; however his kindness was looked at by the gods as weakness, and he was punished for it with an early and abrupt death.**

Obelisk – **Pg. 115, ¶ 3 – An obelisk is a stone tower pointing upwards at the sky. Userkaf placed an obelisk with a miniature pyramid covered in gold in front of the first temple built to Ra.**

Ra – **Pg. 112, ¶ 1 – Ra was the Egyptian sun-god.**

Seheteptawy – **Pg. 116, ¶ 3 – Seheteptawy was the Horus-name of Teti, the first pharaoh of the Sixth Dynasty. Seheteptawy means "He who pacifies the Two Lands."**

ALTERNATE ANSWER: The student may include that the return of north-south hostility marked the decline of the Old Kingdom of Egypt.

Sphinx – **Pg. 110, ¶ 4 – The Sphinx is a limestone sculpture, part lion and part falcon, with a man's face, which may be Khafre's.**

ALTERNATE ANSWER: The student may include that the Sphinx is a statue made from living rock, which means it was carved on a piece of rock already sticking out of the ground (Pg. 110, ¶ 4 – Pg. 111, ¶ 1).

Section II: Comprehension

Write a two/three sentence answer to each of the following questions.

1. Why would Khafre want to guard the place where his soul would rest with the Sphinx? Also, why would Khafre put his face on the monument?
A1. – Pg. 111, ¶ 4 to Pg. 112, ¶ 1 – Khafre wanted to guard his tomb with the Sphinx because it meant that the gods were protecting him. The falcon was identified with the god Horus, and the lion was identified with the sun and thus the sun-god Ra, and Ra's divine colleague Amun. To have a statue half-lion, half-falcon, guarding the place where his soul would exist eternally was to claim the protection of Egypt's most powerful gods. By putting his own face on the Sphinx, Khafre claimed the identity of both of these gods, making him equal to Horus and Ra.

2. Menkaure reopened Egypt's temples and sanctuaries, raised the people from the misery which his predecessors had inflicted on them, and ruled them kindly. Yet, the gods were displeased with Menkaure's rule and sent him a message: he would die before his seventh year of rule. Why, if Menkaure was a benevolent ruler and a god-fearing man, did the gods want to punish him? What does Menkaure's fate tell us about the way a pharaoh was supposed to rule?
A2. – Pg. 113, ¶ 2 – The gods had planned for Egypt to suffer for a hundred and fifty years. Menkaure's acts of reformation did not follow the gods' intentions for Egypt's future. Menkaure's show of compassion to the Egyptian people was also a show of weakness; the pharaoh was supposed to show his god-like status by exploiting his power.

3. In what way did Shepseskaf's burial place mark the end of the Fourth Dynasty?
A4. – Pg. 113, ¶ 3 –Shepseskaf did not have a pyramid. He was buried in a mastaba tomb, an old-fashioned grave at the old graveyard of Saqqara, where his Third Dynasty predecessors lay. Shepseskaf's reversion to the old burial ground marked the end of the Fourth Dynasty.

4. Who could an Egyptian pharaoh marry? Why was this a problem for the continuation of the royal line?
A4 – Pg. 113, ¶ 5 & Pg. 114, ¶ 2 – Since the pharaoh was divine, he needed to marry another divinity to maintain the divinity of his heirs, so the king's siblings were the only possible wives on offer. Intermarriage of blood relations tends to reproduce a limited genetic pool, so damage in the genes is more likely to show up.

5. How does the Egyptian king list support the idea that intermarriage damaged the royal succession?
A5. – Pg. 114, ¶ 3 – The rapid falloff of the pharaoh's power after Menkaure supports the idea that intermarriage damaged the royal succession. Menkaure died very suddenly, his oldest son, Prince Khuenre, lived just long enough to be proclaimed heir, and then succumbed to some unknown illness before his father's death and Menkaure's second son, Shepseskaf, had an entirely undistinguished and brief reign.

6. What are the distinct differences between the 4th and 5th Egyptian dynasties?
A6. – Pg. 115, ¶ 1-4 – In the 5th dynasty of Egypt, the father-to-son succession was broken. Also, power shifted from the palace towards the temple. The pharaoh became more closely identified with the sun-god; he was now the son of Ra.

7. What is the significance of the demotion of 5th dynasty kings from the earthly incarnation of god to the son of a god?

A7. – Pg. 115. ¶ 5 – While the pharaoh was still divine, he was no longer the central and unquestioned conduit of power. This is reflected in his demotion from the earthly incarnation of a god to the son of a god.

8. How do we know that in the Fifth Dynasty, the king was no longer thought to live forever on earth? Where did the Egyptians now believe the king went after his death?

A8. – Pg. 115, ¶ 5 –During the Fifth Dynasty, the entire progression of the spirit after death into another world was laid out in writing for the first time. The last pharaoh of the dynasty, Unas, was buried in a small pyramid with detailed incantations written along the walls that clearly indicated that Unas was leaving his people. The king would now ascend with Ra, rise to the sky and live there forever.

9. Sixth Dynasty pharaoh Pepi II is credited with a ninety-four-year rule, yet he was placed on the throne when he was just six years old. How could Pepi II rule at such a young age, and then hold on to the throne for so long?

A9. – Pg. 116, ¶ 4 – In the Sixth Dynasty, the pharaoh ruled in name only. Noblemen, priests, and palace officials increasingly broke the kingdom apart between them. Pepi II, the last king of the Old Kingdom of Egypt, was able to rule at six, and keep the throne for so long, because he had so little actual power.

10. What were the four factors that brought an end to the Sixth Dynasty, and Old Kingdom, of Egypt?

A10. – Pg. 117, ¶ 2 – The four factors that brought an end to the Sixth Dynasty, and Old Kingdom, of Egypt were: 1) the wasteful squandering of Egyptian lives and money by the Fourth Dynasty, 2) the weakness of the royal family's genes, 3) the natural self-limiting nature of the pharaoh's divinity, and 4) drought.

Section III: Critical Thinking

In this chapter we read about the first collapse of empire – the crumbling of the Old Kingdom of Egypt. The pyramids stand as proof of the exploitation of Egyptian lives and money, and the Pyramid Texts give us a glimpse into the changing relationship between the pharaoh, his people and the gods. We also know that the desert was creeping at the edge of Egypt's cultivable land, meaning a drought most surely occurred. But what about the theory that inbreeding was partly to blame for the downfall of Egypt's empire? While we don't have hard proof, we have some circumstantial evidence that supports this theory.

Explain how each passage below indicates that inbreeding was also part of the collapse of the first Egyptian empire.

- Statues of Menkaure himself show a slightly odd-shaped head with weirdly prominent eyes.

The odd shape of Menkaure's head, and his prominent eyes, could indicate abnormal growth and development because of a birth defect or inbred/weak genes.

• Prince Khuenre lived just long enough to be proclaimed heir, and then succumbed to some unknown illness before his father's death.

A short life and quick death suggest fragility and sickness. Inbreeding causes weak genes, which could lead to both fragility and sickness.

• Shepseskaf had an entirely undistinguished and very brief reign.

The second son of Menkaure left no mark on Egyptian history. The undistinguished and brief reign suggests ineptitude, possibly caused by feeble genetics.

• There is also the survival of a story that Menkaure fell in love with his own daughter and raped her, after which she hanged herself in grief. The story also says that the daughter was Menkaure's only child, which we know is not true. Herodotus remarks, "But this is all nonsense, in my opinion."

Though this story sounds more like gossip, we can still find value in its account. This is the only story that actually mentions incest in relation to Menkaure. The fact that Herodotus believes this story untrue suggests two things: 1) that Menkaure would not need to rape his daughter in order to have sex with her and 2) that his daughter would not become so stricken with grief after sex with her father as to hang herself. While the histrionics of Menkaure's daughter's behavior seem false, especially considering that she is called Menkaure's only child, the mention of incest gives us a clue as to the role of inbreeding as part of the downfall of the Old Kingdom.

CHAPTER SIXTEEN: THE FIRST BARBARIAN INVASIONS

The student may use her text when answering the questions in sections I and II.

Section I: Who, What, Where

Write a one or two-sentence answer explaining the significance of each item listed below.

Barbarian – **Pg. 119, ¶ 5 – A barbarian is someone from outside of a kingdom, whose only purpose is to wreck and destroy.**

Gudea of Lagash – **Pg. 123, ¶ 3 & 4 – Gudea of Lagash was the first Sumerian to rid his city of the Gutians and rebuild temples, re-establish trade with the Elamites, the Indians and with northern Mesopotamia.**

Manishtushu – **Pg. 118, ¶ 1-2 – Manishtushu was Sargon's son. Manishtushu was just as warlike as his father, and continued to expand the Akkadian empire.**

Naram-Sin the Great – **Pg. 118, ¶ 3 to Pg. 119, ¶ 1 – Naram-Sin the Great was the son of Manishtushu, and the grandson of Sargon. Naram-Sin spread the Akkadian empire to its greatest extent, but also faced the invasion of barbarians.**

Third Dynasty of Ur – **Pg. 125, ¶ 3 – The Third Dynasty of Ur started with the reign of Ur-Nammu and the restoration of civilization after the Gutian invasions.**

Ur-Nammu – **Pg. 124, ¶ 3 & 4 – Ur-Nammu married Utuhegal's daughter, and took Utuhegal's throne. Under Ur-Nammu, the Sumerians enjoyed their last renaissance; he restored civilization on the plain.**

Section II: Comprehension

Write a two/three sentence answer to each of the following questions.

1. How do we know Naram-Sin the Great was considered a god? How is this relationship with godliness different from previous Mesopotamian kings?

A1. – Pg. 118, ¶ 4 to Pg. 119, ¶ 1 – Naram-Sin the Great gave himself the titles "King of the Four Quarters of the World" and "King of the Universe." His name in cuneiform appears next to a sign that indicates godship, and the Victory Stele shows his huge figure standing above his battling armies, in the position that the gods occupy in earlier engravings. Unlike previous Mesopotamian kings, Naram-Sin did not need any gods to bless his battles. Naram-Sin was the first Mesopotamian king to lay hold of godlike status during his life.

2. Explain the reason for the bilingualism of the Akkadian empire.

A2. – Pg. 119, ¶ 2 – The people who lived in the Akkadian empire were not all Akkadians. You could live in the Akkadian empire, obeying its Akkadian king, and still be a Sumerian. Sargon's sons and grandson described their victories in Sumerian cuneiform for the sake of the conquered, and in Akkadian, for the sake of themselves.

3. On page 121, an excerpt from a historical text tells us how the Akkadians viewed the Gutians. Use the note reference to correctly fill in the blanks in the sentence below.
In the book _____, translated by _____, which was published in _____, we find out exactly how the Akkadians reacted to the invading Gutians.

Then, write a sentence or two about how the Akkadians felt about the Gutians, making sure to quote the excerpted passage

A3. – a. In the book _The Education of Cyrus_, translated by <u>Wayne Ambler,</u> which was published in <u>2001</u>, we find out exactly how the Akkadians reacted to the invading Gutians.

NOTE TO INSTRUCTOR:
The student will find the reference for this excerpt in the "Notes" section of the text on page 783. In the "Notes" for Chapter 16, we see that the text is referred to as ETC. This text is first mentioned in Chapter 13, note 4 (pg. 782) as The Education of Cyrus, translated by Wayne Ambler (2001).

b. *The excerpted passage from the text reads:*
those who are not part of the Land:
the Gutians, a people with no bridle,
with minds of men, but the feelings of dogs,
with the features of monkeys.
Like small birds, they swooped over the ground in great flocks....
nothing escaped their clutches,
no one escaped their grasp.

The student may use any part of the excerpt in her answer.
Example: **Pg. 121, ¶ 1 – The Sumerians called the Gutians snakes and scorpions and parodies of men. They said the Gutians were a people "with no bridle" and "features of monkeys."**

4. What happened to Naram-Sin's empire once the Gutians attacked? Use examples from the second excerpted passage on page 121.
The second excerpted passage from the text reads:
The messenger could no longer travel the highway,
the boat of the courier could no longer travel the river....
Prisoners manned the watch,
bandits occupied the roads....
They planted gardens for themselves inside the cities,
not, as is usual, on the wide field outside.
The fields gave no grain, the floods no fish,
the orchards no syrup or wine,
the clouds did not bring rain....
Honest men were confused with traitors,

heroes lay dead in heaps on top of heroes,
the blood of traitors streamed over the blood of honest men.
The student may use any part of the excerpt in her answer.
A4. – *Example:* **When the Gutians invaded Naram-Sin's empire, "bandits occupied the roads" and "the messenger could no longer travel the highway." The Gutians turned the empire on its head, planting "gardens for themselves inside the cities/not, as is usual, on the wide field outside." The land went barren; "The fields gave no grain, the floods no fish, the orchards no syrup or wine."**

5. What did Naram-Sin do to make the gods so angry that they would send barbarians upon his empire?
A5. – Pg. 121, ¶ 4 – According to "The Cursing of Agade," Naram-Sin destroyed the great Temple of Enlil in his capital city and stole its gold, silver, and copper. This act doomed his country.

6. In what way is the damage of the Gutians linked to the destruction caused by the Great Flood?
A6. – Pg. 121, ¶ 4 to Pg. 122, ¶ 1 – In "The Cursing of Agade," the Gutian hordes came against Agade like "the roaring storm that subjugates the entire land, the rising deluge that cannot be confronted." In this passage the destructive nature of the Gutians is compared to the devastation caused by the Great Flood. Their invasion of Mesopotamia was as tragic to civilization as the Great Flood.

7. Shar-kali-sharri battled what two forces that sought to destroy the Akkadian empire?
A7. – Pg. 122, ¶ 3 – Shar-kali-sharri continued to fight the invading Gutians. While Shar-kali-sharri was fighting the Gutians, other cities freed themselves from an allegiance to the Akkadian king. Not only was Shar-kali-sharri fighting with barbarians, he was also dealing with anarchy.

8. What historical evidence tells us the Gutians did not have a culture of their own?
A8. – Pg. 123, ¶ 1 – It is actually a lack of historical evidence that tells us the Gutians did not have a culture of their own. The left behind no writing, no inscriptions or statues and no centers of worship.

9. What did Utuhegal do to claim the title "The King of the Four Quarters?"
A9. – Pg. 124, ¶ 1 & 2 – Utuhegal drove the Gutians out of Uruk, Ur, Eridu and Nippur. Freeing Nippur from the Gutians symbolized the final freedom of the plain from the Gutian hordes. Utuhegal captured the strongest Gutian leader, marched him into his court in handcuffs, and "set his foot upon his neck." These actions led Utuhegal to claim the title "The King of the Four Quarters."

10. How did Ur-Nammu use diplomacy to restore order and civilization to Sumer?
A10. – Pg. 125, ¶ 2 – In a diplomatic move, Ur-Nammu married the daughter of the king of the city of Mari. Also, he built temples in cities all up and down the plain, including a new temple to the great god Enlil.

Section III: Critical Thinking

"No one calls himself a barbarian, that's what your enemy call you."

-historian David McCullough

While it is clear from our reading in this chapter that the Gutian invasions of Akkadian lands were terribly destructive, how did they benefit Akkadian culture? Though the Gutians overwhelmed the Akkadian civilization at one point, how did the Akkadians win in the eyes of history?

A good place to start answering this question is to think back to Chapter 1. In Chapter 1 we learn about the distinction between the wandering shepherd and the civilized basketmaker. You will recall that Inanna rejects Dumuzi because he is an uncivilized shepherd. The Gutians provide the same contrast to the whole of civilization on the Mesopotamian plain. While chaos threatened the established order, the cultural identity of the Akkadians became very clear against the Gutians. The world of the Gutians was scattered and chaotic, where the Akkadians were orderly and civilized. Though the Akkadian empire was made up of different peoples – Sumerians and Elamites – all of the civilized people were different than the Gutians. The civilized people were united as one against the evil barbarians.

The second part of this question is meant to push the student to think about historical records. While the Gutians may have disrupted life in Mesopotamia, their legacy exists only in Akkadian history. The Gutians did not leave behind inscriptions or steles – nothing to tell us their story. The Gutian invasions are retold only through the historical record of the civilized Akkadian culture.

CHAPTER SEVENTEEN: THE FIRST MONOTHEIST

The student may use his text when answering the questions in sections I and II.

Section I: Who, What, Where

Write a one or two-sentence answer explaining the significance of each item listed below.

Hagar – **Pg. 133, ¶ 4 – Hagar, Sarai's servant, was borrowed by Abram as a second and unofficial wife in order to make an heir. Hagar gave birth to Ishmael, the father of the Arab people.**

Ishmael – **Pg. 135, ¶ 9 & Pg. 136, ¶ 1 – Ishmael was the son of Abram and Hagar. He is known in history as the father of the Arab people, and, with his father, was the first to worship Allah, the one God, rather than the stars, the moon, or the sun.**

Jericho – **Pg. 130, ¶ 3 – Jericho is one of the oldest cities in the world. There was a huge stone wall around the city, with a circular tower at the corner that rose thirty-five feet high so that watchmen could keep a constant eye on the surrounding land.**

Nuzi Tablets – **Pg. 133, ¶ 4 – The Nuzi Tablets present a set of Sumerian codes, one of which says a second and unofficial wife could be taken by a Sumerian man in order to create a child.**

Terah – **Pg. 127, ¶ 1 & 2 – Terah was the father of Abram, and traced his ancestry back to the Semites. Terah took his family out of Ur during the Gutian invasions.**

YHWH – **Pg. 128, ¶ 2 & 4 – YHWH is the name of God. Abram heard the voice of YHWH, which told him that Abram will be made into a great nation and will be blessed, but that Abram must leave his county and his people and go to Canaan.**

Section II: Comprehension

Write a two/three sentence answer to each of the following questions.

1. Why is it important for YHWH to rename Abram and Sarai, Abraham and Sarah?

A1. – Pg. 128, ¶ 3 – Abram and Sarai, like most Ur natives, most likely worshiped the moon-god Sin and his daughter Inanna. YHWH renames Abram and Sarai as part of the making of a covenant. The new names, Abraham and Sarah, both contain the new syllable *ah,* the first syllable of the covenant name YHWH, a name which reclaims them from the possession of Ur and transfers ownership to the God of Genesis.

2. Where was Shechem? Why was Abram uneasy about carrying out God's covenant in Shechem?
A2. – Pg. 129, ¶ 4 & 5 – Shechem was west of the Jordan River and halfway between the two bodies of water later known as the Sea of Galilee and the Dead Sea. Abram was unsure about God's covenant because Shechem was already full of Canaanites.

3. How did trade with Egypt help the economies of Byblos and Ebla?
A3. – Pg. 130, ¶ 5 – The city of Byblos built its entire economy on shipping cedars down to Egypt in exchange for Egyptian linen and precious metals. Ebla collected taxes from caravans that passed through the city between the Western Semitic cities and Egypt.

4. In what way did the failure of cropland and the fall of the Old Kingdom cause problems for the Western Semites?
A4. – Pg. 131, ¶ 3 – Failure of the cropland because of overplanting and drought meant that the people of Canaan had to disperse in order to find food and water. The collapse of the Old Kingdom meant that the Western Semites lost their wealthiest and most consistent trading partner, further damaging the general economy of the cities.

5. When Abram and Sarai moved to Egypt, why did Abram tell the nameless pharaoh that Sarai was his sister? How did this decision benefit Abram?
A5. – Pg. 133, ¶ 1 & 2 – Abram thought that because of Sarai's beauty, the pharaoh would kill him in order to have Sarai. If Sarai was Abram's sister, there would be no need to kill Abram. When Abram arrived in Egypt, he was right in his assumptions and the pharaoh took Sarai for his own. Abram was given Egyptian sheep, cows, donkey, camels, and servants from the pharaoh as a thank you for bringing Sarai to Egypt.

6. How does Abram's plan to father a child with Hagar as a substitute for the child Sarai had not yet conceived backfire?
A6. – Pg. 134, ¶ 1 – God made his promise of a new nation to Abram and Sarai, not Abram alone. An heir made with Hagar would not count as the birth of a new nation.

7. What happened when a man other than Abram had a physical relationship with Sarai? Why is this important for the story of Abram and Sarai?
A7. – Pg. 133, ¶ 2 & Pg. 134, ¶ 2 & 3 – When a man other than Abram tried to have a physical relationship with Sarai, something would go terribly wrong in his household. In Egypt, Sarai's presence brought the plague to the pharaoh and his household. In Gerar, the king and his harem were rendered barren until Sarai was returned to Abram. God wanted Sarai and Abram to father his new nation, and if another man got in the way, a curse would be brought upon his house.

8. When God's promise to Abram and Sarai is finally fulfilled, how is their child, Isaac, differentiated from the people that came before him?
A8. – Pg. 135, ¶ 4 – When the promise of God is finally fulfilled and Isaac is born, a new race is created and given a physical mark as a sign of the covenant. Abram, Isaac and the rest of their family were circumcised as a sign of their separateness.

9. While Abram turned away from the worship of the moon-god, how did Shulgi trumpet his worship of the celestial divinity?
A9. – Pg. 137, ¶ 1 – In gratitude to the moon-god Nanna, Shulgi built the largest ziggurat of Ur. It was an enormous structure for worship, named in Sumerian "The House Whose Foundation is Clothed in Terror."

Section III: Critical Thinking

- What is race? Consult your dictionary, and record the definition of race as related to humans.

- How is race different from identity? In your answer, use the example of different people in Sargon's empire.

- If Abram was of the same blood as the people that came before him, how could he be of a different race? How is Abram's monotheism inextricable from his race?

- **In the first point the student will look up the definition of race. A generic definition is "a group of persons related by a common descent or heredity."**

- **In the second point, the student should think about the difference between a barbarian and a city dweller. The passage in the chapter that refers to Sargon's empire is on page 135. It reads:**

In Sumer, from the earliest times, the primary identity of its people had not been as "Sumerians." They had been citizens of Ur, citizens of Lagash, citizens of Uruk, each paying primary loyalty to a different deity while acknowledging the existence of the others. The rise of Sargon's Akkadian empire, with its clear differentiation between Sumerians and Akkadians, had brought about a change: two peoples within one set of political boundaries, with a common identity ("subjects of Sargon") that nevertheless had not removed their basic difference. The raiding Gutians had further clarified this: two different peoples could nevertheless share an identity as civilized that set them off, together, against the contrast of a third.

While a citizen of Sargon's empire may have different roots from the artisan next to him, the two are both civilized. Race is hereditary, where identity is a way of relating to a particular way of life; it is a characteristic rather than a bloodline.

- **Third point asks the student to understand the covenant made between Abraham, Sarah and YHWH. On page 129, the text states "By blood Abram was no different from the Semites around him, and not so different from the people who inhabited the land he was headed towards. But by divine fiat, he was separated from the rest and began something new: one Semite out of the rest, one God rising above the chaos of polytheism." Abram was the first man to believe in a single God, and it was this single God that told Abram that both he and his wife, and his future children, would be different from everyone else. Abram's blood was special because it was blood touched by God.**

CHAPTER EIGHTEEN: THE FIRST ENVIRONMENTAL DISASTER

The student may use her text when answering the questions in sections I and II.

Section I: Who, What, Where

Write a one or two-sentence answer explaining the significance of each item listed below.

Shu-Sin – **Pg. 139, ¶ 2 & 3 – Shu-Sin was the grandson of Shulgi, and it was during Shu-Sin's reign that the Sumerian culture began to fall apart. Shu-Sin had to deal with disappearing fertile land and the threat of invasion by Western Semitic nomads.**

The Martu/Amurru – **Pg. 139, ¶ 3 – The Martu, or Amurru, were Western Semitic nomads who roved along the western border between Canaan and the neo-Sumerian realm. The Martu wanted to take control of the remaining fertile land in Sumer.**

Ibbi-Sin – **Pg. 141, ¶ 2 & Pg. 143, ¶ 3 – Ibbi-Sin inherited a crumbling Sumerian empire from his father Shu-Sin. Ibbi-Sin was king when Ur fell to the Elamites, and he could not stop the death of the Sumerian culture.**

Ishbi-Erra – **Pg. 141, ¶ 4 & Pg. 143, ¶ 2 – Ishbi-Erra took advantage of the weakness of the king of Ur, Ibbi-Sin, and usurped the throne of Sumer. Ishbi-Erra called himself the first king of the Isin Dynasty.**

Kindattu – **Pg. 143, ¶ 3 – Kindattu was the king of the Elamites when they destroyed Ur and ended the Sumerian era.**

Nanna – **Pg. 143, ¶ 4 to Pg. 144, ¶ 1 – Nanna was the moon god and the patron deity of Ur. Nanna let his people down when he could not protect Ur from the invading Elamites.**

Section II: Comprehension

Write a two/three sentence answer to each of the following questions.

1. Describe the process of salinization. What happens when the ground is salinized?
A1. – Pg. 139, ¶ 5 to Pg. 140, ¶ 1 – Salinization occurs when salt water evaporates and leaves more salt on the ground than there was before. When ground becomes salinized, crops refuse to grow.

2. Why did Sumerians switch from growing wheat to growing barley?
A2. – Pg. 140, ¶ 1 – Wheat is particularly sensitive to salt in the earth. Sumerians switched over from growing wheat to growing barley because barley can tolerate more salt in the soil.

3. What is weed fallowing? What is the benefit of weed fallowing? What did practicing weed fallowing mean for the food supply of the Sumerian people?
A3. – Pg. 140, ¶ 3 – Weed fallowing is a practice where crops are only planted every other year. The benefit of weed fallowing is that weeds with deep roots have time to grow, which lowers the water table and allows salt to wash back down beneath the topsoil. Weed fallowing did not solve the problem of feeding the Sumerian people. While the earth was replenishing itself, crops could not grow, and the Sumerian people had nothing to eat.

4. Why was the fertile land in Mesopotamia so scarce?
A4. – Pg. 140, ¶ 4 – The Mesopotamian plain did not have an unlimited expanse of fields; it is what anthropologists call "circumscribed agricultural land," sharply defined by surrounding mountains and deserts. This meant that there was only a small part of the land that could actually be used to produce grain.

5. How did the lack of grain in Sumer lead to the Ur III Dynasty's inability to defend itself?
A5. – Pg. 140, ¶ 5 – The growing scarcity of grain made the Sumerian population generally hungrier, less healthy, and less able to defend itself. Without the full grain tax, the Ur III Dynasty could not pay its soldiers, and those who trespassed on the Sumerian land could not be easily driven away.

6. The invading Amorites were not the only threat to Ibbi-Sin's empire. Chronicle the rebellion of the Sumerian people caused by famine and discontent during Ibbi-Sin's early reign.
A6. – Pg. 141, ¶ 2 – When Ibbi-Sin had been on the throne for two years, Eshnunna, in the far north of the remaining empire, rebelled and refused to pay tribute, and Ibbi-Sin did not have the soldiers to bring the city back into the fold. The year afterwards, the Elamite king of Anshan drove the Sumerians back out of Susa. Two years later, Umma broke free. In the eighth year of Ibbi-Sin's reign, the prestigious city of Nippur refused to acknowledge his lordship any longer.

7. In a last resort to feed his people, Ibbi-Sin sent Ishbi-Erra north to get grain and meat. How did Ibbi-Sin's plan backfire?
A7. – Pg. 141, ¶ 4 – While Ibbi-Sin trusted Ishbi-Erra to bring food back from the north, Ishbi-Erra saw this as a time to take advantage of Ibbi-Sin's weakness. Ishbi-Erra blackmailed Ibbi-Sin; he sent a message to the weak king from Isin saying the only way he could bring grain back to Ur was if Ibbi-Sin sent six hundred boats upriver, and if Ishbi-Erra was put in charge of both Isin and Nippur.

8. In what way was the fall of Ur symbolic of the fall of the Sumerian culture? Use the poem on page 143 to help answer this question. **A8. – Pg. 143, ¶ 2-4 – The north of Sumer was taken over by Ishbi-Erra, and the new Isin Dynasty was formed. What was left of Sumer was Ur. The newly reunited Elamites were ready to revenge themselves by destroying Ur, the last remaining mainstay of Sumerian culture. A poem mourning the fall of Ur equates the death of the city to the death of Sumerian cultural practices: "on the streets where festivals had been held, heads lay scattered/where dances had been held, bodies were stacked in heaps."**

The poem on page 143 reads:

Corpses were piled at the lofty city gates,
on the streets where festivals had been held, heads lay scattered,
where dances had been held, bodies were stacked in heaps….
In the river, dust has gathered,
no flowing water is carried through the city,
the plain that was covered in grass has become cracked like a kiln.

The student should at least use the parts of the poem that reflect cultural activity in her answer (Lines 1-3).

9. What did the fall of Ur mean for the relationship of the Sumerians with the moon-god Nanna, and the other patron deities of Sumerian cities?
A9. – Pg. 143, ¶ 4 to Pg. 144, ¶ 1 - Ur's collapse showed the powerlessness of the moon god Nanna and the patron deities of the fallen cities. Nanna could not even protect his own temple against the invading Elamites. The gods had lost their potency.

Section III: Critical Thinking

This chapter is called "The First Environmental Disaster." While you may have expected content that was similar to the flood stories we read about in Chapter Two, this environmental disaster was much more complicated. Write a paragraph, in your own words, explaining how the environment of Sumer during the Ur III dynasty was to blame for the fall of Sumer.

In this critical thinking question, it is important for the student to connect famine with civil unrest. While the title of the chapter, "The First Environmental Disaster" connotes a single devastating event, the disaster was really a series of events that were caused by a major environmental problem. The environmental problem was the very salty soil in Sumer. The disaster was the breakdown of Sumer's bureaucracy because of hungry and unhappy citizens.

When the ground became too salty to grow wheat and barley, the Sumerians faced a grain shortage. They could not easily move to new fertile land because they were walled in by mountains and deserts. A shortage of grain not only meant less bread for the people, it also meant less food for animals. Thus, there was less meat for human consumption. With little to no produce to tax, Sumer's bureaucratic system fell apart. Without money from taxes, Sumer's soldiers were not paid, and so Sumer's defense system was very weak. The only way to compensate the military commanders was with titles, and so the power of the king decreased as different soldiers grew strong. Hungry and angry citizens followed newly powerful military commanders. Invaders could take over small bits of fertile land because there were no soldiers to protect Sumer's fields. Ultimately, the entire Sumerian civilization unraveled because the land could not produce food for its people.

Chapter Nineteen: The Battle for Reunification

The student may use his text when answering the questions in sections I and II.

Section I: Who, What, Where

Write a one or two-sentence answer explaining the significance of each item listed below.

Achthoes/Akhtoy I – **Pg. 147, ¶ 1-2 – Achthoes was the founder of the Ninth Dynasty of Egypt. In reality Achthoes was only the governor of the province centered at Herakleopolis, not the pharaoh of all Egypt.**

Amenemhet I – **Pg. 149, ¶ 7 – Amenemhet I was the first king of Egypt's twelfth dynasty.**

Itj-taway – **Pg. 149, ¶ 7 – Itj-taway, meaning "Seizer of the Two Lands," is the name of the capital city Amenemhet built to celebrate his hold over Egypt.**

Mentuhotep – **Pg. 148, ¶ 4-6 & Pg. 149, ¶ 3-4 – Mentuhotep, the king of Thebes, successfully took over Herakleopolis, and was known as a second Narmer. His reign marked the end of the First Intermediate Period, and the beginning of the Middle Kingdom.**

Nomarch – **Pg. 147, ¶ 4 – A nomarch was the governor of a provincial area of Egypt.**

Nome – **Pg. 147, ¶ 4 – A nome was the territory ruled by a nomarch.**

Section II: Comprehension

Write a two/three sentence answer to each of the following questions.

1. Manetho says that Akhtoy's Ninth Dynasty was followed by a Tenth Dynasty and then neatly by an Eleventh Dynasty. However, in actuality, the Ninth, Tenth, and Eleventh Dynasties ruled simultaneously. How was this possible?

A1. – Pg. 147, ¶ 4 –The Ninth, Tenth, and Eleventh Dynasties could rise simultaneously because each Dynasty corresponded to a different section of Egypt, ruled by a distinct nomarch. Not one of these nomarchs had control over all of Egypt.

2. Why did Intef I call himself "King of Upper and Lower Egypt"?

A2. – Pg. 148, ¶ 3 – Intef I wanted to claim authenticity for his kingship. He called himself "King of Upper and Lower Egypt" because it put him firmly into the tradition of Upper Egyptian pharaohs who had managed to bring the rebellious north back under control.

3. What obstacles did Mentuhotep face as he fought his way into Lower Egypt? What evidence suggests Mentuhotep was a fierce warrior?

A3. – Pg. 148, ¶ 5 – Mentuhotep had to campaign against the soldiers of the northern king. He also had to fight the nomarchs that stood in his way. There is at least one mass grave of sixty soldiers killed in the same battle at Abydos, suggesting the ferocity of Mentuhotep's fighting.

4. What clue do we have from Egyptian portraits of royal officials during Mentuhotep's rise to power that supports the idea that Mentuhotep was a powerful and dangerous man?

A4. – Pg. 149, ¶ 2 –Portraits of Egyptian royal officials during Mentuhotep's rise to power tend to show them carrying weapons, rather than papyri or other tools of office. This supports the idea that Mentuhotep was a powerful and dangerous man because the royal officials had to carry weapons with them to work just in case of attack.

5. What was Mentuhotep's Horus-name, and why was it significant to Egyptian history?

A5. – Pg. 149, ¶ 3 – Mentuhotep's Horus-name was "Uniter of the Two Lands." Referencing the old paradigm of civil war gave Mentuhotep the credibility he needed to be seen as a great pharaoh who had rescued Egypt once again. Mentuhotep eventually was praised as a second Narmer, equal to the legendary king who had first pulled Upper and Lower Egypt together into one.

6. Describe the "Prophecy of Nerferti" - how did it come into being, and where was it from? What did the prophecy predict about the new king and his relationship with the Asiatics? Use at least two lines from the actual prophecy in your answer.

A6. – Pg. 149, ¶ 8 to Pg. 150, ¶ 1 – The Prophecy of Nerferti was commissioned by Amenemhet I. The prophecy was supposedly from the reign of King Snefru five hundred years before. It begins with King Snefru brooding over the possibility that Egypt will fall to Asiatic invaders from the east. However, King Snefru's sage predicted "A king will come from the South/He will take the White Crown, He will wear the Red Crown" and the threatening Asiatics "will fall to his sword."

The prophecy on page 150 reads:

A king will come from the South....
He will take the White Crown,
He will wear the Red Crown....
Asiatic will fall to his sword,
Rebels to his wrath, traitors to his might....
[He] will build the Walls-of-the-Ruler
To bar Asiatics from entering Egypt.

The student can use any part of the inscription, however the student must mention that the prophecy says the Asiatic will fall to the new king's sword, or that the Asiatics will be kept out of Egypt by the Walls-of-the-Ruler.

7. Who was Sinuhe? Write a two/three sentence summary of the "Tale of Sinuhe."

A7. – Pg. 150, ¶ 6 to Pg. 151 ¶ 2 – Sinuhe was a courtier in Amenemhet's court. In the "Tale of Sinuhe," Senusret I learns of his father's death while campaigning down south and quickly returns to Itj-taway. Sinuhe, sure that he will be suspected of involvement in the crime, flees to Canaan. Much later, Sinuhe returns to his native land and is pardoned by Senusret, but not before he is shaved all over, since exile among the Western Semites had made him shaggy.

8. What two practices in the Twelfth Dynasty reflect the continuing transition of the pharaoh from god to man?

A8. – Pg. 152, ¶ 3 – Senusret made his son co-regent a few years before his death, which meant his son had power before Senusret actually died. This overturned the old belief that the king died and then was reborn as his son. Also, Twelfth Dynasty statues of kings looked much more like portraits of real people, unlike the immobile god-faces of the Fourth Dynasty rulers.

9. Why was Senusret III's fortress at Buhen so large, and heavily fortified?

A9. – Pg. 152, ¶ 4 & Pg. 153, ¶ 1 – Senusret III's fortress at Buhen was so large and heavily fortified because of the Egyptian mistreatment of the Nubian people. The Egyptians guarded themselves from any Nubian backlash by living inside the thick walls of the fort at Buhen.

Section III: Critical Thinking

Amenemhet I's rise to power, and what he did while on the throne, were very much in line with the actions of the great pharaohs of the Old Kingdom. However, unlike the pharaohs of the Fourth Dynasty, Amenemhet was not considered a god. Write a short paragraph describing what Amenemhet did while in power that mimicked the great pharaohs of Egypt's past. Then, write a short paragraph detailing how Amenemhet created a divine legacy for himself to make up for the his humanity.

The answer to this question is very straightforward. The parenthetical citations are for parent use only. The student should NOT use his text when answering the question.

Amenemhet I put himself into the line of great unifiers, like Narmer, by building himself a brand-new capital city, Itj-taway. Itj-taway means "Seizer of Two Lands," thus associating Amenemhet with the traditional north-south conflict (Pg. 149, ¶ 7). Near the end of his reign, Amenemhet I built himself a small pyramid near Itj-taway. The pyramid stood as a monument to the return of the old order (Pg. 150, ¶ 3). In this way, Amenemhet was like the great pharaohs Narmer, Khufu and Khafre.

Amenemhet had to do something that would give him a strong link to the divine. Amenemhet

commissioned scribes to write a "prophecy" about him, a document which began to circulate through Egypt very near the beginning of his reign. The prophecy said that a king will come from the South to unite Egypt and keep out Asiatics, rebels and traitors (Pg. 149, ¶ 8 to Pg. 150, ¶ 1). Amenemhet then proceeded to carry out the prophecy. Fulfilling the terms of the vision he had commissioned, Amenemhet's actions seemed to come from the gods. This made Amenemhet appear more divine than human, thus circumventing the transition of the pharaoh from god to man.

Chapter Twenty: The Mesopotamian Mixing Bowl

The student may use her text when answering the questions in sections I and II.

Section I: Who, What, Where

Write a one or two-sentence answer explaining the significance of each item listed below.

1794 BC – **Pg. 161, ¶ 3 – In 1794 BC, the Mesopotamian plain was ruled by two powerful men – Rim-Sin to the south, and Shamshi-Adad to the north.**

Assyria – **Pg. 160, ¶ 4 – Assyria is the empire composed of the triangle of land between the upper Tigris and Lower Zab river, cornered by the three cities of Assur, Arbela and Nineveh.**

Gungunum – **Pg. 156, ¶ 8 to Pg. 158, ¶ 3 – Gungunum was the fifth king of Larsa, and an Amorite. He took control of Susa, Nippur and Ur.**

Hammurabi – **Pg. 161, ¶ 5 & Pg. 162, ¶ 3 – Hammurabi was the great-great-great-grandson of Sumu-abum. Hammurabi used strategic warfare and diplomacy to strengthen his growing kingdom.**

Ishbi-Erra – **Pg. 155, ¶ 1 & Pg. 156, ¶ 4 – Ishbi-Erra, firmly in control of Isin, wished to establish a new Sumerian dynasty. When he died, he was in control of Isin, Nippur, Uruk, and Ur.**

Rim-Sin – **Pg. 159, ¶ 4 & 5 – Rim-Sin, the son of an Elamite warrior-chief, ruled in Larsa on his father's behalf and restored the city's might. He continue to expand his empire until he ruled almost all of southern Mesopotamia.**

Shamshi-Adad – **Pg. 160, ¶ 1 to ¶ 4 – Shamshi-Adad was the first man to rule over Assyria. He had the largest extent of any ancient king's reign, outside of Egypt.**

Section II: Comprehension

Write a two/three sentence answer to each of the following questions.

1. In what ways did the Amorite presence in Mesopotamia hinder Ishbi-Erra from going after Eshnunna and Larsa?
A1. – Pg. 156, ¶ 1 & 2 – Eshnunna was far located far north of Isin, and Amorites stood in Ishbi-Erra's path from his city to the northern defector. Larsa's kingship had been claimed by an Amorite, which made it difficult for Ishbi-Erra to attack the city.

2. Describe Ishbi-Erra's victory over the Elamites and his recapture of Ur. Use the poem on page 156 in your answer.
A2. – Pg. 156, ¶ 2 & 3 – Ishbi-Erra fortified his own city of Isin, and built up his army in

preparation for an attack on Ur. Near the end of his reign, Ishbi-Erra swept down from the north "On a great chariot/he rode into the city in victory," and "he took its gold and jewels." *The poem on page 156 reads:*

Ishbi-Erra approached the enemy,
and they did not escape his power, there on the plain of Urim.
On a great chariot,
he rode into the city in victory,
he took its gold and jewels,
and the news was brought to… [the] king of Elam.

3. What cities made up Ishbi-Erra's kingdom?
A3. – Pg. 156, ¶ 4 – **Ishbi-Erra's four-city kingdom was made up of Isin, Nippur, Uruk, and Ur.**

4. While the Isin dynasty of Ishbi-Erra and the Amorite kings of Larsa fought it out against each other on the southern plain, what were the cities of Assur and Mari doing in the north of Mesopotamia?
A4. – Pg. 156, ¶ 6 – **Up in the north, the cities of Assur and Mari started to reassert their own independence. Assur rebuilt its walls and began trading with the Western Semites near the Mediterranean coast; merchants from Assur even built their own little trading colonies on the eastern edge of Asia Minor. Mari was doing the same.**

5. How was Sumu-abum's rule in Babylon different from the leadership of the other cities of the Sumerian plain at the time of his rule?
A5. – Pg. 158, ¶ 5 to Pg. 159, ¶ 2 – **Sumu-abum built walls around Babylon, made himself king and named his son as heirs. Apart from Sumu-abum, none of the other cities of the Sumerian plain were blessed with distinguished leadership. Petty king succeeded petty king without leaving much in the way of tracks behind.**

6. Recount the embarrassing shift of power at Isin that followed the oracle's prediction that disaster was heading Erra-imitti's way.
A6. – Pg. 159, ¶ 2 & 3 – **Once Erra-imitti learned of the oracle, he decided to follow a scapegoat ritual and hire a groundskeeper to be king-for-a-day, who would be ceremonially executed at the end of the day, fulfilling the omen and leaving the real king unscathed. Unfortunately, during his time off, Erra-imitti went to eat a bowl of soup and died sipping from it – he most probably poisoned. With the king dead, the groundskeeper refused to give up the throne and reigned for twenty-four years.**

7. What was happening in Assur when Rim-Sin took over Uruk?
A7. – Pg. 159, ¶ 7 to Pg. 160, ¶ 1 – **While Rim-Sin was marching to Uruk, the king of Eshnunna decided to take advantage of the southern chaos to extend his own territory northwards. He marched up the Tigris, knocked the Amorite king of Assur off his throne, and entrusted the city to his son. The king of Eshnunna's son was not long in power; Shamshi-Adad marched on Assur and ascended the throne himself.**

8. In what way was Babylon's location on the Mesopotamian plain an advantage to Hammurabi and his expanding empire?

A8. – Pg. 161, ¶ 6 – Babylon was a little too far south of Assur to worry Shamshi-Adad, and too far north of Larsa to threaten Rim-Sin. This allowed Hammurabi to slowly claim control of nearby cities in central Mesopotamia, like Kish and Borsippa.

9. What were the terms of Hammurabi and Shamshi-Adad's official relationship?
A9. – Pg. 162, ¶ 2 –Hammurabi and Shamshi-Adad made a formal alliance, bound by oath. The language of the oath stated that Hammurabi acknowledged Shamshi-Adad as his superior.

10. What diplomatic moves did Hammurabi make after the death of Shamshi-Adad? How did Rim-Sin react to Hammurabi's actions?
A10. – Pg. 162, ¶ 3 & 4 –Hammurabi established friendly relations with Shamshi-Adad's son Yasmah-Adad, who was still ruling as king at Mari. Hammurabi also made friends with the kings of Eshnunna and Aleppo. In response, Rim-Sin built alliances with the Elamites, the king of Malgium, the king of Eshnunna and with the Gutians, hoping to trap Hammurabi from both north and south.

Section III: Critical Thinking

The student may NOT use her text to answer this question.

During the tumultuous time we read about in "The Mesopotamian Mixing Bowl," a king had to take drastic measures to keep his power. This was especially true in the case of Gungunum, the fifth king of Larsa. He declared himself the divine protector of the ancient city of Ur, and commissioned poems that promised the moon-god that he longed to restore the city's ancient ways. Write a paragraph explaining why this was an extreme move. What did Gungunum have to gain by making this declaration? In what way did Gungunum's capture of Ur and his promise to Nanna exemplify "The Mesopotamian Mixing Bowl?"

To answer this question, the student should remember that Sumerians enjoyed their last great time of power and prosperity during the Third Dynasty of Ur. After famine destroyed Ur, invading Elamites sacked the city. The fall of Ur was seen as the fall of the entire Sumerian culture. When Gungunum declared loyalty to the moon-god Nanna, he forsake his Amorite ancestry to protect a Sumerian god. That was a big step to take in order to secure rule over a city.

On page 158 of the text, we are given an excerpt from one of Gungunum's commissioned poems, "You, Nanna, are beloved of the king Gungunum... He will restore your city for you; he will bring back for you the scattered peoples of Sumer and Akkad; in your Ur, the ancient city, the city of the great divine powers, the house which never diminished, may Gungunum live for many days!" It is clear from this passage that Gungunum believes that if he can restore Ur to its former greatness, he will be blessed by Nanna and live for a long time. This suggests that Gungunum believes he will gain protection from Nanna in exchange for his service to Ur.

Gungunum, an Amorite, promises to bring the peoples of Sumer and Akkad back to Ur. The people of Ur are bound by the city, but are disparate in their ancestry and beliefs. In this way, the city of Ur itself becomes a mixing bowl.

CHAPTER TWENTY-ONE: THE OVERTHROW OF THE XIA

The student may use his text when answering the questions in sections I and II.

Section I: Who, What, Where

Write a one or two-sentence answer explaining the significance of each item listed below.

Jie – Pg. 168, ¶ 1 – Jie, the last Xia king, alienated himself from his courtiers, his people and the lords of the Longshan villages. When his throne was attacked, he fled from the capital city and died in exile.

Qi – Pg. 166, ¶ 2 & 3 – Qi was Yü's son. He succeeded his father, ushering in an era of blood succession, beginning the Xia Dynasty.

Shao-Kang – Pg. 167, ¶ 2 & 3 – Shao-Kang was Qi's great-great-nephew. After the chaotic years of the blood succession following Qi's death, Shao-Kang was able to challenge the usurper of the Chinese kingship, kick him off the throne, and restore the Xia Dynasty.

Tang – Pg. 168, ¶ 2 & 3 – Tang was a village patriarch arbitrarily jailed by Jie. Eventually Tang kicked Jie off the throne, and became the first emperor of the Shang Dynasty.

Yi – Pg. 165, ¶ 5 – Yi was the name of the walled settlements along the Yellow River during the age of Yü.

Yü – Pg. 164, ¶ 1 – Yü was the last of the Three Sage Kings.

Section II: Comprehension

Write a two/three sentence answer to each of the following questions.

1. What did Yü do to earn his place as a Sage King?
A1. – Pg. 164, ¶ 3 to Pg. 165, ¶ 1 – Yü was a vassal recruited to solve the problem of the Yellow River floods. Yü worked for thirteen years, planning ditches and canals, building embankments and dikes, directing the Yellow river floods into irrigation and away from the settlements threatened by waters. Yü's efforts earned him his place on the Chinese throne.

2. What was a patriarch in the context of the Longshan culture?
A2. – Pg. 165, ¶ 2 – A Longshan patriarch was the title given to the governors of the walled villages in the valley at the southern bend of the Yellow River. The patriarch was a strong family head who allied himself with other village patriarchs through intermarriage and conquest.

3. Where was Erlitou located? Why was it a good place for Yü's capital city?

A3. – Pg. 165, ¶ 4 – Erlitou was located just below the southern bend of the Yellow River in a valley formed by the Lo River. It was a good place for a capital city because the land around it was unusually good, since it was fertilized by silt deposits. Also, the ring of mountains surrounding the valley on three sides acted as walls and made Erlitou easy to defend.

4. Why did the Chinese move from choosing a worthy successor to be king to an era of blood succession?

A4. – Pg. 166, ¶ 2 – Yü tried to follow the examples of the Sage Kings and pick a worthy heir to his throne, bypassing his son, Qi. Unfortunately the powerful patriarchs of the villages disagreed with his choice and instead supported Qi. The patriarchs wanted to have a hereditary dynasty.

5. What did Qi do to silence his dissenters in the village of Youhu?

A5. – Pg. 166, ¶ 3 – Qi sent his army to round up any dissenters in Youhu. He defeated any Youhu resistance and destroyed the village.

6. Give a brief account of the first years of Xia blood succession and the chaos that followed.

A6. – Pg. 167, ¶ 1 – After Qi's death, his five sons fought over the kingship because there were no conventions to guide the Xia state in the peaceful transfer of the crown from one generation to the next. The son who triumphed did not take his job seriously and spent his time carousing and womanizing, rather than ruling. In response, a powerful village patriarch mounted an attack on the palace and took the throne away from Qi's son. In turn, the patriarch was murdered by a court official, who seized the throne for himself.

7. Explain Jie's last words: "I should have killed Tang when I had the chance."

A7. – Pg. 168, ¶ 1 to ¶ 4 – Jie arrested anyone who might pose a challenge to his rule. One of the village patriarchs arbitrarily jailed was a man named Tang, a member of the Shang clan, who held enough power over the lands east of Erlitou to appear threatening. For some reason, Jie set Tang free. Eventually Tang claimed the divine right to take vengeance against evil, and led his followers against the emperor. Jie fled from the capital city and died in exile. If Jie had killed Tang when he was first jailed, Jie would not have been forced to flee Erlitou.

Section III: Critical Thinking

This chapter introduced two very important ideas about Chinese dynastic rule: 1) the greatest threat to a Chinese king's power came from his own nature, and 2) there was a particular cycle related to the Chinese throne. Explain what each of these important ideas means, and then write a few sentences explaining how these two major points are inextricable from one another. Make sure to include examples from the chapter as proof of your point.

Part Three: Struggle

When China was ruled by the Sage Kings, each king had to earn his place on the throne. When blood succession became the path to power, hard work and virtuosity became less important for a son who was guaranteed the throne. As stated on page 167, "Chinese historians tell us that the right to rule, based on no quality but that of accidental birth, slowly corrupted those who held it." Thus, a king's own nature became his greatest enemy. Drunk with power, a king could threaten his dissenters with death, like Qi, or take money from the palace treasury in order to build palaces for himself, like Jie. Inevitably, the corruption of these blood descendants would be righted by a virtuous man who would start a new dynasty. This man would earn his right to rule by wisdom and virtue, like Tang of the Shang Dynasty; this was the cycle related to the Chinese throne.

The two ideas are inextricable from one another because without a corrupt king to dethrone, a righteous and moral new leader would not have to usurp the crown. While "the ideal of Chinese kingship was rule by wisdom" it was inevitable that "as soon as a king could claim power over those villages along the Yellow River, corruption, oppression, and armed conflict...followed" (167). The cycle was the only way to fix the decay of rule associated with the blood succession within each dynasty.

CHAPTER TWENTY-TWO: HAMMURABI'S EMPIRE

The student may use her text when answering the questions in sections I and II.

Section I: Who, What, Where

Write a one or two-sentence answer explaining the significance of each item listed below.

Ishme-Dagan – **Pg. 170, ¶ 2 – Ishme-Dagan was son to Shamshi-Adad and older brother to Yasmah-Adad. When Shamshi-Adad died, the crown of Assur went to Ishme-Dagan, leaving him to control Shamshi-Adad's entire empire.**

The Kassites – **Pg. 176, ¶ 2 & 3 – The Kassites were nomads that came from over the Zagros mountains into the center of Mesopotamia. At first these nomads hired themselves out as cheap labor, then they banded together to raid the northern borders of Samsuiluna's empire.**

Kutir-Nahhunte – **Pg. 176, ¶ 5 – Kutir-Nahhunte was an Elamite king who came across the Tigris with an army to attack Samsuiluna, driving Samsuiluna out of Elamite territory back to Babylon.**

Samsuiluna – **Pg. 176, ¶ 1-6 – Samsuiluna was Hammurabi's son. Unfortunately, Samsuiluna did not have Hammurabi's gift for warfare and as a result Samsuiluna could not keep his father's kingdom together.**

Yasmah-Adad – **Pg. 170, ¶ 2 & Pg. 171, ¶ 4 – Yasmah-Adad, ruler of Mari, was Shamshi-Adad's younger son. Yasmah-Adad could not live up to his brother Ishme-Dagan's successes.**

Zimri-Lim – **Pg. 171, ¶ 4-6 & Pg. 173, ¶ 3 & 4 – Zimri-Lim reclaimed Mari from Yasmah-Adad. Zimri-Lim then made an alliance with Hammurabi, only to be attacked by his partner. There is no record of Zimri-Lim's fate at the hands of Hammurabi.**

Section II: Comprehension

Write a two/three sentence answer to each of the following questions.

1. How did Shamshi-Adad fuel the distance between his two sons Ishme-Dagan and Yasmah-Adad? Use the excerpt from the correspondence between father and son on page 170 in your answer.

A1. – Pg. 170, ¶ 2 & 3 – Shamshi-Adad favored Ishme-Dagan, and constantly compared Yasmah-Adad to his older brother. Shamshi-Adad wrote to Yasmah-Adad, "Can't you behave like a man? Your brother has made a great name for himself; you should do the same in your own land." Shamshi-Adad's favoritism cemented the wedge between the two brothers.

Part Three: Struggle

The excerpt on page 170 reads:
"[But] you remain there, reclining amongst the women. Can't you behave like a man? Your brother has made a great name for himself; you should do the same in your own land."

2. Who was responsible for Yasmah-Adad's death? Use evidence from the text to support your answer.
A2. – There are two possible answers to this question, both found on pg. 171, ¶ 4 & 5:
1) Zimri-Lim was responsible for Yasmah-Adad's death. Zimri-Lim marched on Mari, and Yasmah-Adad died in the waves of attack.
2) Ishme-Dagan was responsible for Yasmah-Adad's death. Ishme-Dagan did not send any troops to help his brother against Zimri-Lim's attack, leaving Yasmah-Adad weak and vulnerable.

3. Zimri-Lim had a hard time figuring out who to ally himself with, either Ishme-Dagan, Rim-Sin or Hammurabi. Who did he choose? How did his choice affect the shape of Hammurabi's kingdom?
A3. – Pg. 172, ¶ 1, 3 & 5 – Zimri-Lim chose to ally himself with Hammurabi. Because of this alliance, Hammurabi was able to defeat the invading coalition of Assur, Eshnunna and Elam. Hammurabi seized Assur and made it part of Babylon, he took Assur as his own, and he captured Susa and sacked it.

4. Hammurabi, wanting to keep a close eye on Zimri-Lim, demanded the right to examine and control all of Zimri-Lim's correspondence with other powers. What happened when Zimri-Lim refused to allow Hammurabi access to his letters?
A4. – Pg. 173, ¶ 3 – After Zimri-Lim refused to let Hammurabi control his correspondence, Hammurabi marched to Mari and began executing prisoners outside its walls. When the gates stayed closed, Hammurabi besieged the city, broke down its walls, hauled its people off into slavery, and set it on fire. No one knows what happened to Zimri-Lim, or any of his family, after the attack.

5. Give a short account of Rim-Sim's turbulent relationship with Hammurabi and his growing empire.
A5. – Pg. 172, ¶ 3, Pg. 173, ¶ 1, 5 ¶ 6 – When Ishme-Dagan fought against Hammurabi, Rim-Sin decided to stay out of it. Rim-Sin was punished for his neutrality, and was made to pay homage to Hammurabi. After turning on Zimri-Lim, Hammurabi again went after Rim-Sin. Six months later, Larsa fell to Hammurabi and Rim-Sin was taken prisoner.

6. What two purposes did Hammurabi's code serve?
A6. – Pg. 173, ¶ 7 – Hammurabi's laws were intended to embody a divine code of justice, as exemplified by the carving of the god of justice bestowing his authority on Hammurabi at the top of the stele. The showy presence of the code on a stele in conquered cities also kept control over the conquered people.

7. Below, fill in the specific penalty for breaking each of Hammurabi's laws.

robbery _____

aiding in the escape of a slave _____

kidnapping _____

designing a faulty house _____

poor performance of an obligation to the king _____

A7. – Pg. 175, ¶ 1 – Every answer is "death."

8. Write a short sentence for each of the regulations associated with each act: marriage, injury, inheritance and firefighting.

A8. – Pg. 175, ¶ 1 – Marriage: a contract was required; husbands could obtain divorce from a judge, but so could a wife whose husband had disgraced her.

Injury: any man who puts out the eye of another free man will lose his own, but putting out a slave's eye only costs a fine of silver.

Inheritance: widows can inherit land but can't sell it; they must keep it for their sons.

Firefighting: if a man goes to fight a fire at his neighbor's house and pinches any of his neighbor's goods under cover of smoke, he "shall be thrown into the fire."

9. How did control of all shipping routes allow Hammurabi to keep a tight grip on his empire?

A9. – Pg. 175, ¶ 2 – Control of the shipping routes meant that all goods had to pass through Hammurabi's checkpoints, and only ships given a royal passport were allowed to continue on. This guaranteed full payment of taxes, and allowed Hammurabi to keep track of all the goods travelling through his kingdom. This meant that no one could sneak in arms, meaning no secret rebellions were possible.

Section III: Critical Thinking

The student may not use her text to answer this question.

As evidenced by our reading in this chapter, Hammurabi was a fierce warrior and gifted leader. His kingdom extended far and wide, yet it did not last long after his reign ended. Write a short paragraph explaining why Hammurabi's kingdom crumbled almost as soon as the king retired.

As we saw broadly in Chapter Twenty: The Mesopotamian Mixing Bowl, and specifically in our reading for this chapter, conquest was one of the main characteristics of the ancient Mesopotamian plain. The student should understand that fighting was constant in this world. While strategy was important, as exemplified by Hammurabi's patience before attacking Ishme-Dagan, it was no guarantee of safety, as shown by Rim-Sim's demise. The only way to protect yourself and your land was to fight. If someone was not a diligent warrior, like Yasmah-Adad, his kingdom did not stand a chance. What kind of warrior was Samsuiluna? This is the key to answering the critical thinking question.

EXAMPLE ANSWER: In many parts of his kingdom, Hammurabi's rule was almost entirely one of subjection and coercion. Hammurabi had to fight for almost the entire time that he ruled over his hard-won empire. Hammurabi left his kingdom to his son Samsuiluna, who was not a gifted and tireless warrior like his father. Samsuiluna had to fight the nomadic Kassites from the north, he had to put down recurring rebellions in Uruk, Isin, Larsa and Ur, and he had to fight an Elamite invasion under the direction of Kutir-Nahhunte. Samsuiluna couldn't keep his father's empire together while fighting these battles one after another. Without the ruthless warrior Hammurabi fighting to keep his land, the far reaches of the empire could not be held together.

Chapter Twenty-Three: The Hyksos Seize Egypt

The student may use his text when answering the questions in sections I and II.

Section I: Who, What, Where

Write a one or two-sentence answer explaining the significance of each item listed below.

Apepi I – **Pg. 180, ¶ 5 to Pg. 181, ¶ 1 – Apepi I was the fifth Hyksos king. His attempt to pick a fight with the king of Thebes exemplified the long-distance hostility between the Fifteenth and Seventeenth Dynasties.**

Avaris – **Pg. 179, ¶ 3 – The city of Avaris, which lay in the desert just east of the Delta, was where the Fifteenth Dynasty's headquarters were located.**

The student might also include that the name "Avaris" means something like "Desert Mansion" (Pg. 180, ¶ 1).

Hyksos/Hikau-khoswet – **Pg. 179, ¶ 4 – Hyksos is short for Hikau-khoswet which means "Desert Princes." The Hyksos people took over rule of Egypt when Sheshi started the Fifteenth Dynasty.**

Queen Sobeknefru – **Pg. 178, ¶ 3 – Queen Sobeknefru took Egypt's throne after her husband Amenemhet IV died. She was the last ruler of the Twelfth Dynasty.**

Sequenere – **Pg. 181, ¶ 2 – Sequenere, the king of Thebes, died a violent death in battle against the Hyksos.**

Sheshi – **Pg. 179, ¶ 3 – Sheshi, a Hyksos foreigner, was the first Fifteenth Dynasty king. He organized his followers into an army and destroyed both the Thirteenth and Fourteenth Dynasties.**

Section II: Comprehension

Write a two/three sentence answer to each of the following questions.

1. What was the state of Egypt's Nubian holdings at the beginning of the Thirteenth Dynasty? What was it like in the north of Egypt, near the Delta, when the new dynasty began?
A1. – Pg. 178, ¶ 4 to Pg. 179, ¶ 1 – At the beginning of the Thirteenth Dynasty, the Nubian governors who watched over the southern lands for the crown began to act with more and more independence. In the north, the fortresses on the eastern border between the Delta and the "land of the Asiatics" were crumbling. Wandering Semitic nomads came into the Delta in increasing numbers, settling down to live side by side with the Egyptians.

2. Why is the Thirteenth Dynasty considered by most historians to be the end of the Middle Kingdom?

A2. – Pg. 179, ¶ 2 – The Thirteenth Dynasty's hold on Egypt was very shaky. Near the end of the Thirteenth Dynasty a second royal family appeared, claiming the right to rule in the eastern reaches of the Nile Delta. This meant that the relative peace and prosperity of the Middle Kingdom was over.

3. Why did Manetho make such a violent account out of the Hyksos' takeover of Egypt? How do we know that most of the Hyksos had actually been in Egypt for awhile?

A3. – Pg. 180, ¶ 1 – Manetho was a proud Egyptian and believed that his great ancestors could only have been overcome by a sudden and vigorous attack. However, we know that the Hyksos, who were Semites, had been in Egypt for a while because Semitic names begin to appear in Middle Kingdom inscriptions and lists well before the 1663 takeover.

4. What were the Hyksos people like? How did they rule over the Egyptian people?

A4. – Pg. 180, ¶ 2 – The Hyksos people were Semitic, but they adopted Egyptian dress and Egyptian customs. Egyptian continued to be the official language of inscriptions and records during Hyksos rule, and Egyptians served the Hyksos as administrators and priests.

5. How was it that the Fifteenth, Sixteenth, and Seventeenth Dynasties of Egypt could exist simultaneously?

A5. – Pg. 180, ¶ 3 – While the Fifteenth Dynasty ruled from Avaris, a vassal line of kings ruled in the northwest; Manetho calls them the Sixteenth Dynasty. Egyptian governors in the southern city of Thebes would not submit to Hyksos rule, and this faction made up the Seventeenth Dynasty.

6. What happened to Sequenere when he went to fight against the Hyksos? What was the result of this battle?

A6. – Pg. 181, ¶ 2 & Pg. 182, ¶ 2 – During the fight against the Hyksos, Sequenere fell, his skull was crushed by a mace, and while he lay on the ground, he was stabbed and hacked with dagger, spear, and axe. The battle did not turn into war, and both parties retreated. Back in Thebes, Sequenere's older son Kahmose took the throne and began to lay plans to avenge his father's death.

Section III: Critical Thinking

The student may use his text to answer this question.

We have read about some gruesome fights in *The History of the Ancient World,* but Sequenere's severe mutilation might be the most grisly yet. While we can understand the tension between Avaris and Thebes, it seems Apepi I's letter to Sequenere did not foreshadow such a violent battle. In this critical thinking question, write out Apepi I's letter to Sequenere. Then, pull apart the language of the letter and explain how Apepi I's words fueled Sequenere's will to fight against the Hyksos.

This question is about close reading. The piece of the letter reproduced in the text seems playful, yet when read against the results – the slaughtering of Sequenere – it takes on a much heavier tone. The letter on page 181 reads, "Get rid of the hippopotami at Thebes. They roar all night, I can hear them all the way up here at Avaris, and their noise is ruining my sleep." The student should use his imagination when considering why this letter was so insulting to Sequenere. Some questions to get the student going are "What does a hippopotamus look like?," "Do hippopotami live in civilized cities?," and "Why is Apepi I telling Sequenere what to do?"

The letter that Apepi I wrote to Sequenere, the Seventeenth Dynasty king at Thebes, said "Get rid of the hippopotami at Thebes. They roar all night, I can hear them all the way up here at Avaris, and their noise is ruining my sleep." In this letter, Apepi I equates Sequenere and his people to hippopotami, or big, fat, ugly roaring animals. Hippopotami are not civilized – they are smelly, loud and barbaric. Apepi I's claim that he could hear the clatter up in Avaris, and his sleep was being ruined, suggests that he was annoyed by the unsightly presence of the Theban people, and that they were disrupting his civilized nation. Also, it was a direct insult to Sequenere's power for Apepi I, the king of another dynasty, to tell Sequenere what to do. This letter was extremely offensive and it made digs at Sequenere's ability to rule the Theban people. Sequenere was too proud to take these insults, and so he gathered his troops and marched towards Avaris.

Chapter Twenty-Four: King Minos of Crete

The student may use her text when answering the questions in sections I and II.

Section I: Who, What, Where

Write a one or two-sentence answer explaining the significance of each item listed below.

Akrotiri – **Pg. 188, ¶ 5 – Akrotiri was the only large town on Thera, an island that was also an active volcano. After trying to rebuild Akrotiri when tremors shook down the city's walls, the people of Akrotiri ultimately fled the island because of the intense earth-shaking.**

Daedalus – **Pg. 184, ¶ 5 – Daedalus was an architect who helped build a contraption so that Pasiphae could mate with a bull. When Pasiphae gave birth to a deformed child, Minos made Daedalus build a prison, the Labyrinth, for the baby.**

Fresco – **Pg. 187, ¶ 4 – A fresco is a wall painting created by laying bright colors made from carbon, yellow ochre, iron ore, and other minerals directly onto a damp layer of lime plaster.**

Minotaur/Asterius – **Pg. 184, ¶ 5 – The Minotaur was the deformed child with the face of a bull produced by Pasiphae and the bull. Asterius was Pasiphae's name for the child.**

Knossos – **Pg. 183, ¶ 2 & Pg. 184, ¶ 3 – Knossos was home of the king of the island of Crete. Knossos was a strategic place from which to keep tabs on the east and west ends of the island.**

The Labyrinth – **Pg. 184, ¶ 5 – The Labyrinth was the name of the prison Daedalus made for the Minotaur. It was made up of many winding passages so that the Minotaur could never escape.**

Minos – **Pg. 184, ¶ 4 – Minos was a king of Crete who occupied the Second Palace. Minos locked away the Minotaur and sacrificed humans to the creature annually.**

alternate answer:

pg. 186, ¶ 2 – The student may also include that Minos might have been the designation given to a line of kings who governed in Knossos, and lent their name to Crete's earliest civilization.

Pasiphae – **Pg. 184, ¶ 5 – Pasiphae was Minos's wife, and mother to the Minotaur.**

Poseidon – **Pg. 188, ¶ 4 & Pg. 184, ¶ 5 – Poseidon was the king of the sea. Another name for Poseidon was Earthshaker. Poseidon cursed Minos's wife and made her lust after a bull.**

Thera – **Pg. 189, ¶ 3 – Thera was a Minoan island that was turned inside out by a volcano. After the eruption, Thera was a ring of land around a central inland sea.**

ALTERNATE ANSWER: The student might include that this formation, of a ring of land around an inland sea, is called a caldera.

Section II: Comprehension

Write a two/three sentence answer to each of the following questions.

1. How do we know that the people of Crete traded with civilizations outside of the Greek islands?
A1. – Pg. 183, ¶ 3 – We know that the people of Crete traded with civilizations outside of the Greek islands because the brightly painted pottery jars of the Crete people have been found along the Nile river and also on the Mediterranean coast.

2. Why was Poseidon displeased with Minos? How did Poseidon punish Minos? What was the result of Minos's punishment?
A2. – Pg. 184, ¶ 5 – Poseidon was displeased by Minos's greed. Poseidon sent Minos a bull to sacrifice, but instead Minos kept the bull for himself. As a punishment, Poseidon cursed Pasiphae, Minos's wife, with a lust for the bull. Pasiphae and the bull coupled, and the result was a horribly disfigured child, a human figure with the face of a bull.

3. How does the story of the Minotaur, excerpted below, reflect the ongoing international sea trade carried on by the Minoan people?
 Minos fed [the Minotaur] on human flesh; after a battle with the inhabitants of the Greek mainland, he ordered them to send seven young men and seven young women each year to be eaten by the Minotaur
A3. – Pg. 186, ¶ 2 – The passage above shows that there was ongoing trade between Minos and other lands. The seven young men and seven young women are reflections of the cargo that was exchanged between cities.

4. Where do we see traces of the Minoan culture in the epic of Gilgamesh? How might this exchange of stories have happened?
A4. – Pg. 186, ¶ 2 –Some of the pictorial representations of Gilgamesh and his fight with the Bull of Heaven show Gilgamesh grappling with a partly human bull who wears a kind of wrestling belt. The monster has a bull's body and man's head, which is a reversal of the Minotaur's deformity. The resemblance between the monster depicted as the Bull of Heaven and the Minotaur suggests that Minoan and Mesopotamian sailors swapped stories in port.

5. Why was a mastery of the waterways around Knossos necessary for Minos to build and maintain his empire?
A5. – Pg. 186, ¶ 3 – Minos established towns on a number of the nearby islands that served as both trading stops and naval bases. Minos then appointed his own sons governors of these towns, extending his power far beyond Knossos. From these posts, Minos was able to expel the Carians, and to put down piracy in the Hellenic Sea.

6. Explain this statement: As piracy decreased in the sea around Crete, the wealth of the Minoan people increased.
A6. – Pg. 187, ¶ 2 – A decrease in piracy meant that the peoples on the islands stopped worrying about theft, and were therefore able to concentrate on gaining more wealth. As their life became more settled, trade flourished, new buildings went up, and the arts became more sophisticated.

7. What is the Minoan bull-dance? In what way is the story of Minos and the Minotaur a reflection of the bull-dance?

A7. – Pg. 187, ¶ 4 to Pg. 188, ¶ 2 – In the bull-dance, worshippers vault over the horns of the bull on to the animal's back, and from there spring to the ground. The worshippers who took part in this ritual were probably young, athletic, and ready to die, just like the young men and women who were sacrificed to the Minotaur. Excavation of the Bull Courts show an entire network of doors, stairs, and corridors opening onto the courts from the surrounding buildings – a maze similar to the labyrinth built by Daedalus.

8. Describe the possible environmental fallout after the volcano at Thera erupted. Why did the Minoans interpret this as an angry message from Poseidon?

A8. – Pg. 190, ¶ 1 & 2 – After the volcano erupted, ash fall certainly reached the eastern half of Crete, perhaps destroying a season's worth of food. A tsunami submerged islands near Thera, and may still have been over thirty feet high when it crashed against the shores of Crete. Electrical storms, heavy and violent thunderstorms, and sinking temperatures followed, along with deep blood red sunsets. The Minoans believed their prosperity to be linked to divine happiness, so the only way that the Minoans could understand these weird manifestations was to assume that Poseidon was angry.

Section III: Critical Thinking

The student may not use her text to answer this question.

A myth often explains a phenomenon of nature, a cultural practice, or a cultural rite. In this chapter, we read the myth of Minos and the Minotaur. While this story was written hundreds of years after Minos occupied the Second Palace, we find telling details in the legend about life on the ancient Greek islands. First, write a short summary of the story of Minos and the Minotaur. Next, explain how this myth describes a phenomenon of nature that occurred during Minoan life. Finally, answer the question, "How does the story of Minos and the Minotaur tell us about a Minoan cultural practice/rite?"

The first part of this answer is a simple recap of the story of Minos and the Minotaur. The story can be found on page 184, ¶ 4-5. King Minos of Crete wanted to prove to his people his rule was divine, so he asked Poseidon to send him a bull for sacrifice. Minos found the bull too beautiful to kill, so he kept the bull for his own and sacrificed a lesser beast. Poseidon, angered by Minos's greed, cursed Minos's wife Pasiphae, and as a result she mated with the holy bull. Pasiphae then birthed a child that had the face of a bull; she named it Asterius. Minos called the deformed baby the Minotaur, and locked it up in a prison full of winding passages - the Labyrinth. The Minotaur ate human flesh. Each year, Minos would feed the creature seven young men and seven young women.

In the chapter we learned that the island of Crete and the sea around it were constantly shaken by earthquakes and the destructive waves that followed. Minoan fear of the moving earth is reflected in the myth of Minos and the Minotaur: the Minotaur lay hidden underground, pounding away in his Labyrinth, trying to escape. The natural phenomenon of the shaking earth is explained by the stampeding Minotaur.

The Minoans did not know how to stop the earthshaking. It is most likely that they participated in ritual sacrifice to appease the gods. If the gods were happy, the earth might stop rumbling. In the story, Minos annually sacrificed young men and women to the Minotaur. The site uncovered at Knossos indicates sacrifice and a ritual feasting on the dead. The Minoan <u>cultural practice/rite</u> of human sacrifice and feasting on the dead is represented by the Minotaur's need for human flesh.

CHAPTER TWENTY-FIVE: THE HARAPPAN DISINTEGRATION

The student may use his text when answering the questions in sections I and II.

Section I: Who, What, Where

Write a one or two-sentence answer explaining the significance of each item listed below.

Jhukar culture – **Pg. 193, ¶ 3 – The Jhukar culture were the people who lived in the Harappan remains once the Harappan civilization ended. The name comes from the village where the crude pottery was first made.**

Arya – **Pg. 195, ¶ 2 – The invaders that settled over the Harappan ruins called themselves arya. It is an adjective that has been given many different meanings, ranging from "respectable" to "pure."**

Section II: Comprehension

Write a two/three sentence answer to each of the following questions.

1. What archaeological evidence suggests an unexpected natural disaster struck Mohenjo-Daro between 1750 and 1700?

A1. – Pg. 192, ¶ 2 – Archaeological excavation of Mohenjo-Daro from approximately 1750 to 1700 has revealed skeletons lying unburied in streets, and an entire family trapped and killed in their home. Treasured items such as tools for carrying on livelihood, jewelry, and silver were dropped haphazardly so the citizens of Mohenjo-Daro could flee their homes faster. The unburied skeletons and scattered valuable items suggest that the people of Mohenjo-Daro were not prepared for the natural disaster that struck their city.

2. Explain hydrologist R. L. Raikes's theory that a silt dam could have been a cause for the destruction of the Harappan cities. What natural evidence does Raikes have to support his point?

A2. – Pg. 192, ¶ 5 to Pg. 193, ¶ 1 – Hydrologist R.L. Raikes suggests that a silt dam formed upstream from Harappa which stopped the flooding altogether for some time. It is possible that the dam then broke under the accumulated weight of water, sending enormous floods rushing down into the city. In 1818, a silt dam stopped up the Indus for almost two years, forming a block fifty miles long and fifty feet high. This natural evidence supports Raikes's point that a flood caused by the breaking of a silt dam caused the destruction of the Harappan cities.

3. What story do the archaeological findings from the Harappan ruins tell us about the agricultural plight of the Harappan people?

A3. – Pg. 193, ¶ 2 – Many of the skeletons found in the Harappan ruins show evidence of illness, the most common being severe anemia, probably caused by malnutrition. As the Harappan civilization grew, more and more grain was needed to feed its citizens. Also, each building needed wood to fuel its baking oven. As the cities grew, the builders must have deforested larger and larger areas. It seems the Harappans were slowly running out of food and fuel.

4. How do we know that the Harappans didn't reoccupy their cities?

A4. – Pg. 193, ¶ 3 – The archaeological findings above the Harappan layers show crude pottery, little organization, and no attempt to rebuild or use the complicated drainage and sewer systems of the cities. Thus, it is clear that the people who occupied the territory after the disaster were not the organized Harappans.

5. Why did the nomads from the north call the first place they settled in India the "Land of the Seven Rivers?"

A5. – Pg. 193, ¶ 4 – The nomads from the north of India called the place they first settled the "Land of the Seven Rivers" because they probably lived in the Punjab, which is near the upper branches of the Indus. At this point, the Indus divided into six branches flowing into the one main river.

6. What skill did the nomadic invaders of India have that allowed them to survive and defeat their enemies?

A6. – Pg. 194, ¶ 1 – The invaders could fight. They had horses, chariots with spoke wheels, bronze axes and longbows. These weapons, and the ability to fight, helped the nomads defeat their enemies.

7. While the term *arya* is sometimes translated as "pure," how do we know that the early Aryan civilization was anything but pure?

A7. – Pg. 195, ¶ 2 – We know that some citizens of Harappa and Mohenjo-Daro survived and mingled with the Aryans because of words from the two civilizations that show up in the Aryan language. The people of Harappa and Mohenjo-Daro lent the Aryans words for "plough," "threshing floor" and "mortar," and presumably taught the ex-nomads how to use these civilized tools. This exchange proves that the Aryans mixed with other cultures.

Section III: Critical Thinking

In this chapter we see a sophisticated civilization pitted against nomadic adaptability. Prior to our reading in "The Harappan Disintegration," it seems the peoples of the Ancient world championed settled living. Using examples from this chapter, play devil's advocate and argue for the advantages of a nomadic, uncivilized lifestyle.

The key to this answer lies in the question on page 193, "Why weren't they [the Harappan cities] rebuilt?" A natural disaster shouldn't have been enough to stop a civilization from rebuilding - for example, though Hurricane Katrina destroyed much of New Orleans, the population is rebuilding because they have access to the resources necessary to start over. The chapter says "We have to assume that some kind of natural disaster descended on a civilization that was already suffering from internal rot" (193, ¶ 3). If the student is having a hard time coming up with an answer, start there. Ask him, "What kinds of problems did the Harappans encounter that were directly related to their growth?" The chapter tells us that malnutrition and deforestation were a result of the over-extension of the Harappan peoples.

From here, the student can home in on the positive aspects of the nomadic lifestyle. The student should remember this clearly from his reading. On pages 194-5, the text reads: "[The nomads] took advantage of deserted buildings that they found, since they had none of their own...and settled in. The sophisticated and highly organized Harappan civilization had been replaced by roving tribes with less culture, less technology, and no experience in running a city – but infinitely more experience in adapting to strange surroundings." The nomads were able to settle in the Harappan ruins because they could fit their lives to their environment. The adaptability of the nomadic people allowed them to roll with the punches and find a way to live no matter where they ended up, no matter what the circumstances. They did not need to be settled to survive, and in the end that gave the nomads an edge over the civilized culture.

CHAPTER TWENTY-SIX: THE RISE OF THE HITTITES

The student may use her text when answering the questions in sections I and II.

Section I: Who, What, Where

Write a one or two-sentence answer explaining the significance of each item listed below.

Anittas – **Pg. 197, ¶ 3-5 – Anittas was the chief of the Hittite city of Kussara. Anittas created a Hittite nation through wars of conquest.**

Ht & Hatti – **Pg. 197, ¶ 2 – Ht was the Egyptian name for the kingdoms in Asia Minor that were settled by Indo-Europeans. Hatti was the Hittite name for the peoples' homeland, Ht.**

Hattusilis I – **Pg. 198, 3 to Pg. 199, ¶ 2 – Hattusilis I expanded the Hittite territory down into the Western Semite kingdoms. He made the Hittite nation into an empire that ruled over more than one people.**

Mursilis – **Pg. 199, ¶ 4-5 & Pg. 200, ¶ 4 – Mursilis, a nephew of Hattusilis, became king of Hittites. Mursilis used his power to conquer Aleppo and Babylon, but he could not protect himself from assassination plots against him; he was murdered by his cupbearer.**

Pimpira – **Pg. 199, ¶ 4 – Pimpira was a Hittite prince that watched over Mursilis before he ascended to the throne. Pimpira was concerned that Mursilis be a just and compassionate king.**

Purushkhanda – **Pg. 197, ¶ 5 – Purushkhanda was an important Hittite city. It was seen by the Hittite people as a capital of the mind and a place of moral authority.**

Section II: Comprehension

Write a two/three sentence answer to each of the following questions.

1. How was the Mesopotamian plain divided in the years immediately following Samsuiluna's death?
A1. – Pg. 196, ¶ 1 – In the years immediately following Samsuiluna's death, Babylon had lost most of its holdings to the south and east. These destroyed, infertile and deserted lands were ruled by the Sealand Dynasty. Babylon still ruled to the north and west, but only as far over as Mari. Past Mari, the king of Aleppo kept his independence.

2. In what way did trade with Assur help advance Hittite culture?
A2. – Pg. 197, ¶ 3 – The Hittites learned to write from the merchants of Assur who lived nearby. This skill allowed the Hittites to keep their own records. The Hittites now could keep a written history of their people and culture.

3. Describe the kingdom Anittas inherited from his father, and his war campaign against Hattusas and Purushkhanda.

A3. – Pg. 197, ¶ 4 – Anittas inherited a small two-city kingdom from his father. The two cities he first ruled were Kussara and Nesa. After his father died and Anittas became king, he attacked Hattusas. Hattusas resisted Anittas's conquest, so he finally sacked and cursed the city. The king of Purushkhanda did not want his city to suffer the same fate, so he turned his power over to Anittas without a fight.

4. Why did Hattusilis I risk moving the Hittite capital from Kussara to Hattusas?

A4. – Pg. 198, ¶ 2 – Hattusilis I moved the Hittite capital to Hattusas because there were seven springs nearby, fertile land surrounded the area, and there was a cliff where a palace could be built and easily defended.

5. What happened when Mursilis and his troops reached Babylon? Why didn't Mursilis add Babylon to his empire? Why did Mursilis sack Babylon?

A5. – Pg. 200, ¶ 1 & 2 – When Mursilis arrived at Babylon, he overran the city, took its people prisoner and put the king in chains. Mursilis didn't add Babylon to his empire because it was too far away from Hattusas to be governed with any security. Mursilis sacked Babylon to prove a point, that he was the most powerful conqueror in the world.

Section III: Critical Thinking

The student may not use her text to answer this question.

There was something rotten in the state of Hattusas around 1500 BC. We learn at the end of the chapter that "the dynastic succession of the Hittites had settled into a game of hunt-the-king."

• What happened on Hattusilis I's deathbed? In your answer, make sure to include all the people Hattusilis scorned, and list who ended up on the throne.

Pg. 199, ¶ 2 – When Hattusilis I was on his deathbed, he condemned his son and daughter because he believed their minds were poisoned against him by Hittite noblemen. He then disregarded the nephew he lined up for the throne, and finally turned on his sister. Hattusilis I ended up picking another nephew named Mursilis for the throne.

• How did the transfer of power from Hattusilis I to Mursilis foreshadow the coming turbulence of the Hittite throne?

The student should come up with an answer that links Mursilis's troubled inheritance of the throne with his murder. Mursilis was not first, second or even third in line for king. This gives us the impression that some people in the royal court did not think that Mursilis had a right to be king. If the Hittite people questioned Mursilis's right to rule (not his ability), it suggests that anyone could be king. This foreshadows Mursilis's death at the hands of his cup-bearer.

• What does the phrase "hunt-the-king" mean? Give an example from the chapter to support your answer.

The phrase "hunt-the-king" refers to the brutality associated with the Hittite king and his family. It seems that someone was always on the hunt for the king and his throne. For example, when Hantili died, a court official killed Hantili's son and all of his grandsons and seized the throne. The court official wanted to be king of the Hittites, and the weakness of the Hittite succession system allowed the official to muscle his way onto the throne.

The student may also include details about the court official's abrupt end and the series of murders that followed. This can be found on page 200, ¶ 5: "[The court official], in turn, was killed by his own son, who was later murdered and replaced by a usurper, who then fell victim to assassination himself."

CHAPTER TWENTY-SEVEN: AHMOSE EXPELS THE HYKSOS

The student may use his text when answering the questions in sections I and II.

Section I: Who, What, Where

Write a one or two-sentence answer explaining the significance of each item listed below.

Ahmose – **Pg. 204, ¶ 2 & Pg. 205, ¶ 3 – Ahmose succeeded Kahmose as the king of Thebes. Ahmose drove the Hyksos out of Egypt, and was named by Manetho as the first king of the Eighteenth Dynasty, which marked the New Kingdom of Egypt.**

Kahmose – **Pg. 202, ¶ 1 – Kahmose was the son of Sequenere. He vowed to avenge the death of his father, who was slaughtered at the hands of the Hyksos.**

Queen Ahhotep – **Pg. 203, ¶ 4 & 5 – Queen Ahhotep acted as regent for her son Ahmose when he was very young. Queen Ahhotep took advantage of northern weakness and continued a successful campaign against the Hyksos.**

Sharuhen – **Pg. 205, ¶ 1 – Sharuhen was a Canaanite city that had become a center for the Western Semitic Kingdom. When Ahmose conquered Sharuhen, Ahmose was able to claim the south of Canaan as an Egyptian province.**

Section II: Comprehension

Write a two/three sentence answer to each of the following questions.

1. Why did Kahmose see Nubia as an obstacle in the path of his campaign against the Hyksos?
A1. – Pg. 202, ¶ 2 – Kahmose saw Nubia as an obstacle because the Nubians were allied with the Hyksos. The Hyksos kings of the Fifteenth Dynasty had made a treaty with them. The Nubians agreed to come to the aid of the Hyksos against Theban Egypt, which would mean the Egyptians would be fighting on both north and south fronts.

2. How did Kahmose plan to intercept communication between the northern Hyksos and the southern Nubians? Did his plan work?
A2. – Pg. 202, ¶ 3 to Pg. 203, ¶ 2 – Kahmose spread out spies all across the south in order to intercept communication between Hyksos and their Nubian allies. Kahmose's plan worked just as planned; his men were able to intercept the Hyksos messenger on his way down to Nubia.

3. After marching on Thebes, why did Kahmose time his arrival back in Thebes with the Nile flood?
A3. – Pg. 203, ¶ 3 – Kahmose timed his arrival back in Thebes with the flooding of the Nile to remind everyone he was the rightful king of all Egypt and responsible for the rising of the

waters. **This move reasserted his divine right to rule.**

4. How did Queen Ahhotep help her son Ahmose reunify Egypt? How did Ahmose use the military head start given to him by his mother?
A4. – Pg. 203, ¶ 5 to Pg. 204, ¶ 2 – Ahmose was too young to rule when he inherited the throne, so his mother acted as regent. She started a military campaign to pacify Upper Egypt and expel her rebels. Ahmose used this head start to battle the Hyksos, capturing Heliopolis, Tjaru, Sharuhen and eventually Avaris.

5. Why did Ahmose's general say that he "brought away a hand" from Avaris?
A5. – Pg. 204, ¶ 4 – Egyptian scribes used amputated hands to tally enemy casualties. When Ahmose's general said he "brought away a hand" from Avaris, he meant that he was successful in beating his enemy.

6. Describe the archaeological and historical evidence that supports the theory that the Hyksos people fled from Avaris en masse.
A6. – Pg. 204, ¶ 5 – The ruins of Avaris show no evidence of a general slaughter, which is usually the final phase of a long siege. Also, there are very few Semitic names in servant lists for the next fifty years, so it is unlikely that many Hyksos were enslaved. This archaeological and historical evidence suggests that there was a mass exodus of people from Avaris.

7. Why did Manetho name Ahmose the first king of the Eighteenth Dynasty?
A7. – Pg. 205, ¶ 3 – Manetho named Ahmose the first king of the Eighteenth dynasty because Ahmose reunified Egypt and reasserted the power of native rule over the Egyptian kingdom.

8. What cultural changes marked the New Kingdom of Egypt?
A8. – Pg. 205, ¶ 3 – The cultural changes that marked the New Kingdom of Egypt were a new phase of building, peace and prosperity, and the creation of new art and literature.

Section III: Critical Thinking

The major point of this chapter is clear: the Hyksos were kicked out of Egypt. The events leading up to the flight of the Hyksos remain somewhat unclear. Write a paragraph that explains how Manetho's account of Ahmose's attack of Avaris differs from the Egyptian version. In your answer, make sure to explain why each version of the story is possible.

Manetho's account of the attack on Avaris at the hands of Ahmose is presented on page 204, in paragraph 2. Manetho recounts that the Hyksos built a thick wall around Avaris. Ahmose surrounded the city with thousands of men. With the threat of siege looming, the Hyksos made a treaty with the Egyptians and agreed to leave Egypt forever. Manetho's account is very peaceful. Egyptian accounts describe much more bloodshed, as detailed on page 204 in paragraph 4. The tomb inscriptions of the general that led the siege describe at least three different savage battles at Avaris. Also, the Egyptians commemorated the event with relief sculptures of battles, and herds of Hyksos led captive.

Part Three: Struggle

There is evidence that each version of the story is possible. Ruins show that Avaris was sacked, the Hyksos palace was flattened, and other traces of Hyksos occupation were so thoroughly obliterated that it is exceedingly difficult to see any details of their reign over Lower Egypt at all. This disappearance, coupled with the Egyptian stories of the brutal attacks, supports the idea that the Egyptians aggressively captured Avaris and destroyed everything – the palace and the people – inside of it. However, while the ruins of Avaris do show that it was sacked, there is no evidence that general slaughter took place within the walls of the city. Also, the lack of Semitic names in the servant lists after the downfall of the Hyksos suggests that few of their people were enslaved. While the lack of Semitic servant names could suggest that all the Hyksos were killed, it is more likely that a mass exodus of the surrendered Hyksos occurred.

CHAPTER TWENTY-EIGHT: USURPATION AND REVENGE

The student may use her text when answering the questions in sections I and II.

Section I: Who, What, Where

Write a one or two-sentence answer explaining the significance of each item listed below.

Amenhotep I – **Pg. 206, ¶ 1 & 2 – Amenhotep I, the son of Ahmose, regained control of Egypt's Nubian territories. Amenhotep was childless, and appointed his general to be the next king of Egypt.**

Hatshepsut – **Pg. 207, ¶ 3 & Pg. 209, ¶ 1 – Hatshepsut, wife of Tuthmosis II, was considered co-ruler during her husband's reign, and acted as regent to his successor, Tuthmosis III. While Hatshepsut never actually deposed Tuthmosis III from the throne, she portrayed herself as the premier ruler of Egypt.**

Tuthmosis I – **Pg. 206, ¶ 3, Pg. 207, ¶ 1 – Tuthmosis I succeeded Amenhotep I as king of Egypt. He was the first pharaoh to build a tomb in the Valley of the Kings.**

Tuthmosis II – **Pg. 207, ¶ 3 and Pg. 208, ¶ 1 – Tuthmosis II was the son of Tuthmosis I by his lesser wife. Tuthmosis II was married to Princess Hatshepsut, however he had an illegitimate son with a woman named Iset, who Tuthmosis II named heir to the throne.**

Tuthmosis III – **Pg. 208, ¶ 2 and Pg. 210, ¶ 3 & 4 – Tuthmosis III was only a child when he was appointed King of Egypt. He lived most of his life in Hatshepsut's shadow; when she finally died Tuthmosis III went on a great war campaign though the territories north of Egypt.**

Senenmut – **Pg. 208, ¶ 5 & 6 – Senenmut was the Chief Steward of Amun. He was Hatshepsut's advisor, and it was rumored that their relationship was based on more than just business.**

NOTE TO INSTRUCTOR: Graffiti found near Hatshepsut's temple suggests a sexual relationship between Hatshepsut and Senenmut. While reference to the graffiti is not necessary, the student's answer should include that Hatshepsut and Senenmut may have been more than friends.

Section II: Comprehension

Write a two/three sentence answer to each of the following questions.

1. What circumstances made Tuthmosis I build a hidden tomb instead of a conspicuous pyramid for his burial place? Though it was underground, how was the tomb still like a pyramid? How was it different?

A1. – Pg. 207, ¶ 1 – Tomb robbers had managed to break into almost every pyramid in Egypt, so to avoid losing his treasures, Tuthmosis I planned a new, secret burial place. The tomb was

like a pyramid because it had ornate painted walls. It was not like a pyramid because it had a hidden entrance.

2. Why did Tuthmosis I appoint his son by his lesser wife heir to the Egyptian throne? What did Tuthmosis I do to strengthen his son's dynastic position?

A2. – Pg. 207, ¶ 3 – Tuthmosis I appointed his son by his lesser wife heir because the two sons he had with his first wife died before Tuthmosis I left the throne. In order to strengthen the son by the lesser wife's dynastic position, Tuthmosis I arranged for him to be married to one of the daughters of his primary wife: the princess Hatshepsut.

3. What did Hatshepsut have carved on the mortuary temple she had built in honor of the sun-god Amun? What was the meaning of the carving?

A3. – Pg. 208, ¶ 3 – Hatshepsut had a relief carved of Amun paying a visit to Hatshepsut's mother. The carving was meant to show Egyptians that Hatshepsut's birth was a product of Hatshepsut's mother's meeting with Amun, implying that Hatshepsut was conceived by the god himself.

4. To what lengths did Hatshepsut go, in addition to claiming she was Amun's daughter, in order to prove she was the true ruler of Egypt?

A4. – Pg. 208, ¶ 4 and Pg. 209, ¶ 1– Hatshepsut had an engraving commissioned that stated Tuthmosis I ordered her crowned the true ruler of Egypt, allowing her to claim a Horus-name, and rule as King of Upper and Lower Egypt. Hatshepsut had statues built showing her with the royal headdress and also the formal square beard of a crowned pharaoh. In her mortuary temple, Hatshepsut had her figure carved celebrating the heb-sed festival, a ritual reserved for the Egyptian pharaoh.

5. While Hatshepsut did not depose Tuthmosis III, she did keep him far away from her throne. What was Tuthmosis III doing while Hatshepsut reigned?

A5. – Pg. 209, ¶ 2 – Tuthmosis III was sent far away from Memphis by Hatshepsut to fight in one military campaign, or another, mostly in the new northern province of Egypt.

6. How did Tuthmosis III get rid of the obelisks Hatshepsut built in honor of Amun? Why did he deal with them in this way?

A6. – Pg. 209, ¶ 5 – Tuthmosis III had walls built around the obelisks so that they could not be seen. Tuthmosis III most likely feared punishment from Amun if he was to smash the monuments, so he obscured their visibility while leaving the obelisks intact.

7. Why didn't the Egyptian army attack Kadesh? How did they eventually win the fight versus the city?

A7. – Pg. 210, ¶ 3 – The Egyptians did not have the experience necessary to attack the walls that surrounded Kadesh. Instead, the Egyptian army starved the enemy out. After seven months, the king of Kadesh surrendered.

8. What made the Egyptian invasion of Joppa unique?

A8. – Pg. 210, ¶ 4 – The Egyptians used trickery to invade Joppa. Joppa's king's charioteer was made to believe that Egypt had surrendered to Joppa. When the queen of Joppa heard the news, she allowed baskets of Egyptian plunder to enter the city.
However, each basket contained an armed Egyptian warrior. Once the queen of Joppa opened the gates, the warriors burst out of their baskets and forced the city to surrender.

Section III: Critical Thinking

The student may not use her text to answer this question.

Hatshepsut and Tuthmosis III had very different ruling styles. In fact, the chapter states that Tuthmosis III was the "anti-Hatshepsut." Write a paragraph contrasting the way Hatshepsut showed her strength as ruler of Egypt versus the way Tuthmosis III proved he was a great pharaoh. Explain why Hatshepsut and Tuthmosis III may have chosen these different styles of leadership.

The prompt is composed of 4 questions:
1) What was the marker of Hatshepsut's rule?
2) Why did she rule this way?
3) What was the marker of Tuthmosis III's rule?
4) Why did he rule this way?

The student's paragraph should address each of these questions. She can answer in the order above, or address the ruling styles of Hatshepsut and Tuthmosis III and then consider why each ruled in that particular way. The answer to each question is listed separately below.

1) What was the marker of Hatshepsut's rule?
On page 209, the chapter states, "Certainly Hatshepsut put almost all of her energy into domestic projects, particularly buildings; in the ancient world the number of buildings a king put up was considered a direct index of his success, and Hatshepsut wanted no question as to her greatness." Hatshepsut showed her strength as ruler of Egypt by building temples and monuments.

2) Why did she rule this way?
Hatshepsut was not heir to the Egyptian throne, but she really wanted to be the one in power. As regent to the young Tuthmosis III, Hatshepsut saw her chance. She had to prove that she was meant to be the leader of Egypt, so she spent her time erecting monuments that supported her claim to the throne.

3) What was the marker of Tuthmosis III's rule?
The text states that Tuthmosis III's campaigns "were Napoleonic in their intensity" (209). Tuthmosis III proved he was a great pharaoh through massive war campaigns. Under his rule, Egypt's borders stretched almost to the Euphrates, a northern border never matched again (212).

4) Why did he rule this way?
After so many years in exile, Tuthmosis III needed to prove he was strong and potent. In order to show he was nothing like his guardian, he had to display his strength in a way that was very different from Hatshepsut. Under Hatshepsut, Egypt's army was stagnant. Tuthmosis III revived Egypt's forces and fought like a mad man, extending Egypt's borders to places they had never been before. By showing he could fight fiercely, Tuthmosis III proved both his right to the throne, and his manhood.

CHAPTER TWENTY-NINE: THE THREE-WAY CONTEST

The student MAY USE his text when answering the questions in sections I and II.

Section I: Who, What, Where

Write a one or two-sentence answer explaining the significance of each item listed below.

Hurrians – **Pg. 213, ¶ 2 – The Hurrians, a mountain tribe from the slopes of the Zagros, settled in the northern reaches of Mesopotamia and in the Hittite lands.**

Maryannu – **Pg. 213, ¶ 3 – Maryannu was the name of the Hurrian ruling class. This class of people was comprised of a group of Aryans that travelled west into Mesopotamia and forced their way into Hurrian life.**

Mitanni – **Pg. 213, ¶ 3 – The Mitanni was a kingdom made of upper class Maryannu and lower class Hurrians that was located northeast of Egypt.**

Parattarna – **Pg. 213, ¶ 4 and Pg. 214, ¶ 1 – Parattarna is the first Mitanni king to surface in written records. Parattarna guided Hurrian troops down through Mesopotamia, where they claimed Assur as a province of the Mitanni kingdom.**

Saustatar – **Pg. 215, ¶ 1 & 2 – Saustatar, king of the Mitanni people, sought to build a great Mitanni empire. However, his push brought him into conflict with both the Hittites and the Egyptians.**

Telepinus – **Pg. 215, ¶ 3 – Telepinus tried to heal internal Hittite struggle so that the king could actually rule over his people. He wrote the Edict of Telepinus, which did not last long after the ruler's death.**

Washukkanni – **Pg. 213, ¶ 4 – Washukanni was the capital of the Mitanni kingdom.**

Section II: Comprehension

Write a two/three sentence answer to each of the following questions.

1. Who ruled Assur before the Mitanni claimed the city? How did Assur fit into the Mitanni kingdom?
A1. – Pg. 214, ¶ 1 – Since the disintegration of Hammurabi's empire, Assur was ruled by whatever warlord could hold onto it. When the Mitanni marched down into Mesopotamia, Assur became a province of the Mitanni kingdom, with its king a vassal serving the Mitanni king.

2. How did the political unrest of the Hittite people affect the nation's ability to protect itself?
A2. – Pg. 215, ¶ 2 – Each time a new Hittite ruler came to the throne he had to beg for support from government officials and the Hittite people, which was very time-consuming. The king

had little time and energy to guard the borders of his empire, meaning cities on the edge were able to break away.

3. What was the Edict of Telepinus?
A3. – Pg. 215, ¶ 4 to 216, ¶ 2 – The Edit of Telepinus laid out detailed rules for the orderly conveying of the crown from one generation of Hittites to the next. The Edict also prescribed penalties for various crimes from sorcery to murder.

4. Why was Tuthmosis III able to take Carchemish from the Hittites so easily?
4. – Pg. 216, ¶ 3 – After Telepinus's rule, the Hittites reverted to another 100 years of "kill the king." When Tuthmosis III marched on Carchemish, the Hittite army was divided and disorganized as a result of internal struggle; the Hittites had no choice but to retreat and give up their land.

5. Describe Saustatar's invasion of Hittite territory.
A5. – Pg. 216, ¶ 5 – Saustatar invaded Hittite territory just after Tuthmosis III took Carchemish. Saustatar pushed westward to Tarsus with little difficulty. Aleppo then paid tribute to him, followed by the cities of Alalakh and Ugarit.

6. How did Saustatar help the Western Semitic cities revolt against the Egyptians after Tuthmosis III's death?
A6. – Pg. 216, ¶ 6 – Saustatar encouraged the Western Semitic cities to revolt against Egypt, even going so far as sending his own army to help the rebels in Kadesh.

7. Why did Amenhotep II make a treaty with Saustatar? How did the alliance between Egypt and the Mitanni benefit both kingdoms?
A7. – Pg. 217, ¶ 2 & 5 – Under Saustatar, the Mitanni kingdom had grown strong enough to cause Amenhotep II serious trouble. A treaty between the two nations offered peace, and posed a threat to any city outside the alliance. The alliance benefited both kingdoms because no Western Semitic city dared revolt against either Egypt or the Mitanni.

Section III: Critical Thinking

How do outside forces galvanize people or cities to become part of an empire? Write two paragraphs, one related to the Hurrians, and one about Assur, that describe how outside forces worked to put these people within the boundaries of the Mitanni kingdom.

The key to this critical thinking question lies in the will of the invader. As empires grow, cities are added to a kingdom at the will of the powerful invader, not at the decision of the conquered. The Hurrians and the people of Assur were both conquered, but in different ways. The Hurrians were not a coherent nation until the Aryans arrived. The Aryans brought the Hurrians together into a particular class, and then made them part of a larger nation. The Mitanni took Assur against its will, and forced the city to remain in the Mitanni kingdom.

Part Three: Struggle

Example: The Hurrians

The Hurrian people, descendants of a mountain tribe from the slopes of the Zagros, lived happily scattered in small groups on the edge of Mesopotamian cities. When a new batch of invaders showed up, a splinter group of Aryans, they settled into life with the Hurrians, and intermarried with them. Eventually this outside group bullied their way into becoming the Hurrian ruling class, the Maryannu. The Hurrians became subservient to the Maryannu. Maryannu and Hurrians together became the upper and lower class of a kingdom called by the surrounding rulers "the Mitanni." If the Aryans hadn't shown up and invaded Hurrian life, the Hurrians would have continued to live in scattered villages. Instead, the Hurrians became part of the Mitanni kingdom.

Example: Assur

Assur was an independent city until it was taken over by Hammurabi. When Samsuiluna lost his grip on the Babylonian kingdom, Assur was left to fend for itself. Various war lords had claimed the city, and then Parattarna came in with his Mitanni army and took Assur for his empire. Assur did not want to be part of the Mitanni kingdom. When the opportunity arose, the people of Assur tried to revolt against their Mitanni overlord. The current king, Saustatar, quickly put down the revolt, and took the gates of Assur to the Mitanni capital Washukkanni as a reminder of the Mitanni's power over Assur. Parattarna's outside troops, and Saustatar's continued tyranny, forced Assur into the Mitanni kingdom.

Chapter Thirty: The Shifting Capitals of the Shang

The student may use her text when answering the questions in sections I and II.

Section I: Who, What, Where

Write a one or two-sentence answer explaining the significance of each item listed below.

P'an Keng – **Pg. 222, ¶ 2 & 3 – P'an Keng was the nineteenth Shang king. He moved the capital city to Yin, and declared the move the carrying on of Chinese tradition. He was adored by his subjects.**

Po – **Pg. 219, ¶ 4 – Po was the capital of the Shang dynasty while Tang and Yi Yin were in power.**

T'ai Jia – **Pg. 220, ¶ 3 & 4 – T'ai Jia was Tang's grandson. Too young to rule on his own, T'ai Jia was chained to his court advisor, Yi Yin.**

Yi Yin – **Pg. 219, ¶ 4, Pg. 221, ¶ 2 – Yi Yin was Tang's most powerful official, and stayed in office through the rein of T'ai Jia, Tang's grandson. Yi Yin manipulated the young ruler and was able to continue his veiled rule of the kingdom.**

Section II: Comprehension

Write a two/three sentence answer to each of the following questions.

1. Where was the capital city of the Shang dynasty between 1766 until 1400?

NOTE TO INSTRUCTOR: This is a trick question. The student should know that the Shang capital moved frequently. The student does not have to list each capital. If the student does list each capital, please refer to the alternate answer.
A1. – Pg. 219, ¶ 2 – The capital city of the Shang rulers moved five different times between 1766 and 1400. Archaeologists believe that all of these sites fell within a circle drawn around the Yellow River, east of the Xia capital.

ALTERNATE ANSWER: Pg. 219, ¶ 2 & Pg. 221, ¶ 4 & 5, Pg. 222, ¶ 3 – Under Tang, the capital city was Po. Under Chung Ting the capital was found at Hsiao. The twelfth Shang king moved the capital to Hsiang. Tsu Yi moved it to Keng. When Keng was destroyed by a flood, Tsu Yi moved the capital to Yen. Under P'an Keng, the capital was moved to Yin.

2. What makes Yi Yin's longevity in the house of Shang seem odd?

A2. Pg. 219, ¶ 5 to Pg. 220, ¶ 1 & 2 – It is odd that Yi Yin was part of the Shang dynasty's official court for so long because he was rumored to have temporarily defected and joined the Xia enemy before returning to Tang's court. What is even more odd is that the first and second heirs to the Shang dynasty died before they could rule, while Yi Yin was still in court.

3. Why couldn't Yi Yin be considered for the Chinese throne?

A3. – Pg. 220, ¶ 3 – Yi Yin could not be enthroned because he was not royalty, he was an ex-cook (or an ex-farmer).

4. How did Yi Yin use T'ai Jia's enthronement to his advantage?

A4. – T'ai Jia was only a child when he was appointed ruler, so Yi Yin acted as his advisor and guided T'ai Jia's actions. Yi Yin could not be the official king, but he could make all of the child king's decisions; he was working his way towards a kingship in all but name.

5. What was the result of Yi Yin's declaration that T'ai Jia be sent to a detention center out of town?

NOTE TO INSTRUCTOR – The chapter offers two answers to this question; both should be listed here.

A5. – Pg. 221, ¶ 2 & 3 – As a result of sending T'ai Jia away, Yi Yin stayed in power. At the detention center, T'ai Jia became obedient and then returned to Po ready to be guided by Yi Yin. A variation on this story is that T'ai Jia escaped from his detention center in order to return to Po, where he assassinated Yi Yin.

6. Why might the capital have moved so many times during the Shang dynasty's rule?

A6. – Pg. 221, ¶ 6 & 7 – Yellow River flooding might have motivated the frequent movement of the capital. Invasions from nearby village patriarchs may also have caused the moves.

Section III: Critical Thinking

The student may use her text to answer this question.

A strong king finds ways to strengthen his country, even in the worst of times. While the Hittites were tearing their kingdom apart, fighting over the seat of power, the rulers of the Shang dynasty used turmoil to their advantage. This is particularly true in the case of P'an Keng. Using the passage on page 222, recounting P'an Keng's response to his suspicious courtiers, to support your response, write a paragraph that answers the following questions:

- Why did P'an Keng move the capital city to Yin?

- What did the oracle tell P'an Keng?

- How was P'an Keng able to use the history of Shang's moving capital to his advantage?

- What argument did P'an Keng make against having a fixed capital city?

Passage from page 222:

I have consulted the [oracle] and obtained the reply: "This is no place for us." When the former kings had any important business, they gave reverent heed to the commands of Heaven. In a case like this especially they did not indulge the wish for constant repose; they did not abide ever in the same city. Up to this time the capital has been in five regions… [We must] follow the examples of these old times…following the meritorious course of the former kings.

P'an Keng moved the capital city to Yin because he was told to do so by an oracle. The oracle told P'an Keng that the current capital city, Yen, was "no place for us." P'an Keng focused on the tradition of the moving Shang capital rather than suggesting the movement was a sign of weakness. P'an Keng said "Up to this time the capital has been in five regions…[We must] follow the example of these old times…following the meritorious course of the former kings." P'an Keng made it seem that moving the capital city was an important part of the Chinese culture, and it was the will of the gods that the movement occur. Finally, P'an Keng argued that a fixed capital city would mean "constant repose" or laziness. The moving capital city reflected an active and able government that followed the traditions of its culture.

CHAPTER THIRTY-ONE: THE MYCENAEANS OF GREECE

The student may use his text when answering the questions in sections I and II.

Section I: Who, What, Where

Write a one or two-sentence answer explaining the significance of each item listed below.

Aegeus – **Pg. 225, ¶ 2 – Aegeus, king of Athens, was helpless against Minos and sent Athenian boys and girls to be sacrificed to the Minotaur. He leapt to his death because he thought his son Theseus was killed by the Minotaur.**

Ariadne – **Pg. 226, ¶ 1 – Ariadne, daughter of Minos, helped Theseus defeat the Minotaur by giving him a ball of string. The ball of string helped Theseus to find and kill the Minotaur, and to find his way out of the Labyrinth.**

Linear A/B – **Pg. 227, ¶ 1 – Linear A was the type of writing used by the Cretans. Linear B was the more sophisticated form of writing, based on Linear A, used by the Mycenaeans.**

Theseus – **Pg. 226, ¶ 1 & 2 – Theseus, son of Athenian king Aegeus, beat the Labyrinth and killed the Minotaur. Theseus was able to escape Minos by sabotaging the Cretan navy**.

Section II: Comprehension

Write a two/three sentence answer to each of the following questions.

1. What were the four major cities on the Greek peninsula around 1600? Why did each of these cities have its own royal palace?
A1. – Pg. 224, ¶ 2 – The four major cities on the Greek peninsula around 1600 were Mycenae, Thebes, Pylos and Athens. The cities were divided by mountain ridges, which caused each to rule over itself, meaning each city had its own royal palace.

2. Why do historians call the people of ancient Thebes, Pylos and Athens, "Mycenaeans?"
A2. – Pg. 224, ¶ 3 – The people of Thebes, Pylos, Athens and Mycenae shared trade, a language and a culture. Historians viewed all of the ancient Greeks as part of the same people, and named this group after the largest city on the peninsula, Mycenae.

3. Why did Aegeus give his son both a black and white flag when he sailed to Knossos?
A3. – Pg. 225, ¶ 3 – Aegeus sent his son to fight the Minotaur on a black-sailed tribute ship, because he was sure his son would die in battle. Keeping a bit of hope alive, Aegeus also gave his son a sail of white, which Theseus promised to hoist if he overcame the Minotaur.
4. How did Theseus find his way out of the Labyrinth?

A4. – Pg. 226, ¶ 1 – Ariadne gave Theseus a ball of string, which he tied to a door post before entering the Labyrinth. After Theseus found the Minotaur at the center of the Labyrinth and killed the beast, he traced the string back out of the maze to safety.

5. How did the body of water near Athens come to be called the "Aegean Sea?"
A5. – Pg. 226, ¶ 2 – When Theseus set sail for Athens after defeating the Minotaur, he forgot to hoist the white flag of triumph, instead sailing with the black flag of defeat. Seeing the black flag, Aegeus threw himself off of the cliff near Athens into the sea. The city mourned Aegeus's unfortunate death, and the surrounding waters became known as the Aegean Sea, in the king's memory.

6. What is the importance of a Mycenaean cup found buried with an official of Tuthmosis III?
A6. – Pg. 226, ¶ 4 – The Mycenaean cup found with one of Tuthmosis III's officials proves that the Mycenaeans were skillful sailors, using the water to transport merchandise as far south as Egypt.

7. Why did trade with Egypt exacerbate the division between Cretans and the Greeks?
A7. – Pg. 227, ¶ 3 – Both the Cretans and the Greeks sailed on the Mediterranean, and wanted a monopoly on trade with Egypt, which had gold and ivory. The Cretans had an advantage, though, as the island was located right on the trade route south to Egypt.

8. How did the eruption of Thera affect the cultural relationship between Crete and Greece?
A8. – Pg. 227, ¶ 4 – After the eruption of Thera, the Mycenaean culture had more influence in Crete. Mycenaean pottery and cups appeared with great frequency in Minoan houses, and Cretan tombs began to show a distinctively Mycenaean design that had not appeared on the island before the natural disaster.

Section III: Critical Thinking

Exchange, both cultural and commercial, was rampant between the Minoans of Crete and the Mycenaeans of Greece. However, after the eruption of Thera, the cultural flow between the two kingdoms went primarily one way: the Mycenaeans had a stronger influence on the Minoans. How might the environment and location of Crete have influenced this cultural shift?

To answer this question, the student must recall what he learned about ancient Crete from Chapter Twenty-Four. Crete was an island in an unstable sea. After Thera erupted, the ash cloud from the volcano covered the sun for an extended period of time. Minoans may have felt doomed, fearing the electrical storms and violent waters that came after the eruption.

Though located on a peninsula, Mycenae was part of the mainland, and therefore had access not only to the goods from the adjacent waters but also from the dry land surrounding the city. We know from the chapter that sometime around 1450 Knossos was sacked. Across Crete, towns were abandoned, or they shrank. The people of Crete were disappearing, and taking their culture with them. The attack on the island, coupled with the volcanic climate of the area, meant that the Minoan culture did not have the room to grow or move like its mainland neighbors. This allowed the Mycenaeans to exert more influence over the stunted Minoan culture.

CHAPTER THIRTY-TWO: STRUGGLE OF THE GODS

The student may use her text when answering the questions in sections I and II.

Section I: Who, What, Where

Write a one or two-sentence answer explaining the significance of each item listed below.

Akhen-aten – **Pg. 234, ¶ 2 – Akhen-aten was the name Amenhotep IV gave himself to show his devotion to Aten. The name means "worshipper of the sun."**

Akhet-aten – **Pg. 234, ¶ 2 – Akhet-aten was the name of the city Amenhotep IV had built in honor of the single sun god Aten.**

Amenhotep III – **Pg. 229, ¶ 1 & Pg. 232, ¶ 1 – Amenhotep III was the son of a Mitanni princess and the Egyptian pharaoh Tuthmosis IV. Amenhotep III created alliances with all the empires surrounding Egypt through negotiation, scheming and marriage.**

Amenhotep IV – **Pg. 233, ¶ 3 – Amenhotep IV, son of Amenhotep III, started a new religion, the worship of the sun itself. He is also known as Akhenaten.**

Aten – **Pg. 233, ¶ 4 – Aten was name of the disk of the sun itself. It is a force, the sun god itself.**

Suppululiuma – **Pg. 231, ¶ 3 – Suppululiuma, king of the Hittites, made an alliance with Amenhotep III against the Mitanni.**

Section II: Comprehension

Write a two/three sentence answer to each of the following questions.

1. How was Amenhotep III's reign like Hatshepsut's? Use at least two examples from the chapter to support your answer.

NOTE TO INSTRUCTOR – There is no direct comparison between Amenhotep III's reign and Hatshepsut's rule in the chapter. The student should remember that Hatshepsut showcased her power through building.

A1. – Pg. 230, ¶ 2 – Amenhotep III's reign was like Hatshepsut's because he chose to show his power through building rather than through military conquest. He added to the Temple of Amun and built a virgin temple to the sun-god.

ALTERNATE ANSWER (the student can list any two of these examples):

- *He dug a lake a mile long for his chief wife.*
- *He added to the Temple of Amun.*
- *He opened new quarries and mines.*
- *He constructed a mortuary temple for himself.*
- *He built a huge new palace for his own use.*
- *He built a virgin temple to the sun-god.*
- *He built a Memphis residence for himself.*
- *He erected various shrines along the Nile.*

2. List all the ways Tushratta of Mitanni and Amenhotep III of Egypt were related. How did these entanglements benefit Egypt?

A2. – Pg. 230, ¶ 5 – Tushratta of Mitanni was the brother of one of Amenhotep's daughters, making him Amenhotep III's cousin. He was also the brother of one of Amenhotep's wives, and the father of another, making him simultaneously Amenhotep III's brother-in-law and father-in-law. All of these entanglements strengthened the Egyptian and Mitanni alliance.

3. Why wasn't Assur supposed to negotiate with foreign powers? How was Amenhotep's businesses with Assur a violation of his treaty with the Mitanni?

A3. – Pg. 231, ¶ 1 & 2 – As a vassal of the Mitanni kingdom, Assur was not supposed to do business with other nations as if it was independent. Amenhotep III was secretly helping Assur strengthen its fortifications in preparation for a revolt against the Mitanni, thus violating Egypt's treaty with the Mitanni empire.

4. What were the arrangements of the Egyptian and Babylonian alliance?

A4. – Pg. 231, ¶ 4 & 5 – Amenhotep III was allied to Babylon through marriage. He wed the daughter of the Kassite king of Babylon.

5. Why was it politically advantageous for Amenhotep III to align himself with the sun-god, Ra?

A5. – Pg. 232, ¶ 5 – By worshipping Ra as his personal deity, Amenhotep III freed himself from the authority of Amun's priests. He also avoided contributing any more land or wealth to Amun's temple.

6. How did Amenhotep IV choose to outshine the power of his father? What made Amenhotep IV's worship of the sun different than the traditional worship of Ra?

A6. – Pg. 233, ¶ 4 – Amenhotep IV chose to outdo his father in devotion. Amenhotep IV started an entire new religion, the worship of the sun itself. While Ra was a god shaped like a mortal being, the sun-disk was an abstract representation of the divine self. The sun was not the chief power, like Ra, it was the only power.

7. Why did Abraham's descendants, the Hebrews, settle in Egypt?

A7. – Pg. 235, ¶ 2 – Abraham's descendants faced famine in the Western Semitic lands where they had lived as shepherds, so they moved down to Egypt where water and fertile land was abundant.

8. How did the Egyptian pharaoh treat the Hebrew people, according to the book of Exodus?

A8. – Pg. 235, ¶ 4 – According to the book of Exodus, the pharaoh of Egypt made the Hebrews slaves that would complete his building projects. When the population of the Hebrews did not decrease after enslavement, the pharaoh ordered all male Hebrew children thrown into the river.

9. Though Sargon lived 1,000 years before Moses, how did the ancient cupbearer help the Hebrew child?

A9. – Pg. 235, ¶ 5 & 6 – Rather than being thrown into the river to die, Moses was sealed in a papyrus basket and set in the reeds of the Nile in the hopes that someone would find and rescue him. A princess found Moses, and even though she recognized him as a Hebrew, she chose to adopt him anyway. The princess may have known the story of Sargon, who floated down the Euphrates as a baby, was saved and then came into power. Sargon's story served as proof of his chosenness and divinity, and so the princess may have believed her found baby was also divinely chosen.

9. What kind of plagues descended on Egypt during the Exodus of the Hebrews? How did these plagues affect the power of the Egyptian gods?

A9. – Pg. 236, ¶ 3 – During the Exodus of the Hebrews, the Nile turned to blood and became foul and poisonous. Frogs, usually sacrificed to Osiris, appeared in numbers so great they became pestilent and the sun-disk was blotted out by darkness. The plagues made a mockery of the Egyptian gods, and showed that they were helpless against the will of YHWH.

Section III: Critical Thinking

The student may not use her text to answer this question.

Akhenaten's worship of Aten was like Moses's worship of YHWH in one way only: both religions were based on monotheism. While both Abraham and Moses felt the call of God, Akhenaten's move to follow Aten seems more political. Write a short paragraph arguing how we might understand Amenhotep IV's conversion to monotheism as a play for power rather than a true spiritual calling.

To answer this question, the student must remember how important it was for an Egyptian ruler to show his/her power. Hatshepsut and Amenhotep III used copious building to flaunt their might; Tuthmosis III displayed his strength through conquest. Amenhotep IV decided to outdo his father's prosperous rule by focusing on devotion. Amenhotep IV's creation of a new religion was a way to show his power over the Egyptian people.

As we read in the chapter, Amenhotep III devoted himself to the sun-god Ra in order to avoid paying tribute to the priests of Amun. Similarly, Amenhotep IV rid himself of all allegiance to the Egyptian gods and their earthly demands by declaring the superiority of a new god: Aten. On page 234, the text reads, "Aten needed no priests, no religious bureaucracy that might thwart the pharaoh's aims. Neither the god nor the god's representative on earth would tolerate shared power." As the only living person able to receive Aten's message or wield his power, Akhenaten was able to elevate himself above all of Egypt and rule as a supreme and untouchable power.

The student should start her answer by recounting the different ways power was displayed by the pharaohs of Egypt. This should lead to the question, "How did Amenhotep IV show his power?" The chapter makes it clear: he created a new religion. Then, the student should compare the decision of Amenhotep III to ally himself with Ra to avoid paying tribute to the earthly priests of Amun to the untouchable nature of Amenhotep IV's devotion to Aten. Worshipping Aten made Amenhotep IV untouchable, religiously and politically.

CHAPTER THIRTY-THREE: WARS AND MARRIAGES

The student may use his text when answering the questions in sections I and II.

Section I: Who, What, Where

Write a one or two-sentence answer explaining the significance of each item listed below.

Ankhesenamun – **Pg. 243, ¶ 3 to Pg. 244, ¶ 2 – Ankhesenamun was the wife of Tutankhamun. When Tutankhamun died, she tried to marry a Hittite prince, but ended up married to her grandfather, Ay.**

Assur-uballit – **Pg. 239, ¶ 3 & 4 – Assur-uballit was the Assyrian king that fought against the Mitanni and reclaimed the title of Great King.**

Ay – **Pg. 244, ¶ 6 – Ay was the maternal grandfather of Ankhesenamun. He married Ankhesenamun after Tutankhamun died, and served as pharaoh until his death four years later.**

Burnaburiash I – **Pg. 242 ¶ 4 – 6 – Burnaburiash I was the Kassite king of Babylon. He allied himself with Assur by marrying his son to an Assyrian princess.**

Horemheb – **Pg. 244, ¶ 1, ¶ 5, ¶ 7 – Horemheb was a member of the Egyptian army since the days of Amenhotep III. He thwarted the marriage of Ankhesenamun to a Hittite prince, and named himself pharaoh after the death of Ay.**

Karaindash – **Pg. 242, ¶ 6 to Pg. 243, ¶ 2 – Karaindash was the son of Burnaburiash. He was passed over as heir to the Babylonian throne; his son was named heir to the kingship.**

Tushratta – **Pg. 238, ¶ 1 & 2 – Tushratta, king of the Mitanni, was allied to Egypt through marriage. He looked to Egypt for help against the threatening Hittites.**

Tutankhaten/Tutankh-Amun – **Pg. 241, ¶ 8, Pg. 242 ¶ 3 – Tutankhaten became pharaoh of Egypt after the plague killed most of the royal family. Tutankhaten changed his name to Tutankh-Amun in order to reflect his devotion to Amun.**

Section II: Comprehension

Write a two/three sentence answer to each of the following questions.

1. What were the signs of Egypt's gradual backing away from the Mitanni alliance?

A1. – Pg. 238, ¶ 3 & 4 – Signs of Egypt's backing away from the Mitanni alliance include sending a small amount of gold as the bride-price for Tushratta's daughter, ignoring the Mitanni envoys in the Egyptian court and refusing to answer a query sent down to Egypt by a Mitanni messenger.

2. Why did Akhenaten choose to honor his alliance with the Hittites over his alliance with the Mitanni?
A2. – Pg. 239, ¶ 1 – Akhenaten chose to honor his alliance with the Hittites because the Hittites had a better chance of winning in a war against the Mitanni. The Hittite army was strong, and

their king, Suppiluliuma was a cunning strategist.

3. How did Assur-uballit take advantage of the Hittite attack on the Mitanni?
A3. – Pg. 239, ¶ 3 & 4 – Assur-uballit took advantage of Mitanni weakness due to the Hittite attack, and marched on Mitanni land himself. When Tushratta retreated, Assur-uballit claimed the territory for Assur, making it a kingdom once again.

4. What happened to the Mitanni kingdom after the fall of Washukkanni? Where did the Hurrians go?
A4. – Pg. 241, ¶ 2 – After the fall of Washukkanni, the Mitanni kingdom no longer existed. The Hurrians retreated to the Zagros mountains, from where they first descended.

5. How did the plague affect the Egyptian royal family?
A5. – Pg. 241, ¶ 5 – 7 – The plague killed most of the Egyptian royal family. Akhenaten's chief wife was the first to go, followed by his second wife, then his middle daughter and eldest daughter. Akhenaten himself died, followed just days after by his heir.

6. Why did the Egyptians dismiss Aten's power? What happened to Aten, the god, and Aten, the city, when Tutankhamun came into power?
A6. – Pg. 242, ¶ 3 – The Egyptians believed the gods were angered by Akhenaten's betrayal and worship of Aten. Tutankhamun restored faith in Amun, and destroyed any trace of Aten's name. He even renamed the city of Aten "Amarna."

7. Why did Ankhesenamun ask Suppiluliuma of the Hittites to send one of his sons down to Egypt?
A7. – Pg. 244, ¶ 2 & 3 – Ankhesenamun asked Suppiluliuma to send one of his sons to Egypt because she was afraid of the powerful men in the Egyptian court - in particular Ay, her grandfather and Horemheb, a longstanding Egyptian military leader. She thought if she married a Hittite prince, she would be guaranteed protection.

8. How did Horemheb end up as the Egyptian pharaoh? How did he get past Ankhesenamun, the Hittite prince, and Ay on his way to the throne?
A8. – Pg. 244, ¶ 5-7 – Horemheb stopped the Hittite prince that was supposed to marry Ankhesenamun from arriving in Egypt by meeting him at the Egyptian border and doing away with him. Ankhesenamun ended up marrying Ay, who only lived for a few more years after becoming pharaoh. As soon as Ay was buried, Horemheb declared himself pharaoh.

Section III: Critical Thinking

While marriage was a typical way for a king to ally himself with a powerful nation, a marital bond between kingdoms did not grant absolute peace. Burnaburiash I was able to make a tenuous peace with Assur-uballit by marrying his daughter to a Babylonian prince. Explain how this alliance fell apart when Burnaburiash died, and how, if not for Assur-uballit, the Babylonian government may have fallen apart. *In order to get a strong answer from the student, ask him "Who did Burnaburiash appoint as his heir? How did the Babylonians react to this appointment?" This answer is straight from the reading on page 243, ¶ 2 & 3.*

• Just before his death, Burnaburiash decided to appoint Karaindash's son heir to the throne. The young boy was half-Assyrian and half-Babylonian. The Kassites of the Babylonian army revolted against this new heir. They saw the king as a half-breed with no right to the throne. The Assyrian princess and her Babylonian husband were done away with, and a military government was put into place.

Then, ask the student, "How did Assur-uballit react to the Babylonian revolt? How were his actions both a violation of the peace treaty, as well as the possible salvation of the Kassite throne?"

• Assur-uballit, as father of the Assyrian princess married to Karaindash, claimed the right to straighten out the Babylonian government. His interference in the Babylonian government can be understood as a violation of the peace treaty between Assur and Babylon. However, Assur-uballit helped restore a Kassite king to the throne, thus saving Babylon from a tyrannical military government.

CHAPTER THIRTY-FOUR: THE GREATEST BATTLE IN VERY ANCIENT TIMES

The student may use her text when answering the questions in sections I and II.

Section I: Who, What, Where

Write a one or two-sentence answer explaining the significance of each item listed below.

Adad-nirari – **Pg. 250, ¶ 2 – Adad-nirari, king of Assyria, claimed much of the land fractured by the Mitanni flight for Assyria, and even took some of Babylon's northern territory for his empire. Adad-nirari called himself "King of the World" because of his successful conquests.**

Battle of Kadesh – **Pg. 248, ¶ 5 – The Battle of Kadesh was fought between the Egyptians and Hittites over the city of Kadesh. Kadesh remained property of the Hittites after the battle, but Rameses II claimed victory for Egypt nonetheless; the Battle of Kadesh became an emblem of Egyptian superiority.**

Hattusilis III – **Pg. 250, ¶ 3 – Hattusilis became king of the Hittites after usurping the throne from Muwatalli's son. His spent his time as king struggling to win a civil war.**

Muwatalli – **Pg. 247, ¶ 2 – Muwatalli, Suppiluliuma's grandson, was king of the Hittite nation when Rameses II was in power in Egypt.**

Rameses I – **Pg. 246, ¶ 2-3 – Rameses I was the first pharaoh ever with absolutely no blood connection to any previous royal line. His kingship marked the beginning of Egypt's Nineteenth Dynasty.**

Rameses II – **Pg. 247, ¶ 1 – Rameses II, son of Seti, earned fame for the length of his reign, the number of his building projects, the legendary strength of his army, and for surviving the battle of Kadesh.**

Seti – **Pg. 246, ¶ 3 to Pg. 247, ¶ 1 – Seti succeeded his father Rameses I as king of Egypt. Seti is remembered mostly for building temples all over Egypt.**

Shalmaneser I – **Pg. 250, ¶ 5 – Shalmaneser I succeeded Adad-nirari as king of Assyria, and he continued to take the Mitanni territory for the empire. He was an aggressive fighter, blinding his captives, which later became standard in Assyrian warfare.**

Section II: Comprehension

Write a two/three sentence answer to each of the following questions.

1. Why did Rameses II want to fight the Hittites and win back Kadesh for the Egyptian kingdom?
A1. – Pg. 247, ¶ 3 – Rameses II wanted to win back Kadesh to prove that Egypt was more powerful than the Hittites. Kadesh was too far north for easy control by the Egyptians, and too far south for easy administration by the Hittites. Whichever empire claimed it could boast of superior strength.

2. How did Rameses II organize his army of twenty thousand men?
A2. – Pg. 247, ¶ 4 – Rameses II organized his army into four companies named after the Egyptian gods: Amun first, Ra second, Ptah third, and Set fourth.

3. How did Muwatalli trick Rameses II into attacking Kadesh?
A3. – Pg. 247, ¶ 4 & Pg. 248, ¶ 1 – Rameses II heard a rumor that Muwatalli was nowhere near Kadesh, so the Egyptian pharaoh thought the time was perfect for an attack. Rameses II gathered his men and marched on Kadesh, reassured by captured Hittite guards that the Hittite army was still very far away. This was actually a trap set up by Muwatalli so that Rameses II would march right into the Hittite army that was waiting just behind Kadesh.

4. Describe Muwatalli's first attack on the invading Egyptian troops.
A4. – Pg. 248, ¶ 1 – While Rameses II and his men set up camp at Kadesh, the Hittite army came out from behind the city and attacked the second division of Egyptian men, Ra, cutting off Rameses II from the rest of his army.

5. What strategic military move of Rameses II helped the Egyptian army recover after the attack on the men of Ra?
A5. – Pg. 248, ¶ 2 – Rameses II had a backup plan in place before the disastrous Egyptian march into Kadesh. Rameses II had sent reinforcements up the coast, probably by sea, in case the main body of the army ran into trouble on land. The two-front battle between land and sea confused the Hittite army.

6. How did the Battle of Kadesh end? Who claimed victory?
A6. – Pg. 248, ¶ 3-5 – The Battle of Kadesh ended in a stalemate, and Rameses II returned to Egypt with prisoners and booty. Kadesh was still claimed by the Hittites, however, Rameses II claimed victory and had flattering accounts of the battle carved onto the walls of Egyptian temples.

7. Why can we assume, at the time of Muwatalli, that the Hittites had a treaty with Babylon?
A7. – Pg. 249, ¶ 2 to Pg. 250, ¶ 1 – We can assume the Hittites had a treaty with Babylon because, according to a letter that has survived, Muwatalli sent down to Babylon for a doctor to come and help him with some personal medical problem, and the Babylonians responded by actually sending a doctor.

8. How did Hattusilis III end up on the Hittite throne?

A8. – Pg. 250, ¶ 3 – Hattusilis had to fight his way to the Hittite throne. When Muwatalli died, he left his throne to his son, who promptly stripped the next most powerful man at court – his uncle, Hattusilis – of his court positions and attempted to exile him. Hattusilis declined to be exiled, rounded up his followers, put the king under guard, and pronounced himself King Hattusilis III.

9. Why did Rameses II agree to a peaceful alliance with Hattusilis III, rather than taking over the Hittite empire?

A9. – Pg. 251, ¶ 3 – Rameses II agreed to an alliance with Hattusilis III rather taking over his nation because Egypt did not have the power to conquer another people. Rameses II was no longer in control of most of the Western Semitic territories that had once belonged to Egypt, and the petty kings along the Mediterranean coast believed Rameses II lost at Kadesh, and had been revolting ever since. There was no way that the Egyptian army could fight, and win, against the Hittite people, while also dealing with Egyptian defectors.

Section III: Critical Thinking

The student may not use her text to answer this question.

We've all heard the adage, "your reputation precedes you." In this chapter we learn that Egypt had become an empire that depended on reputation as much as actual strength to keep its position as a world leader. Similarly, Hattusilis III needed to fix his reputation in order to keep his position as King of the Hittites. Write two paragraphs below describing how Rameses II of Egypt and Hattusilis III of the Hittites manipulated their public perception in order to stay powerful.

The student has a choice of two accounts when writing about Egypt's reliance on its reputation to secure its power in the world: the Battle of Kadesh, or the treaty with Hattusilis III and the Hittites. The most important point to be made in either story is that if Egypt was still truly a great power, Hittite land would have been seized. At Kadesh, the Egyptians would have taken the city, and when Hattusilis III came to Rameses II asking for an alliance, a truly powerful Egypt would have attacked and conquered the weak Hittite empire.

<u>Questions to ask the student (Choice 1):</u>

Why did Rameses II take his army to Kadesh?
What happened at Kadesh?
Why didn't Rameses II take Kadesh for Egypt?
What did Rameses II do to make the Egyptian people believe Egypt won at Kadesh?
Why did Rameses II need to make his people believe Egypt triumphed over the Hittites?

<u>Choice 1:</u>

When Rameses II went to battle against the Hittites at Kadesh in order to prove Egypt's might, his army couldn't secure a win. Fortunately, neither could Muwatalli's. Wanting to avoid eternal battle, Muwatalli suggested a truce. Rameses II did not agree to this peace, but did leave the battle with prisoners and booty. If Egypt was truly strong, however, Rameses II would have taken Kadesh from the Hittites. Returning to Egypt, Rameses II needed to make his people believe Egypt had beat the Hittites, so he carved the battle into the walls of temples at least nine times, showing graphic illustrations of Egyptians slaughtering Hittites. Rameses II turned the Battle of Kadesh into an myth, a story that boasted of Egyptian superiority. We know, however, that this was not the case.

Why did the Hittites ask Egypt for an alliance?
Why didn't Rameses II take advantage of Hittite weakness and attack the nation?
How did Rameses II portray the alliance between the Hittites and Egypt on the walls at Karnak?
Why didn't Rameses II send a daughter to marry a Hittite prince?

Choice 2:
Muwatalli's son, kicked off the throne by Hattusilis III, went to Egypt for asylum. At the same time, Hattusilis III suggested an alliance between the Hittites and Egyptians. This was the perfect opportunity for Rameses II to take over the Hittite territories and claim them for Egypt. Unfortunately, Egypt did not have the power to fight the Hittites, the rebellious Western Semitic territories, and the petty kings on the Mediterranean coast. Rameses II kicked Muwatalli's son out of Egypt and made peace with Hattusilis III. In order to save Egypt's reputation, Rameses II had the treaty, which promised that Egypt would not attack the Hittites, carved on the temple walls at Karnak, with an introductory note explaining that the Hittites had come to him begging for peace. Also, Rameses II refused to send a daughter north to marry a Hittite prince. Rameses II, unable to send an army to conquer Hittite land, had to make it look like Egypt still had the upper hand.

The second half of the answer will be about Hattusilis III's "The Apology." Hattusilis III struggled to clean up his reputation after taking the throne from Muwatalli's son. Hattusilis III, not wanting to be part of a new game of "Kill the King," needed his people to believe he had the right to rule.

Questions to ask the student:

How did Hattusilis III come to be king of the Hittites?
What did he write in order to justify his kingship?
What did it say?
How did the people react to Hattusilis III's reign?

Hattusilis III came to the Hittite throne by usurping power from his nephew, the rightful heir. Wanting to show his people that he was truly meant to rule, Hattusilis III wrote "The Apology," which explains that the gods had given him the right to rule, and that his successful seizing of the throne proved that the gods approved of his kingship. Unfortunately, this argument was not entirely convincing to the Hittites; fragmentary records from Hattusas show that Hattusilis III spent most of his reign struggling to win a civil war. Hattusilis III's reputation as a usurper, even though he did the best he could to change the public's view of his reign, made him a disliked king.

Chapter Thirty-Five: The Battle for Troy

The student may use his text when answering the questions in sections I and II.

Section I: Who, What, Where

Write a one or two-sentence answer explaining the significance of each item listed below.

Achilles – **Pg. 254, ¶ 6 – Achilles was a great warrior from Thessaly. His behavior is the central drama of the Iliad.**

Agamemnon – **Pg. 254, ¶ 4-5 – Agamemnon was the high king of the Greeks, and Menelaus's brother. He called all of the Greek cities to join forces and attack Troy to avenge Paris's insult to Menelaus.**

Helen – **Pg. 254, ¶ 4 – Helen, a princess from Argos, was married to Menelaus. Helen was seduced by Paris and taken to Troy.**

Menelaus – **Pg. 254, ¶ 4 – Menelaus was the king of the Greek city of Sparta. Menelaus vowed revenge on Paris of Troy for taking away his wife, Helen.**

Nestor – **Pg. 255, ¶ 5 – Nestor was the king of Pylos, the Mycenaean city credited with sending sixty ships to the anti-Troy alliance. In the Iliad, Nestor drinks from a cup topped with two doves, linking the fictional Iliad with the real ruins of Mycenae.**

Paris – **Pg. 254, ¶ 4 – Paris, son of the king of Troy, seduced Menelaus's wife, Helen, and carried her off to Troy.**

Priam – **Pg. 254, ¶ 6 – Priam was the king of Troy, and father to Paris.**

Section II: Comprehension

Write a two/three sentence answer to each of the following questions.

1. What was the city of Troy like in its seventh incarnation?
A1. – Pg. 253, ¶ 3 to Pg. 254, ¶ 1 – Troy, in its seventh incarnation, was a wealthy city, without much need of imported food or goods; Troy stood on a plain with plenty of fertile farmland. There were fish in the nearby waters, sheep in the meadows, and Troy was famous for the herds of horses which ate its surplus grain.

2. What thwarted Agamemnon's attack on Troy? How long did the Greeks attack Troy without success?
A2. – Pg. 254, ¶ 5 – When he arrived on the shores of Asia Minor, Agamemnon found that Troy was protected by high walls and mighty soldiers. The Greeks attacked Troy for ten years, with no progress.

3. Why is Homer's inclusion of historical detail in the Iliad, like Pylos's use of the cup topped with

two doves, important for our understanding of the real-life tensions that fueled the writing of the poem?

NOTE TO THE INSTRUCTOR: This question is a little tricky. Like so many of the myths our text addresses, the fictional Iliad is a story that reflects real tensions of the ancient Greek world. The cup topped with two doves was an actual relic found in Mycenaean ruins. The text refers to this as "historical fiction." The details of the story show us that "Homer was telling the story of an older time" (255). This points us to a specific time in history, and the real conflict during this time is what is reflected in the Iliad.

A3. – Pg. 255, ¶ 5 – While Troy did not fall during Homer's lifetime, he uses real details of an older time to make his account authentic. A cup identical to the one Pylos uses in the Iliad was found in the ruins of Mycenae. The date of this cup, 1260 BC, points us to a particular period in Greek history, allowing us to uncover what real tensions fueled the fictional Iliad.

4. What were the Mycenaean cities of Mycenae, Thebes, Athens and Pylos like in 1260 BC?
A4. – Pg. 255, ¶ 6 to Pg. 256, ¶ 1 – By 1260 BC, the kings of Mycenae, Thebes, Athens, and Pylos had built their cities into small kingdoms, surrounded by walls and connected by chariot-smooth roads. Mycenae claimed the largest territory, and Pylos was so big that it was divided into sixteen districts, each with a governor and deputy governor who sent the king a tax of bronze each year. The cities carried on active trade with the Hittites and the Egyptians.

5. How may a captive princess actually sparked a battle between the Mycenaean cities and the Trojans?
A5. – Pg. 256, ¶ 2 – As we have seen in previous chapters, diplomatic marriages were taking place all over the ancient world. There was a great deal of pride involved in the delicate negotiations; those who sent princesses were inferior, those who accepted them boasted the greater power. Thus, it may well have been a captive princess that sparked the battle between the Mycenaeans and the Trojans.

6. How does historian Robert Graves explain the war between the Mycenaeans and the Greeks?
A6. – Pg. 256, ¶ 4 – Historian Robert Graves suggests that the hostility between Greece and Persia, as written by Herodotus, reflects a longstanding dislike between the cities of the Greek peninsula and those in Asia Minor. He argues that Helen's kidnapping was real, but it was actually an act of revenge for a previous Mycenaean raid on Trojan land. Her abduction fanned a hostility which had existed for years already.

7. Why, according to Thucydides, did the siege against Troy by the Mycenaeans last for so many years?
A7. – Pg. 257, ¶ 2 –Thucydides tells us that the war lasted for so many years because the Mycenaean attackers didn't have enough money to supply themselves properly; since they ran out of food, they had to spend part of their time growing food and making piratical raids into the Aegean, rather than fighting nonstop.

8. Why is the Mycenaean victory over Troy tinged with sadness? Use pieces of the excerpt from the Odyssey in your answer.

The following excerpt from the Odyssey is provided in the text on page 257:

This is the story of the woe we endured in that land,
we sons of the Achaeans, unrestrained in fury,
and of all that we bore....
There the best of us were slain...and many other ills
we suffered beside these...
After we had sacked the steep city of Priam,
and had departed in our ships...
even then, Zeus was fashioning for us a ruinous doom.

A8. – Pg. 257, ¶ 1 & 3-4 – After the victory at Troy, Mycenaean cities shrank, grew shabby and were less secure. The Trojan war cost the Mycenaeans everything – "the best" of the Mycenaeans "were slain," and they suffered "many other ills." The Mycenaeans faced "ruinous doom" once they left Troy. The peak of Mycenaean glory had passed, and after Troy, would not come again.

Section III: Critical Thinking

The student may use his text to answer this question.

The Trojan Horse is perhaps one of the most famous ruses in history. Using the excerpt from the poem the Aeneid, by Virgil, describe in detail how the Greeks used a wooden horse to finally break through Troy's walls and destroy the city.

This is a close reading response. Instead of retelling the story in his own words, the student should use as much of the poem as possible in his answer.

The following excerpt from the Aeneid is provided in the text on pages 254-55:

> *Broken in war and foiled by fate*
> *With so many years already slipping away, the Greek staff*
> *Constructed a horse....*
> *It was high as a hill, and its ribs were made from planks of pinewood....*
> *... Choosing warriors by lot they secretly*
> *Put them in on the blind side of the horse, until its vast*
> *And cavernous belly was crammed with a party of armed men.*
> *They broke out over a city drowned in a drunken sleep;*
> *They killed the sentries and then threw open the gates, admitting*
> *Their main body, and joined in the pre-arranged plan of attack...*
> *... The city's on fire; the Greeks are masters here.*

EXAMPLE ANSWER: The Greek army "constructed a horse" that was "high as a hill" with "ribs made from planks of pinewood." Greek warriors then got in "on the blind side of the horse" until the horse's "cavernous belly was crammed with a party of armed men." The Greek army pretended to depart the shores of Troy, and the Trojans, taking the horse as an offering, hauled it into the city.

The Trojans had a big party where they feasted in triumph over the Greeks, and then fell asleep dead drunk. The warriors in the horse then "broke out over a city drowned in a drunken sleep." They "killed the sentries" and called in the ships waiting just off shore. The Greeks "threw open the gates" of Troy, "admitting/Their main body," and then sacked the city. The invaders burned the city, "The city's on fire," and declared victory over the Trojans: "the Greeks are masters here."

CHAPTER THIRTY-SIX: THE FIRST HISTORICAL KING OF CHINA

The student may use her text when answering the questions in sections I and II.

Section I: Who, What, Where

Write a one or two-sentence answer explaining the significance of each item listed below.

I ching – **Pg. 261, ¶ 5 – The I ching is an ancient Chinese philosophical text, whose name means "Book of Changes."**

Ideogram – **Pg. 261, ¶ 2 – An ideogram is a pictorial sign used to represent a thing.**

Composite Ideogram – **Pg. 261, ¶ 2 – A composite ideogram is a sign that represented not a thing, but an abstraction or an idea. A composite ideogram was formed when pictorial signs, or ideograms, were combined.**

Fu Yueh – **Pg. 263, ¶ 1 – Fu Yueh was a common laborer working in a city near Yin who was chosen by Wu Ting to be his assistant in ruling the Shang kingdom.**

Shih ching – **Pg. 261, ¶ 5 – The Shih ching is an ancient Chinese philosophical text, whose name means "Book of Songs."**

Shu ching – **Pg. 259, ¶ 2 – The Shu ching is a book of ancient Chinese history, written before the Sima Qian.**

Wu Ting – **Pg. 259, ¶ 1 & Pg. 261, ¶ 5 – Wu Ting was the twenty-second Shang king. He was known for his hard work, refusal to sink into luxury, and the contentment he brought to his people.**

Section II: Comprehension

Write a two/three sentence answer to each of the following questions.

1. In what way did the casting of bronze showcase the power of the Shang king?
A1. – Pg. 260, ¶ 2 – The casting of bronze needed a king who could force multitudes of men to dig ore out of the mines that lay in the hilly country north of the Yellow River. Only a king with great power could make men do such a labor-intensive and nasty job.

2. Why are the bronze products of the Shang called "one of humankind's great artistic achievements"? Describe some of the great bronze works of ancient China.
A2. – Pg. 260, ¶ 3 to Pg. 261, ¶ 1 – The bronze products of the Shang were called "one of humankind's great artistic achievements" because no other ancient nation was able to cast bronze into such sophisticated forms. Some of the bronze works include: bronze-hafted spears

set with turquoise and topped with blades of white jade, ornate bronze buckles, bronze masks with snarling or comic faces, vessels for food and wine shaped like dragons, oxen or other creatures, finished with elaborate patternings and handles.

3. What do the inscriptions, names and signs engraved on some of the Shang's bronze pieces tell us about Shang culture?
A3. – Pg. 261, ¶ 2 – **The inscriptions, names and signs engraved on the bronze pieces from the Shang dynasty tell us that the Shang people had progressed to using writing.**

5. How was the development of Chinese writing different from the development of writing in other parts of the ancient world?
A5. – Pg. 261, ¶ 2 – **Ancient Chinese writing differed from other ancient writing development because the Chinese were the first to move beyond the pictorial by combining pictures: putting pictorial signs together into composite ideograms which represented abstractions and ideas.**

6. Describe the process of divination used by Shang priests to answer the questions of Chinese men and women.
A6. – Pg. 261, ¶ 3 – **A Shang priest would bring out a clean and dried shoulder bone of a cow or sheep, carved with patterns or marked with an inscription, and then touch the bone or shell with a heated metal point. When the bone cracked, the path of the crack through the pattern or inscription was "read" by the priests and interpreted as a message sent by ancestors who now passed their wisdom back to the living. The priest carved the results of the inquiry into the bone or shell, in signs cut by a knife and filled with paint.**

7. What do the *I ching* and the *Shih ching* tell us about Wu Ting? How do these descriptions conflict with the representation of Wu Ting as spiritual leader?
A7. – Pg. 261, ¶ 5 – **The *I ching* tells us that Wu Ting went on a three-year campaign against rebellious tribes to the northwest. The *Shih ching* credits Wu Ting with rule over an enormous amount of land. Wu Ting is praised for his hard work, and the contentment of his people during his reign. The image of Wu Ting as a tough warrior fighting rebels and conquering massive amounts of land conflicts with the image of a peaceful, taciturn king.**

8. What do the burial grounds of the Shang kings tell us about the rising power of Chinese rulers?
A8. – Pg. 262, ¶ 3 & 4 – **Chinese kings were buried in massive graves lined with human sacrifices. The people who were buried with the king were decapitated, most likely on a sacrificial altar. This suggests a great deal of authority on the part of the king; he was able to compel death even after he was no longer on this earth.**

Section III: Critical Thinking

During the Shang Dynasty, the king was known to be a spiritual leader, but the *Shih ching* suggests he was also a fierce warrior. Write two or three paragraphs explaining how the Chinese king could be both holy leader and strict overlord. In your answer, make sure to explain why Wu Ting needed Fu Yueh to rule. Also, make clear the connection between a king and his noblemen, and the large number of human sacrifices in the royal burial pits.

To start the student off, ask her to recall what the chapter says about the Chinese king ruling his widespread provinces. He needed men to act as his representatives. Did these men act exactly like the king, or did they act on their own accord? Then ask her to recall the story of Wu Ting and Fu Yueh. If Wu Ting would not break his three year silence until he found a good assistant, what does this prove about the ruling style of the Chinese king? Finally, thinking about all of the help the Chinese king needed, how might the decapitated bodies in the burial pits be a result of the actions of the king's many noblemen, rather than simple, voluntary sacrifices?

The Sima Qian makes constant mention of court officials and ruling noblemen with power of their own in the Chinese territories outside of Yin. The noblemen and officials governed in the king's name, but acted more or less as they pleased. Tributes sent to the king to avoid his anger were most likely demanded by the governors, not the king himself. Chinese villagers knew the king only through the noblemen that seized goods in the king's name. The Shang king was the spiritual head of all his people, but his real and earthly power existed inside a much smaller domain. His governors ruled all the land outside of the king's center.
We know that Wu Ting needed help ruling his land, and would not break his silence and start his reign until he found the perfect person to help him. Only when Wu Ting found Fu Yueh, a common laborer, to be his sage assistant, was Wu Ting able to take up his role as king. This proves that the Chinese king did not rule alone. Wu Ting needed more help than Fu Yueh could give, so he also relied on his noblemen to control the farther-flung provinces of the Shang kingdom. It is possible, then, that the numerous decapitated bodies in the burial pits were not devoted subjects willing to follow their king into death, but rather people sacrificed by the noblemen in deference to their king.

CHAPTER THIRTY-SEVEN: THE RIG VEDA

The student may use his text when answering the questions in sections I and II.

Section I: Who, What, Where

Write a one or two-sentence answer explaining the significance of each item listed below.

Grama – **Pg. 264, ¶ 2 – Grama is a Sanskrit word for a settled and walled village. It originally meant a wandering wagon-centered clan.**

Mandala – **Pg. 265, ¶ 2 – A mandala is a single cycle of the Rig Veda; there are ten mandalas all together. Each mandala contains hymns in praise of the gods, and chants to be said during sacrifices and other rituals.**

Rig Veda – **Pg. 264, ¶ 3 – The Rig Veda was the earliest collection of Indian hymns, created by the arya to make sense of their new incarnation as a settled people.**

*The student might also include that the Rig Veda was devoted to explaining the nature and requirements of the Indian gods.

Section II: Comprehension

Write a two/three sentence answer to each of the following questions.

1. How does the Sanskrit word "grama" reflect the changes in the culture of the arya people once they settled along the Indus River?
A1. – Pg. 264, ¶ 2 – The Sanskrit world "grama" once meant a wandering wagon-centered clan. The meaning then changed to the name for a settled and walled village. This change reflects the shift in the lifestyle of the arya from the nomadic, tribal roamings of their past to the settled lives they lived along the Indus.

2. What place did the priests of the arya hold in society?
A2. – Pg. 265, ¶ 1 – Priests were the first true aristocracy of the arya. The priests of the arya were not simply specialists in god-care, but a hereditary class of specialists.

3. To what was the Rig Veda almost exclusively devoted?
A3. – Pg. 265, ¶ 1 – The Rig Veda was devoted almost entirely to explaining the nature and requirements of the Indian gods.

4. What type of gods did the Indians worship?
A4. – Pg. 265, ¶ 2 – The Indians worshiped nature-gods.

5. What can we learn from the presence of Indra, Varuna, and Mitra as witnesses in a treaty between the Mitanni king and the Hittite empire-builder Suppululiuma?

A5. – Pg. 256, ¶ 2 – The presence of Indra, Varuna, and Mitra as witnesses in a treaty between the Mitanni king and Suppululiuma shows us not only that the Mitanni were arya, but that the arya were worshipping these gods long before they separated and went their different ways to the west and south.

6. How does the Rig Veda help us to understand the military structure of the arya?

A6. – Pg. 265, ¶ 3 – The Rig Veda shows us a glimpse of the warring side of the arya. In the oldest part of the Rig Veda, the fire-god Agni is credited with attacking "walls with his weapons," which suggests that the arya flourished and spread, and they made war on wooden-walled villages in their path by burning them.

7. What does the Rig Veda tells us about internal struggles among the arya?

A7. – Pg. 265, ¶ 3 – One hymn of the Rig Veda mentions a battle between "dark-hued" peoples and the arya, a description that suggests an inferior native people had been wiped out by light skinned "Aryans." Also, the seventh mandala describes a battle among ten arya kings. These two examples suggest that the arya struggled for dominance among their own people.

Section III: Critical Thinking

The student may use his text to answer this question.

The text tells us that the arya worshiped nature-gods, as was common to people who lived in harsh environments and along fierce rivers. The nature-gods reflect the anxieties the arya had about their natural environment. Below, list the name of each god mentioned in the text and the god's duty. Then, use the text to explain how Agni, Parjanya and Indra were manifestations of the arya's worries about their livelihood.

List of the gods and their duties.

Varuna: the sky-god
Ratri: spirit of the night
Agni: the god of fire
Parjanya: the rain-god
Mitra: the god of the sun
Indra: the ruler of the pantheon, the calmer of chaos

The student will use the text to answer this question, but he will also have to call upon what he has learned from other ancient cultures to answer the prompt fully.

Agni

Agni, the god of fire, attacks "walls with his weapons" (Pg. 265, ¶ 3). Agni reflects the use of arms by the arya to conquer other villages. Agni needed to be on the side of the arya if their people wanted to expand successfully.

Parjanya

If the student gets stuck here, ask him to think about the Egyptians and the Nile River. How much of Egypt's early fate relied on the controlled waters of the Nile? Similarly, what happens to a civilization when there is drought?

Parjanya, the rain-god, "'shatters the trees' and pours down water on cattle, horses, and men as well" (Pg. 265, ¶ 2). While the rain Parjanya gave to the arya was necessary for the growth of their crops, too much rain meant the Indus River would flood, possibly destroying their crops, livestock and villages. The arya prayed to Parjanya to deliver just the right amount of rain to nourish their lands. Similarly, if Parjanya decided not to give the arya any rain, everything would dry up, followed most certainly by famine and death.

Indra

The student may recall the story of the Minotaur and the Labyrinth here. The myth reflects the Greek fear of earthquakes and volcanic explosions. How might these same fears manifest themselves in the worship of Indra? Also, rebellious villagers can cause massive chaos. How might a god help the arya avoid internal conflict?

Indra, the ruler of the pantheon, the calmer of chaos, "made firm the shaking earth, who brought to rest the mountains when they were disturbed…in whose control are the horses, villages and all chariots" (Pg. 265, ¶2). Indra reflected the desire of the arya people to have peace. Perhaps the shaking earth and moving mountains point to the threat of severe thunderstorms and earthquakes. In addition, in order for the growing arya to stay peaceful, order was necessary, from the temperament of the horses to the behavior of the villagers. The seventh mandala describes a battle among ten arya kings against each other. If Indra can calm villages, it means he has control over the actions of men. It is possible that in addition to the mirroring the arya's fear of natural disasters, Indra also reflected the arya people's fear of internal struggle and revolt.

CHAPTER THIRTY-EIGHT: THE WHEEL TURNS AGAIN

The student may use her text when answering the questions in sections I and II.

Section I: Who, What, Where

Write a one or two-sentence answer explaining the significance of each item listed below.

Marduk – **Pg. 270, ¶ 5, Pg. 271, ¶ 5 & Pg. 273, ¶ 2 – Marduk was a Babylonian god whose statue was removed from Babylon when Tukulti-Ninurta sacked the city. Marduk was returned to Babylon, only to be carried off to Susa by the Elamites.**

Merneptah – **Pg. 267, ¶ 2 – Merneptah, the thirteenth son of Rameses II, succeeded his father as Egypt's pharaoh. He was the last pharaoh of the Nineteenth Dynasty.**

Tudhaliya – **Pg. 267, ¶ 4 – Tudhaliya, son of Hattusilis III, served as his father's Chief of Bodyguards before inheriting the throne and becoming King Tudhaliya IV.**

Tukulti-Ninurta – **Pg. 268, ¶ 6 – Tukulti-Ninurta succeeded his father Shalmaneser I as king of Assyria. Tukulti-Ninurta took advantage of Hittite weakness and launched an attack on the neighboring empire.**

Section II: Comprehension

Write a two/three sentence answer to each of the following questions.

1. How did the drought rattle Hittite security?
A1. – Pg. 268, ¶ 2 – The Hittite drought caused a massive shortage of grain. A country without grain is a country without money, and a country without money inevitably delays paying its soldiers until the last possible moment. Underpaid soldiers are always less disciplined than well-fed and satisfied ones.

2. Why was Tudhaliya worried about his position as king of the Hittites?
A2. – Pg. 268, ¶ 3 – Hattusilis III forcefully took the throne. Tudhaliya was the son of a usurper, and he feared one of the many men with royal blood who still lived in the kingdom might attempt to reclaim the throne.

3. What did Tudhaliya do to prove his power as rightful king of the Hittites?
A3. – Pg. 268 ¶ 4 – To prove that he was the rightful king, Tudhaliya gave orders for the most massive building program of any Hittite king ever: new shrines; additions to the already-large palace complex; a new suburb of the capital city Hattusas that included twenty-six new temples and doubled the size of the old city.

4. What was inherently wrong with Tudhaliya's massive building program?
A4. – Pg. 268, ¶ 4 – What was inherently wrong with Tudhaliya's plan was that these building projects drained the Hittite treasury. In a kingdom already suffering from famine and poverty, Tudhaliya IV was pouring money into construction, and this left him even less royal silver with which to pay his soldiers.

5. How did Tukulti-Ninurta know that Tudhaliya was unsure that the Hittites could beat the Assyrians at Erbila?
A5. – Pg. 269, ¶ 1 – Tukulti-Ninurta knew that Tudhaliya was unsure of the strength of the Hittite army because of the mixed messages Tudhaliya sent to the Assyrian king. First, Tudhaliya challenged Tukulti-Ninurta, then three more tablets appeared from a Hittite messenger. Two were hostile, but the third suggested a truce.

6. What was the result of the Hittite-Assyrian battle at Erbila?
A6. – Pg. 269, ¶ 2-3 – Tukulti-Ninurta won the battle at Erbila against the Hittite army. He carried off thousands of Hittites and brought them back to Assyria.

NOTE TO INSTRUCTOR: The student might also include that the conquest made enough of a splash in the ancient Near East to figure in the oldest Greek chronicles.

7. In what ways were Babylon and Assyria alike?
A7. – Pg. 270, ¶ 3 – Babylon and Assyria were twins in culture. They had once been part of the same empire, under Hammurabi, and the essentially Babylonian stamp on the whole area linked the two kingdoms. They shared the same gods with the same stories, and the Assyrians used Babylonian cuneiform in their inscriptions and annals.

8. How did Tukulti-Ninurta react to Babylonian king Kashtiliash IV's attempted conquest of disputed land between the Assyrian and Babylonian borders?
A8. – Pg. 270, ¶ 5 – Tukulti-Ninurta was angered by Kashtiliash IV's attempt to seize Assyrian land. In response, Tukulti-Ninurta marched down into to Babylon and plundered the temples. He even took the images of the gods away. Tukulti-Ninurta then captured Kashtiliash and marched him back to Assur naked and in chains.

9. Why might Tukulti-Ninurta have wanted to barricade himself in the little city he built, away from the people of Assur? Was the walled mini-city able to keep Tukulti-Ninurta safe?
A9. – Pg. 271, ¶ 3-4 – The Assyrian people were not happy with Tukulti-Ninurta's sacking of Babylon, nor did they approve of the removal of Babylonian sacred images and their transport to Assur. Tukulti-Ninurta could not hide in his mini-city from his enemies; he was cast from the throne, imprisoned, and then killed with a sword.

Section III: Critical Thinking

The student may use her text to answer this question.

In this chapter, we see very drastic and important changes happening across the ancient world. How has the turning wheel of fortune treated these great empires? Using your text for reference, write a short paragraph for each empire, describing how the empire fared during this tumultuous time. Each paragraph should begin, "As the wheel of fortune turned..."

The student will write a paragraph for each of the following: Hittites, Assyrians, Elamites, Babylonians, and Egyptians. If the student does not know where to start, suggest to her that she think of this as writing a summary of what happens to each empire in this chapter.

HITTITES
As the wheel of fortune turned, the Hittites were struck by drought. Tudhaliya IV had to ask Egypt for food. Instead of trying to fix the drought problem, Tudhaliya spent an incredible amount of money on construction, hoping to prove his power through the buildings he erected. No show of power could help Tudhaliya and his troops at Erbila, however, and the Hittites suffered a crushing defeat at the hands of Tukulti-Ninurta. After the battle against Assyria at Erbila, Hittite military strength faded quickly, many ships at Carchemish were no longer able to sail, and Tudhaliya was worried about internal rebellion. The edges of the Hittite kingdom were cracking away.

ASSYRIANS
As the wheel of fortune turned, the changing climate favored Assyrian king Tukulti-Ninurta for a short period of time. He fought against the Hittites at Erbila and won. Then, he fought against the king of Babylon, Kashtiliash IV. Tukulti-Ninurta victoriously sacked Babylon, brought the city's sacred images to Assur, and proclaimed himself king of Babylon. To celebrate his expanding empire, Tukulti-Ninurta built himself a new mini-city, for the king only. Unfortunately, both Babylonians and Assyrians were upset by Tukulti-Ninurta's sacking of Babylon. Tukulti-Ninurta's sacrilege brought about his end – he was dethroned and murdered. After Tukulti-Ninurta's death, the statue of the god Marduk was returned to Babylon. This did not stop a Babylonian rebellion, and the city was declared free from Assyrian domination once again. Soon after, Elamites began to attack the borders of the Assyrian empire.

ELAMITES
As the wheel of fortune turned, the Elamites took advantage of Assyrian and Babylonian weakness. After the Babylonian revolt against Assyria, the Elamites began to prod at the eastern border of Assyrian land. They came as far in as Nippur, and knocked the Assyrian king of that city off the throne two separate times. The Elamites also invaded Babylon. They stole Marduk, Hammurabi's law stele, and the Babylonian king, carrying them all off to Susa.

BABYLONIANS
As the wheel of fortune turned, Babylon did not have much luck. Babylon was invaded by Assyrian forces, sacked, plundered and claimed by Tukulti-Ninurta as part of the Assyrian empire. Things looked up briefly when Tukulti-Ninurta was killed; his son returned the statue of Marduk to Babylon and the city declared itself sovereign once again. But soon after, the Elamites invaded and stole

Marduk, Hammurabi's law stele, and the king himself. The Second Isin Dynasty took possession of the throne, but the kings didn't have much power. In just fifteen years, four kings rose and fell without much fanfare.

EGYPTIANS

As the wheel of fortune turned, Egypt's king Merneptah helped out the struggling Hittites by sending them grain. Egypt's strength was challenged soon after Merneptah's death. The succession of Egyptian kings failed, and anarchy followed. The chaos was aggravated by wandering raiders who came down into the Delta attempting to seize Egyptian land for themselves. This chaos marked the end of the Nineteenth Dynasty.

CHAPTER THIRTY-NINE: THE END OF THE NEW KINGDOM

The student may use his text when answering the questions in sections I and II.

Section I: Who, What, Where

Write a one or two-sentence answer explaining the significance of each item listed below.

Herihor – **Pg. 280, ¶ 1 – Herihor was a general under Rameses XI who named himself the High Priest of Amun. He was later known as Viceroy of Kush, Vizier of Egypt and then co-ruler of the entire country.**

Rameses III – **Pg. 275, ¶ 3 – Rameses III, who took the name in imitation of Rameses II, was Setnakhte's son. Despite his worship of Amun, Rameses III could not avoid a great battle against invaders from the north.**

Setnakhte – **Pg. 275, ¶ 1-2 – Setnakhte came to power at the end of the Nineteenth Dynasty, drove off Asiatic invaders and restored order to Egypt.**

Sea People – **Pg. 277, ¶ 5 – Sea People was the name the Egyptians gave to the alliance of sailors from the Aegean who expertly attacked Egypt from the water.**

Wenamun – **Pg. 279, ¶ 5 – Wenamun, a court official, was robbed on his way to Byblos, where he was going to negotiate a good price for cedar logs. Once Wenamun reached Byblos, the king of Byblos refused to do business with Egypt.**

Section II: Comprehension

Write a two/three sentence answer to each of the following questions.

1. According to the papyrus from the reign of Setnakhte's grandson, how did Setnakhte right the mess of the Nineteenth Dynasty?
A1. – Pg. 275, ¶ 2 – According to the ancient papyrus, Setnakhte fought off the "vile Asiatics;" he restored law and order so that local noblemen were no longer fighting with each other over control of land, he reopened temples which had closed out of fear or poverty, and he put priests back on duty.

2. Why did Rameses III have the Libyan tribes that wandered into Egypt from the western desert slaughtered or enslaved?
A2. – Pg. 276, ¶ 2 – Rameses III had wandering Libyan tribes slaughtered or taken into slavery because they showed signs of gathering and appointing a king of their own. Since the Hyksos disaster, no foreign people had been allowed to rule themselves within Egypt's borders. Rameses III wanted to squash any threat of internal rebellion before it started.

3. Describe the "general seething mess" of the Western Semitic lands that threatened Rameses III's Egypt.

A3. – Pg. 276, ¶ 3 – From Troy all the way over to Assur and down to Babylon, the Western Semitic lands were disorganized and full of strife. Local chiefs were asserting their independence, Hittite borders were shrinking, Assur and Babylon were at odds, the Elamites were rampaging along the eastern borders and a growing migration of tribal peoples from past the Aegean and the Black Sea were moving south.

4. Why was Egypt a popular destination for wanderers during the time of Rameses III?

A4. – Pg. 276, ¶ 4 – When Rameses III was on the throne, most of the ancient world had been suffering through a decade of drought, which inevitably caused famine. To hungry and thirsty wanderers, Egypt, with its always-watered lands, looked like the perfect place to resettle.

5. Who were the Weshesh, the Shekelesh and the Peleset? Why were these groups of people particularly threatening to Rameses III?

A5. – Pg. 277, ¶ 1 – The Weshesh were probably African tribes; the Shekelesh were most likely invaders from the Aegean; the Peleset were a seafaring folk who were of vaguely Aegean origin who probably came over by way of Crete. While invasions of the Delta were nothing new, these groups of people swore allegiances to each other, making their threat to Rameses III particularly fierce.

6. Why do historians think the Peleset were responsible for arming the force of allied tribes that invaded Egypt?

A6. – Pg. 277, ¶ 1 – Historians think the Peleset, who were from Crete, were responsible for arming the force because Egyptian reliefs of the attackers show the whole force in crested helmets of Cretan style.

7. What is the meaning of the carvings of piles of hands in Rameses III's mortuary temple?

A7. – Pg. 277, ¶ 3 – When Weshesh, the Shekelesh and the Peleset first invaded Egypt, Rameses III met the invasion at the border and beat the force back. It was customary for Egyptian soldiers to sever the right hands of the dead and bring them back to the scribes, so that an accurate count of enemy casualties could be recorded. The carvings of hands in Rameses III's temple symbolize the countless invaders that Rameses III put down at the first battle.

8. How did Rameses III configure his army to beat the Sea People?

A8. – Pg. 277, ¶ 6 to Pg. 278, ¶ 1 – Knowing the Egyptians could never meet the Sea People on equal terms, Rameses III filled his riverboats with soldiers until they were full of valiant warriors and then clogged the harbor entrances in the Delta with them, like a strong wall. He then lined his foot soldiers along the banks with orders to pelt the incoming enemy ships with arrows and spears.

9. Why did one of Rameses III's lesser wives want to assassinate the king and his appointed successor? What was the result of her assassination plot?

A9. – Pg. 278, ¶ 4 to Pg. 279, ¶ 1-3 – One of Rameses III's lesser wives wanted to assassinate the king and his appointed successor so that her own son would inherit the throne. The plot was discovered and almost every person involved took his or her own life, or was executed. Three conspirators had their noses and ears cut off and there was a single acquittal. The lucky man, Hori, a standard-bearer, was the only one who survived the purge.

10. How were the priests of Amun able to prosper while the rest of Egypt slowly lost its territories and riches?
A10. – Pg. 279, ¶ 6 – Since the reenthronement of Amun as chief god by Tutankhamun, the priests of Amun continued to grow richer because of the tributes of Egypt's kings. Pharaoh after pharaoh made rich offerings to the Temple of Amun. Rameses III gave Amun so much land that at the time of his death, the priests of Amun controlled almost a third of all the cropland in Egypt.

11. How did Horemheb's appointment of military officers to the priesthood – done in order to assure loyalty to the throne – eventually backfire?
A11. – Pg. 280, ¶ 1 – During the reign of Rameses XI, a general called Herihor had himself appointed High Priest of Amun. Herihor wanted more and more power, until he was challenging the throne itself; his name eventually began to appear as co-ruler of Egypt. Herihor was not at all loyal to the throne, in fact, he wanted to take it for himself.

12. What caused the civil war that started Egypt's Third Intermediate Period? Who claimed the north? Who claimed the south?
A12. – Pg. 280, ¶ 2-3 – Neither Rameses XI nor Herihor left an heir to the throne, so their sons-in-law began a civil war. Rameses XI's son-in-law enthroned himself in the north, while Herihor's son-in-law claimed a divine right to rule the south from the city of Thebes.

Section III: Critical Thinking

This chapter covers the slow decline of the New Kingdom of Egypt. While Egypt's military power had been weakening for a long time, its reputation as a world power quickly plummeted after the death of Rameses III. Using the excerpted passage below, write a paragraph explaining how Wenamun's story reflects the fall of both Egypt's military power and reputation.

A court official named Wenamun, attempting to travel up the coast in order to negotiate a good price for cedar logs from Byblos, was set upon and robbed of his money; the thieves had no fear of Egyptian reprisals. Wenamun finally did reach Byblos, but his mission failed. The king of Byblos was not inclined to accept Egyptian credit, which was no longer any good up north. "I am not your servant," he remarked to Wenamun, "nor am I the servant of the one who sent you. The logs stay here on the shore." (279)

The student needs to identify how this story reflects 1) the loss of Egypt's military power and 2) the loss of Egypt's reputation as a world power. It is clear that Wenamun's robbers had no fear of persecution by Egyptian law. This shows that Egypt's military was weak and could not punish criminals. The king of Byblos's refusal to trade with Egypt exemplifies the decline of Egypt's reputation as a world power. The king of Byblos did not want to do business with Egypt. Egypt could no longer count on its reputation to seal a business deal; with its mines silent, Egypt was no longer eligible for credit.

EXAMPLE ANSWER: Wenamun's misfortune on his business trip to Byblos exemplifies Egypt's fading military strength and the loss of its reputation as a great world power. First, Wenamun's robbers show no fear of Egyptian reprisals, meaning they had no fear of punishment from Egyptian officials for their crimes. This makes it clear that Egypt was turning into a lawless land with a weak military. Second, when the king of Byblos refused to give credit to Egypt, we see that Egypt no longer had the reputation of being a great world power. The king of Byblos's scorn towards Egypt displays just how little the foreign king thought of Egypt. With its mines closed and borders crumbling, Egypt could no longer pretend it was a powerful country.

CHAPTER FORTY: THE DARK AGE OF GREECE

The student may use her text when answering the questions in sections I and II.

Section I: Who, What, Where

Write a one or two-sentence answer explaining the significance of each item listed below.

Apollo Sminthian – **Pg. 283, ¶ 4 – Apollo Sminthian was the name of the Apollo who spread bubonic plague; he was also called "Lord of the Mice." The name Apollo Sminthian was specific to Asia Minor.**

Bubonic Plague – **Pg. 283, ¶ 4 – Bubonic plague was a deadly sickness spread by rodents. It killed both domestic animals and humans.**

Dorians – **Pg. 281, ¶ 4 – Dorians were a group of people from the northern part of the Greek peninsula that settled in the Mycenaean cities. They had no writing, no skill in building with brick or stone, and no grasp of bronzeworking.**

Peloponnese – **Pg. 282, ¶1 – The Peloponnese is Thucydides's name for the southernmost part of the Greek peninsula.**

Section II: Comprehension

Write a two/three sentence answer to each of the following questions.

1. What was happening on the Greek peninsula around 1200 BC? How did Sparta, Mycenae and Pylos fare?
A1. – Pg. 281, ¶ 3 – Around 1200 BC, a rash of fires spread across the Greek peninsula. The city of Sparta burned to the ground. The fortresses at Mycenae survived, but the houses outside the walls of the city were in ashes. Pylos was also swept by fire.

2. Explain how Codrus, king of Athens, sacrificed himself in order to save Athens from Dorian invasion.
A2. – Pg. 281, ¶ 5 – An oracle at the Dorian camp told the savage invaders that they would win the battle for Athens, as long as they didn't kill the Athenian king Codrus. Codrus then disguised himself and headed to the Dorian camp, where he picked a fight with armed Dorian warriors. In the brawl afterwards, he was killed, thus fulfilling the oracle and saving his city.

3. What is the significance of the ninety year gap between the burning of Pylos and Mycenae?
A3. – Pg. 282, ¶ 2 – If Pylos and Mycenae were burned ninety years apart, that means the Dorian influx spread slowly down over the peninsula over the course of a century, rather than through a violent takeover as chronicled by Thucydides and Herodotus.
4. How could a ship carrying only healthy people on board spread bubonic plague?

A4. – Pg. 283, ¶ 5 – A ship with no sick people on board, docking on an uninfected shore, might still have plague-carrying rats in its hold.

5. Why did the plague seem to follow famine?
A5. – Pg. 283, ¶ 5 – Plague tended to follow famine because grain shipments from one part of the world to another also carried rats from one city to the next.

6. Describe the circumstances that led the Egyptians to hire troops from the Aegean to fight *for* Egypt *against* the Libyans of the western desert.
A6. – Pg. 283, ¶ 6 to Pg. 284, ¶ 1 – Driven out of their homeland, Mycenaeans, Cretans and Aegeans looked for new homes, and hired themselves out as mercenaries for work. Before the Sea People and Libyans were allied, the Egyptians actually hired some of these Aegean Sea People to help put down an early Libyan skirmish.

7. While we don't know much about Dorian culture, what <u>do</u> we know about their life on the peninsula after the decay of the Mycenaean cities?
A7. – Pg. 284, ¶ 2 – We do know that the Dorian settlers had no king and court, no taxes and tributes, and no foreign sea trade. They farmed, they survived, and they had no particular need to write anything down.

8. When is the term "dark age" generally used?

Note to INSTRUCTOR: The answer to this question is in the note at the bottom of page 284.
A8. – Pg. 284, Note – The term "dark age" tends to be used only when written records have been kept and then trail off, rather than for times before written accounts are widely used.

Section III: Critical Thinking

The student may not use her text to answer this question.

After the war with Troy, the Mycenaean cities began to slowly decay. Though Thucydides and Herodotus blame the Dorian invasion, we know this is not accurate. If the Dorians didn't kick the Athenians out of their city, and Sparta was already empty when the invaders set fire to it, what is to blame for the decline of the Mycenaean cities?
In this critical thinking section, write three short paragraphs explaining how each of the conditions listed below played a part in the evacuation of the peninsula by the Mycenaean people.

- *WAR*
- *DROUGHT*
- *PLAGUE*

In each paragraph, the student should first describe the condition, and then explain how it affected the Mycenaeans. The explanation should conclude with the condition's role in driving the Mycenaeans out of their homes.

• *WAR*

*The ten year battle against Troy was very costly for the Mycenaeans. They ran out of money and food, and the best Mycenaean men were slain. In addition, when the Mycenaean ships returned to the mainland of Greece after the war with Troy, they found their homes poor and troubled (Pg. 281, ¶ 1). The strife was so severe, that many Mycenaeans were driven from their own cities (Pg. 283, ¶ 1). *The information in this first sentence comes from Chapter Thirty-Five, "The Battle for Troy." The student should remember that "the victory damaged the winner almost as much as the vanquished." For review, the student can look at page 257, ¶s 2-4.*

• *DROUGHT*

Two or three years of bad weather in a row resulted in a crop shortage. This came at the same time when the old reliable sources of grain from Egypt and Asia Minor had also been disrupted by wars in both places (Pg. 283, ¶ 1). With no grain at home, and no grain coming in from other sources, the Mycenaeans were on the brink of starvation. The hunger the Mycenaeans faced either sparked war between the cities, or the able-bodied moved away and looked for new homes (Pg. 283, ¶ 6).

• *PLAGUE*

The bubonic plague spread quickly, and killed the men in its path. The plague spread not just by human contact, but also surreptitiously by rodent. If a man was not killed by the plague, he most likely fled his contaminated home and tried to find a place to settle that was untouched by disease (Pg. 283, ¶ 4).

CHAPTER FORTY-ONE: THE DARK AGE OF MESOPOTAMIA

The student may use his text when answering the questions in sections I and II.

Section I: Who, What, Where

Write a one or two-sentence answer explaining the significance of each item listed below.

Erra – **Pg. 289, ¶ 4 – Erra was a god who could not resist afflicting the city of Babylon with death and destruction. His mischief is recorded in the ancient Babylonian poem, the Erra Epic.**

Mushki – **Pg. 287, ¶ 4 – Mushki is the name given to the Phrygians by Tiglath-Pileser.**

Nebuchadnezzar – **Pg. 288, ¶ 2 & Pg. 288, ¶ 5 – Nebuchadnezzar was the first powerful king of Babylon since Burnaburiash, two hundred years earlier. Having rescued Marduk, the chief god of Babylon, Nebuchadnezzar claimed divine favor had been set on him, thus he had the god-given right to rule.**

Phrygians – **Pg. 286, ¶ 1 – The Phrygians were a tribe of people from the area north of the Greek peninsula called Thrace. They crossed over the Bosphorus Strait and attacked the Hittites.**

Suppiluliuma II – **Pg. 285, ¶ 2 – Suppiluliuma II was the second son of Tudhaliya IV. Suppiluliuma took the throne from his elder brother and claimed rule of the Hittite empire for himself.**

Tiglath-Pileser – **Pg. 287, ¶ 2 & 3 – Tiglath-Pileser was the first warlike king of Assyria since Shalmaneser, a hundred years earlier. Tiglath-Pileser turned against the invaders of surrounding empires and used their attacks to take more land for Assyria.**

Section II: Comprehension

Write a two/three sentence answer to each of the following questions.

1. From where did the wandering people pressing into Asia Minor originate?
A1. – Pg. 285, ¶ 4 & Pg. 286, ¶ 1 – Some of the people wandering to Asia Minor came from the direction of Troy. Others came from the sea; these people gathered at Cyprus, the island south of the Hittite coast, and then moved into Asia Minor. Other wanderers came from over the Bosphorus Strait, from the area north of the Greek peninsula called Thrace.

2. Describe the Phrygian attack that ended the Hittite kingdom.
A2. – Pg. 286, ¶ 2 – The Phrygians came from Thrace across the Bosphorus Strait and overwhelmed the Hittite army. The invaders moved right through Suppiluliuma's troops, scattered his defenses, and arrived in the heart of his kingdom. The capital city Hattusas burned to the ground. The Hittite people fled, and the royal court dispersed like dust.

3. What part of the Hittite culture survived the Phrygian attack?
A3. – Pg. 286, ¶ 3 – The Hittite language survived in a few separated cities around the southern edge of the old empire; Carchemish was the largest.

4. What cities make the points of the upside-down triangle known as the Assyrian heartland? Why did the kings of Assyria want to keep the heartland safe?
A4. – Pg. 287, ¶ 2 – The upside-down triangle known as the Assyrian heartland had Assur at its bottom point, Erbila on the west and Nineveh on the east. The kings wanted to keep the heartland safe because it was prosperous, with the richest corn-growing land in all of Mesopotamia.

5. When Nebuchadnezzar came to Babylon's throne, why was the statue of Marduk still in the hands of the Elamites of Susa?
A5. – Pg. 288, ¶ 3 – Since its capture, a hundred years before Nebuchadnezzar came to the throne, the statue of Marduk rested in the hands of the Elamites of Susa. No king of Babylon had proved himself mighty enough to get it back.

6. What plan of attack did Nebuchadnezzar implement in order to attack Susa and, ultimately, retrieve the statue of Marduk?
A6. – Pg. 288, ¶ 4 – Nebuchadnezzar marched his men into Elam at the very height of summer, a time when no commander with any sense would force an army to march anywhere. The Babylonian soldiers caught the Elam border patrols by surprise and made it to the city of Susa before anyone could raise the alarm. They raided the city, broke down the temple doors, kidnapped the statue, and departed to march in triumph back to Babylon.

7. How did Marduk become the chief god of the Babylonians?
A7. – Pg. 288, ¶ 5 – Marduk became the chief god of the Babylonians after the rescue of the statue of Marduk from the Elamites by Nebuchadnezzar. Nebuchadnezzar hired scribes to compose tales about the rescue and to compose hymns in Marduk's honor. Stories and songs and offerings streamed from the royal palace to the Temple of Marduk until the god stood at the top of the Babylonian pantheon.

8. Why did Tiglath-Pileser burn the king's palace at Babylon? In what way was this a symbolic act, rather than a true act of war?
A8. – Pg. 288, ¶ 6 to Pg. 289, ¶ 1 – After a couple of Assyrian frontier towns were sacked by Babylonian soldiers, Tiglath-Pileser retorted by marching to Babylon and burning the king's palace. This was a symbolic act because most of the Babylonian government offices had been moved elsewhere since Babylon was so close to the Assyrian border. The city was a sacred site, but no longer a center of power, so no real harm was done to the Babylonian people.

9. Who were the Aramaeans? In what way did the Aramaeans threaten Tiglath-Pileser's kingdom?
A9. – Pg. 289, ¶ 2 – The Aramaeans were people from the northwest of the Western Semitic lands, pushed onwards by an influx of people from farther west. The Aramaeans threatened Tiglath-Pileser's kingdom because they were rapidly moving into Babylonian territory; Tiglath-Pileser made something like twenty-eight different campaigns to the west, each aimed at beating back Aramaean invasions.

10. What evidence do historians have that proves Assyria was not immune to the same famine and drought that plagued the rest of the known world?
A10. – Pg. 289, ¶ 3 – Historians know that Assyrians faced the same hardships as the rest of the known world because court records describe the last years of Tiglath-Pileser's reign as desperate and hungry.

11. What is the Erra Epic? What story does it tell?
A11. – Pg. 289, ¶ 4 – The Erra Epic is a long poem in which the god Marduk complains that his statue is unpolished, and that his temple is in disrepair. Marduk can't leave Babylon long enough to do anything about it, because every time he departs the city, something horrendous happens to it. The current problem Marduk faces is the wrath of Erra, who wants to ruin Babylon and its people.

12. How does the Erra Epic reflect the hardships Babylon faced at the end of Nebuchadnezzar's reign?
A12. – Pg. 289, ¶ 4-5 – In the Erra Epic, Babylon is described as a luxuriant orchard whose fruit had withered before ripening. This reflects the crop failure Babylon faced due to drought. Erra says he will "fell the cattle" and "fell the people." The falling of people and cattle suggests death because of famine, and slaughter at the hands of the invading Aramaeans.

13. Why did Tiglath-Pileser's son make a treaty with the new king of Babylon? Was the treaty effective?
A13. – Pg. 289, ¶ 5-6 – By the time Tiglath-Pileser's son succeeded his father as king of Assyria, the Aramaean problem had become so acute that he was forced to make a treaty with the new king of Babylon in hopes of beating off their common enemy. The treaty failed. Not long after the treaty was made, Aramaeans rampaged across Assyria, seizing for themselves all but the very center of the empire. They invaded Babylon as well and the son Nebuchadnezzar lost his throne to an Aramaean usurper.

Section III: Critical Thinking

The student may use his text to answer this question.

Tiglath-Pileser came from a long line of kings who, each in turn, ruled over the Assyrian heartland. Keeping this treasured upside-down triangle safe was not enough for Tiglath-Pileser, so he gathered his men and went out to conquer more land for Assyria. Write a paragraph, using quotes from the Assyrian king's inscriptions and annals, to describe how Tiglath-Pileser restored, even if for just a short time, Assyria's greatness.

The student should find these phrases for himself in the text. If he is having trouble, you can point out what he should be looking for, and how each phrase relates to Tiglath-Pileser's warring attitude and restoration of Assyrian greatness.

Tiglath-Pileser on defeating an army of Phrygians in the former Hittite territory:

Pg. 287, ¶ 4 - _"I made their blood flow down the ravines and pour from the heights of the mountains."_

Pg. 287, ¶ 4 - _"I cut off their heads and piled them like grain heaps."_

Tiglath-Pileser on facing another wave of Phrygians further northwest:

Pg. 287, ¶ 5 - _"[I set out for] the lands of the distant kings who were on the shore of the Upper sea, who had never known subjection."_

Pg. 287, ¶ 5 - _"I took my chariots and my warriors and over the steep mountain and through their wearisome paths I hewed a way with pickaxes of bronze; I made passable a road for my chariot and my troops. I crossed the Tigris....I scattered warriors...and made their blood to flow."_

Tiglath-Pileser on taking Hittite Carchemish:

Pg. 287, ¶ 6 – _"[I took it] in one day."_

In this paragraph, the student should describe Tiglath-Pileser's conquests, how the conquered treated the king, and the ways in which Tiglath-Pileser publicly declared his greatness. This paragraph will resemble the text on page 287 of the chapter (¶s 2-6), however it should not be copied directly from the text.

Tiglath-Pileser took advantage of the crumbling Hittite empire, fighting against the Phrygian invaders to take Hittite land for Assyria. As the Phrygians, or Mushki, as Tiglath-Pileser called them, approached Assyria on the northwest, the Assyrian king rallied his army in the valley of the northern Tigris and slaughtered the invaders, making "their blood flow down the ravines" after he "cut off their heads and piled them like grain heaps." Tiglath-Pileser continued, setting out for "the lands of the distant kings who were on the shore of the Upper sea, who had never known subjection." He would make these kings pay taxes and send their laborers to the Assyrian palace, and finally know subjection and suffering under the rule of Assyrian governors. Tiglath-Pileser carved his way northwest, making "passable a road for my chariot and my troops." He "crossed the Tigris," "scattered warriors...and made their blood to flow." He even got to Carchemish, and took the old Hittite stronghold "in one day." Some cities fought against Tiglath-Pileser's takeover, and others met the king with their heads down, begging to kiss his feet. The pharaoh of Egypt even sent Tiglath-Pileser a crocodile for a present. Tiglath-Pileser celebrated his victories on the walls of newly built shrines and temples, proclaiming that Assyria once again had a great king.

CHAPTER FORTY-TWO: THE FALL OF THE SHANG

The student may use her text when answering the questions in sections I and II.

Section I: Who, What, Where

Write a one or two-sentence answer explaining the significance of each item listed below.

Chou – **Pg. 292, ¶ 3 & Pg. 293, 1 – Chou inherited the Shang throne from his great-grandfather Wu-yi. Chou's weird frivolity gave way to tyranny, and he was resented and hated by both the Shang and Zhou people.**

"Lord of the West" – **Pg. 291, ¶ 4 – "Lord of the West" was the name of the chief of the Zhou tribe.**

Wen – **Pg. 293, ¶ 2 & 4 – Pg. 293, ¶ 4 – Wen, chief of the Zhou people, was known as a warrior-king who was both good and mighty. After being jailed by Chou, Went started a rebellion against the tyrannous Shang king.**

Wu – **Pg. 293, ¶ 5 – Wu, son of Wen, took his father's place as the leader of the Zhou rebellion against the Shang king. Wu killed the evil Shang king Chou, and solidified Zhou rule in China.**

Wu-yi – **Pg. 291, ¶ 6 to Pg. 292, ¶ 3 – Wu-yi was the fifth Shang ruler to follow Wu Ting. Wu-yi mocked the gods. His death seemed to be punishment for this crime: he was struck by lightning while out hunting.**

Section II: Comprehension

Write a two/three sentence answer to each of the following questions.

1. What threat did the Shang kings and their people face at the beginning of the 11th century BC?
A1. – Pg. 291, ¶ 3 – The Shang kings and their people were threatened by cousins of their own people: the Zhou tribe from across the Wei River valley.

2. If the Zhou tribe were "not exactly subjects of the Shang king," how were the Zhou connected to the Shang? To whom were the Zhou people most loyal?
A2. – Pg. 291, ¶ 4 – The Zhou's chief paid lip service to the authority of the crown, and oracle bones travelled back and forth between the Lord of the West and the Shang palace, keeping a path of shared language and customs open. The Zhou noblemen were loyal first to their own lord, not to the distant Shang monarch.

3. Why was Wu-yi's production of idols a serious breach of his royal responsibilities?
A3. – Pg. 292, ¶ 2 – The oracle-bone ritual, which was taken very seriously by the Shang people, was based on the king as conduit for the message from the divine powers. For Wu-yi to mock the gods by producing idols for play was appalling, and thus a serious breach of his royal responsibilities.

4. In what way did Chou's love of wine and pleasure lead to the exploitation of the Shang people?
A4. – Pg. 292, ¶ 4 – Chou's love of wine and pleasure led him to raise taxes so that he could stock his hunting forests and pleasure parks with game.

5. Give two examples of Chou's cruel methods of punishment in his court.
A5. – Pg. 293, ¶ 1 – Chou forced noblemen suspected of disloyalty to lie on a red-hot rack. He also carved up one court official into meat strips and then hung them up to dry.

ALTERNATE ANSWER:
Pg. 293, ¶ 1 – Chou had one court official flayed.
Pg. 293, ¶ 1 – Chou cut out the heart of his uncle after remarking that since the heart of a wise man had seven chambers, he would need to examine his uncle's heart with his open eyes before heeding his advice.

6. Why did Chou have Wen jailed?
A6. – Pg. 293, ¶ 2 – Chou had Wen arrested and thrown into jail after Chou's spies overheard Wen sighing over the behavior of the Shang king.

7. What prompted Wen's release from jail?
A7. – Pg. 293, ¶ 3 – Wen was released from jail after the Zhou tribes brought Chou a tribute of fine objects and beautiful women.

8. What kind of deal did Wen make with Chou before returning home to the Wei River valley?
A8. – Pg. 293, ¶ 3 – Wen, making an effort to shield Chou's oppressed subjects from the king's brutality, told Chou that if he would promise to stop using his red-hot rack, Wen would gift him with the fertile Zhou land around the Lo River, which flowed south to join the Wei. Chou agreed to the deal, took ownership of the land, and Wen went home.

9. What caused the Zhou people to rebel against Chou? Describe the forces that gathered against Chou.
A9. – Pg. 293, ¶ 4 – When Wen returned to his own lands, he began quietly to round up opposition to the king. Feudal lords rebelled, and were joined by the sages of the court who read the oracle bones and divine prophecies.

10. What happened at the Battle of Muye? What weapon did the Zhou have that gave them an advantage over the Shang? Why did the Shang forces retreat?
A10. – Pg. 293, ¶ 5 & Pg. 294, ¶ 1-2 – At the Battle of Muye, the Zhou army of fifty thousand met the Shang army of seven hundred thousand. Zhou noblemen had provided three hundred war-chariots, and this gave them an advantage over the royal army, who had no war-chariots. The Shang king's men, disgusted with their king's cruelty, reversed the direction of their attack and retreated of their own volition.

Section III: Critical Thinking

The student may not use her text to answer this question.

Wisdom, not military might, was the force that held together ancient Chinese culture. Knowing this, explain why ancient Chinese historians did not celebrate Wu's overthrow of the Shang king, and why the Zhou dynasty starts with Wen, rather than Wu.

Use the prompts below to answer this question fully.

• Were the Zhou people subjects of the Shang kingdom?

While the Zhou looked at the Lord of the West as their king, Chou was able to put Wen in jail. This suggests that the Zhou were subjects of the Shang people. However, Wen was able to offer Chou a gift of land, and while Chou could have said the land belonged to him, Chou accepted it as a gift. This meant Wen was the primary ruler of the land that was gifted.

• Was the aggression against the Shang king a rebellion?

While the oppressed Shang people were happy to revolt against the ruling tyrant, the troops led by the Zhou were not regularly subject to Chou's brutality. This makes the Zhou fight against the Shang neither a rebellion nor an empiric conquest.

• Why isn't Wen given credit for his military success against the Shang?

Chinese historians did not celebrate the overthrow of a tyrant; this would glorify the violence of the event. Wen's military actions were the physical manifestation of the spiritual grievances aired by his father, Wu, and so Wen is credited for his restoration of the proper order.

• How did ancient Chinese historians justify the Zhou defiance?

The Zhou and Shang, sibling cultures, both had to have lawful and good kings. When Chou brought disgrace to the Shang throne, it was the responsibility of the virtuous Zhou king to set things right.

• Why does the Zhou Dynasty begin with Wen, rather than with Wu?

Though Wen actually brought Chou down, it was the actions of his father that started the movement against the Shang. According to historians, the Zhou rule begins when Wen was unjustly imprisoned, and shortly after he willingly sacrificed Zhou land for the good of his people. Wu may have killed Chou, but it was under his father that the Shang rule is said to have ended, when the noblemen and the oracle-readers gathered under the leadership of the Lord of the West.

While the Zhou looked at the Lord of the West as their king, Chou was able to put Wen in jail. This suggests that the Zhou were subjects of the Shang people. However, Wen was able to offer Chou a gift of land, and while Chou could have said the land belonged to him, Chou accepted it as a gift. This meant Wen was the primary ruler of the land that was gifted. The oppressed Shang people were happy to revolt against the ruling tyrant, however the troops led by the Zhou were not regularly subject to Chou's brutality. This makes the Zhou fight against the Shang neither a rebellion nor an empiric conquest. Chinese historians did not celebrate the overthrow of a tyrant; this would glorify the violence of the event. Wen's military actions were the physical manifestation of the spiritual grievances aired by his father, Wu, and so Wen is credited for his restoration of the proper order. The Zhou and Shang, sibling cultures, both had to have lawful and good kings. When Chou brought disgrace to the Shang throne, it was

the responsibility of the virtuous Zhou king to set things right. Though Wen actually brought Chou down, it was the actions of his father that started the movement against the Shang. According to historians, the Zhou rule begins when Wen was unjustly imprisoned, and shortly after he willingly sacrificed Zhou land for the good of his people. Wu may have killed Chou, but it was under his father that the Shang rule is said to have ended, when the noblemen and the oracle-readers gathered under the leadership of the Lord of the West.

CHAPTER FORTY-THREE: THE MANDATE OF HEAVEN

The student may use his text when answering the questions in sections I and II.

Section I: Who, What, Where

Write a one or two-sentence answer explaining the significance of each item listed below.

Ch'eng – Pg. 302, ¶ 4 & Pg. 303, ¶ 3 – Ch'eng was Wu's son. Ch'eng fought a continual battle o keep the edges of his empire safe, always careful to connect this use of force to his divine right to rule.

Feng & Hao – Pg. 301, ¶ 1 – Feng & Hao was the double city, separated by the Fenghe River, that served as the new capital of the Zhou dynasty.

K'ang – Pg. 303, ¶ $4 & 5 – K'ang followed his father Ch'eng as Zhou king of China. K'ang subjugated the northern tribe, the Guifang, extending the northern edge of his kingdom.

Loyang – Pg. 302, ¶ 7 to Pg. 303, ¶ 1 – Loyang was a city built on the eastern edge of the Zhou empire, on the Yellow River ford. The city was built around a fortress that was meant to protect the eastern approach to the Zhou capital, and to watch over the remnants of the old Shang tribe.

Lu-fu – Pg. 301, ¶ 1 to Pg. 302, ¶ 3 – Lu-fu was the deposed heir to the Shang dynasty. In order to show respect for the old dynasty, Wu installed Lu-fu as lord of Yin. Lu-fu and his brothers organized a Shang uprising after Wu died; Lu-fu was killed in battle.

Mu – Pg. 304, ¶ 2 – Mu took the Zhou throne after his father Zhao was killed in battle.

The Nine Cauldrons – Pg. 300, ¶ 2 – The Nine Cauldrons were nine bronze ceremonial vessels that represented the Zhou position at the top of the power ladder. The Nine Cauldrons resided in the Zhou capital city.

Tan – Pg. 302, ¶ 2 & 5 – Tan was Wu's brother. Tan served as Ch'eng's regent because Ch'eng was too young to rule China. After turning over the throne to Ch'eng, Tan became known as the "Duke of Zhou."

Zhao – Pg. 303, ¶ 6 to Pg. 304, ¶ 1 – Zhao, son of K'ang, was the 5th king of the Zhou dynasty. Zhao died in battle while trying to expand the southern border of his kingdom.

Section II: Comprehension

Write a two/three sentence answer to each of the following questions.

1. Why did Wu put away his weapons and discharge his soldiers at the start of his reign?
A1. – Pg. 299, ¶ 3 – Wu had to show that he would be a peaceful ruler in order to keep his throne. The Shang king had been unable to fight off the united force of the feudal lords. Wu knew these forces could turn against him; to stay in power, Wu had to rule by influence and tact, not sheer force.

2. Who were the "Lords of the Nine Rings?" Why was this a misnomer?
A2. – Pg. 299, ¶ 3 – The "Lords of the Nine Rings" were noblemen who governed their own territories, while still owing loyalty to the king This is a misnomer because there were many more than nine lands; the *Record of Rites* counts up to a total of 1,763 separately governed territories at the beginning of the Zhou period.

3. What did it mean if a Chinese nobleman was "enfeoffed" by the king of the Zhou? What kind of gifts was an "enfeoffed" lord given?
A3. – Pg. 300, ¶ 2 – When a nobleman was "enfeoffed" by the king of the Zhou, he was given gifts as a symbol that the Zhou king had awarded him a portion of sacred authority. Most often, these gifts were bronze vessels with inscriptions.

4. What did a gift of bronze stand for in ancient China?
A4. – Pg. 300, ¶ 2 - A gift of bronze symbolized both wealth and power, in particular power to control the miners who dug the metal out of the earth, the craftsmen who cast it into shape, and the priests who inscribed it.

5. What is the biggest difference between the feudalism practiced in later times and the Zhou system of power and authority?
A5. – Pg. 300, ¶ 2 to Pg. 301, ¶ 1 – The big difference between feudalism as practiced in later times and the Zhou power system was that later feudal lords claimed actual possession over their kingdom's far-reaching lands, not mere moral authority over it. The Zhou king did claim the right to run Chinese land properly, but he did not claim to own it.

6. How did Wu plan to keep the peace at newly pacified Yin? How did his plan backfire?
A6. – Pg. 301, ¶ 1 to Pg. 302, ¶ 3 – Wu planned to keep the peace at Yin by installing Lu-fu, the former Shang king's son, as lord of the city. Wanting to make sure Lu-fu behaved himself, Wu installed Lu-fu's two brothers as watchdogs. The plan backfired when Wu died; the two brothers organized an armed uprising in the middle of old Shang territory, intending to put Lu-fu back on the throne.

7. What was the result of the Shang loyalist uprising?
A7. – Pg. 302, ¶ 3 – In response to the Shang loyalist uprising, Tan turned out the royal army and overwhelmed the rebel fighters. Lu-fu and one of his brothers were killed in the fight. Tan then did his best to break up the Shang resistance by deporting the Shang loyalists to other parts of the empire.

8. How did the Chinese people view Tan? Why were the Chinese people able to accept Ch'eng's authority after Tan turned over his authority to the young king?

A8. – Pg. 302, ¶ 4 – Tan was praised across the country for both his wisdom and virtue. In Chinese culture, a virtuous man gave his power only to a more virtuous man; this action cleared Ch'eng of his insurgent heritage and legitimized his kingship.

9. What were the responsibilities of the Duke of Zhou? Why was it necessary for him to compile a book of ritual?

A9. – Pg. 302, ¶ 5 – The Duke of Zhou managed the proper oversight of land, a tax system, appointments of officials, and the gathering together of all the ceremonies surrounding the royal court into a book of ritual. A book of ritual was necessary to display the divine authority of the Zhou king; the rituals that surrounded him would be the outward show of his moral authority.

10. What are the five rings of the Zhou king's domain?

A10. – Pg. 304, ¶ 2 – The five rings of the Zhou domain, starting in the capital, were 1) the supply domain, 2) the warning domain, 3) the subordinated domain, 4) the reinforcing domain, and 5) the wild domain.

11. List the frequency of sacrifices each domain sent to the capital city. If a domain did not send sacrifices, how was loyalty displayed? How does this schedule reflect each domain's level of responsibility to maintain the Mandate of Heaven?

A11. – Pg. 304, ¶ 3 – The supply domain was expected to offer daily sacrifices. The warning domain was expected to offer monthly sacrifices, while the subordinated domain only had to offer seasonal sacrifices. The reinforcing domain and the wild domain did not offer sacrifices; instead the reinforcing domain paid tribute once a year, and the wild domain did homage only once for each king, at his funeral. The closer to the capital, the more responsibility a domain had to recognize the Mandate, which is reflected in the frequency of sacrifices sent to the capital.

12. Why didn't Mu attack the northern Chuan-Jung tribe?

A12. Pg. 304, ¶ 2-4 – Mu did not attack the northern Chuan-Jung tribe because his noblemen told him the Mandate of Heaven did not stretch out that far. The Chuan-Jung tribe were out in the wild domain, and the Mandate did not dictate that they be treated in the same way as people at the center of the kingdom. Attacking them was bound to be fruitless, and could result in defeat.

Section III: Critical Thinking

The student may use his text to answer this question.

While the Chinese people valued peace, at times war was necessary to protect the Chinese king, his divine powers, and his land. In a sort of circular reasoning we have seen before, the Mandate of Heaven gave the Chinese king the right to protect his empire through war, and the success of the Chinese in battle verified the Mandate of Heaven. Write a paragraph explaining how this circular reasoning worked. First define the Mandate of Heaven. Second, describe how King Zhao's death explains the limits of the Mandate of Heaven. Third, explain why a Chinese king could only go to war if he was certain he would win. Finally, explain how the Mandate of Heaven hurt the growing Chinese empire.

First define the Mandate of Heaven. (Reference: Pg. 303, ¶ 3)
The Mandate of Heaven gave the king a right to take up arms against outside enemies. While a king was given the divine right to rule because of his virtue, heaven did not expect the Chinese king to sit back and wait for acknowledgment of his power from outsiders. The Mandate allowed the Chinese king to go to war with other peoples.

Second, describe how King Zhao's death explains the limits of the Mandate of Haven. (Reference: Pg. 303 ¶ 6 to Pg. 304, ¶ 1)
King Shao planned a campaign of expansion to the south. He was encouraged by a comet, which seemed a fortunate sign. The comet was deceptive, however, and both the king and his men were lost. Sima Qian writes that Shao's death was not announced to the feudal lords; to admit that a Chinese king could lose to outside enemies weakened the perception of the king as divinely protected.

Third, explain why a Chinese king could only go to war if he was certain he would win. (Reference: Pg. 304, ¶ 5)
While the Mandate of Heaven justified war, the king had a sacred responsibility to protect his divinely granted powers. But defeat in battle cast doubt on the Mandate itself. In order to preserve it, the monarch could only go to war with the absolute certainty he would win.

Finally, explain how the Mandate of Heaven hurt the growing Chinese empire. (Reference: Pg. 304, ¶ 5)
The Mandate of Heaven strengthened the king's power at the center of his kingdom. However, not wanting to lose in battle, the king hesitated to defend the outer reaches of his empire. While the supply domain performed daily rituals that recognized the king's hallowed status, the edges of the Chinese empire slowly tore away.

CHAPTER FORTY-FOUR: THE BHARATA WAR

The student may use her text when answering the questions in sections I and II.

Section I: Who, What, Where

Write a one or two-sentence answer explaining the significance of each item listed below.

Bhisma – **Pg. 308, ¶ 2 – Bhisma was the brother of the king of the Kuru clan. Bhisma made a vow to give up any claim to his brother's throne; also Bhisma could not provide an heir to the throne because he had taken another vow: a vow of celibacy.**

Doab – **Pg. 306, ¶ 1 – The Doab was a curved area of land lying between the northern flow of the Ganga and the Jamuna branch of the river. The Aryan-Harappan mixture settled in the Doab after wandering farther and farther from the Indus.**

Draupadi – **Pg. 310, ¶ 3 – Draupadi was the daughter of the king of Pancala, a clan which lay to the east of Hastinapura. Draupadi married all five sons of Pandu.**

Hastinapura – **Pg. 310, ¶ 3 – Hastinapura was the Kuru capital which stood on the upper Ganga. Hastinapura was at the center of the quarrel between the Kauravas and the Pandavas.**

Indo-Gangetic Plain – **Pg. 308, ¶ 1 & Pg. 311, ¶ 5 – The Indo-Gangetic plain was an area north of the Ganga, east of the Indus and just south of the Himalaya mountain range. The Bharata War was fought on the Indo-Gangetic Plain.**

The "Kauravas" – **Pg. 310, ¶ 2 – The "Kauravas" was the group name for Dhritarashtra's one hundred sons. The sons were led by the eldest prince, Duryodhana.**

Mahabharata – **Pg. 306, ¶ 1 – The Mahabharata is a sacred Indian text. It is a mythical work that may preserve an earlier tradition.**

The "Pandavas" – **Pg. 310, ¶ 2 – The "Pandavas" was the group name for the five sons of Pandu, led by their oldest brother Yudhishtra.**

Vyasa (Krishna) – **Pg. 308, ¶ 3 to Pg. 309, ¶ 1 – Vyasa (Krishna) was a mysterious wise man who impregnated both wives of the dead king of Kuru, and the maid-servant of the older wife. Vyasa's three sons eventually battled over the throne.**

Section II: Comprehension

Write a two/three sentence answer to each of the following questions.

1. Who are the *dasa* people? Why is it unlikely that "dasa" is another name for the Harappan people? **A1. – Pg. 306, ¶ 2 & 3 – The *dasa* are a group of people the Rig Veda makes reference to who lived in fortified cities which advancing Aryans broke down. The *dasa* became servants of the conquerors. Most likely *dasa* is a general term used to describe tribes encountered during**

the Aryan spread. It is unlikely that the *dasa* and Harappan people are the same because Harappan cities had crumbled before the Aryan advance.

2. What evidence supports the notion that invading Aryans married *dasa* people? Why is this intermarriage culturally important?
A2. – Pg. 306, ¶ 3 – It seems likely that the Aryans occasionally married *dasa* people because the related forms *dasa* and *daha* pop up in the names of legendary Aryan kings. Intermarriage between the *dasa* and Aryans is culturally important because it shows that there is no simple racial division between Aryans and others.

3. What type of terrain did the settlers of the Ganga encounter when they arrived between 1000 and 6000 BC? Why were the forests thought to be populated with demons?
A3. – Pg. 306, ¶ 4 to Pg. 307, ¶ 1 – The fertile lands of the Ganga were tropical forest and swamp, covered over with thick, mysterious, tangled green. The earliest tales of the forests populate them with demons because the forest was full of hardship and danger. Trees had to be felled, roots thicker and deeper than the settlers had ever seen had to be dug out of the ground, and poisonous snakes and unfamiliar animals lurked in the dark thickets.

4. How did the Indian warrior clans clear the forests of the Ganga River valley?
A4. – Pg. 307, ¶ 2 & 3 – The warrior clans used axes and thick plows made of iron to break up the dense green of the forest. It is possible the warriors also used fire to clear the woods.

5. What are the names of Vyasa's three sons? What are the distinct talents of each son?
A5. – Pg. 309, ¶ 2 – Vyasa's three sons were called Vidura, Pandu and Dhritarashtra. Vidura grows to be one of the wisest and most devout of men; Pandu excels in archery; and Dhritarashtra becomes immensely strong and heir to the Kuru throne.

6. How did Dhritarashtra come to have 100 sons? Who is the acknowledged oldest son?
A6. – Pg. 309, ¶ 4 – Wanting to ensure that her husband's royal line would forever be secure, Gandhari appeals to the magical Vyasa. Her pregnancy is supernatural, and lasts for two years; when Gandhari's child is finally born, it is not a baby but a lump. Vyasa cuts it into a hundred pieces, and they become children. Duryodhana is the acknowledged oldest son.

7. Why was Yudhishtra able to lay claim to the Indian throne?
A7. – Pg. 309, ¶ 5 – Because of Gandhari's two-year pregnancy, Yudhishtra was born before Gandhari's baby-lump; thus Yudhishtra could also claim to be the oldest royal heir in the family.

8. In what way was the marriage of the Pandavas to Draupadi a strategic alliance?
A8. – Pg. 310, ¶ 4 & 5 – Draupadi was from the eastern clan Pancala, which was made up of mostly indigenous people. By marrying Draupadi, the Pandavas were firmly allied with the native peoples.

9. Describe the Pandavas' palace at Indraprastha. How was the Kaurava king Duryodhana embarrassed at the palace?
A9. – Pg. 310, ¶ 7 – The palace at Indraprastha was filled with golden pillars that glowed like the moon, and the assembly hall featured an enormous aquarium stocked with different

birds as well as with tortoises and fish. When visiting the palace, Duryodhana mistook the mirrorlike floor for water and drew his clothes up to his waist before realizing his error. Then, he fell in a pond because he thought it was made of glass. Everyone at the palace, including Bhisma laughed at the Kaurava king.

10. What did Yudhishtra lose to Duryodhana in a game of dice?
A10. – Pg. 311, ¶ 2 – Yudhishtra lost his jewels, his wealth, his army, his wife and his territory to Duryodhana, all in a game of dice.

11. What hostility between the Kauravas and the Pandavas caused the Bharata War?
A11. – Pg. 311, ¶ 5 – After being in exile for twelve years, the Pandavas returned to their former kingdom and demanded their palace and land. Duryodhana refused to give any of it back. This was the hostility that broke out in open war: the Bharata War.

12. Who won the Bharata War? How is the conflict between the Pandavas and the Kauravas reconciled in heaven?
A12. – Pg. 312, ¶ 4 & 5 – The Pandava brothers, with the help of the indigenous people, won the Bharata War. Despite so much earthly blood shed, the Pandavas and Kauravas find each other in heaven, free from human wrath, and enjoy each other's company without strife, for eternity.

Section III: Critical Thinking

The student may not use her text to answer this question.

The Bharata War was a battle fought between two clans who were not so far away from their old days as nomadic warriors. The transition from a network of warriors who watched over the good of the clan towards a more hierarchical idea of kingship was a bumpy one.

In order to make sense of this messy transition, <u>make a genealogical chart for the Kuru clan</u>.

These are the names that must be included in the chart:

Queen Mother	King of Kuru
Older Wife	Younger Wife
Maidservant of Older Wife	Bhisma
Vyasa (Krishna)	Vidura
Pandu	Dhritarashtra
Gandhari	Duryodhana
Yudhishtra	The Pandavas
The Kauravas	Draupadi
Pancala Clan	

Part Four: Empires

Queen Mother
|
King of Kuru – Bhisma (Celibate)
|

Maidservant of Older Wife - Older Wife - Younger Wife   + Vyasa

=

Vidura - Dhritarashtra -   Pandu   + Gandhari   + Older Wife

=

The Kaurava, led by eldest son Duryodhana   The Pandavas, led by eldest son Yudhishtra
Draupadi
Pancala Clan

KEY FOR INSTRUCTOR-

The student MAY NOT use her text to answer the question – you can give her hints, however.

Queen Mother – King of Kuru's Mother

King of Kuru – Dead

Older Wife – Older Wife of Kuru

Younger Wife – Younger Wife of Kuru

Maidservant of Older Wife (of Kuru)

Bhisma – Kuru's Celibate Brother

Vyasa (Krishna) – Mystical Being, Impregnates Older Wife of Kuru, Younger Wife of Kuru and Maidservant of Older Wife (of Kuru)

Vidura – Son of Vyasa by Maidservant

Pandu – Son of Vyasa by Younger Wife

Older Wife – Older Wife of Pandu

Dhritarashtra – Son of Vyasa by Older Wife

Gandhari – Dhritarashtra's Wife

Duryodhana – Eldest of 100 Sons by Dhritarashtra and Gandhari

Yudhishtra – Eldest of 5 Sons by Pandu and his Older Wife

The Pandavas – Name of Pandu's Group of Sons

The Kauravas – Name of the Dhritarashtra's Group of Sons

Draupadi – Wife of the Pandavas, Primary Wife of Yudhishtra

Pancala Clan – Draupadi's People

CHAPTER FORTY-FIVE: THE SON OF DAVID

The student may use his text when answering the questions in sections I and II.

Section I: Who, What, Where

Write a one or two-sentence answer explaining the significance of each item listed below.

Dagon – **Pg. 318, ¶ 1 – Dagon was the chief god of Philistines. Dagon was a fish-god, which reflected the Aegean seafaring roots of the Philistine people.**

David – **Pg. 319, ¶ 5 – David, a member of Saul's army, fought against the Philistine giant Goliath. David knocked Goliath out with a stone to the head, and then cut off the giant's head with his own sword. David became the king of the Israelites, and turned the twelve tribes into a kingdom.**

Delilah – **Pg. 318, ¶ 1 – Delilah, a Philistine prostitute who lived on the border between Philistine and Israelite territory, was hired by the Philistines to betray Samson. Delilah was successful in her seduction of Samson.**

Goliath – **Pg. 319, ¶ 4 & 5 – Goliath was a Philistine giant: three meters tall, armed to the teeth and a superior fighter. Goliath was killed and decapitated by David, who knocked Goliath out with a well-placed stone to the head.**

Hiram – **Pg. 320, ¶ 6 – Hiram was king of Tyre, a city on the northern Mediterranean coast. Hiram had a friendly alliance with David, and the Israelite nation.**

Israel – **Pg. 317, ¶ 1 – Israel was the name of the nation made up of the Hebrew tribes that descended from Abraham, who under the leadership of Joshua, invaded Western Semitic lands.**

Joshua – **Pg. 315, ¶ 3 to Pg. 316, ¶ 2 – Joshua, Moses's aide and assistant, became the leader of the Hebrew people when Moses died. Under Joshua, the Hebrew tribes laid claim to the land along the Mediterranean coast from Lebanon to the Euphrates, all the Hittite country, and all the way over the Great Sea on the west.**

Meshwesh – **Pg. 325, ¶ 4 – Meshwesh was the name of the hired mercenaries from Libya used by the Egyptian priests of Amun to back up their authority against the pharaohs of Dynasty 21.**

Pentapolis/Peleset/Philistines – **Pg. 314, ¶ 1 – The Pentapolis was the alliance of five powerful cities that grew from settlements of scattered Sea People in the Western Semitic lands: Gaza, Ashkelon, Ashdod, Gath and Ekron. The Egyptians called this alliance the Peleset; this grouping was also known as the Philistines.**

Samson – **Pg. 317, ¶ 3 and Pg. 318, ¶ 1 – Samson was one of the chief judges of Israel, known for his supernatural strength. After being captured by the Philistines and put on display during a festival, Samson pulled down the Temple of Dagon, killing himself, as well as over three thousand Philistines.**

Saul – **Pg. 318, ¶ 3 – Saul was an impressively tall Benjamite who was made the first king of the Israelite nation.**

Queen of Sheba – **Pg. 322, ¶ 4 & 5 – The Queen of Sheba is the first personality to come out of the Arabian peninsula. She went to visit Solomon, and brought him gifts of spices, gold and precious gems.**

Sheshonq – **Pg. 325, ¶ 4 – Sheshonq, a Libyan warrior, was the Great Chief of the Meshwesh, hired by Egyptian powers in the north. He created an alliance with southern Egyptian royals by marrying one of the daughters of the pharaoh at Tanis. When the pharaoh died, Sheshonq asserted his right to power over both the north and south of Egypt.**

Section II: Comprehension

Write a two/three sentence answer to each of the following questions.

1. From where did the Philistines borrow their culture? What archaeological evidence supports this theory?
A1. – Pg. 314, ¶ 2 – The Philistines borrowed their culture from the Mycenaeans and the Egyptians. Philistine pottery was Mycenaean in style. The Philistines buried their dead in coffins carved to look like Egyptian sarcophagi. The faux Egyptian coffins were decorated with meaningless hieroglyphs, meaning someone had seen the signs often but had no idea what they meant.

2. Why were the 40 years the Hebrews wandered in the desert crucial to their culture?
A2. – Pg. 315, ¶ 1 & 2 – During the 40 years the Hebrews wandered in the desert, God gave them the Ten Commandments. This was the bedrock of Hebrew national identity, and led to a political reorganization.

3. How did Moses reorganize the Hebrews?
A3. – Pg. 315, ¶ 2 – Moses took a census and listed all the Hebrew clans and families. They were divided into twelve tribes, each known by the name of the great-grandson of Abraham who served as its ancestor.

4. Why did Joshua order all adult Hebrew men circumcised?
A4. – Pg. 316, ¶ 2 – Joshua ordered all adult Hebrew men circumcised because the circumcision ritual had been much neglected during the four decades in the desert. Joshua needed his men to understand what they were about to do: the conquest of Canaan was the fulfillment of the promise made to Abraham, the first Jew and the first to circumcise his sons, six hundred years before.

5. Who succeeded Joshua as commander of the Israelites?
A5. – Pg. 317, ¶ 1 – Joshua was not succeeded by a person, but rather by a series of chief judges – prophets who told the nation of Israel what God required.

6. What happened when Saul led his men into Philistine territory? What kind of forces did the Israelites face?
A6. – Pg. 319, ¶ 2 – The Israelite forces, led by Saul, were met by three thousand Philistine chariots, six thousand charioteers, and soldiers too great to count. The Israelite forces, badly outnumbered and completely outarmed, scattered and hid.

7. How did David's defeat of Goliath affect the Israelite push against the Philistines? Why did Saul want to get rid of David after his success?

A7. – Pg. 319, ¶ 5 to Pg. 320, ¶ 1 – After David killed Goliath, the Philistines turned and ran. The men of Israel and Judah surged forward and pursued the Philistines to the entrance of Gath and to the gates of Ekron; Philistine dead were strewn along the road. Saul wanted to get rid of David because he was threatened by his success, and saw David as a competitor for the throne.

8. Describe how David expanded the Israelite kingdom when he first came to power.

A8. – Pg. 320, ¶ 3 & 4 – When David first came to power, he besieged the city of Jerusalem. Then, he marched down to the southeast and defeated the Edomites, who controlled the land as far as the Red Sea; he defeated the tribes of Moab, on the other side of the Dead Sea, and the tribes of Ammon to their north, just across Jordan. Finally he defeated the Philistines, who had marched on Israel as soon as they heard David was in power.

9. Who were the Phoenicians? What united the Phoenicians? What type of trade did the Phoenicians control?

A9. – Pg. 320, ¶ 6 to Pg. 321, ¶ 2 – The Phoenicians were a particular mix of Western Semites and people of Aegean descent that resided in Tyre, Sidon and Byblos. The Phoenicians were united by a common culture and language. The Phoenicians controlled the trade of cedar logs, which they cut from the local hills and sent abroad to Egypt, Israel and even father away.

10. How did Solomon reorganize David's Israel? Why did he choose to restructure the kingdom?

A10. – Pg. 321, ¶ 3 – Solomon reorganized David's kingdom into twelve administrative districts which did not always fall along the traditional tribal boundaries. Solomon chose to restructure the kingdom because he wanted to break up old tribal divisions and any infighting they might have encouraged.

11. How did Solomon's ruling style differ from David's?

A11. – Pg. 321, ¶ 3 & 4 – Unlike David, who was a charismatic leader who wasn't afraid to get his hands dirty, Solomon was business-oriented, concerned only with turning Israel into a cushy and well-organized empire. Solomon wanted to do everything bigger and better than his father, and wielded great power over his subjects.

12. How did Solomon fuel his massive building projects and court?

A12. – Pg. 323, ¶ 4 – Solomon conscripted thirty thousand Israelite men as laborers, who spent one out of every three months working for the king while also maintaining their own fields and vines. Solomon provided food for his court by demanding that each district feed the group for one month of the year.

13. Why was Solomon in debt? How did Solomon propose to pay off his debts to Hiram?

A13. – Pg. 324, ¶ 2 – Solomon's building programs ran him into tremendous debt. Lacking enough cash to pay off shipments of cedar, pine and gold, Solomon proposed to give Hiram twenty towns in Galilee – a large section of the northern edge of the Israelite kingdom.

14. How did Jeroboam come to be king of the northern part of Israel? What kingdom was Rehoboam left to rule over?

A14. – Pg. 324, ¶ 5 & 6 – When Solomon died, Jeroboam asked the next king of Israel, Rehoboam, to lower taxes and demand less conscripted labor. Rehoboam refused to change the cruel treatment of the Israelites that his father made common. The northern tribes, already unhappy, seceded and proclaimed Jeroboam as king. Rehoboam was left to rule over the tribes of Judah and Benjamin.

15. Why did Sheshonq invade the Western Semitic lands? In what way did Sheshonq's attack on the Western Semitic lands reinforce the division between Israel and Judah?

A15. – Pg. 326, ¶ 4 & 5 – Sheshonq invaded the Western Semitic lands to prove that under his rule Egypt's strength had been renewed. Sheshonq's invasion of the Western Semitic lands left a quivering and thoroughly demoralized divided kingdom behind him. The vigorous attack reinforced a division between southern Judah and northern Israel that would last centuries.

Section III: Critical Thinking

Samuel, an old and weary Israelite, believed kingship to be an enormous mistake. He warned "[A king] will draft your sons to be soldiers in his army…. He will take them to plow his fields….He will take the best of your harvest…. You will cry out for relief from the king you have chosen." Considering the exploits of Solomon, and his son Rehoboam, Samuel was right. However, as we know, kingship is also tied with the success of a nation. Below you will find a description of two particular circumstances we read about in this chapter. Write a short paragraph for each explaining how kingship was necessary in order for the nations featured to progress.

#1 – Around 1050, Philistines raided Israelite villages, Israelites burned Philistine fields, both sides knocked off the odd hunting party caught out of bounds, and neither kingdom triumphed.
Neither the Philistines, nor the Israelites, had a king that could lead their nation to supreme greatness. There was no Philistine warlord to pull the armies of all five Pentapolis cities together, nor was there a king of Israel to lead the nation, only a number of judges who advocated for action based on each judge's own beliefs. There were too many voices making decisions for each group; there was not one person taking decisive and strategic action on behalf of the Philistines, or the Israelites. Around 1050 BC, if either nation had a king, one may have been able to triumph over the other.

#2 – Around 950, Sheshonq headed up the armed forces of the north of Egypt, and also managed to create an alliance with the south by marrying one of the daughters of the pharaoh at Tanis. When the pharaoh died, Sheshonq had asserted his right, by marriage, to the throne of Egypt in Tanis.
Sheshonq was a strong, and smart, warrior. By allying himself with the south of Egypt, while leading forces in the north, Sheshonq made sure he had power in both parts of divided Egypt. When his wife's father died, Sheshonq asserted his right to the Egyptian throne at Tanis. Coupled with Sheshonq's power over the priests of Thebes, it did not take him long to assert himself as king of all of Egypt. Sheshonq reunited a divided Egypt, and his descendants held the north and south together for some years. A strong king was necessary to reunite north and south Egypt, renewing Egypt's overall strength and power.

CHAPTER FORTY-SIX: FROM WESTERN TO EASTERN ZHOU

The student may use her text when answering the questions in sections I and II.

Section I: Who, What, Where

Write a one or two-sentence answer explaining the significance of each item listed below.

Hsiao – **Pg. 329, ¶ 5** – Hsiao was King Yih's brother. Hsiao seized the throne from King Yi, and took power away from Yih's son and living heir, Yi.

Duke of Mi – **Pg. 329, ¶ 2 & 3** – The Duke of Mi had collected three beautiful girls for his harem, and did not offer any of the girls to King Kung during Kung's royal visit. A year after visiting Mi, Kung had Mi executed; no lord would live in greater luxury than the king.

P'ing – **Pg. 333, ¶ 1** – P'ing was the deposed son of Yu. After the fall of the Zhou house, P'ing was reinstated to the throne, moving the center of the Zhou kingdom east to the city of Loyang.

Duke of Qi – **Pg. 329, ¶ 6** – The Duke of Qi was lord of a strong state up on the north Yellow River, which bickered with and defied King Yi. Yi mounted an attack on Qi, the Duke was captured, and then boiled in a bronze cauldron.

Quan Rong – **Pg. 332, ¶ 7** – The Quan Rong were barbarians that lived north and west of the Zhou lands. They attacked the capital city with the help of the relatives of King Yu's first wife, angry that she had been deposed in favor of a harem woman.

Xianyun – **Pg. 331, ¶ 2** – Xianyun was the designation given to a coalition of different nomadic groups from the area west of China, who had joined together to try to gain some of the Zhou prosperity for themselves.

alternate answer:

Pg. 331, ¶ 3 – Xianyun is the name of a poem from the Minor Odes section of the Shi jing, which laments the Invasion of Zhou territory by the nomadic tribes from the west.

King Yih – **Pg. 329, ¶ 4 & 5** – King Yih, able to beat off barbarian tribes from outside Zhou land, was not able to defend himself against his usurper brother, Hsiao. King Yih fled the capital city and died in exile.

Section II: Comprehension

Write a two/three sentence answer to each of the following questions.

1. What archaeological evidence shows us that around 900 BC, the "Lords of the Nine Lands" were beginning to act with more and more independence?
A1. – Pg. 328, ¶ 2 – Archaeologists have uncovered bronze vessels cast and inscribed by the lords of the lands themselves, meaning the Zhou emperor had lost the royal monopoly over bronze casting. The inscriptions on these vessels show that these same local governors were also beginning to celebrate their own feasts and rituals, reflecting the growing independence of the outlying Chinese lands.

2. In what way did the growing bureaucracy of the Zhou administration, which was meant to protect the king, actually reflect the king's weakening power?
A2. – Pg. 328, ¶ 3 to Pg. 329, ¶ 1 – As the Zhou kingdom expanded, the administration became more structured, putting strict rules in place to ensure the king's power. The growing Zhou bureaucracy made it clear that the king could not compel all-encompassing heartfelt obedience through the force of his character. He needed rules and lords to make sure his subjects would remain loyal.

3. How was Yi able to recapture the Zhou throne?
A3. – Pg. 329, ¶ 6 – After Yih died in exile, and the usurper Hsiao died as well, Yi was able to recapture the Zhou throne with the help of a coalition of lords who enthroned him.

4. What was the purpose of Li's Grand Inquisitor? What were the consequences of speaking against King Li? How did the people in the capital react to the Grand Inquisitor?
A4. – Pg. 329, ¶ 7 – Li, disturbed by the criticisms of his people, ordered a Grand Inquisitor to go out and listen for disloyal speech. Dissenters were arrested and executed. Fearing death, the criticisms subsided because no one in the capital dared to say a word.

5. In addition to Li's repressive politics, what environmental circumstance made the people of China more miserable than ever?
A5. – Pg. 330, ¶ 2 – During Li's reign, the people of China suffered because famine and drought, punctuated by flooding rains, destroyed the harvest.

6. What did the Duke of Shao sacrifice in order to save Li's heir Hsuan? What were the circumstances of this sacrifice? Why the Duke of Shao make this sacrifice?
A6. – Pg. 331, ¶ 4 & 5 – The Duke of Shao sacrificed his own son in order to save Li's heir, Hsuan. When rebellion broke out in the capital, Li managed to get away to the countryside, leaving Hsuan stuck in the city. After the Duke of Shao swapped the living heir with his son, the fake heir was killed, and the Duke of Shao was able to raise the prince in his household until Hsuan was ready to take the throne and continue the Zhou Dynasty.

7. Describe the barbarians Hsuan faced.
A7. – Pg. 330, ¶ 8 to Pg. 331, ¶ 1 – The barbarians that Hsuan faced were probably Indo-European. They lived a horse-oriented nomadic culture, travelling across the high steppes

on horseback, hunting game with bows. When they grew hungry, they came down to raid the fields and granaries of the Zhou farmers. The most threatening tribes Hsuan faced were to the west; the Zhou called them "Xianyun."

8. What made the Xianyun particularly meddlesome invaders?
A8. – Pg. 331, ¶ 3 – The Xianyun were particularly meddlesome invaders because they used chariots in battle, and the wars against them dragged on and on.

9. In what way was Yu's concubine responsible for the collapse of the royal family?
A9. – Pg. 332, ¶ 4 – Yu became obsessed with a harem woman, and together they had a son. Yu then tried to depose the queen and crown prince on behalf of the concubine and her bastard son. Though his advisors resisted the suggestion, Yu insisted, and the queen was thrown out of the palace.

10. When King Yu ordered the beacon fires lit to signal the invasion of the Quan Rong, why did the feudal lords choose to ignore his cry for help?
A10. – Pg. 332, ¶ 6-8 – Yu's concubine was not easily amused, so Yu decided to entertain his mistress by lighting all the beacon fires and beating the alarm drums as if the capital was being attacked, only to have the nearby lords turn up with their armies to find out it was prank. When the Quan Rong did attack the city, the feudal lords simply shrugged off the beacon fires; they had no intention of being made fools of twice in order to entertain the concubine-queen.

11. When P'ing made Ch'in a duke as a show of gratitude for safe passage to the new capital, how was this action also an admission that the king no longer was protected under the Mandate of Heaven?
A11. – Pg. 334, ¶ 2 – Though the Zhou dynasty survived the fall of the western Zhou house, the Zhou homeland was no longer protected by the king. Knowing the Mandate of Heaven no longer protected the royal house, the king now had to lean on the support of lesser lords, like the Duke of Ch'in, in order to keep his kingdom intact.

Section III: Critical Thinking

The student may not use her text to answer this question.

Li's Grand Inquisitor may have stopped audible criticism of the king, but feelings of resentment against the royal house could not be quelled. The Duke of Shao warned Li that an explosion was coming: "To block people's mouths is worse than blocking a river…. When an obstructed river bursts its banks, it will surely hurt a great number of people." Write a paragraph explaining how this prophecy came true during Li's grandson Yu's reign. In your answer, make sure to include the consequences of the earthquake that shook the capital, and the results of Yu's decision to make his harem woman his queen.

A discussion of the earthquake that hit the capital when Yu took the Zhou throne can be found on page 331, ¶ 5 to page 332, ¶ 3. The action and consequence of Yu making his harem woman queen can be found on page 332, ¶ 4-8. The student should be able to parallel Li's action of blocking the mouths of his people with the landslides that blocked the river; his actions were mimicked in nature.

Part Four: Empires

Later, Yu deposed the royal queen and heir because of his own personal wish to make his harem woman queen. Yu suppressed the opinions of his people and followed his own desires when he kicked the queen off of the throne. It is no surprise that when given the chance, the relatives of King Yu's first wife helped take down the Zhou house as retribution for her humiliation, much like the river that finally burst in the warning originally given to Li.

When Yu inherited the throne, an earthquake shook the Zhou capital city, resulting in landslides that choked the river channels that supplied fresh water to the city. Soon after the earthquake, the three river channels dried up, and cut the city off from its water source. Just as Li blocked the mouths of his people from speaking, landslides blocked the rivers. The evils of the Zhou overflowed into the earth itself. The troubles continued when Yu deposed his queen so that a harem woman could sit on the throne. This action upset many people in the kingdom. Like the Zhou kings before him, Yu had to fight off outside invaders, and depended on the armies of the lords in his kingdom to defend the capital. When the Quan Rong attacked the Zhou, they were joined by the relatives of King Yu's first wife. The second part of the Duke of Shao's prophecy had come true: Yu had not listened to the voices of his people and did what he wanted – he put his harem woman on the throne. The retribution was battle, which hurt many people, and caused the fall of the house of Zhou.

CHAPTER FORTY-SEVEN: THE ASSYRIAN RENAISSANCE

The student may use his text when answering the questions in sections I and II.

Section I: Who, What, Where

Write a one or two-sentence answer explaining the significance of each item listed below.

Aram – **Pg. 335, ¶ 2 – Aram was the name given to the entire area west of the Euphrates by the Assyrians. Aram was a blanket term for the cities governed by Aramaean chiefs.**

Black Obelisk – **Pg. 342, ¶ 2 & Pg. 343, ¶ 1 – The Black Obelisk was Shalmaneser III's victory monument, commemorating his triumph over Israel. On it, dozens of conquered kings come with tribute for Shalmaneser; on the second panel of one side, Jehu of Israel touches his forehead to the ground before Shalmaneser, the first Assyrian king to enter Israel.**

Caleh – **Pg. 336, ¶ 2 to Pg. 337, ¶ 2 – Caleh was the center of Assyrian king Ashurnasirpal II's government. Ashurnasirpal resurrected the old village; he laid out orchards, put a wall around the city, and built a massive and ornate palace within its boundaries.**

Damascus – **Pg. 335, ¶ 1 – Damascus, a city in the middle of the plain that lay across the Euphrates from Assyria, was the strongest of the independent states settled by the Aramaeans.**

Elijah – **Pg. 339, ¶ 2 – Elijah, a wild man in animal skins, was a prophet of Israel who escaped Jezebel's attempts to assassinate him. Elijah anointed Jehu to be God's choice as the next king of Israel, and gave him divine permission to assassinate Ahab, Jezebel, and the entire royal house.**

Jehu – **Pg. 339, ¶ 2 & Pg. 341, ¶ 5-8 – Jehu was chosen by Elijah to take down Ahab's royal house. Jehu finally fulfilled his calling when Ahab's son was on the throne; Jehu killed Joram, Jezebel, her Phoenician prophets, and the rest of Ahab's family.**

Joram – **Pg. 341, ¶ 3 – Joram, son of Ahab, tried to conquer Ramoth-Gilead after his father's first attempt, and was also unsuccessful. Shortly after returning to Jezreel to recover from a battle wound, Joram was killed by Jehu.**

Omri – **Pg. 337, ¶ 4 – Omri, king of Israel, built Samaria to be the new capital of the north, and was the first Israelite king to be mentioned with awe in the inscriptions of another country.**

ALTERNATE ANSWER: The student might include that the inscription in which Omri was mentioned was called the Mesha Inscription. The Mesha Inscription was a stone found across the Jordan river in the territory of the tribe known as the Moabites; the inscription mourns that Omri "humbled Moab for many years."

Section II: Comprehension

Write a two/three sentence answer to each of the following questions.

1. What steps did Ashur-dan II take to help bring Assyria out of its dark age, into its new renaissance?
A1. – Pg. 335, ¶ 3 – Ashur-dan II burned the Aramaean cities which had been built on land that had once been Assyrian. He secured the Assyrian heartland by ringing it with his troops, and he brought back from the mountains the Assyrian villagers who had been driven from their town and resettled them in their own land.

2. Why did Aramaic replace Akkadian as the common language spoken in Babylon?
A2. – Pg. 336, ¶ 1 – Aramaeans had infiltrated the old Babylonian territory to such an extent that their language, Aramaic, was beginning to replace the ancient Akkadian which had once served Babylonians as a common tongue.

3. Describe one instance of cruelty from Ashurnasirpal II's "reign of terror."
A3. – Pg. 338, ¶ 3 – Ashurnasirpal put a pillar up at the gate of a city which had revolted against its Assyrian-appointed governor, and then he skinned the chiefs who were responsible for the revolt, so that he could cover the pillar with their skins.

ALTERNATE ANSWER – any combination of these instances, found on pg. 338, ¶ 3, is acceptable: Ashurnasirpal put a pillar up at the gate of a city which had revolted against its Assyrian-appointed governor, and walled those who revolted against Assyria in the pillar. He also impaled some of the dissenters and arranged them around the pillar itself. Ashurnasirpal II skinned those who revolted against Assyria and covered the walls of the city with their skins. Sometimes he cut the private parts off of the disloyal royal officials, or he cut off their noses and ears, gouged out their eyes, or decapitated them and tied their heads to vines throughout the gardens of conquered cities like decaying fruit. In one city he made a pillar out of living people, piling them one on top of the over and covering them in plaster to make a column. He also cut off the ears and fingers of villagers, put out their eyes, and burned young men and maidens in the fire.

4. What was the political motive behind Ahab's marriage to Jezebel?
A4. – Pg. 338, ¶ 5 – Ahab, king of Israel, saw the spreading of the Assyrian threat to his east and north. In order to ally himself with the Phoenicians, Ahab negotiated a strategic marriage with the daughter of the Phoenician king of Sidon, Jezebel.

5. Why did Ahab choose to worship Baal, chief god of the Phoenicians?
A5. – Pg. 339, ¶ 1 – The Phoenicians were not the only ones who worshiped Baal as their chief god. A number of other Western Semitic tribes and cities worshiped Baal as well. Worshipping Baal would have won Ahab the friendship not only of Tyre and Byblos, but also the cities that lay between Israel and the advancing Assyrian front.

6. What did Jezebel do to the prophets of the God of Abraham? What happened to those who escaped the queen's purge?

A6. – Pg. 339, ¶ 1 – Jezebel rounded up and slaughtered the prophets of the God of Abraham. Some of the prophets escaped in the mountains, where they called for the Israelites to rebel against their evil king.

7. When Shalmaneser met Israelite forces at Qarqar in 853, who did he find allied with Ahab's army? How did Ahab manage to get all this support?
A7. – Pg. 339, ¶ 6 – Shalmaneser faced not only Ahab's Israelite forces, but also Phoenician troops, men sent by the king of Damascus, and Egyptian troops. Ahab was able to get help from Phoenician troops because they were allies, and he was supported by Damascus and Egypt because both feared becoming victims of Assyrian expansion.

8. What is the Monolith Inscription? How did the Monolith Inscription differ from the account of the battle at Qarqar depicted in Assyrian reliefs?
A8. – Pg. 339, ¶ 8 – The Monolith Inscription is an inscription in which Shalmaneser III declared victory over Ahab and his allied troops. However, Assyrian reliefs depict enemy soldiers charging over the bodies of the Assyrian dead, suggesting Shalmaneser was not as successful as he claimed to be.

9. After hearing Phoenician advisors predict certain victory for Ahab over the city of Ramoth-Gilead, why did Jehoshaphat suggest that Ahab consider asking a Hebrew prophet what Yahweh thought about the plan?

NOTE TO INSTRUCTOR: This question is asking the student to identify two major points: that the Phoenician advisors were mystics, not prophets, and that Ahab should have turned to his first faith's God, Yahweh, for a true prophecy.

A9. – Pg. 340, ¶ 6 – Jehoshaphat did not trust the Phoenician advisors; they were fortune-tellers, not conduits for the word of God. Jehoshaphat suggested Ahab ask a Hebrew prophet for advice, because the prophet would be able to relay an opinion about the attack from Yahweh himself.

10. What were the details of Jezebel's death?
A10. – Pg. 341, ¶ 6 & 7 – When Jezebel heard that Jehu had killed Joram and was coming to the royal palace, she put on her royal robes and waited at a window for his approach. As Jehu drew near he called out for help and three eunuchs from the queen mother's own household came up behind the old woman and threw her from the window. She fell to the pavement, Jehu rode over her body, and then half-wild dogs ate all but her hands and feet and her skull.

11. At what cost did Jehu purify the house of Israel?
A11. – Pg. 343, ¶ 2 – After purifying the house of Israel, Jehu found that he had lost Ahab's old allies. Also, the Aramaeans were against him, as well as the Phoenicians. Jehu had to submit to Assyrian power, as he had no more allies to fight on his side.

Section III: Critical Thinking

As we know from our textbook, alliances in the ancient world were both a blessing and a curse. While the longevity of some alliances was remarkable, even by today's standards, it was more common for an alliance to be broken prematurely. Write two or three paragraphs explaining how Ahab's opportunist tendencies showed when he decided to turn on the king of Damascus. In your answer, describe how Ahab and the king of Damascus came to make a treaty, why Ahab thought it would be opportune for him to break the treaty, and how the king of Judah probably had a secret alliance that protected his own neck in the advance on Ramoth-Gilead.

To start, you can break up the question into four parts. Once the student comes up with an answer to each part, he can then put the pieces together to form 2-3 paragraphs. The student is retelling the story of Ahab's alliance with the king of Damascus, his turn against the Aramaean leader, and Jehoshaphat's involvement in Ahab's plan of attack. The student should recognize that alliances are strategic, and while it might seem like one leader is allied with another, there could always be another plan in the works.

How did Ahab and the king of Damascus come to make a treaty?
Pg. 339, ¶ 1-4 – When Ahab married Jezebel, he allowed his Phoenician wife to round up and slaughter all the prophets of the God of Abraham. This made Ahab very unpopular with his own people. The Aramaean king of Damascus chose to use this internal unrest as an opportunity to launch an attack on Israel. Surprisingly, Ahab fought the Aramaeans to a draw, and the king of Damascus made a treaty with Ahab.

Why did Ahab think it would be opportune for him to break the treaty with the king of Damascus?
Pg. 339, ¶ 5 to Pg. 340, ¶ 9 – When Shalmaneser marched against the Israelite border, he expected victory. Instead, he was met with a strong opponent made up of Israelites, Phoenicians, Aramaeans and Egyptians. The battle ended in a draw, and was devastating enough to Assyria that Shalmaneser decided to withdraw. Ahab, exalted by the successful defense of his country, decided he was strong enough to take on his ally, the king of Damascus. Also, Ahab's Phoenician advisors predicted certain victory against the Aramaeans.

How was the king of Judah involved in Ahab's plan to attack Ramoth-Gilead? What evidence suggests that the king of Judah had a secret alliance with the Aramaeans?
Pg. 340, ¶ 4 to Pg. 341, ¶ 1 – Ahab asked Jehoshaphat, the king of Judah, to travel north and join with him in an attack against the Aramaean border city of Ramoth-Gilead. Jehoshaphat had no enormous military might, but since Ramoth-Gilead lay almost exactly on the north-south border, Jehoshaphat's alliance would have allowed Ahab to perform a pincer move on the city. Jehoshaphat agreed to join in the attack, though he had reservations about the Phoenician dominated house of Israel, and had been warned by a Hebrew prophet that the attack would fail, and Ahab would be killed. It seems Jehoshaphat made his own alliance with the Aramaean government because when the battle commenced, the Aramaean chariot commanders, who were headed directly for him, reversed direction and left him alone after he called out, "I am the king of Judah, not the king of Israel!"

What was the end result of Ahab's attack on Ramoth-Gilead?

Pg. 341, ¶ 2 – Like the Hebrew prophet predicted, Israel's attack on Ramoth-Gilead was a failure, and Ahab died in battle.

Example Answer:

  When Ahab married Jezebel, he allowed his Phoenician wife to round up and slaughter all the prophets of the God of Abraham. This made Ahab very unpopular with his own people. The Aramaean king of Damascus chose to take advantage of Israel's internal unrest and attack. Surprisingly, Ahab fought the Aramaeans to a draw, and the king of Damascus made a treaty with Ahab.

  A few years later, Shalmaneser marched against the Israelite border expecting victory. Instead, he was met with a strong opponent made up of Israelites, Phoenicians, Aramaeans and Egyptians. The battle ended in a draw, and was devastating enough to Assyria that Shalmaneser decided to withdraw. Ahab, exalted by the successful defense of his country, decided he was strong enough to take on his ally, the king of Damascus. Also, Ahab's Phoenician advisors predicted certain victory against the Aramaeans.

  Ahab asked Jehoshaphat, the king of Judah, to travel north and join with him in an attack against the Aramaean border city of Ramoth-Gilead. Jehoshaphat had no enormous military might, but since Ramoth-Gilead lay almost exactly on the north-south border, Jehoshaphat's alliance would have allowed Ahab to perform a pincer move on the city. Jehoshaphat agreed to join in the attack, though he had reservations about the Phoenician dominated house of Israel, and had been warned by a Hebrew prophet that the attack would fail, and Ahab would be killed. It seems Jehoshaphat made his own alliance with the Aramaean government because when the battle commenced, the Aramaean chariot commanders, who were headed directly for him, reversed direction and left him alone after he called out, "I am the king of Judah, not the king of Israel!" Ultimately, the battle was a failure, and Ahab died in battle.

CHAPTER FORTY-EIGHT: NEW PEOPLES

The student may use her text when answering the questions in sections I and II.

Section I: Who, What, Where

Write a one or two-sentence answer explaining the significance of each item listed below.

Adad-nirari III – **Pg. 349, ¶ 4 – Adad-nirari III was the son of Shamshi-Adad V and Sammu-amat. Adad-nirari III was still a child when his father died, so his mother took his place on the Assyrian throne.**

Arcadia – **Pg. 350, ¶ 1 – Arcadia, in the center of the southern Greek peninsula called the Peloponnese, was home to the surviving remnants of Mycenaean civilization.**

Barbaro-phonoi – **Pg. 353, ¶ 4 – Barbaro-phonoi means "strange speakers." Homer gave those who lived outside the triple circle of Greeks this name; it was a simple division between those who spoke a dialect of Greek and those who didn't.**

Gordium – **Pg. 345, ¶ 4 – Gordium was the capital city of the Phrygians.**

Mada – **Pg. 347, ¶ 4 & 5 – The Mada, nomadic peoples wandering all along the north of the Zagros mountains, acted as a buffer against Elamite power for the Assyrian kingdom. Later the Mada would be named the Medes by the Greeks.**

Marduk-zakir-shumi – **Pg. 344, ¶ 1 & 2 – Marduk-zakir-shumi was the eldest son of the king of Babylon. When Marduk-zakir-shumi's kingship was challenged by his younger brother, Shalmaneser III of Assyria marched down to help the prince reclaim his throne.**

Marduk-balassu-iqbi – **Pg. 348, ¶ 5 & 6 – Marduk-balassu-iqbi, son of Marduk-zakir-Shumi, took Babylon's throne when his father died. Not too many years after his accession, Marduk-balassu-iqbi was defeated by Shamshi-Adad V of Assyria, and taken captive by Assyrian forces.**

Parsua – **Pg. 347, ¶ 4 & 5 – The Parsua, a group of northern mountain-dwellers who were settled just across the Zagros mountains on the western side of Elam, acted as a buffer against Elamite power for the Assyrian kingdom. Later the Parsua would be named the Persians by the Greeks.**

Phrygians – **Pg. 345, ¶ 4 – The Phrygians were invaders from southern Europe who crossed over the Bosphorus Strait and settled in the area of Asia Minor previously occupied by the Hittites.**

Que – **Pg. 345, ¶ 6 to Pg. 347, ¶ 1 – Que was a neo-Hittite kingdom that lay in a strategic position on the path through the Taurus Mountains, the best gateway into Asia Minor and also the road to the silver mines north of the mountains. Shalmaneser attacked Que, marched into its capital, and claimed the silver mines for himself.**

Ring Composition – **Pg. 352, ¶ 1 – A ring composition is a writing structure where the poet gives himself a convenient mental anchor for an episode by beginning in the middle of the story, going back to the beginning, and then forward to the end.**

Sammu-amat – **Pg. 349, ¶ 4 – Sammu-amat was Shamshi-Adad V's queen. She stepped into the place of power because her son, Adad-nirari III, was too young to rule.**

Shamshi-Adad V – **Pg. 347, ¶ 6 – Shamshi-Adad V, Shalmaneser III's second son, was appointed heir to the Assyrian throne by his father. Shamshi-Adad V was forced to flee Assyria because of a revolt led by his brother Assur-danin-apli.**

ALTERNATE ANSWER: Pg. 348, ¶ 5-6 & Pg. 349, ¶ 3 – Shamshi-Adad V planned and completed a campaign that no Assyrian king had undertaken for generations: the invasion of Babylon. After successfully defeating Marduk-balassu-iqbi and taking Babylon for Assyria, Shamshi-Adad V declared himself "King of Sumer and Akkad."

NOTE TO INSTRUCTOR: The alternate answer to this term is covered in Comprehension question number 4. You may suggest to the student that she think of answering the "Who, What, Where" by identifying Shamshi-Adad V's parentage and succession.

Section II: Comprehension

Write a two/three sentence answer to each of the following questions.

1. Why was Shalmaneser III unwilling to attack Babylon?
A1. – Pg. 344, ¶ 3 & 4 – Shalmaneser III was unwilling to attack Babylon because he was worried about offending Marduk, Babylon's chief god.

2. Where were each of the Semitic tribes at the head of the Persian Gulf, known collectively to the Assyrians as the Chaldeans, specifically located? Under whose control were the Chaldeans?
A2. – Pg. 344, ¶ 5 to Pg. 345, ¶ 1 – The Semitic tribes known to the Assyrians as Chaldeans, claimed the land which had once formed the far southern edge of Sumer. The tribe of Bit-Amukanni dominated the land near the old Sumerian city of Uruk; Bit-Dakkuri lay a little to the north, closest to Babylon; the tribe of Bit-Yakin dominated Ur and the marshy land bordering the Gulf itself; and two smaller tribes lay under the protection of these three. They paid nominal allegiance to the king of Babylon, but they were only sketchily under any Babylonian control.

3. Why did Marduk-zakir-shumi make Shamshi-Adad V sign a treaty as a condition of getting Babylonian troops to fight against Assur-danin-apli? What were the terms of the treaty?
A3. – Pg. 348, ¶ 2 – Marduk-zakir-shumi did not trust his Assyrian son-in-law Shamshi-Adad V, and that is why he made the Assyrian heir sign a treaty. The treaty required Shamshi-Adad V to acknowledge Babylon's superiority. In the treaty, only Marduk-zakir-shumi is referred to as king, and the accompanying oaths were sworn in front of the Babylonian gods only.

4. How was Shamshi-Adad V able to avenge the humiliation of Marduk-zakir-shumi's treaty? In your answer, be sure to explain the significance of the title "King of Sumer and Akkad."

A4. – Pg. 348, ¶ 6 & Pg. 349, ¶ 3 – Shamshi-Adad V was able to avenge the humiliation of Marduk-zakir-shumi's treaty by successfully invading Marduk-balassu-iqbi's Babylon. Shamshi-Adad V then declared himself, in ancient terms, "King of Sumer and Akkad." By using these ancient terms, Shamshi-Adad V was denying Babylon existed; there was only Assyria, the proper guardian of Babylonian culture and Babylonian gods.

5. How did Sammu-amat assert her right to the Assyrian throne?
A5. – Pg. 349, ¶ 4 – Sammu-amat asserted her right to the Assyrian throne by building a stele that linked her to every available Assyrian king. Not only does she make sure to link herself to her dead husband, Shamshi-Adad V, but also to her father-in-law, "Shalmaneser, king of the four regions."

6. Who were the Ionians? Where did they come from, and what peoples made up their culture?
A6. – Pg. 350, ¶ 2 – The Ionians were a culture of people made up of migrating Mycenaean Greeks who sailed across the Aegean Sea over to the coast of Asia Minor. They settled along the shore, in villages that grew into cities: Smyrna, Miletus, Ephesus, and others. The mixture of Mycenaean and Asian language and ways resulted in a distinctive Ionian culture.

7. Where did the Ionians go during the Dorian occupation?
A7. – Pg. 350, ¶ 2 – During the Dorian occupation, the Ionians spread back across the nearby islands, settling in Lesbos, Chios, and Samos, among others, and finally returning to the eastern coast of Greece itself.

8. Explain how the Ionians, Mycenaeans and the Dorians were, more or less, from the same race.
A8. – Pg. 351, ¶ 2 – The Ionians were Mycenaean at the root, and the Mycenaeans and Dorians came from the same Indo-European stock; both of them were descended from wanderers who had come south into the Greek peninsula centuries before.

9. Who was Homer? Where did he come from?
A9. – Pg. 351, ¶ 5 – Homer was the composer of the poems the Iliad and the Odyssey. Some people think Homer was a single genius, while others think "Homer" was the single penname for a school of poets. He was an Ionian that came either from the Asia Minor city of Smyrna, or from the island of Chios just off the Ionian coast.

10. How do the Iliad and the Odyssey reflect both a pre-800 BC world, and the world after the Dorian invasion?
A10. – Pg. 352, ¶ 2 – The Iliad and Odyssey reflect a pre-800 BC world in their use of Mycenaean details; particulars of armor, like a boar's tusk helmet, and treasure reflect a world before the coming of the Dorians. However, the language of the epic is itself that of the eighth century, and the name of Priam, king of Troy, belongs to the neo-Hittite language spoken by the inhabitants of Que and other scattered descendants of the Hittite empire.

Section III: Critical Thinking

The student may not use her text to answer this question.

In the ancient world, the mingling of different peoples often occurred as a result of war and conquest. In ancient Greece, literature acted as another type of galvanizing force. Write a paragraph explaining how peace brought together the Ionians, Dorians and Arcadians. Then address how the blending of these cultures is reflected in Homer's writing. Finally, explain how the Iliad and Odyssey gave these three different peoples a shared past.

This question is addressed specifically in the chapter, page 351, ¶ 4 and page 352, ¶ 3-5. This is the first time we see a great epic bringing together different peoples and combining them into a single culture. This question reinforces the importance of narrative as part of the fabric of culture. Another example of narrative as a piece of a people's particular culture is the flood story. As seen in Chapter 2, there was no universal flood story, but rather many variations, one for each particular ancient civilization.

As the Dorian disruption receded into the distant past, the cities of the Greek peninsula entered into a period of relative peace. During this time, the Ionians, Arcadians and Dorians acted as allies. Sometime around 800 BC, the growing sense of a single cultural identity led to the weaving together of a number of different historical traditions into two related epic poems, Homer's Iliad and Odyssey. The Iliad offered the Dorians, Arcadians and Ionians a mythical shared past in that, in the Iliad, each city sent its ships instantly in response to Agamemnon's call. This was a unity of action that the Greeks never actually managed to achieve. Also, in the Iliad, for the first time, Homer calls those who live outside of the triple circle of Greeks *barbaro-phonoi*, meaning "strange speakers." The story expresses the beginnings of a growing identification between Greek cities that separated them from other peoples. The history presented in the Iliad and the Odyssey soon was claimed as the shared history of every city on the Greek peninsula.

CHAPTER FORTY-NINE: TRADING POSTS AND COLONIES

The student may use his text when answering the questions in sections I and II.

Section I: Who, What, Where

Write a one or two-sentence answer explaining the significance of each item listed below.

Alba Longa – **Pg. 358, ¶ 2 – Alba Longa, a town built along the ridge of the Alban hills, was planted as a colony for Lavinium. Alba Longa was ruled by king Numitor.**

Amphictyonys – **Pg. 357, ¶ 2 – Amphictyonys was a Greek term for associations which shared responsibility for the upkeep of a temple or shrine.**

Amulius – **Pg. 358, ¶ 3 – Amulius, the wicked younger brother of Numitor, forced Numitor into exile. Amulius then seized the thrones of Lavinium and Alba Longa, murdered his brothers' sons, and declared that the daughter of Numitor, Rhea Silvia, should be a perpetual virgin.**

Apennine Culture – **Pg. 355, ¶ 1 – Apennine culture was the assignation archaeologists gave to the ancient people who lived on the Italian peninsula because so many settlements lay along the ridge of the Apennine mountains.**

Lavinium – **Pg. 358, ¶ 2 – Lavinium was a Latin town on the Italian peninsula, just south of the Tiber, ruled over by Numitor.**

Numitor – **Pg. 358, ¶ 2 & 3 – Numitor was the king of two Latin towns, Lavinium and Alba Longa. Numitor was forced into exile by his younger brother, Amulius.**

Rhea Silvia – **Pg. 358, ¶ 3 & 4 – Rhea Silvia was Numitor's daughter. She was ordered by Amulius to remain a virgin; however, claiming she was raped by the god Mars, Rhea Silvia gave birth to twin boys.**

Titus Tatius – **Pg. 360, ¶ 4 – Titus Tatius was the king of the Sabines. After the Sabines attacked Rome in order to retrieve their women, Titus Tatius agreed to a truce with Romulus, and the two kings brought their states together under a single government.**

Section II: Comprehension

Write a two/three sentence answer to each of the following questions.

1. Where did Greek merchants sail in order to trade during Homer's time?
A1. – Pg. 354, ¶ 1 – Greek merchants sailed across the Aegean Sea from island to island, to the Asia Minor coast, down to Crete and to the southern shores of the Italian peninsula.

NOTE TO INSTRUCTOR:
The text reads, "By the time of Homer, ships from Greek cities were also making regular calls at the southern shores of the peninsula to the west, to trade with the peoples there." The student should look at the map on page 356 to discern that the "peninsula to the west" is the Italian peninsula.

2. What clue do we have that the scattered settlements of people on the Italian peninsula were of the same descent?
A2. – Pg. 354, ¶ 2 – Despite the distance between them, the people scattered on the Italian peninsula made the same kinds of pots, which suggests they were all of the same descent.

3. How do archaeologists distinguish early Italian settlements from one another? List the different settlements and how they were grouped.
A3. – Pg. 355, ¶ 3 – Archaeologists can distinguish early Italian settlements from one another based on how the villages treated their dead. The groups of villages that still buried their dead were: the Fossa, the Apulian, and the Middle Adriatic. The groups of villagers who cremated their dead were divided into four groups: the Golasecca, the Este, the Villanovan and the Latial.

4. What did the Latial peoples do with their dead? How was the burial ritual a reflection of everyday Latial culture?
A4. – Pg. 355, ¶ 4 – The Latial people put their ashes not just in urns, but in tiny huts that were replicas of homes for the living, made as dwellings for the dead. The huts reflected the simple and unprotected huts of the living Latial people.

5. Why did the Latial peoples build their villages on the top of hills? What united these tiny villages?
A5. – Pg. 355, ¶ 4 – The Latial villages were built on the top of hills to ensure their safety. The tiny villages were united by a common language called Latin.

6. What does "pan-Hellenic" mean? Give an example of pan-Hellenism from the chapter.
A6. – Pg. 357, ¶ 2 – "Pan-Hellenic" is the term for a site that belonged not just to the nearest Greek city, but to all speakers of Greek. An example of pan-Hellenism is the oracle at Delphi – the shrine attracted distant Greek visitors, all of whom sought guidance from the gods.

ALTERNATE ANSWERS for an example of pan-Hellenism:
Pg. 357, ¶ 1 & 2 – Chalcis and Eretria set up a trading post together on the bay of Naples for their mutual good.
Pg. 357, ¶ 2 – The temple of Zeus and Hera at Olympia grew in size thanks to pilgrimages made to it by Greeks from much farther away.
Pg. 357, ¶ 2 – On the island of Delos, the temple of Apollo and Artemis expanded due to visits from Greeks from much farther away.

7. How did the Olympic festival come into existence? When would the games be held, and how did the Olympic truce work?
A7. – Pg. 357, ¶ 4 – In 776, the king of Elis journeyed to the oracle at Delphi to ask how battles between Greek cities might be brought to an end. The oracle told him to make the games at Olympia into an official festival, during which time a truce must be declared. From then on, official games were held at Olympia every four years; during the games an Olympic truce was declared so that Greeks could travel to and from the games safely.

8. While the Olympics did not bring about sustained peace between Greek cities, how was the festival successful in galvanizing the ancient Greeks?

A8. – Pg. 358, ¶ 1 – While the Olympic games may not have actually brought about sustained peace, they did remind the Greek cities that they were united by the same language, they worshiped the same gods, and that war was not the only possible relation between them.

9. Who found Rhea Silvia's twin sons once they were dropped off on the banks of the Tiber? What were the boys named, and who paid for their education?

A9. – Pg. 358, ¶ 5 & 6 – When the boys were dropped off on the banks of the Tiber, they were found by a she-wolf who nursed them, and not long after the king's herdsman found them and carried them off to raise them with his wife. The herdsman named the boys Romulus and Remus. From his exile, Numitor sent money to fund the boys' education.

10. How did Romulus make up for Rome's shortage of women?

A10. – Pg. 360, ¶ 2 – Romulus threw a huge festival for Neptune and invited the Sabines. At the height of the festivities, when the Sabine men were distracted, the Roman men kidnapped all of the young Sabine women and carried them off.

11. How did the formation of colonies help the growing cities of the ancient Greeks?

A11. – Pg. 361, ¶ 2 & 3 – As the population of the ancient Greek cities grew, the Greek people needed more metal, more stone, more grain and more pastureland. The formation of colonies allowed the Greeks to set up numerous trade posts where they could barter for more metal and stone, and to farm new land for grains and livestock.

12. What happened to a Greek family's land when it was passed down to the next generation? Why was this problematic?

A12. – Pg. 361, ¶ 3 – In a Greek family, land was traditionally divided between the sons equally. However, because land on the Greek peninsula was limited, a family's property shrank as it was divided between each son, and in the end there was simply no more land to give to the next generation.

13. How did the limited amount of land on the Greek peninsula cause corruption in Greek land-owners and officials?

A13. – Pg. 361, ¶ 4 & 5 – The limited land available to Greek sons caused corruption because the judges who handled land disputes could be bribed in exchange for unjust rulings. Rights to the land because of inheritance no longer mattered; one could have the land if he could pay the judges for it.

14. What Greek cities sent out colonists? What were the names of the new Greek colonies, and where were they located?

A14. – Pg. 362, ¶ 3 – Chalcis and Eretria sent colonists to the Bay of Naples, where they built Cumae. Other colonists from Chalcis and Eretria were sent to the southern Italian coast, where they formed Naxus, Lentini, Catana, and Rhegium. Also, the city of Corinth sent Archias as the head of an expedition to Sicily, where he founded Syracuse.

Section III: Critical Thinking

In this chapter we find many instances of conflict associated with the formation of ancient Rome. Using the list of pairings below, write a short description of each and its association with Rome's origins. Then, write a paragraph describing how division was inextricable from ancient Rome's actual formation.

• Lavinium/Alba Longa
• Numitor/Amulius
• Romulus/Remus
• Romans/Sabines

• Lavinium/Alba Longa

Pg. 358, ¶ 2 & 6 – Lavinium and Alba Longa were two cities on the Italian peninsula. Lavinium was the first and older town. Alba Longa was a colony for Lavinium. Numitor was the king of these two cities. He was the grandfather of Remus and Romulus, the quarrelling sons who founded Rome.

• Numitor/Amulius

Pg. 358, ¶ 3 & 4 – Numitor was chased into exile by his usurper brother, Amulius. The rivalry between Numitor and Amulius is later echoed in the tumultuous relationship between Romulus and Remus.

• Romulus/Remus

Pg. 358, ¶ 7 & Pg. 359, ¶ 1 & 2 – Remus and Romulus were the twin sons of Numitor's daughter Rhea Silvia. After surviving a murder attempt made by Amulius, they wanted to pay homage to their survival by founding a new settlement where they had been left to drown as infants. However, the twins could not decide who would be the ruler of this new settlement. Their conflict lead to a battle, in which Remus was killed. The newly built city was named after Romulus, who fortified the Palatine hill and made it the center of his new city of Rome.

• Romans/Sabines

Pg. 360, ¶ 1-4 – When Rome was finally built under the authority of Romulus, it faced a dire lack of women. When the city's neighbors, the Sabines, refused to send women over to Rome, the Romans forcefully took the Sabine women themselves. This led to a battle, but the Sabine women begged both sides to stop. A treaty was made between the Sabines and the Romans; the two states were united under one government, with Rome as the seat of power.

Write a paragraph describing how division was inextricable from ancient Rome's actual formation.

Pg. 359, ¶ 4 & 5 and Pg. 360, ¶ 5 – The tale of Romulus and Remus tells a story about war between two related peoples. Ancient remains tell us that Rome began as two settlements, one on the Palatine hill, the other on the Esquiline, each hill held by a different Latial tribe. Possibly one tribe did come down, like Romulus, from the Alban ridge, perhaps to feed a growing population with grain from the fertile Tiberian plain. Very likely the other group

came from the Sabine hills, providing fodder for the story about the Romans kidnapping all of the Sabine women. Ancient Rome, then, was formed by two different peoples. These people – of the same basic stock, with similar customs and languages and gods – were nevertheless divided at the core.

CHAPTER FIFTY: OLD ENEMIES

The student may use her text when answering the questions in sections I and II.

Section I: Who, What, Where

Write a one or two-sentence answer explaining the significance of each item listed below.

Kar Assur – Pg. 366, ¶ 3 – Kar Assur, meaning "Wall of Assur," was a city located to the north of Babylon, just under the Assyrian border. Ostensibly this city was to help protect Babylon against nomads trying to infiltrate Nabonassar's land, but in reality it became an Assyrian outpost in Babylonia.

Nabonassar – Pg. 365, ¶ 5 & Pg. 366, ¶ 2 – Nabonassar took the throne of Babylon at the same time that Tiglath-Pileser III came to Assyria's throne. Nabonassar and Tiglath-Pileser III became allies, and Babylon and Assyria remained at peace until Nabonassar's death.

Merodach-baladan – Pg. 369, ¶ 4 – Merodach-baladan was a local Babylonian warlord that swore allegiance to Tiglath-Pileser III when he became king of Babylon. Merodach-baladan brought the Assyrian king lovely presents of gold necklaces, precious stones, logs of valuable wood, dyed garments and livestock.

Pul – Pg. 365, ¶ 3 & 4 – Pul, the governor of Caleh, led an insurrection against Ashur-nirari V, and murdered the king and his family. Pul then claimed the Assyrian throne for himself and took a new name: Tiglath-Pileser III.

Sapea – Pg. 369, ¶ 2 – Sapea, a city with three very high walls, was the refuge for the Chaldean chief who fled Babylon upon Tiglath-Pileser III's arrival. Tiglath-Pileser III followed the chief to Sapea and swarmed the city with Assyrian troops; an Assyrian relief shows Sapean bodies piled in the stream and weeping women and children that are being carried off into exile.

Sarduri I – Pg. 365, ¶ 1 & Pg. 367, ¶ 2 & 3 – Sarduri I, king of Urartu, extended Urartu's rule south into Assyria and west into ancient Hittite territory. After Tiglath-Pileser III drove Sarduri out of his capital city, Sarduri regathered his remaining peoples and ruled over a smaller Urartu in the northern part of the old kingdom.

Syria – Pg. 363, ¶ 1 – Syria was an Aramaean kingdom that had its capital at Damascus. When Shalmaneser IV ruled Assyria, the Syrians posed a great threat to Assyria's borders.

Urartu – Pg. 363, ¶ 2 & 3 – Urartu was the name of the mountain peoples that lived in old Mitanni territory. Constantly attacked by Assyrian raiding parties, the scattered people were forced to organize themselves into a coalition that turned into a large kingdom.

Section II: Comprehension

Write a two/three sentence answer to each of the following questions.

1. How did Shalmaneser IV lose hold of Babylon?
A1. – Pg. 364, ¶ 1 – Babylon had become increasingly restless under its Assyrian governor. When Chaldean warlords began to fight over the throne, the Assyrian governor of Babylon fled, meaning that Shalmaneser IV no longer controlled Babylon.

2. How was the governor of Mari's decision to date events by the years of his own rule a sign of waning power at Caleh?
A2. – Pg. 364, ¶ 2 – The governor of Mari's decision to date the events of his city by the years of his own rule was clearly made without consulting the seat of Assyrian power at Caleh. He was just one example of a governor ignoring his real king, instead acting like a petty king himself.

3. Why did the Greeks come to associate the term "astronomer" with "Chaldean"?
A3. – Pg. 365, ¶ 6 – The Greeks associated "astronomer" with "Chaldean" because it was during a Chaldean king's – Nabonassar's – reign that Babylon's strength and prosperity allowed the science of astronomy to flourish.

4. Why was the conquest of Arvad important to Tiglath-Pileser III's expanding empire? How did the fall of Arvad help Tiglath-Pileser III defeat the Urartu?
A4. – Pg. 366, ¶ 5 & Pg. 367, ¶ 1 & 2 – Arvad, technically bound to Assyria by treaty, had joined the growing Urartu kingdom as an ally. Taking down Arvad was the first step in Tiglath-Pileser III's campaign against his northern enemy. Once Arvad fell, Tiglath-Pileser III used the city as his military headquarters to fight against Que, Carchemish and finally Urartu's capital city.

5. What happened to the Phrygians after Tiglath-Pileser III conquered the Urartu?
A5. – Pg. 367, ¶ 4 – After Tiglath-Pileser III conquered the Urartu, his new province swallowed the eastern tribes of the Phrygians, in central Asia Minor. As a result, the western tribes regathered themselves into a new Phrygian kingdom.

6. According to legend, how did Midas come to be king of Phrygia?
A6. – Pg. 367, ¶ 5 – According to legend, the Phrygian people asked an oracle who should become their king; the oracle answered that the first man who drove up in a wagon was the divine choice, whereupon a farmer named Midas came into sight, riding a wagon. He was at once crowned king.

7. What historical evidence suggests that Midas did a great deal of trade with the Ionian cities on the Asia Minor coast?
A7. – Pg. 367, ¶ 5 to Pg. 368, ¶ 1 – Historical narratives tell us that Midas dedicated his wagon to Zeus just after he was made king, and that Midas married a Greek woman from Cyme. Also, according to Herodotus, Midas sent an offering to the oracle at Delphi. These stories reveal that the Phrygians had a lot of contact with the Greeks, and presumably did a great deal of trade with Ionian cities on the Asia Minor coast.

8. Describe the submission of Judah and Israel to Tiglath-Pileser III.

A8. – Pg. 368, ¶ 3 & 4 – When Menahem, the king of Israel, saw the Assyrian forces on the horizon, he sent forty tons of silver to buy Tiglath-Pileser III's favor. Judah's king Ahaz raided Solomon's temple and sent all the sacred items to Tiglath-Pileser III as a gesture of submission, and then offered to become Assyria's ally against Israel. With Judah willingly subservient to Assyria, Tiglath-Pileser III was then able to take most of Israel's northern parts.

9. Why did Tiglath-Pileser III choose to invade Babylon after the death of Nabonassar?
A9. – Pg. 368, ¶ 5 – When Nabonassar died, Babylon fell into a frenzy of civil war. The unrest in the kingdom made it an easy target for Tiglath-Pileser III's rapidly expanding empire.

10. Why was it seemingly effortless for Tiglath-Pileser III to sway the citizens in the north of Babylonia to join the Assyrian empire?
A10. – Pg. 368, ¶ 6 – Tiglath-Pileser III was able to garner support from the north of Babylonia effortlessly because the cities just south of the Assyrian border tended to be pro-Assyrian; it was in their best interest to get along with their northern neighbors. In addition, the northern Babylonians had more in common with Assyrian customs and gods than with the ways of the Semitic Chaldeans who were fighting over the throne.

11. Why was Tiglath-Pileser III's role as king of Babylon groundbreaking?
A11. – Pg. 369, ¶ 5 – Tiglath-Pileser III's rule in Babylon was groundbreaking because he was the first Assyrian monarch to appear in Babylon's own king lists, and the first foreigner to be recognized by the people of Babylon as their own king.

Section III: Critical Thinking

The student may not use her text to answer this question.

The relationship between Assyria and Babylon was like a rollercoaster; up one minute, down the next. First, explain why Tiglath-Pileser III chose to make Babylon an ally when he first came to the throne, instead of trying to conquer his southern neighbor. Second, explain why Nabonassar did not challenge Assyria when Tiglath-Pileser III claimed to have conquered Babylon. In your answers, make sure to include how Babylon's prosperity and peace may have factored into both acts.

First, explain why Tiglath-Pileser III chose to make Babylon an ally when he first came to the throne, instead of trying to conquer his southern neighbor. Note: The underlined sentences fulfill the requirement to explain how Babylon's strength may have factored into Tiglath-Pileser III's decision to act as an ally to Nabonassar.

Tiglath-Pileser III took the throne of Assyria at almost the same time that Nabonassar took the throne of Babylon (Pg. 365, ¶ 5). <u>Nabonassar quelled the revolts in Babylon, and soothed the discontented (Pg. 365, ¶ 6). Tiglath-Pileser III, with enemies to the north, east, and west, did not need another enemy to the south, especially not a king who had the support of his people</u>. Instead, Tiglath-Pileser III chose to offer himself as an ally to Nabonassar, and sent Assyrian soldiers to help the new king of Babylon wipe out any Chaldean and Aramaean resistance to his reign.

Second, explain why Nabonassar did not challenge Assyria when Tiglath-Pileser III claimed to have conquered Babylon. Note: The underlined sentences explain how astronomical study under Nabonassar exemplified Babylon's strength and prosperity.

When Tiglath-Pileser III called himself "King of Sumer and Akkad," he claimed to have rule over Babylon (Pg. 366, ¶ 3). <u>The strength of Babylon during Nabonassar's reign allowed the science of astronomy to flourish (Pg. 365, ¶ 6). During Nabonassar's years on the throne, Babylonian scribes kept tables that correlated astronomical observations to daily records of the weather, the levels of the Tigris and Euphrates, and the price of grain and other important supplies. This was a sign that Babylon was not only at peace, but it was a city with enough leisure time to search for ways to make itself more prosperous (Pg. 366, ¶ 1)</u>. It seems that Nabonassar did not mount an attack on Tiglath-Pileser III in retaliation because Babylon was doing very well, even if it was supposedly controlled by Assyria.

CHAPTER FIFTY-ONE: KINGS OF ASSYRIA AND BABYLON

The student may use his text when answering the questions in sections I and II.

Section I: Who, What, Where

Write a one or two-sentence answer explaining the significance of each item listed below.

Dur-Sharrukin – **Pg. 376, ¶ 2 – Dur-Sharrukin, or "Sargon City," was the capital city built by Sargon II, northeast of Nineveh. Dur-Sharrukin was just beyond the foothills of the Taurus Mountains where the Urartu hovered as a threat.**

Hoshea – **Pg. 371, ¶ 4 & Pg. 375, ¶ 1 – Hoshea, king of Israel, asked Egypt for its alliance in a war against Assyria. No help came, Israel was destroyed, and Hoshea was put in jail by Sargon II.**

Kush – **Pg. 373, ¶ 2 – Kush was the name given to the Egypt-governed section of Nubia by the Egyptian overlords.**

Napata – **Pg. 373, ¶ 2 – Napata was the name of the kingdom inhabited by a mixture of native African tribes and the Egyptians that had settled among them. Napata was ruled by its own king from a Nubian palace at Jebel Barkal.**

Nubia – **Pg. 373, ¶ 2 – Nubia was an African country that was occupied in part by the Egyptians.**

Piankhe – **Pg. 373, ¶ 3 to Pg. 374, ¶ 2 – Piankhe, a Nubian native and king of Napata, successfully fought off a coalition of Egyptian cities that wanted to push Egypt's border back into Nubian territory. After this attack, Piankhe chose not to wipe out his enemies, but rather to see Egypt as a set of kingdoms, with himself as High King over them.**

Rusas – **Pg. 376, ¶ 3 & Pg. 378, ¶ 2 – Rusas, king of Urartu, fled from Sargon II's troops when they arrived just south of Tabriz. When Rusas found out that Sargon II had sacked the Mushashir, Rusas stabbed himself through the heart and ended his life.**

Samaritans – **Pg. 375, ¶ 2 – Samaritans was the label given to the mishmash of Israelites and exiles from elsewhere who lived in northern Israel. They were of mixed religions and bloodlines, and were despised as half-breeds.**

Sargon II – **Pg. 374, ¶ 5, Pg. 375, ¶ 1, Pg. 378, ¶ 3 and Pg. 380, ¶ 2 – Sargon II, a younger son of Tiglath-Pileser III, seized the Assyrian throne from his older brother Shalmaneser V. Sargon II was responsible for the destruction of Israel, the conquest of Urartu, and the restoration of Babylon to Assyria.**

Shutruk-Nahhunte – **Pg. 379, ¶ 2 & ¶ 4 – Shutruk-Nahhunte, king of Elam, fled when Sargon II marched into Elam. When Merodach-baladan asked for refuge in Elam, Shutruk-Nahhunte said yes, but then barred Merodach-baladan from entering, fearing the wrath of Assyria.**

Section II: Comprehension

Write a two/three sentence answer to each of the following questions.

1. What did Hoshea, king of Israel, do that made Shalmaneser V want to wipe out Israel?
A1. – Pg. 371, ¶ 4 – Shalmaneser V decided to attack Israel for two reasons; first, Hoshea no longer paid tribute to the king of Assyria. Second, Shalmaneser V's spies reported to him that Hoshea had sent envoys down to So, king of Egypt, suggesting that Israel was planning a war against Assyria, and was searching for allies.

2. How did Egypt come to have three separate capitals? In your answer, make sure to list the three capitals.
A2. – Pg. 371, ¶ 5 to Pg. 373, ¶ 1 – After the battle of Qarqar, Egypt split not only into north and south, but also into east and west kingdoms. This yielded an array of pharaohs at three separate capitals: Thebes, Tanis and Leontopolis.

3. How did Manetho organize Egypt's ruling families in the century since the battle of Qarqar? Why was Manetho's categorization problematic?
A3. – Pg. 373, ¶ 1 – Manetho attempted to organize the multiple claims to Egypt's throne by sorting the kings into the Twenty-Second, Twenty-Third and Twenty-Fourth Dynasties. This was problematic because all three dynasties were actually ruling simultaneously from different cities, and the local power of the Twenty-Second Dynasty lingered on into the dominance of the Twenty-Fifth Dynasty.

4. What traditions did the Napatans have in common with the Egyptians?
A4. – Pg. 373, ¶ 2 – The Napatan culture bore unmistakable traces of the Egyptian people: they worshiped the god Amun, and Nubian rulers followed the ancient tradition of brother-sister marriages.

5. Why didn't Piankhe help Israel fight against the Assyrians?
A5. – Pg. 374, ¶ 2 – Piankhe didn't help Israel because he probably didn't even know Israel had asked for aid. Hoshea may not have known exactly who was in charge down in Egypt, and with a political scene so complicated that even the Egyptians were confused, it is possible Piankhe did not even know that Israelite ambassadors had arrived in his country.

6. Why did Sargon II admire the Urartian king Rusas?
A6. – Pg. 376, ¶ 3 – Sargon II admired king Rusas of Urartu for many reasons. Sargon admired the network of canals and wells Rusas built, and his herds of well-bred and guarded horses. He also admired the efficiency and speed of Urartian communication, where beacon fires were lit to signal news of an invasion faster than a messenger could ride.

7. What was Sargon II's strategy for the invasion of Urartu?
A7. – Pg. 376, ¶ 4 – Sargon II decided that rather than marching straight north into Urartian territory, which would have brought his army against the strongest of the Urartian fortresses, he would lead the army east towards the Zagros, intending to reach the relatively flat land on the other side and march up towards the weaker eastern border of the Urartu.

8. What happened when Sargon II and his army met Urartian forces at Tabriz?

A8. – Pg. 377, ¶ 3 & 4 – When Sargon II and his army met Urartian forces at Tabriz, the exhausted Assyrian soldiers refused to follow Sargon II into battle. Only when Sargon II flung himself into the line of the nearest wing of Rusas's men did the Assyrian troops take courage and follow him into battle. The Urartian army eventually wavered, then broke and began to retreat.

9. How did Merodach-baladan hope to persuade northern Babylonians to turn away from Assyria and support his rule?

A9. – Pg. 378, ¶ 6 – Merodach-baladan attempted to persuade northern Babylonians to support his kingship by claiming he was the country's liberator, the restorer of an ancient Babylonian tradition long trampled under the foot of northern, meaning Assyrian, invaders.

10. In what ways did Sargon II's southern attack on Babylon trap Merodach-baladan?

A10. – Pg. 379, ¶ 3 – By attacking Babylon from the south, Sargon II cut Merodach-baladan off from his Elamite allies and also made it very dangerous for him to retreat to his homeland at the head of the Gulf, since Sargon's soldiers were actually nearer to Bit-Yakin than they were to Babylon. Also, Merodach-baladan faced opposition in the north, where the northern cities of Babylon welcomed Sargon with relief.

11. What happened to Merodach-baladan after his surrender to the Assyrians?

A11. – Pg. 381, ¶ 1 – After surrendering to the Assyrians, Sargon II allowed Merodach-baladan to remain as vassal chief of Bit-Yakin.

Section III: Critical Thinking

Ancient historical narratives tell us that the Israelites have always had a strong national identity based on Abraham's divine call from Yahweh. Though Israel had become part of Assyria's growing kingdom, the Israelites were still culturally separate from the Assyrians. Write a paragraph explaining why Sargon II, after hearing of Hoshea's attempt to revolt against him, chose to scatter the peoples of Israel in addition to physically destroying the nation. In your answer make sure to include why Israel became known as the "lost 10 tribes."

• *The student should remember that Abraham was given a promise and a command from Yahweh – the promise was that Abram would be made into a great nation and be blessed; the command was that he leave his country and his people and go to the land of Canaan and start a new race. Abraham did as he was told, had a son called Isaac, and started a new race of people.*

• *You might ask the student why the Israelites felt tied together as a single people. As the descendants of Abraham, the Israelites were united by their closeness to God.*

• *Why would Israel's closeness to Yahweh threaten Sargon II? The fierceness with which the Israelites held on to their divine cultural identity could have been more threatening to Sargon II than their actual military power. The only way Sargon II could attempt to break apart the Israelites' cultural unity would be to scatter them apart.*

• *The text defines the "lost ten tribes" on page 375, ¶ 1: "These Israelites became known as the 'lost ten tribes,' not because the people themselves were lost, but because their identity as descendants of Abraham and worshippers of Yahweh was dissipated into the new wild areas where they were now forced to make their homes."*

EXAMPLE ANSWER: **Israel may have become property of Assyria, but they were far from becoming Assyrians. The national identity of the Israelites was based on a power bigger than the Assyrian king – they were Yahweh's chosen people. Sacking Israel's buildings and temples would not be enough to destroy the fierce sense of cultural identity shared by the people of Israel. Scattering the people of Israel around the ancient world was one way that Sargon II could ruin the nation's sense of self. This scattering led the people of Israel to be called the "lost ten tribes." The people were not actually lost, but their identity as descendants of Abraham and worshippers of Yahweh was dissipated into the new wild areas where they were forced to make their homes.**

CHAPTER FIFTY-TWO: SPECTACULAR DEFEAT

The student may use her text when answering the questions in sections I and II.

Section I: Who, What, Where

Write a one or two-sentence answer explaining the significance of each item listed below.

Ashur-nadin-shumi – **Pg. 387, ¶ 5 & Pg. 388, ¶ 2-4 – Ashur-nadin-shumi, Sennacherib's son, was sent by his father to rule Babylon after Merodach-baladan was finally expelled from the city. Ashur-nadin-shumi's kidnapping by the Elamites started a four-year war between Assyria, Babylon and Elam.**

Bel-ibni – **Pg. 384, ¶ 4 and Pg. 387, ¶ 4 – Bel-ibni was the puppet-king Sennacherib installed in Babylon. Bel-ibni's rule was challenged by the continuously anarchic Merodach-baladan.**

King Kahllushu – **Pg. 388, ¶ 2 – King Kahllushu led the Elamite army into Babylon, where they captured the crown prince Ashur-nadin-shumi.**

Marduk-apla-iddina II – **Pg. 383, ¶ 1 and Footnote – Marduk-apla-iddina II was Merodach-baladan's royal Babylonian name.**

Musezib-Marduk – **Pg. 388, ¶ 3 – Musezib-Marduk was a Chaldean who seized Babylon's throne after Ashur-nadin-shumi was taken captive by the Elamites. Musezib-Marduk stripped Babylon's temple of gold, and hired more Elamites to fight with Babylon against Assyria.**

Nineveh – **Pg. 387, ¶ 2 – Nineveh was appointed to be the capital of Assyria by Sennacherib, a position it held for the rest of Assyrian history. Sennacherib built new palaces in it, and decorated the walls with tremendous reliefs of battles won and cities besieged.**

Sennacherib – **Pg. 382, ¶ 2 – Sennacherib inherited the Assyrian throne from his father, Sargon II. Sargon II let the world know that he thought Sennacherib was a weakling; Sennacherib spent his life in battle proving his father wrong.**

Section II: Comprehension

Write a two/three sentence answer to each of the following questions.

1. How did Sennacherib insult the Babylonian court? What was the result of this insult?
A1. – Pg. 382, ¶ 4 – Sennacherib, during his Babylonian coronation ceremony, did not go through the ritual of "taking the hand of Marduk" in formal submission to the god; he simply announced himself to be king of Babylon, an insult to both Babylon and its chief deity. The result of this was that almost as soon as Sennacherib's coronation ceremonies had ended, the son of a Babylonian official declared himself king of Babylon.

2. How did Merodach-baladan become king of Babylon once again?
A2. – Pg. 382, ¶ 5 to Pg. 383, ¶ 1 – Hearing that the son of a Babylonian official declared himself king after Sennacherib's coronation ceremony, Merodach-baladan returned to Babylon with his kinsmen and removed the new king from the throne. Once again, Merodach-baladan called himself king, and claimed he was the true restorer of ancient Babylonian traditions.

3. What prompted Sennacherib to first send troops down to attack Babylon? What drove him to go down to Babylon himself?
A3. – Pg. 383, ¶ 2 & 3 – Sennacherib first sent troops down to Babylon to restore order after Merodach-baladan's turnover of the Babylonian throne. When Assyrian forces found that Merodach-baladan was supported by the Chaldeans, Aramaeans and Elamites, Sennacherib came down to Babylon to deal with Merodach-baladan himself.

4. Who was Tirhakah, and how did he come to be known as Egypt's pharaoh?
A4. – Pg. 384, ¶ 6 & 7 – Tirhakah was the younger son of the dead pharaoh Piankhe. Though his older brother was on the throne, Tirhakah served him as general, and was appointed the next heir. Tirhakah took the Egyptian army into battle against Assyria, and was called pharaoh because of his future appointment to the throne.

5. How did the imprisoned king of Ekron end up in Jerusalem?
A5. – Pg. 385, ¶ 4 – King Hezekiah of Jerusalem decided to join Egypt and Babylon in the fight against Assyria. His first anti-Assyrian gesture was to take charge of the imprisoned king of Ekron. The leaders of the Ekron rebellion feared that the king's continued presence in the Ekron dungeons might encourage other pro-Assyrian forces in the city to mount a counter-rebellion, so they moved the imprisoned pro-Assyrian king to Jerusalem.

6. What made Hezekiah bow out of the coalition against Assyria?
A6. – Pg. 385, ¶ 6 to Pg. 386, ¶ 2 – Hearing about Hezekiah's act of defiance, Sennacherib sent his own general, chief officer and field commander to Jerusalem to intimidate the king. The men stood outside of Jerusalem's walls and threatened the city's very existence so that the king, and all of his people, would quake in fear. The plan worked; Hezekiah freed the king of Ekron and sent Sennacherib eleven tons of silver and nearly a ton of gold as a bribe.

7. In what way did Merodach-baladan have the last word in his battle against Assyria?
A7. – Pg. 387, ¶ 4-6 – Failing to take Babylon's throne from Bel-ibni, Merodach-baladan was once again chased out of the city. Hearing that Merodach-baladan had crossed the sea to Elam, Sennacherib hired Phoenician shipbuilders to make him a fleet of ships that would sail to Elam, manned by mercenaries on the hunt for Merodach-baladan. Though Sennacherib successfully captured every city where his ships docked, Merodach-baladan was never caught because he died of old age just before arriving in Elam.

8. Why did Sennacherib retreat from Babylon in the three way war between Assyria, Elam and Babylon? What shifted in the war that prompted Sennacherib to attack Babylon one more time?
A8. – Pg. 388, ¶ 6 to Pg. 389, ¶ 2 – Sennacherib chose to retreat from Babylon because there was simply a limit to how many men he could throw at the Babylon problem over and over again. When Sennacherib heard that the Elamite king had been struck by illness and could no longer give commands, he took the opportunity of Elamite absence to attack Babylon once again.

9. What did Sennacherib do to Babylon once he finally broke down the city's gates?

A9. – Pg. 389, ¶ 3 – When Sennacherib finally broke down Babylon's gates, he ordered the city razed. After burning the city, he turned it into a lake, building canals so he could flood the civilized lands with water.

10. What was the fate of Sennacherib's son, Ashur-nadin-shumi? What was the fate of Sennacherib himself?

A10 – Pg. 389, ¶ 4 & 5 – The fate of Ashur-nadin-shumi is unknown. The Elamites made no demands for ransom; in all likelihood they tortured him to death. Seven years later, Sennacherib was killed by two of his younger sons while sacrificing to the god Nabu in the god's temple at Nineveh.

Section III: Critical Thinking

The student may not use her text to answer this question.

When Sennacherib came to Assyria's throne, he had the reputation of being "boneless and inadequate." Like his father, Sennacherib made prolific military strides, and secured Assyria's great empire. Yet, Sennacherib is most famously remembered for his inability to capture Jerusalem. Was Sennacherib's defeat caused by old-world disease, or was it God's will that protected Jerusalem? Using evidence from the chapter, explain how the plague could have been responsible for Sennacherib's retreat from Jerusalem. Then, using Lord Byron's words, explain how God's will may have been behind Jerusalem's triumph.

• *On page 386, ¶ 7, we find out that according to 2 Kings, an angel of the Lord struck 185,000 of Sennacherib's men dead in the middle of the night. This made Sennacherib withdraw from Jerusalem. We also learn that the priests of Egypt thought Sennacherib chose to retreat because of a rodent problem: "Sennacherib decided to give up and go home because the Assyrian camp was overrun by mice, who 'gnawed quivers and bows and the handles of the shields.'" On page 387, ¶ 1, the text explicitly states, "the combination [of dead men and mice] suggests that the plague had arrived outside Jerusalem's walls, and that the king of Assyria retreated in the face of mounting deaths." Another tidbit of information comes from page 385, ¶ 1. We find out that Hezekiah fell sick with boils around the time he decided to support the anti-Assyrian alliance. This does not necessarily mean that he had the plague, but does give us another connection between sickness and Jerusalem.*

• *The last stanza of Lord Byron's poem reads:*

And the widows of Ashur are loud in their wail,

And the idols are broke in the temple of Baal;

And the might of the Gentile, unsmote by the sword,

Hath melted like snow in the glance of the Lord!

The first two lines of the poem describe the breadth of Sennacherib's destruction: the women of Ashur who have lost their husbands in battle wail with sorrow, and the temple of Baal has been sacked, its statues broken. The third line tells us about Sennacherib's power; in all this fighting, he has remained untouched by the sword. In the fourth line, the poem says Sennacherib's might is inconsequential, the Lord can take Sennacherib's power away as easily as snow melts. Lord Byron's poem suggests that no matter how strong Sennacherib was, he was no match for God's will.

EXAMPLE ANSWER: **The plague was most likely responsible for Sennacherib's retreat from Jerusalem. Egyptian priests told Herodotus that the Assyrian camp was overrun by mice. 2 Kings says that 185,000 of Sennacherib's men died in the middle of the night. The combination of rodents and dead men points to the plague as the reason for the deaths, and for Sennacherib's return to Nineveh. While the plague may have been the practical reason Sennacherib gave up on an invasion of Jerusalem, Lord Byron suggests that it was God's will that kept the city safe. Sennacherib may have been very powerful, making "the widows of Ashur" weep, sacking sacred sites like the temple of Baal where "the idols are broke," but he was no match for God's authority: "And the might of the Gentile, unsmote by the sword,/ Hath melted like snow in the glance of the Lord!" Once God showed the previously unharmed Sennacherib how little power he actually had, Sennacherib backed off from Jerusalem and returned to Nineveh.**

CHAPTER FIFTY-THREE: THE DECLINE OF THE KING

The student may use his text when answering the questions in sections I and II.

Section I: Who, What, Where

Write a one or two-sentence answer explaining the significance of each item listed below.

"Central States" – Pg. 394, ¶ 2 – The "Central States" were Cheng, Wey, Jin, and Zhou land: the center of China.

Chuang – Pg. 393, ¶ 3-5 – Chuang, Duke of Cheng, was insulted by King Huan when he did not pay him proper respect. In retaliation, Chuang seized the royal residence at Hsü, claiming authority over both Hsü and the king's religious observances.

Hegemon – Pg. 394, ¶ 5 and Pg. 395, ¶ 2 – Hegemon is another word for overlord. Hegemon was the title given to the military leader of ancient China.

Huan – Pg. 393, ¶ 1, 4 & 6 – Huan, P'ing's grandson, took the Zhou throne when his grandfather died. The Duke of Cheng threatened the king's ceremonial role; when Huan finally took action against Chuang, he was wounded by an arrow and forced to retreat.

"Square Wall" – Pg. 398, ¶ 2 – The "Square Wall" was erected by the Duke of Chu along the northern border of his kingdom. It was a huge wall which served to keep barbarians out, and that blocked the route that a Jin army might take it if were to march straight down to the east of the Zhou land into Chu territory.

Wen – Pg. 397, ¶ 1 & 2 – Wen, the Duke of Jin, rounded up his own Jin soldiers to drive Shu Tai and the Ti out of the Zhou palace. Duke Wen of Jin was recognized as Hegemon by Hsiang, the king he helped to reenthrone.

Section II: Comprehension

Write a two/three sentence answer to each of the following questions.

1. Why was it advantageous for P'ing to hand over the old western Zhou territory to the Duke of Ch'in?
A1. – Pg. 391, ¶ 3 – It was advantageous to hand over the old Zhou territory in western China to the Duke of Ch'in because now it was his responsibility to deal with invading barbarians; P'ing was off the hook.

2. How did P'ing earn the name "P'ing the Peaceful?"
A2. – Pg. 391, ¶ 3 to Pg. 392, ¶ 1 – During P'ing's reign, various noblemen were jockeying for power while also keeping an eye on the king's throne. In the fifty years of his reign, P'ing

did nothing to interfere in spats between noblemen, earning him the nickname "P'ing the Peaceful."

3. List the twelve major centers of power that were in existence during P'ing's reign.
A3. – Pg. 392, ¶ 3 – 1) Qi, 2) Chu, 3) Ch'in, 4) Jin, 5) Yen, 6) Lu, 7) Wey, 8) Wu, 9) Yueh, 10) Sung, 11) Cheng, 12) Loyang.

4. Who were the Yi and Ti? Why were they a threat to China?
A4. – Pg. 393, ¶ 8 to Pg. 394, ¶ 1 – The Southern Yi and the Northern Ti were nomadic tribes that had never accepted the authority of either lord or king. While feudal lords fought between themselves, the Yi and Ti took advantage of this weakness and began attacking China's Central States.

5. Why did the Duke of Qi declare himself Hegemon in 679 BC?
A5. – Pg. 394, ¶ 3 & 4 – If the Yi and the Ti barbarians chose to attack the long western border of Qi, the results would be disastrous for the Duke of Qi. Knowing that King Hsi was incapable of keeping the Central States safe, the Duke of Qi declared himself Hegemon first to protect his own land and second for the common good of China.

6. How did the Duke of Qi use his power as Hegemon to fight the Yi and the Ti?
A6. – Pg. 394, ¶ 5 – The Duke of Qi used his power as Hegemon to force other Chinese states into submission for the common good. Leading the Qi army with his minister Kuan Chung, The Duke of Qi got the bickering lords to stop fighting among themselves long enough to donate soldiers to a coalition force which would march along the borders and beat back barbarian invasions.

7. Why did the Hegemon choose to ignore Shu Tai's treachery after King Hsiang ordered Shu Tai arrested and killed for plotting a revolt with the Ti and the Jung?
A7. – Pg. 395, ¶ 6 & 7 – Ignoring Shu Tia allowed the Hegemon to deal with the mess Shu Tai created without giving up any of his power, or offending the king. If the Hegemon refused to give Shu Tai sanctuary, he would be admitting he feared the king's power. If Duke Huan granted Shu Tai protection, he would be proclaiming hostility towards the king.

8. How did King Hsiang and Shu Tai come to marry the same Ti princess?
A8. – Pg. 396, ¶ 4 – Hoping to gain back the power of the Hegemon, King Hsiang made a treaty with the Ti; if the Ti barbarians would help him invade and punish the disloyal Cheng, then Hsian would marry the daughter of the Ti leader and make her queen. After the barbarians failed to destroy the Cheng state, Hsian decided to do away with his new wife. This caused the Ti to invade the Zhou capital and install Shu Tai on the throne; Shu Tai then married the same Ti princess.

Section III: Critical Thinking

The student may use his text to answer this question.

The Mandate of Heaven was weak in 7th century BC China. While the king was still the nation's figurehead, he could no longer protect his kingdom. The new role of Hegemon, or military overlord was created, making the king obsolete. Despite his lack of power, the king was still shown respect, and the formalities of the Chinese government were preserved. Write a short paragraph explaining why the role of king was not done away with, and how a "two-headed country with both a military and religious leader" worked.

We learn in this chapter that "the tenuous identity that linked the states of China together into a single people depended in large part on their willingness to accept the nominal lordship of the Son of Heaven. Without his unifying rule, cast like a net around the territories, they would break apart; and the northern and western barbarians would move in and destroy the separate states, one by one" (page 393, ¶ 6). Although the king was no longer capable of keeping the Central States safe, his spiritual power was necessary to keep the Chinese people unified. Belief in the king's power, however, could not actually stop barbarians from invading. China was in need of an overlord, and so the position of Hegemon, or military leader, was born. In order to keep a coherent Chinese identity based on the belief in the ceremonial king, a military leader was needed to ensure the safety and protection of the land, thus creating a "two-headed country with both a military and religious leader."

EXAMPLE ANSWER: **In 7th century BC China, the weakness of the Mandate of Heaven meant that the king had no real power. China was now protected by a Hegemon, or military leader. Though the king's power was only ceremonial, it was necessary to continue to believe in the king because he unified the disparate Chinese states into one people. If the states were not unified, barbarians could come in and destroy the separate states one by one. The strength of China depended on its nature as a "two-headed country with both a military and religious leader." The Hegemon ensured the safety of the states, and the king kept the states unified under a single cultural and spiritual identity.**

CHAPTER FIFTY-FOUR: THE ASSYRIANS IN EGYPT

The student may use her text when answering the questions in sections I and II.

Section I: Who, What, Where

Write a one or two-sentence answer explaining the significance of each item listed below.

Bit-Dakkuri – **Pg. 401, ¶ 4** – Bit-Dakkuri was the brother-tribe to the Bit-Yakin of Merodach-baladan. When the Bit-Dakkuri sent a letter to Esarhaddon offering loyalty, the Assyrian king rebuffed their offer of friendship and sent troops down to the southern lands of Babylonia to push them back into their own territory.

Cimmerians/Gimirrai – **Pg. 402, ¶ 1** – The Cimmerians, or Gimirrai as they were called by the Assyrians, were nomadic tribes who had long roamed around the shores of the Caspian Sea. As the Cimmerians gathered together above the tribes of the Medes and Persians they began to pose a threat to Assyria.

Gyges – **Pg. 404, ¶ 5** – Gyges was king of the Lydians when Phrygia was destroyed. Once the Phrygian kingdom was out of the way, Gyges found that he was the strongest power in all of Asia Minor.

Façade monument – **Pg. 404, ¶ 2** – A façade monument was a slab of stone jutting up into the air, one side carved into the likeness of a wall, with a sculpted door that could never be opened. The Midas Monument is an example. It faces the rising sun, as do all the other facade monuments, and for a few moments at dawn, its gray surface turns bright and the false door glows.

Nabu-zer-ketti-lisher – **Pg. 400, ¶ 3** – Nabu-zer-ketti-lisher, son of Merodach-baladan, led a Chaldean army through Ur in order to recapture Babylon. Nabu-zer-ketti-lisher was arrested and put to death in Elam after fleeing from Esarhaddon.

Prism – **Pg. 399, ¶ 3** – A prism was a stone pillar with six to ten sides used for recording important events and information.

Psammetichus – **Pg. 406, ¶ 2** – Psammetichus, son of Necho, was taken captive by Esarhaddon when the Assyrian king invaded Egypt. Psammetichus was then installed in the Egyptian city of Athribis and, along with his father, was given the responsibility of overseeing all of Egypt in the name of Assyria.

Rusas II – **Pg. 399, ¶ 2** – Rusas II succeeded his grandfather Rusas I as king of Urartu. Rusas II was building an army to fight Assyria, and welcomed the former king's assassins into his kingdom.

Scythians – **Pg. 402, ¶ 3** – The Scythians were a tribe of nomads who filtered down from the Caucasus Mountains, north of the Black Sea. Esarhaddon made an alliance with the Scythians in order to protect Assyria from the Cimmerian/Urartian threat.

Shamash-shum-ukin – **Pg. 406, ¶ 1 – Shamash-shum-ukin was one of Esarhaddon's younger sons. Shamash-shum-ukin was appointed crown prince of Babylon, a sovereign ruler under his older brother's supervision.**

Tantamani – **Pg. 406, ¶ 3-5 & Pg. 407, ¶ 4 – Tantamani, cousin to Tirhakah and heir to the Egyptian throne, had a dream that he was to take Egypt back from the Assyrians. At first Tantamani was victorious, but once Ashurbanipal returned to protect his territory, Tantamani fled.**

Teushpa – **Pg. 404, ¶ 4 – Teushpa, king of the Cimmerians, led his army all the way through Phrygia. When Teushpa came up against the Assyrian troops, his luck failed, and he was killed by Esarhaddon's own hands.**

Tirhakah – **Pg. 405, ¶ 1, 3 & 4 – Tirhakah, once an Egyptian prince who fought off Sennacherib, faced Esarhaddon as king of Kush. Though Tirhakah was able to fend off Esarhaddon's troops at first, he was not as successful the second time Assyria attacked; he fled to his ancestral lands.**

Section II: Comprehension

Write a two/three sentence answer to each of the following questions.

1. Why was it somewhat problematic for Esarhaddon to claim he was rebuilding Babylon out of affection for Marduk?
A1. – It was problematic for Esarhaddon to claim he was rebuilding Babylon out of affection for Marduk because if he spent too much time appeasing the god, that would suggest his father acted impiously when he drowned Babylon. If Sennacherib was not faithful to Marduk, then Esarhaddon's divine royal succession could potentially be destroyed.

2. On what did Esarhaddon blame the destruction of Babylon? Why did he start his account with the phrase "Before my time?"
A2. – Pg. 400, ¶ 7 to Pg. 401, ¶ 2 – Esarhaddon claimed that the gods deserted Babylon out of divine anger. He also said the appeal to Elam against Assyria had made Marduk particularly furious, and also that the Arahtu overflowed on its own, drowning the city. Starting the account with the phrase "Before my time" removed blame from Esarhaddon without pinning the destruction on his father.

3. Why did the statue of Marduk remain in Assyria after Esarhaddon rebuilt Babylon?
A3. – Pg. 401, ¶ 3 – The statue of Marduk remained in Assyria as a reminder to citizens of Babylon that their god had taken up residence with the rightful king of Babylon.

4. What made Esarhaddon cautious of the Cimmerians?
A4. – Pg. 402, ¶ 2 – Esarhaddon became cautious of the Cimmerians when they made friends with the Urartian King, Rusas II. The Cimmerians were very good at fighting, and a Cimmerian/Urartian alliance could be very dangerous to Assyria.

5. Who were the Lydians, and how did they come to have so much power after Phrygia's destruction?
A5. – Pg. 404, ¶ 5 – The Lydians were people who lived in the villages farther west than Phrygia. When Phrygia was destroyed by the Cimmerians, their trade routes were taken over by the Lydians, making them the strongest power in all of Asia Minor.

6. Why did Esarhaddon retreat from the battle against the Egyptians at Ashkelon?
A6. – Pg. 405, ¶ 2 & 3 – On the long march south from Nineveh to Ashkelon, Esarhaddon's men were tired and weakened from fighting off thieving Arabian tribes. Tirhakah's men quickly beat the Assyrians, and Esarhaddon took his worn-out men home.

7. Who was the governor of Sais, and why did he remain loyal to Assyria after Esarhaddon left his newly conquered Egypt?
A7. – Pg. 405, ¶ 5 – The governor of Sais was a man named Necho. Necho remained loyal to Assyria after Esarhaddon left Egypt because the Assyrian king had taken his son captive.

8. What did Ashurbanipal do with all of the Egyptian noblemen his father Esarhaddon had taken captive?
A8. – Pg. 406, ¶ 2 – Ashurbanipal, storming through Egypt after his father's death, killed every king that had forgotten his Assyrian allegiance and replaced them with the Assyrian-trained Egyptians that his father had taken back to Nineveh.

9. What was the impact of the destruction of Thebes on the ancient Near East?
A9. – Pg. 407, ¶ 4 – In the ancient Near East, the destruction of Thebes served as a warning to anyone who might think of crossing Assyria; it was proof of what would happen to those who defied Assyrian might.

10. Why was it a mistake for Ashurbanipal to appoint Psammetichus sole pharaoh of Egypt?
A10. – Pg. 407, ¶ 5 to Pg. 408, ¶ 1 – Despite his Assyrian indoctrination, Psammetichus was only willing to fight on the side of Ashurbanipal to preserve himself. As soon as Psammetichus was on the throne, he slowly cleansed his cities of Assyrian soldiers, and with the help of troops sent by king Gyges of Lydia, successfully rebelled against Assyria.

11. What happened to king Gyges after he helped Psammetichus regain control of Egypt?
A11. – Pg. 408, ¶ 5 – After Gyges helped Psammetichus gain control of Egypt, he found that his own kingdom was in danger: the Cimmerians were on the march west. With no help from Ashurbanipal, the Lydian army was driven back by the Cimmerians, Gyges was killed and Sardis was sacked.

Section III: Critical Thinking

The student may not use her text to answer this question.

Chapter after chapter we read about the military conquests and subsequent losses of the kingdoms in the ancient Near East. The last few chapters, in particular, have focused on Assyria's constant war state. Write a paragraph explaining why king after Assyrian king comes to his throne with a voracious appetite for war. To substantiate your answer, consider what would have happened if Egypt had taken over Assyria, and what that would mean for Assyria's religious practice.

In Chapter 53, the text contrasts the power struggles within ancient China with those of the ancient Near East: "The kings of the ancient Near East were caught in a spiraling contest; any king who did not immediately set out to conquer territory risked losing some of his own to an opponent who was likely to speak a different language and worship a different god" (Pg. 395, ¶ 5). The student does not need to remember this passage exactly, but should be cognizant of the impetus behind Assyria's constant warring state: <u>if an Assyrian king did not defend what the previous ruler conquered, another kingdom would snatch the territory up. Not only would this affect the kingdom's reputation, but also its basic fabric. For example, if the Egyptians were to have taken over Assyria, Marduk would no longer be the chief god of worship; the temples would become places to praise Egypt's chief god Amun. If an Assyrian king did not come to the throne ready to at least defend the edges of his kingdom, he risked losing both the kingdom's land and cultural identity.</u>

To start the student off, you may want to refer her back to the passage in Chapter 53 mentioned above. This should make clear why the chapters she's been reading about Assyria have mostly been narratives of war. You can also ask the student to recall how Esarhaddon was able to talk about the destruction of Babylon without blaming his father, or how the destruction of Thebes acted as a warning to other kingdoms about the consequences of turning against Assyria. Both of these examples point to the importance of war and to Assyria's reputation; conquest defined Assyria. Finally, you can ask the student who the Assyrians would worship if Psammetichus had not only taken Egypt back, but somehow conquered Ashurbanipal's kingdom as well. The student's final answer should resemble the underlined parts of the passage above.

CHAPTER FIFTY-FIVE: MEDES AND PERSIANS

The student may use his text when answering the questions in sections I and II.

Section I: Who, What, Where

Write a one or two-sentence answer explaining the significance of each item listed below.

Ashur-etillu-ilani – **Pg. 415, ¶ 3 & Pg. 416, ¶ 3 – Ashur-etillu-ilani, son of Ashurbanipal, governed the Assyrian empire in his father's name from 630 until Ashurbanipal's death in 627. When Ashurbanipal died, Ashur-etillu-ilani became king of Assyria, and immediately had to defend his hold over Babylon against his brother and the Chaldean, Nabopolassar.**

Bastions – **Pg. 412, ¶ 2 – Bastions were the defensive positions on a city's protective walls, built out from the wall itself in a fortified wedge so that archers could stand on them.**

Cuthah – **Pg. 413, ¶ 4 – Cuthah was an Assyrian outpost just north of Babylon. Shamash-shum-ukin attacked Cuthah in an open attempt to drive Ashurbanipal's forces out; this led to a three-year Assyrian siege on Babylon.**

Cyarxes – **Pg. 416, ¶ 5 – Cyarxes was the son of Phraortes, leader of Medes. Cyarxes killed the Scythian overlord of the Medes, and became high king over the Medes and Persia.**

Cyrus – **Pg. 415, ¶ 2 – Cyrus succeeded his father Teispes as King of Anshan, though he was still under the umbrella rule of Madius the Scythian.**

Deioces – **Pg. 412, ¶ 1 – Deioces was a village judge who had gained a reputation for fairness and integrity among the Median tribes, and they proclaimed him leader of them all. Deioces insisted that the Medes build a single city and maintain it; the city was Ecbatana.**

Ecbatana – **Pg. 412, ¶ 1 & 2 – Ecbatana was the central city of the emerging nation of the Medes. The city was built on the eastern slopes of Mount Orontes, and was considered one of the great sights of the ancient world because of its seven circular walls.**

Madius – **Pg. 413, ¶ 3 – Madius was the warrior chief of the Scythians. After Phraortes was killed, Madius declared himself not only leader of the Scythians, but also King of the Medes and the Persians.**

Phraortes – **Pg. 413, ¶ 1 – Phraortes inherited his role as leader of the Medes from his father, Deioces, in 675. Phraortes was able to make Parsua a subject of the Medes, but he was not able to conquer Nineveh; while attempting to attack Assyria, Phraortes was killed by the Assyrian sympathizers, the Scythians.**

Teispes – **Pg. 415, ¶ 1 – Teispes was the Persian overlord who moved into the old Elamite territory of Anshan and claimed it for his own. Though Teispes was called "King of Anshan," he still had to answer to Madius the Scythian, with a submissive attitude and payment of tribute.**

Section II: Comprehension

Write a two/three sentence answer to each of the following questions.

1. Why did the Elamite king Teumann expect a warm welcome at Babylon around 650 BC?
A1. – Pg. 411, ¶ 3 & 4 – Though Shamash-shum-ukin, viceroy of Babylon, names Ashurbanipal, king of Assyria, his favorite brother, it seems that Ashurbanipal was micromanaging Babylon's affairs. Teumann expected a warm welcome because the Elamite army could help Shamash-shum-ukin shake free from Ashurbanipal's dominance.

2. What happened to Teumann and his army as they marched toward Babylon?
A2. – Pg. 411, ¶ 5 – When Ashurbanipal received news that the Elamites were on the march, he crossed the Tigris and met the Elamites on their own land. His army drove the Elamites back to Susa, inflicting a great slaughter on them. Teumann was tracked down by Ashurbanipal and beheaded.
NOTE TO INSTRUCTOR:
The student might add that Ashurbanipal hung the heads of Teumann and his son in the royal garden, where he and his wife dined underneath them (Pg. 411, ¶ 6).

3. Describe the layout of Ecbatana's walls, and the decoration of its bastions.
A3. – Pg. 412, ¶ 2 – Ecbatana was surrounded by seven circular walls, the outermost lying downhill from the next and so on, so that the top of each wall could be seen above the previous wall. The city's bastions were painted with bright colors; the bastions of the outer wall were white, the next black, then red, blue, and orange; the bastions of the penultimate circle were gilded with silver, and the final circle, within which lay the royal palace itself, gilded with gold.

4. What did Ashurbanipal do to Babylon's inhabitants after his three-year siege on the city? What was Shamash-shum-ukin's fate?
A4. – Pg. 413, ¶ 6 to Pg. 414, ¶ 1 – When the three-year siege against Babylon ended, Ashurbanipal showed no mercy on the rebels who defended the city. Ashurbanipal killed any surviving Babylonians. Shamash-shum-ukin died in a fire he set in his own palace in order to avoid his brother's vengeance.

5. In what way was civil war responsible for the obliteration of Elam?
A5. – Pg. 414, ¶ 3 – Ashurbanipal saw Elam's weakness because of the civil war which had broken out over the succession to the throne. Ashurbanipal attacked Elam with ferocity; cities were burned, the temples and palaces of Susa were robbed and the royal tombs opened and the bones of the kings bundled off into captivity – all because the Elamites couldn't figure out who would rule their kingdom next.

6. What did Ashurbanipal do to the people of Elam in order to ensure that the nation would not rise again?
A6. – Pg. 414, ¶ 4 – Ashurbanipal took anyone who could lay future claim to the throne of Elam back to Nineveh in chains, and deported huge groups of Elamite citizens far away from their homeland.

7. How did Teispes's move into the old Elamite territory of Anshan affect Persian culture and history?

A7. – Pg. 415, ¶ 1 – When the Persians moved into Anshan, they adopted the Elamite dress of long ceremonial robes, that later on were identified as distinctively Persian. Also, Anshan became known as the Persian homeland, rather than Parsua.

8. What archaeological evidence found in ancient Urartian territory suggests aggressive Scythian attacks on Urartu?
A8. – Pg. 415, ¶ 4 – The walls of excavated Urartian citadels had Scythian arrowheads dug into them like a spray of musket balls. Collapsed wooden roofs of the city of Teishabani were discovered, studded with charred Scythian arrowheads; burning arrows, fired into the town, had set it ablaze. Both archaeological discoveries suggest aggressive Scythian attacks on Urartu.

9. Who was involved in the three-way battle over Babylon after the death of Ashurbanipal?
A9. – Pg. 416, ¶ 3 – After Ashurbanipal died, the three-way battle for Babylon was fought by Assyrians based in Nineveh under Ashur-etillu-ilani, the Assyrians in Babylon, and the Chaldeans under their chief Nabopolassar.

Section III: Critical Thinking

The student may use his text to answer this question.

In general, Assyrian kings were known for their brutality and unmerciful ruling tactics. Ashurbanipal, however, was not interested in constant warfare that yielded only a small increase in territory. The Assyrian king spent his energies on something else, building a library. Write a paragraph explaining the assembly of Ashurbanipal's library, and how this collection offered Ashurbanipal a legacy that would last longer than the constantly changing imperial borders of the ancient world.

On page 410, ¶ 2 you will find a detailed explanation of how Ashurbanipal gathered the materials for his library. The passage reads: "He was not the first Assyrian king to collect clay tablets, but he was the first to make their collection a priority all over his empire. He went about this in an organized fashion: he sent officers all over the kingdom to make an inventory of every library anywhere in the empire, and collected copies of every tablet he could find: spells, prophecies, medical remedies, astronomical observations, stories and tales (including a compilation of a thousand years' worth of stories about the ancient hero Gilgamesh), all put together. Eventually the library at Nineveh had almost thirty thousand tablets in it." The student does not have to remember every kind of tablet Ashurbanipal collected, nor does he have to remember the exact number of tablets stated in the text that were collected at Nineveh.

We are all familiar with the old saying "the pen is mightier than the sword." As we know from our reading, if an Assyrian king was not fighting constantly, he would most likely lose the territory gained by a previous king to another ambitious leader. Ashurbanipal's library was not a piece of land that could switch empires in a moment's notice. It was, as Ashurbanipal wrote himself, a way "to sustain the foundations of my royal throne" (Pg. 410, ¶ 1). The text states that while Esarhaddon might have managed to keep Egypt, "Ashurbanipal's realm of the mind would last forever" (Pg. 411, ¶ 1). It is clear from our text that the stories of the ancient world have lasted far longer than its borders and buildings. Ashurbanipal, investing in a library, was creating a lasting legacy for himself as both a great and powerful ruler; not only did Ashurbanipal need to wield the manpower to copy and collect all of those tablets, he also had the vision to invest in something other than land, which could be easily conquered.

EXAMPLE ANSWER: **Ashurbanipal made the collection of clay tablets a priority. He sent officers all over the kingdom to make an inventory of every library in the empire, and collected copies of every tablet he could find. He collected spells, prophecies, medical remedies, astronomical observations, stories and tales, including many stories about Gilgamesh. Eventually the library had tens of thousands of tablets.**

Investing in a library was wise because a library was not as changeable as a border. If an Assyrian king was not fighting constantly, he would most likely lose the territory gained by a previous king to another ambitious leader. Ashurbanipal's library showcased his power as much as any victorious battle – he needed great manpower to copy and collect all of those tablets. Also, Ashurbanipal's intelligence is proven in that he had the vision to invest in something other than land, which could be easily conquered. It is clear from our text that the stories of the ancient world have lasted far longer than its borders and buildings. Ashurbanipal, investing in a library, created for himself a lasting legacy.

CHAPTER FIFTY-SIX: CONQUEST AND TYRANNY

The student may use her text when answering the questions in sections I and II.

Section I: Who, What, Where

Write a one or two-sentence answer explaining the significance of each item listed below.

Acropolis – **Pg. 424, ¶ 4 – The Acropolis was the high rock at the center of Athens on which the palace of the mythological ruler Theseus once stood. The Acropolis was known as the high point of the city.**

Archon – **Pg. 424, ¶ 7 to Pg. 425, ¶ 3 – Archon was the name of the ruler of Athens; it meant a chief justice. When the role of archon was first introduced, power passed from father to son, and lasted a lifetime; later the archon's term was reduced to ten years, in 684 the term of the archon was only one year, and 683 the archon role was played by a board of nine landowners.**

Chalcidice – **Pg. 418, ¶ 1 – Chalcidice was the area north of the Aegean Sea settled by a large number of Greek colonists from Chalcis.**

Cylon – **Pg. 425, ¶ 5 & 6 and Pg. 426, ¶ 4 – Cylon attempted to alter the archonship of Athens, but chose the wrong time to occupy the Acropolis. Athenians attacked Cylon and his followers; Cylon managed to escape, but his conspirators were killed.**

Cyrene – **Pg. 419, ¶ 3 – Cyrene was the Greek settlement of Theran colonists on the North African coast. Conditions in Cyrene during the first fifty-six years that the first two kings ruled were so difficult that the colony barely survived.**

Note to INSTRUCTOR – The student might also include that the original colonists had been so hungry and hard-pressed that they tried to return to Thera, only to be refused entry and told to return to the colony. Also, the student might note that the African Coast south of Thera was also called Libya.

Draco – **Pg. 427, ¶ 4 – Draco, a councilor, took down the most important of Athens' massive oral traditions, systematized them, and turned them into a written code. Draco prescribed death as the punishment for almost all crimes.**

Ekklesia – **Pg. 425, ¶ 3 – The ekklesia was an assembly of all Athenians who confirmed the elections of the board of nine landowners.**

Eusebius – **Pg. 424, ¶ 6 & 7 – Eusebius, the bishop of Caesarea in Palestine, put together a chronological table of ancient times which describes a seven-hundred-year succession of Athenian kings. While the list may not be factual, it does tell us that Athens once had kings.**

Messene – **Pg. 421, ¶ 3 – Messene, which was located on the western side of the Taygetus mountain range, was attacked by Spartans because it was good for ploughing and planting. After twenty years of war, Messene became a subject city of Sparta.**

Metropolis – **Pg. 418, ¶ 2** – A metropolis was the home city, or mother city, of a Greek colonist. Once a Greek settler ventured out to a new city, he was forced to give up citizenship in his metropolis.

Polemarch – **Pg. 425, ¶ 1** – Polemarch was the title given to the Athenian who controlled the military.

Solon – **Pg. 428, ¶ 3 to Pg. 429, ¶ 1** – Solon, a respectable middle-class merchant, was elected archon around 600 BC. He attempted to establish a fair law code by first revoking the laws of Draco, except the penalty for homicide, and then writing new regulations that covered everything from the qualifications for holding public office, to acceptable boundaries for mourning the dead, and the redistribution of land.

Section II: Comprehension

Write a two/three sentence answer to each of the following questions.

1. How were Greek colonists able to maintain their Greek identity and culture in their new cities?
A1. – Pg. 418, ¶ 2 – Greek colonists maintained their identity and culture in their new land by establishing a Greek enclosure in each new land. For example, they took with them baskets of Greek grain to plant, and firepots with Greek brands to light the hearthfire. They built Greek temples, told Greek tales, and sent their delegations to the Greek games.

2. Once Messene was conquered by Sparta, how were the Messenians treated by the Spartans? What place did the Spartans hold in the new class system?
A2. – Pg. 421, ¶ 4 – Once Messene was conquered by Sparta, the Messenians became a whole class of slaves, who grew food for their captors under harsh terms. The Spartans themselves became the aristocracy, a master race of warrior men and mothers of soldiers.

3. Why did the Spartan people prefer to be ruled by two kings at odds rather than a singular king with unchallenged power?
A3. – Pg. 421, ¶ 5 to Pg. 422, ¶ 1 – The two-king system preferred by the Spartans prevented the rise of a Mesopotamian-style monarchy. The Spartans thought the idea of a singular king ordained by the gods to exercise sovereignty was foreign and repulsive. In Sparta, inherited and limitless royal power was feared.

4. What were the three primary powers of any ancient kingdom? In what way did Israel fix this three-way power into law?
A4. – Pg. 422, ¶ 2 – Any ancient kingdom had three primary powers: the military power to declare war and lead the army; the judicial power to make laws and enforce them; and the priestly power to maintain good relationships with the gods. Israel fixed this three-way power into law by making a formal division between the official state roles of prophet, priest and king.

5. While the kings of Sparta held all three primary powers, how was their ability to use them limited?
A5. – Pg. 422, ¶ 2 – While the kings of Sparta were priests of Zeus and received oracles from the gods, they could not keep an evil omen from the people because four state officials also had the right to hear the prophecies. In matters of war, the kings had the right to declare war, but they were required to be first in the charge and last in the retreat, which kept them from sending the army into needless battles.

6. How did one put a question to the Delphic oracle? Why was it difficult to get a straight answer from the oracle?

A6. – Pg. 425, ¶ 6 – In order to ask the Delphic oracle a question, one had to climb to the top of Sibylline Rock, where a priestess sat next to a large crack. One would then put a question to the priestess, who then asked the earth-goddess Gaia for an answer and received it by way of the crack. She then delivered the answer in a trance to a set of attendant priests, who cast it into hexameter verse and delivered it back to the questioner. The crack, the trance and the hexameters combined to produce generally puzzling answers that could be interpreted in numerous ways.

7. Define "tyrant" in terms of Greek politics.

A7. – Pg. 426, ¶ 2 – "Tyrant" was a technical term in Greek politics; it referred to a politician who leapfrogged the normal routes of power (election and then confirmation) and took control of a city's government by force. Tyrants were not necessarily cruel, although they tended to be autocratic in order to keep hold of their power.

8. What grave mistake did the archons make when they dealt with Cylon's conspirators after the rebels occupied the Acropolis?

A8. – Pg. 426, ¶ 4 & 5 – The archons agreed to spare the lives of Cylon's conspirators, but when the men began to come out of the Acropolis, the archons ordered them killed. Several flung themselves against the altars of the goddesses Demeter and Persephone, but were murdered anyway – a dreadful breach of protocol, since anyone who begged for the protection of a god at his altar was supposed to be spared. The archons who had ordered the massacre were exiled for their crime.

9. What was a "Sixth-Part-Tenant?" In what way does a "sixth-part-tenant" exemplify the false nature of Athenian democracy?

A9. – Pg. 427, ¶ 2 – "Sixth-Part-Tenant" refers to the rent farmers paid for the rich men's land which they cultivated. If they ever failed to pay their rents, they themselves and their children were liable to arrest. Though Athens was supposed to be a democracy, the poor were actually in slavery to the rich.

10. Why did Draco assign the penalty of death to so many crimes in his newly written law?

A10. – Pg. 427, ¶ 4 & 5 – Draco assigned the penalty of death to so many crimes because he believed even petty crimes deserved death, and he could not find a more severe punishment for greater crimes. By assigning the penalty of death to even the smallest of crimes, Draco believed he could scare men into saintly living.

11. How did Solon set about righting the inequalities of the wealth in Athens? Why were the debtors unhappy with Solon's redistribution plan?

A11. – Pg. 428, ¶ 6 to Pg. 429, ¶ 2 – In order to right the inequalities of wealth in Athens, Solon cancelled the overwhelming debts of the poor and redistributed the land so that the farmers who had cultivated it for generations now owned it. The debtors hoped for a good deal more than debt cancellation; they had wanted land redistributed equally to all, but the poorest still had no holdings of their own.

12. What was Solon's reason for leaving Athens as soon as his laws were enacted? Why was leaving the city advantageous for Solon?

A12. – Pg. 429, ¶ 4 to Pg. 430, ¶ 1 – Solon left Athens as soon as his laws were enacted to prove that no one would break them. He left in order to let the laws do their own work, free from any appeals to his person. Leaving the city was advantageous for Solon because this meant he would not be present in order to repeal any of the laws he had made, nor would he have to deal with the daily complaints and questions he received about his laws.

Section III: Critical Thinking

The student may not use her text to answer this question.

Though Spartans wanted to avoid the tyranny often associated with Mesopotamian kings, they managed to create a society oppressed by an unwritten yet incredibly strict code of laws. Write a paragraph that first gives two examples of severe Spartan law. Next, explain the overall purpose of Spartan laws. In your answer, make sure to explain why Spartan laws were never written down. Finally, explain how the laws that were meant to free Spartans from sin actually trapped Spartans in a cage of fear.

Examples of Spartan law:

• *Children did not belong to their families but to the city of Sparta; the council of elders had the right to inspect each baby and give it permission to live, or else order it laid out to die (Pg. 422, ¶ 4).*

• *Boys were assigned at the age of seven to "boy herds" which ran in packs, learning to fight and forage for food (Pg. 422, ¶ 4).*

• *Any husband could choose to impregnate another woman, or hand his wife over to another man, as long as the decision was made for the good of the master race (Pg. 422, ¶ 4).*

• *Spartans had most of their meals in common messes in order to prevent them from spending time at home reclining at the table on expensive couches (Pg. 423, ¶ 2).*

• *Eating meals together ensured that the Spartans were not ruining themselves physically by gorging themselves (Pg. 423, ¶ 2).*

• *Girls, who were the future mothers of Spartan warriors, were required to dance naked in front of crowds of young men, giving them additional motivation to stay slim (Pg. 423, ¶ 2).*

• *The doors and roofs of Spartan houses could be shaped only by axe and saw; to use more refined tools was illegal. This was meant to prevent a longing for fine furniture and fabrics (Pg. 423, ¶ 2).*

Purpose of Spartan laws and why Spartan laws were never written down:

• *Spartan laws were intended to eliminate all wrongdoing (Pg. 428, ¶ 1). The only way this could work is if the laws were written on the character and hearts of the citizens (Pg. 423, ¶ 3).*

• *Spartan laws were never written down because they were engraved on Spartan hearts (Pg. 428, ¶ 1).*

Laws that were meant to free Spartan hearts from sin actually trapped Spartans in fear:

• _Because Spartan law was never written down, the Spartans themselves continually watched each other for violations of unwritten regulations (Pg. 423, ¶ 3). The Spartans lived in a culture of fear as the state policed the citizens, and the citizens policed each other._

• _The Spartan Demaratus explained that although Spartans seemed free, they were not free, "Their master is the law, and they're far more afraid of this than your men are of you" (Pg. 423 ¶ 4). The Spartan state was designed to escape the absolutism of monarchy, but in fact it exceeded it._

EXAMPLE ANSWER: The Spartans lived by strict and unforgiving laws. For example, children did not belong to their families but to the city of Sparta. If the council of elders found a baby to be unfit for the Spartan race, they would order it laid out to die. Girls, who would one day be the mothers of Spartan warriors, were required to dance naked in front of crowds of young men to ensure they stayed attractive and fit. The purpose of Spartan laws was not to make Spartans miserable; the laws were intended to help Spartans eliminate all wrongdoing from their lives. The only way this would work was if the laws were written on the character and hearts of the Spartans, thus the laws were not allowed to be written down. While this seems like a good idea, what actually happened was that Spartans began to police each other. The constant fear of wrongdoing created a society in which Spartans, though not bound by written law, were paralyzed by the law inscribed on their hearts.

CHAPTER FIFTY-SEVEN: THE BEGINNINGS AND END OF EMPIRE

The student may use his text when answering the questions in sections I and II.

Section I: Who, What, Where

Write a one or two-sentence answer explaining the significance of each item listed below.

Assur-uballit – **Pg. 439, ¶ 2 – Assur-uballit, an army officer and royal cousin, took the title of king of Assyria after the death of Sin-shum-ishkun.**

Dionysius of Halicarnassus – **Pg. 433, ¶ 4 – Dionysius of Halicarnassus was a Greek historian who went to Rome in the reign of Augustus Caesar and spent twenty-two years writing a history of the city.**

Estruscans – **Pg. 432, ¶ 1 – The Estruscans were a meld of Villanovans and newcomers from the east. The Estruscans were strong builders and wealthy merchants who did not intend to let Rome and its Latial inhabitants expand without challenge.**

Haran – **Pg. 439, ¶ 2 & 3 & Pg. 440, – Haran, a city west of Assur and Nineveh, became the new capital of Assyria after the fall of Nineveh. After Assur-uballit fled the city upon hearing of advancing Babylon troops, the city remained under Babylon's control.**

Josiah of Judah – **Pg. 440, ¶ 4 – Josiah of Judah took advantage of the Assyrian disintegration to reassert his own independence. Not wanting to answer again to Assyria, or to Egypt, Josiah attempted to stop Necho II from helping the Assyrians; he was killed by Necho II in battle.**

Lucumo (Lucius Tarquinius Priscus/Tarquin the Elder) – **Pg. 434, ¶ 4 – Lucumo (or Lucius Tarquinius Priscus, or Tarquin the Elder as later historians knew him) was an Etruscan who moved to Rome and became the right-hand man of the king. Lucumo was elected to the Roman throne in 616, after sending the rightful heirs off on a very long hunting expedition.**

Nebuchadnezzar – **Pg. 441, ¶ 2 - Nebuchadnezzar was the son of Nabopolassar. In 605 BC, Nebuchadnezzar was sent to Carchemish by his father to get rid of the Assyrian remnant stationed there.**

Necho II – **Pg. 439, ¶ 5 – Necho II succeeded his father Psammetichus I as the Egyptian pharaoh. Unlike his father, Necho II was not averse to friendly relations with the Assyrians.**

Numa Pompilius – **Pg. 433, ¶ 3 – Numa Pompilius was the first Sabine king of Rome, picked by the senate. Numa Pompilius was famous for his justice; his rule stood for a transition in Rome, from a colony established by war towards a settled and mature city.**

Servius Tullius – **Pg. 434, ¶ 5 – Servius Tullius, an Etruscan, was the son-in-law of Lucumo. When Servius Tullius was a child, his head burst into flames, a sign that he was to become the future king of Rome.**

Section II: Comprehension

Write a two/three sentence answer to each of the following questions.

1. What was the cause of King Romulus of Rome's death?
A1. – Pg. 433, ¶ 1 – King Romulus of Rome died one day when reviewing his troops; a storm burst, and the senators of Rome claimed that he had been carried away up high by a whirlwind. However, a few dissenters claim that once in the thick cloud, the king had been torn to pieces by the senators.

NOTE TO INSTRUCTOR: The student should both include Romulus's death by storm and his suspected death by senators.

2. Why were the gates to the Temple of Janus, god of war, closed under Numa Pompilius?
A2. – Pg. 433, ¶ 3 – The gates to the Temple of Janus were closed under Numa Pompilius as a symbol of Rome's peace with the outside world.

3. In 650 BC, Rome seemed to be a city at peace; what division was still present within the city's walls?
A3. – Pg. 433, ¶ 4 – Though Rome seemed to be at peace around 650 BC, its citizens were still divided by race. In particular, the Sabine population felt that they stood in an inferior position to the founding Alban element.

4. How did Numa Pompilius's successors, Tullus Hostilius and Ancus Marcius, change the shape of Rome?
A4. – Pg. 433, ¶ 6 to Pg. 434, ¶ 1 – Tullus Hostilius and Ancus Marcius both led campaigns against the cities and tribes that surrounded Rome. Numa Pompilius's successors doubled the size of Rome by force.

5. What was Sin-shum-ishkun's next move once the three-way fight at Babylon broke out?
A5. – Pg. 437, ¶ 1 – After years of fighting, Sin-shum-ishkun of Babylon could no longer defend his city, and Nabopolassar marched into the city. After his surrender, it seems that Sin-Shum-ishkun went north and seized his brother Ashur-etillu-ilani's throne in the Assyrian heartland; Ashur-etillu-ilani disappears from the accounts from this point on.

6. Who helped Nabopolassar in his fight against Assyria? What agreement was made between the two allies?
A8. – Pg. 437, ¶ 3 – Nabopolassar was able to pull the Assyrian empire apart with the help of Cyarxes, the Median king of Medes and the Persians. In exchange for Cyarxes's help, Nabopolassar married off his son, the Babylonian crown prince, Nebuchadnezzar, to Cyarxes's daughter, Amytis, the Median princess.

7. Describe how Nabopolassar and Cyarxes worked together to take down Assur.
A7. – Pg. 437, ¶ 6 – Nabopolassar tried to take down Assur, but after a month of fighting was forced to retreat. Cyarxes came back from Medes and laid siege to Assur himself. He captured the city and raided it for captives and goods; afterwards, he permitted the Median troops to massacre everyone left inside.

8. How was Necho and Cyarxes's army able to get through the wall surrounding Nineveh? Why was this act a particularly fitting way for the Babylonians to attack the city?
A8. – Pg. 438, ¶ 3 & Pg. 439, ¶ 1 – Necho and Cyarxes's invading armies most likely built a dam to divert more of the waters from the Tigris into the Nineveh, carrying away the foundations of the walls and breaking them away. Babylon had been flooded by Assyrians a hundred years earlier; now the Babylonians were returning the favor.

9. After the fall of Nineveh, how did the Medes and Babylon split the territory that was once Assyria?
A9. – Pg. 439, ¶ 2 – After the fall of Nineveh, the Medes claimed the eastern territory, including the land which had once belonged to the Scythians. Babylon took over the old western provinces.

10. – Considering Egypt's tumultuous relationship with Assyria, why did Necho II want to help the dying empire?
A10. – Pg. 439, ¶5 to Pg. 440, ¶ 1 – Necho II had plans to make Egypt more important in world affairs, and the logical place for expansion was the Western Semitic lands along the Mediterranean. The rise of a strong Babylonian empire would not allow for Egyptian takeover of those Mediterranean territories. Also, if the Assyrians fell, one more barrier between Egypt and the Scythians, who had already attempted an Egyptian invasion, would be gone.

11. After failing to take Babylon, how did Necho II avenge Josiah of Judah's surprise attack on his Egyptian troops?
A11. – Pg. 440, ¶ 7 to Pg. 441, ¶ 1 – After failing to take Babylon, Necho II focused his attentions on Jerusalem, and took Josiah's son and heir Jehoahaz captive. Jehoahaz died in exile, and his younger brother, Eliakim became Necho II's puppet ruler of Jerusalem. Necho II renamed Eliakim as Jehoiakim, a traditional act of dominance and ownership.

12. Why didn't Nebuchadnezzar follow the fleeing Necho II all the way into Egypt after the battle at Carchemish?
A12. – Pg. 441, ¶ 4 – Nebuchadnezzar began to follow the retreating Necho II back towards the Delta, but when he received news of Nabopolassar's passing, he knew he had to return to Babylon immediately to claim his rightful place on the throne.

Section III: Critical Thinking

The student may use his text to answer this question.

Rome was a city built on division. The racial division within Rome could cause tension, but it also allowed those of mixed race to find worth outside of their bloodline. Write a paragraph explaining how Rome's mix of races gave citizens the opportunity for success no matter their origins, and how the slow takeover of Roman life by Etruscans only added to Rome's strength.

Rome was made up of two types of people: the Latins and the Sabines. Though the Latins thought of themselves as better than the Sabines, there was no one noble blood. Lucumo is a good example of racial mobility in Rome. Lucumo was mixed race by birth; his mother was Etruscan and his father was a Greek. Lucumo found himself facing the scorn of the full-blooded Etruscans, and so he decided to move to Rome with his wife, where race mattered less than opportunity. Lucumo worked hard and eventually became the right-hand man of the king himself. He was even appointed guardian of the royal princes. When Ancus Marcius died, Lucumo took advantage of the young age of the princes and managed to have himself elected to the throne. Lucumo's mixed race did not stop him from becoming king of Rome.

Lucumo's ascent is only one example of the Etruscan infiltration of Roman life. Another example of the good brought to Rome by Etruscans is the architectural work of <u>Tarquin the Elder</u>. Tarquin the Elder is credited with the planning of Circus Maximus, the great Roman stadium that lay between the Palatine and Aventine hills, and the laying of the foundations for the Temple of Jupiter, on the Capitol. He also squared off the walls and began the digging of the sewers to drain Rome's waste. In addition, Tarquin the Elder introduced Rome to the Etruscan symbols of kingship.

The Etruscan <u>Servius Tullius</u> is praised for claiming the Quirinal and Viminal hills, and building trenches and earthworks to reinforce Rome's walls. Under Servius Tullius, the size of Rome was greatly increased, and he reigned for forty-four years as king, an Etruscan monarch over a mixed population of Etruscans, Latins and Sabines.

In the student's response, he should use Lucumo to demonstrate how success was possible in Rome despite one's race. Then, he should use one example from each great Etruscan, Tarquin the Elder and Servius Tullius (underlined), to exemplify the benefits of the Etruscan infiltration of Rome.

EXAMPLE ANSWER: The citizens of Rome identified themselves as Latin or Sabine. The mix of races in the city meant that race had less to do with success than hard work. Half-Etruscan and half-Greek Lucumo saw an opportunity to do well in Rome because race mattered less than opportunity. Lucumo worked diligently and eventually became the Ancus Marcius's right-hand man, and he was even appointed guardian of the royal princes. When the king died, Lucumo managed to have himself elected to the throne. Lucumo's mixed race did not stop him from becoming king of Rome. The Etruscan influence in Rome was good for the city. The Etruscan Tarquin the Elder planned Circus Maximus, and started the production of sewers to drain the city's waste. Lucumo's son-in-law, Servius Tullius, also an Etruscan, built trenches and earthworks that fortified the city's walls. The work of Etruscans in Rome helped it to become a well-planned and protected city.

CHAPTER FIFTY-EIGHT: A BRIEF EMPIRE

The student may use her text when answering the questions in sections I and II.

Section I: Who, What, Where

Write a one or two-sentence answer explaining the significance of each item listed below.

Alyattes – **Pg. 452, ¶ 3 & 4 – Alyattes, king of the Lydians, led his army to meet the Median army as they fought their way towards Asia Minor. The Lydians fought the Medians for five years; the stalemate was eventually broken with some help from Nebuchadnezzar II.**

Apries – **Pg. 451, ¶ 1 – Apries succeeded his father Psammetichus II as ruler of Egypt. Apries made no challenge to Nebuchadnezzar II's power.**

Carthage – **Pg. 446, ¶ 2 – Carthage was a Phoenician-built city on the North African coast. It was founded by Jezebel's great-niece, Elissa, and was growing rapidly.**

Hanging Gardens – **Pg. 448, ¶ 1 to Pg. 449, ¶ 2 – The Hanging Gardens were built by Nebuchadnezzar II for his wife, and also to show his strength as king of Babylon. The Hanging Gardens acquired their name from Diodorus of Siculus's description of their upside-down ziggurat formation, with each level of the garden overhanging the one below.**

Ishtar Gate – **Pg. 447, ¶ 4 – Ishtar Gate was a ceremonial gate on the north side of Babylon. Nebuchadnezzar II built a ceremonial road, seventy-feet wide, from the central temple complex to the Ishtar Gate, so that Marduk could progress along it in the New Year's festival.**

Note to INSTRUCTOR: The student might include that walls on either side of the ceremonial path were glazed blue and decorated with carved lions.

Jehoiachin – **Pg. 446, ¶ 5 to Pg. 447, ¶ 1 – Jehoiachin, Jehoiakim's son, was only a teenager when he was set on Jerusalem's throne in 597. Jehoiachin, along with his mother, his court, the noblemen and Jerusalem's officials, surrendered to Nebuchadnezzar II, and spent the next forty years in comfortable captivity paid for by the Babylonian treasury.**

Jehoiakim – **Pg. 443, ¶ 3 and Pg. 444, ¶ 3 – Jehoiakim, ruler of Israel, was first loyal to Necho II of Egypt, and then to Nebuchadnezzar II of Babylon. His allegiance to Nebuchadnezzar was false, however, and as soon as Necho II was ready, he joined the Egyptians in an attack against Babylon.**

Psammetichus II – **Pg. 450, ¶ 3 & Pg. 451, ¶ 1 – Psammetichus succeeded his father Necho II as the king of Egypt. After success at Napata, Psammetichus II was prompted by Zedekiah of Jerusalem to attack Nebuchadnezzar II; the Egyptians were defeated and Psammetichus died just a few weeks later in 589.**

Zedekiah – **Pg. 447, ¶ 2 – Zedekiah was the name given to Mattaniah, Jehoiachin's uncle, by Nebuchadnezzar II. Zedekiah was put on Jerusalem's throne, but in fact was no more than a Babylonian governor.**

Section II: Comprehension

Write a two/three sentence answer to each of the following questions.

1. What caused Jehoiakim to drop his alliance to Necho II in order to become a vassal for Nebuchadnezzar II?
A1. – Pg. 443, ¶ 3 – Jehoiakim swapped alliances away from Necho II to Babylon after Nebuchadnezzar II posted a garrison outside the walls of Jerusalem. By buying Babylon's alliance, Jehoiakim kept his nation from being completely taken over by Nebuchadnezzar II's growing empire.

2. Describe the pet project Necho II worked on after drawing against Babylon twice, in 602 and 601.
A2. – Pg. 444, ¶ 6 to Pg. 446, ¶ 1 –After fighting unsuccessfully against Babylon in 602 and 601, Necho II worked on a canal that ran from the eastern Nile river through to the Red Sea. The canal took four days to sail, and was thirty feet wide. Necho II built a fortress called Pelusium to guard the canal's entrance to the Nile.

3. Who did Necho II hire to help him train an Egyptian navy?
A3. – Pg. 446, ¶ 2 – Necho II hired two sets of mercenaries to come down and help him train a navy: Greek sailors from the Ionian cities around the Aegean Sea, and Phoenician seamen, probably from one of the Phoenician cities like Tyre, Sidon, or maybe Carthage.

4. Following in the tradition of Mesopotamian kings, what did Nebuchadnezzar II build to establish his position as a great king?
A4. – Pg. 447, ¶ 3-5 – In order to establish his position as a great king, Nebuchadnezzar II restored and added to temple after temple in Babylon, all dedicated to Marduk. He built a ceremonial road for the festival of Marduk, a seventy-foot-wide path from the central temple complex to the ceremonial Ishtar Gate. He built himself three palaces, gilded with glazing, gold and silver, and in one of these palaces be built the Hanging Gardens of Babylon.

5. What did Nebuchadnezzar II build in order to strengthen Babylon's walls? Against what threat was Nebuchadnezzar trying to protect the city?
A5. – Pg. 449, ¶ 3 – Nebuchadnezzar II reinforced the inner wall of Babylon until it was twenty-one feet thick, and he placed watchtowers on the outer wall at every sixty feet. Nebuchadnezzar II built a forty foot belt of water around the city, and then built another wall on the city's east side to ensure that the Tigris could not be diverted and flood the city.

6. What brought an end to the two-year Babylonian siege against Jerusalem, and to Zedekiah's reign?
A6. – Pg. 451, ¶ 4 – The two-year Babylonian siege against Jerusalem was finally ended by famine. Zedekiah had had enough and tried to escape, without thought for the rest of the people. The city's walls were broken down, and Zedekiah was eventually captured in the plains of Jericho.

7. What did Nebuchadnezzar II do to Jerusalem and its inhabitants in order to ensure the city would never again plot against Babylon?
A7. – Pg. 452, ¶ 1 –In order to ensure that Jerusalem would never again be a nuisance, Nebuchadnezzar II had all of Zedekiah's chief officials and chief priests executed. Jerusalem was set on fire, the walls were broken down and the city's people were marched off into exile.

8. What did Nebuchadnezzar II do to resolve the stalemate between the Lydians and the Medians? How was the peace between the two quarrelling nations sealed?
A8. – Pg. 452, ¶ 4 – Nebuchadnezzar II sent a Babylonian officer named Nabonidus to help arrange a cease-fire between the Lydians and the Medians. The two kings agreed to a peace, which was sealed by the marriage of Alyattes of Lydia's daughter, Aryenis, to Cyarxes of Medes's son, Astyages.

Section III: Critical Thinking

The student may not use her text to answer this question.

If the epic "Hanging Gardens" of Babylon were symbolic of Nebuchadnezzar II's rule, then we could assume that he was a king who could wield great power, but who also valued peace and serenity. However, Nebuchadnezzar II's treatment of Zedekiah of Jerusalem, and stories of the king's madness, suggest that he was far more tyrannical that exemplified by the beautiful gardens. How did kingship change Nebuchadnezzar II? Write a passage that first describes Nebuchadnezzar II's transformation from man to animal, then use Nebuchadnezzar II's treatment of Zedekiah as an example of the king's turn, and finally explain what this transformation was meant to symbolize in terms of the way Nebuchadnezzar II ruled.

Descriptions of Nebuchadnezzar II's transformation from man to animal:
(The student need only use two or three details from these descriptions.)
• Pg. 453, ¶ 2 – Nebuchadnezzar II was driven away from people and ate grass like cattle… His hair grew like the feathers of an eagle and his nails like the claws of a bird.
• Pg. 454, ¶ 1 – Nebuchadnezzar II's head and foreparts were those of an ox, his legs and hinder parts those of a lion.

Nebuchadnezzar II's treatment of Zedekiah of Jerusalem:
Jerusalem's alliance to its more powerful neighbors was fickle; it seems somewhat justified that by the time of Zedekiah's revolt against Nebuchadnezzar II, the Assyrian king had had enough. Nebuchadnezzar II's treatment of Zedekiah was incredibly cruel: Zedekiah was made to watch his sons killed in front of him, and then Nebuchadnezzar II had Zedekiah's eyes put out so that the last sight he ever witnessed was the execution of his family.

What Nebuchadnezzar II's transformation from man to beast was meant to symbolize:
Nebuchadnezzar II was not known to be cruel like the Assyrian kings before him. The Lives of the Prophets *states that "It is the manner of tyrants that… in their latter years they become wild beasts." Nebuchadnezzar II's treatment of Zedekiah exemplifies this turn; mad with power, Nebuchadnezzar II began to resemble the tyrannical beast that lived in his heart.*

EXAMPLE ANSWER: It is said that Nebuchadnezzar II went a little mad towards the end of his reign. This madness was paired with descriptions of the king as an animal. Supposedly, he ate grass like cattle, grew feathers and had a head like an ox. Like Nebuchadnezzar II's appearance, his treatment of conquered subjects also changed. When the rebellious Zedekiah of Jerusalem was taken captive, he was made to watch his sons killed in front of him. Then Nebuchadnezzar II had Zedekiah's eyes put out so that the last sight he ever witnessed was the execution of his family. Nebuchadnezzar was not known to be cruel like the Assyrian kings before him, but his treatment of Zedekiah tells a different story; mad with power, Nebuchadnezzar II began to resemble the tyrannical beast that lived in his heart.

CHAPTER FIFTY-NINE: CYRUS THE GREAT

The student may use his text when answering the questions in sections I and II.

Section I: Who, What, Where

Write a one or two-sentence answer explaining the significance of each item listed below.

Astyages – **Pg. 455, ¶ 1** – Astyages was the high king of the Medes and the Persians. He tried to have the baby Cyrus killed, out of fear for his own position.

Aryenis – **Pg. 455, ¶ 1** – Aryenis was the wife of Astyages, high king of the Medes and the Persians, and the mother of Mandane, who gave birth to Cyrus.

Belshazzar – **Pg. 464, ¶ 3** – Belshazzar was named co-regent by his father Nabonidus, and put in charge of Babylon while the king travelled to Arabia in order to worship the moon-god Sin.

Cambyses – **Pg. 455, ¶ 3** – Cambyses was a Persian vassal to king Astyages, and was chosen by the Median king to marry his daughter, Mandane. With Mandane, Cambyses fathered Cyrus II.

Croesus – **Pg. 459, ¶ 4** – Croesus, son of Alyattes, ruled over the Lydians of Asia Minor. Croesus extended the Lydian empire: he made the Phrygians subject to Lydia, and allied Lydia with the Greek Ionian cities on the coast.

Harpagus – **Pg. 456, ¶ 2 and Pg. 457, ¶ 4** – Harpagus was Astyages's cousin, and chief official. Harpagus's punishment by Astyages for not doing away with Mandane's baby was to be served his own son's body for dinner.

Mandane – **Pg. 455, ¶ 1** – Mandane was the daughter of Astyages and Aryenis, and mother of Cyrus II.

Nabonidus – **Pg. 458, ¶ 4** – Nabonidus, the army officer who helped negotiate the treaty between the Medes and the Persians, ended up as king of Babylon after the multiple short reigns of Nebuchadnezzar II's kin.

Pasargadae – **Pg. 468, ¶ 1** – Pasargadae was the new capital city Cyrus II built for the administration of his new empire.

Section II: Comprehension

Write a two/three sentence answer to each of the following questions.

1. How did Astyages's wise men interpret the king's dream in which his daughter Mandane urinated so much that she not only filled his city, but even flooded the whole of Asia?
A1. – Pg. 455, ¶ 1 – Astyages's wise men interpreted the king's disturbing dream about his daughter Mandane and her urine to mean that a child of Mandane's would grow up to take Astyages's kingdom.

2. Why did Astyages choose Cambyses of Persia to be Mandane's husband?
A2. – Pg. 455, ¶ 2 & 3 – Because the prophecy about Mandane's child meant that Mandane's husband would not be king, Astyages wanted to make sure Mandane married a man who would be willing to watch the crown pass directly from grandfather to grandson. Astyages chose Cambyses because the Persian vassal did not have grand ambitions, and thus he would not threaten the future of Astyages's grandchild.

3. What interpretation did Astyages's wise men give the king of his second dream concerning Mandane's child, where a vine grew out of his daughter and curled itself all around his territory?
A3. – Pg. 455, ¶ 4 – Astyages's wise men interpreted the second dream about Mandane and her vine to mean that her son would not only succeed Astyages, but rule in his place.

4. Give a short chronicle of the men who wore the crown of Babylon between Nebuchadnezzar II and Nabonidus.
A4. – Pg. 458, ¶ 3 – Nebuchadnezzar II's son Amel-Marduk took the Babylonian throne when his father died. Amel-Marduk was then murdered by his brother-in-law after six years on the throne. Amel-Marduk's brother-in-law died after only four years on the throne, then his son Labashi-Marduk became king. Labashi-Marduk was beaten to death by his kinsman after only nine months as king.

5. How was Cyrus II able to get both the Persians and most of the important Median officials on his side in an attack against Astyages, the high king of Media and Persia?
A5. – Pg. 460, ¶ 1 & 2 – Cyrus II belonged to the Persian Pasargadae tribe, which was the largest and most powerful of all the Persian clans. Cyrus II used his Pasargadae backing to convince the other Persian tribes to fight with him against his grandfather. Cyrus II also had Harpagus on his side; Harpagus was able to convince the important Median officials of the necessity of setting up Cyrus II as their leader.

6. How did Cyrus II manage to lay siege to Sardis and take control of Lydia?
A6. – Pg. 460, ¶ 6 – Cyrus II met Lydian king Croesus at the Halys river and fought to a draw. As Croesus drew back in order to get outside aid, Cyrus II pushed forwards into Lydia and scattered the Lydian cavalry by bringing in camels, which frightened the horses into bolting. Cyrus II laid siege to the city, Croesus was taken prisoner, and Cyrus II's troops plundered the city's fabled wealth.

7. To which god was Nabonidus devoted? Why was Nabonidus's faith at odds with his kingship?
A7. – Pg. 464, ¶ 2 & 3 – Nabonidus was devoted to the moon-god Sin; his own inscriptions attribute his rise to power to the blessings of Sin. Marduk, however, was the god of Babylon, and the priests of Marduk had gained enormous influence under the reign of Nebuchadnezzar II. Nabonidus found the hostility of the priests serious enough to make Babylon uninhabitable for him, so he left his son Belshazzar in charge of the city.

8. Why did Nabonidus choose to settle in Tema after he left Babylon?
A8. – Pg. 464, ¶ 3 – Nabonidus chose to settle in Tema after leaving Babylon because Tema was a city through which valuable gold and salt passed continually. From Tema's busy trade routes, Nabonidus could keep his hand on Babylonian commerce, and could communicate with his son and co-regent Belshazzar.

9. How was Cyrus II able to take Babylon once Nabonidus and his people were barricaded inside?

A9. – Pg. 465, ¶ 7 to Pg. 466, ¶ 1 – Cyrus II had trenches dug all along the Tigris, upstream from Babylon, and during one night, he had his men open all the trenches simultaneously. This diverted the water away from its main stream and the level of the Tigris that ran through the city sank at once. Persian soldiers marched through the mud of the riverbed, under the walls of the city, and took the palace by storm.

10. Why was Nabonidus blamed for the fall of Babylon?

A10. – Pg. 466, ¶ 3 – Nabonidus was blamed for the fall of Babylon because, by worshipping Sin, it was said that he slighted Marduk. Because Nabonidus did not venerate Marduk, the city was punished and given to Cyrus II.

11. What was the political strategy behind Cyrus II's restoration of the temple of Yahweh at Jerusalem in Judah, and his returning of the valuables from the Temple of Solomon that were in the Babylonian treasury?

A11. – Pg. 466, ¶ 4 to Pg. 467, ¶ 1 – Cyrus II rebuilt the temple of the Yahweh at Jerusalem in Judah, and returned the valuables from the Temple of Solomon, so that he would gain the favor of the Jewish exiles. For this, he earned himself the title from the Jews "Anointed of the Lord."

Section III: Critical Thinking

The student may use his text to answer this question.

In this chapter, we read that Xenophon, author of *The Education of Cyrus,* saw Cyrus II as a new kind of emperor, whose reasons for success were ultimately justice, benevolence and fairness. While there was some "newness" to Cyrus II's rule, it was not the "newness" to which Xenophon referred. Write a passage detailing both what <u>was</u> new about Cyrus II's rule and what about his rule seems to be pulled straight from China's ancient history.

What <u>was</u> new about Cyrus II's empire was that Cyrus II did not try to make conquered peoples into Persians. His empire had many different peoples together under one rule. He did not try to destroy national loyalties or identities. Cyrus II portrayed himself as a benevolent guardian of those very identities, and would protect them as long as they praised him as king.

The purpose of Cyrus II's Eyes and Ears should ring a bell to the student – their purpose was the same as King Li of China's Grand Inquisitor (Chapter 46). King Li hired a Grand Inquisitor to go out and listen to disloyal speech. You might ask the student: why did Li and Cyrus II have spies? The motivation behind Li's Grand Inquisitor and Cyrus II's Eyes and Ears was the same: perpetuating fear in one's subjects in order to make sure they would be obedient. Just as criticisms in Li's capital city subsided because no one dared say a word against him, the people in Cyrus II's empire were afraid to say what was not advantageous to the king, just as if he were listening. Like Li, Cyrus II excelled primarily in creating terror. As Xenophon remarked, "He was able to extend fear of himself to so much of the world that he intimidated all."

Cyrus II was clever, and masked his controlling ways by giving gifts. Ask the student to recall why people liked Cyrus II so much. Xenophon writes, "Who else, by the magnitude of his

gifts, is said to make people prefer himself to their brother, to their fathers and to their children?"
Bribery can be a powerful tool; by giving his subjects food and other gifts, Cyrus II was able to trick
them into doing his dirty work. In this way Cyrus II convinced people all over his empire to become
"the so-called Eyes and ears of the King," and to report to him anything "that would benefit the
king." This was not reporting, but surveillance, and like those in the Zhou capital of Hao, Cyrus II's
people would not dare speak out against the king.

EXAMPLE ANSWER: What was new about Cyrus II's rule was not his justice, benevolence
and fairness. Cyrus II employed force and fear as much as any other great king before him.
What was new was that Cyrus II did not try to make conquered peoples into Persians. His
empire had many different peoples together under one rule. He did not try to destroy national
loyalties or identities. Cyrus II portrayed himself as a benevolent guardian of those very
identities, and would protect them as long as they praised him as king.

But Cyrus II was not benevolent. He used gifts to mask his controlling ways. He gave his people
food and gifts, convincing them to become his Eyes and Ears, and to report to him anything that
would benefit the king. In this way, he turned his people into spies. Who would dare speak out
against Cyrus II? Cyrus II made his people fear him. His actions were very similar to those of
King Li of China. King Li hired a Grand Inquisitor to go out and listen to disloyal speech. Just
as criticisms in Hao subsided because no one dared say a word against Li, the people in Cyrus
II's empire were afraid to say anything bad about the king, as if he were present. Like Li before
him, Cyrus II excelled primarily in creating terror. This was nothing new.

CHAPTER SIXTY: THE REPUBLIC OF ROME

The student may use her text when answering the questions in sections I and II.

Section I: Who, What, Where

Write a one or two-sentence answer explaining the significance of each item listed below.

Alalia – **Pg. 469, ¶ 3** – Alalia was the name of the trading post the Phocaeans built for themselves on the island of Corsica, or as the Greeks called it, Cyrnus.

Celt/Gaul – **Pg. 470, ¶ 3** – Celt is an anachronistic name for the tribes who roamed around in western central Europe between 600 and 500 BC. Referred to later as Celts, or "Gauls," by the Greeks and Romans, in 600 and 500 BC they were merely a scattering of tribes with no ethnic identity.

Carthage – **Pg. 471, ¶ 5** – Carthage was a city on the northern coast of Africa at the bottom of the Mediterranean Sea. Carthage was about three hundred years old in 550 BC, and was ruled by Mago, the first Carthaginian monarch of whom we have any historical record.

Hallstatt – **Pg. 470, ¶ 5** – Hallstatt is a name for the civilization of people who spread from modern Austria across to the southern Loire River who buried their dead in a very particular style. The name Hallstatt comes from the best-known of these burial sites south of the Danube.

Horatius – **Pg. 476, ¶ 9 to Pg. 477, ¶ 2** – Horatius was a Roman soldier who single-handedly held off Etruscan forces lead by Lars Porsena on the bridge that connected the Janiculum to the city. Horatius fought courageously until Roman demolition forces arrived to destroy the bridge; Roman legend claims he went down with the bridge, plunged into the Tiber, and then swam across.

Janiculum – **Pg. 476, ¶ 7** – The Janiculum was the name for the eastern lands that lay on the other side of the Tiber outside of Rome.

Lars Porsena – **Pg. 476, ¶ 5 and Pg. 477, ¶ 3** – Lars Porsena, king of the Etruscan city of Clusium, led an attack against Rome to reinstate Estruscan dominance after the fall of Tarquin the Proud. Lars Porsena besieged the city, but was not able to claim victory; Porsena agreed to withdraw after swearing out a peace treaty with Rome.

Massalia – **Pg. 469, ¶ 4 to Pg. 470, ¶ 1** – Massalia was a colony built by the Phocaeans on the coast of southern France. The colony acted as a trading post to the west, where the Phocaeans could exchange goods with the Celts.

Penteconter – **Pg. 469, 2-4** – A penteconter was a ship with fifty oars and square mainsail that was particular to the Phocaeans. A penteconter was perfect for trade because it carried a large crew, all of whom could fight, which made it much more daunting to pirates than a merchant ship.

Phocaea – **Pg. 469, ¶ 1 & 2 – Phocaea was a Greek city on the Ionian coast that had once been an ally of the Lydians.**

Stonehenge – **Pg. 479, ¶ 4 – Stonehenge was one of a set of many huge rings of standing stones found in England used for something that had to do with the sky. Construction of Stonehenge began sometime around 3100 BC and continued over the next two thousand years.**

Tarquin the Younger/Tarquin the Proud – **Pg. 474, ¶ 4 & 5 and Pg. 475, ¶ 3 – Tarquin the Younger/ Tarquin the Proud usurped the Roman throne from his uncle Servius Tullius. After his son raped a noblewoman, rebellion broke out in Rome, and Tarquin the Proud was forced to flee into Etruria.**

Section II: Comprehension

Write a two/three sentence answer to each of the following questions.

1. From where did the Celts originate? How are the Celts connected to the Hittites, Mycenaeans, and the Aryans?
A1. – Pg. 470, ¶ 4 – The origin of the Celts was Indo-European, which means they came from the same homeland between the Caspian and the Black seas once occupied by the peoples later known as Hittites, Mycenaeans, and Aryans. The Celts are not only connected to the Hittites, Mycenaeans and Aryans by their point of origin, but also by similarities in their languages.

2. What did the Hallstatt tribes include in the graves of their dead? What was the configuration of graves for dead Hallstatt chiefs and soldiers?
A2. – Pg. 470, ¶ 6 to Pg. 471, ¶ 1 – The Hallstatt tribes filled their graves with gold jewelry, swords and spears, food and drink, and dishes for use by the dead. Their dead chiefs were surrounded by the graves of warriors. Dead warriors were buried with their long iron swords, their most precious possession.

3. What was the Etruscan League, and why was it formed?
A3. – Pg. 471, ¶ 2 & 3 – The Etruscan League was an association of twelve Etruscan cities. It was formed in order to stop the spread of Greek colonies along the northern coast of the Mediterranean, territory the Etruscans considered their own to exploit.

4. What prompted the Carthaginians to join the Etruscans in an alliance against the Phocaeans at Alalia?
A4. – Pg. 471, ¶ 6 and Footnote – The Carthaginians were planting trading colonies around the Mediterranean at the same time as the Phocaeans. Excavations suggest that Phoenician settlers built a trading post of their own at Massalia before the Phocaeans arrived. Carthaginians teamed up with the Etruscans because they wanted to make sure their own territories on the Mediterranean were protected, and to get back at the Phocaeans for taking over Massalia.

5. What was the outcome of the sea battle at Alalia between the Etruscans, Carthaginians and the Phocaeans?

A5. – Pg. 473, ¶ 2-5 – **After the sea battle at Alalia, the Phocaeans admitted defeat, loaded up their womenfolk and children and retreated to Rhegium. The Etruscans became top dog; they took over Corsica, cut Massalia off from Alalia, and built trading posts as far west as the coast of Spain. The Carthaginians made a treaty with the Etruscans, took Sardinia for themselves, and also extended their reach to the Spanish coast.**

6. On what criteria did Servius Tullius base his division of the Roman people into different classes, and how did this division translate into defense of the city?
A6. – Pg. 474, ¶ 1 – **Servius Tullius divided the people of Rome into six classes based on wealth. When it came to battle in defense of the city, the richest Romans were expected to defend the city with bronze helmet, greaves, breastplate, sword and spear, while the poorest were required to bring only slings and stones.**

7. Describe the events that led up to the rebellion against the Roman monarchy.
A7. – Pg. 474 ¶ 5 to Pg. 475, ¶ 2 – **After Tarquin the Younger took the Roman throne by force from his uncle Servius Tullius, he had the old man and his loyal supporters killed. Tarquin the Younger had innocent people convicted of capital crimes so he could confiscate their money, he did not consult the Senate on matters of public business and he made and unmade alliances with whom he pleased. The last straw came when his son raped a Roman noblewoman, Lucretia, who subsequently killed herself because of the shame of the crime. Indignation over the rape and death of Lucretia, and anger over the tyrannical acts of Tarquin the Younger, led to rebellion against the monarchy.**

8. Who took power in Rome after the collapse of the monarchy? How did the new system of government work? In your answer, make sure to define the term "consuls."
A8. – Pg. 475, ¶ 4 – **After the fall of the Roman monarchy, Lucretia's husband and one of his trusted friends were elected leaders of the city by popular vote. They were called consuls: the highest office in Roman government. The two men were given kinglike powers to declare war and make decrees, however their time in power would only last a year, and each man could veto the other's decrees.**

9. What did Tarquin the Proud's expulsion from Rome signify in terms of the relationship between the Etruscans and the Romans? How was this solidified by the treaty made with Lars Porsena?
A9. – Pg. 476, ¶ 2 & 4 and Pg. 477, ¶ 4 – **Tarquin the Proud's expulsion from Rome signified the throwing off of Etruscan dominance. The treaty made with Lars Porsena revealed that the Romans and Etruscans were now balanced in power.**

10. Describe the details of Rome's treaty with Carthage.
A10. – Pg. 477, ¶ 5 to Pg. 478, ¶ 1 – **Rome and Carthage agreed that no Roman ships were to sail father west than Fair Promontory, and if a Roman captain was blown off course and did land in the forbidden territory, he was to repair his ship and leave within five days, without buying or carrying anything away, and any trade that took place east of Fair Promontory had to be carried out in the presence of a town clerk. In return, Carthaginians agreed to leave the entire Latin population alone, to build no forts near them, and to refrain from entering Latin territory with weapons.**

11. Why did the Gauls move further and further into Etruscan land? To where did the Gaulish people spread?

A11. – Pg. 478, ¶ 3 & 4 – The Gauls moved into Etruscan land because of a population explosion; Gaul had become so rich and populous that its people could not be effectively controlled. The Gaulish people went north into southern Germany, south into the Alps, down into the Po River valley, and finally they crossed the Po and moved into the area between the Po and the Apennine ridge.

12. How did internal strife cause the spread of the Celtic culture?

A12. – Pg. 479, ¶ 3 & 4 – Internal strife amongst the Celts caused the Celts to search for new areas to settle. This search led to the spread of Celtic culture throughout Italy, over on the western coast of Europe, and perhaps even to the island of Britain.

13. Who had the right to vote in Rome? For what reasons did the voting populace elect to have a dictator just eight years after the Republic began?

A13. – Pg. 480, ¶ 3 – In Rome, citizens in the army had the right to vote. The voting populace elected to have a dictator because of a whole constellation of military emergencies: war with various nearby cities, hostility from the Sabines, looming attack from other Latin towns, unrest from within the city, and threat from invading Gauls.

14. How did a Roman dictator come to power, and how long did his rule last? What powers were granted to the dictator? How did the presence of a dictator keep Rome's unruly population under control?

A14. – Pg. 480, ¶ 4 & 5 – The Roman dictator had to be appointed by ruling consuls, and was in power only for six months at a time. The dictator was allowed to exercise the power of life and death inside Rome, with no obligation to consult the people. The dictator's presence scared Rome's unruly population straight; fear of death meant an obedient public.

Section III: Critical Thinking

The student may use her text to answer this question.

Sometimes, ancient cultures can speak to us from the grave. For example, in the case of the Hallstatt civilization, archaeologists have learned much about these ancient peoples from the clues left behind in their graves. This is also true of the Celts. Write a paragraph first explaining what "Celt" means, and second, how the artifacts found in Celtic graves help us to understand why the Celts were given this name by the Greeks and Romans. Finally, describe what we know about the Celtic takeover of the Hallstatt civilization, as evidenced by the stories their gravesites tell.

The student should first look up what "Celt" means. On page 478, ¶ 5, the text reads "The Celts must have been a fearsome sight, charging down the mountain slopes towards the walls of the Etruscan cities. The word 'Celt,' given to these tribes by the Greeks and Romans, comes from an Indo-European root meaning 'to strike.'" The weapons found in Celtic graves testify to their skill at war: seven-foot spears, iron swords with thrusting tips and cutting edges, war chariots, helmets and shields.

The Celts left other signs of their dominance in the layers of earth near their settlements. The Celts used knots, curves, and mazelike lines as decorations, and these began to overlay the old Hallstatt settlements, suggesting Celtic dominance.

The leaders of the Celts were buried with two-wheeled war chariots, and these show up in Britain around 500 BC, further evidence of the Celts' breadth and power.

The spreading Celtic culture was given the name La Tène, and the style of art found in La Tène graves is what we now identify as "Celtic." The characteristics of La Tène culture replaced those of the Hallstatt, as testified by the sites of Celtic living that overwhelmed and spread beyond the remains of the Hallstatt civilization.

EXAMPLE ANSWER: The word "Celt" comes from an Indo-European root meaning "to strike." The Celts were buried with seven-foot spears, iron swords with thrusting tips and cutting edges, war chariots, helmets and shields, supporting the idea that the Celts were skilled and well-equipped warriors. The Celts clearly used their power to overwhelm the Hallstatt civilization, as evidenced by artifacts found in both Celtic and Hallstatt sites. Hallstatt graves, identified by the two-wheel war chariots buried with Celtic leaders, show up in Britain around 500 BC, meaning the Celts were spreading far across the ancient world. In the phase of Celtic culture known as "La Tène," the signature decoration of the Celts, knots, curves, and mazelike lines, overlay the old Hallstatt settlements, suggesting Celtic dominance. The characteristics of La Tène culture replaced those of the Hallstatt, as testified by the sites of Celtic living that overwhelmed and spread beyond the remains of the Hallstatt civilization.

CHAPTER SIXTY-ONE: KINGDOMS AND REFORMERS

The student may use his text when answering the questions in sections I and II.

Section I: Who, What, Where

Write a one or two-sentence answer explaining the significance of each item listed below.

Bimbisara – **Pg. 489, ¶ 5 – Bimbisara, crowned king of Magadha in 544 BC, was the first Indian empire builder. He conquered the city of Anga, married his way into control over part of Kosal, and he built roads all across his kingdom, which allowed him to travel around easily and to police the payment of taxes.**

Brahman – **Pg. 483, ¶ 2 – Brahman was the term given to a person born into a priestly family. A person born into the brahman class inherited the privilege to make sacrifices.**

Gana-sangha – **Pg. 485, ¶ 1 & 2 – Gana-sangha were tribes with roots in the Ganga valley that resisted being enfolded into any one of the sixteen mahajanapadas. Because the gana-sanghas did not share the ritual practices of the Indians in the mahajanapada they were most likely of non-Aryan descent.**

Jainism – **Pg. 487, ¶ 2 – Jainism was the name of the doctrine taught by the Mahavira, and followers of Jainism were called Jains. Jainism taught extreme self-denial, and the obligation to respect all life.**

Kshatriya – **Pg. 483, ¶ 1 – Kshatriya was the term given to a person born into the ruling clan of a mahajanapada. To be born into the kshatriya was to belong, by right, to the elite and powerful of the kingdom.**

Mahajanapada – **Pg. 482, ¶ 1-3 – Mahajanapada was the term for the sixteen semi-stable Indian kingdoms formed between the mythical battle of the Mahabharata and the middle of the sixth century BC. These kingdoms are mentioned in tales preserved by Buddhist oral tradition.**

Nataputta Vardhamana/The Mahavira – **Pg. 486, ¶ 3 to Pg. 487, ¶ 1 – Nataputta Vardhamana, or the Mahavira, was born into a gana-sangha as a prince and rich man, but he rejected the wealth and privilege of his birth and spent twelve years in silence and meditation. After this period of meditation, Nataputta Vardhamana taught that man should free himself from the chains of the material universe by rejecting the passions that chain him to the material world. His followers became the sect known as "Jains."**

Nirvana – **Pg. 488, ¶ 4 – According to Buddhist teachings, Nirvana is a state achieved by an enlightened person, such as Siddhartha Gautama. It is the knowledge of a truth which is caused by nothing, dependent on nothing, and leads to nothing, a way of existence impossible to define in words.**

Shudra – **Pg. 485, ¶ 5 to Pg. 486, ¶ 1 – Shudra was the name of the fourth and subordinate class of people in India during the time of the sixteen mahajanapadas. The shudra, most likely a conquered people, were slaves and servants that could be killed or exiled at the whim of their** master, and were barred from hearing the sacred Vedas when they were read.

Siddhartha Gautama/Buddha – Pg. 487, ¶ 3 and Pg. 488, ¶ 3 – Siddhartha Gautama, or the Buddha, was a reformer born into a gana-sangha family of great wealth. Siddhartha Gautama rejected this way of life, and after many attempts to reach enlightenment, came to the answer that the only freedom from desire was the freedom from existence itself.

Vaishyas – Pg. 483, ¶ 3 – Vaishyas was name of the class of common people in India during the days of the sixteen kingdoms.

Section II: Comprehension

Write a two/three sentence answer to each of the following questions.

1. List and define the roots of the word "mahajanapada."
A1. – Pg. 483, ¶ 1 – Mahajanapada is a word with roots from several other words; the early nomadic Aryan warrior clans had called themselves "jana," meaning tribe. The warrior clans that settled in the Ganga River valley and claimed land for themselves called themselves "janapada," meaning tribes with land. The sixteen mahajanapada, or "great mahajanapada" were tribes with land who absorbed other tribes and had become kingdoms.

2. Why did priests have so much power in sixth century BC India?
A2. – Pg. 483, ¶ 2 – The power of priests in sixth century BC India came from an Aryan tradition of daily sacrifices and offerings; they had been performing these rituals since their journey south into India. The priests who performed the sacrifices had been the first aristocracy of Indian society, and they continued to hold their influence in the sixteen mahajanapadas.

3. How could a man born into the vaishya class become a king? How could a common man become a priest?
A3. – Pg. 483, ¶ 4 – A man born into the vaishya class could become a king if the priests carried out a ritual to bestow sacred power upon him. A common man could not become a priest, only a man born into the Brahman class could take up the job of a priest.

4. With animal sacrifices out of favor in the growing urban populations of India, what services did priests perform in order to keep their central role in society?
A4. – Pg. 484, ¶ 2 – Rather than sacrificing, the priests governed the proper performance of bloodless rituals which occupied the place of offerings: rituals carried out to honor the flame of the hearth, to acknowledge the coming of dusk, to honor deities by caring for their images, and rituals to mark marriages and funerals.

5. What five principles did the Mahavira teach? In your answer, make sure to explain each principle.
A5. – Pg. 486, ¶ 5 – The Mahavira taught ahisma, nonviolence against all living things; satya, truthfulness; asteya, refraining from theft of any kind; brahmacharya, the rejection of sexual pleasure; and aparigraha, detachment from all material things.

6. What experiences caused Siddhartha Gautama to set out on a self-exposed exile?
A6. – Pg. 487, ¶ 5 to Pg. 488, ¶ 1 – One day Siddhartha Gautama went for a drive in the park

and saw an ancient man with broken teeth and a curved back, trembling. Another day, he went for a drive and saw a man riddled with disease, and a corpse. Finally, one night as they slept, Siddhartha looked at the women in the palace who were paid to entertain him and saw their bodily excretions and loathsome nakedness, which seemed like a cemetery filled with dead, rotting bodies. It was after these brushes with mortality that Siddhartha set out on his own self-imposed exile.

7. Why did Bimbisara want to conquer Anga and make it part of Magadha?
A7. – Pg. 489, ¶ 5 – Bimbisara wanted to absorb Anga into Magadha because Anga controlled river access to the ocean by way of the Bay of Bengal. Also, Anga contained the important city of Campa, the primary port from which ships sailed out for trade and down the coast to the south.

Section III: Critical Thinking

While it is common to associate the teachings of the Buddha with religion, it is less frequent that we think of Buddha as a political figure. Explain how the Buddha's religious beliefs were also a political position. In your answer, make sure to include the political ramifications of self-reliance. *Towards the end of the chapter (page 488, ¶ 5 to page 489, ¶ 2), the text states that the Buddha's position was not merely a spiritual discovery, but also a political position. If the student is stuck at the beginning of this question, ask him to recall the definition of nirvana. The Buddha's teachings were meant to bring a follower to nirvana, a truth that lies outside of any material ties. Nirvana lies outside of existence itself, meaning that no earthly bounds exist in nirvana.*

Ask the student how nirvana is different from the concept of reincarnation associated with brahmanical Hinduism. The caste system at work in the mahajanapadas meant that an Indian born into, for example, the shudra class of slaves and servants, would most likely be born into that subordinate class again and again. How did one move up in social class if he was constantly reborn into the class of his origins? The Buddha's teachings offered an escape from this endless cycle of suffering; if you believed in nirvana, you could escape from the caste system by reaching enlightenment. To believe in Buddhism meant that one no longer believed in the perpetuation of a class system fueled by reincarnation.

The Buddha also taught that man must rely on himself, not on the power of a leader, to solve his problems. Self-reliance resists authority, lessening the power of a king and increasing the power of an individual. Again, this is a political choice that shifted power away from traditional Indian leaders, kings and priests, to individuals who were historically dominated, the shudra.

EXAMPLE ANSWER: The Buddha's teachings were meant to bring his followers to nirvana, a truth that lies outside of any material or earthly ties. Conversely, brahmanical Hinduism taught reincarnation, which meant that an Indian born into, for example, the shudra class of slaves and servants, would most likely be born into that subordinate class again and again. The Buddha's teachings offered an escape from this endless cycle of suffering; if you believed in nirvana, you could escape from the caste system by reaching enlightenment. To believe in Buddhism meant that one no longer believed in the perpetuation of a class system fueled by

reincarnation. This political position took power away from the rigid classifications between the castes.

Similarly, the Buddha's insistence on self-reliance was a rebellion against the standing political structure of India at the time of the sixteen kingdoms. Self-reliance resists authority, lessening the power of a king and increasing the power of an individual. Self-reliance shifted power away from traditional Indian leaders, kings and priests, to individuals who were thought to have no power at all.

CHAPTER SIXTY TWO: THE POWER OF DUTY AND THE ART OF WAR

The student may use her text when answering the questions in sections I and II.

Section I: Who, What, Where

Write a one or two-sentence answer explaining the significance of each item listed below.

King Ching – Pg. 493, ¶ 6 – **King Ching succeeded his great grandfather King Ting on the Zhou throne. King Ching wanted to appoint his favorite son, not the eldest son, as his successor, but died in 521 BC before he made the appointment formal.**

Duke of Chu/King of Chu – Pg. 493, ¶ 1 & 4 – **The Duke of Chu became the King of Chu after attacking a band of Jung barbarians outside of Zhou, and inquiring about the Nine Cauldrons of the Zhou. After battling the Jung, the King of Chu defeated the Ts'ai and became leader of the Cheng state.**

Prince Kai/King Ching II – Pg. 494, ¶ 2 & 3 – **Prince Kai believed he was the rightful heir of the Zhou throne after the death of King Ching. With the help of the Duke of Jin, who declared Kai King Ching II, the rightful king in exile, Ching II attacked Zhou and reduced King Tao to a vassal.**

Kong Fuzi/Confucius – Pg. 494, ¶ 5 & 8, page 497, ¶ 3, 4, 5 – **Kong Fuzi, better known as Confucius, was a Chinese philosopher. He knew hundreds of Chinese rituals, rites, ceremonies, poems and songs by heart, and he treasured order and stability. He drew on the wisdom of the past to show people and rulers of the present how to live dutifully and harmoniously.**

Li ching – Pg. 495, ¶ 5 – **The Li ching was a collection of Chinese rituals and ceremonies put together by Confucius. The Li ching regulated everything from the proper attitude of mourners to the orderly succession of monthly tasks.**

Lun yu – Pg. 495, ¶ 5 – **The Lun yu was a collection of Confucius's sayings gathered together by his followers. The Lun yu is also known as the Analects.**

King Tao – Pg. 494, ¶ 1 – **King Tao was supposed to succeed King Ching on the Zhou throne, but when his older brother took the throne, Tao killed him and took the throne for himself. King Tao was eventually dethroned by another older brother, King Ching II.**

Shi jin – Pg. 495, ¶ 5 – **The Shi jin, or the Classic of Poetry, was a collection of the oldest poems and songs of China complied by Confucius.**

Sun-Tzu – Pg. 497, ¶ 4 and Pg. 498, ¶ 2 – **Sun-Tzu, a general who fought for the Duke of Wu, was also a philosopher who wrote the *Art of War*. Sun-Tzu's philosophy was to break the resistance of one's enemy without fighting, through the art of deception.**

Ting – Pg. 491, ¶ 3 – **Ting was the second grandson of King Hsiang, and he took the ceremonial Zhou throne in 606 BC.**

Section II: Comprehension

Write a two/three sentence answer to each of the following questions.

1. Name the Chinese states that were part of the Five Hegemonies. What four other states had major power at this time, and what were their locations in relation to the Five Hegemonies?
A1. – Pg. 491, ¶ 1 and Pg. 492, Map – The Chinese states that were part of the Five Hegemonies were Jin, Qi, Chu, Ch'in and Yueh. The four other major powers at this time were Lu and Wu, both east of the Five Hegemonies, with borders on the coast of the Yellow Sea; Cheng which bordered the Zhou land to the east; and the Sung, which followed Cheng on the eastern side.

2. Who were the Jin fighting in the north? What was the result of this ongoing battle?
A2. – Pg. 491, ¶ 2 – The Jin were fighting against the northern barbarian tribes known as the Ti. The war that continued for decades gradually extended the Jin border farther and farther to the north.

3. Describe the conquests of the southern state of Chu in the two and half centuries since the Zhou move.
A3. – Pg. 492, ¶ 1 – Chu soldiers had marched steadily to the north and east since the Zhou move. The Chu took over several states that are now disappeared from the map, first Deng, then Shen and Xi, next Jiang and Huang, followed by Chen and Cai, until finally the Chu were knocking at Zhou's door.

4. What is the significance of the Duke of Chu calling himself "King of Chu?" How is this title connected to the Duke of Chu's retreat from Zhou?
A4. – Pg. 493, ¶ 1 & 3 – The Duke of Chu's self-title "King of Chu" was significant because there had never been a duke who had been given the royal title. It seems that the Zhou king agreed to let the Duke of Chu keep his royal title, and so the King of Chu returned south without waging battle with the Zhou.

5. Why did the Lu court first call on Confucius? What did Confucius do for the court after he was hired away from his record-keeping job?
A5. – Pg. 494, ¶ 9 to Pg. 495, ¶ 2 – The Lu court first called on Confucius to make sure that visitors to the court were received with the proper rites. The Duke of Lu consulted Confucius on a regular basis, and he was hired away from his record-keeping job to tutor the sons of at least one high Lu official.

6. While Confucius was not the inventor of the philosophy laid out in the Analects, how were his teachings innovative?
A6. – Pg. 495, ¶ 6 to Pg. 496, ¶ 1 – Confucius was innovative in his belief that turning back to the past was necessary in order to find a way forwards. His study of China's past told him that, in a fractious China, both tranquility and virtue lay in the orderly performance of duties. He believed that it was through the rules of propriety that order and character were established.

7. What happened to Confucius after he was forced to flee from Lu because the duke was driven out by a rival aristocratic family?

A7. – Pg. 496, ¶ 4 – After being forced to leave Lu, Confucius followed the exiled duke into Qi, but while the duke was welcomed, jealous Qi courtiers blocked Confucius from the duke, putting him out of a job. Confucius returned to Lu, declaring himself out of politics, devoting most of his time to writing the history of Lu, now known as the Spring and Autumn annals.

8. How did constant war against barbarians affect the Jin state, particularly by 505 BC?

A8. – Pg. 497, ¶ 1 – In the constant campaigning against the barbarians, several large families of Jin had grown steadily richer; one family claimed by birth the hereditary right to command the army; another claimed a huge amount of barbarian land and made alliances and treaties with the barbarian tribe. By 505 BC, the divisions hampered Jin fighting against the barbarians, and the Jin had to retreat from a siege against a barbarian town without success.

9. Briefly describe the period of turmoil and war in China around 493/492 BC.

A9. – Pg. 497, ¶ 2 & 3 – In 493, Cheng and Jin waged a brief and vicious war with each other; in 492 Qi, Lu and Wey agreed to join with one of the Jin aristocrats and marched into Jin itself to push another Jin family off the map. At the same time, Chu was fighting against the invasions of Wu and Yueh, and the Zhou monarch had ceased to matter.

10. On what did Sun-Tzu believe war was based? Considering the warring Chinese states that surrounded Sun-Tzu, why did he think this way about war?

A10. – Pg. 498, ¶ 2 – Sun-Tzu believed that all warfare was based on deception; the only way to win at war was to be more deceptive than your enemy. Sun-Tzu lived in a country where friends were as likely to be plotting against one another as their enemies; deception became a way of life.

Section III: Critical Thinking

The student may not use her text to answer this question.

The further away we move from the beginnings of ancient Chinese history, the looser the grasp of Zhou power on the Chinese states becomes. In this chapter, we read about the first visible crack in the Zhou's stronghold. Write a paragraph explaining why the King of Chu's demand to see the Nine Tripods was actually an assault on Zhou dominance. In your answer, make sure to first explain how the Duke of Chu came to be called the King of Chu, and the significance of this name change.

The student will first explain how the Duke of Chu came to be known as the King of Chu. This is a reiteration of Comprehension question 4. The Duke of Chu was the leader of a rapidly growing state. After multiple conquests, the Duke of Chu attacked the Jung, a barbarian tribe stationed outside of Zhou territory, and styled himself as "King of Chu." The Duke did this to show the Zhou his power.

After his campaign against the Jung, the King of Chu sent a messenger to inquire about the Zhou's Nine Tripods. The Nine Tripods, or Nine Cauldrons, were a symbol of the Zhou's kingly power. Asking about the Tripods was like asking to see an opposing player's hand in a game of poker; the

King of Chu wanted to see the hidden power of the Zhou. While we don't know what happened between the King of Chu and the court official King Ting sent to talk his way out of answering Chu's question about the Tripods, we do know that Chu left the Zhou state without waging war, and that his title of "king" went unchallenged. Something must have been up in order for the subordinate state to challenge the power of their leader without punishment; whether the Chu could destroy Zhou, or King Ting was feeling kind, both scenarios suggest the end of Zhou dominance.

EXAMPLE ANSWER: **The Duke of Chu was the leader of a rapidly growing state. After multiple conquests, the Duke of Chu attacked the Jung, a barbarian tribe stationed outside of Zhou territory, and styled himself as "King of Chu." The Duke did this to show the Zhou his power. After his campaign against the Jung, the King of Chu sent a messenger to inquire about the Zhou's Nine Tripods. The Nine Tripods, or Nine Cauldrons, were a symbol of the Zhou's kingly power. While we don't know what happened between the King of Chu and the court official King Ting sent to talk his way out of answering Chu's question about the Tripods, we do know that Chu left the Zhou state without waging war, and that his title of "king" went unchallenged. The Zhou may not have shown the source of their power, but the concession of the kingly title to the Duke of Chu was evidence of the Zhou's waning power.**

CHAPTER SIXTY-THREE: THE SPREADING PERSIAN EMPIRE

The student may use his text when answering the questions in sections I and II.

Section I: Who, What, Where

Write a one or two-sentence answer explaining the significance of each item listed below.

Ajatashatru – **Pg. 509, ¶ 6 and Pg. 511, ¶ 4 – Ajatashatru mounted a rebellion against his father, Bimbisara, king of Magadha, in order to become king himself. Ajatashatru is credited with inventing a huge rock-throwing catapult and a new kind of war chariot and with creating India's first standing military force.**

Amasis – **Pg. 502, ¶ 6 & 8 and Pg. 503, ¶ 3 – Amasis, Apries's chief general, was called upon to put down the rebellion against the pharaoh. Instead, Amasis offered himself as king, and usurped the throne from Apries.**

Bardiya – **Pg. 505, ¶ 3 & 4 – Bardiya was the younger brother of Cambyses II. Bardiya, en route to Persia after leaving Cambyses II on campaign, disappeared without explanation.**

Battus the Prosperous – **Pg. 502, ¶ 3 – Battus the Prosperous was the third king of the Greek settlement of Cyrene, on the North African coast. Battus begged for settlers from Greece, promising everyone who came a plot of land, to which a considerable mass of people from the mainland responded.**

Massagetae – **Pg. 500, ¶ 2 – Massagetae was the name Herodotus gave to the mountain tribes in central Asia who lived near the Aral Sea and Oxus River. The Massagetae were known as fierce fighters who used bronze-tipped bows and spears, worshiped the sun, and lived off cattle and fish.**

Patizeithes – **Pg. 505, ¶ 3-5 – Patizeithes was the household manager for Cambyses II. Upon hearing of Bardiya's disappearance, Patizeithes suggested his younger brother, Smerdis, who looked so much like the lost royal brother, take Bardiya's place and declare himself king of Persia.**

Psammetichus III – **Pg. 504, ¶ 4 – Psammetichus III, pharaoh of Egypt after his father Amasis, unwisely left the waterways of the Delta undefended, allowing the Persians to besiege Memphis by land and sea. Psammetichus III was forced to surrender less than a year into his reign as Egyptian pharaoh.**

Smerdis – **Pg. 505, ¶ 5 & 7 – Smerdis, younger brother of Patizeithes, pretended to be Bardiya and usurped the Persian throne from Cambyses II. He was able to hold onto the throne for seven months by never leaving the palace compound in Susa, or calling any of the Persian noblemen who knew the real Bardiya.**

Tomyris – **Pg. 500, ¶ 3 – Tomyris, queen of the Massagetae, turned down Cyrus the Great's offer of marriage, and subsequently sent her son to attack against the Persian army. When her** son committed suicide after the failed attack on Persia, Tomyris vowed revenge on Cyrus the Great, wiped out the Persian army, and shoved the head of the fallen king into a sack of blood.

Wajet – Pg. 504, ¶ 6 – Wajet was the cobra goddess of Lower Egypt whose likeness had appeared on the Red Crown since the days of the unification.

Section II: Comprehension

Write a two/three sentence answer to each of the following questions.

1. In what kind of building was Cyrus laid to rest? How was he prepared for the afterlife? Who would watch over Cyrus's final resting place?
A1. – Pg. 501, ¶ 3 – Cyrus's tomb was a gabled stone house, carved to look like timber, that stood on the top level of a seven-level ziggurat of steps. His body was dressed in royal robes and ornaments, provided with weapons, and placed on a couch of gold. A cadre of Persian priests was given the task of living in a small house nearby as guardians of Cyrus's final resting place.

2. What was Cambyses II's first act as king? What was the motivation behind this act?
A2. – Pg. 502, ¶ 1 – Cambyses II's first act as king was to move his palace and the center of the administration from his father's capital at Pasargadea to the old Elamite capital of Susa, closer to the middle of the empire. Cambyses II did this in order to step out of his father's shadow and to establish his own power as king.

3. Why did the Egyptians rebel against Apries after the decimation of the Egyptian army by the Greeks in North Africa?
A3. – Pg. 502, ¶ 5 – The Egyptians rebelled against Apries after the Egyptian loss in North Africa because the Egyptians thought Apries had deliberately sent the troops to certain death. It was believed that Apries, who was already unpopular, sent the troops to slaughter so that there would be fewer subjects left for him to rule, thus making his reign more secure.

4. Who fought with Apries at Momemphis against the rebellious Egyptian army? What was the result of this battle?
A4. – Pg. 503, ¶ 2 & 3 – Ionian Greeks and Carians, hired mercenaries, fought with Apries against the Egyptian army. The Egyptians were victorious at Momemphis, and Apries was taken captive.

5. What was the advantage of creating a Persian navy from the resources of the Ionians and Phoenicians?
A5. – Pg. 503, ¶ 7 and Pg. 504, ¶ 1 – The Ionians of the Asian Minor coast and the Phoenician cities under Persian control both had sea-faring cultures. The Persian navy combined the skills of the Greeks and Phoenicians, two cultures familiar with, and comfortable on, the water.

6. Why did Cambyses II want to dismember the body of Amasis?
A6. – Pg. 504, ¶ 6 & 7 – While Herodotus claims Cambyses II wanted to dismember the body of Amasis as an act of gratuitous sacrilege, Cambyses II most likely attempted to get rid of the body in order to identify himself as the successor of Apries.

7. Describe Darius's professional Persian army. What did the foot soldiers in Darius's army call themselves?

A7. – Pg. 508, ¶ 6 – Darius's professional army was better fed, better trained, and more loyal than the previous Persian army. He created a professional standing core of ten thousand foot soldiers and ten thousand cavalry, with no mercenaries. The troops were bound together by a national feeling, with loyalty so strong that the foot soldiers called themselves the Companions.

8. Define satrapy and satrap. What was the risk of being a satrap?

A8. – Pg. 509, ¶ 1 – Satrapy was the name for a Persian province under Darius. A satrap was the governor of the satrapy. Each satrap was assigned a tribute which had to be sent to Susa each year, and if a satrap did not send the proper amount, or did not manage to keep his satrapy in order, he was liable to be executed.

9. How did Bimbisara's death cause a Kosal rebellion against Magadha?

A9. – Pg. 510, ¶ 2 – When Bimbisara died, his wife grieved so harshly that she died. Her brother, king of Kosal, mounted a rebellion against Magadha to reclaim the land given to Magadha as part of his sister's dowry.

10. What caused the twelve-year war between Ajatashatru and his brother, vice-regent of Anga? How was Ajatashatru able to take Kosal at the same time that he was fighting against his brother?

A10. – Pg. 511, ¶ 2 & 3 – Ajatashatru's brother, vice-regent of Anga, decided to become king of Anga. He made an alliance with the Licchavi, the gana-sangha to the north, to fight Ajatashatru; this started the war between the two brothers. Ajatashatru was able to take Kosal while also fighting his brother in Anga because a flash flood wiped out most of the army of Kosal, which had unwisely camped in a river bed.

11. How did Ajatashatru handle the Buddha's death? What did he make sure to do in order to secure the Buddha's legacy?

A11. – Pg. 511, ¶ 5 – When the Buddha died, Ajatashatru claimed that Magadha had the right to guard the Buddha's sacred legacy. In order to secure the Buddha's legacy, Ajatashatru ordered a council held at Rajagriha to collect and set down into writing the Buddha's sayings, the suttas.

12. What precious materials did Persia gain from Darius's expeditions and conquests in India?

A12. – Pg. 512, ¶ 3 – Persia gained timbers from the Gandhara and a yearly tribute of gold dust from the Hindush satrapy as a result of Darius's expeditions and conquests in India.

13. What is the significance of the Babylonian inscription about a woman from India who kept an inn in the city of Kish?

A13. – Pg. 513, ¶ 2 – The Babylonian inscription about a woman from India living in Kish is significant because it shows how Persia had become a bridge between India and peoples farther west. The woman did not move from India to Babylon, rather she moved from one part of Darius's Persian empire to another.

Section III: Critical Thinking

In this chapter, we found out that the successful and skilled warrior Cambyses II, king of expanding Persia, died suddenly, supposedly from a self-inflicted sword wound that turned gangrenous. Cambyses II's death and the events that followed were surrounded by mystery. Write a brief description of how Cambyses II came to fatally wound himself, followed by an explanation of what you think really happened to his brother, Bardiya. In your answer, argue for only one scenario related to Bardiya's disappearance.

A. How Cambyses II came to fatally wound himself (Pg. 505, ¶3-6):
The oldest sources say that Cambyses II, when he began the Egyptian campaign, took his brother Bardiya with him, but then changed his mind and sent Bardiya back to Persia. On his return home, Bardiya disappeared. Patizeithes, in charge of Cambyses II's household, took advantage of Bardiya's disappearance and convinced his brother, Smerdis, who looked like the lost heir, to take the throne. Patizeithes sent word to the front that Bardiya had usurped his brother's throne. When Cambyses II heard the news, he immediately ran to his horse and vaulted onto it, but in the process he knocked the scabbard off his sword and sliced himself in the thigh. The wound turned into gangrene and three weeks later Cambyses II was dead.

B1. Cambyses II (Pg. 507, ¶ 7):
Darius claims that Cambyses II killed Bardiya. If Bardiya really did have designs on the Persian throne, perhaps Cambyses II killed him to remove any threat to his kingship.

B2. Darius (Pg. 507, ¶ 2 & 3):
If Bardiya did not disappear and arrived safely at Susa, where he did mount a coup against his brother and seize the throne, then Darius had the most to benefit from Bardiya's death. If it was Bardiya on the throne, the man Darius killed was the legitimate heir to the Persian throne, the son of Cyrus the Great. Getting rid of legitimate heirs meant that Darius could claim the throne without the challenge of a royal bloodline, and start a new dynasty.

B3. Patizeithes (Pg. 507, ¶ 7):
If Patizeithes's brother Smerdis really did look like Bardiya, then Patizeithes would do best out of Bardiya's disappearance. Patizeithes could put his brother on the throne, and relax in the spoils of royalty, instead of just watching over them.

EXAMPLE ANSWER: Cambyses II took Bardiya with him on campaign against Egypt, but then changed his mind and sent Bardiya back to Susa. On his return home, Bardiya disappeared. Patizeithes, in charge of Cambyses II's household, took advantage of Bardiya's disappearance and convinced his brother, Smerdis, who looked like the lost heir, to take the throne. Patizeithes sent word to the front that Bardiya had usurped his brother's throne. When Cambyses II heard the news, he immediately ran to his horse, and when he jumped on it, he managed to stab himself in the leg. The wound turned into gangrene and three weeks later Cambyses II was dead.

Option B1:

I think Cambyses II killed his brother. If he heard even a little murmur that his brother wanted to take his throne, it would be easiest for Cambyses II to simply kill him off. This makes sense because Cambyses II dragged Bardiya out into the middle of nowhere, only to send him home, during which time he could have had him killed en route and then claim his disappearance was a mystery.

Option B2:

I think Darius killed Bardiya. It is unlikely that a prince would simply disappear, so Darius probably made up the story about the usurper so that he could murder Bardiya without question. Even if it was Bardiya on the throne, Darius would still benefit from his death. With Bardiya out of the way, Darius was one step closer to the throne: without a bloodline to contest, Darius could become king of Persia and start a new dynasty.

Option B3:

I think Bardiya really did disappear, and Patizeithes took advantage of his good luck to put his look-alike brother on the throne. After all, Patizeithes's job was to watch over Cambyses II's household, meaning he could look at, but not touch, the spoils of royalty. With his brother on the throne, Patizeithes could live the lifestyle that had been dangled in front of him.

CHAPTER SIXTY-FOUR: THE PERSIAN WARS

The student may use her text when answering the questions in sections I and II.

Section I: Who, What, Where

Write a one or two-sentence answer explaining the significance of each item listed below.

Aeschylus – **Pg. 532, ¶ 3** – Aeschylus was a Greek playwright who witnessed and wrote about the Persian Wars. In his play *The Persians*, Aeschylus recounts the Greek and Persian battles in the Peloponnese.

Amyntas I – **Pg. 518, ¶ 3** – Amyntas I was the ninth Argead king of Macedonia. Instead of fighting against the invading Persians, Amyntas I made an alliance with the Persian king and offered his daughter in marriage to Megabazus's son.

Argead – **Pg. 517, ¶ 6 to Pg. 518, ¶ 1** – The Argead was a warrior-chief clan that spawned the first Macedonian kings. When the mostly Greek Argead moved from the south to the land around the Thermaic Gulf, they built a capital city at Aegae, organized an army, and collected taxes.

Battle of Marathon – **Pg. 529, ¶ 5 & 6** – The Battle of Marathon, where a small number of Athenian hoplites fought a large Persian army and navy, was a staggering victory for Athens. Herodotus claims that 6,400 Persians died, as opposed to only 192 Athenians.

Battle of Thermopylae – **Pg. 531, ¶ 2-5** – The Battle of Thermopylae was fought between the Persians, who had been given the location of a hidden mountain road around the Thermopylae pass, and three hundred Spartans. The Spartans fought until they were wiped out; later, the heroism of the soldiers who fell at the Battle of Thermopylae would become one of the most famous acts of heroism in history.

Cleomenes – **Pg. 523, ¶ 3** – Cleomenes, king of Sparta, marched towards Athens in 508 to overthrow the tyrannous Hippias.

Helot – **Pg. 523, ¶ 4** – Helot was the name of the huge underclass of Spartans who were viewed by the native Spartans to be untrustworthy as citizens. The helots were slaves and laborers.

Hoplite – **Pg. 529, ¶ 4** – Hoplite was the term for an Athenian foot soldier. The hoplites were named after their shields, the Athenian hoplons.

Hoplon – **Pg. 529, ¶ 4** – A hoplon, the shield used by the Athenian hoplites, had grips at the side rather than the center. The hoplon was designed to leave the right arm free for spear use, which meant that it exposed part of the user's right-hand side, but it jutted out to the left far enough to cover the right side of the next hoplite over.

Leonidas – **Pg. 531, ¶ 2 & 5** – Leonidas succeeded Cleomenes as king of Sparta. Leonidas died fighting against the Persians at Thermopylae; his body was beheaded and nailed up on a cross by Xerxes.

Mandrocles – **Pg. 515, ¶ 3 & 4** – Mandrocles, an Ionian engineer who worked for Darius, built a bridge made of low, flat-decked ships, roped together to from a floating foundation for a plank road covered with dirt and stones, across the Bosphorus Strait. This was the first pontoon bridge in history.

Marathonomachoi – **Pg. 529, ¶ 8 to Pg. 530, ¶ 1** – Marathonomachoi was the name for the men who fought at the Battle of Marathon. They were honored veterans who were revered for their role in guaranteeing Athenian freedom from Persia.

Mardonius – **Pg. 534, ¶ 2** – Mardonius, son-in-law of Xerxes, was put in control of the Persian army in Greece after Xerxes left to squash a Babylonian rebellion. Mardonius was killed during battle at Plataea; his body was never recovered.

Megabazus – **Pg. 517, ¶ 2 & 3 and Pg. 518, ¶ 4** – Megabazus was Darius's most trusted general, and was responsible for the Persian conquest of Thrace. Because of his success at Thrace, Megabazus was able to take Macedonia for Persian with no coercion; the general was received with honor.

Miltiades – **Pg. 529, ¶ 4 and Pg. 530, ¶ 1** – Miltiades was the commander of the Athenian hoplites during the Battle of Marathon. Though Athens was victorious, Miltiades was viewed as a failure because he was unable to capture the Persian-loyal island of Paros, and he died shortly after of a gangrenous wound.

Pausanias – **Pg. 534, ¶ 2** – Pausanias, nephew of Leonidas, was both a general and the regent for Leonidas's young son, king of Sparta. Pausanias led the victorious assault on the Persians at Plataea.

Peisistratus – **Pg. 519, ¶ 5 and Pg. 522, ¶ 4 & 5** – Peisistratus was the democratic leader of the Men of the Hills, and would stop at nothing to gain power in Athenian government. After working in silver mines for about ten years, Peisistratus hired an army of mercenaries and forcefully took over Athens, ruling as tyrant to a generally accepting public until his death.

Pheidippides – **Pg. 528, ¶ 7 and Footnote** – Pheidippides, a trained runner, was sent from Marathon to Sparta for assistance against approaching Persian troops. Pheidippides was said to have covered the 140 miles between Sparta and Athens in barely twenty-four hours, a feat of endurance still remembered in the name of the longest Olympic footrace, the marathon.

Royal Road – **Pg. 514, ¶ 4 to Pg. 515, ¶ 1** – The Royal Road was built by Darius of Persia to connect Susa to Sardis, his secondary center of administration. The Royal Road was dotted with post stations for the change of horses, so that a messenger could rapidly get from the west to the capital and back again.

Skudra – **Pg. 517, ¶ 4** – Skudra was the name of the Persian satrapy composed of conquered Thracian cities.

Themistocles – **Pg. 532, ¶ 4 and Pg. 534, ¶ 1** – Themistocles sent a message to Xerxes encouraging the Persian leader to attack the Peloponnese, a trick designed to help the Greeks triumph over the Persians. After the Persian defeat, Themistocles sent another message to Xerxes, this time telling the king that the Greek fleet intended to sail up to the Hellespont and rip up the Persians' pontoon bridge, which caused the Persians to retreat from Greece.

Section II: Comprehension

Write a two/three sentence answer to each of the following questions.

1. Why was it hard to pinpoint a homeland for the ancient Scythians? Where was the Scythian homeland in 516 BC?
A1. – Pg. 514, ¶ 2 – It was hard to pinpoint a homeland for the ancient Scythians because they moved constantly. In 516 BC, the center of their homeland lay between the two great rivers that ran into the Black Sea: the Danube to the west, and the Don River to the east.

2. How did the Scythians avoid war with the invading Persians around 516 BC?
A2. – Pg. 516, ¶ 2 – The Scythians avoided war with the Persians by constantly retreating in front of the invading troops. As the Scythians moved, they filled in wells and springs, and torched trees and grasslands, meaning the Persians had to constantly forage for food and water. Eventually, tired and hungry, Darius turned his men around and headed back to Persian territory without a fight.

3. Who were the Illyrians and the Paeonians, and what made them give up attacking Macedonian borders?
A3. – Pg. 518, ¶ 2 & 4 – The Illyrians were a loose alliance of tribes west of Macedonia, and the Paeonians were Thracian tribes found north of Macedonia, both of which caused troubles at Macedonia's borders. The Illyrians and Paeonians left Macedonia alone once an alliance was made between Amyntas and King Darius; neither group would attack Macedonia since doing so might be to risk Persian wrath.

4. How was the Athenian government organized under Solon's reforms? How could a man with no land eventually gain the right to vote?
A4. – Pg. 519, ¶ 2 & 3 – The Athenian government was organized into three levels under Solon's reforms: the archons; the Council of Four Hundred, drawn by lot from the middle- and upper-class citizens of Athens; and the Assembly, made up of the citizens, or property owners, of Athens. Solon had legislated that the sons of citizens inherited citizenship, so if one's father lost his land, the son could still inherit citizenship.

5. List the three groups that squabbled over Solon's reforms, and the political beliefs of each group.
A5. – Pg. 519, ¶ 5 – The three groups that squabbled over Solon's reforms were the Men of the Coast, the Men of the Plain and the Men of the Hills. The Men of the Coast wanted to keep Solon's reforms, the Men of the Plain wanted to return all power to the hands of the richest Athenians, and the Men of the Hills wanted complete democracy, with the poor and landless granted exactly the same privileges as everyone else.

6. What were the circumstances of Hipparchus's death? How did Hippias react to his brother's death?
A6. – Pg. 522, ¶ 6 to Pg. 523, ¶ 2 – Hipparchus fell madly in love with Harmodius, but when Harmodius rebuffed Hipparchus, Hipparchus publicly remarked that Harmodius was a degenerate. Infuriated, Harmodius murdered Hipparchus, and as a result, Hippias tortured Harmodius's murderous accomplice. The young man, maddened by pain, accused all sorts of

Athenian citizens of plotting against Hippias, to which Hippias responded by killing everyone named by the young accomplice, and anyone else who got in his way.

7. Why did Cleomenes help Athenians get rid of Hippias?

A7. – Pg. 523, ¶ 5 – Cleomenes helped the Athenians get rid of the divisive Hippias because of the advancing Persian juggernaut. If Athens fell apart into squabbling factions, it would scarcely be able to resist the Persian march south, meaning Sparta's biggest barrier between itself and the advancing Persian army would disappear.

8. What motivated Athens to attempt an alliance with the Persians? What was the outcome of this negotiation?

A8. – Pg. 524, ¶ 1-4 – After getting rid of Hippias for the Athenians, the Spartans began to interfere with Athenian politics, attempting to get someone in power that would help make Athens into a subject city of Sparta. It seemed to someone in the Athenian assembly that the only way to check Spartan arrogance would be to make an alliance with the Persians. The Persians were open to the alliance if Athens agreed to complete submission; the Athenians, however, had no intention of giving up their liberties and went about attacking the Spartan problem on their own.

9. Describe the Athenian custom of ostracism. How did ostracism help prevent tyranny?

A9. – Pg. 525, ¶ 2 – According to the Athenian custom of ostracism, any citizen of Athens could be exiled from the city for ten years, should six thousand of his compatriots write his name on an ostraka, a piece of pottery used as a ballot. This was another defense against tyranny because if one man became greater in power than appropriate, the citizens of Athens could vote to have the man exiled.

10. How did Aristagorus manage to start war between the Greeks and the Persians?

A10. – Pg. 526, ¶ 1, 5 & 6 – Aristagorus wanted to lead the Greek cities of Asia Minor in a rebellion against the Persian overlords, but he had no money to start a war against Persia. Aristagorus arrived in Athens with a proposal of rebellion at the same time that a message from Artaphranes was received, threatening invasion if the city did not reinstate Hippias. Athens, indignant at the Persian ultimatum, agreed to send twenty ships to help with Aristagorus's rebellion, then Athens's ally Eretria sent five, and war with Persia began.

11. What was Aristagorus's first coup against Darius in the Persian Wars? What was the "conflagration of Sardis?"

A11. – Pg. 527, ¶ 2 & 3 – Aristagorus managed to surprise Sardis early in battle, and enter the city. The Greeks had only planned on looting the city, but they burned the whole thing down instead. The conflagration of Sardis happened when a soldier torched a single house which turned into a widespread fire; since the buildings of Sardis were mostly made of reeds, the flames quickly spread throughout the whole city.

12. For what reason did Sparta refuse to help Athens fight the Persians at Marathon?
A12. – Pg. 529, ¶ 2 – Sparta knew that the Persians attacking Marathon were looking for payback for the Ionian rebellion. By staying out of the battle, the Spartans were attempting to avoid war with Persia.

13. What was the purpose of the Hellenic League? Who was in the League?
A13. – Pg. 530, ¶ 6 – The Hellenic League was a coalition of Greek cities joined together specifically for the defense of Greece against the Persians. Athens, Sparta and twenty-nine other Greek cities were in the League.

14. How were the Greek forces able to defeat the Persians once they sailed into the narrows around Salamis?
A14. – Pg. 533, ¶ 2 – The Greeks were waiting in the narrows around Salamis in triremes, which were fast, narrow and could flight effectively in the tight waters. When the Persians sailed into the narrows, they were unable to get out of the way of the ramming triremes. Also, Persians were not swimmers, and almost every Persian that fell overboard, drowned.

15. What were the Persians relying on to defeat the Greeks at Mycale? Why did the Persians lose the battle?
A15. – Pg. 534, ¶ 4 – The Persians were relying on the Ionian fighters in their ranks to back them up against the Greeks at the battle of Mycale. However, when the Greeks approached, the Ionians melted away, back towards their cities, and left the Persians standing alone. Without the help of the Ionians, the Persians were unable to defeat the advancing Spartans and Athenians.

16. In what way did the Persian Wars galvanize Greek culture?
A16. – Pg. 534, ¶ 5 – The Persian Wars galvanized Greek culture by creating a voluntary alliance between Greek cities, from Sparta all the way over to the Ionian coast, to defeat a common enemy. It was the first joint action taken by the entire Greek world.

Section III: Critical Thinking

The student may not use her text to answer this question.

In this chapter, we read about battle after battle between Persia and Greece based on accounts culled from Greek histories. Where are the Persian accounts? Write a short explanation of why the Persian Wars register barely a blip in Persian history. In your answer, use the example of how the Persians treated the failed invasion of the Scythian homeland to explain how the Persians dealt with unfavorable histories.

There are various examples from our book of the use of written text to rewrite history. A common example is the changing of one's name once he becomes king in order to reflect both the divine right to rule and inclusion in a royal bloodline. The choice to <u>not</u> acknowledge the inability of Persia to take Greece in Persian history is a way to hide that blemish on Persia's military record.

The Scythian Example:

In 516 BC, Darius began a campaign against the Scythians. Though Persian troops were able to cross the Bosphorus Strait and make it into Scythian territory, their attack was unsuccessful. The text on page 516, ¶ 3 to page 517, ¶ 1 reads: "The entire Persian force marched <u>back</u> to the south, back over the pontoon bridge across the Danube, leaving the unconquered Scythians behind. Persian court historians, and later Persian kings, dealt with this problem by only writing the history of the lands south of the Danube. For all practical purposes, the land on the other side of the river simply ceased to exist. If the Persians couldn't take it, it clearly wasn't important." Ignoring the Scythian triumph over Persian troops allowed the Persians to save face; if they didn't acknowledge it, it didn't happen.

EXAMPLE ANSWER: The Persian histories do not give detailed stories about the Persian Wars because there was little to brag about. By ignoring the wars, the Persians did not have to acknowledge their failures. This is exactly what the Persians did when it came to their loss against the Scythians. The Scythians outsmarted the Persians, and Darius was forced to head home without a victory. The Persians simply left this defeat out of their history. Ignoring the Scythian triumph over Persian troops allowed the Persians to save face; if they didn't acknowledge it, it didn't happen.

CHAPTER SIXTY-FIVE: THE PELOPONNESIAN WARS

The student may use his text when answering the questions in sections I and II.

Section I: Who, What, Where

Write a one or two-sentence answer explaining the significance of each item listed below.

Alcibiades – **Pg. 550, ¶ 1 & 5 and Pg. 552, ¶ 3** – Alcibiades, an extravagant Athenian libertine with an obsessive need for public acclaim, dragged Athens into battle with Syracuse, betrayed Athens for Sparta, and found asylum in Persia once he was kicked out of Sparta.

Chiliarch – **Pg. 544, ¶ 1** – A chiliarch was a Persian army commander who was in charge of a thousand of the elite Persian fighters.

Delian League – **Pg. 541, ¶ 5** – The Delian League was an alliance of Greek cities, with Athens at his head, formed after the dismantling of the Hellenic League.

Inaros – **Pg. 544, ¶ 4** – Inaros, one of Psammetichus III's sons, attempted to rebel against Persia after the death of Xerxes. With the help of Athens, Inaros managed to hold off Persian troops for eleven years - ultimately the rebellion failed and Inaros was crucified.

Long Walls – **Pg. 545, ¶ 2** – Long Walls, the pet project of Pericles, were walls built out from Athens down to the port of Pireus, a distance of eight miles. The walls were built so that goods and soldiers could get to the water without fear of attack.

Lysander – **Pg. 553, ¶ 1-5** – Lysander was admiral of the Spartan army during the time of Alcibiades and Tissaphernes's scheming. Lysander destroyed the Athenian fleet and besieged Athens; Lysander ordered the Long Walls knocked down and that Athens give up all influence over the cities which had once belonged to the Athenian empire.

Nicias – **Pg. 549, ¶ 4 and Pg. 551, ¶ 1-4** – Nicias, an Athenian leader, negotiated a six year peace with Sparta in 421. Nicias was dragged into battle against Syracuse because of his colleague Alcibiades, was forced to fight and surrender and was ultimately murdered by the Syracusean commander.

Ochus/Darius II – **Pg. 549, ¶ 3** – Ochus was the illegitimate half-brother of Xerxes II, the son of Artaxerxes. After Xerxes II's death, Ochus took the throne from another half-brother, and gave himself a proper royal name, Darius II.

Pericles – **Pg. 545, ¶ 2 and Pg. 546, ¶ 2** – Pericles, son of Xanthippus, was a great orator and military leader. He built a new temple to Athena on top of the Acropolis: the Parthenon, and he proposed the building of Athens's Long Walls.

Plataea – **Pg. 547, ¶ 2** – Plataea, under Athenian protection, was attacked in 431 by Thebes, a Spartan ally. This was the first attack in the skirmishes between Athens and Sparta since the Battle of Sybota that threatened a city's actual walls, an overt action that made both the Athenians and the Spartans prepare for all out war.

The Thirty Years' Peace – Pg. 545, ¶ 5 – The Thirty Years' Peace was a treaty made between the Spartans and the Athenians in 446 BC. The terms of the treaty were that Athens would give up some of the land seized on the Isthmus of Corinth and along the shore of the Peloponnese for an end to fighting, and both cities agreed not to interfere with the other's allies.

Thurii – Pg. 546, ¶ 1 – Thurii was a new pan-Hellenic colony that was drawing citizens from all across Greece. Herodotus moved to Thurii after he left Athens.

Tissaphernes – Pg. 552, ¶ 3 – Tissaphernes, satrap in charge of Asia Minor, plotted with Alcibiades, and devised a plan to work the ongoing war between Athens and Sparta in a way that might benefit Persia. When Darius II found out about the scheme, Tissaphernes was put in his place and sent back to Susa.

Xanthippus – Pg. 540, ¶ 3, Pg. 541, ¶ 4 – Xanthippus was an Athenian general who backed up Pausanias and the soldiers of the Hellenic League to successfully restore Byzantium to the Greeks. Later, Xanthippus replaced Pausanias as commander of Byzantium, and refused to give up his control to the Spartans, an action that broke up the Hellenic League.

Section II: Comprehension

Write a two/three sentence answer to each of the following questions.

1. Why did the Spartans agree to fight the Persians with the rest of the Hellenic League?
A1. – Pg. 540, ¶ 2 – The Spartans did not want to fight the Persians, however, if they did not join the Hellenic League in battle, Athens would gain power as head of the League. By agreeing to fight, the Spartans were guaranteed that their own commander, Pausanias, would remain the supreme commander of the League.

2. In what way did Athens get in the way of the Spartans claiming the overall lordship of Greece?
A2. – Pg. 540, ¶ 7 & 8 – After the Persians laid waste to Athens, the Athenians wanted to restore their city, while the Spartans demanded that the building stop. If Athens ceased to exist, it would no longer be in the way of the Spartans claiming clear leadership of the cities in Greece.

3. How did Themistocles ensure that Athens was rebuilt despite Spartan resistance?
A3. – Pg. 540, ¶ 8 to Pg. 541, ¶ 2 – Themistocles agreed to travel to Sparta in order to discuss the problems surrounding the rebuilding of Athens. While he deliberately traveled as slowly as possible to Sparta, he told the Athenians to rebuild the city's walls as fast as they could, with whatever materials they could find. When he finally got to Sparta, the wall was up, and Themistocles was able to tell the Spartans that Athens now had defenses and wasn't going to give the Spartans permission to run its affairs.

4. What were the circumstances related to Pausanias's dismissal from command of Ionian Byzantium?
A4. – Pg. 541, ¶ 3 – The Ionians in Byzantium complained that Pausanias was acting like a tyrant, and that he was carrying on secret negotiations with Xerxes of Persia. In response, the Spartan assembly summoned Pausanias home to stand trial, and Xanthippus took supreme command in his place.

5. Why wouldn't Xanthippus give up control of Byzantium? How was this action the "death knell" for the old Hellenic League?

A5. – Pg. 541, ¶ 4 & 5 – Xanthippus would not relinquish his control of Byzantium to the replaced commander sent by the Spartans because control of Byzantium gave Athens a one up over Sparta. The Spartans were angered by Xanthippus's actions, so they left Byzantium, and the other soldiers from the Peloponnesian cities did as well. When the Spartans left Byzantium, the old Hellenic League fell apart; the alliance was broken.

6. How did Themistocles's ostracism lead the Athenian to offer himself as an advisor to Xerxes?

A6. – Pg. 543, ¶ 1 - After Themistocles was ostracized, the Spartans sent a message to Athens telling them it was discovered that Themistocles, like Pausanias, was conspiring with the Persians. The Athenians sent an assassin after the exiled general, but Themistocles managed to evade his hunters. He eventually arrived at the Persian court and offered himself as an advisor on Greek affairs, on the condition that Xerxes pay the reward for Themistocles's capture.

7. Who killed Xerxes? Who killed Darius II? Who killed Artabanos? Who killed Hystaspes? Who ended up as king of Persia?

A7. – Pg. 544, ¶ 1-3 – Artabanos probably killed Xerxes, though he blamed Xerxes oldest son, Darius II, of the crime. Artaxerxes, believing Artabanos's claim against Darius II, killed his brother. Artaxerxes, attacked by Artabanos, killed the captain. Hystaspes tried to take the throne from Artaxerxes, but Artaxerxes killed his other brother, and emerged as king of Persia.

8. What caused the Delian League to turn into something like an Athenian empire?

A8. – Pg. 544, ¶ 6 to Pg. 545, ¶ 2 – The Delian League, headed by Athens, had not been easy to hold together, and as a consequence, Athens was using more and more force against its own allies. Forcing cities to stay in the league turned the coalition from an alliance into something like an empire.

9. What led the Athenians to propose a peace treaty with the Spartans in 446 BC?

A9. – Pg. 545, ¶ 4 & 5 – The Athenians and Spartans fought at Boeotia, and it seemed that the Spartans won the battle. However, just two months later the Athenians claimed the area for themselves, subverting the Spartan victory. The two cities were matched in power, so in 446 Athens proposed a peace to stop the constant fighting.

10. How did fighting begin between Athens and Corinth in 433? What was the significance of the Battle at Sybota?

A10. – Pg. 546, ¶ 6 to Pg. 547, ¶ 1 – The Athenian assembly had agreed to aid the Corinthian colony Corcyra in a rebellion against Corinth, with the stipulation that the Athenians were not to attack the Corinthians unless the Corinthians landed in Corcyra, or threatened Corcyra's ships. Once in battle, the Athenian captain held back until the Corinthians were inflicting casualties, and as soon as this happened, Athenian ships joined the battle and sent for reinforcements. The Battle of Sybota was significant because it broke The Thirty Years' Peace; Corinth was an ally of Sparta, and the treaty had stated that neither Sparta nor Athens would interfere with the other's allies.

11. In what ways did the plague affect order and custom in Athens?

A11. – Pg. 548, ¶ 1 & 2 – The plague made men in Athens desperate and dejected; the city was in complete disorder. Piles of bodies burned in the street, petty thieves had free range through deserted households, and no one bothered to sacrifice or observe any rituals. What was once sacred in the city was displaced by the need for survival.

12. Describe the plan hatched by Alcibiades and Tissaphernes in which Sparta and Athens would destroy one another.

A12. – Pg. 552, ¶ 4-6 – Tissaphernes sent word to the Spartans, offering to fund their ongoing war with Athens on the condition that, once Athens fell, the Spartans would abandon the Ionian cities to Persia. At the same time, Alcibiades wrote to Athens, offering to come and join them with plenty of Persian gold, as long as they would agree to reinstate him in his previous position in the Athenian government. The plan was supposed to end with a huge sea battle in which the Athenians and the Spartans would, theoretically, destroy each other's fleets.

13. Who were the Thirty? How were the Athenians able to overthrow the Thirty?

A13. – Pg. 553, ¶ 5 to Pg. 554, ¶ 1 – The Thirty, a group of aristocrats set in place by Lysander to rule Athens, were infamous for the bloodbath which they instituted, putting to death anyone who wanted democracy restored, anyone they feared, and anyone whose possessions they wanted. The Athenians who survived the Thirty's reign of terror came together, sent to nearby Thebes for help, and attacked them, as well as the Spartan garrison that protected the men. The Spartans were not interested in starting another war; the king of Sparta overruled Lysander and pulled the garrison out of Athens.

Section III: Critical Thinking

In this chapter, we are introduced to narratives related to Athenian patriotism. In Athens, citizens were not coerced to fight, but rather called on to defend their blooming culture. How was this rising sense of patriotism related to the harsh treatment of the great Athenian leader Thucydides? Write a brief description of Athenian culture just before the start of the Peloponnesian Wars, and Pericles's call for the ideological support of the war from the people of Athens. Then, write a sentence or two considering how Athenian pride might have lead to Thucydides's exile.

A description of Athenian life just before the Peloponnesian War can be found on page 546, ¶ 2. The text reads: "The commander Pericles, who had gained more and more popularity as a public speaker, oversaw the building of a new temple to Athena on top of the Acropolis. This temple, the Parthenon, was decorated with sculpted stone friezes showing legendary Greek victories over semihuman centaurs: a celebration of Greek triumph over non-Greek enemies. A forty-foot seated statue of Zeus was carved from ivory and placed at the temple at Olympia, where it became so well known that later list-makers called it one of the seven wonders of the ancient world. The philosopher Socrates spent his days talking and teaching, attracting scores of followers; like the Buddha, evolving a coherent and influential philosophy without writing a word, since all of his teachings were set down by his students."

The speech given to the people of Athens by Pericles calling for Athenian pride is on page 547, ¶ 3. The text reads: "When the first Athenians died in battle, Pericles gave a funeral oration to honor them, a speech in which he listed the superiorities of Athenian civilization: Athenian freedom, Athenian education (which gives its men "knowledge without effeminacy"), the ongoing Athenian war against poverty, the ability of its citizens to understand public matters. He ended with a patriotic call unlike any in history so far: "You must yourselves realize the power of Athens," he told them. "Feed your eyes on her from day by day till love of her fills your hearts; and then, when all her greatness shall break upon you, you must reflect that it was by courage, sense of duty, and a keen feeling of honor in action that men were enabled to win all this." It was a call for loyalty not to a king, but to a concept; to identify themselves as Athenians, based not on race, but on a willing and voluntary association with an <u>idea</u>."

After the plague swept through Athens, and Thucydides recovered from his own battle against the sickness, he was put in command of the Athenian force protecting Thrace. Thucydides's soldiers were driven into retreat, another Spartan victory in the war. Thucydides was sent into exile as punishment for this loss. Thucydides's exile is indicative of the power of Athenian patriotism; Pericles's call for Athenian pride meant that any act that did not benefit Athens could be seen as criminal. When Thucydides lost the battle for Thrace, he did his city a disservice, and therefore betrayed the trust of his fellow Athenians.

EXAMPLE ANSWER: Just before the Peloponnesian War, Pericles celebrated Athenian history when he oversaw the building the Parthenon, which was decorated with sculpted stone friezes showing legendary Greek victories over semihuman centaurs. Athenians could worship at a giant statue of Zeus that was built at the temple at Olympia, and they could learn from the philosopher Socrates, who was walking around Athens and disseminating his teachings to anyone who would listen. Citizens of Athens were proud of their city's thriving culture.

Pericles took advantage of the Athenians' love of their culture after the first Athenians died in battle against the Spartans. He gave a funeral oration to honor the fallen Athenians, in which he listed the superiorities of Athenian civilization, like Athenian education and the Athenian war against poverty. Pericles called upon the people of Athens to "realize the power of Athens" and to "feed your eyes on her from day by day till love of her fills your hearts." Pericles introduced the idea of fighting for the love of Athens, which was very different from fighting because a king gave you orders to do so, or because of racial hierarchies. Pericles was suggesting that the Athenians fight for the city because they wanted to, because protecting the culture of the city was worth one's life.

When Thucydides was charged with protecting Thrace, he was given the responsibility of protecting Athenian pride. Unfortunately, Thucydides was unable to beat the Spartans, and his soldiers were driven into retreat. Thucydides was sent into exile as punishment for this loss. Thucydides's exile is indicative of the power of Athenian patriotism; Pericles's call for Athenian pride meant that any act that did not benefit Athens could be seen as criminal. When Thucydides lost the battle for Thrace, he did his city a disservice, and therefore betrayed the trust of his fellow Athenians.

CHAPTER SIXTY-SIX: THE FIRST SACK OF ROME

The student may use her text when answering the questions in sections I and II.

Section I: Who, What, Where

Write a one or two-sentence answer explaining the significance of each item listed below.

Citizens – **Pg. 555, ¶ 4 – Citizens was the Spartan term for the people of power, the conquerors.**

Decemvirs – **Pg. 557, ¶ 3 to Pg. 558, ¶ 1 – The decemvirs were a board of ten lawmakers appointed to replace the regular Roman officers during the year 450. The decemvirs were charged with both running the Roman government and drawing up the first set of written Roman laws.**

Helots – **Pg. 555, ¶ 4 – Helots was the term for the conquered people of Sparta, those with no power.**

Patricians – **Pg. 555, ¶ 4 – Patricians, from the Latin word pater, "father," were the Roman people of power. They were by tradition descendants of the Roman council of advisors that served the old kings.**

Plebians – **Pg. 555, ¶ 4 – Plebians was the term for the people in Rome who were not patricians.**

Tribune – **Pg. 557, ¶ 4 – A tribune was a special magistrate in the Roman court, always appointed from the ranks of the plebians, whose job it was to protect the plebs from injustice.**

The Twelve Tables – **Pg. 558, ¶ 1 & 2 – The Twelve Tables were wood tablets upon which the first written Roman law was recorded. Because the Twelve Tables were lost, what we know of them is assembled from quotes found in various Roman documents.**

Volscii – **Pg. 556, ¶ 6 – The Volscii were a tribe of people who lived south of Rome that marched on the city during the debt slave uprising in 495. The Volscii were thoroughly thrashed by the army of debtors that were sent to put down the invasion.**

Section II: Comprehension

Write a two/three sentence answer to each of the following questions.

1. Why is it hard to define the Roman term "plebian?"
A1. – Pg. 555, ¶ 4 to Pg. 556, ¶ 1 – It is hard to define the Roman word "plebian" because it is a negation, meaning "not patrician." This included conquered peoples living in Rome, as well as men who traced their ancestry back to the lowly inhabitants of the original city.

2. Though the plebians largely outnumbered the patricians, why did the patricians have so much power?

A2. – Pg. 556, ¶ 2 – Though the plebians outnumbered the patricians, the patricians were more powerful because they held a disproportionate amount of land and wealth. Not only did the patricians own most of the land, they were also the ones who held positions of authority in Rome; they were the magistrates and priests, landowners and generals.

3. Under what circumstance might a plebian and his dependents become slaves? How did this increase the power of the patrician class?

A3. – Pg. 556, ¶ 3 – A plebian and his dependents became slaves if, after borrowing money in a time of famine or while away at war, the plebian did not pay back his debts. This increased the power of the patricians because they gained not only the land and money of the plebian and his family, but also ownership over the plebians themselves.

4. What caused the 495 BC debt slave uprising in Rome?

A4. – Pg. 556, ¶ 4 & 5 – In 495 BC a famous old soldier spoke at the Forum, telling the crowd, "While I was on service, during the Sabine war, my crops were ruined by enemy raids, and my cottage was burnt. Everything I had was taken, including my cattle. Then, when I was least able to do so, I was expected to pay my taxes, and fell, consequently, into debt." In response, debt slaves from all over the city thronged into the streets, shouting for the Senate to decide at once how to give them relief from their slavery.

5. Explain the terms of the hasty resolution made by the Roman Senate regarding debt slaves while the Volscii tribes advanced on Rome, and why the resolution was made.

A5. – Pg. 556, ¶ 6 to Pg. 557, ¶ 1 – Hearing that Volscii tribes were marching on Rome, the Senate passed a hasty resolution that no man could in the future be reduced to debt slavery as long as he was on active military duty. This resolution caused almost everyone in the streets to join the army so as to avoid debt slavery, guaranteeing a victory over the invading Volscii tribes.

6. Describe the world's first recorded strike, the Plebian Secession.

A6. – Pg. 557, ¶ 3 – In 494, the plebians went on the world's first recorded strike: they took themselves off in a body to the Sacred Mount, three miles from the city and made a camp. The Plebian Secession threw off both the patricians, because they lost most of their slaves and their army, and the plebians who did not strike, because they lost the safety generally ensured by the number of plebians in the city. The Plebian Secession caused Rome to freeze up and made it vulnerable for attack.

7. How did the Senate respond to the Plebian Secession?

A7. – Pg. 557, ¶ 4 & 5 – The Senate responded to the Plebian Secession by creating special magistrates called tribunes, who would always be appointed from the ranks of the plebians. It was the first Roman office blocked off to patricians. The first two tribunes were appointed in the same year as the Plebian Secession.

8. When thousands of Celts showed up at Clusium's city gates waving weapons, why couldn't Rome send aid to its northern neighbor?

A8. – Pg. 559, ¶ 2 & ¶ 4 and Pg. 560, ¶ 3 – Since the internal stability that followed the Twelve Tables, Rome turned its sights outward and had been busy warring with Fidenae and Veii.

Its soldiers had been all over the countryside, terrorizing farmers and seizing villages to add to the growing Roman territory. Though Rome was expanding, it was at a great cost; when Clusium sent to Rome for help against the invading Celts, the Senate had no troops to give.

9. Why did the Gaulish army hold back when it first met the Roman defense at the Tiber?
A9. – Pg. 560, ¶ 5 – The Gauls held back when they first met the Romans on the Tiber because they suspected a trap. The Roman soldiers were so few that the Gauls thought they were being tricked.

10. How did the Massalians end the wretched standstill between Rome and the Celts who had invaded Rome?
A10. – Pg. 561, ¶ 3 & 4 – The Massalians, who had had their own encounter with invading Gauls, sent envoys to the shrine at Delphi to thank Apollo for their deliverance. On their way back, the envoys heard of the siege at Rome and took the news back to Massalia, where city leaders felts that good relations with Rome were worth cultivating. Massalia came up with enough booty to buy off the Celts for the Romans.

11. In what way did the first sack of Rome leave a permanent mark on the city?
A11. – Pg. 561, ¶ 5 – After the Gauls left Rome, the Romans emerged from the Capitol to rebuild, hastily, in case the enemy should return. Nobody bothered to make sure the streets were straight, and houses went up wherever there was room for them. The hodge-podge layout of the city was a permanent reminder of the first barbarian sack of Rome.

Section III: Critical Thinking

The student may not use her text to answer this question.

In the 5th century BC, Rome was a city divided between patricians and plebians. Sanctions made on the behalf of the plebians after the debt slave uprising and the Plebian Secession were not enough to mend the ill feelings of the second class. In what way did the Twelve Tables attempt to combine the people with great power, and those with no power, into a harmonious whole? While the Twelve Tables gave more protection to the rights of the plebs, how did the newly written law continue to reinforce the differences between the high and low peoples of Rome?

To answer the first part of the question, the student should describe the relatively democratic process by which the Twelve Tables were created. This can be found in ¶ 7 on page 557 though ¶ 1 on page 558. Though a council of ten lawmakers was put to the task of writing the laws, the Twelve Tables were not accepted until they were presented for public discussion. When the laws had been amended by the discussion, an assembly of all the people was held to approve them. There was a general feeling that a little more regulation was still in order, so decemvirs were appointed for the following year also to draw up two more tables. The ability for the public to discuss and amend the laws incorporated the views of both the patricians and plebians. All men were invited to contribute to the creation of Roman law.

Next, the student should think about the list of laws presented on pages 558-559 in order to support the rest of her answer. The text reads:

…"You who admit to or have been judged to owe money have thirty days to pay for it." After that, the debtor can be taken to court, and if he has no surety or income, he can be put in chains; but his accuser must pay for his food (which might end up being more costly than forgiving the debt). Anyone who makes a false claim, according to Table XII, can be brought in front of three judges; if they decide that he has lied, he as to pay a substantial penalty. And then there is Table IX, the bedrock of the whole arrangement: "Privilegia ne irroganato," "No private laws can be proposed." No longer could patricians simply impose their will on plebians without their agreement.

Along with these are regulations of injury and harm that recall the laws of Hammurabi: a man who breaks another's bone must pay a fine, but the fine is halved if the bone broken belongs to a slave; if roads are not kept up by those who own the property through which they pass, the users are permitted to trespass and drive their cattle alongside the road instead; a son who is sold into slavery three different times can declare himself emancipated from his father.

And along with these are hints that although the Laws of the Twelve Tables were a step in the right direction, there was still plenty of injustice in Rome. Some of the injustices are standard ancient practice: "A deformed child shall be killed," reads Table IV, baldly, and Table V explains, "Women, because of their light dispositions, shall always have guardians even when they are grown." And others are particular to Rome itself. "No one may hold meetings in the city during the night," reads Table VIII, a regulation meant to protect that patricians from another plebian plot; and, most infamously, Table XI decrees, "Marriage between a patrician and a plebian is forbidden." This particular law was finally repealed in 445 after savage debate in the Senate; not everyone was convinced that Rome would prosper if the blood of noble and common Romans mingled.

The student should note that although laws were in place to protect plebian rights, like the law that stopped the formation of private laws, there were laws in place that continued to reinforce class differences. For example, meeting at night was barred, which was meant to defer secret plebian plots, suggesting that the plebians might still want to gather to protest against the injustices imposed upon them by the patricians. Also, a law was passed to bar the marriage of a patrician to a plebian. Though this law was eventually revoked, the fact that it was first passed demonstrates the lingering feelings of patricians that the plebians were not their equals.

EXAMPLE ANSWER: The Twelve Tables were written by a council of ten lawmakers, the decemvirs. After the decemvirs wrote a version of the laws, they presented them to the public for discussion. The laws were then amended and put up for approval by the people. Still, the public wasn't happy, so the decemvirs were appointed for another year to draw up two more tables. The process by which the Tables were created demonstrates that both the plebians and the patricians were instrumental in creating Roman law. All men were invited to contribute.

The newly written Roman law did protect plebian rights in some ways; for example, a law was passed that barred patricians from creating private laws, meaning a patrician could not create a law that manipulated a plebian without public approval. However, laws were passed that continued to show the class difference between the patricians and the plebs. Though it was later repealed, a law was passed that barred the marriage of a patrician to a plebian. This law proved that even though the lawmaking process was somewhat democratic, the plebians were not seen as equal to the patricians.

CHAPTER SIXTY-SEVEN: THE RISE OF THE CH'IN

The student may use his text when answering the questions in sections I and II.

Section I: Who, What, Where

Write a one or two-sentence answer explaining the significance of each item listed below.

343 BC – Pg. 567, ¶ 1 – 343 BC marks the year that the Eastern Zhou king formally recognized Duke Hsiao of Ch'in as the Hegemon. It was the first time in a century that a duke could lay claim to the title, and the first time in history that a Ch'in lord had won it.

403 BC – Pg. 563, ¶ 1 & 2 – In 403 BC, the Nine Tripods shook, and the northern state of Jin finally cracked apart. Han, Wei and Chao, three battling families of the Jin state, were appointed feudal lords.

Chuang Tzu – Pg. 568, ¶ 4 to Pg. 569, ¶ 2 – Chuang Tzu, born in the same year that Duke Hsiao inherited the rule of Ch'in and welcomed Shang Yang into his country, was the most famous of Taoists. By practicing the Tao-Teh-Ching, Chuang Tzu was able to let go of the material world around him and remain as unconcerned as a butterfly.

Duke Hsiao – Pg. 565, ¶ 2 and Pg. 567, ¶ 1 – Duke Hsiao of Ch'in hired Shan Yang to shape up the state of Ch'in. The success of Shang Yang's reforms made the Ch'in state so powerful that Duke Hsiao was formally recognized as Hegemon.

Huiwen – Pg. 565, ¶ 4 and Pg. 567, ¶ 5 – Huiwen, son of Duke Hsiao, violated one of Shang Yang's laws, and his tutors paid the price; one was executed and the other was branded. When Huiwen took his father's place as leader of Ch'in, he enacted revenge on Shang Yang for the death of the tutors and had the minister killed.

alternate answer: Pg. 567, ¶ 6 – Huiwen decided not to revoke any of the minister's reforms since they had made Ch'in more powerful than it had ever been; so powerful, in fact, that in 325 BC Huiwen declared himself king.

Mencius/Meng-tzu – Pg. 567, ¶ 9 – Mencius/Meng-tzu, the most famous pupil of Confucius, paid particular attention to the relationship between a ruler and his people. Mencius claimed that a ruler had to measure whether or not he was carrying out the will of Heaven by listening to the opinions of the people.

Shang Yang – Pg. 565, ¶ 4 to Pg. 566, ¶ 2 – Shang Yang instituted a set of reforms that turned Ch'in into the most powerful of the Chinese states. These reforms included instituting a meritocracy and officially sanctioned private ownership of land.

Note to INSTRUCTOR: Shang Yang's life and his reforms are the subject matter of Comprehension Questions 5-9, as well as the Critical Thinking Question, so the student does not have to list all details associated with Shang Yang in this ID.

Section II: Comprehension

Write a two/three sentence answer to each of the following questions.

1. What happened in the twenty-fourth year of King Wei-lieh that caused the final destruction of the Jin?
A1. – Pg. 563, ¶ 1 & 2 – In the twenty-fourth year of King Wei-lieh, Han, Wei, and Chao, three battling families of the Jin state, claimed part of the Jin territory for themselves. They demanded that the Eastern Zhou monarch recognize them as lords over their three newly defined lands, and he had no power to refuse. The Eastern Zhou king lost his last bit of authority over his own land.

2. Which state benefitted the most from the end of the Jin state, and why?
A2. – Pg. 563, ¶ 4 – The Ch'in state benefitted the most from the end of the Jin state. After the dissolution of the Jin state, Ch'in quadrupled in size. Eventually the eastern border of Ch'in stretched from the Yellow River all the way down to the Yangtze.

3. What were the strengths of each of the following states by 361 BC: Qi, Wei and Ch'in? Despite its size, why was Ch'in looked down upon by the Qi and Wei?
A3. – Pg. 564, ¶ 2 – The Qi state was powerful because it was the most prosperous; it had a run of competent dukes, who collected taxes in an orderly manner and also managed to corner a salt monopoly. Wei was powerful because it had a strong military. The Ch'in state was powerful because it had a huge amount of territory. However, because Ch'in was a backwater state, far from the center of power, with a ridge of high lands separating it from the older Chinese states, it was regarded by the Qi and Wei as semibarbaric.

4. Where was Shang Yang from, and how did he end up in the Ch'in court?
A4. – Pg. 565, ¶ 2 – Shang Yang was born in Wei, the son of a royal concubine. Shang Yang was barred from rule because of his parentage; he felt himself deserving of more power than his birth allowed, so when he found out that Duke Hsiao of Ch'in had sent out an invitation to all capable men to join him in making Ch'in stronger, Shang Yang left his native land and journeyed to Duke Hsiao's court.

5. How did Shang Yang feel about merchants? What happened to those who occupied themselves with trade under Shang Yang's reforms?
A5. – Pg. 565, ¶ 5 to Pg. 566, ¶ 1 – Shang Yang felt that merchants were parasites who sold goods made by other men and took a cut of the proceeds. Those who occupied themselves with trade, under Shang Yang's reforms, were enslaved.

6. Why did the residents of Ch'in have to get official permission to move to a new home?
A6. – Pg. 566, ¶ 2 – The residents of Ch'in had to get official permission before moving to a new home because Shang Yang wanted to make sure farmers did not exhaust their land in one area and then shift to a new farm. The rule ensured the proper management of one's land.

7. Why did Sima Qian call Ch'in, under the rule of Duke Hsiao and Shang Yang, a terrible place to live?

A7. – Pg. 566, ¶ 5 – Sima Qian called Ch'in a terrible place to live because, though Shang Yang's reforms made the people of Ch'in prosperous, they were slaves to the law. Anyone who spoke out against the reforms was banished, music and poetry were banished, and philosophy was scorned.

8. What were the circumstances of Shang Yang's death?
A8. – Pg. 567, ¶ 5 – After Duke Hsiao died, his son, Huiwen, became the ruler of Ch'in. Huiwen hated Shang Yang ever since the minister had Huiwen's tutors executed and disfigured. Huiwen ordered Shang Yang arrested; though Shang Yang tried to hide, he was caught and taken to the capital, where he died after being tied to four chariots which were driven off in different directions, tearing him apart.

9. Why was Huiwen's proclamation of his kingly title anti-climactic?
A9. – Pg. 567, ¶ 6 & 7 – After Huiwen proclaimed himself king in 325 BC, all other feudal lords also declared themselves kings. Now, the wars of the Warring States were conducted by kings rather than dukes.

10. For what reason was Mencius most likely turned down when he offered himself as an advisor to the dukes of several states?
A10. – Pg. 567, ¶ 9 to Pg. 568, ¶ 1 – Mencius believed that though a duke governed by the will of Heaven, Heaven did not speak, so the ruler had to measure whether or not he was in fact carrying out the will of Heaven by listening to the opinions of the people. If he listened closely enough, he would learn that warfare was never Heaven's will. This was not a philosophy welcomed by kings, and most likely the reason Mencius was never taken up on his offer to become a royal advisor.

11. What is the philosophy of the Tao-Teh-Ching? How was the Tao-Teh-Ching a practical philosophy to adopt during the Warring States period?
A11. – Pg. 568, ¶ 3 & 4 and Pg. 569, ¶ 2 – The Tao-Teh-Ching taught that the way to peace lay in a passive acceptance of the way things were. To withdraw from chaos and wait in the faith that what will be, will be was a practical philosophy to adopt in evil times. When one had no control over the laws imposed upon him, removing himself from the material world was one way to ensure happiness.

Section III: Critical Thinking

The student may use his text to answer this question.

Shang Yang was not a well-liked guy; his brutal death speaks to his unpopularity. Yet, he transformed the backwater and semibarbaric state of Ch'in into the home of the Hegemon. How was Shang Yang able to bring order to the previously lawless state of Ch'in? Write a paragraph describing Shang Yang's reforms: the network of squares, efficient agriculture, officially sanctioned land and meritocracy. Then, write a paragraph explaining how these reforms worked together to turn Ch'in into the most powerful of the Warring States.

The student will find Shang Yang's reforms listed on pages 565 and 566. You can find the text that explicitly details Shang Yang's reforms below:

Pg. 565, ¶ 3 – At once, Shang Yang began a new regime by instituting strong penalties for treason and feuds; even private quarrels were punishable by law. To enforce this, he ordered Ch'in divided into a whole network of small squares, each containing not more than ten households, with each household given the responsibility of informing on any wrongdoing committed by others...Nor was anyone allowed to escape the watchful eye of officials and neighbors by disappearing into the distance; innkeepers were forbidden to offer rooms to travelers unless those travelers carried official permits.

Pg. 565, ¶ 4 – With this control mechanism in place, Shang Yang set about making Ch'in into a meritocracy....Titles would from now on be awarded by the duke solely on the basis of "military merit," and aristocrats who couldn't fight would be aristocrats no longer.

Pg. 565, ¶ 5 to Pg. 565, ¶ 1 – Furthermore, from now on no Ch'in citizen would be allowed to duck the task of performing useful labor for the good of the state... "Everyone had to assist in the fundamental occupations of tilling and weaving," writes Sima Qian, of Shang Yang's reforms, "and only those who produced a large quantity of grain or silk were exempted from labour on public works. Those who occupied themselves with trade were enslaved, along with the destitute and lazy."

Pg. 566, ¶ 2 – [T]hose who worked hard could look forwards to being rewarded tracts of land. This was a new idea, and probably the first officially sanctioned private ownership of land in all of China. This new private ownership was backed up with its own set of regulations: no one could now move to a new home without official permission, meaning that farmers could not exhaust their land and then shift to new farms. They had to manage their land properly of else starve.

The significance of Shang Yang's reforms is described as follows:

Page 566 in ¶ 3 – [T]he new importance given to farming meant that much of the Ch'in land now lying waste could be put into crops. And despite the severity of Shang Yang's penalties, his policies (which also allowed convicted criminals to earn their freedom by farming previously untilled land) attracted more and more poor peasants from other Chinese states. In Ch'in, they at least had the opportunity to rise in the hierarchy through military service.

Pg. 566, ¶ 4 – Most ancient historians dislike Shang Yang intensely, but even Sima Qian had to admit that all this legislation established a kind of stability in a previously lawless state. He writes that, ten years into the new regime, "there were no robbers in the mountains; families were self-supporting and people had plenty.... great order prevailed throughout the countryside and in the towns."

Not only did Shang Yang's reforms produce a well-fed and growing population, they had made military service one of the most attractive careers for the new crop of young Ch'in men. When Huiwen became duke, he got rid of Shang Yang, but kept his reforms because they had made Ch'in more powerful than it had ever been.

EXAMPLE ANSWER: Shang Yang imposed a strict set of reforms on the Ch'in state that brought it from lawlessness to order and prosperity. First, the minister divided Ch'in into a whole network of small squares, each containing not more than ten households, with each household given the responsibility of informing on any wrongdoing committed by others. Then, Shang Yang set about making Ch'in into a meritocracy. Titles would be awarded by the duke solely on the basis of military merit, and aristocrats who couldn't fight would no longer be aristocrats. Furthermore, Shang Yang outlawed tradesmen; everyone had to assist in the fundamental occupations of tilling and weaving. Finally, Shang Yang instituted a policy of officially sanctioned private ownership of land; those who worked hard could look forward to being rewarded with tracts of land.

Shang Yang's network of small squares ensured order within Ch'in; Sima Qian even goes so far to write that ten years into the new regime, "there were no robbers in the mountains." A military meritocracy turned Ch'in's greatest weakness, its lack of aristocracy and its blended heritage of Chinese and non-Chinese, into a strength. Poor peasants from other Chinese states were attracted to Ch'in because they had the opportunity to rise in the hierarchy through military service. Shang Yang's agricultural reforms made land that was previously worthless into valuable farmland. Also, since no one could move into a new home without official permission, a farmer couldn't exhaust his land and move on, meaning he had to become an efficient manager of his crops and soil. All of these factors combined meant the Ch'in had a well-fed and growing population, one that could conquer its neighbors, and claim the power of the Hegemon.

CHAPTER SIXTY-EIGHT: THE MACEDONIAN CONQUERORS

The student may use her text when answering the questions in sections I and II.

Section I: Who, What, Where

Write a one or two-sentence answer explaining the significance of each item listed below.

Achoris – **Pg. 573, ¶ 4 & 5 – Achoris, pharaoh of Egypt after Nepherites I, sent up to Greece to ask Athens for help against Persian attempts to retake Egypt.**

Alexander – **Pg. 577, ¶ 5 & 6, Pg. 581, ¶ 3 and Pg. 582, ¶ 4 – Alexander was born in 356 to Philip of Macedonia and Olympias of Greece. Though Attalus challenged Alexander's right to rule because the heir was only half-Macedonian, Alexander promptly inherited the throne after his father's murder in 336.**

Artaxerxes II – **Pg. 570, ¶ 3, Pg. 574, ¶ 6 and Pg. 575, ¶ 2 – Artaxerxes II inherited the Persian throne from his father Darius II in 404 BC. Artaxerxes claimed power over Sparta, Athens and the Ionian cities through the King's Peace, but he was unable to reclaim Egypt as part of Persia's kingdom.**

Artaxerxes III/Ochus – **Pg. 576, ¶ 4 and Pg. 580, ¶ 4 – Artaxerxes III/Ochus, after poisoning his older brother, succeeded his father Artaxerxes II as king of Persia in 359 BC. His greatest achievement was the retaking of Egypt for Persia in 343 BC.**

Attalus – **Pg. 581, ¶ 3 and Pg. 582, ¶ 6 – Attalus, the uncle of Philip's last wife, questioned Alexander's right to rule Macedonia. Attalus was later killed by an assassin sent on the request of Alexander, who never forgot an insult.**

Bagoas – **Pg. 580, ¶ 5 to Pg. 581, ¶ 1 – Bagoas, one of Artaxerxes III's commanders in the victory over Egypt, seems to have poisoned the Persian king. Bagoas ran Persia as vizier after Artaxerxes III's death, and ensured his position as ruler by poisoning all three of Artaxerxes III's sons.**

Bucephalas – **Pg. 578, ¶ 3 – Bucephalas was an unmanageable Greek stallion from Thessaly that was tamed by Philip's young son, Alexander. The story of Alexander's handling of Bucephalas became famous throughout Macedonia and, later, Greece.**

Corinthian League – **Pg. 580, ¶ 3 – The Corinthian League, a league of Greek city-states, was formed by Philip of Persia after the Battle of Chaeronea. The Corinthian League was formed with the intent of attacking the Persians.**

Cyrus – **Pg. 570, ¶ 3 and Pg. 572, ¶ 1 – Cyrus, Artaxerxes II's younger brother and satrap of Sardis, attempted to usurp his brother's throne. Rejoicing after he thought he had killed Artaxerxes II, Cyrus was killed by a stray arrow that went through his temple.**

Isocrates – **Pg. 575, ¶ 4 to Pg. 576, ¶ 1 and Pg. 579, ¶ 3 – Isocrates, an Athenian orator and teacher of rhetoric, published *Panegyricus*, a written speech begging for all Greek cities to** recognize their common heritage in a new surge of pan-Hellenism, to be led by Athens. Later, Isocrates wrote a speech called *To Philip*, asking the Macedonian king to take the lead of the pan-Hellenic league.

Philip II – Pg. 577, ¶ 2 and Pg. 581, ¶ 3 – Philip II became king of Macedonia in 359 BC, after his brother Perdikkas was killed in war against the Illyrians. After a great career of empire building, Philip was killed by his jealous lover Pausanias, who stabbed the king in the back.

Section II: Comprehension

Write a two/three sentence answer to each of the following questions.

1. Describe the state of Athens and Sparta just before 400 BC.
A1. – Pg. 570, ¶ 1-3 – Around 400 BC, as many as seventy thousand Athenians were dead because of plague, war, or political purge. No one had a plan for the future, and the city was filled with widows and women who would never marry because so many men had died. Sparta wasn't doing much better; planting and harvesting had been thrown entirely off schedule, the armies storming through the Peloponnese had crushed vines, flattened olive trees and killed flocks, and thousands of Spartans left the city and became mercenaries, fighting for the Persian royal family.

2. Why was the March of the Ten Thousand an extraordinary feat?
A2. – Pg. 573, ¶ 3 – The March of the Ten Thousand was an extraordinary feat because Artaxerxes II's Persian army could not capture the retreating Greeks, who managed to escape from the very center of Persian power.

3. How did Artaxerxes II lose his grip on Egypt?
A3. – Pg. 573, ¶ 4 – Artaxerxes II lost his grip on Egypt when an Egyptian nobleman from Sais named Amyrtaeus declared himself pharaoh, and the Persian satrap was unable to get enough support from the Persian king to quell the revolt. Amyrtaeus then gained enough power to title himself as first pharaoh of the Twenty-Eighth dynasty.

4. What was the cause of the Corinthian War, and how was it resolved?
A4. – Pg. 574, ¶ 2 & 3 – The Corinthian War started when Sparta decided not to give up the Ionian cities to the Persians. Athens, Thebes, Corinth and Argos banded together to force Sparta to give up its claims. After three years of battle, Sparta backpedaled to the Persians, offering to give up the Ionian cities if the Persians would support the Spartan army once again.

5. Why did Artaxerxes II need to declare a cease-fire between Sparta and Athens? What was the name of this peace treaty?
A5. – Pg. 574, ¶ 5 & 6 – Artaxerxes II, seeing that both the Athenian and Spartan armies were exhausted, decreed that unless the two cities agreed to a peace, the Persians would step in and Artaxerxes would war against the aggressor. The treaty made by Artaxerxes II between Sparta and Athens was called the "King's Peace."

6. How did Nectanebo, founder of the Thirtieth Dynasty of Egypt, fight off the Persians and Athenians led by Artaxerxes II?

A6. – Pg. 575, ¶ 2 – Nectanebo made a stand at each stream in the Delta, fighting for a while before retreating a little bit farther south, pulling the Athenian and Persian forces further and further into Egypt. Nectanebo waited until the Nile flooded to make a quick retreat south; startled and overwhelmed by the flooding, the Persians and Athenians retreated back out of the Delta.

7. Why did Artaxerxes II have his oldest son, Darius, killed? Who succeeded Artaxerxes II as king of Persia?

A7. – Pg. 576, ¶ 2 – Artaxerxes II had his oldest son Darius killed after Darius attempted to assassinate the old king. Ochus, Artaxerxes II's youngest son, poisoned his other brothers after his father's death, and became the next king of Persia.

8. Why did Alexander II of Macedonia send his ten-year-old brother, Philip, to live in Illyria?

A8. – Pg. 576, ¶ 8 – When Alexander II became king, Illyrian tribes were threatening to invade Macedonia. Alexander II had to avoid conquest by paying the Illyrians off and sending Philip to live in Illyria as a hostage.

9. How did Philip end up as a hostage in Thebes? How was Perdikkas able to rescue his younger brother?

A9. – Pg. 576, ¶ 8 to Pg. 577, ¶ 1 – When Philip returned home from his time as a hostage in Illyria, he was then sent off to Thebes as a hostage by Ptolemy, his mother's lover, who became king after Alexander II was murdered. Perdikkas, too young to rule on his own when Ptolemy first took power, waited until the age of accession and then, with the support of Macedonian noblemen, had the usurper executed. Once Perdikkas was on the throne, he negotiated Philip's release from Thebes.

10. Why did Isocrates write the speech, *To Philip*? What was the result of this speech?

A10. – Pg. 579, ¶ 3 & 4 – Isocrates wrote the speech *To Philip* because he had given up on his hopes for willing cooperation between Greek cities to form a pan-Hellenic union. The speech resulted in the agreement of the association of Greek cities that looked after the shrine of Delphi to invite Philip into Greece.

11. What two things made the Battle of Chaeronea remarkable?

A11. – Pg. 580, ¶ 1 – The Battle of Chaeronea was remarkable because 1) Alexander courageously led his wing of the Macedonian army against the Athenian army, making his first attempt at military command a success, and 2) because it marked the end of the era of Athenian, and Greek, sovereignty. The Greek city-states would never again be free from the bonds of empire.

12. To what did Attalus toast at the wedding of his niece to Philip? Why was this toast so offensive to Alexander?

A12. – Pg. 581, ¶ 3 & 4 – Attalus made a toast at the wedding of his niece to Philip proclaiming that the gods could now send Macedonia a legitimate heir to the throne. This was offensive to Alexander, who was a legitimate heir, because it implied that his half-Macedonian and half-Greek heritage made him unfit to rule.

13. Who killed Philip, and why? What were the circumstance that led to Philip's murder?
A13. – Pg. 581, ¶ 6 to Pg. 582, ¶ 2 – Pausanias killed Philip because he was humiliated and broken hearted due to Philip's rejection of him as a lover. Pausanias insulted Philip's new lover, and in response, the young man committed suicide. After a brutal punishment by Attalus, a trusted and valuable general to Philip, and a friend of the dead man, Pausanias went mad and stabbed Philip to death.

Section III: Critical Thinking

The student may use her text to answer this question.

Often, disparate groups come together when faced with a common enemy. In the case of Philip II and the Greeks, he forced the sparring nations to come together as one. Write a paragraph describing Philip II's Greek conquests. Then, write a second paragraph explaining how Philip II's strategy in subsuming the Greek nations under Macedonian rule was different from the strategies of other conquerors in the history of the ancient world.

The student may look back over her text when writing about the sequence of Philip II's battles in Greece. The description of Philip II's battles against the Greeks starts on page 577, ¶ 2 and ends on page 580, ¶ 3.

EXAMPLE ANSWER, Paragraph 1:
When Philip inherited Macedonia's throne, Macedonia was at war against the Illyrians, and Athens was making an attempt to put a candidate of their own on the Macedonian throne. Philip handled the Athenians by surrendering a border city to their control, and then, after teaching his soldiers how to fight in a Greek phalanx, Philip II triumphed against the Illyrians. Philip II continued his conquests through marriage, allying or dominating the territories along the Thermaic Gulf, the border between Macedonia and Thrace, and the north and northwest borders of Macedonia. Philip then went to Greece. When the ruler of the Greek city of Pherae was assassinated, Philip restored order, and then kept control of the city. He took Thrace, the city he had previously yielded to Athens, and then Athens itself. Philip then made a speech at Corinth suggesting that Greek submission to his kingship would be good for Greece. Though Sparta refused, the rest of the Greek cities agreed to join Philip in the Corinthian League.

The key to the second part of the question is found on page 578, ¶ 2: "Philip went right on swallowing bits of Greece. His push southwards was not so much against a Greece that he wanted to conquer, as a Greece that he wanted to absorb. His infantry, his cavalry, his very court were salted with Greeks." Unlike other conquerors, Philip did not want to destroy Greek culture. When Philip took Athens, he treated the city and its people with great respect, releasing his prisoners and even putting together an honor guard to accompany the Athenian dead back to the city. Though some Athenians may not have agreed, Philip felt he was helping the Athenians by taking control of their city. Philip's speech at Corinth made it clear that he wanted to help all of the Greek cities by putting them under Macedonian rule. Many other conquests that we've read about relied on breaking apart old associations and alliances, erasing native cultures and replacing them with the habits of the ruling king. Philip did not treat the Greek cities this way. Philip II wanted the Greek cities to be under Macedonia's rule while keeping their Greek identities.

EXAMPLE ANSWER, Paragraph 2:
Philip II's strategy in subsuming the Greek nations under Macedonian rule was different from the strategies of other conquerors in the history of the ancient world in that he wanted to absorb the Greek cities rather than conquer them. When Philip took Athens, he treated the city and its people with great respect, releasing his prisoners and even putting together an honor guard to accompany the Athenian dead back to the city. Philip then made a speech at Corinth suggesting that Greek submission to his kingship would be good for Greece, uniting the previously squabbling cities under one leader. Philip II's conquest of Greece was different from previous conquerors in the ancient world because he did not want to destroy Greek culture and rebuilt the cities as Macedonian. He wanted the Greek cities to exist as they were, but under Macedonia's rule.

CHAPTER SIXTY-NINE: ROME TIGHTENS ITS GRASP

The student may use his text when answering the questions in sections I and II.

Section I: Who, What, Where

Write a one or two-sentence answer explaining the significance of each item listed below.

Agathocles – **Pg. 588, ¶ 2 & 4 – Agathocles was a Sicilian ex-potter who married well, hired himself an army, and made himself tyrant of Syracuse. Though he could not conquer Carthage, Agathocles was able to conquer most of the rest of Sicily.**

Appian Way – **Pg. 589, ¶ 1 – The Appian Way was a road which ran from the coast of Rome all the way down to Capua in Campania. The road was named after consul Appius Claudius Caecus, who began the project in 312.**

Latin League – **Pg. 584, ¶ 1 – The Latin League was the name of the alliance made between the cities in the old territory of Latium. The Romans called this league the *Nomen Latium*, and while relations between the Latin League and Rome were friendly, Rome never joined.**

Samnites – **Pg. 585, ¶ 4 – The Samnites were an alliance of tribes from the southern Apennines, who lived in a mesh of farms and villages below Rome and east of the coastal area of Campania. The Samnites were known as great fighters.**

Section II: Comprehension

Write a two/three sentence answer to each of the following questions.

1. What decision was made in 367 BC that ended the plebian and patrician standoff in Rome?
A1. – Pg. 584, ¶ 2 – In 367 BC, the decision was made to open the consulship of Rome to plebians, a concession that ended the most recent plebian and patrician standoff. The first plebian consul was installed in the same year that the decision was made.

2. Describe the terms of the Cassius treaty. In what way did the Cassius treaty legitimate Rome's power in the middle of the 4th century BC?
A2. – Pg. 585, ¶ 1 and Footnote – The Cassius treaty, made between Rome and the Latin League, stated that the two sides were obliged to defend each other in attack. All booty from joint campaigns would be divided equally between the two sides, meaning Rome would get as much out of the victory as all the cities of the League combined. This showed that Rome had as much power as the whole of the Latin League, legitimating its place as a force to be reckoned with.

3. What were the terms of the renegotiated treaty between Carthage and Rome?

A3. – Pg. 585, ¶ 2 – As per the old treaty, Roman ships weren't supposed to sail farther west than Fair Promontory, and the Carthaginians still promised not to build any forts in the territory of the Latins. A new condition was made in 348 BC; if the Carthaginians captured any city in Latium which was not subject to Rome, the Carthaginians would keep the goods and the men, and Rome would get the city. The treaty made Carthage and Rome partners in conquest.

4. For what reason did Rome claim to go to war with the Samnites in 343? What was the real reason Rome decided to attack their neighbors?

A4. – Pg. 585, ¶ 5 – Rome claimed that the Samnites had unjustly attacked the people who lived in the region of Campania, on the southwestern coast, and so Rome attacked the Samnites in retaliation. Really, Rome saw Campania as a piece of land to be subsumed by the Samnites or the Romans, and so the Romans attacked the Samnites to ensure their stake on Campania.

5. Despite just having fought in the First Samnite War against the Romans, why did the Samnites fight on Rome's side in the Latin War?

A5. – Pg. 587, ¶ 2 – The Samnites fought on Rome's side in the Samnite War in order to keep Latin power from spreading farther to the south.

6. What did Rome do to cut ties between the cities of the Latin League after victory in the Latin War?

A6. – Pg. 587, ¶ 5 – The Romans barred the Latins from intermarriage and trade with each other, and they were not allowed to hold councils amongst themselves. These rules were put in place in order to cut ties between the cities of the Latin League.

7. What is the meaning of *civitas sine suffragio*? Who was given this label?

A7. – Pg. 587, ¶ 5 – *Civitas sine suffragio* means citizens without the vote. The people of Campania who had fought on Rome's side in the Latin War were given this label; they were protected by the Laws of the Twelve Tables, but given no voice in Rome's decisions.

8. What caused the second Samnite War?

A8. – Pg. 587, ¶ 7 to Pg. 588, ¶ 1 – The cause of the second Samnite War was Roman aggression against the Samnites. When the Romans crossed the Liri River, the boundary between the Romans and the Samnites, to build a colony in Samnite land, the Samnites once again rose up in arms.

9. What archaeological evidence supports Diodorus's claim that Carthaginians sacrificed hundreds of children in order to assure victory over Syracuse?

A9. – Pg. 588, Footnote – Excavation near the ancient ports of Carthage has revealed the remains of victims, supporting Diodorus's claim that Carthaginians sacrificed children in their religious practice.

10. How did Rome manage to reduce its opponents in the Third Samnite War from Etruscans, Umbrians, Samnites and Gauls to just Samnites and Gauls?

A10. – Pg. 589, ¶ 3 – In order to increase their chances of victory, Rome sent a detachment to raid Etruscan and Umbrian land, hoping to break up the four-way alliance that waited for them

in Sentinum. The plan worked; the Etruscan and Umbrian contingents went home to defend their families and farms and the Romans were left to face only the Samnites and the Gauls.

11. Why did the Roman cavalry scatter in terror when the Gauls charged at them during the battle in Sentinum? How did the battle at Sentinum end?
A11. – Pg. 589, ¶ 3 – The Roman cavalry scattered when the Gauls charged at them because the Gauls were in chariots, which many Romans had never seen before. Despite the skittish start of the battle, the Romans were able to break the Gaulish and Samnite line, invade their camp, and block their enemy's retreat.

Section III: Critical Thinking

The student may use his text to answer this question.

Chapter Sixty-Nine begins with an account of Rome's refusal to join the Latin League, and ends with this phrase: "the Roman fist, closing over the countryside, was armored." Yet, as we read, Rome did not win every battle it started, and most of the time Rome had to sign a treaty in order to end a stalemate war. What, then, made Rome such a threat to its neighbors? Write a paragraph explaining how Rome could cause so much turmoil without the clout of numerous conquests and successes on its side.

To get the student started on his answer, you might want to ask how Rome saw itself among its peers. The chapter opens, explaining, "...while they had been reasonably friendly with the Latin League cities for over a century...Rome never joined. The city was not inclined to become one among equals" (Pg. 584, ¶ 1). In 358, Rome renegotiated its treaty with the Latin League, and was able to demand that any spoils of war be divided equally between the two sides. The text states, "Rome was no longer simply another city on the peninsula; it was a power as great as the League itself" (Pg. 585, ¶ 1). Because Rome always saw itself as a great, singular power, its leaders demanded that it be treated as such. The student should next think about Rome's persistence in war. Rome went to war with the Samnites numerous times, they won the Latin War, and after the stalemate of the Third Samnite War, "Roman soldiers marched out every year to fight in the north and center of the Italian peninsula" (Pg. 590, ¶ 1). Though the Romans had to sign several treaties to end stalemate wars, the country's military ambition cannot be denied. The Romans never saw themselves as part of a league because Rome's officials had ambitions to dominate its neighbors. Rome's constant willingness to attack its neighbors for more land made it a threat, despite the fact that Rome did not always win. Rome's iron fist kept punching out, ceaseless in its ambition for more territory and more power.

EXAMPLE ANSWER: Rome always saw itself as exceptional. While Rome was friendly with the Latin League, it did not become part of the League because it did not see itself as one among equals. Eventually, Rome demanded as much power as the League, and in the renewed treaty between the Latin League and Rome, it was agreed upon that any spoils of war be divided equally between Rome and the cities of the League. Rome had made itself as powerful as the combined cities in the League. To further increase its power, Rome was constantly going to

war. In the Latin War, Rome was successful, and acquired an empire's worth of Italian land. However, each of the three wars Rome fought against the Samnites ended in either a stalemate or bad peace. Rome's threat, then, didn't come from its ability to win wars, but its ceaseless desire to go to war. Rome's iron fist kept punching out, incessant in its ambition for more territory and more power.

Chapter Seventy: Alexander and the Wars of the Successors

The student may use her text when answering the questions in sections I and II.

Section I: Who, What, Where

Write a one or two-sentence answer explaining the significance of each item listed below.

Arthashastra – **Pg. 605, ¶ 6 to Pg. 606, ¶ 1 – Arthashastra was a political handbook written by Kautilya, which stated that the Indian ruler was to enforce internal order by making sure his subjects properly observed the caste system. The Arthashastra also taught that the Indian ruler was to preserve outside order by suspecting every neighbor of planning conquest, and taking the proper precautions against invasion.**

Chandragupta – **Pg. 605, ¶ 5 – Chandragupta, Indian king of Maurya, made war on the last Nanda king of Magadha and captured the kingdom, turning Maurya into an empire.**

Cleitus the Black – **Pg. 593, ¶ 4 and Pg. 597, ¶ 3 – Cleitus the Black, one of Alexander's commanders, saved Alexander's life by cutting off an attacker's arm at the shoulder before the enemy could strike. Later, Cleitus accused Alexander of taking credit for victories won by the blood of loyal Macedonians, a taunt which cost Cleitus his life.**

Drypetis – **Pg. 599, ¶ 2 and Pg. 600, ¶ 6 – Drypetis, younger daughter of Darius III, was married to Hephaestion in Alexander's mass wedding. Drypetis was poisoned by Roxane after Alexander and Hephaestion's deaths.**

Hephaestion – **Pg. 599, ¶ 2 and Pg. 600, ¶ 1-2 – Hephaestion, Alexander's closest friend and most trusted general, died when his stomach burst after eating a huge meal of chicken, most likely caused by a bout of typhoid. Alexander never recovered from Hephaestion's death, grew ill himself, and died shortly after.**

Kautilya – **Pg. 605, ¶ 6 – Kautilya, Chandragupta's closest advisor, is given credit for writing the ancient political handbook *Arthashastra*.**

Kodomannos/Darius III – **Pg. 592, ¶ 4 & 5 – Kodomannos was the puppet-king installed by Bagoas. Kodomannos poisoned Bagoas, and then declared himself Darius III, King of Persia.**

Mahapadma Nanda – **Pg. 597, ¶ 5 & 6 – Mahapadma Nanda was an illegitimate son of the Indian royal line who had taken the royal crown from the direct descendants of the King Ajatashatru of Magadha in 424 BC. Mahapadma Nanda lived to be the greatest Indian conqueror the nation had seen; he pushed the territory of Magadha all the way down to the northern edge of the dry southern desert, the Deccan.**

Parmenio – **Pg. 596, ¶ 4 and Pg. 597, ¶ 1 – Parmenio was one of Alexander's commanders. Parmenio was put to death, along with his son, after his son was convicted of plotting against Alexander's life.**

Philip Arrhidaeus – **Pg. 601, ¶ 1 & 2 – Philip Arrhidaeus, Alexander's feeble minded half-brother, was installed in Babylon, where Alexander brought him in order to keep him safe. Philip Arrhidaeus was named king after Alexander's death.**

Roxane – **Pg. 597, ¶ 2 and Pg. 600, ¶ 5 & 6 – Roxane, a beautiful princess from Sogdiana, was Alexander's first wife. Fearing that her child would be replaced by the heir Alexander produced with Persian born Stateira, Roxane poisoned Alexander's other wife, and her sister, Drypetis.**

Stateira – **Pg. 599, ¶ 2 & Pg. 600, ¶ 6 – Stateira, daughter of Darius III, wed Alexander and became pregnant with his heir. Stateira and her unborn baby were poisoned by Roxane after Alexander's death.**

King Taxiles – **Pg. 598, ¶ 3 – King Taxiles of India made an alliance with Alexander, giving him gifts and tribute soldiers, in exchange for Alexander's help in fighting Taxila's enemy, Hydaspes.**

Wars of the Diadochi/Wars of the Successors – **Pg. 601, ¶ 5 – Wars of the Diadochi, or, Wars of the Successors, were the wars that broke out after Alexander's death, caused by the division of his kingdom into satrapies.**

Section II: Comprehension

Write a two/three sentence answer to each of the following questions.

1. Why was Athens so quick to surrender to Alexander after its secession from the Corinthian League? **A1. – Pg. 591, ¶ 2 & 3 – Athens quickly surrendered to Alexander after its secession from the Corinthian League because the Athenians saw what would happen if they did not do as Alexander wished. The Thebans refused to give in to Alexander and, as a result, the city was sacked and razed, thirty thousand Thebans were sold as slaves and around six thousand were killed. Fearing Alexander's wrath, the Athenians did whatever they could to get on Alexander's good side as fast as possible.**

2. Where was Alexander when he charged his men to attack Persia? How did this influence the performance of Alexander's army? **A2. – Pg. 593, ¶ 4 – When the Macedonian army attacked the Persians, Alexander was right in the middle of the first charge and fought on the front line until the end of battle. Alexander's presence showed his courage, and this in turn made his men even more ferocious.**

3. Why, despite having a massive force behind him, was Darius III defeated at Babylon? **A3. – Pg. 595, ¶ 2 & 3 – Darius III expected to fight Alexander in open country near the old Assyrian heartland, but instead marched on Asia Minor and confronted the enemy at the Issus River, in Syria. The small battlefield could not accommodate all of Darius III's soldiers, so his mass of soldiers gave the Persians no advantage.**

4. How did Darius III's actions after Alexander's success in Syria reinforce Bagoas's characterization of the puppet-king as mild-mannered?**A4. – Pg. 595, ¶ 3 to Pg. 596, ¶ 3 – After Alexander's troops broke through the Persian line at the Issus River in Syria, Darius III fled, leaving behind his wife, aged mother and all his children. Darius III then sent a letter to Alexander asking for the release of his family if he offered himself as an ally. Alexander declined, and Darius III never retrieved his family. Bagoas was right; Darius must have been really frightened of Alexander if he was willing to desert his family and leave them in Macedonian company.**

5. Why did Alexander encourage his men to sack Persepolis? What command did Alexander give his men?**A5. – Pg. 596, ¶ 5 – When Alexander arrived at Persepolis, he found a whole contingent of Greek prisoners of war, some of whom had been taken captive decades before in older wars, but all of whom had been made slaves. To keep them from escaping, their Persian masters has amputated whatever arms and legs they didn't need to fulfill their tasks. Alexander was moved to fury; he ordered his men to sack the city, they could burn what they wanted and kill or enslave who they wanted, but they were not to rape any women.**

6. What stopped Alexander from killing the constantly-fleeing Darius III?**A6. – Pg. 596, ¶ 6 – Alexander wasn't able to kill Darius III because Darius III's own men turned against him. His cavalry commander and one of his satraps stabbed him, and left him in a wagon to die in the hot July sun.**

7. Why did Alexander's men turn against him after he was called "Great King?"
A7. – Pg. 597, ¶ 1 & 2 – Alexander's men thought that once Alexander was Great King, their tour of duty would be over, but Alexander wanted to take the northeastern satrapies for Macedonia, and made his men campaign over rough terrain for another three years. Alexander also married a princess from Sogdiana, a tribe that was thought of as slaves and barbarians, and he increasingly dressed like a Persian and followed Persian customs. Alexander's men believed he was becoming less and less Macedonian as he took more and more territory.

8. Why did the Macedonians turn around and head home after their victory against Porus, king of Hydaspes?**A8. – Pg. 598, ¶ 6 – Though the Macedonians were victorious, Alexander's army suffered heavy losses against Porus and his elephants. Alexander III's men refused to face more hostile Indians and elephants, and demanded that Alexander lead them back home.**

9. What happened to Alexander during his trek home from India?**A9. – Pg. 598, ¶ 8 to Pg. 599, ¶ 1 – On the march back to Macedonia, Alexander was struck in the chest by an arrow during a fight with the Mallians, a hostile riverside town along the Indus. Alexander seemed to be dead for some hours; when they resumed the march home Alexander could barely sit on a horse, and the wound never completely healed.**

10. Describe the two strategies Alexander employed to bring together the Macedonians and Persians, and their outcomes.**A10. – Pg. 599, ¶ 3 & 4 – Alexander hosted a mass wedding between Macedonian noblemen and hundreds of Persian noblewomen in an attempt to end hostilities between the two peoples. Alexander also rounded up thousands of Persian boys and put them under the command of Macedonian officers, to be trained in Macedonian fighting. Both experiments backfired – most of the mass marriages fell apart and the**

Macedonian foot soldiers hated the Persian youths so much that they threatened to go back to Macedonia.

11. Who were the men that wanted a piece of Alexander's conquests after the king died? **A11. – Pg. 601, ¶ 2 – The men who wanted a piece of Alexander's conquests after he died were: Ptolemy, a Macedonian who was rumored to be a bastard son of old Philip himself; Antigonus, one of Alexander's trusted generals; Lysimachus, one of Alexander's companions on the Indian campaign; and Perdiccas, who had served as commander of cavalry and then, after Hephaestion's death, as second-in-command.**

12. What were the terms of the "Partition of Babylon?" **A12. – Pg. 601, ¶ 3 & 4 – By the "Partition of Babylon," Alexander's kingdom would be divided into satrapies: Ptolemy would govern Egypt; Antigonus, most of Asia Minor; Lysimachus would rule Thrace; Antipater, one of Alexander's trusted officers, would rule over Macedonia and keep tabs on Greece, and Cassender, Antipater's son, would ruler over Caria, which was the southern Asia Minor coast, and five other officers were granted control of other parts of the empire. Perdiccas would stay in Babylon and act as regent for Philip and his possible co-ruler, Roxane's unborn baby.**

13. What became of Pyrrhus after he was driven out of Macedonia by Lysimachus? **A13. – Pg. 607, ¶ 3, 5-7 – After Pyrrhus was driven out of Macedonia, he was allowed to keep his rule over Epirus. As ruler of Epirus, Pyrrhus helped the people of Tarentum fight off the Romans by hiring elephants and mercenaries, and he followed up on this success by helping Asculum keep the Romans away. Then, still looking for glory, while fighting in a Spartan civil war, an old woman threw a tile at him from a roof top and knocked him unconscious, after which he was killed at once by his opponent.**

Section III: Critical Thinking

The student may use her text to answer this question.

There is no question that Alexander was a great warrior and strategist. His headstrong nature, however, meant that Alexander would not stop until he had what he wanted, be it a horse, or a kingdom. Alexander's forceful ways may have created a larger-than-life empire, but that also meant the ties that bound the conquered territories together were weak. The "Partition of Babylon," created to keep all the parts of Alexander's kingdoms safe, was actually the quickest way to ensure the breakup of the empire. Write a brief summary of the seven scenes of the Wars of the Diadochi, showing each phase of the destruction of Alexander's kingdom.

This chapter is packed with information about Alexander and his empire. For this critical thinking exercise, the student is expected to synthesize the information presented about the Wars of the Diadochi succinctly. No summary should be more than three sentences, except for scene 7, which is particularly dense. The scenes of the Wars of the Diadochi are clearly labeled in the text on pages 603 to 607. For the ease of reference, the page and paragraphs that are being summarized are listed before each example.

EXAMPLE ANSWER: Scene 1 - Pg. 603, ¶ 1-3 – Ptolemy kidnapped Alexander's body and buried it in Egypt, an attempt to show Egypt's power as the strongest of all the satrapies. Perdiccas's forces marched against Egypt only to be embarrassed by Ptolemy's army. As a result Perdiccas was assassinated by one of his officers, Seleucus, who was then named satrap of Babylon by Ptolemy.

Scene 2 - Pg. 603, ¶ 4 to Pg. 604, ¶ 1 – When Antipater died, Cassender gained control of Macedonia with some help from Ptolemy and Antigonus. Olympias, Alexander's mother, made a play for the throne herself, but unable to fight off Ptolemy and Antigonus, took concession in stabbing King Philip to death, for which she was then stoned to death for murder. Roxane and her son, young Alexander, were put under house arrest.

Scene 3 - Pg. 604, ¶ 2 & 3 – Cassender poisoned Roxane and young Alexander. For the next half-decade the five generals pretended Alexander IV was still alive, and no one named himself king for fear of having the other four generals allied against him.

Scene 4 - Pg. 604, ¶ 4 to Pg. 605, ¶ 1 – After defeating Cassender's troops in Greece and Ptolemy's ships in a naval battle at Salamis, Antigonus took the title of king. Rather than allying themselves with Antigonus, Lysimachus and Seleucus began to call themselves kings as well, as did Ptolemy and Cassender.

Scene 5 - Pg. 605, ¶ 2 & 3 - After the Battle of Ipsus in 301 BC, five kings remained, but the borders had shifted: Antigonus was dead, but his son lived on and became king of Greece, Lysimachus took the western part of Asia minor for his own, adding it to Thrace; Seleucus took the rest of Antigonus's old territory; Cassender and Ptolemy remained in control of Macedonia and Egypt, respectively.

Scene 6 - Pg. 605 ¶ 4 to Pg. 606, ¶ 3 – Chandragupta, the Indian king of the Mauryan empire, made a treaty with Seleucus: he would give Seleucus war elephants if Seleucus would give the Indian territories once claimed by Alexander back to India. Seleucus agreed, and in 299 the two swore out a peace.

Scene 7 – Pg. 606, ¶ 4 to Pg. 607, ¶ 3 – Demetrius took Macedonia after Cassender died. Pyrrhus, first cousin of Alexander the Great himself, married Ptolemy's stepdaughter, and appealed to his father-in-law to get his old kingdom of Epirus back, which he did, as well as driving out Demetrius and overrunning the rest of Macedonia. Demetrius then started a fight with Seleucus, who put Demetrius under house arrest where he drank himself to death. Lysimachus came down from Thrace and drove Pyrrhus out of Macedonia. Now there were three kings and three kingdoms: Ptolemy ruled the Ptolemaic, Seleucus ruled the Seleucid and Lysimachus ruled the Thracian-Macedonian domain.

CHAPTER SEVENTY-ONE: THE MAURYAN EPIPHANY

The student may use his text when answering the questions in sections I and II.

Section I: Who, What, Where

Write a one or two-sentence answer explaining the significance of each item listed below.

Aparigraha – **Pg. 609, ¶ 1 – Aparigraha is the Jainist belief in the detachment from all material things. Chandragupta Maurya died when he starved himself to death in an extreme demonstration of aparigraha.**

Bindusara – **Pg. 609, ¶ 2 – Bindusara, Chandragupta Maurya's successor, spent his reign empire-building, expanding the Mauryan empire down south into the Deccan, as far as Karnataka. The Greeks called him *Amitrochates*, which means "slayer of enemies," a name for a conqueror.**

Devi – **Pg. 611, ¶ 2 – Devi was a beautiful woman from Ujjain with which Asoka fathered two children. One of Devi's sons became a Buddhist missionary, which suggests that Devi was a Buddhist.**

Section II: Comprehension

Write a two/three sentence answer to each of the following questions.

1. What were the locations and names of the kingdoms of India during Bindusara's reign?**A1. – Pg. 609, ¶ 3 – During Bindusara's reign, the Mauryan empire was centered in the north of India. In the southeast, one could find Kalinga, Andhra lay in the center of the southern peninsula, Chera was to the west and a little to the south, and at the very top of the subcontinent was the land of the Pandyas.**

2. How might we explain the difference between the language spoken in the north and south of India?
A2. – Pg. 609, ¶ 4 to Pg. 610, ¶ 1 – We can explain the difference between the language in the north and south of India because the people of southern India had a different heritage than the people of northern India. It is possible the people in the south descended from intrepid sailors who made it across the Arabian Sea from Africa millennia earlier.

3. Where did King Asoka carve inscriptions about his life? What names were given to the places where the inscriptions were carved? **A3. – Pg. 610, ¶ 3 – King Asoka carved inscriptions about his life all around his empire, first on rocks and then on sandstone pillars. The rock carvings were called the Rock Edicts, and the pillar carvings were called the Pillar Edicts.**

4. What major events defined King Asoka's early life? **A4. – Pg. 610, ¶ 3 to Pg. 611, ¶ 1 – As a young man, Asoka was sent to Taxila to put down a rebellion. After that, he was sent to Ujjain to govern one of the five janapadas into which the Mauryan empire had been divided.**

5. Describe King Asoka's 206 BC campaign against Kalinga. **A5. – Pg. 611, ¶ 4 – In 206 BC, King Asoka took an army down south to campaign against Kalinga. A hundred and fifty thousand people were deported, a hundred thousand were killed, and many times that number perished.**

6. What is dhamma?
A6. – Pg. 611, ¶ 6 – While it is very difficult to define dhamma, it is a way of thinking that means something like "the Way, the Rightness, the Duty, the Virtue."

7. What was Asoka's most lasting achievement?
A7. – Pg. 611, ¶ 8 – Asoka's most lasting achievement was his calling together of a Buddhist council to reassert the principles of dhamma. The Third Buddhist Council, held around 245 in the city of Pataliputra, gave birth to one of the books of the Pali Canon.

Section III: Critical Thinking

King Asoka attempted to build his empire the traditional ancient world way by conquering his enemies. Seeing the destruction caused by his military campaigns, Asoka shifted his perspective and tried to build his empire by other means. Write a paragraph explaining King Asoka's attempt to find a new unifying principle to build his empire. In your answer, explain whether or not this principle actually worked.

The first thing the student should recognize is that though King Asoka renounced the violent ways of his past, he still had ambitions to build an empire. The student should then state how King Asoka approached empire building without war. King Asoka hoped his new beliefs would also combat the old clan loyalties that divided India. As written on page 612, ¶ 2, "The clan system that had survived for so long in India…was not one that lent itself easily to the establishment of empire; clan loyalties tended to pull the country apart into smaller political units, each negotiating friendship or hostility with those around it…In place of the old clan loyalties, or loyalties enforced by conquest, Asoka tried for a third kind of loyalty: a common belief system that would make all Indians 'my children' (as the Kalinga inscription puts it)." King Asoka wanted to build an empire that was tied together by peace and good feeling, and he wanted his sons to follow in his serene footsteps. The text states, "Any sons or great-grandsons that I may have should not think of gaining new conquests…delight in dhamma should be their whole delight, for this is of value in both this world and the next" (Pg. 611, ¶ 6). Finally, the student should address the results of Asoka's reforms. We learn at the end of the chapter that Asoka's attempt to create an empire united by dhamma failed. After Asoka's death, the Mauryan empire crumbled, and its history is dark to us. Asoka's descendants "lost hold of their kingdom and it separated again into smaller battling territories" (Pg. 612, ¶ 3).

EXAMPLE ANSWER: Though King Asoka renounced the violent ways of his past, he still had ambitions to build an empire. His idea was to build an empire unified by dhamma rather than by bloodshed. Also, King Asoka had to combat old clan loyalties. He thought a common belief system could be stronger than clan ties. King Asoka wanted his descendants to follow in his footsteps, practicing dhamma as a unifying principle that would benefit Indians in both this world and the next. Unfortunately, after his death, King Asoka's reforms were abandoned, and his empire fell apart. The history of the Indians grows dark, Asoka's sons and grandsons lost hold of the Mauryan kingdom, and it separated again into smaller battling territories.

CHAPTER SEVENTY-TWO: FIRST EMPEROR, SECOND DYNASTY

The student may use her text when answering the questions in sections I and II.

Section I: Who, What, Where

Write a one or two-sentence answer explaining the significance of each item listed below.

221 BC – **Pg. 614, ¶ 5 & 6** – 221 BC is the date from which we can actually speak of China, a country unified by Cheng.

Cheng/Shi Huang-ti – **Pg. 614, ¶ 2 & 6** – Cheng became king of Ch'in at only thirteen, and he was kept safe by his official guardians until he was old enough to rule. Cheng unified China under one rule, and became Shi Huang-ti, or "First Emperor."

Han Dynasty – **Pg. 620, ¶ 5** – The Han Dynasty was the first lasting dynasty of China, unified under Liu Pang/Gao Zu. The Han Dynasty would last for four hundred years.

Hu-hai/Second Emperor – **Pg. 618, ¶ 2 and Pg. 619, ¶ 4** – Hu-hai, Shi Huang-ti's son, became the Second Emperor after his father's death. Hu-hai, constantly afraid of rebellion, killed himself when he found out his chancellor had plotted against him.

Hsiang Yu – **Pg. 619, ¶ 6** – Hsiang Yu, a Chu general, killed Tzu Ying, massacred the court, burned the palace and handed the royal treasures out to his allies, all in an effort to wipe out the pretentions of the Ch'in.

Liu Pang/Gao Zu – **Pg. 620, ¶ 2** – Liu Pang, an official in Hsiang Yu's rebellious army, was awarded the leadership of the Han territory in exchange for his service. Liu Pang fought his way into control of all of China, and claimed the title of emperor, and gave himself the name Gao Zu.

Tzu-Ying/Third Emperor – **Pg. 619, ¶ 5 & 6** – Tzu Ying, the Second Emperor's nephew, was installed by the Second Emperor's chancellor as ruler after the Second Emperor's suicide. Though his rule only lasted for forty-six days, he did have time to kill the scheming chancellor that put him on the throne.

Yen Lo – **Pg. 619, ¶ 3 & 4** – Yen Lo, son-in-law to the Second Emperor's chancellor, was used by the chancellor to dethrone Hu-hai. Yen Lo, thinking the Second Emperor was holding his mother hostage, stormed the palace and let the Second Emperor know his reign was coming to an end.

Section II: Comprehension

Write a two/three sentence answer to each of the following questions.

1. How did Ch'in handle the rising ambitions of the Chao kingdom?

A1. – Pg. 613, ¶ 2 – The Ch'in aggressively attacked the growing Chao kingdom. The armies met on the wide plains of China, and tens of thousands of Ch'in and Chao men died in the battle. When the Chao army surrendered, the captives were massacred by the Ch'in in huge numbers.

2. What happened to the Nine Tripods after the end of Zhou rule?

A2. – Pg. 613, ¶ 4 to Pg. 614, ¶ 1 – After the Ch'in invaded Zhou territory, the Nine Tripods were removed by the Ch'in from their sacred site and paraded in triumph along the river. One of the tripods fell into the water, and all attempts to get it back out again failed. The sign of the Chinese king's divinely bestowed power would remain forever incomplete.

3. Why did Cheng start recording the age of boys in Ch'in in 231 BC?

A3. – Pg. 614, ¶ 4 – Cheng started having the age of boys recorded in 231 BC because he was probably starting a draft. Cheng had ambitions to take all of China for his own, and he needed a massive army in order to do so.

4. What were the circumstances around the crown prince of Yen's death?

A4. – Pg. 614, ¶ 4 – The crown prince of Yen was worried about Cheng's growing power, so he sent an assassin disguised as an ambassador to Cheng's court. Cheng discovered the false ambassador's real purpose and had the man dismembered. The following year Cheng marched into Yen, captured the crown prince, and beheaded him.

5. How did Shi Huang-ti break down old lines of family influence, inherited wealth, and clan loyalties of the former Chinese states?

A5. – Pg. 615, ¶ 1 – Shi Huang-ti broke down old loyalties by dividing his empire into thirty-six areas of command called jun, with each jun divided into smaller counties called xian. A paired military commander and civilian administrator governed each jun, and a government spy would keep tabs on each pair. Also, no relatives of officials were handed jobs and former noblemen from every state were brought to the capital and settled in new homes so that the king could keep an eye on them.

6. What other reforms, outside of breaking up old alliances, did Shi Huang-ti put in place to create an efficient society?

A6. – Pg. 615, ¶ 2 to Pg. 616, ¶ 1 – Shi Huang-ti built roads out to every edge of China; he built canals for transportation and irrigation, and he restarted the calendar, so that everyone in his domain would follow the same system. He also created universal measurements, and he tightened up Chinese writing by standardizing characters.

7. Why did Shi Huang-ti have all the records in the Scribes' offices which were not Ch'in's, as well as any books that were not books of medicine, divination, or gardening, destroyed?

A7. – Pg. 616, ¶ 3 – Shi Huang-ti destroyed old records and books from the days before his rule because he was trying to create a new China in which there could be no rejection of the present based on the past. By erasing any proof that China had once been divided, Shi Huang-ti hoped to pull his empire together.

8. Why was Shi Huang-ti buried with almost seven thousand life-size pottery soldiers and horses?
A8. – Shi Huang-ti was buried with thousands of pottery soldiers and horses in order to represent his earthly power. Shi Huang-ti could no longer express his power by compelling hundreds of courtiers to follow him to the grave, so he substituted men made of terracotta for real ones.

9. What prompted the Second Emperor to slaughter scores of people across China? What was the result of these deaths?
A9. – Pg. 618, ¶ 2 to Pg. 619, ¶ 1 – The Second Emperor felt that the recently unified states were not yet fully subordinate to his central authority. His chancellor suggested that he demonstrate his authority by force, eliminating all jun commanders and ex-nobles who seemed too reluctant to the Second Emperor's authority. The Second Emperor took his chancellor's advice, but his violent actions had the reverse effect; soon after the slaughter, revolt spread from jun to jun and the old states reemerged.

10. Why did Liu Pang claim a right to punish Hsiang Yu after the slaughter of the Ch'in court and redistribution of Chinese territories?
A10. – Pg. 620, ¶ 2 & 3 – After the slaughter of the Ch'in court, Hsiang Yu claimed a territory in the old Chu and settled down to rule it, that is, after he had the man with the best claim to be the real Duke of Chu murdered. Liu Pang claimed that it was his righteous duty to punish the murderer of a king, and so he marched towards Hsiang Yu with his own army.

11. What was the course of events that led to Liu Pang's reunification of China?
A11. – Pg. 620, ¶ 2-5 – Liu Pang began his reunification of China in the Han territory, which he was given by Hsiang Yu. Liu Pang then took Hsiang Yang, and from there he fought an ongoing battle against other kingly claimants, rewarding his officers with captured land. By 202 he had managed to fight his way into control of almost every one of the old kingdoms of China, finally taking Chu when Hsiang Yu killed himself instead of surrendering to Liu Pang's approaching army.

Section III: Critical Thinking

The student may not use her text to answer this question.

The Great Wall of China is a famous landmark that many believe Shi Huang-ti built during his time as First Emperor. This is not the case, however. Write a paragraph or two explaining how the Great Wall really came into existence. Then, draw a parallel between the building materials used to link together the pieces of the wall, and Shi Huang-ti's unification of China.

Part Five: Identity

In the first part of this answer, the student should easily recall from her reading that the states of China had been building walls to protect themselves from barbarians, and ambitious neighbors, for generations (Pg. 616, ¶ 4). Shi Huang-ti's idea was to link all of the walls together.

In the second part of the answer, the student should recall that the wall was composed of separate, already existing pieces (Pg. 616, ¶ 4 to Pg. 617, ¶ 1). The connecting walls were built with whatever materials lay at hand, for example, stone in the mountains, packed earth in the plains, sand and pebbles in the desert. The cost of connecting the walls was thousands of Chinese lives, peasants, prisoners, soldiers and farmers, all sent to labor for the good of the country (Pg. 617, ¶ 2). Like the already existing pieces of the wall, Shi Huang-ti had to pull together the already existing states into a unified Chinese whole. The customs of the various territories were molded into a single Chinese identity, much like the building materials of sand and pebbles were no longer just sand and pebbles, but a strong fortification against outsiders. And like the lives cost to make the wall, thousands of soldiers were killed in China's wide fields during the battles fought by Shi Huang-ti for power over all of the states. The wall, made of many different parts to create one whole, was the earth-and-stone embodiment of Shi Huang-ti's vision of China, formerly separate states bound together into a single, unified nation.

Chapter Seventy-Three: The Wars of the Sons

The student may use his text when answering the questions in sections I and II.

Section I: Who, What, Where

Write a one or two-sentence answer explaining the significance of each item listed below.

Aetolian League – **Pg. 634, ¶ 6 to Pg. 635, ¶ 1 – The Aetolian League was an alliance of cities in the center of the Greek peninsula, south of Macedonia and north of the Gulf of Corinth. This league was allied with the Romans against the Macedonians and Carthaginians.**

Agathocles – **Pg. 622, ¶ 3 and Pg. 623, ¶ 2 & 3 – Agathocles, son of Lysimachus from his first marriage, was heir to Thrace's throne. Agathocles was imprisoned after he was accused by Ptolemy Ceraunus and Arsinoe of plotting to assassinate Lysimachus; Agathocles died in prison, where he was most likely killed by Ptolemy Ceraunus.**

Antiochus I/Antiochus the Savior – **Pg. 623, ¶ 9 and Pg. 625, ¶ 2 – Antiochus I, son of Seleucus, became ruler of the Seleucid empire after his father's death. Antiochus I became known as Antiochus the Savior after he fought the Gauls from the border of his empire.**

Antiochus III – **Pg. 628, ¶ 4, Pg. 629, ¶ – Antiochus III, just fifteen when he became king of the Seleucids in 223 BC, was able to put down rebellions in Media and Persia, and make lasting peace with Bactria and Parthia. He also took Judea and the Western Semitic territories away from Egypt.**

Antigonus II – **Pg. 623, ¶ 8 – Antigonus II, grandson of Antigonus the One-Eyed, took the Macedonian-Thracian throne after Ptolemy Ceraunus's death.**

Arsinoe – **Pg. 622, ¶ 2 and Pg. 623, ¶ 6 – Arsinoe, Ptolemy's daughter, was married to Lysimachus of Thrace. She married Ptolemy Ceraunus when he claimed the Macedonian-Thracian throne, but then fled to Egypt and married her other brother Ptolemy II after Ptolemy Ceraunus killed her two sons.**

First Macedonian War – **Pg. 634, ¶ 6 to Pg. 635, ¶ 1 – The First Macedonian War was fought between the Carthaginians and Philip V of Macedonia on one side, and Rome and its allies, which included Sparta and the cities of the Aetolian League, on the opposing side.**

First Punic War – **Pg. 626, ¶ 3 and Pg. 627, ¶ 2 – The First Punic War was fought between the Romans and the Carthaginians over Sicily. The war, which lasted for twenty-three years, came to an end when Hamilcar Barca submitted to a treaty with the Romans that required Carthage to give up all of Sicily, to release all prisoners, and to pay a sizable fine over the next ten years.**

Gadir – **Pg. 630, ¶ 2 – Gadir was the center of Hamilcar Barca's operations on the Iberian peninsula.**

Galatians – **Pg. 625, ¶ 2 – Galatians was the name the Gauls eventually were called once they settled in Asia Minor.**

Hamilcar Barca – **Pg. 626, ¶ 6 and Pg. 627, ¶ 2, Pgs. 629-630 – Hamilcar Barca was a young general put in charge of Carthaginian forces seventeen years into the First Punic War. Though Hamilcar Barca won many battles for the Carthaginians in Sicily, he was unable to take the island and had to surrender to the Romans in 241 BC. He made his son, Hannibal, swear never to be a friend of the Romans.**

Hasdrubal – **Pg. 635, ¶ 2 & 5 – Hasdrubal, Hannibal's brother, sent a letter to his brother arranging to meet in Umbria in order to combine forces to fight the Romans. The letter was intercepted by Roman officers, Hasdrubal's troops were massacred in a surprise attack, and Hasdrubal died fighting.**

Peace of Phoenice – **Pg. 636, ¶ 2 – The Peace of Phoenice, an agreement signed by Philip V of Macedonia with the Greek cities to his south, ended the First Macedonian War. The treaty gave the Romans control of a few smaller cities, turned over other territories to Macedonia, and halted all hostilities between Macedonia and the Aetolian League.**

Ptolemy II – **Pg. 622, ¶ 1 – Ptolemy II, Ptolemy's younger son, succeeded his father as king of Egypt in 285 BC.**

Ptolemy IV – **Pg. 628, ¶ 5 to Pg. 629, ¶ 1 – Ptolemy IV was a cruel man who poisoned his mother so that she wouldn't plot against him, scalded his younger brother to death because he was popular with the army, and neglected the business of the state in order to get drunk and carouse with women.**

Ptolemy Ceraunus – **Pg. 622, ¶ 2 and Pg. 623, ¶ 6 & 8 – Ptolemy Ceraunus, Ptolemy's older son, left Egypt after Ptolemy II was given the throne by their father. Ptolemy Ceraunus then schemed his way into the Macedonian-Thracian throne, but his reign was short lived; two years later, Ptolemy Ceraunus died in battle against the Gauls.**

Scipio/Scipio Africanus – **Pg. 635, ¶ 3 and Pg. 637, ¶ 1 – Scipio, an official whose father died fighting the Carthaginians on the Iberian peninsula, lived to avenge his father's death. After successfully taking New Carthage, Scipio went on to triumph against Hannibal in Carthage, earning him the title Scipio Africanus.**

Seleucia – **Pg. 625, ¶ 1 – Seleucia was the largest and most favored city of Antiochus I in the Seleucid empire. Seleucia was on the western bank of the Tigris and linked with the Euphrates by a canal.**

Section II: Comprehension

Write a two/three sentence answer to each of the following questions.

1. In what way was Lysimachus's marriage to Arsinoe insurance against an attack from Seleucus?
A1. – Pg. 622, ¶ 3 – Seleucus's presence to the east of Lysimachus was growing, and Lysimachus wanted to hang on to Thrace, Macedonia and Asia Minor. Lysimachus's marriage to Arsinoe, daughter of the king of Egypt, allied Lysimachus with Egypt. This alliance would make Seleucus think twice before attacking Lysimachus and his territories.

2. How did Ptolemy Ceraunus get Lysimachus to turn against his son, Agathocles? Then, how did Ptolemy Ceraunus get Seleucus to turn against Lysimachus?
A2. – Pg. 622, ¶ 4 to Pg. 623, ¶ 4 – Ptolemy Ceraunus accused Agathocles of plotting with Seleucus to assassinate Lysimachus and take the Thracian-Macedonian throne away from him. Lysimachus then tried to poison his son, and when that failed, Lysimachus threw Agathocles into prison, where he died. Ptolemy Ceraunus then showed up in Seleucus's court, asking Seleucus to join with him against the son-poisoning Lysimachus. Seleucus then marched on Lysimachus; the two men met in battle, and Seleucus killed Lysimachus.

3. How did Ptolemy Ceraunus get hold of the Macedonian-Thracian throne? How did he lose it just two years later?
A3. – Pg. 623, ¶ 6 & 8 – Ptolemy Ceraunus murdered Seleucus just after the old king killed Lysimachus, and claimed the Macedonian-Thracian throne for himself. Just two years later, the Gauls attacked Macedonia. Ptolemy Ceraunus went out to fight them and died in battle.

4. For what reason did Roman soldiers attack the Carthaginian troops that were occupying the Sicilian city of Messina?
A4. – Pg. 625, ¶ 4 to Pg. 626, ¶ 2 – When Rome responded to a call for help from the Sicilian city of Messina, a Greek colony that was invaded by renegade Italian mercenaries from Campania, they found that the Carthaginians had joined the tyrant of Syracuse, Hiero II, in driving out the previous invaders and occupying the city themselves. The Romans refused to give up the project of besieging Messina and simply attacked the Carthaginian occupying forces instead.

5. What was the second "first" of the First Punic War? How did the Romans learn to build ships?
A5. – Pg. 626, ¶ 4 – The second "first" of the First Punic War was the Roman attempt to learn to build ships and have a competent navy. The Romans learned to build ships by pulling apart a Carthaginian warship that ran aground on Roman shores, and then modeling their own ships after it.

6. In what way was the marriage between Antiochus II and Ptolemy III's daughter meant to solve the problems of Antiochus II's disintegrating empire? Did the marriage solve Antiochus's problems?
A6. – Pg. 627, ¶ 6 to Pg. 628, ¶ 2 – Antiochus II lost the satrapies of Bactria and Parthia early in his reign because he was preoccupied in a fight with Egypt over control of the old Western Semitic lands. The marriage between Antiochus II and Ptolemy III's daughter was meant to seal a temporary peace between Egypt and the Seleucid empire. The plan failed, however; Bactria and Parthia were not reunited with the Seleucid empire, and Antiochus II was poisoned by his indignant first wife.

7. What happened to Ptolemy IV's sister, her brother Agathocles, his young son Ptolemy V and Egypt's reputation, after Ptolemy IV's death?
A7. – Pg. 629, ¶ 2 & 3 – After Ptolemy IV's death, Agathocles forged a document claiming to be the regent to young Ptolemy V. Shortly after, Agathocles and his sister were torn to pieces by an angry mob, and Ptolemy V was enthroned in Memphis with a proper Egyptian council of advisors. However, when Ptolemy V was twelve, Antiochus III marched on Egypt and the

Seleucids took hold of its Western Semitic territories, marking the end of Egypt's greatness.

8. Why did Hamilcar Barca want to plant a Carthaginian colony in Iberia?
A8. – Pg. 629, ¶ 5 – Hamilcar Barca wanted to plant a Carthaginian colony in Iberia in order to replace the losses suffered at Sicily. The Iberian colony would be a new center for Carthaginian might, as well as an excellent base from which to launch retaliatory strikes against Rome.

9. For what reason did the Romans sail to the Greek island of Corcyra? Why did some Romans remain on the island?
A9. – Pg. 630, ¶ 3 – The Romans sailed to the Greek island of Corcyra because they were invited to protect the island from the double threat of invasion by other hostile Greeks and the ongoing attacks of the northern Gauls. After the intervention, a Roman garrison remained on the island, ostensibly as a peacekeeping force.

10. What was Hannibal's first act as Carthage's new chief general? How did this act start the Second Punic War?
A10. Pg. 630, ¶ 5 to Pg. 632, ¶ 2 – When Hannibal became commander, he immediately began to prepare for an overland invasion of Roman territory, fighting his way along the coast in order to clear a safe passage towards the Alps. When he drew near to Massalia, the city appealed to Rome for help against Hannibal. Rome warned Hannibal that if he passed the town of Saguntum, it would be considered an act of war. Hannibal besieged and sacked the town, prompting the Romans to present a final ultimatum: surrender Hannibal, or face a Second Punic War. Needless to say, Hannibal did not surrender.

11. Why happened to Roman forces during the battles fought against Hannibal and his army at the Trebbia River and Lake Trasimene? Why were these battles so damaging to Roman morale?
A11. – Pg. 633, ¶ 4 & 5 – When the Romans met the Carthaginians at the Trebbia River, a full third of the Roman troops fell. During the battle at Lake Trasimene, fifteen thousand Romans died, as well as their commander Gaius Falminus. These defeats were damaging to the Roman morale because the people of Rome had an unrealistic confidence in their troops; when the men of Rome stopped coming home, the city went into a panic and women roamed the street asking anyone they met the meaning of the dreadful tidings which had so suddenly come.

12. How did Hannibal defeat the Roman army of over one hundred thousand soldiers at Cannae?
A12. Pg. 634, ¶ 3 & 4 – When Hannibal heard of Rome's massive force heading for Cannae, he arranged a thin front line to meet the Roman attack, and placed, on his far left and right, his strongest and fiercest men. When the Romans advanced, the thin front line of Carthaginians fought ferociously while slowly retreating, drawing the Romans into a V as they moved back. Then, the troops on either side of the Romans attacked, surprising the Romans, who were not equipped to fight on three sides at once.

13. What were the terms of the peace treaty made between Carthage and Rome at the end of the Second Punic War?
A13. – Pg. 637, ¶ 1 - The terms of the peace treaty made between Carthage and Rome that ended the Second Punic War required Carthage to surrender itself to the Roman official Scipio. In addition, Carthage was forced to give up its fleet, bringing an end to its ambitions

to spread across the west; under Roman orders, five hundred of the ships were towed away from the shore and set ablaze, where they all burned to the waterline and then sank.

Section III: Critical Thinking

The student may use his text to answer this question.

The oath Hannibal made to his father as a young boy to never become a friend to the Romans motivated his entire military career. It also tied him more closely to the Romans than it did to his home country of Carthage. Explain how Hannibal's vendetta against Rome stopped him from making a strong connection to his own country, and how this may have influenced his defeat at Zama.

To start the student off, ask him to recall where Hannibal was raised. Hannibal left Carthage when he was nine to live with his father, Hamilcar Barca, in Iberia. Hamilcar Barca moved to Iberia in order to build a colony whose primary purpose was to serve as a base from which to launch retaliatory strikes against Rome. The student should understand that from his youngest days, Hannibal was raised in an environment that centered around Carthaginian and Roman hostilities. Then ask the student what Hannibal first did when he became a Carthaginian commander. Hannibal immediately began to prepare for an overland invasion of Rome. Hannibal spent most of his adult life on a campaign against Rome, far away from the nation of his birth. Next, ask the student to recall why Hannibal returned to Rome. When Scipio invaded the North African coast in 204 BC, Hannibal returned home to protect his country. Yet, it wasn't really his country. Livy writes, "Seldom has any exile left his native land with so heavy a heart as Hannibal's when he left the country of his enemies." Hannibal felt more at home fighting in Rome than he did on the ground of his home country. Ask the student "Who did Hannibal recruit to fight for Carthage against Scipio?" The student should recall that Hannibal did not have a cohesive army. Hannibal put together a hodgepodge defense against Rome, made up of reluctant Carthaginians, African mercenaries, and a few veterans brought back from Italy. The men Hannibal led shared nothing in common, and had no common reason for fighting. Most of the men were fighting for money. Finally, ask the student why money was not as powerful a motivator in war as patriotism. When Scipio's army stormed Hannibal's troops, many men retreated in fear, for after all, what good is money to a dead man? If the men had been inspired to fight for something they all believed in, sacrificing their lives in the name of Carthage would have meant something. However, these men did not believe in Carthage, nor did Hannibal. He could not inspire his troops with patriotism, because he had none himself. Hannibal only knew hatred for Rome, not love for Carthage. Because of this lack of heart, Hannibal lost all control at the Battle of Zama, and was forced to surrender to the Romans.

EXAMPLE ANSWER: Hannibal left Carthage at nine to live with his father in Iberia, in a colony built to fight Rome. When Hannibal became a Carthaginian commander at twenty-six, he immediately began to prepare for a Roman invasion. He spent most of his adult life on a campaign against Rome, far away from the nation of his birth. The only reason Hannibal returned to Carthage proper was because of Scipio's invasion of the North African coast. Away from his regular troops, who were stationed in Italy, Hannibal pulled together a motley crew to fight against Rome, made up of reluctant Carthaginians, African mercenaries, and a few veterans brought back from Italy. The men Hannibal led shared nothing in common,

and had no common reason for fighting. Most of the men were fighting for money. This meant that when Scipio attacked, many men retreated in fear. Money would be no good to them if they were dead. Perhaps if the men had been inspired to fight for a common cause, they would have been willing to sacrifice their lives for Hannibal. But Hannibal could not inspire his troops with patriotism, because he had none himself. Hannibal only knew hatred for Rome, not love for Carthage. Because of this lack of heart, Hannibal lost all control at the Battle of Zama, and was forced to surrender to the Romans.

CHAPTER SEVENTY-FOUR: ROMAN LIBERATORS AND SELEUCID CONQUERORS

The student may use her text when answering the questions in sections I and II.

Section I: Who, What, Where

Write a one or two-sentence answer explaining the significance of each item listed below.

Antiochus Epiphanes (Antiochus IV) – **Pg. 643, ¶ 3, Pg. 645, ¶ 1 & 2 – Antiochus Epiphanes took the Seleucid throne after murdering the rightful heir, his brother's son, for whom Antiochus was to act as regent. Antiochus Epiphanes had designs on Egypt, but when he was told by the Romans to leave Egypt alone, he took his army to Coele Syria where he waged war on Jerusalem.**

Antiochus the Great (Antiochus III) – **Pg. 638, ¶ 1 – Antiochus the Great was the title earned by Antiochus III of the Seleucid empire for pushing the Seleucid border down through the old Egyptian holdings, and forcing both Parthia and Bactria to a peace.**

Artaxias I – **Pg. 640, ¶ 3 – Artaxias I, satrap of the Asia Minor province called Armenia, set himself up as king around 190 BC. Artaxias's break from the Seleucid empire showed Antiochus III's increasing weakness after the defeat at the Pass of Thermopylae.**

Asiaticus (Scipio) – **Pg. 640, ¶ 3 – Asiaticus was the title earned by Scipio after he defeated Antiochus's army at Magnesia.**

Brhadratha – **Pg. 641, ¶ 5 – Brhadratha, the last Mauryan king of India, was a devout Buddhist. While on a thousand-day penance in search of truth, during which he left his oldest son in charge of the throne, Brhadratha was murdered by the commander of his army.**

Coele Syria – **Pg. 644, ¶ 3 – Coele Syria was the name for the Seleucid satrapy made up of the old kingdoms of Israel, Judah, Syria, and some of the surrounding land.**

Demetrius I (of Bactria) – **Pg. 641, ¶ 3 and Pg. 641, ¶ 6 to Pg. 642, ¶ 1 – Demetrius I, the Greek king of Bactria, invaded India after Antiochus III's downfall. Though there is no written record of his invasion, we can guess by the trail of coins left behind from the Bactrian king, that Demetrius I took Purushapura and Taxila, and by 175 BC, he seems to have fought through the Punjab.**

Demetrius I (of Seleucid Empire) – **Pg. 646, ¶ 4 to Pg. 647, ¶ 1 – Demetrius I became king of the Seleucid empire after the death of his uncle Antiochus Epiphanes. Demetrius I reconquered Jerusalem and reinstalled it as part of Coele Syria under the Seleucid crown, but he did not enforce his uncle's religious reforms.**

Eumenes – **Pg. 643, ¶ 4 – Eumenes, ruler of the city of Pergamum in Asia Minor, went to Rome to complain about the aggressive behavior of Macedonian king Perseus. Perseus tried, and failed, to have Eumenes assassinated, which further justified Eumenes's complaints against the Macedonian king.**

Jonathan – **Pg. 647, ¶ 1 – Jonathan, Judas's brother, was given a fair amount of freedom by Demetrius I to govern the Jews as he saw fit, as long as he remained a faithful subject governor of the Seleucid empire. Jonathan paid polite deference to the Seleucid authorities, and managed to stay in power in Jerusalem for almost twenty years.**

Judas – **Pg. 646, ¶ 2 and Pg. 646, ¶ 4 – Judas, the oldest of five brothers that descended from the old tribe of Jewish priests, led a rebellion against the Seleucid occupiers of Jerusalem. After Antiochus Epiphanes's death, Judas declared himself the first king of the Hasmonean Dynasty of Jerusalem.**

Maccabean War – **Pg. 646, ¶ 2 – The Maccabean war was fought between the Seleucid occupiers of Jerusalem, under the leadership of Antiochus Epiphanes, and the Jews of Jerusalem, led by Judas. Judas made an alliance with Rome that helped him prolong the rebellion, but fighting fizzled out when Antiochus Epiphanes died and no one had energy to send more soldiers down to Jerusalem.**

Perseus – **Pg. 643, ¶ 1 and Pg. 643, ¶ 6 to Pg. 644, ¶ 1 – Perseus, the younger son of Philip V, convinced his father that his older brother Demetrius had been brainwashed by the Romans, who intended to put him on the throne of Macedonia as a Roman puppet. As king, Perseus tried to take Greece for Macedonia and failed; he ended up as a captive in Rome, and the Macedonian monarchy ended.**

Pusyamitra Sunga – **Pg. 641, ¶ 5 – Pusyamitra Sunga, a devout Hindu, murdered the reigning Mauryan king of India, Brhadratha, and took control of what was left of the empire. Pusyamitra Sunga founded a new dynasty, and began to expand the old kingdom of Magadha.**

Third Macedonian War – **Pg. 643, ¶ 6 to Pg. 644, ¶ 1 – The Third Macedonian War, fought between Perseus of Macedonia and Rome, lasted about three years and ended at the battle of Pydna. The Romans defeated the Macedonians and the Roman consul oversaw the division of Macedonia into four separate subject countries.**

Treaty of Apamea – **Pg. 640, ¶ 3 – The Treaty of Apamea was signed by Antiochus III after his defeat at Magnesia, forcing him to give up most of his navy as well as his territory north of the Taurus Mountains.**

Section II: Comprehension

Write a two/three sentence answer to each of the following questions.

1. What caused the Second Macedonian War?
A1. – Pg. 638, ¶ 3 to Pg. 639, ¶ 1 – The Second Macedonian War was caused by Philip V's secret treaty with Antiochus III to divide up Egyptian territories which had once belonged to the Ptolemies. Philip V's alliance with Antiochus III made him a threat to Rome, who did not want the Greek peninsula, which they were sure Philip V planned to invade, under the control of a pro-Seleucid king.

2. Describe the conditions of, and reasoning behind, the peace made between Rome and Macedonia at the end of the Second Macedonian War.
A2. – Pg. 639, ¶ 2 – The Romans offered Philip V a peace that would allow the king to stay in

Macedonia if he gave up all of his warships, pay a fine and withdraw all of his soldiers from Greek territory. By allowing Philip V to keep Macedonia, the Romans were able guarantee that Philip V would stay out of Greece. If he wanted to keep fighting, he would then be kicked out of his own kingdom, and he would have nothing.

3. What kind of relationship did Rome have with Greece after the Second Macedonian War? What did the skeptics say about this relationship? What did the people say who were in favor of Roman and Greek relations?
A3. – Pg. 639, ¶ 2 & 3 – After the Second Macedonian War, Rome claimed to have liberated the Greeks from Macedonian oppression. A few skeptics claimed that the Greeks were not liberated, they just had new Roman masters. Those in favor of Rome's intervention were happy to sign a treaty that was anti-Macedonian.

4. Why was Antiochus III more inclined to go to war with Rome after the Second Macedonian War, despite Rome's new alliance with the cities of the Achaean League?
A4. – Pg. 639, ¶ 4 – Antiochus III was more inclined to go to war with Rome after the Second Macedonian War because he had Hannibal of Carthage as a new military advisor. Hannibal's loathing for Rome was so strong, he said there was nothing that lay in his power that he would not do to harm the Romans.

5. What did the Roman consul say to the troops from Rome and the Aegean League to inspire them to fight hard at the Pass of Thermopylae against the Seleucids and Aetolian League?
A5. – Pg. 640, ¶ 2 – The Roman consul told the troops from Rome and the Aegean League that they were fighting for the independence of Greece from the Aetolians and Antiochus. He also proclaimed that beating Antiochus and his allies would open up Asia, Syria and all the known wealthy kingdoms to Rome.

6. Explain why both Philip V and Seleucus IV had to send their sons to Rome as hostages?
A6. – Pg. 640, 4 & 5 – Philip V had to send his son to Rome as a hostage as part of his punishment for his friendship with Antiochus. Seleucus IV, Antiochus III's son and heir, had to send his oldest son to Rome as hostage as a sign of Rome's continued dominance over the Seleucids.

7. What evidence is there that Pusyamitra Sunga failed to reestablish Hindu orthodoxy in India during his reign?
A7. – Pg. 641, ¶ 5 – It seems Pusyamitra Sunga failed to reestablish Hindu orthodoxy in India during his reign because there are several stupas, Buddhist sacred monuments, that have been dated to his reign. If the Buddhists could still create monuments, then that meant not everyone was practicing Hinduism during Pusyamitra Sunga's reign.

8. Why did Antiochus Epiphanes back away from his invasion of Egypt? Why did the Romans want to stop Antiochus Epiphanes from gaining more territory?
A8. – Pg. 644, ¶ 4 to Pg. 645, ¶ 1 – Antiochus Epiphanes backed away from his invasion of Egypt because a Roman ambassador demanded that he leave Egypt to the Ptolemys. If Antiochus Epiphanes did not leave Egypt, he would face war with Rome, and he was not ready to do so. Rome did not want the Seleucid empire to gain more territory because more territory meant more resources, more men for the army and in general, more power for the Seleucids.

9. What was Antiochus Epiphanes's plan for keeping the Jews in Jerusalem loyal? Why did his plan backfire?

A9. – Pg. 645, ¶ 4-6 – Antiochus Epiphanes's plan for keeping the Jews in Jerusalem loyal was to change the temple cult so that their Yahweh became identified with Zeus, and Antiochus Epiphanes would then be worshiped as the human manifestation of the hybrid god. The plan backfired because the Jews believed in a single God who was different from man, so to worship a human god was blasphemy.

10. How did Judas earn the nickname "Judas Maccabeus," or "Judas the Hammer?"

A10. – Pg. 646, ¶ 2 – Judas led an army of six thousand men in guerilla warfare against the Seleucid occupiers of Jerusalem. His leadership of the rebellion against Antiochus Epiphanes and the invader's religious reforms earned the nickname "Judas Maccabeus" or "Judas the Hammer."

Section III: Critical Thinking

The student may not use her text to answer this question.

Over the course of the text, we've read about countless conquerors who took drastic measures to dismantle the cultures of the peoples in their newly acquired lands, and the struggles of these conquered peoples to keep their own cultural identities. Conversely, we've read about conquerors who left the cultures of their new conquests alone. In this chapter, we read about a conquered city that *asked* its overlord to make official changes in its home culture so it could be more like its conqueror. Write a paragraph explaining why, in 180 BC, the city of Cumae in Campania, asked Rome for permission to change its official language from its old dialect of Oscan to Latin.

The student should start her answer by restating the Cumae's seemingly puzzling action of asking Rome for permission to change its official language from its old dialect of Oscan to Latin. Next, ask the student what kind of relationship Cumae had with Rome. The people of Cumae already had the privilege of civitas sine suffragio, *which allied Cumae to Rome, but their original culture remain unchanged. Now, ask the student how Cumae could strengthen its alliance with Rome. By adopting Latin as their official language, the Cumaeans were making a willing identification not just with Roman politics, but with Roman culture. Make sure the student notes that the Cumaeans did not give up speaking Oscan, nor did they become full Romans. Making Latin their official language allowed the Cumaeans to participate more fully in Roman politics, commerce and culture without sacrificing their identity as Cumaeans. As stated on page 647, ¶ 5, "the official status of Latin allowed Cumae to* remain *Cumaean. Latin would not be their only language, but it would be used for commerce and administration, binding Cumae together with other cities and peoples who retained their own identities, but glossed another above them."*

EXAMPLE ANSWER: In 180 BC, the city of Cumae, in Campania, asked Rome for permission to change its official language from its old dialect of Oscan to Latin. The people of Cumae already had the privilege of *civitas sine suffragio*, which allied Cumae to Rome, but their original culture remain unchanged. By adopting Latin as their official language, the

Cumaeans were making a willing identification not just with Roman politics, but with Roman culture. The Cumaeans did not give up speaking Oscan, nor did they become full Romans. Once Latin was their official language, the Cumaeans could participate more fully in Roman politics, commerce and culture without sacrificing their native cultural identity. Sharing an official language strengthened the alliance between the Rome, Cumae, and the other nations under Rome's domain, without destroying the native Cumaean culture.

CHAPTER SEVENTY-FIVE: BETWEEN EAST AND WEST

The student may use his text when answering the questions in sections I and II.

Section I: Who, What, Where

Write a one or two-sentence answer explaining the significance of each item listed below.

Chanyu – **Pg. 650, ¶ 2 – Chanyu was the term for the man appointed to be the king of the association of tribes called the Xiongnu.**

Ctesiphon – **Pg. 656, ¶ 2 – Ctesiphon was the location of a Parthian camp used by the Parthians to penetrate further and further into Seleucid land.**

Demetrius II/Nicator – **Pg. 655, ¶ 2 to Pg. 656, ¶ 1 – Demetrius II, also called Nicator, the third king of the Seleucid Empire after Antiochus Epiphanes, was captured by Mithridates I and hauled back to Parthia. While Demetrius Nicator was treated well and held in comfortable confinement, his captivity was horrendously embarrassing for the king of the once-great Seleucids, and he most likely died in captivity.**

Heliocles – **Pg. 653, ¶ 6 to Pg. 654, ¶ 1 – Heliocles was the last Bactrian king of Greek descent. His reign was brought to an end around 130 BC by the invading Yuezhi.**

Hui-ti – **Pg. 650, ¶ 6 to Pg. 651, ¶ 1 – Hui-ti succeeded his father Gao Zu as emperor of China in 195 BC. Hui-ti died at twenty-three by drinking himself to death while watching his regent-mother kill countless royal sons and wives.**

Kao-hou – **Pg. 650, ¶ 6 to Pg. 651, ¶ 2 – Kao-hou, Gao-Zu's first wife, ruled as empress dowager and regent for her son, Hui-ti. Kao-hou poisoned an array of royal sons and wives and then installed her own family members in important government positions, a method of appointment that made her extremely unpopular.**

Lucius Cornelius Sulla – **Pg. 656, ¶ 3 – Lucius Cornelius Sulla was sent from Rome to keep an eye on Mithridates II, the Great, of Parthia. Sulla was the first Roman the Parthians reached out to for alliance and friendship.**

Mao-tun – **Pg. 650, ¶ 4 – Mao-tun, the Xiongnu chanyu in the earliest years of the Han dynasty, had organized his confederation to the point where they had a regular annual gathering and something like a voting system. Mao-tun was seen as a threat to Gao Zu, and after a failed invasion, the Han emperor made peace with Mao-tun by sending him gifts and one of his daughter's to be the warrior-king's bride.**

Menander I – **Pg. 654, ¶ 3 – Menander I became king of the Indo-Greeks around 150 BC, and is remembered in a Buddhist sacred text, the Milinda Panha for his conversion to Buddhism.**

Mithridates I – **Pg. 655, ¶ 1 & 2 – Mithridates I, king of Parthia, captured the king of the Seleucids, Demetrius Nicator, in 139 BC.**

Mithridates II, the Great – **Pg. 656, ¶ 3 and Pg. 658, ¶ 1 – Mithridates II, the Great, the greatest Parthian king of all time, came to the throne in 123 BC. Mithridates II sent merchants to Rome and to China, acting as a bridge between the two great and growing empires of the west and east.**

Wendi – **Pg. 651, ¶ 4 – Wendi, son of Gao Zu by a concubine, was proclaimed emperor after Kao-hou's family had been cleared out of the government.**

Wudi – **Pg. 653, ¶ 2-4 – Wudi, the grandson of Wendi, began his reign as emperor of the Han Dynasty by campaigning against the Xiongnu. Wudi reshaped China into an empire by reintroducing taxes, rebuilding a bureaucracy and sending ambassadors out of China to explore the rest of the world.**

Xiongnu – **Pg. 650, ¶ 2 – The Xiongnu were a loose association of nomadic tribes to the north of China.**

Yuezhi – **Pg. 652, ¶ 2 to Pg. 652, ¶ 1 – The Yuezhi were nomads north of China that were driven west by the Xiongnu. The Yuezhi ran into Bactria, and around 160 BC settled along its northern border.**

Zhang Qian – **Pg. 653, ¶ 4 & 5 – Zhang Qian, an ambassador sent by Wudi to find out what lay beyond the western Chinese border, lived for ten years as a Xiongnu captive before he was able to escape and complete his exploratory travels. He returned to China in 126, after visiting Bactria, Parthia and witnessing the movement of the Yuezhi nomads.**

Section II: Comprehension

Write a two/three sentence answer to each of the following questions.

1. Describe Gao-Zu's ruling style, and explain how, by using this ruling style, Gao-Zu was able to hold his empire together.
A1. – Pg. 649, ¶ 2 – Gao-Zu's ruling style was a combination of heavy-handed authority and the promise of independence. By using this ruling style, Gao-Zu was able to march with his army against any dukes who showed signs of revolt, securing his power. But he also proclaimed that all noble families who were not currently planning rebellion could live free from fear of random arrest and execution, thus gaining approval from the general public.

2. How were the so-called barbaric Xiongnu like the "Chinese proper?"
A2. – Pg. 650, ¶ 2 & 3 - The Xiongnu, like the "Chinese proper," had a king that ruled over each association of tribes with its own leader, modeled after the Chinese system of government. Also, Sima Qian revealed that the Xiongnu were descended from a member of the Hsia Dynasty, meaning the blood of the Xiongnu was no different than the blood of the "Chinese proper."

3. What happened to Kao-hou's family after her death? Why was the Han Dynasty able to survive this crisis?
A3. – Pg. 651, ¶ 3 – After Kao-hou's death, the court rose up and slaughtered every relative of Kao-hou that they could get their hands on. Despite her ruthlessness, Kao-hou kept her ambitions within the court, and did not micromanage the common people. Without internal

war or the threat of barbarian invasion, farming could continue undisturbed, and the result was a prosperous nation with abundant food and clothing who were disinclined to revolt against a system that seemed to be working.

4. What policies did Wudi enforce in China to create a more established empire?
A4. – Pg. 653, ¶ 3 – Wudi's policies to create a more established empire were numerous: he reintroduced taxes; he took control of the trade of iron, salt and alcohol as government monopolies; he cut back down to size local officials who had taken advantage of the hands-off policies of the Han; and he introduced for the first time the requirement that officials take, and pass, a qualifying examination.

5. How did Zhang Qian described the land of Shen-tu? What was this land, and who lived there?
A5. – Pg. 654, ¶ 2 – Zhang Qian described the land of Shen-tu as a kingdom settled on a river in a hot and damp region several thousand li southeast of Bactria. He said the people in Shen-tu cultivated the land and rode elephants when they go into battle. This land was the new Indo-Greek kingdom settled by the Greek Bactrians who had fled the Yuezhi and crossed the mountains to settle in India.

6. What historical evidence suggests Menander I of India did not become a Buddhist pilgrim? Why, if he was not a Buddhist pilgrim, is Menander remembered fondly by the Buddhist sacred texts?
A6. – Pg. 654, ¶ 4 & 5 – It seems that Menander I did not become a Buddhist pilgrim because he is also remembered for his extension of the Indo-Greek border almost all the way to Pataliputra, a campaign which must have involved years and years of fighting. Despite his questionable status as a pilgrim, Menander I pushed back the Hindus and extended the Buddhist kingdom, which preserved his greatness in the Buddhist texts.

7. According to Zhang Qian, what was the Parthian kingdom like? How did Zhang Qian describe T'iao-chih, or the Mesopotamian valley?
A7. – Pg. 656, ¶ 2 –According to Zhang Qian, the Parthian kingdom had several hundred cities of various sizes, some of which were walled. Parthian farmers grew rice, wheat, and grapes for wine, and Parthian merchants travelled far to trade with distant countries. Zhang Qian described T'iao-chih, or the Mesopotamian valley, as hot and damp, where there were great birds which lay eggs as large as pots, and where the people were ruled by petty chiefs who in turn paid attention to the king of Parthia, and recognized themselves as vassals.

Section III: Critical Thinking

As we move closer to the medieval world, we see the kingdoms of the ancient world growing more confident in their own identities, and more curious about the outside world. There is no better example of this than the trade between Parthia and China. Write a paragraph explaining how the walls around these two kingdoms actually opened up each empire to cultural exchange.

If the student is stumped, you can start by asking him what the walls contributed to the morale of the people in each kingdom. We know that Parthia had walled cities, meaning the people that lived in those cities felt protected from outside invasion. In China, the Great Wall was built not just to keep barbarians out, but also to tie together the various Chinese states into one cohesive whole. The Great Wall gave the Chinese a sense of united cultural identity. Each of the kingdoms felt they had a safe place to retreat if danger ever struck. This sense of security allowed both Parthia and China to explore outside the walls of their kingdoms.

The student should then give examples of the types of trading that went on between Parthia and China. China's Zhang Qian had a successful trip abroad, bringing back to the Han court stories of different peoples and goods that lay outside of China's borders. Similarly, Mithridates sent envoys to China, and after he heard about the kingdom's breadth and might, he sent the Han court some of the eggs of the great birds that lived in the region as gifts. This initial contact expanded into regular trade. The Parthians bought silks and lacquer, which they did not make themselves, from the Chinese. The Chinese emperor bought Parthian horses, which he admired for their speed and beauty. Only because each kingdom felt protected within its walls, sure of its identity as a great kingdom, could these exchanges have occurred.

EXAMPLE ANSWER: Both Parthia and China had walls protecting their kingdoms. In Parthia, cities were walled, meaning the people that lived in those cities felt protected from outside invasion. In China, the Great Wall kept barbarians out while uniting the Chinese people behind the wall. Each kingdom felt they had a safe place to retreat if danger ever struck. This sense of security allowed both Parthia and China to explore outside the walls of their kingdoms. China sent envoy Zhang Qian to explore the western world. He had a successful trip abroad, bringing back to the Han court stories of different peoples and goods that lay outside of China's borders. Similarly, Mithridates of Parthia sent envoys to China, and after he heard about the kingdom's breadth and might, he sent the Han court some of the eggs of the great birds that lived in the region as gifts. This initial contact expanded into regular trade. The Parthians bought silks and lacquer, which they did not make themselves, from the Chinese. The Chinese emperor bought Parthian horses, which he admired for their speed and beauty. Only because each kingdom felt protected within its walls, sure of its identity as a great kingdom, could these exchanges have occurred.

CHAPTER SEVENTY-SIX: BREAKING THE SYSTEM

The student may use her text when answering the questions in sections I and II.

Section I: Who, What, Where

Write a one or two-sentence answer explaining the significance of each item listed below.

Gaius Gracchus – **Pg. 666, ¶ 1 to Pg. 667, ¶ 1 – Gaius Gracchus, younger brother of Tiberius Gracchus, proposed reforms even more radical than Tiberius's had been. Frustrated by the consuls' block on his changes, Gaius rounded up his own supporters and started a riot that ended in bloodshed; Gracchus was murdered, and three thousand other rioters fell as well.**

First Servile War – **Pg. 662, ¶ 3-5 and Pg. 665, ¶ 2 – The First Servile War started after a rebellion broke out in Enna, led by Eunus, where four hundred slaves killed a slaveowner notorious for his cruelty. Publius Rupilius ended the war three years later when he besieged the leadership of the revolt in the city of Tauromenium.**

Marcus Cato – **Pg. 659, ¶ 3 – Marcus Cato, an elderly Roman statesman who was a vehement anti-Carthaginian, called for war against Carthage after seeing the thriving and well-armed city.**

Masinissa – **Pg. 659, ¶ 2 – Masinissa, king of the African kingdom of Numidia, was a Roman ally. Masinissa had been carrying on armed attacks against Carthaginian territory and claiming them for himself since the end of the Second Punic War.**

Mummius – **Pg. 661, ¶ 1 – Mummius, Roman consul, led a successful attack on Corinth. He set the city on fire, and Romans overran it; after the fall of Corinth, Rome ruled all of Greece.**

Publius Rupilius – **Pg. 665, ¶ 2 – Publius Rupilius, a Roman consul, brought a crushing end to the First Servile War in Sicily by refusing to lift his siege on the city of Tauromenium until conditions inside became unspeakable. When the city surrendered, only after those inside the city began to eat each other, Rupilius tortured the slaves inside and then threw them, still living, over a cliff.**

Third Punic War – **Pg. 660, ¶ 3 – The Third Punic War started in 149 BC, when Roman ships sailed for the North African coast under the command of Scipio Aemilius. A three-year siege was fought against Carthage because of its questionable loyalty to Rome.**

Tiberius Sempronius Gracchus – **Pg. 663, ¶ 4 & Pg. 664, ¶ 5 – Tiberius Sempronius Gracchus was a tribune and son of a consul who was determined to reform Rome's treatment of its soldiers. Unfortunately Tiberius Sempronius Gracchus broke the law in order to, supposedly, do good, and ultimately was murdered in a riot when he stood for reelection.**

Section II: Comprehension

Write a two/three sentence answer to each of the following questions.

1. Why did Rome continue to trade with Carthage, despite their uneasy relationship?
A1. – Pg. 659, ¶ 1 – Rome continued to trade with Carthage because the city was a good source for gold, silver, wine and figs.

2. Why did Scipio Aemilius sail on Carthage in 149 BC?
A2. – Pg. 660, ¶ 3 – Scipio Aemilius sailed on Carthage in 149 BC because the city's inhabitants refused to desert Carthage and rebuild it ten miles from the coast. Marcus Cato's constant questioning of Carthage's loyalty caused the Senate to make continual demands on the city to prove its trustworthiness. Carthage's refusal to move and rebuild was understood as an act of aggression against Rome, and the city had to be punished.

3. What was the cause of the dispute between Sparta and the Achaean League around 148 BC?
A3. – Pg. 660, ¶ 5 & 6 – Sparta, unhappy with a decision made by the Achaean League, announced its intention to appeal directly to Rome. The other League cities immediately passed a regulation saying that only the League as a whole could appeal to Rome. The Spartans reacted to this by drawing their swords against the cities of the Achaean League.

4. What was the last city Rome took before it finally swallowed Greece? What were the circumstances of this fight?
A4. – Pg. 660, ¶ 8 to Pg. 661, ¶ 1 – Corinth was the last city Rome had to conquer before it had swallowed all of Greece. Roman ships sailed for Corinth after the Corinthians attacked Romans in a riot against the Spartans. When indignant Romans returned to Rome and put the worst possible spin on the situation, consul Mummius sailed to Greece with twenty-six thousand men and thirty-five hundred cavalry. Mummius pitched camp at the Isthmus of Corinth, broke the Greek line, set Corinth on fire and the Romans overran it.

5. Why does historian M.I. Finley describe Roman slavery as a "very odd institution indeed"?
A5. – Pg. 661, ¶ 6 to Pg. 662, ¶ 1 – Historian M.I. Finley describes Roman slavery as a "very odd institution indeed" because while under the rule of their master, Roman slaves could be beaten, raped or starved. However, as soon as a Roman master set his slave free, that slave became a Roman citizen, with all the rights of citizenship. Roman slaves came in all shades, meaning freedmen could melt into the population within one or two generations, with no mark of their former servitude.

6. Who led the Sicilian slave revolt? What was the cause of the uprising?
A6. – Pg. 662, ¶ 2 & 3 – The Sicilian slave revolt was led by a slave named Eunus, who was rumored to have magical powers. The Sicilians were particularly cruel to their slaves, granting them the most meager care, and giving them the bare minimum for food and clothing. The slaves, distressed by their hardships, frequently outraged and beaten beyond all reason, got together and planned the uprising.

7. Where were the conditions for life in Rome for free hired men? Why were they so bad?
A7. – Pg. 663, ¶ 2 & 3 – Conditions in Rome for free hired men were very bad: Rome's

constant warfare meant that hundreds of thousands of Roman foot soldiers had marched off to fight, and had returned, poorly paid and sometimes disabled, to badly kept farms, crumbling houses, and unsettled debts. Conquered lands were bought up by the wealthy, who used slaves to work their land rather than hired men that were free, because these men could be drafted into military service. This meant that free men were held down by poverty, taxes, and military service.

8. How did Tiberius Sempronius Gracchus react to the veto of his reform bill?
A8. – Pg. 664, ¶ 2 – When Tiberius found out his bill was vetoed, he breached Rome's constitution, blocked a whole range of public services and announced that they would not start again until his bill was brought up for popular vote.

9. Why did Romans - both those who did not support Tiberius Sempronius Gracchus and those who did - begin to worry when his bill was passed and Tiberius put himself in charge?
A9. – Pg 664, ¶ 4 – When Tiberius's bill passed, he not only put himself in charge, but also put his father-in-law and his younger brother Gaius in power. Tiberius had bypassed the authority of his fellow tribunes, and the office of the tribune was supposed to serve as a protection for the common people. They wanted his reforms passed, but many of them were worried about his methods.

10. What started the Roman riot in 132 that ended in the death of Tiberius Sempronius Gracchus and three hundred other Romans?
A10. – Pg. 664, ¶ 5 – When Tiberius Sempronius Gracchus stood for reelection to the office of tribune, rumors spread that the wealthy would not allow a vote for him to be cast; assassins were coming to find him. Tiberius then put his hand to his head, a sign for his followers that it was time to resort to violence in order to get him into office. It is not known who struck the first blow, but the whole crowd erupted into a violent riot.

Section III: Critical Thinking

The student may not use her text to answer this question.

As the Roman general Scipio Aemilius watched the city of Carthage burn to the ground, he said, "[I]t is a grand thing, but I know not how, I feel a terror and dread, lest someone should one day give the same order about my own native city." In this chapter, we begin to see the destruction of Rome, not from arson, but from the manipulation of power within the seat of government. Write a paragraph explaining how Tiberius Sempronius Gracchus, thinking he was doing good, actually made a choice in his political actions that dealt a death blow to the Republic.

One of the most important sentences in this chapter comes on page 664 in ¶ 3: "This was breaking the law in order to do good, and it was this action which began to turn more and more Roman lawmakers against Tiberius Gracchus." The student must recognize that Gracchus broke the law to get his own way.

To start, you might ask the student to summarize Tiberius Gracchus's story. He felt it was an outrage that Roman soldiers fought for hearth and home, and yet when they returned to Rome, they were on the edge of losing all their property. Gracchus proposed reforms that would take care of the soldiers and crimp the estate-building of the rich. When Tiberius Gracchus's bill was vetoed, he blocked a whole range of public services and announced they would not start again until his bill was brought up for the popular vote, breaking the law in order to get his bill passed.

Then, you can ask the student why it was so dangerous for Gracchus to break the law. The Republic of Rome was built on a system that depended on the participation of the people, through tribunes, the Senate and consuls, in order for it to run as a Republic. Tiberius Gracchus, breaking the law to follow his own will, even if he thought he was doing something for the good of the people, broke the system that held up the Republic. As is written in the text, "No matter what his intentions were, he was introducing a dangerous precedent: he was using his personal popularity with the masses to get his own way" (page 664, ¶ 3). When Gracchus decided to bypass his fellow tribunes for the sake of the poor, he corrupted Rome's mechanics in a way that could never be fixed. The text notes that "He lost his life...because he followed up an excellent plan in too lawless a way" (page 665, ¶ 1). If Tiberius Gracchus could break the law, even if it was for the benefit of the people, anyone could now break the law and claim it was for the good of Rome -- even if it was for their own despotic interests.

EXAMPLE ANSWER: Tiberius Gracchus wanted to make reforms in the Roman government that would protect soldiers from losing their homes. Gracchus proposed reforms that would take care of the soldiers and crimp the estate-building of the rich. When Tiberius Gracchus's bill was vetoed, he blocked a whole range of public services and announced they would not start again until his bill was brought up for the popular vote, breaking the law in order to get his bill passed. Even thought Gracchus felt he was doing the right thing in order to protect the common people of Rome, he set a dangerous precedent that would later cripple the Republic. Rome ran on an intricate system of representation, through tribunes, the Senate and consuls. When Gracchus bypassed the system, he corrupted Rome's mechanics in a way that could never be fixed. Now any man in power could break the law, claiming it was to benefit the people, even if it was only to benefit himself.

CHAPTER SEVENTY-SEVEN: THE PROBLEM OF PROSPERITY

The student may use his text when answering the questions in sections I and II.

Section I: Who, What, Where

Write a one or two-sentence answer explaining the significance of each item listed below.

Lucius Cinna – **Pg. 673, ¶ 4, Pg. 676, ¶ 3 and Pg. 677, ¶ 3** – Lucius Cinna, elected consul after Sulla invaded the pomerium and ousted Marius Gaius and Sulpicius, was promptly thrown out of Rome after Sulla left the Italian peninsula. After Cinna and Marius Gaius were reinstated in Rome, Cinna planned to face Sulla in battle, but was killed in a mutiny before he could go very far.

Crassus – **Pg. 677, ¶ 4 and Pg. 678, ¶ 2** –Crassus was a young officer who aided Sulla in his fight back to Rome after Gaius Marius and Lucius Cinna's disastrous rule. When Sulla was in power, Crassus set fire to houses in Rome that Sulla wanted to claim, urging owners to sell their burning homes for a bargain price, only to have a firefighter put out the flames before any real damage was done.

Erh-shih – **Pg. 675, ¶ 6** – Erh-shih was the capital city of Ferghana's ruling lord. Once the Han took Erh-shih, the Xiongnu could no longer stop the Han advance, or claim Ferghana as their own.

Eupator Dionysius – **Pg. 671, ¶ 5** – Eupator Dionysus was king of Pontus, a northwestern kingdom in Asia Minor which was threatening to swallow more Asia Minor territory than Rome was comfortable with.

Jugurtha – **Pg. 668, ¶ 3 to Pg. 669, ¶ 2 and Pg. 670, ¶ 3** – Jugurtha, nephew to King Micipsa of Numidia, usurped the Numidian throne when Micipsa died, and ensured his kingship by buying protection from Rome. Jugurtha was finally dethroned by Gaius Marius, and was taken back to Rome in chains.

Pomerium – **Pg. 673, ¶ 2** – The pomerium was the domestic space set off from the outside world by Rome's walls. The inside of the city was solely the domain of the Senate, and no consul awarded military powers was supposed to exercise them within the pomerium.

Pompey – **Pg. 677, ¶ 4 and Pg. 678, ¶ 2** – Pompey was a young officer who aided Sulla in his fight back to Rome after Gaius Marius and Lucius Cinna's disastrous rule. When Sulla was in power, Pompey tracked down allies of Marius in Sicily and in North Africa, and was so successful in murdering them all that he demanded a victory parade when they returned to Rome.

The Social War – **Pg. 671, ¶ 2-5** – The Social War started in 91 BC, when indignant Italians, sick of being denied the Roman right to vote, killed a Roman official in the city of Asculum. Rome slowly bargained and beat the Italian cities back into its fold, at first granting citizenship to any Italian allies who refused to join the rebellion, and then granting all Italian cities the right of full Roman citizenship.

Sulpicius – Pg. 672, ¶ 2 and Pg. 673, ¶ 4 – Sulpicius, a tribune bribed by Marius Gaius, gathered himself a troop of armed men which he called the "Anti-Senate"; with these men Sulpicius strong-armed the Senate into giving the generalship of the troops headed to fight Eupator Dionysius Marius Gaius. After Sulla stormed the pomerium in anger over Gaius's bribe, Sulpicius was taken prisoner and sentenced to death.

Section II: Comprehension

Write a two/three sentence answer to each of the following questions.

1. What were the first signs of anti-Roman sentiment shown by Roman allies that were not granted voting rights in Rome?
A1. – Pg. 671, ¶ 2 – The first sign of anti-Roman sentiment shown by the allies and the Latins was a rejection of Roman customs and the Latin language, in favor of the old tongues of Italy. This was followed by the joining together of a number of Italian cities into a new association which they called Italia.

2. How did Lucius Cornelius Sulla prove his worth in the Social War, compared to Gaius Marius?
A2. – Pg. 671, ¶ 3-5 – Unlike Gaius Marius, who was hesitant in battle and incapacitated by ill health, Lucius Cornelius Sulla was able to stand up to the rigors of camp life, and won victory after victory against the Italians. Sulla stood for consul and was elected, thanks to his reputation as a great general.

3. Why did Marius Gaius want so badly to lead troops against Eupator Dionysus of Pontus?
A3. – Pg. 672, ¶ 1 – Marius Gaius knew that leading troops in a successful campaign against Eupator Dionysius would be a sure path to glory. Jealous of Sulla, Marius Gaius was desperate to take the generalship despite age and ill health.

4. How did Sulla take back control of the Senate after Gaius Marius bribed his way into the generalship? How did Sulla justify breaking the constitution and invading the pomerium?
A4. – Pg. 673, ¶ 2-4 – Sulla called his legions together and asked them to march on Rome. Sulla justified breaking the constitution and invading the pomerium by countering that Marius had already violated this restriction by employing Sulpicius and his armed men, who strong armed the Senate into giving Marius more power. Sulla burst through the gates of Rome, setting fire to the houses of his enemies. Sulpicius and Marius (though he fled) were sentenced to death and Sulla allowed a free election for a consul.

5. How was Li Kuang treated by Emperor Wudi upon his return from his failed attempt at conquest of Ferghana?
A5. – Pg. 675, ¶ 3 – As Li Kuang made his way back to Han land after failing to take Ferghana, Emperor Wudi sent messengers to stand at the pass that led from Ferghana down into the Han territory, the Jade Gate, and declared that anyone who came across the path would be cut down on the spot. Li Kuang was in limbo – unable to go home, but without the necessary tools to continue to fight.

6. What did Emperor Wudi believe was at stake in the conquest of Ferghana? How did Wudi attempt to help the problem?

A6. – Pg. 675, ¶ 4 – Emperor Wudi believed that the reputation of his empire was in jeopardy, and now that the paths to the west had been opened, he could not afford to look like a laughingstock with a defeat at Ferghana. To help the cause, Wudi emptied the royal treasury, hired soldiers, rounded up tribute soldiers from his allies and freed all the criminals in prison, getting everyone to help in the fight to win Ferghana.

7. Why was Li Kuang's first campaign against Ferghana unsuccessful? What did Li Kuang do differently in his second campaign against Ferghana?

A7. – Pg. 675, ¶ 1 & 5 – In his first attempt to take Ferghana, Li Kuang was unprepared to take care of his men as they marched across the Salt Swamp. Their only source of food and water came from the walled cities along the way to Yu-ch'eng, and most of these cities shut their gates tight and refused to come out. In his second attempt, Li Kuang besieged, conquered, sacked and slaughtered the inhabitants of the first walled city that refused to supply provisions for the passing soldiers; after this first act of aggression, Li Kuang's path was unhindered.

8. Why was the conquest of Ferghana so important for the Han?

A8. – Pg. 675, ¶ 7 to Pg. 676, ¶ 1 – The conquest of Ferghana was so important for the Han because it demonstrated Han superiority over the Xiongnu, and also put the states to the west, along the Silk Road, on notice that they had better yield to any Han parties passing through. The Han emperor had protected and proved his empire's claim to greatness – its power to buy and sell with the west.

9. How did Marius and Cinna manage to get themselves back into the Roman senate after they were both ousted?

A9. – Pg. 676, ¶ 4 & 5 – After Cinna was thrown out of the city, he began to collect an army, intending to fight his way back in. Marius, hearing this news, returned at once and met Cinna outside of the city with a large army of North African mercenaries. During his exile, Marius had dressed in rags and refused to cut his hair; when news of his humility reached Rome, the Senate, upset with the current consul, invited both Cinna and Marius to return to Rome.

10. Describe the scene as Sulla addressed the Senate once he was back inside Rome after Marius and Cinna's departure. How did the Romans feel about their new leader?

A10. – Pg. 677, ¶ 5 to Pg. ¶ 1 – At the same time as Sulla addressed the Senate upon his return to Rome, he had six thousand prisoners herded into the Circus and slaughtered. Sulla continued to address the Senate calmly as screams began to rise from the Circus. The people of Rome came to understand that they had merely exchanged one monstrous tyranny for another.

Section III: Critical Thinking

The student may use his text to answer this question.

In this chapter, we continue to discover holes in the fabric of the Republic of Rome. Write a paragraph recounting the Jugurthine War. Then, write a paragraph explaining how the war, and its aftermath, were both examples of corruption inside of Rome.

A complete account of the Jugurthine War runs from page 668, ¶ 2 through pages 670, ¶ 5. The student may consult his text as he summarizes the events of the war.

The two ways corruption manifests itself in the events of the Jugurthine War are 1) Jugurtha was continuously able to bribe Rome to safeguard his throne, and 2) after Gaius Marius took down Jugurtha, he was elected consul five more times in a row, a direct violation of Rome's constitution.

The first of these offenses, Jugurtha's ability to buy his safety, seems to be the more heinous of the two crimes. Yet it was Roman officers who first convinced Jugurtha to usurp Numidia's throne, telling him, "At Rome money could buy anything." Jugurtha saw this for himself, and remarked after he paid off a consul and a tribune in two different bribes, "There is a city put up for sale, and if it finds a buyer, its days are numbered." While Jugurtha did steal the Numidian throne from his cousin, he was only able to keep his title as king because of Rome's corruption. If it was not so easy to buy one's way into the good graces of Rome's government, Jugurtha would have been dethroned almost as soon as he claimed his title.

The second offense, Gaius Marius's long term as consul, is reminiscent of the liberties taken by Tiberius Sempronius Gracchus. Gaius Marius once again ignored the delicate mechanics of the Roman constitution because he thought he was doing well by the people. Gaius Marius's defeat of Jugurtha was seen as the triumph of common honesty over aristocratic corruption, yet Marius himself broke the rules and accepted the title of consul year after year because he believed it was the people's will for him to be in that position. Gaius Marius's actions mark the second obvious weakening of Rome's constitution, and the possibility for a man to gain singular power within the Republic.

EXAMPLE ANSWER: The Jugurthine War started when Jugurtha, nephew to Micipsa, King of Numidia, stole the Numidian throne after Micipsa's death. Jugurtha ensured his place as the new King of Numidia by sending large quantities of silver and gold to Roman senators. However, one of Jugurutha's cousins, Adherbal, the rightful heir to the throne, showed up in Rome asking for help to get his crown back. Since Jugurtha had already bought his safety, the next best thing Rome could do was to split the kingdom between the two men. Once Adherbal was back in Numidia, Jugurtha mounted a war against him, trapped him in his own capital city, and tortured him to death. Jugurtha's actions could not be ignored by Rome. A consul sent to Numidia with an army to punish Jugurtha was easily bought off, and once Jugurtha was dragged to court, he was able to pay off a tribune to halt the trial. Eventually, a "new man" named Marius Gaius was elected consul, and after three years of campaigning in Numidia, he was finally able to capture Jugurtha and bring him back to Rome in chains. Marius Gaius was lauded for his ability to put an end to aristocratic corruption, and was elected consul five more times in succession.

The war and its aftermath displayed corruption inside of Rome in two ways: 1) the ability to buy Roman favor through bribes and 2) the ability of one man to stay in power as long as his reelection was couched in the terms of the people's will. Though Jugurtha's actions as a usurper were heinous, he was only able to stay on his throne because of Roman officials' desire for money over propriety. Marius Gaius showed the flimsy nature of Rome's constitution when he continued to allow himself to be reelected as consul. Though he believed the people wanted him in power, he violated the terms of the constitution in order to keep his power. Both events were signs that the Republic of Rome was disintegrating from the inside out.

CHAPTER SEVENTY-EIGHT: NEW MEN

The student may use her text when answering the questions in sections I and II.

Section I: Who, What, Where

Write a one or two-sentence answer explaining the significance of each item listed below.

44 BC – **Pg. 693, ¶ 6 – In 44 BC, the Roman Senate, out of fear of the army's retaliation and of public resistance, named Caesar dictator for life.**

Brutus of Britain – **Pg. 688, ¶ 2 – Brutus, according to Monmouth, was the great grandson of Aeneas. He set out on an expedition and stumbled upon an island, which he named Britain, after himself.**

Carrhae – **Pg. 689, ¶ 6 to Pg. 689, ¶ 1 – Carrhae, old Haran, the city where Nabonidus was born and where Terah, father of Abraham, had died, was where Crassus and his Roman army were defeated by Parthian troops. Publius, son of Crassus, Crassus, and almost all of his men were killed in battle at Carrhae.**

Cassivelaunus – **Pg. 688, ¶ 2 and Pg. 689, ¶ 3 & 4 – Cassivelaunus, whom Geoffrey of Monmouth called "king of the Britains," appeared in Julius Caesar's account as a rogue warrior who usurped the throne of the ancient British Trinovantes tribe. Cassivelaunus went to war with Julius Caesar after he usurped the Trinovantes throne, but was defeated and forced to give the crown back to its rightful heir.**

Cicero – **Pg. 683, ¶ 1, Pg. 685, ¶ 3 and Pg. 691, ¶ 3 – Cicero was a young politician who campaigned against senatorial corruption with zeal; in 63 BC, Cicero was elected consul. Eventually, Cicero joined Pompey against Caesar.**

Cleopatra VII – **Pg. 692, ¶ 4 and Pg. 693, ¶ 1 & 2 – Cleopatra VII, sister of Ptolemy XIII, was named rightful heir to Egypt's throne by her lover, Caesar.**

Gladiator War/Third Servile War – **Pg. 681, ¶ 2 & 3 – The Gladiator War started in 73 BC when seventy-eight gladiators broke out of their quarters. They raided a butcher's shop for weapons, headed out of Capua, and then killed the troops that came after them and took their weapons away.**

Historia Regum Britannia – **Pg. 688, ¶ 1 – Historia Regum Britannia is Geoffrey of Monmouth's history of ancient Britain, which combined a mix of Roman and medieval place names with Welsh legend, a thin thread of fact and a strong patriotic bent. Besides Julius Caesar's own accounts of conquest, Monmouth's Historia is the only account that tells us anything about the tribes that settled down into little kingdoms in the south of Britain.**

Hyrcanus II (John Hyrcanus) – **Pg. 685, ¶ 1 – Hyrcanus II (John Hyrcanus) was appointed to be "High Priest and Ethnarch" of Jerusalem once it became part of the Roman province of Palestine. Hyrcanus II, both priest and government official, would report to a Roman** governor who had charge over all of Syria.

The Ides of March – Pg. 694, ¶ 2 – The Ides of March refers to March 15 of 44 BC, the day Caesar would next enter the Senate, and the day his assassination would take place.

Lud – Pg. 688, ¶ 3 – Lud, king of the Trinovantes tribe in Britain, was best known for expanding and walling in the main settlement on the river Thames, which became known as Lundres in his honor.

Mandubracius – Pg. 689, ¶ 1 – Mandubracius, son and heir to King Lud's throne, was displaced by Cassivelaunus after Lud's death. After Julius Caesar defeated Cassivelaunus, Mandubracius was put back in charge of the Trinovantes as a subject king of Rome.

Marcus Brutus – Pg. 694, ¶ 2 and Pg. 695, ¶ 1 – Marcus Brutus, Caesar's cousin and one of the heirs to Caesar's wealth, was part of the plot to assassinate the Dictator for Life. As Caesar died, he called out to Brutus, "Even you, my son?"

Mark Antony – Pg. 692, ¶ 2 and Pg. 694, ¶ 2 – Mark Antony, Caesar's aide, ran Rome as Caesar's deputy while Caesar was in Egypt chasing down Pompey. Mark Antony was not in on the plans to murder Caesar.

Novus homo (new man) – Pg. 685, ¶ 3 – A novus homo, or new man, was a man elected to be consul from a family where no man had ever been consul before.

Octavian – Pg. 694, ¶ 1 – Octavian, son of Caesar's sister's daughter, was named by Caesar as his legal heir in his will.

Orodes – Pg. 690, ¶ 2 & 3 – Orodes, king of Parthia, was given Crassus's head by the Parthian general Surena, which Orodes used as a prop in a victory play. After Crassus's failed siege, King Orodes ruled over a Parthia which stretched across much of the old Seleucid territory, from the Euphrates almost all the way to the border of China.

Pompeia – Pg. 683, ¶ 3 – Pompeia was the daughter of Pompey, and the wife of Julius Caesar.

Ptolemy XIII – Pg. 692, ¶ 4 & Pg. 693, ¶ 2 – Ptolemy XIII, brother of Cleopatra VII, was stopped from attacking his sister in order to secure his position as pharaoh by Caesar. Ptolemy XIII died fighting against the Roman troops who arrived to enforce Caesar's decision that Cleopatra was the rightful ruler of Egypt.

Ptolemy XV Caesarion – Pg. 694, ¶ 1 – Ptolemy XV Caesarion was the son of Caesar and Cleopatra VII.

Spartacus – Pg. 681, ¶ 3 and Pg. 682, ¶ 4 – Spartacus, a captured Thracian, was the gladiator elected to lead the rebellion known as the Gladiator War. Though Spartacus was a brilliant strategist, he was eventually brought down by Crassus and Pompey.

Transalpine Gaul – Pg. 686, ¶ 3 – Transalpine Gaul, the western part of the province on the other side of the Alps, was where, as governor, Julius Caesar built himself a reputation as a conqueror. From Transalpine Gaul, Caesar pushed back the Celtic tribes of the Helvetii and the Tigurini, and he took war into enemy territory towards the Rhine River, against the tribes known collectively as "German."

Trinovantes – Pg. 688, ¶ 3 – Trinovantes was the name of one of the most powerful tribal kingdoms in southern Britain.

Section II: Comprehension

Write a two/three sentence answer to each of the following questions.

1. Why was much of the Roman army off of the Italian peninsula after the death of Sulla in 78 BC?
A1. – Pg. 680, ¶ 2 – Much of Rome's army was off of the Italian peninsula after the death of Sulla because of various battles being fought in Rome's name. Pompey led an army over to the Iberian peninsula to fight against one of Marius's allies, another army went west to wrap up the war against the king of Pontus, and Romans were fighting pirates in the Mediterranean.

2. Who were the gladiators, and where did they come from? How were gladiators treated by Roman society?
A2. – Pg. 680, ¶ 4 – Gladiators were Roman slaves that fought for the entertainment of onlookers. Gladiators were usually captive soldiers from Gaul, the Iberian peninsula, Thrace, Syria and Greece. While a successful gladiator could attract his share of hero worship, he remained a despised member of society.

3. What is the practice of "decimation?" What were the circumstances of Crassus's use of decimation?
A3. – Pg. 682, ¶ 1 – "Decimation" was a vicious punishment where foot soldiers were chosen by a lottery to be put to death in from of the rest of the army. The intention of decimation was to make the army stronger. Crassus used decimation after his troops first failed to defeat Spartacus and the gladiators.

4. Why is Pompey given the credit for ending the Gladiator War, and not Crassus?
A4. – Pg. 682, ¶ 4 & 5 – Though Crassus was in charge of the troops that beat the gladiators in an ill-timed attack, and killed Spartacus, Pompey caught and killed many slaves fleeing the disastrous battle. Pompey himself sent a letter to the Senate saying that while Crassus had managed to win a battle, he himself had won the war.

5. What made Pompey and Crassus popular consuls, even though they constantly quarreled and got nothing done?
A5. – Pg. 683, ¶ 1 & 3 – Pompey and Crassus were popular with the people because they gave out grain, which made them seem like champions of the common man. Pompey's biggest offense while consul was taking credit for things others had done, and Crassus's shady money-making activities had taken a back seat to his duties as consul. After Pompey successfully commanded all of Rome's ships and over a hundred thousand Roman troops in a war against piracy in the Mediterranean, he became even more popular.

6. What were the terms of the arrangement made by Julius Caesar, Crassus and Pompey upon Caesar's return from Hispania? What were the terms of the second stage of the arrangement, made in 56 BC?
A6. – Pg. 685, ¶ 4 to Pg. 686, ¶ 1 – When Julius Caesar returned to Rome after paying off his debts while in Hispania, he called together Crassus and Pompey suggested that if they would give him enough public support and money to make his run for the consulship of 59 a success, he would push for whatever laws they wanted once he was in power. The three men agreed, and the alliance was cemented when Caesar's daughter married Pompey. In 56 BC, the three

men decided that Crassus and Pompey would run for the consulship of 55; once they were in power they would award Caesar another five years in Gaul. After the consulship ended, Crassus, in search of military glory, would make himself a general of an expedition to the east against the Parthians, and Pompey would give himself the governorship of Hispania and make a profit from it.

7. What were the circumstances that led to the Senate's decision to bar Caesar from entering Rome unless he surrendered his army upon his return from Gaul?
A7. – Pg. 690, ¶ 4-6 – After Caesar put down a serious rebellion in Gaul, he prepared to march back into Rome richer than Pompey and with more triumphs to his credit. In the Senate's eyes, this meant that Caesar would act as a dictator. Pompey, jealous of Caesar, convinced the Senate to deny Caesar entrance into Rome unless he surrendered his army, meaning his threat to Pompey would be significantly diminished.

8. Despite Pompey and the Senate's ban, how did Caesar come to power in Rome after he returned from his years in Gaul? What were the events that led up to Caesar's appointment as consul?
A8. – Pg. 691, ¶ 4 to Pg. 692, ¶ 2 – When Caesar returned to Rome, he simply took control of the city and scared the resistance out of everyone by sheer force of personality. After two years of fighting Pompey in Greece, Caesar's troops finally came out victorious, and Caesar was proclaimed first dictator and then, after eleven days, consul.

9. Why did the Egyptian plan to present a dead Pompey to Caesar backfire? At the same time, how did the presentation of Pompey's head benefit Caesar?
A9. – Pg. 692, ¶ 5 to Pg. 693, ¶ 1 – The Egyptians thought that if they caught and killed Pompey before Caesar arrived in Egypt, they would get on the Roman consul's good side. However, when Caesar arrived, he was furious that Pompey was dead: he had intended to humiliate his old ally but not kill him. Caesar was able to use the foible as an excuse for taking control of Egypt, which he could now do by way of punishment.

10. Describe Caesar's homecoming in 46 BC, after his years of travel in Egypt, along the African border and the Iberian peninsula.
A10. – Pg. 693, ¶ 4 – In 46 BC, Caesar's supporters gave him a victory parade when he returned to Rome. Statues of him were placed around the city, alongside those of the ancient kings, he was allowed to wear a purple robe and was hailed with the ceremonial title Imperator. The parade was led by a placard that read "Veni, vidi, vici!," meaning "I came, I saw, I conquered!"

11. Though the public was indignant to having a king, what concession did the Senate make regarding Caesar and his crown? How was this also Caesar's kiss of death?
A11. – Pg. 694, 2 – The Senate agreed that Caesar could wear a crown, but only when he was out of Rome campaigning against Parthia – because myth said that only a king could conquer Parthia. But Caesar's crown was the last straw for those senators who were increasingly worried about the Republic and its myth of being ruled by the people; consequently, plans for Caesar's assassination were in the works.

Section III: Critical Thinking

The student may not use her text to answer this question.

As we continue to read about Rome, we see the growing division between the ideals of the Republic and the actions of its rulers. However, did these rulers see the widening gap themselves? Explain why, when Caesar was murdered, he cried out in surprise, "But this is force!"

The critical thinking question in this chapter follows the trend of the previous two chapters, where Rome's leading men believed they were acting for the good of the people, even though they acted unconstitutionally. Caesar is certainly the most exaggerated case of this delusion that we have encountered so far. Caesar had a loyal army and was believed by the people to be their benevolent guardian, even as he garnered more and more power for himself, "appointing magistrates, passing laws, and generally behaving as Senate, Tribune, Assembly, and Council all wrapped into one" (page 693, ¶ 5).

On page 696 in ¶ 1, the text states, "Rome is a place where the people have power." However, this had not been true since the breaking of the constitution by the Gracchi. Somehow, the people of Rome believed they still had power, even as they were led by a "Dictator for Life" that was to wear a crown as he represented Rome while abroad. The fantasy of the living Republic was so strong that Caesar believed his autocratic ways were a reflection of the will of the people. When Caesar cried out "But this is force!" he made it clear that even he, a dictator in everything but name, believed in the myth of the Republic.

EXAMPLE ANSWER: Caesar acted like a dictator. He appointed officials and passed laws, performing by himself all the duties of the Senate, tribunes, consuls and assembly. However, he had a loyal army, and he was liked by his people – they saw him as their benevolent guardian. Even though he acted unconstitutionally, Caesar believed his actions were sanctioned because he was following the will of the people. When Caesar cried out "But this is force!" he made it clear that even he, a dictator in everything but name, believed in the myth of the Republic.

CHAPTER SEVENTY-NINE: EMPIRE

The student may use his text when answering the questions in sections I and II.

Section I: Who, What, Where

Write a one or two-sentence answer explaining the significance of each item listed below.

30 BC – Pg. 704, ¶ 1 & 2 – 30 BC is the year Mark Antony stabbed himself in the stomach after hearing of Octavian's approach on Alexandria. It is also the year Cleopatra died, as well as her son by Caesar, leaving Octavian, alone, in control of the Roman territories.

Herod – Pg. 700, ¶ 7 and Pg. 702, ¶ 2 & 4 – Herod, son of Antipater, took over rule as Roman governor of Syria after his father was poisoned. Herod fled to Rome when the Parthians invaded Palestine in 40 BC, and in 37 BC, Antony installed Herod as a vassal king of Rome in Palestine.

Julia – Pg. 708, ¶ 4 & 5 – Julia, daughter of Octavian, was put under pressure by her father to sire a son so that he would have an heir. Julia, married off three times, produced no son, and was eventually confined on Pandateria, a prison island, because of her promiscuous and drunken ways.

Marcus Aemilius Lepidus – Pg. 698, ¶ 2 and Pg. 699, ¶ 7 – Marcus Aemilius Lepidus was the leader of Mark Anthony's armed guard and was then appointed by Antony to the position of Pontifex Maximus, High Priest of Rome. Lepidus then joined a triumvirate with Octavian and Mark Antony, and was given control of one third of Rome.

Modena – Pg. 699, ¶ 3 – Modena was the site of the first battle between Mark Antony and Octavian in 43 BC. Mark Antony's line was broken, but he remained unharmed, unlike both Roman consuls and many of Octavian's men, who were all killed in the battle.

Phraates IV – Pg. 702, ¶ 3 – Phraates IV, son of Orodes II, killed his father, brothers, and his oldest son, to ensure his place as king of Parthia.

Phraates V – Pg. 709, ¶ 3 – Phraates V, the son of Phraates IV by his slave girl, murdered his father and took the Parthian throne. Phraates V co-ruled with his mother, possibly in marriage, and because of this they were so unpopular that they were driven into exile.

Praetorian Guard – Pg. 705, ¶ 1 – The Praetorian Guard was a large, standing army that was stationed in Italy itself. The Praetorian Guard, established by Octavian, was in effect a private army, and broke the tradition that Rome did not keep an army close to home.

Tiberius – Pg. 708, ¶ 5 and Pg. 710, ¶ 1 & 2 – Tiberius, Octavian's wife's cold and distant son by a previous marriage, was married to Julia in a last-ditch attempt to create a blood-heir for Octavian. Tiberius was formally adopted by Octavian, and in AD 13, the Senate confirmed Tiberius as proconsul and princeps alongside Augustus, which eliminated the problem of a hereditary transfer of power.

Vonones I – **Pg. 709, ¶ 4 & 5 – Vonones I, one of Phraates IV's Roman-educated sons, took the Parthian throne after Phraates V's exile. Vonones I's Roman ways made him unpopular, and he was driven away (or killed) by the patriot Artabanus.**

Section II: Comprehension

Write a two/three sentence answer to each of the following questions.

1. How did Brutus and Cassius treat Caesar's memory after his death? Why did they act this way?
A1. – Pg. 697, ¶ 1 & 2 – Brutus and Cassius, fearing Caesar's public would rebel against the government, made speeches about Caesar's death as a tragic necessity that would allow the people of Rome to 'resume their liberty.' Then, they reassembled the Senate and suggested that Caesar be given a big honorable funeral, and also to be honored as divine. Honoring Caesar, now that he was safely dead and no longer a threat, ensured public support for the two men.

2. Why did the public riot when they saw the mutilation of Caesar's body?
A2. – Pg. 697, ¶ 3 to Pg. 698, ¶ 1 – Caesar, though tyrannical, had been a champion of the people; when his will was made public, it was found that he had divided his huge private fortune among the citizens of Rome. As his body was carried through the streets as part of his honorable burial, the citizens to whom he had been so generous were outraged by his mutilation and consequently started a riot.

3. How did Brutus gain public support from his exile at Antium? With all of this work to improve his image, why didn't Brutus return to Rome?
A3. – Pg. 698, ¶ 6-9 – While in exile at Antium, Brutus was wooing the public by sending money back to Rome for public festivals. Also, Brutus had Cicero make continual speeches in the Senate about his generosity and his willingness to fight tyranny. However, when Octavian showed up, Cicero allied himself with Caesar's adopted son, which naturally headed off any support for Brutus; he gave up and went to Athens.

4. How did Octavian and Cicero drive Mark Antony out of Italy?
A4. – Pg. 699, ¶ 2 – Octavian began to make friends with all of Antony's detractors and opponents, causing a rumor to spread that Octavian was planning to have Antony assassinated. As a result, Mark Antony gathered up troops to protect himself. Cicero then was able to convince the Senate to declare Antony a public enemy of the Roman people, which meant that Roman troops could drive him out of Italy.

5. Why did Octavian, after the defeat of Mark Antony at Modena, cease to regard Cicero? Who did Octavian ally himself with after his desertion of Cicero?
A5. – Pg. 699, ¶ 5 to Pg. 700, ¶ 2 – Octavian realized that Cicero and the Senate had hopes for the return of the Republic, but Octavian didn't want the return of the Republic, he wanted Caesar's power. Octavian turned his back on Cicero and made an alliance with Mark Antony and Lepidus instead. The triumvirate signed an official pact of allegiance, and Rome's empire was divided among them.

6. Why did Mark Antony stay in the east after the campaign against Brutus and Cassius was complete? Why did Mark Antony leave Syria for Alexandria in 41 BC?
A6. – Pg. 700, ¶ 7 to Pg. 702, ¶ 1 – Antony stayed in the east after Brutus and Cassius were dead because the Roman province of Syria was facing a possible invasion by the Parthians, under the command of their king, Orodes II. Herod was new to his position as the Roman governor of Syria; Antony stayed to help protect the Roman border. In 41 BC, Mark Antony met, and immediately was mesmerized by, Cleopatra, and instead of remaining in Syria to protect the province, he followed Cleopatra to Alexandria.

7. Explain how Lepidus was forced to give up his title of Triumvir, and how he ended up under life-long house arrest.
A7. – Pg. 702, ¶ 5 & 6 – Lepidus sailed with troops to Sicily, a clear message that he wanted more power. Octavian landed on the shores of Sicily and convinced Lepidus's troops to desert the cause, which eventually forced Lepidus to surrender to Octavian and beg for mercy. Octavian spared Lepidus's life, but took his provinces, his soldiers, his title of Triumvir, and put him under house arrest, where he remained for the rest of his life.

8. What excuse did Octavian use to declare war on Antony? How was Octavian able to turn the Senate against Mark Antony, too?
A8. – Pg. 703, ¶ 2 & 3 – After Antony gave up fighting against the Parthians and returned to Alexandria, Octavian used Antony's desertion as an excuse to declare Antony an enemy of Rome. In 32 BC, Octavian illegally read Antony's will to the Senate. When the Senate heard that Antony had left most of his money to the half-Egyptian children that Cleopatra had borne him, and also had asked to be buried in Egypt, they agreed to a formal pronouncement of war against Antony.

9. What were the details of the compromise made between Octavian and the Senate in 27 BC?
A9. – Pg. 704, ¶ 6 to Pg. 705, ¶ 2 – In 27 BC, Octavian formally announced the laying down of all powers the had been granted to him in the years of crisis. In return, once Octavian demonstrated that he respected the Republic, he was allowed to remain consul, and the Senate gave him control over the outlying provinces. Since most of the soldiers were stationed in these provinces, Octavian had control of the army. He was also allowed to establish a private army that was stationed in Italy itself, and he retained the title of Imperator.

10. What were the possible reasons that, in 23 BC, Augustus/Octavian declined to be elected for a tenth time as consul?
A10. – Pg. 705, ¶ 4 – One reason that Augustus declined to be elected consul again is because he may have realized that, if he were elected consul every year, a lot of senators were not getting the chance to run for office, which was bound to produce discontent. Another reason he may not have run was because he was struck by a serious illness, and didn't want to display himself at election while suffering from unsightly blemishes.

11. What were the powers given to Octavian when he was made proconsul by the Senate?
A11. – Pg. 706, ¶ 1 – As proconsul, Octavian was above the consuls in the power structure. Octavian could legally dabble in senatorial and consular affairs whenever he pleased, and he could also exercise military power – the imperium – inside the city.

12. How did both Parthia and Rome benefit from Phraates IV sending all four of his sons to Rome as hostages?

A12. – Pg. 706, ¶ 5 – Parthia benefitted from sending all four of the king's sons to Rome because it ensured the king would stay on his throne for at least a little while longer without threat of an internal usurper. Rome benefitted from receiving Parthian hostages because it gave Romans the chance to teach Roman ways to the Parthians. Also, continued peace with the Parthians meant that the trade route to India and perhaps even further west was now passable, ensuring Roman prosperity.

13. In what ways did the Senate surreptitiously rebel against Octavian and his false republic? How did Octavian deal with these rebellious acts?

A13. – Pg. 706, ¶ 6 and Pg. 708, ¶ 2 – Rome's senators started trailing into the Senate later and later and in response, Octavian announced in 17 BC that senators who came in late would have to pay a fine. Some senators stopped showing up, and the senators, who traditionally spoke in order of seniority, developed the habit of getting up one at a time and saying, "I agree with the last speaker." Octavian changed the regulations of the Senate so business could be carried on even if the minimum of four hundred of six hundred senators didn't show up, and he started calling on the senators to speak at random in order to keep them on their toes.

14. How was Palestine divided after Herod the Great's death?

A14. – Pg. 709, ¶ 1 – After the Herod the Great died, Palestine was divided into three parts, one for each son. Herod Antipas got Galilee, next to the Sea of Galilee; Archelaus got Samaria and Judea; Philip got the north. Archelaus turned out to be so cruel that in AD 6 Augustus yanked him from his throne and put a Roman official, a procurator, on the throne, to keep an eye on the area.

Section III: Critical Thinking

Augustus is the first Roman leader we have read about that could admit to the farce of the Republic. However, Octavian went to extreme lengths in order to preserve the façade of a Rome run by its people. Write a paragraph explaining what the title "Augustus" meant to Octavian, and why it was important for Octavian not to think of himself as a "prince" but as First Citizen.

The text tells us that Augustus technically meant consecrated, set apart and different. For Octavian, Augustus meant a fresh start – it was a brand-new name with no political baggage, so it could take on any shade of meaning Octavian gave it. Like the Roman leaders before him, Octavian thought his increasingly dictatorial actions were approved because they were in line with the will of the people. As such, Octavian believed the title Augustus was a reward for his virtue, given to him by the Senate in recognition of his refusal to grasp power. However, Octavian did not actually give up any of his power – he remained a consul, he controlled the military and he retained the title of Imperator. He would eventually be given the title of proconsul, and he would assume the office of the high priest. For Octavian, Augustus was a title that meant the power of an emperor under the guise of yielding to the Republic.

Tacitus says that Augustus "subjected the world to empire under the title of princeps: fessa nomine principis sub imperium accepit." *Augustus could not think of himself as a monarch because he knew that in order to stay in power, he had to pretend the Republic still worked as it was traditionally supposed to. The word "citizen" means a member of a state who owes allegiance to its government and is entitled to its protection. As "First Citizen," Augustus remained part of the contract between a people and its state, allied to the ideals of the Republic even if they ceased to exist in reality.*

EXAMPLE ANSWER: For Octavian, the name "Augustus" meant a fresh start – it was a brand-new name with no political baggage, so it could take on any shade of meaning Octavian gave it. Like the Roman leaders before him, Octavian thought his increasingly dictatorial actions were approved because they were in line with the will of the people. As such, Octavian believed the title Augustus was a reward for his virtue, given to him by the Senate in recognition of his refusal to grasp power. However, Octavian did not actually give up any of his power – he remained a consul, he controlled the military and he retained the title of Imperator. For Octavian, Augustus was a title that meant the power of an emperor under the guise of yielding to the Republic.

While Tacitus may have called Augustus a "prince," Augustus would have called himself "First Citizen." A citizen is in a relationship with the state - the state will protect a citizen as long as he follows the state's laws. In order to stay in power, Augustus had to pretend the Republic still worked as a government of the people. By thinking of himself as "First Citizen," Augustus remained part of the contract between a people and its state, allied to the ideals of the Republic even if they ceased to exist in reality.

CHAPTER EIGHTY: ECLIPSE AND RESTORATION

The student may use her text when answering the questions in sections I and II.

Section I: Who, What, Where

Write a one or two-sentence answer explaining the significance of each item listed below.

Cheng-chun – **Pg. 712, ¶ 3 – Cheng-chun was the empress dowager for her son Chengdi. Cheng-chun used her regent-like powers over Chengdi to instill Wang family members in government until the highest posts in the Han government were overloaded with them.**

Chengdi – **Pg. 712, ¶ 2 – Chengdi, son of Xuandi and great grandson of Yuandi, became Han emperor in 33 BC at the age of 18. He died after a reign of two decades, but with no son to succeed him.**

Liu Xiu/Guang Wudi – **Pg. 714, ¶ 4 – Liu Xiu won the Han throne after Wang Mang fled in AD 23.**

Mingdi – **Pg. 715, ¶ 2 – Mingdi, Guang Wudi's son with his second southern wife, succeeded Guang Wudi as emperor.**

The Red Eyebrows – **Pg. 714, ¶ 3 – Pg. 714, ¶ 3 – The Red Eyebrows were one of the first secret societies in Chinese history. The Red Eyebrows, men organized into a band to fight against the soldiers who came out into the countryside to enforce Wang Mang's decrees, painted their foreheads red so that, in battle, they could distinguish friend from foe.**

Ruzi – Pg. 713, ¶ 1 & ¶ 5 – **Ruzi, the great-great-grandson of the earlier emperor Xuandi, was a distant Han cousin that came to the throne after the very short reigns of Aiti and Ping. He was sent away to be raised elsewhere when Wang Mang took the throne.**

Sutta in Forty-two Sections – **Pg. 715, ¶ 6 – The Sutta in Forty-two Sections, Buddhist sayings presented in much the same way as the Analects of Confucius, were gathered by men Mingdi sent to India to learn more about the Buddha. Mingdi, pleased by the Sutta, adopted its teaching for himself and for his court.**

Wang Mang – **Pg. 713, ¶ 1 & ¶ 3 and Pg. 714, ¶ 4 – Wang Mang, nephew of Cheng-chun, and regent for emperor Ruzi, used his power to convince the people of the capital city that Heaven had turned against the Han and that it was time for a new dynasty, the Xin. In AD 23, Wang Mang gave up his throne and fled, ending the Xin Dynasty.**

Xin Dynasty – **Pg. 713, ¶ 4 – The Xin Dynasty was created by Wang Mang in AD 9, and replaced the Han Dynasty as the ruler of China.**

Section II: Comprehension

Write a two/three sentence answer to each of the following questions.

---

1. List the succession of Han emperors that followed Chengdi.
A1. – Pg. 712, ¶ 4 to Pg. 713, ¶ 1 – Chengdi died in 7 BC, with no son to follow his reign. His nephew Aiti succeeded him. Aiti ruled for only six years, also without children; Ping followed with a seven year rule, and did not produce an heir. Ruzi, a distant Han cousin that could claim to be the great-great-grandson of Xuandi then came to the throne.

2. Who protested Wang Mang acting as regent for Ruzi? How did Wang Mang manage to stay regent despite the opposition?
A2. – Pg. 713, ¶ 2 – Noblemen who resented the Wang power in government protested Wang Mang's appointment. One nobleman insisted that Wang Mang had poisoned at least one of the previous kings, and another nobleman led a short-lived, armed uprising against the minister. Wang Mang promised that he would hand the crown over to the baby king as soon as he was old enough, and that enabled him to keep his position as regent.

3. How was Wang Mang able to convince the people of the capital city to turn against the Han?
A3. – Pg. 713, ¶ 3 – Wang Mang convinced the people of the capital city that the extraordinary bad luck of the Han succession showed that the Will of Heaven had turned against the Han. He also claimed that the absence of an adult emperor on the throne was encouraging banditry, murder, and all sorts of crimes.

4. How did Wang Mang introduce the "New" Xin Dynasty to the Chinese people?
A4. – Pg. 713, ¶ 3 & 4 – Wang Mang claimed that omens favored a new government, such as a white stone discovered at the bottom of a well that had written on it "Tell Wang Mang that he must become Emperor!" He then declared that the Han had ended, and that he was now emperor of China. He claimed to be the descendant of the Yellow Emperor, and in AD 9 introduced the Xin Dynasty – the "New" Dynasty.

5. Describe the sweeping and sudden changes Wang Mang made once he was emperor. How did the people react to these changes?
A5. – Pg. 713, ¶ 5 to Pg. 714, ¶ 1 – Wang Mang pronounced himself restorer of the old and honorable ways. He gave noble families some of their feudal powers back, which meant peasants lost some of their power. Wang Mang also revived the ancient idea that all of China belonged to the emperor, and claimed some of the territories of the aristocrats for himself. The rich had no means to protect themselves from Wang Mang, and the poor had no way to stay alive, and as a result the people rose up and became thieves and bandits.

6. Why did Guang Wudi move the capital city from Chang'an to Loyang? What was this part of the Han empire called as a result of the move?
A6. – Pg. 714, ¶ 5 – When Guang Wudi became Han emperor after Wang Mang's short-lived Xi Dynasty, he set himself to reverse the damage caused by the previous emperor. However, he also wanted to distance himself from the earlier Han kingdom, so he moved his capital city from Chang'an to Loyang, two hundred miles east. As a result of the move, the second half of

the Han empire was called the Eastern Han in order to distinguish it from earlier Han rule.

7. What changes did Guang Wudi make in order to stop the nepotism of previous Han rulers?
A7. – Pg. 714, ¶ 6 – Guang Wudi made several changes to fight the tradition of nepotism sustained by previous Han rulers: he divided the old Han territory up into new counties, and gave more of the government posts to less important families. He built over one hundred training schools for future bureaucrats, in which government-paid teachers taught the skills that government officials needed to run the empire properly. He also put into effect a system of examinations; candidates who passed the examinations could win government posts, regardless of family background.

8. Why were the new counties of Guang Wudi's China filled with fewer people than the previous Han dynasty?
A8. – Pg. 715, ¶ 1 – The new counties of Guang Wudi's China had less people in them because of famine, civil war and flooding. As many as ten million people had died in the last years of the Western Han and the years of the New Dynasty.

9. Why, and how, did Mingdi have to make peace with the north of China upon his enthronement?
A9. – Pg. 715, ¶ 3 & 4 – Mingdi was not the original heir to Guang Wudi's throne. Guang Wudi had first married a noblewoman of the north and named their son heir. However, twenty years later Guang Wudi felt in control of the north, so he married a southern woman and produced another son, Mingdi, that he then pronounced to be his heir. Mingdi solved the problem of northern resentment by sending his general Pan Ch'ao north to campaign against the ongoing threat of the Xiongnu. Pan Ch'ao's campaigns whipped the Xiongnu into submission and gratitude from the north ensured Mingdi of their loyalty.

Section III: Critical Thinking

The student may not use her text to answer this question.

The Eastern Han brought many changes to China, including a new religion: Buddhism. Explain how Buddhism made its way into Chinese culture, both Mingdi's account and the more probable version. Then, explain how Buddhism reinforced the new Eastern Han power structure.

The student should remember from her reading that Mingdi claimed to have a dream where he saw a golden god in the sky asking to be honored. This god was identified by Mingdi's advisors as Buddha from India. The text states on page 715, ¶ 5, "This is a poetic expression of the reality of migration. Both merchants and missionaries from India had begun to travel regularly to China." The Silk Road enabled easy travel between China and other countries, meaning both goods and customs were exchanged. The movement of peoples between countries for commerce allowed cultures to blend. Mingdi's dream was a romanticized way of bringing attention to gradual change.

To get the student thinking about the use of Buddhism in the Chinese culture, you might ask the student, what did Mingdi do after his revelatory dream? Mingdi sent men to India to learn more about the Buddha. According to Chinese tradition, they came back with the Sutta in Forty-two Sections, which were Buddhist sayings presented in much the same way as the Analects of

Confucius. Mingdi then adopted its teaching for himself and for his court. The student should recall that Confucianism was prevalent in the Chinese court during the years of the Western Han. The text reminds us on page 715, ¶ 6 into page 716, ¶ 1 that "Confucianism, now set into the structures of Han bureaucracy by Guang Wudi's schools, had begun among the people and had run along the grass roots of Chinese society, promising ordinary men and women principles that would get them through their day-to-day lives: a republican ethic." Confucianism, a belief system for the people, did not reinforce the governing power structures of the Han Dynasty. Buddhism, however, coming from Mingdi's dream and then given out to the people via the Suttas, came from the top of China's social tree. From the king, the religion spread downwards. Buddhism linked the Eastern Han Dynasty with a religious practice of its own, both of which were to be worshiped by the Chinese people.

EXAMPLE ANSWER: The second emperor of the Eastern Han, Mingdi, claimed to have a dream where he saw a golden god in the sky asking to be honored. Mingdi's advisors identified the god as Buddha from India. Mingdi then sent men to India to learn more about the Buddha. According to Chinese tradition, they came back with the *Sutta in Forty-two Sections*, a book of Buddhist sayings. Mingdi adopted its teachings for himself and for his court. This is the romantic version of how Buddhism was introduced to China, giving credit to the Han emperor. More likely what happened is that merchants and missionaries from India had begun to travel to China regularly, sharing both their goods and their customs. This is the more probable version of how Buddhism was introduced into Chinese culture.

Buddhism, unlike Confucianism, came from the top of the social ladder and worked its way down. Confucianism promised ordinary men and women principles that would get them through their day-to-day lives, where Buddhism was adopted by the king and then was taught to the people. Buddhism linked the Eastern Han Dynasty with a religious practice of its own, both of which were to be worshiped by the Chinese people.

CHAPTER EIGHTY-ONE: THE PROBLEM OF SUCCESSION

The student may use his text when answering the questions in sections I and II.

Section I: Who, What, Where

Write a one or two-sentence answer explaining the significance of each item listed below.

Agrippina – **Pg. 727, ¶ 2-4** – Agrippina, Caligula's younger sister, married Claudius. After her son Nero was declared Claudius's heir, Agrippina ensured her own survival by poisoning her husband.

Artabanus III – **Pg. 722, ¶ 1 & 4** – Artabanus III, king of Parthia, restored nationalism to his country; appeared on his coins with the ancient square-cut Persian beard, and he created a ruling system copied from the old Persian satrapies. Artabanus III avoided war with Rome by partially withdrawing his troops from Armenia, leaving it as a buffer state.

Boudiccea – **Pg. 728, ¶ 6 to Pg. 729, ¶ 2** – Boudiccea, wife of the dead king of the British Iceni tribe, led a revolt against the Romans after Roman soldiers stormed into Iceni territory, raped Boudiccea's daughters and beat the widow up. With the help of the Trinovantes, Boudiccea successfully attacked the partially built city of Camulodunum; Boudiccea's revolt was squelched after the Roman commander Paulinus led a violent retribution, to which Boudiccea responded by taking poison.

Caligula – **Pg. 721, ¶ 1-3** – Caligula, princeps of Rome after Tiberius, started his reign by pardoning all those imprisoned under Tiberius, inviting exiles to return to the city and making a few tax reforms that helped out poorer Romans. Caligula quickly turned sour, committing a list of shocking crimes, and in 39 AD, he fired both of the consuls and dissolved the Senate by force.

Caratacus – **Pg. 726, ¶ 5 & 6** – Caratacus was the king of a British tribe that challenged the power of the Romans when he had gained enough power in the south of Britain to threaten Roman control of the Channel. Caratacus's power was stunted when Claudius sent four legions to fight against the British tribal leader in 43 AD.

Claudius – **Pg. 726, ¶ 1 and Pg. 727, ¶ 1** – Claudius, brother of Germanicus and uncle to Caligula, bribed the Praetorian Guard and was consequently given the power of princeps, Pontifex Maximus, and imperator after Caligula's death. The establishment of Roman power in Britain was the greatest political accomplishment of Claudius's reign.

Galba – **Pg. 731, ¶ 3 & 6 to Pg. 732, ¶ 2** – Galba, governor of Hispania, was given full support of the Praetorian Guard if he wanted to claim the imperium from Nero. Once Galba claimed the title, he declined to pay off the soldiers who had supported him, and seven months after claiming the power of imperator, Galba was replaced by Otho, murdered, and his head was stuck on a pole.

Germanicus – Pg. 717, ¶ 3 & 4 – Germanicus, Tiberius's nephew, was serving as general in command of the legions at the Rhine when he was appointed as his uncle's heir and subsequently given the responsibility of governing Syria. Germanicus died shortly after arriving in Syria, leaving behind him his wife and young son Caligula.

Germany – Pg. 717, ¶ 3 – Germany was the name given to the province at the Rhine by the Romans. The Celtic tribes that roved through the province were known as Germans.

Gondophernes – Pg. 723, ¶ 2 to Pg. 724, ¶ 4 – Gondophernes, an ancient Indian ruler, conquered the area of the Punjab that was under Kushan's control, and spread his kingdom up as far as the modern valley of Kabul. The discovery of Gondophernes's coins prove his existence, despite the centuries old belief that the biblical story of Gondophernes and Doubting Thomas was entirely mythical.

Jesus – Pg. 720, ¶ 1 & 4 – Jesus was a wandering prophet that challenged the power of the priests in Galilee, who were controlling the religious life of the Jews. Jesus was sentenced to execution by crucifixion because he called himself "King of the Jews," thereby threatening Roman power in Palestine.

Kujula Kadphises – Pg. 722, ¶ 7 to 723, ¶ 1 – Kujula Kadphises became ruler of Kushan around AD 30, and held the throne for about fifty years. During his reign, Kushan grew west far enough to push on Parthia's eastern border, absorbing territories like Gaofu that had not been a full part of the Parthian system.

Lucius Aelius Sejanus – Pg. 718, ¶ 4 & 5 – Lucius Aelius Sejanus, the commander of the Praetorian Guard, was ordered arrested and tried by Tiberius after the princeps found out the guard was not only the lover of Tiberius's dead son Drusus's wife, but also that the two of them had conspired to poison Drusus. After Sejanus was convicted, a purge ensued that swept up hundreds of citizens of Rome.

Lucius Domitius/Nero – Pg. 727, ¶ 2 & 5 and Pg. 730, ¶ 3 – Lucius Domitius, or Nero, son of Agrippina, was adopted by Claudius when he married Agrippina mother, and was named Claudius's heir. Nero was blamed for the great fire that burned through Rome in 64 AD, and in an effort to clear his name, put to death all suspected conspirators against him and began to persecute Christians.

Otho – Pg. 731, ¶ 3 and Pg. 732, ¶ 3 & 4 – Otho, former husband of Poppea, supported Galba's stab at princeps, and then replaced his former ally as imperator and princeps after Galba's murder. When Otho was challenged by Vitellius for his power, Otho decided that a civil war would do Rome no good, so he killed himself instead of going to battle.

Pontius Pilate – Pg. 720, ¶ 3-5 – Pontius Pilate, the Roman procurator, agreed to execute Jesus after the prophet did not deny that he claimed to be the king of the Jews. After Pilate executed a bunch of rebelling Samaritans and caused a backlash of anti-Roman sentiment in Palestine, the Roman governor of Syria yanked Pilate off the job and sent him back to Rome in disgrace.

Vespasian – Pg. 732, ¶ 6 and Pg. 734, ¶ 2 – Vespasian, governor of Syria, known for his strong command of Roman forces in the wars in Britain, became princeps of Rome without ever stepping foot into the city. Vespasian was busy dealing with the siege of Jerusalem, and did not want to leave go to Rome before the affairs in his own province were settled.

Vitellius – Pg. 732, ¶ 3 & 5 and Pg. 734, ¶ 1 – Vitellius, commander of Roman forces in Germany, challenged Otho for the role of imperator, supported by a vast army at his back. Vitellius's first act as imperator was to dissolve the existing Praetorian Guard and to recreate it with his own loyal troops, an act that caused outraged troops to storm Rome, kill Vitellius, and throw his body into the Tiber.

Section II: Comprehension

Write a two/three sentence answer to each of the following questions.

1. Why did Tiberius leave Rome for Campania? What did Tiberius do once he settled in Capri?
A1. – Pg. 717, ¶ 4 to Pg. 718, ¶ 3 – Tiberius left Rome for Campania because he lost heart after both his appointed successors – Germanicus and Drusus – died. Then he moved on to Capri, where he managed Rome from afar, and never even visited the mother city. While in Capri, Tiberius indulged himself in the indiscriminate fulfillment of all his desires.

2. Describe the special circumstances around Caligula's appointment as leader of Rome.
A2. – Pg. 721, ¶ 1 and footnote – When Tiberius was still alive, Caligula was given the job of quaestor, or financial official, but he never got any other title. Caligula was appointed joint heir with Tiberius Gemellus in Tiberius's will, but Caligula had the will declared void and had Gemellus killed. Once Tiberius was dead, the Senate awarded Caligula the title of princeps, the authority of the Pontifex Maximus, and the military power of the imperium without recognizing him first as the surviving member of a joint proconsulate, and without the formality of his surrendering his powers.

3. How did Caligula maintain loyal followers during his reign of terror?
A3. – Pg. 721, ¶ 4 – Caligula's wrath did not terrorize everyone equally; he lavished money and privileges on those who managed to stay on his good side. This meant that there were always people ready to carry reports of treason back to Caligula. Caligula's informants wouldn't dare turn on him either – his punishments were so inventively painful that few wanted to risk them.

4. How did Artabanus III keep tight control over Parthia?
A4. – Pg. 722, ¶ 1 & 2 – Artabanus III kept control over Parthia by putting his kinsmen, now princes of a royal family, on minor thrones to rule over the eighteen regions of his kingdom and report to him, in a system copied from the old Persian satrapies.

5. What did it mean for a kingdom to be "Roman protected?"
A5. – Pg. 722, ¶ 2 – If a kingdom was "Roman protected," it meant that Roman troops were propping up rule of that kingdom with a Roman-sympathizing king.

6. What was the result of Parthia's Armenian attack?
A6. – Pg. 722, ¶ 3-5 – Fighting in the capital city of Armenia ended with Artabanus's son Arsaces dead, but Artabanus was unwilling to give up and made another assault on the kingdom. Soon after, Artabanus agreed to meet a Roman diplomat, and both sides committed to a partial withdrawal. Armenia would remain as a buffer state between Parthia and Rome.

7. Who were the Kushan people? Describe the coins used by the Kushan, and explain what the details of the coins tell us about the Kushan culture.

A7. – Pg. 722, ¶ 6 – The Kushan people originated from Yuezhi tribes that had invaded and broken down Greek Bactria. The Kushan people were Asian, but they used Greek script on their coins, which had Zeus on one-side and a cross-legged seated figure who may be Buddha on the other. The Kushan culture was woven through with influences from both west and south.

8. What did the Senate want to do with the office of princeps after Caligula's death? In what way was the Praetorian Guard responsible for Claudius's installment as princeps?

A8. – Pg. 726, ¶ 1 & 2 – After the death of Caligula, the Senate considered doing away with the office of princeps altogether, and dividing the power which had been temporarily united in the person of the princeps back into their old republican offices. Because the restoration of the Republic would probably end in the dissolution of the Praetorian Guard, the guard was willing to be bribed by Claudius, who had set his sights on the power of the princeps, in order to secure their own livelihood. The Praetorian guard, once bribed, ensured Claudius was installed at princeps.

9. How did Nero begin his reign? Give an example of how the course of Nero's actions changed after he turned 20 years old.

A9. – Pg. 727, ¶ 6 to Pg. 728, ¶ 3 – Nero began his reign by paying off the Praetorian Guard, and promising the Senate that he would give them back some of their powers. Once Nero turned twenty, his actions turned towards the overindulgent. For example, after he fell in love with Poppea, the wife of his friend Otho, Nero sent Otho away and invited Poppea to stay in the palace, even though Nero was already married.

Other examples of Nero's dark actions are listed below:

Pg. 728, ¶ 4 – Nero tried to get rid of his mother by building her a collapsible boat that was meant to fold in upon her and drown her. When this plan failed, he ordered a servant to stab his mother.

Pg. 728, ¶ 4 – Nero divorced his wife and then had her murdered and her head brought back to Poppea as a trophy.

Pg. 728, ¶ 4 – Nero declared a divorce between Poppea and her husband Otho, and married Poppea himself.

Pg. 729, ¶ 3 – Nero had affairs, drank tremendously, raised taxes in the provinces to pay for his indulgences, and started once again to hold the infamous treason trials as Caligula had done.

10. Why did Nero give up Armenia to Parthia?

A10. – Pg. 730, ¶ 4 to Pg. 731, ¶ 1 – A long and draining war in Armenia that started when the Parthian king Vologases I refused to honor the agreement made between Parthia and Rome, coupled with Roman provinces that were restless and unhappy under too much tax, had spread the Roman army thin. Unwilling to continue to fight a battle sure to end in Roman destruction, Nero decided to make peace with Parthia by recognizing Vologases's brother, Tiridates, as king of Armenia.

11. Where did the real power of princeps lie? How did the princeps ensure his power in this area, and in what way did this fundamentally differ from the way the Republic of Rome was meant to be ruled?

A11. – Pg. 731, ¶ 5 – The real power of the princeps lay in the imperium, the supreme command of the army. To ensure his power over the imperium, the ruler of Rome needed the support of the Praetorian Guard. The Republic was no longer run by the people; it had become an empire run by a band of powerful soldiers would could put up or remove a figurehead ruler, but who held the real power themselves.

12. Once he was nominated as a rival for the power of princeps, why didn't Vespasian go immediately to Rome? What were the circumstances of the battle Vespasian had to clean up?

A12. – Pg. 732, ¶ 7 to Pg. 733, ¶ 1 – Vespasian did not go to Rome after he was nominated to challenge Vitellius as princeps because he was busy in Syria putting down trouble in Palestine. In 66, a group of freedom fighters called Zealots had proclaimed war on the Roman soldiers stationed in Jerusalem. The local governor had marched troops in but had been defeated, and the situation had grown serious enough for Vespasian himself, with the help of his son and commander Titus, to drive the rebels back inside Jerusalem.

13. What happened in the fighting between the Roman troops that supported Vespasian and the troops that were loyal to Vitellius when they met at Cremona, and then in Rome?

A13. – Pg. 733, ¶ 2 – When the two sets of Roman troops met at Cremona, the Vespasian-loyal troops eventually won a victory, but the victory resulted in a four-day rampage of burning and destruction that stretched down into Rome itself. Vespasian's supporters in the city tried to seize the Capital from Vitellius, and in the battle that followed both the Capital and the great Temple of Jupiter Optimus Maximus burned to the ground.

14. What does *damnatio memoria* mean? Why were the names of the five princeps who ruled prior to Vespasian erased from the record?

A14. – Pg. 734, ¶ 3 – *Damnatio memoria* means erased from the record. In order to continue the illusion that Rome was run by the people, and not by the strongest man with the most armed support, the Senate struck the names Caligula, Nero, Galba, Otho and Vitellius from the record. By not listing the names of these men, the Senate denied their existence and continued the illusion that Rome was still a Republic.

Section III: Critical Thinking

As the Roman empire spread, it subsumed provinces that contained people who were torn between the identities of their birth and their new identities as Romans. While the struggle between these two ends was difficult for some, Christians were able to be both Roman and Christian because of the very nature of Christianity. Write a paragraph that explains the dualism inherent in the origins of Christianity, and that describes why Christianity would endure through Rome's unstable times.

Christianity was an off-shoot of Judaism, where the death and resurrection of Jesus was believed to be a process repeated in the lives of Christian believers. The Jewish theologian Paul, a Roman citizen, said that conversion to Christianity brought death to an old corrupt self, and the power of Christ raised it back up and restored it anew. Once converted, one was "dead to sin, but alive to God." The text tells us that "the spreading cult of Christianity gave its adherents a brand-new identity in place of the old."

The duality of the Christian identity had its roots in the origins of the religion. We learn on page 725, ¶ 3 that "Christianity had, after all, originated in a conquered land – Judea – which had been allowed to keep its identity while donning another one at the same time. The Jews of Judea were Jews, not Roman; but they were also subjects of Rome, and some of them were even Roman citizens." While a Jew was obliged to follow Rome's laws, his spiritual allegiance was to God. Christianity, a sect of Judaism, had the same rules of allegiance. Christians could believe in God and believe in Rome, meaning they were adaptable to any changes in Roman government because their true allegiance was to God's other-worldly kingdom.

As the tides of Roman politics swayed, Christianity gave its followers a way to be true to their identity as Romans, while also being true to their spiritual identities as followers of Christ. On page 725, ¶ 2, the text reads, "But the old identity, though it may be transformed, does not completely disappear. In another letter, to Christians in Galatia, Paul writes, 'There is neither Jew nor Gentile, slave nor free, not to mention male and female, for all are one in Jesus Christ.' Yet elsewhere his letters make quite clear that Christians remained Jews and Gentiles, slave and free, not to mention male and female. A Christian had his (or her) core identity as a follower of Jesus Christ, but orthodox Christians did not relinquish their old nationalities, or their gender, or their place in the social hierarchy." The adaptability of Christians to their earthly circumstances meant the religion was suited for a constantly changing world.

EXAMPLE ANSWER: The duality of the Christian identity had its roots in the origins of the religion. Christianity was a sect of Judaism, a religion that originated in a conquered land – Judea. The people of Judea were allowed to keep their own identity as Jews while also being subjects, or even citizens, of Rome. Christianity had the same rules of allegiance; Christians could believe in God and believe in Rome. Once converted to Christianity, a believer received a brand-new identity as a follower of Christ. His old identity did not completely disappear – a Christian had his core identity as a follower of Jesus Christ, but he did not relinquish his old nationality. As the tides of Roman politics swayed, Christianity gave its followers a way to be true to their identity as Romans, while also being true to their spiritual identities as followers of Christ.

Chapter Eighty-Two: The Edges of the Roman World

The student may use her text when answering the questions in sections I and II.

Section I: Who, What, Where

Write a one or two-sentence answer explaining the significance of each item listed below.

Domitian – **Pg. 738, ¶ 4, Pg. 739, ¶ 1 and Pg. 740, ¶ 1 – Domitian, who became imperator and princeps after the death of his brother Titus, adopted the title *dominus et deus,* or "Lord and God," and became the first Roman ruler to recognize his power as emperor. Though he paid the army for their support, Domitian's oppressive ruling style led to his murder.**

Hadrian – **Pg. 743, ¶ 3 & 4 and Pg. 744, ¶ 3 & 4 – Hadrian, who followed Trajan as emperor of Rome, was a middle-ground emperor who fought his biggest war against rebellious Jews when he tried to build a new capital city atop the ruins of Jerusalem. Hadrian had a wall built across Roman Britain, from the North Sea to the Irish Sea, in order to delineate the edge of the Roman kingdom.**

Mount Vesuvius – **Pg. 737, ¶ 3 to Pg. 738, ¶ 1 – Mount Vesuvius, found on the southwest coast of Italy not far from the Bay of Naples, erupted on August 24, 79 AD. Over two thousand people in the city of Pompeii, which was located at the foot of the mountain, died either by being buried in twenty-five feet of ash, or by choking on the heat and gasses from the eruption.**

Nerva – **Pg. 740, ¶ 1 & 2 – Nerva, declared emperor after Domitian's murder, named Trajan his heir because he was afraid the Praetorian Guard would kill him out of loyalty to Domitian. Nerva died only a few months into his reign from fever.**

Pliny the Younger – **Pg. 737, ¶ 4 – Pliny the Younger, a Roman writer, was in Pompeii the day before the eruption of Mount Vesuvius. He fled the city, and lived to write an account of his flight from Pompeii.**

Simon Bar Kochba – **Pg. 743, ¶ 5 – Simon Bar Kochba was the leader of the Jewish resistance against Hadrian's plan to build a new capital city over the ruins of Jerusalem. Kochba, described as a man with the character of a robber and a murder, wrongly promised the Jews he would bring them light in the midst of their misfortunes.**

Titus – **Pg. 735, ¶ 5 to Pg. 737, ¶ 1 and Pg. 738, ¶ 2 & 3 – Titus, son of Vespasian, became princeps in 79 AD and followed his father's orderly and decent example. After three major disasters hit the Roman empire – the eruption of Mount Vesuvius, fire in Rome, and a deadly epidemic – Titus died from fever, having only ruled for three years.**

Trajan – **Pg. 740, ¶ 6 – Trajan, elected emperor after the death of Nerva, was known as a good emperor because of his basic fairness, his lack of paranoia, his decent administration of the capital city, and his willingness to campaign for the greater glory of Rome. Trajan was also well liked because he observed the traditional empty forms of cooperation with the Senate.**

Section II: Comprehension

Write a two/three sentence answer to each of the following questions.

1. When Vespasian finally arrived in Rome, how did he make sure the army would not destroy his power?
A1. – Pg. 735, ¶ 2 – When Vespasian arrived in Rome, his first action was to reassign commanders and divide troops so that old loyalties would be destroyed, and the army would not pose a threat to his power.

2. What events led to Syria's absorption of Palestine?
A2. – Pg. 735, ¶ 3 – In 73 AD, the last members of the Jewish rebellion in Jerusalem were trapped in their fortress of Masada. Rather than finally surrendering to the Romans, they killed their children and then themselves. The last Jewish stronghold was gone, as was Judea and all the remnants of the old nation of Israel, leaving Syria to take Palestine as a province.

3. Though Domitian ruled with general disregard for Rome and the Senate, why was Domitian's severity not necessarily a bad thing? Give one example of how Domitian's harsh policies were actually good for Rome.
A3. – Pg. 738, ¶ 5 – Domitian may have ruled severely, but his severity was generally exercised in the interests of law and order. For example, he degraded jurors and their associates who accepted bribes, meaning he was trying to get corruption out of Rome.

Other examples of good that came from Domitian's harsh policies are listed below:

Pg. 738, ¶ 5 – Domitian's close watch over the city officials and governors of the provinces meant that they were honest and just.

Pg. 738, ¶ 5 – Domitian kept a severe eye on public morals, and made an example of an ex-quaestor by expelling him from the Senate because he was given to acting and dancing.

Pg. 738, ¶ 5 – Domitian kept a severe eye on public morals, and made it illegal for prostitutes to receive inheritances, and he put to death one of the Vestal Virgins that had been having multiple flings.

4. Why did Roman historians bestow praise upon Trajan?
A4. – Pg. 740, ¶ 5 to Pg. 741, ¶ 1 – Roman historians bestowed praise upon Trajan because he was a fair and diligent ruler; he repaired the roads and harbors, built libraries, dug canals, repaired sewers, and his military campaigns added land to the Roman empire without excessive bloodshed. Trajan also treated the Senators with dignity, and upheld the traditions of senatorial regulations that had been ignored by Rome's most recent rulers.

5. Define the Roman philosophy of stoicism. How did Epictetus apply stoic principles to the problem of emperor?
A5. – Pg. 741, ¶ 2 & 3 – The Roman philosophy of stoicism taught that the stoic man was not dominated by his appetites; he was able to detach himself from both pleasure and pain in order to decide with objectivity what course of action was good. Epictetus applied stoicism to the problem of emperor by explaining that man had never been free in the eyes of the constitution, he was only free in his soul. The emperor was just another real-world obstacle men had to endure, but he did not hamper the freedom of a man's spirit.

6. What was different about the threat posed to Rome by Christians as opposed to the threat that was posed by the Jews?

A6. – Pg. 741, ¶ 4 to Pg. 742, ¶ 2 – The Christians were seen as a threat to Rome because they talked about belonging to a kingdom in another dimension with no earthly ruler. The Jews, who also worshiped an otherworldly ruler, were tied to Israel, which meant their faith had to have a political dimension and that they would defend the land promised to them by God. Because the Christians had never had a country of their own, the Romans could not extinguish the Christian homeland, and therefore could not extinguish the Christians.

7. In what way did Trajan choose to deal with the growing number of Christians in Rome?

A7. – Pg. 742, ¶ 5 – Trajan chose to deal with the growing number of Christians in Rome by instituting a don't ask-don't tell policy. Public professions of Christianity were discouraged, but Christians were not sought out. If they were behaving peacefully, the Christians were left in peace.

8. How far did the Roman Empire reach under Trajan's rule? How did Trajan himself help the growth of the empire?

A8. – Pg. 742, ¶ 6 – Under Trajan's rule, the Roman Empire reached its greatest extent. His final campaign was against Parthia, which he led himself. Armenia fell as Roman troops marched towards Parthia. Parthians were forced to retreat; Trajan marched into Mesopotamia, occupied Babylon, and captured the Parthian capital Ctesiphon.

9. How did the Jews take advantage of Roman fighting in Parthia? What did Trajan do to stop the Jewish rebellions?

A9. – Pg. 742, ¶ 7 to Pg. 743, ¶ 1 – The Jewish communities scattered across the empire took advantage of Trajan's preoccupation with Parthia by rebelling and trying to win back the land given to them by God. Trajan put a temporary stop to the rebellions by giving permission to the non-Jews in the troubled areas to kill their Jewish neighbors.

10. What caused the huge Jewish uprising, led by Simon Bar Kochba, against Rome? How did Hadrian put down the revolt?

A10. – Pg. 743, ¶ 4-6 – A huge Jewish uprising against Rome was caused by Hadrian's plan to build himself a new capital city overtop of the ruins of Jerusalem and a temple to Jupiter on the site of the Second Temple. Hadrian put a stop to the revolt by sending his most experienced generals to mount small battles against the Jewish guerrilla outposts across the country, intercepting small groups, depriving them of food and shutting them up.

11. What was the practical reason for Hadrian to build a wall across Roman Britain? What was the ideological reason behind the creation of the wall?

A11. – Pg. 744, ¶ 2-5 – The practical reason for Hadrian to build a wall across Roman Britain was to keep the Celts from the north from raiding Rome's province. The ideological reason for building the wall was to seal Rome's borders and to clearly delineate that those on the Roman side of the wall were Romans, and those outside of the wall were Rome's enemies.

Section III: Critical Thinking

The student may not use her text to answer this question.

As we've read about the growth of the kingdom of Rome, we've read about the continued struggle to keep up the façade that Rome was a republic of the people. For years imperators laid down their powers to the Senate in a play-act, and the names of rulers who had claimed the power of princeps but acted as tyrants were stricken from the record, their existence denied by the Senate. How is it, then, that with one simple phrase Domitian turned the Roman Republic into an empire? In your answer, define the meaning of the title *dominus et deus,* and explain how, with the adoption of this title, Domitian changed the very fabric of Roman government.

The phrase dominus et deus *is defined on page 739, ¶ 1: it means "Lord and God." Not only did Domitian take this title, but he also ordered that all official letters be headed "Our Lord and our God commands that this be done." The Senate did not mount a sustained objection to this change, nor did the Praetorian Guard immediately try to kill Domitian. Domitian made Romans acknowledge the truth behind the princeps – that he alone ruled Rome.*

By accepting Domitian as "Lord and God," the Senate accepted the rule of Rome by an emperor. As the text states, "Domitian was not the first Roman ruler to wield kingly powers, but he was the first to <u>say</u> so. The first Citizen had finally become emperor." Domitian's new title marked the end of the transition period in which republican ideals were slowly buried, and the ruler of Rome was no longer First Citizen, but emperor. Now, the Senate could no longer deny the fact that the ruler of Rome did not need the sanction of the people to stay in power. Unlike the days when Rome was a republic, any traditions carried on between the princeps and Senate were merely formalities.

EXAMPLE ANSWER: For years, the imperators of Rome had been acting like kings. When Domitian adopted the title *dominus et deus*, or "Lord and God," he forced the people of Rome to acknowledge that they were ruled by an emperor, not a chosen First Citizen. Domitian's official letters were headed, "Our Lord and our God commands that this be done." Neither the Senate nor the Praetorian Guard challenged "Lord and God," and thus it became clear that Rome was no longer a republic. Domitian's new title marked the end of the transition period in which republican ideals were slowly buried. Now, the Senate could no longer deny the fact that the ruler of Rome did not need the sanction of the people to stay in power. Unlike the days when Rome was a republic, any traditions carried on between the princeps and Senate were merely formalities.

CHAPTER EIGHTY-THREE: CHILDREN ON THE THRONE

The student may use his text when answering the questions in sections I and II.

Section I: Who, What, Where

Write a one or two-sentence answer explaining the significance of each item listed below.

Andi – **Pg. 747, ¶ 1 & 2** – Andi followed Hedi as China's ruler. Without Pan Ch'ao to watch over the young ruler, Andi was married while still a child to the daughter of an ambitious official, and was encouraged to leave the political decisions to his wife's family.

Chang Chueh – **Pg. 749, ¶ 5 to Pg. 750, ¶ 2** – Chang Chueh, a Daoist teacher, was the leader of the Yellow Turbans. Chang Chueh's claim that he could do magic resulted in hundreds of thousands of Chinese following the Yellow Turbans.

Empress Dowager Dou – **Pg. 748, ¶ 5 to Pg. 749, ¶ 1** – The Empress Dowager Dou was Huandi's third wife, and she served as her son Lingdi's regent. Empress Dowager Dou was put under guard by the palace eunuchs when they found out she had received advice to wipe all of the eunuchs out.

Hedi – **Pg. 746, ¶ 1 & 2** – Hedi, at just nine years old, followed Zhangdhi as emperor of China. When Hedi was twelve, he ordered the palace eunuchs to kill off his mother's relatives because they were trying to take advantage of his youth and muscle their way into government positions.

Huandi – **Pg. 747, ¶ 4-7** – Huandi, made king of Han China at just fourteen, retreated into the palace when his wife's older brother, Liang Ji, took power. In an attempt to restore his own power, Huandi charged five eunuchs with the job of killing Liang Ji in 159.

Liang Ji – **Pg. 747 ¶ 4-7** – Liang Ji was the older brother of Huandi's wife, and he ran China for Huandi. Liang Ji killed himself when he found out that five eunuchs had been sent to murder him by Huandi.

Lingdi – **Pg. 748, ¶ 4 and Pg. 749, ¶ 1** – Lingdi, Huandi's son, became king of China when he was twelve years old. Lingdi was convinced by the Ten Regular Attendants that his mother was dangerous and that the palace eunuchs would keep him safe.

Ten Regular Attendants – **Pg. 748, ¶ 5** – The Ten Regular Attendants was the name for a group of palace eunuchs who were committed to getting as much as they could from the emperor for themselves. The Ten Regular Attendants were like a voluntary clan, crossed with a secret society.

Yellow Turbans – **Pg. 749, ¶ 5** – The Yellow Turbans were a millennial sect of rebels who looked forward to the coming of a golden age. They were led by Chang Chueh.

Zhang Rang – **Pg. 749, ¶ 2** – Zhang Rang, a much-hated member of the Ten Regular Attendants, was given the honorary title "My Foster Father" by Lingdi.

Section II: Comprehension

Write a two/three sentence answer to each of the following questions.

1. Why did Hedi order the palace eunuchs to kill off his mother's relatives?

A1. – Pg. 746, ¶ 2 – Hedi ordered the palace eunuchs to kill of his mother's relatives because they were trying to take advantage of his youth and muscle their way into government offices. Hedi's regent, Pan Ch'ao, most likely prompted the young king to give the order, since Pan Ch'ao remembered that the Han Dynasty had once been overthrown by relatives of a dowager empress.

2. What role did the palace eunuchs serve, and why weren't they considered a threat to the royal family?

A2. – Pg. 746, ¶ 3 – The palace eunuchs were trusted loyal servants of the royal family. Because they were castrated, it was presumed that the eunuchs had no ambitions to seize land, wealth or power on behalf of their children or clan.

3. List the succession of rulers that followed Andi until AD 146 – make sure to list the age of each ruler at the time he came to power.

A3. Pg. 747, ¶ 3 – Andi was succeeded by his son Shundi, who was crowned in 125 at the age of ten. Shundi's son Chongdi was crowned when he was barely a year old; Chongdi died before he was three and was succeeded by his third cousin, the seven year old Zhidi. Zhidi was poisoned when he was eight and was replaced by another cousin, the fourteen-year-old Huandi.

4. Who ran Han China during the succession of child-kings? Who made the decisions for Huandi when he was a child, and how did this affect Huandi's behavior?

A4. – Pg. 747, ¶ 4 – During the years child-kings were on the throne, uncles, cousins, aunts and anyone else who wiggled their way into the government ran Han China. Huandi's wife's older brother, Liang Ji, made decisions for the young king. Deprived of his power, Huandi retreated into the palace and cultivated a friendship with the palace eunuchs.

5. What two important rulings were made in favor of the eunuchs that allowed eunuchs to create their own ruling clan?

A5. – Pg. 747, ¶ 5 – Two important rulings were made in favor of the eunuchs that allowed them to create their own ruling clan: first, a decision was made that allowed the adopted son of an eunuch to keep the land left to him by his adopted father when he died. Second, another eunuch was permitted to pass down an honorary title to his adopted son.

6. What happened when Chen Fan, an advisor to the Empress Dowager Dou, suggested that all the palace eunuchs be wiped out?

A6. Pg. 749, ¶ 1 – When Chen Fan suggested all the eunuchs be wiped out, word got back to the eunuchs and, together with their allies, they stormed the palace. They put the empress dowager under guard, and told the young king Lingdi that they had come to free him from his mother's influence and keep him safe.

7. Describe the disasters that hit China between the years of 172 and 179 AD.

A7. – Pg. 749, ¶ 3 – In 172 widespread sickness hit China, followed first by flooding and then by an invasion of locusts. In 177, an army campaign against the barbarians ended in disaster,

and then in 179, another epidemic swept across the country.

8. What did Chang Chueh claim his magical powers could do for the people of China? Why did so many Chinese people believe in Chang Chueh?

A8. – Pg. 749, ¶ 5 to Pg. 750, ¶ 1 – Chang Chueh claimed he had the power to do magic. He said he could heal sickness and that if the Chinese people took his medicines, they would be immune from wounds and could fight in battle without fear. The Chinese people, who had just suffered through an epidemic and were vulnerable, underarmed and weak with hunger, were marveled by Chang Chueh's promises of health and strength.

Section III: Critical Thinking

How did ambition drive the shape of China between 88 and 182 AD? Great leaders are often driven by ambition, but their success always comes at a price. In this chapter, we read about the ambitious and able men of China making a place for themselves in a Han Dynasty ruled by children and extended family. Write a paragraph describing how the men who governed China's provinces made a successful life for themselves while simultaneously creating a new kind of feudal system in Han China. Then, write a paragraph explaining how ambitious merchants were able to change their position in society from parasitic middlemen to traders that made a vast fortune at the cost of China's poor laboring class.

In this chapter, the student read about several different groups of people gaining power during the final years of the Han Dynasty: eunuchs, the men who governed China's provinces, merchants and the Yellow Turbans. This question addresses the men who governed China's provinces and the merchants specifically because these two groups had to take advantage of the laboring class in order to advance themselves in society.

On page 748, ¶ 1 the text reads, "Unwatched, the merit system instituted by Guang Wudi had started to backfire. It had put the government of China's provinces into the hands of trained and able men instead of aristocrats. But those able men were also ambitious. Many of them, over time, had seized the land of those who could not pay their taxes, and then had allowed the debtors to continue farming it." While the debtors could have been thrown into prison, government officials were smart and had the debtors continue to farm the land they once owned, with the profits now going to the government rather than the former land owner. Over time, government officials accumulated huge tracts of previously-owned land, which they then handed down to their sons. The debtors, unable to pay their dues, became a new kind of feudal peasant class. The result was that "wealthy landowners ran vast estates, and the poor farmers who worked the land had no power to protest their own low wages." The rise of the ambitious government officials and their families came at the cost of the men who used to own the land they now slaved over for someone else's profit.

While the men who governed China's provinces were increasing the amount of land they owned, the merchants were thriving because of increased trade along the Silk Road. On page 748, ¶ 3, the text reads, "under the original Han system, [merchants] had been scorned as parasites and middlemen." However, the vast amounts of trade between east and west meant that Han merchants were able to make tremendous fortunes. This also cost the laboring class: "the trade was built partly on the back

of the poor laboring farmworkers, who had to pay higher and higher taxes so that the Silk Road could be kept up all the way west, and staffed with garrisons to keep merchant caravans safe from bandits."
The merchants profited from the taxes paid by the farmworkers, and the new wealthy landowners were ensured their indentured servants would never gain their freedom because they would not be able to pay their taxes on top of their previous debts.

EXAMPLE ANSWER: **The ambitions of the men who ruled China's provinces and the merchants who traded on China's Silk Road were fueled by the hard work of the laboring class. The governors of the provinces may have earned their positions in government by merit, but they soon took advantage of those who could not pay their taxes and seized the land of these debtors. The men in power then allowed the debtors to continue farming the land in an effort to pay back their taxes, but the governors were the only ones who saw the profits from the laborers' work. Over time, government officials accumulated huge tracts of previously-owned land, which they then handed down to their sons. The debtors, unable to pay their dues, became a new kind of feudal peasant class. The result was that wealthy landowners ran huge estates while the poor farmers who worked the land had no power to protest their own low wages. The men who used to own the land now slaved over it for the ambitious governors' profits.**

Merchants were also taking advantage of the laboring class during this time. Increased trade along the Silk Road meant that merchants were no longer seen as parasitic middlemen but as ambitious traders with great fortunes. Just as the governors exploited the laboring class, the merchants relied on the taxes paid by farmworkers to maintain the condition and security of the Silk Road. As the merchants grew more wealthy, farmworkers went deeper into debt and were driven further and further away from freedom.

CHAPTER EIGHTY-FOUR: THE MISTAKE OF INHERITED POWER

The student may use her text when answering the questions in sections I and II.

Section I: Who, What, Where

Write a one or two-sentence answer explaining the significance of each item listed below.

Antonius Pius – **Pg. 751, ¶ 1 & 3 – Antonius Pius was the adopted heir and successor of Hadrian. He had a relatively long and uneventful rule; the most exciting event during his twenty-three years was a big festival, in 148, celebrating Rome's 900th anniversary.**

Caracalla – **Pg. 756, ¶ 2, Pg. 760, ¶ 1 & 2 – Caracalla, son of Septimus Severus, was appointed as his father's heir in 198. Caracalla murdered his brother, co-emperor Geta, bought the loyalty of the Praetorian Guard, and in 212 AD announced that all free men in his empire were now Roman citizens.**

Commodus – **Pg. 754, ¶ 2 & 5, and Pg. 755, ¶ 3 – Commodus, the son of Marcus Aurelius, was made co-emperor by his father when he was fifteen years old. Commodus's bad behavior as emperor led to widespread agreement that he should be done away with; he was murdered in 192.**

Elagabalus – **Pg. 762, ¶ 5 to Pg. 763, ¶ 1 - Elagabalus, Caracalla's first cousin once removed, was proclaimed emperor in Macrinus's place after Macrinus paid off the Parthians. Elagabalus was a weak minded individual who likely went insane shortly after his accession; the Praetorian Guard had him killed in 222 AD.**

Geta – **Pg. 756, ¶ 3 and Pg. 759, ¶ 3 – Geta, the younger son of Septimus Severus, was appointed as heir with his brother Caracalla two years before Septimus Severus died. Once he was ruling as co-emperor, Geta was the victim of joint rule with his brother and was murdered by the command of Caracalla.**

Jian Shi – **Pg. 757, ¶ 2 & 3 – Jian Shi, a palace eunuch who had been given control of the armed forces by Lingdi, was given the task, along with the empress dowager, of naming Lingdi's heir. After Jian Shi appointed Shaodi, Lingdi's son, to the throne, he plotted to kill the Han chief general in order to increase his own power.**

Jiao (Jue), Bao and Liang – **Pg. 756, ¶ 6 – Jiao (Jue), Boa and Liang were three brothers of the Zhang family that led the revolt of the Yellow Turbans in 184. Their slogan was "The Han has perished, the rebellion will rise; let there be prosperity in the world!" and they hoped to take away the land of the wealthy and share it out evenly, among all the Chinese.**

Macrinus – **Pg. 762, ¶ 4 & 5 – Macrinus was declared emperor of Rome after Caracalla's murder. Instead of continuing the fight against Artabanus V, Macrinus chose to pay off the Parthians, an act which cost him his life.**

Marcus Aurelius – **Pg. 751, ¶ 3 to Pg. 752, ¶ 1 and Pg. 754, ¶ 2 – Marcus Aurelius, one of two heirs adopted by Antonius Pius, made his adopted brother Lucius Verus co-emperor when he was** appointed by the Senate to rule Rome. Marcus Aurelius spent the majority of his reign away from Rome, and before he died he appointed his son, Commodus, co-emperor.

Meditations of Marcus Aurelius – Pg. 754, ¶ 1 – The *Meditations of Marcus Aurelius* is the name of the philosophical writings of Marcus Aurelius. The book, one of the classics of Stoicism, contains the musings of a man trapped by his own duty, carrying the weight of an empire that he was happiest when farthest from.

Lucius Verus – Pg. 751, ¶ 3, Pg. 752, ¶ 1 and Pg. 753, ¶ 1 – Lucius Verus, one of two heirs adopted by Antonius Pius, was made co-emperor of Rome by his adopted brother Marcus Aurelius. Lucius Verus successfully beat the Parthians in Syria, and took back Armenia for Rome.

Septimus Severus – Pg. 755, ¶ 4 to Pg. 756, ¶ 1 – Septimus Severus, a man born in North Africa that served in the Senate during the rule of Marcus Aurelius, became emperor of Rome after the ousting of Commodus. Septimus Severus ensured loyalty from the Praetorian Guard by replacing anyone that didn't support him with men from his own army.

Shaodi – Pg. 757, ¶ 3 & 7 – Shaodi, Lingdi's fifteen-year-old son, was named heir to the throne after his father's death. Shaodi fled the royal palace during the slaughter of the eunuchs and was promised sanctuary after the chaos by Tung Cho; the general was lying and killed the young man when he returned to the palace.

Sima Guang – Pg. 756, ¶ 7 – Sima Guang, Chinese scholar and statesman, wrote a complete account of the Yellow Turban revolt and its aftermath in the history *Zizhi Tongjian*. Though he wrote the history in the middle of the eleventh century, Sima Guang made heavy use of the official records that stretched back for centuries.

Tung Cho – Pg. 757, ¶ 5 and Pg. 758, ¶ 1 – Tung Cho, a Han general, took control of the Han palace after the slaughter of the eunuchs. Tung Cho was forced to retreat from Loyang by Ts'ao Ts'ao, who cornered the general in Chang'an and killed him.

Ts'ao Ts'ao – Pg. 758, ¶ 1, 2 & 5 – Ts'ao Ts'ao, an able fighter, took the leadership of the Han army from Tung Cho, married Xiandi to his daughter, and recaptured the north of China for his new son-in-law. After much fighting, Ts'ao Ts'ao was unable to reunify China, and he retreated with only the north remaining to the Han king.

Vologases IV – Pg. 752, ¶ 2 to Pg. 753, ¶ 1 – Vologases IV, king of Parthia, seized Armenia and invaded Syria when Marcus Aurelius and Lucius Verus became co-emperors of Rome. Vologases IV was defeated in Syria by Lucius Verus, and his palace in Ctesiphon was destroyed by the Romans.

Xiandi – Pg. 757, ¶ 7 and Pg. 758, ¶ 2 – Xiandi, younger son of Lingdi and brother of Shaodi, was made emperor by the chief general of the Han army, Tung Cho. When Ts'ao Ts'ao ousted Tung Cho from the generalship, Xiandi was married to Ts'ao Ts'ao's daughter.

Section II: Comprehension

Write a two/three sentence answer to each of the following questions.

1. Why did Roman emperors adopt heirs instead of leaving the throne to their actual sons?
A1. – Pg. 751, ¶ 2 – Roman emperors adopted heirs because it was a useful way to combine the great advantage of father-to-son succession with the great republican notion that only the deserving should have power. Adoption created a "blood relationship" by law, and it allowed each emperor to pass his throne not to the son he had, but to the son he had hoped for.

2. Describe the plague that Roman troops brought back with them from Syria. Why did Marcus Aurelius outlaw the building of new tombs after the plague hit?
A2. – Pg. 753, ¶ 2 & 3 – The plague that hit Rome when troops returned from successfully beating the Parthians in Syria gave Romans a sore throat, fever and pustules. The epidemic was severe, and went on for three years. At the plague's height, two thousand people a day were dying, so Marcus Aurelius outlawed the building of new tombs in order to force Romans to haul their dead out of the city.

3. How did Marcus Aurelius stay popular with his people, even though he chose to spend most of his reign stationed along the Danube rather than in the capital city?
A3. – Pg. 753, ¶ 6 – Though Marcus Aurelius chose to stay stationed along the Danube for the better part of his reign, he nevertheless earned a reputation for keeping the empire safe and for dealing gently with his people. When the treasury was drained, instead of raising taxes, Marcus Aurelius sold off goods from the imperial palace to replenish Rome's funds; this made him even more beloved.

4. Why did the Roman system of adopted-heirs work so well? Why did Marcus Aurelius break the system?
A4. – Pg. 754, ¶ 3 & 4 – The system of Roman emperors adopting their heirs worked so well because it avoided the worst pitfalls of hereditary kingship; once a wise and efficient ruler had the throne, he tended to appoint an heir of the same quality. Marcus Aurelius did not want to be emperor, so he spent his time away from Rome and out of touch with its people. Since he did not develop any close friendships, Marcus Aurelius did not find any man to replace him, so he defaulted to his blood heir.

5. How did the Romans justify the murder of Commodus?
A5. – Pg. 755, ¶ 3 – Commodus was so decadent and badly behaved that all of Rome decided that he must have been the product of one of his mother's affairs with a gladiator, rather than the son of the great Marcus Aurelius. If Commodus was not Marcus Aurelius's son, then he had no right to the throne, and could be done away with without hesitation.

6. How did Septimus Severus ensure the Praetorian Guard's loyalty?
A6. – Pg. 755, ¶ 5 to Pg. 756, ¶ 1 – When Septimus Severus arrived in Rome, he summoned the Praetorian Guard to a ceremonial parade and then brought his own army out to surround them. Every guard suspected of preferring someone else for the position of emperor was warned to leave the city. After they fled, Septimus Severus at once appointed his loyal men to replace those that left.

7. What happened when the chief general of the Han army found out that Jian Shi was plotting to have him murdered?

A7. – Pg. 757, ¶ 4 – When the chief general of the Han army found out about Jian Shi's plans, he began to plot a wholesale extermination of the palace eunuchs. The eunuchs found out about the plot, seized the chief general and beheaded him. In response, one of the other commanders ordered the gates of the palace locked and all of the eunuchs slaughtered; altogether some two thousand people died, both eunuchs and "whole men."

8. Why, when Xiandi was finally returned to Loyang and placed on the throne by Ts'ao Ts'ao, was he considered powerless and unimportant?

A8. – Pg. 758, ¶ 3 – When Xiandi was finally returned to Loyang and placed on the throne, he was considered powerless and unimportant because the decades of mismanagement and misconduct prior to his rule had destroyed the country and effectively ended the Han dynasty. Wars between would-be kings broke out all around the imperial territory. Though Ts'ao Ts'ao had been successful in recapturing the north, he had no allies in his quest to reunify the Han lands and too many rival generals did not want to see Loyang become powerful again.

9. Who made up the Three Kingdoms that replaced the Han Dynasty, and where were these new kingdoms located?

A9. – Pg. 759, ¶ 2 – The Three Kingdoms that replaced the Han Dynasty were the Wu Dynasty, led by Sun Ch'uan; the Shu Han Dynasty, led by Liu Pei; and the former Han Dynasty, led by Ts'ao Ts'ao's son, Ts'ao Pei. Sun Ch'uan was in the Yangtze valley and had a royal capital at Chien-yeh; Liu Pei ruled over the south-west from his own capital on the Min River, Chengdu; and Ts'ao Pei controlled the old Han land in the north.

10. How did Caracalla manage to win back the loyalty Praetorian Guard after Geta's murder? What did he do to anyone whose loyalty he still questioned?

A10. – Pg. 760, ¶ 1 – Caracalla managed to win back the loyalty of the Praetorian Guard after Geta's murder by complaining to the soldiers that Geta was going to poison him, and that Geta had been disrespectful to their mother. Caracalla publically rendered thanks to those who killed Geta, and he bought back the loyalty of the Praetorian Guard who were still smarting over Geta's death. Caracalla then began a purge of anyone who might resent Geta's murder.

11. What was going on in Parthia in 212 that led Caracalla to believe he could reduce the Parthians to vassals? How did Caracalla's plan backfire?

A11. – Pg. 761, ¶ 4 to Pg. 762, ¶ 2 – In 212, Parthian vassal king Ardashir was waging small campaigns against the vassal kingdoms around him, and the Parthian king Artabanus V didn't notice because he was busy trying to regain control of the lower Mesopotamian valley, which had been taken from him by one of his own relatives. Caracalla, seeing a chance to reduce the Parthians to vassals, offered Artabanus V help in exchange for a marriage alliance with Artabanus's daughter. When Artabanus refused, Caracalla attacked Parthia but his plans backfired: Caracalla was assassinated during the spring campaign.

Section III: Critical Thinking

The student may not use her text to answer this question.

When Rome was a republic, citizenship was a privilege that gave a man the ability to vote. In 212 AD, Rome was no longer a republic. Since the vote no longer mattered, what advantages were there to being a Roman citizen? Write a paragraph explaining what a free man had to gain from Caracalla's declaration that all free men in his empire were now Roman citizens, and explain what the government had to gain by accepting all of these new citizens.

In 212 AD, a free man might not have a say in the running of Rome's government, but he did enjoy certain privileges by being called a citizen of Rome (the text addresses the explanation of Roman identity and the rights of citizens on page 761, ¶ 2 & 3). First, if he was sentenced to death for a crime, he could appeal to Rome; second, his marriage and other contracts could be upheld in Roman courts; third, his children were guaranteed to get their inheritance under his will. While there was some feeling of protection attached to being a citizen of Rome, it was really the government that benefited from Caracalla's declaration.

The text makes it very clear that as the Roman empire grew, the loyalty of its new provinces was an issue: "Hadrian's wall and the turning of client kingdoms (with a kind of independence and national pride of their own) into tightly controlled provinces both pointed to the same inevitable end, for those peoples enclosed within Rome's borders. They could not be allowed to remain a collection of countries 'under Roman rule,' like marbles in a jar; their first loyalty would always be to their first identity, and when crisis broke the jar, the marbles would escape. They had to be pulled away from the past, and pointed towards a new loyalty. They had to be made Roman."
As Rome claimed provinces full of people raised in different cultures, the declaration of citizenship forced these diverse peoples to be loyal to Rome first, and loyal to their home cultures second. More importantly, as a citizen it was your duty to be obedient to the emperor, and being obedient to the emperor meant paying your taxes. When Caracalla declared all free men in his empire to be citizens, he increased the number of people he could tax, and therefore increased Rome's purse.

EXAMPLE ANSWER: In 212 AD, a free man might not have a say in the running of Rome's government, but he did enjoy certain privileges by being called a citizen of Rome. First, if he was sentenced to death for a crime, he could appeal to Rome; second, his marriage and other contracts could be upheld in Roman courts; third, his children were guaranteed to get their inheritance under his will. While there was some feeling of protection attached to being a citizen of Rome, it was really the government that benefited from Caracalla's declaration. As Rome claimed provinces full of people raised in different cultures, the declaration of citizenship forced these diverse peoples to be loyal to Rome first, and loyal to their home cultures second. More importantly, as a citizen it was your duty to be obedient to the emperor, and being obedient to the emperor meant paying your taxes. When Caracalla declared all free men in his empire to be citizens, he increased the number of people he could tax, and therefore, he increased Rome's treasury.

CHAPTER EIGHTY-FIVE: THE SAVIOR OF THE EMPIRE

The student may use his text when answering the questions in sections I and II.

Section I: Who, What, Where

Write a one or two-sentence answer explaining the significance of each item listed below.

Ardashir I – **Pg. 764, ¶ 1-4** – Ardashir I, King of Kings, was the royal name of the Persian Ardashir, who defeated Artabanus V and ended the Parthian empire. Ardashir I created a new Persian empire that was divided up into provinces laid out across old kingdom borders.

Aurelian – **Pg. 769, ¶ 5** – Aurelian, Roman emperor at the time of the barbarian invasions in 271, had the reputation of being able in war, but also inclined to cruelty. Aurelian directed Roman troops into a series of well-planned campaigns that almost restored Rome's old borders, and this temporary reversal of Rome's disintegration made Aurelian respected, if not popular.

Constantine – **Pg. 773, ¶ 2 & 5, Pg. 775, ¶ 1 & 3** – Constantine, Constantius's son, was elected by Constantius's army to rival Severus for Roman rule. After Constantine had a vision of God, and inscribed the chi and rho onto his helmet, he defeated his current rival, Maxentius, and became master of the Roman empire.

Constantius – **Pg. 771, ¶ 5 and Pg. 773, ¶ 2** – Constantius, Diocletian's Caesar, became emperor of Gaul, Italy and Africa after Diocletian abdicated his throne. Constantius died only a year after his accession.

Daevas – **Pg. 765, ¶ 2** – Daevas were demonic spirits that represented the forces of wickedness in Zoroastrianism.

Decius – **Pg. 767, ¶ 4** – Decius was made Roman emperor after Philip failed to protect Rome from the invading Visigoths. Just two years after his appointment, Decius was killed in battle, the first Roman emperor to fall while fighting an outside threat.

Galerius – **Pg. 771, ¶ 5 and Pg. 773, ¶ 2** – Galerius, Maximian's Caesar, became emperor of the eastern Roman empire when Maximian abdicated his throne. In the debacle following Constantius's death, Galerius supported Severus's taking of the western throne.

Gallienus – **Pg. 767, ¶ 6 and Pg. 769, ¶ 3** – Gallienus, son of Valerian, commanded legions in the west against the Goths, while his father attacked the approaching Persians. Gallienus, who acted as emperor while his father was in captivity, was murdered by one of the men in the small circle of soldiers he trusted.

Goths – **Pg. 766, ¶ 3 to Pg. 767, ¶ 2** – Goths were a large group of barbarians from north of Rome, made up of a wide array of tribes: Screrefennae, Finnaithae, Finns, Dani, Grannii and more. These tough and resilient people fought their way through the Germanic tribes down to the Danube, with some making their way east, towards the old territory of the Scythians.

Maxentius – **Pg. 773, ¶ 4 & 5 and Pg. 775, ¶ 3** – Maxentius, son of Maximian, took control of Rome after the mayhem that followed the death of Constantius. Maxentius lost his battle for the throne when he drowned in the Tiber while retreating from Constantine's troops.

Maximian – **Pg. 771, ¶ 3 and Pg. 773, ¶ 3-5** – Maximian, an army officer Diocletian knew well, was named Augustus and made Diocletian's co-emperor. When his junior died, Maximian tried to reclaim his role as emperor of the west; when he failed, he committed suicide.

Ostrogoths – **Pg. 767, ¶ 2** – Ostrogoths were a faction of the invading northern Goths that were overflowing into the old eastern lands of Thrace and Macedonia.

Philip – **Pg. 767, ¶ 3** – Philip, the Roman emperor during the Visigoth invasion, tried to buy the Goths off with tribute payments; when he fell behind on his installments the Visigoths crossed the Danube and ravaged the countryside. Philip's poor leadership lost him the title of emperor.

Sassanian – **Pg. 764, ¶ 3 & 4** – Sassanian was the name of the new dynasty started by Ardashir I in the resurrected Persian empire. The name Sassanian came from Ardashir I's native Persian clan; the shahs of Persia's provinces were members of Ardashir I's own royal Sassanian clan.

Severus – **Pg. 773, ¶ 3 & 4** – Severus, Constantius's junior, was challenged by Constantine (via the wishes of Constantius's army) and Maximian when he was up to take the role of emperor of the west. With the support of Constantine, Maximian marched on Severus and killed him.

Shah – **Pg. 764, ¶ 4** – Shah was the honorary Persian title given to the military governors of the new provinces, or satrapies, laid out by Ardashir I.

Shapur – **Pg. 764, ¶ 5, Pg. 765, ¶ 4 to Pg. 766, ¶ 1, Pg. 767, ¶ 5 and Pg. 769, ¶ 1** – Shapur, son of Ardashir I, continued to strengthen the new Persian empire by capturing the Roman garrisons in Mesopotamia, marching into Syria and, on his second attempt, taking Syria for Persia and sacking Antioch. Shapur captured the Roman emperor Valerian and kept him captive, further reinforcing Persia's strength.

Valerian – **Pg. 767, ¶ 6 to Pg. 769, ¶ 1** – Valerian, a former consul and general, made emperor of Rome at nearly sixty years old, was called "Restorer of the World" on a coin from 257. Despite his successes, Valerian was captured by Shapur I of Persia and humiliated, depicted as a footstool for the Persian king.

Visigoths – **Pg. 767, ¶ 2** – Visigoths, or "Goths of the Western Country," were a faction of the invading northern Goths that threatened the Danube, and the Roman territory near it.

Zoroastrianism – **Pg. 765, ¶ 2** – Zoroastrianism was a mystical religion first preached by the prophet Zoroaster (or Zarathustra) that taught that the universe was divided into two equally powerful opposing forces of good and evil. Good emanated from the being of the great god Ahuramazda, and evil resided in the opposing deity Ahriman.

Section II: Comprehension

Write a two/three sentence answer to each of the following questions.

1. What happened when Ardashir met Artabanus V at the plain of Hormizdagan?

A1. – Pg. 764, ¶ 1 & 2 – When Ardashir and his Median/Persian troops met Artabanus V at the plain of Hormizdagan, Artabanus V met his end. After the death of Artabanus V, Ardashir moved into the palace at Ctesiphon and declared himself to be Ardashir I, King of Kings.

2. How do we know Ardashir I made Shapur co-ruler before his own death? Why would Ardashir crown his son before he died?

A2. – Pg. 765, ¶ 1 – We know Ardashir I made Shapur co-ruler before his own death from two different sources: first, coins from the end of Ardashir I's reign show the king facing a younger prince. Second, Arab historian Abu al-Mas'udi says that Ardashir I put his crown upon Shapur's head with his own hands, and then withdrew so that Shapur could rule alone. Ardashir I most likely crowned his son while he was alive because he had the future on his mind – he wanted to make sure his new kingdom was being passed into able hands.

3. In what way did Zoroastrianism bring the new Persian empire together?

A3. – Pg. 765, ¶ 2 & 3 – When Ardashir made Zoroastrianism the state religion of his new empire, he essentially drew every one of his subjects together into a holy community with a single purpose: to fight evil. When Shapur I began his career as king by calling on the great god Ahuramazda to support his claim to the throne, he reinforced the importance of Zoroastrianism in Persia. Every subject of Shapur I was a soldier against the daevas; the loyalty of every man and woman to Persia was also a commitment to the constant fight against evil.

4. How did church historians from after Valerian's time characterize Valerian's capture by the Persians?

A4. – Pg. 768, ¶ 3 – Church historians from a time after Valerian's loathed the Roman emperor because he hated Christians, so they depicted his capture by the Persians as God's judgment. They said that God punished Valerian in a new and extraordinary manner, and that Valerian was made to be a footstool for the Persian king.

5. What happened to the Roman empire while Valerian was in Shapur I's captivity?

A5. – Pg. 769, ¶ 2 – While Valerian was in captivity, the Roman empire began to fall apart. The Roman army was scraped thin dealing with rebellion and with more invasions from the north: the Germanic Alemanni tribe was making intrusions into Italy, the Germanic Franks were ravaging the Roman provinces on the Iberian peninsula, and the Gauls had broken away and announced themselves a kingdom in their own right.

6. Why did Aurelian have a wall built around the city of Rome? What did the construction of the wall say about the nature of Rome's army?

A6. – Pg. 770, ¶ 1 & 2 – Aurelian had a wall built around Rome in order to protect the city. Previously, Romans boasted that they didn't need a wall because they were protected by the power of Rome's army, but now the army's loyalties were too changeable and could not be relied upon. Rome had too many armies on too many frontiers for there to be any stability.

7. Though Carus seems to have escaped the fate of the five other emperors who were murdered in the nine years following Aurelian's death, why might we believe his bodyguard Diocletian was involved in Carus's death? In what way does the death of Numerian, and Carus's other son, suggest that Diocletian was behind all three deaths?

A7. – Pg. 770, ¶ 2-5 – Carus's men, including his bodyguard Diocletian, claimed he was struck dead by lightning. Carus's son Numerian, the next king, then died mysteriously while travelling with the army. Diocletian claimed to know who killed Numerian, and stabbed the man in the sight of the army in order to do away with the necessity of investigation. When Carus's other son was acclaimed emperor, Diocletian killed him, too, and took charge of the Roman empire. It seems that Diocletian had his eyes on the Roman throne the whole time, and was responsible for all three deaths.

8. What happened to Diocletian's system of managing the Roman empire's succession when Constantius died?

A8. – Pg. 773, ¶ 2 & 3 – When Constantius died, his army demanded that his young son Constantine take his place, rather than his junior, Severus. The eastern emperor, Galerius, insisted that Severus take his rightful place as emperor of the west. At the same time, Maximian threw his hat back into the ring because he never wanted to abdicate in the first place. Diocletian's system had fallen apart.

9. Why did Constantine engrave the first two Greek letters in the name of Christ, the chi and rho, onto his helmet and standard?

A9. – Pg. 774, ¶ 3 to Pg. 775, ¶ 1 – Constantine engraved the chi and rho onto his helmet and standard because God told him to do so. Constantine claimed that one afternoon he saw a cross of light in the heavens, above the sun, bearing the inscription, *Conquer by this.* Then God appeared to him in his sleep bearing the same sign and commanded Constantine to make a likeness of the sign and to use it as a safeguard in all engagements with his enemies.

10. Why did Constantine believe Christianity would help to reunite the Roman empire?

A10. – Pg. 776, ¶ 1 to Pg. 777, ¶ 2 – Constantine saw in Christianity hope for Rome because, over the past three centuries, the Christian identity – an identity that became absolutely central to those who held onto it, yet did not wipe out the other identities that came before it – proved itself stronger than any other identity. Christians survived bloody wars and spread across a good part of the known world. Christianity did what Rome never managed: it spread out from its land of origin and became an identity which drew many different cultures into a single fold. Constantine believed that Christianity would be the key to holding Rome together.

Section III: Critical Thinking

Histories of Rome written by church fathers depict Diocletian in a negative light because he persecuted Christians. They accuse him of almost ruining Rome because of his idea to divide up the rule of the empire. However, Diocletian's idea of breaking up Roman rule actually saved the empire. Explain how, under Diocletian, Rome went from recognizing one emperor to recognizing four men in power. Why did Diocletian think this division would save Rome? In your answer, explain what Diocletian hoped to achieve by abdicating his throne to his junior.

Diocletian was an ambitious man, but unlike many emperors before him, his ambitions were actually good for Rome. Diocletian wanted Rome to succeed, and he realized that it could not survive in its current unwieldy state. The student should first identify why Diocletian decided to break up the empire. On page 771, ¶ 4, the text reads, "He had come to the conclusion that the biggest problem of the empire was one of size. It was impossible for any one man to keep a hand on all the regions without autocratic tyranny, and autocratic tyranny led to death. Anyway, even the most autocratic emperor could not remain the favorite of the troops spread from Gaul all the way over to the Euphrates. The legions were bound to favor the man who was closest to them; Diocletian gave both halves of the empire an emperor who could remain near." Realizing that men would be loyal to an accessible leader, Diocletian saw the salvation of Rome in its division: two rulers would serve the Romans better than one.

Diocletian recognized that Rome's problems were not just based on its size, but also on its unstable armies. Army loyalties were constantly changing, and the best interests of the people were no longer the army's priority. By making the co-emperors name their successors, or Caesars, Diocletian took the power of choosing the emperor away from the army. This is how Rome went from having one emperor to four men in power.

It was important for Diocletian that the Roman people realize that the emperor was only a figurehead – it didn't matter who the emperor was, as long as he was a faithful and conscientious representative of Rome. Ask the student to recall Diocletian's attempt to get Romans to understand the idea of imperial authority. On page 773, ¶ 1, the text reads, "Diocletian was attempting to demonstrate that the emperor represented Rome, for a time, but that the task of representative was greater than the personality who undertook it." By making a show of abdication, taking off imperial robes and changing into civilian clothes at the end of a victory parade to celebrate the emperors' reigns, Diocletian asked Romans to accept the next kings not for who they were, but what they stood for – Rome. Diocletian thought if he could get his people to believe in the power of the emperors, and not the people who were the emperors, then Rome would remain stable no matter who was sitting in its thrones.

EXAMPLE ANSWER: Diocletian saw Rome's massive size as its downfall. He knew that men would remain loyal to a leader close to them, so he decided, for the good of Rome, to name a co-emperor. In order to solve the problems of succession that had plagued Rome in the past, Diocletian decided that each co-emperor would appoint a Caesar, or a man to take the co-emperor's place once his reign was through. By naming the juniors, Diocletian limited the fickle army's involvement in the change of power. With two men on the throne, and two successors on deck, Rome now had four men in power.

Diocletian decided to abdicate his throne to his junior before he died, and insisted that his co-emperor do the same. Diocletian wanted Romans to realize that the emperors were just figureheads, or representatives, of Rome. By making a show of abdication, taking off imperial robes and changing into civilian clothes at the end of a victory parade to celebrate the emperors' reigns, Diocletian asked Romans to accept the next kings not for who they were, but what they stood for – Rome. Diocletian thought if he could get his people to believe in the power of the emperors, and not the people who were the emperors, then Rome would remain stable no matter who was sitting in its thrones.

STUDENT STUDY GUIDE

for

The History of the Ancient World

STUDY GUIDE for The History of the Ancient World

HOW TO USE THIS STUDY GUIDE

For each chapter of *The History of the Ancient World,* you will see three or four sections of exercises.

I. Who, What, Where

This section is designed to check your grasp of basic information presented in the chapter: prominent characters, important places, and foundational ideas. You should explain the significance of each person, place or idea in **one or two complete sentences**.

II. Comprehension

This section requires you to express, in your own words, the central concepts in each chapter. You may use two to three complete sentences to answer each question.

III. Critical Thinking

This section requires you to produce a brief written reflection on the ideas presented in the chapter. Some preliminary exercises are also provided.

IV. Map Work

This section uses a traditional method to improve your geography. In his *Complete Course in Geography* (1875), the geographer William Swinton observed:

> That form is easiest remembered which the hand is taught to trace. The exercise of the mind, needed to teach the hand to trace a form, impresses that form upon the mind. As the study of maps is a study of form, the manner of studying them should be by map-drawing.

Section IV asks you to go through a carefully structured set of steps: tracing repeatedly, then copying while looking at the original, and finally, where appropriate, reproducing from memory. You will be asked to use a black pencil (one that does not erase easily) as well as a regular pencil with an eraser, as well as colored pencils of various kinds. Large amounts of tracing paper are needed!

CHAPTER ONE: THE ORIGIN OF KINGSHIP

You MAY USE your text when answering the questions in sections I and II.

Section I: Who, What, Where

Write a one or two-sentence answer explaining the significance of the items listed below.

11,000 BC
Alulim
Dumuzi
Eridu
Fertile Crescent
Sumerian king list

Section II: Comprehension

Write a two or three-sentence answer to each of the following questions.

1. How did the Mesopotamian climate change as the earth warmed and the ice caps melted? What happened in the winter and the summer? What happened to the streams and fields?

2. What types of materials did the Sumerians use to build their homes, and where did the materials come from? What else did they make with the materials? Why were the Sumerians "people of the earth?"

3. Define the term "Semite-influenced Sumerians."

4. Explain how Sumerian hunters turned into farmers. In your answer, make sure to include how the changing climate influenced this transition.

5. Why did civilization begin in the Fertile Crescent? Explain what had to be done in order for the farmers and the non-farmers to survive, and how this led to the need for a king.

6. Why did the goddess Inanna reject King Dumuzi's approaches? Use part of "The Wooing of Inanna" in your answer. How were shepherds perceived by Sumerian city dwellers?

Section III: Critical Thinking

You may NOT use your text to answer this question.

In this chapter we learned that Sumerians developed the first civilization. We also learned that even though all Sumerians needed to work together to survive, "mutual need didn't produce mutual respect." As the Sumerian civilization developed, so did inequality among men.

***

Farmer / Shepherd / King / Basketmaker

A. Order the occupations above from most civilized to least civilized:

B. Order the occupations above from most important to least important:

C. Write a paragraph explaining how you ordered the occupations in part A. Then, write a paragraph explaining how you ordered the occupations in part B.

Section IV: Map Exercise: The Persian Gulf

1. Using a black pencil, trace the rectangular outline of the frame for Map 1.1: Very Ancient Mesopotamia.

2. Using a blue pencil, trace the Persian Gulf. Repeat until the contours are familiar.

3. Trace the rectangular outline of the frame in black. Remove your tracing paper from the original. Using a regular pencil with an eraser, draw the Persian Gulf within the map frame while looking at Map 1.1. Be sure to look at the distance between the lines on the map and the lines of the framework as a guide. Erase and redraw as necessary.

4. When you are pleased with your Persian Gulf, lay your map over the original. Erase and redraw any lines which are more than 1/4 inch off the original.

5. Trace the modern course of the Tigris and Euphrates rivers in blue.

6. With a contrasting color, lightly trace the 6000 B.C. coastline of the Persian Gulf and the possible waterways at the time of Alulim.

CHAPTER TWO: THE EARLIEST STORY

You MAY USE your text when answering the questions in sections I and II.

Section I: Who, What, Where

Write a one or two-sentence answer explaining the significance of the items listed below.

Akkadian
"Poem of Atrahasis"
Enlil
Ea

Section II: Comprehension

Write a two or three-sentence answer to each of the following questions.

1. Why is the story of the Great Flood important to historians?

2. Briefly list all the Great Flood stories mentioned in the chapter. List where the story came from, the title (if listed in the text) and write a short summary of each story, making sure to name its key figures. Follow the format of the example provided.

Example:
Sumeria, no title. Enlil, the king of the gods, attempts to wipe out mankind, but the god Ea warns the wise man Utnapishtim of Enlil's plan. Utnapishtim escapes the flood in a boat with his family, a few animals and as many others as he can save.

3. In the Akkadian creation story, why is half of the sea-being Tiamat's body tossed into the heavens?

4. The Akkadian creation story, the Mixtec creation legend, the Indian Satapatha-Brahamana, the Bantu myth, and the beginning of Genesis are all related. What are these stories, and what narrative detail do they have in common?

5. Describe the lost paradise that is the subject of the very ancient Sumerian poem "Enki and Ninhusag." Use at least two examples from the poem in your answer.

Section III: Critical Thinking

You may NOT use your text to answer this question.

Early in Chapter 2, the author writes, "The historian cannot ignore the Great Flood; it is the closest thing to a universal story that the human race possesses" (11). Write a paragraph in response to each of the following questions concerning the flood and its existence.

A. What can a historian learn from ancient stories about the flood? In your answer, explain this passage from the text, "Three cultures, three stories: too much coincidence of detail to be dismissed" (12).

B. What can a historian learn from physical evidence related to the flood? In your answer, explain this passage from the text, "If these American flood stories are related to the Mesopotamian tales, the flood could not have happened in 7000 BC; as the historian John Bright suggests, the shared disaster must have taken place before 10,000 BC, when hunters migrated across the Bering Strait" (14).

C. What conclusion can we come to about the Great Flood?

Chapter Three: The Rise of Aristocracy

You MAY USE your text when answering the questions in sections I and II.

Section I: Who, What, Where

Write a one or two-sentence answer explaining the significance of each item listed below. For questions marked with *, use the map on page 19 to supplement your answer.

2700 BC
Aristocracy
Etana
Kish
*Euphrates (Uruttu)
*Tigris (Idiglat)
"The First Dynasty of Kish"

Section II: Comprehension

Write a two or three-sentence answer to each of the following questions.

1. Describe the ways that all of these cities were alike: Eridu, Ur, Uruk, Nippur, Adab, Lagash, and Kish.

2. Define "streaming-in" (make sure to include a date in your answer).

3. How is Etana's entry on the king list different from those of his predecessors? What do we learn about Etana's reign and legacy from the entry?

4. What is the significance of Atab's succession by his son and grandson? How does this fundamentally change the way kings come to rule?

5. A later poem helps us understand the terms of Etana's rule. Summarize the later poem, and explain how it helps us understand the passage related to Etana on the king list.

6. Explain how Mesopotamia shifted from an egalitarian society (a society that believes in the equality of all people) to an aristocracy. Make sure to incorporate what you learned from Chapter 1 into your answer.

7. Explain the organization of a typical Mesopotamian walled city, and what pilgrims, shepherds and herdsmen did in the city.

8. Why was the city of Kish so powerful around 2500 BC?

Section III: Critical Thinking

You may NOT use your text to answer this question.

"The Rise of Aristocracy" ends with this thought, "The difficulty of moving armies up and down the length of the plain may have dissuaded the kings of Kish from actually conquering other cities; or perhaps they simply had, as yet, no thought of imperial leadership to complement the ideas of kingship and aristocracy" (21).

First, look up "empire" and write down its definition. Second, using what you know about "streaming-in," the beginning of aristocracy, and the power struggle between rising cities in Mesopotamia, write a paragraph explaining how creating empires is the next logical step in our history of the ancient world.

Section IV: Map Exercise: The Tigris and Euphrates

1. Using a black pencil, trace the rectangular outline of the frame for Map 3.1: Early Cities of Sumer.

2. Using a blue pencil, trace the Persian Gulf and the courses of the Tigris and Euphrates Rivers, including all tributaries. Repeat until the contours are familiar.

3. Trace the rectangular outline of the frame in black. Remove your tracing paper from the original. Using a regular pencil with an eraser, draw the Persian Gulf, the Tigris, and the Euphrates within the map frame while looking at Map 3.1. Be sure to look at the distance between the lines on the map and the lines of the framework as a guide. Erase and redraw as necessary.

4. When you are pleased with your map, lay it over the original. Erase and redraw any lines which are more than 1/4 inch off the original. Trace over your pencil lines in blue.

5. Remove your map. Without looking at the book, label the Tigris, the Euphrates, and the Persian Gulf.

6. Look back at Map 3.1 and study carefully the location of the cities of Kish and Ur. When you are familiar with them, close the book. Using your regular pencil, mark and label Kish and Ur on your own map. Check your map against the original. If you are more than 1/8 inch off, erase and re-mark the cities while looking at the original.

Chapter Four: The Creation of Empire

You MAY USE your text when answering the questions in sections I and II.

Section I: Who, What, Where

Write a one or two-sentence answer explaining the significance of each item listed below.

3200 BC
Dynasteia
Herodotus
Menes (Narmer)
Palette
Turin Canon

Section II: Comprehension

Write a two or three-sentence answer to each of the following questions.

1. What have archaeologists discovered beneath the sands of the Sahara? What do these findings suggest about the climate of the Sahara?

2. Which way did the Nile River flow? How did this affect the Egyptians' view of all other rivers?

3. How did the first Egyptians manage the overflow of water from the Nile?

4. Why did the Egyptians give their country two different names? In your answer make sure to identify the names of each land, the color associated with each land, and the significance of each color.

5. What kingdom were the cities of Nubt and Hierakonpolis a part of? How is the ruler of this kingdom identified?

6. How does the construction of the oldest Egyptian king lists vary from the construction of the Sumerian king list?

7. How do we know that the White King and the Scorpion King are the same person? In your answer, name and describe the object that links the two kings. Make sure to include where the object was found, and what markings on the object tell us that the two kings were the same person.

8. When did the first Egyptian dynasty begin according to Manetho's revised king list?

9. What did Narmer build to celebrate his victory over Lower Egypt? Why did he choose Memphis? What does "Memphis" mean?

Section III: Critical Thinking

You MUST USE your text to answer this question.

Doubleness has deeply influenced the development of Egyptian culture. Find two passages in the text where doubleness appears and write them down, noting where a reader can find the passage by putting the page number after the quote. Then, write a few sentences for each example, explaining what each section means in the context of early Egyptian culture.

Section IV: Map Exercise: The Nile River

1. Using a black pencil, trace the rectangular outline of the frame for Map 4.1: Upper and Lower Egypt.

2. Using a blue pencil, trace the Red Sea, the Nile River, and the Mediterranean Sea. Keep the orientation of the original map (with the south at the top). Repeat until the contours are familiar.

3. Trace the rectangular outline of the frame in black. Remove your tracing paper from the original. Using a regular pencil with an eraser, draw the Red Sea, the Nile River, and the Mediterranean Sea within the map frame while looking at Map 4.1. Be sure to look at the distance between the lines on the map and the lines of the framework as a guide. Erase and redraw as necessary.

4. When you are pleased with your map, lay it over the original. Erase and redraw any lines which are more than 1/4 inch off the original. Trace over your pencil lines in blue.

5. Remove your map. Without looking at the book, label the Nile, the Mediterranean Sea, and the Red Sea.

6. Look back at Map 4.1 and study carefully the location of the city of Memphis and the kingdoms of Upper Egypt and Lower Egypt. When you are familiar with them, close the book. Using your regular pencil, mark and label Memphis, Upper Egypt, and Lower Egypt on your own map. Check your map against the original. If the city or the labels are more than 1/8 inch off, erase and re-mark while looking at the original.

CHAPTER FIVE: THE AGE OF IRON

You MAY USE your text when answering the questions in sections I and II.

Section I: Who, What, Where

Write a one or two-sentence answer explaining the significance of each item listed below.

3102 BC
Baluchistan
Kali Yuga
Khyber Pass
Manu
Manu Vaivaswata
Vindhya and Satpura

Section II: Comprehension

Write a two or three-sentence answer to each of the following questions.

1. Why do we know so little about the first centuries of India? Why do we look at Indian epics written thousands of years after the first settlements for clues about ancient Indian civilizations?

2. Why is the upper end of the Indus River called the Punjab?

3. Why did the people of south India, east India and northwest India live independent of each other?

4. Why did the settlers of the Indus valley bake their clay in kilns?

5. How do we know the people of the Indus valley participated in trade outside of the valley?

Section III: Critical Thinking

You may NOT use your text to answer this question.

The people of ancient India have much in common with the early civilizations of Mesopotamia and Egypt. The following passages from the chapter connect in some way to your previous reading. Describe what each passage is about, and then explain how each passage about ancient Indian history relates to either Mesopotamia or Egypt.

"In the Iron Age, the sacred writings warned, leaders would commandeer the goods that belonged to their people, pleading financial need. The strong would take property from the vulnerable, and seize hard-won wealth for themselves. Rich men would abandon their fields and herds and spend their days protecting their money, becoming slaves of their earthly possessions rather than free men who knew how to use the earth" (34).

"[Manu] was washing his hands one morning when a tiny fish came wriggling up to him, begging for protection from the stronger and larger fish who preyed on the weak, as was 'the custom of the river.' Manu had pity and saved the fish. Past danger of being eaten, the fish repaid his kindness by warning him of a coming flood that would sweep away the heavens and the earth. So Manu built a wooden ark and went on board with seven wise sages, known as the Rishis. When the flood subsided, Manu anchored his ship to a far northern mountain, disembarked, and became the first king of historical India" (33).

"The earliest houses in the Indus River valley were built on the river plain, perhaps a mile away from the river, well above the line of the flood. Mud bricks would dissolve in river water, and crops would wash away" (32).

Section IV: Map Exercise: India

1. Using a black pencil, trace the rectangular outline of the frame for Map 5.1: India.

2. Using a black pencil, trace the coastline of India, the island to the south (Sri Lanka), and the northern mountain ranges (you do not need to trace the Vindhya and Satpura ranges). Repeat until the contours are familiar. (You may draw simple peaks to represent the mountains; you do not need to shade them as the mapmaker does.)

3. Trace the rectangular outline of the frame in black. Remove your tracing paper from the original. Using a regular pencil with an eraser, draw the coastline of India, the southern island, and the northern mountain ranges while looking at Map 5.1. Erase and redraw as necessary.

4. When you are pleased with your map, lay it over the original. Erase and redraw any lines which are more than 1/4 inch off the original

5. Trace the courses of the Indus and Ganga rivers in blue. Remove your map from the original.

6. Look back at Map 5.1 and study carefully the location of the Ganga and Indus River, the Himalaya mountain range, and the Khyber Pass. When you are familiar with them, close the book. Using your regular pencil, label the Ganga, the Indus, the Himalaya, and the Khyber Pass. Check your map against the original. If your labels are misplaced, erase and re-mark while looking at the original.

Chapter Six: The Philosopher King

You MAY USE your text when answering the questions in sections I and II.

Section I: Who, What, Where

Write a one or two-sentence answer explaining the significance of each item listed below.

2850 BC
Eight Trigrams
Fu Xi
Huangdi (The Yellow Emperor)
Shennong (The Farmer King)
Sima Qian (The Grand Historian)
Yangtze River
Yellow River

Section II: Comprehension

Write a two/three sentence answer to each of the following questions.

1. List the four early Chinese settlements, and where these settlements were located.

2. How can we differentiate between the various early Chinese settlements?

3. What is culture?

4. The following passage is given to us on page 38 in Chapter Six. Explain what happens in the passage, and why it is significant to Fu Xi's historical legacy.

5. What did Shennong do to earn the label "The Farmer King"?

6. What two things did Huangdi do to secure his title as one of the great kings of China?

7. Explain what qualified one to rule in China. What did not guarantee kingly power in ancient China?

Section III: Critical Thinking

You MAY USE your text to answer this question.

We learn in this chapter that "excavations show Longshan ruins overtop Yang-shao remains, suggesting that the Longshan may have peacefully overwhelmed at least part of the Yellow River culture" (38). This is not our first encounter with the Longshan and Yang-shao cultures, however. Look back over your notes and lessons and explain where you first heard about the Longshan and Yang-shao. Then write a few sentences explaining how this information supports the idea that the Longshan mingled with the Yang-shao culture.

Section IV: Map Exercise: China

1. Using a black pencil, trace the rectangular outline of the frame for Map 6.1: China's Early Settlements

2. Using a black pencil, trace the southern and eastern coastlines of China and the three large islands, and then trace the courses of the Yangtze and Yellow rivers. Repeat until the contours are familiar.

3. Trace the rectangular outline of the frame in black. Remove your tracing paper from the original. Using a regular pencil with an eraser, draw the coastlines of China, the three islands, and the two rivers while looking at Map 6.1. Be sure to look at the distance between the lines on the map and the lines of the framework as a guide. Erase and redraw as necessary.

4. When you are pleased with your map, lay it over the original. Erase and redraw any lines which are more than 1/4 inch off the original.

5. Remove your map from the original. Looking at Map 6.1, study carefully the locations of the Plateau of Tibet, the Yangtze, the Yellow, the East China Sea, and the Yellow Sea. When you are familiar with them, close the book. Using your regular pencil, label all five. Check your map against the original. If your labels are misplaced, erase and re-mark while looking at the original.

CHAPTER SEVEN: THE FIRST WRITTEN RECORDS

You MAY USE your text when answering the questions in sections I and II.

Section I: Who, What, Where

Write a one or two-sentence answer explaining the significance of each item listed below.

3000 BC
Cuneiform
Determinant
Hieroglyph
Hieratic script
Pictogram
Protosinaitic script
Rosetta Stone
Thoth

Section II: Comprehension

Write a two or three sentence answer to each of the following questions.

1. Why did people start writing?

2. How did pictograms develop?

3. What is the difference between a mark and a seal? In ancient Sumer, how did a seal protect one's property?

4. Describe the transition from pictograms to a phonetic system.

5. What happened to Sumerian cuneiform?

6. What power did the Egyptians believe writing had? How did this help to preserve the pictorial form of hieroglyphs?

7. How did the defacement of the carved name of an Egyptian king kill the king eternally?

8. What were the benefits of using papyrus as a writing material?

9. Why do we know so little about the daily life of pharaohs and their officials after the invention of papyrus?

Section III: Critical Thinking

You may NOT use your text to answer this question.

Explain how writing developed in Ancient Sumeria. In your answer, incorporate and explain the following four statements:

* "From its earliest days, literature was tied to commerce."

* "A step had been made towards triumphing over space."

* "The relationship between *thing* and *mark* had begun to grow more abstract."

* *"Ilshu, who was here, watched this transaction and can explain it, if you have any questions."*

CHAPTER EIGHT: THE FIRST WAR CHRONICLES

You MAY USE your text when answering the questions in sections I and II.

Section I: Who, What, Where

Write a one or two-sentence answer explaining the significance of each item listed below.

2800 BC
Elamites
Enmebaraggesi
Enmerkar
Gilgamesh
Mesannepadda
Meskiaggasher
Nippur

Section II: Comprehension

Write a two/three sentence answer to each of the following questions.

1. What is bronze?

2. Why is the period of Sumerian history between 4000 and 3200 BC called the Uruk period? (See footnote on page 51.)

3. What piece of information is strong evidence that Meskiaggasher seized the throne of Uruk?

4. Explain why it was necessary for Uruk to find a southern trade route in order to declare war on Kish.

5. Describe a Sumerian reed boat and its purpose.

6. What made Aratta special, and why did Enmerkar want to conquer this city?

7. How do we know that Enmerkar was unsuccessful in his attempt to conquer Aratta?

8. What was Gilgamesh's first step in preparing for war against his neighbors?

9. Describe the double parliamentary assembly of Sumerian city governments.

10. How did Gilgamesh finally conquer Kish?

11. What four cities were in the four-cornered kingdom of Sumer?

Section III: Critical Thinking

You may NOT use your text to answer this question.

We can see ancient roots in the familiar saying "the pen is mightier than the sword." In this chapter, we find that epic tales "were written by scribes who were paid by the kings whose achievements they recorded, which naturally tends to tilt them in the king's favor." However, we can compare these fantastic stories to "accounts of battles won, trades negotiated, and temples built" to piece together what events actually occurred in the ancient world.

Explain how each passage below is related to the function of the written history of Ancient Sumer.

1. "At the tale's end ['Enmerkar and the Lord of Aratta'], the Elamites of Aratta are still free from Enmerkar's rule. Given that the story has come down to us from the Sumerians, not the Elamites, the ambiguous ending probably represents a shattering Sumerian defeat" (55).

2. "In an epic tale told not long after his reign, we find Gilgamesh claiming Lugulbanda, the warrior-companion of Enmerkar, as his father. On the face of it, this is silly; Lugulbanda had occupied the throne decades (at least) before Gilgamesh's birth. But from the view point of a man rewriting his personal history, Lugulbanda was a fine choice....By Gilgamesh's day, Lugulbanda – perhaps thirty years dead, or even more – was well on his way to achieving the status of a Sumerian hero. A hundred years later, he would be considered a god. He lent Gilgamesh a sheen of secular power" (55-56).

3. Gilgamesh's first attack on Kish was a failure. "We know this because the king lists record Enmebaraggesi's death from old age, and the peaceful succession of his son Agga to the throne of Kish" (57).

4. "Why did Gilgamesh retreat? In all the legends that accrue around Gilgamesh, the central figure remains vividly the same: a young, aggressive, impetuous man of almost superhuman vitality... In the story of Gilgamesh's expedition to the north, he has to seek the approval of a council of elders before he sets off.... They were not likely to suffer a king's encroachments for long without objecting, and in this case, they declined to go to war anymore" (57).

Section IV: Map Exercise: The Ancient Near East Trade World

1. Using a black pencil, trace the rectangular outline of the frame for Map 8.1: Meskiaggasher's Trade.

2. Using a black pencil, trace the borders of the Persian Gulf, the Gulf of Oman, the southern and western coastlines of the Arabian peninsula, and the Caspian Sea. At this time, you do not need to trace the edges of the Black Sea (in the upper left-hand corner of the map) or coastline of Africa (in the lower left-hand corner). Repeat until the contours are familiar.

3. Trace the rectangular outline of the frame in black. Remove your tracing paper from the original. Using a regular pencil with an eraser, draw the Persian Gulf, the Gulf of Oman, the Caspian Sea, and the southern and western coastlines of the Arabian peninsula while looking at Map 8.1. Erase and redraw as necessary.

4. When you are pleased with your map, lay it over the original. Erase and redraw any lines which are more than 1/4 inch off the original.

5. Using a blue pencil, trace the courses of the Tigris and Euphrates Rivers.

6. Using a black pencil, trace the Elburz and Zagros Mountains.

7. Remove your map. Study carefully the locations of the Tigris, the Euphrates, the Elburz and Zagros, the Persian Gulf, the Gulf of Oman, the Caspian Sea, and the Arabian Sea. When you are familiar with them, close the book. Using your regular pencil, label all eight. Check your map against the original. Correct any misplaced labels.

CHAPTER NINE: THE FIRST CIVIL WAR

You MAY USE your text when answering the questions in sections I and II.

Section I: Who, What, Where

Write a one or two-sentence answer explaining the significance of each item listed below.

2890 BC
Abydos
Djer
Horus
Khasekhem
Osiris
Saqqara
Shabaka Stone

Section II: Comprehension

Write a two/three sentence answer to each of the following questions.

1. What brought an end to predynastic Egypt, and why?

2. Why do we think that the kings of the First Dynasty of Egypt were going to join the sun in his passage across the sky?

3. Write a short summary of the "Memphite Theology."

4. What does it mean when we say the kings of the First Dynasty of Egypt were not simply individuals, they were the bearers of a Power?

5. Adjib, the fourth king of the First Dynasty, added a new descriptive title to his royal appellations: the *nesu-bit* name. What does *nesu-bit* mean?

6. How did Semerkhet attempt to rewrite Egypt's past?

7. What do archaeological findings tell us about the annual Nile floods toward the beginning of the Second Dynasty? How did this change in the floods affect Semerkhet's power?

8. Why did sacrificial burials stop in the Second Dynasty?

9. What suggests that Sekemib, a southerner, might have been a northern sympathizer?

10. How does the sibling rivalry between Set and Horus reflect the hostility between north and south Egypt?

11. How did Khasekhem's name change to Khasekhemwy temporarily reconcile the Horus and Set problem?

Section III: Critical Thinking

You may NOT use your text to answer this question.

In Chapter 7 we learned about the fragility of papyrus. Though papyrus enabled Egyptians to communicate quickly and effectively, the brittle paper on which Egyptians wrote their important records crumbled soon after they were created. Explain each passage below, and how the circumstances presented can be viewed as historical evidence in place of the written histories that long ago turned to dust.

What these eight kings were up to, in the six hundred years that they governed over unified Egypt, is more than a little obscure. But we can glimpse the growth of a centralized state: the establishment of a royal court, the collection of taxes, and an economy that allowed Egypt the luxury of supporting citizens who produced no food: full-time priests to sacrifice for the king, skilled metalworkers who provided jewelry for the court's noblemen and women, scribes who kept track of the growing bureaucracy (62).

Possibly, the pharaoh would continue his royal rule; we have no Egyptian proof for this, but Gilgamesh, once dead, joined the gods of the underworld to help run the place. If the early pharaohs were believed to continue their kingly functions in the afterworld, the sacrificial burials make a kind of sense. After all, if a king's power only lasts until death, he must be obeyed during his life, but there is no good reason to follow him into death. If, on the other hand, he's still going to be waiting for you on the other side, his power becomes all-encompassing. The passage to the undiscovered country is simply a journey from one state of loyalty to the next (64).

Section IV: Map Exercise: Ancient Egypt

1. Using a black pencil, trace the rectangular outline of the frame for Map 9.1: Egyptian Expansion.

2. Using a black pencil, trace the Red Sea, the Nile River, and the Mediterranean Sea. Keep the orientation of the original map (with the south at the top). You do not need to include the bend of the Euphrates (in the lower left-hand corner). Repeat until the contours are familiar.

3. Trace the rectangular outline of the frame in black. Remove your tracing paper from the original. Using a regular pencil with an eraser, draw the Red Sea, the Nile River, and the Mediterranean Sea within the map frame while looking at Map 4.1. Erase and redraw as necessary.

4. When you are pleased with your map, lay it over the original. Erase and redraw any lines which are more than 1/4 inch off the original.

5. Remove your map. Study the locations of the Second Cataract, the First Cataract, Memphis, Heliopolis, the Red Sea, Upper Egypt, Lower Egypt, and the Sinai Peninsula on the original. When you are familiar with them, close the book. Using your regular pencil, mark and label the First Cataract, the Second Cataract, Memphis, and Heliopolis on your own map. Label Upper Egypt, Lower Egypt, and the Sinai Peninsula. Then, check your map against the original. If the city or the labels are more than 1/8 inch off, erase and re-mark while looking at the original.

CHAPTER TEN: THE FIRST EPIC HERO

You MAY USE your text when answering the questions in sections I and II.

Section I: Who, What, Where

Write a one or two-sentence answer explaining the significance of each item listed below.

626 BC

Ashurbanipal

Enkidu

Humbaba

Shulgi

Section II: Comprehension

Write a two/three sentence answer to each of the following questions.

1. List the 7 parts of the Epic of Gilgamesh, and write a short description of each section.

2. What makes the clay tablets of the tales of Gilgamesh written by Shulgi's scribe different from the copy of the Epic found in the library of Ashurbanipal? How do the two copies differ in form, and in accuracy?

3. What were the two most important duties of a Sumerian king?

4. What two threats to Sumerian life were represented by the monster Enkidu?

5. Why does Gilgamesh want to slay the Giant Hugeness? Cite a passage from the Epic of Gilgamesh that refers to Gilgamesh's battle in the cedar forest. Explain what the section of the poem you quoted means.

6. Use the footnote on page 76 to answer this question: Why was the world of the dead so horrifying for Sumerians?

7. The Epic of Gilgamesh ends with a lament. Gilgamesh is unsuccessful in his quest for immortality; "He has gone into the mountain; he will not come again" (77). How does this impact the idea of Sumerian kingship?

Section III: Critical Thinking

You may NOT use your text to answer this question.

Poems, epics, records and king lists give us great views into ancient cultures. To learn from these texts, we must be careful readers, piecing together significance from what we learned previously and what we are currently reading. The three questions below will test your skill as a reader, and historical sleuth.

1. Explain how the passage below asserts that the story of Agga and Gilgamesh was written within striking distance of Gilgamesh's life.

   "Outside of the Epic, though, Gilgamesh's life is chronicled by a couple of inscriptions, the Sumerian king list, and a poem or two. The story of Agga's fruitless peace-mission to Gilgamesh…is one such poem; it is written in Sumerian, and was likely told orally for some decades (or centuries) before being written down on clay tablets" (71).

2. Using the passage below, explain why historians think "The Story of the Flood" was not originally included in the Epic of Gilgamesh.

   "The story of the flood, which existed in a number of different versions well before 2000 BC, was likely shoehorned into Gilgamesh's story, as the fifth tale, at least a thousand years after Gilgamesh's death; it is clearly independent from the rest of the epic. ("Sit down and let me tell you a story," Utnapishtim orders Gilgamesh, and launches into the tale as though he's had little opportunity to tell it since getting off the boat.)" (72).

3. In the chapter, look up the term "droit de seigneur." How does "droit de seigneur" relate to the fine line between kingly privilege and kingly corruption, and the possible destruction of the king's realm?

CHAPTER ELEVEN: THE FIRST VICTORY OVER DEATH

You MAY USE your text when answering the questions in sections I and II.

Section I: Who, What, Where

Write a one or two-sentence answer explaining the significance of each item listed below.

Heb-sed

Imhote

Mastabas

Red Pyramid

Sadd al-Kafara

Serdab

Step Pyramid

Ziggurats

Section II: Comprehension

Write a two/three sentence answer to each of the following questions.

1. What is another term for the beginning of the pyramid age in Egyptian history?

2. In what way did the construction of the Step Pyramid represent the beginning of a new, peaceful and united kingdom of Egypt?

3. How was Djoser's tomb different from the tombs of the pharaohs in the Second Egyptian Dynasty?

4. Describe Sekhemkhet's vision for his pyramid. Why is Sekhemkhet's pyramid called the "Unfinished Pyramid"?

5. How can we distinguish the Fourth Dynasty of Egypt from the Third Dynasty of Egypt?

6. The Meydum Pyramid, started by Third Dynasty king, Huni, and finished by Fourth Dynasty king, Snefru, is surrounded by heaps of rubble. What does this rubble indicate about the intended construction of the Meydum Pyramid?

7. Describe the purpose of the causeway in the Meydum Pyramid, and the function of the mortuary temple.

8. What did Snefru figure out while building the Bent Pyramid that allowed him to construct the Northern Pyramid successfully? What is the Northern Pyramid like now, four thousand years later?

9. Herodotus said that Khufu "was a very bad man" (83). Describe one story that illustrates Khufu's evil.

10. What is "monumental architecture?" Why is it said that monumental architecture is a universal sign for power?

11. How do we know that Erich von Däniken's theory that "the pyramids suddenly appeared without any precedent, which meant that they had most likely been built by aliens," is not true?

Section III: Critical Thinking

You may NOT use your text to answer this question.

In *Chapter Nine: The First Civil War*, we read about the first two Egyptian dynasties and the evolution of pharaohs from men to gods. In the First Dynasty, a king's reign continued after death. The Second Dynasty held the same fortune for a king, but a pharaoh's power in the afterlife was questioned by Egyptians due to the lessening of the Nile floodwaters. In the Third and Fourth Dynasties, we see two more devolutions of divine power. However, an Egyptian king's earthly power was on the rise. Arrange the selected passages so that they reflect the correct transition of Egyptian beliefs about the afterlife and the king's power in the Third and Fourth Dynasties. When you are finished, write a short essay, in your own words, describing the changes from the First to Fourth Dynasties in Egyptian thought and culture as related to the pharaoh and his power.

PART I:

A. By Khufu's day, the original purpose of that first necropolis built by Imhotehad been well obscured. The Great Pyramid and the monuments that came after are the oldest surviving example of what we call "monumental architecture"…The less necessary and useful the pyramids were, the more they testified to the power of their builders. The house of the spirit had become the glittering testament to power.

B. The Step Pyramid, the first of the great Egyptian pyramids, shows more than an effort to redefine death as the absence of the body and the presence of the spirit. It shows the beginning of a new kingdom of Egypt, a peaceful and unified one with an orderly bureaucracy…Pyramid building required prosperity, peace and tax money…Only a strong and well-to-do state could order workers to the quarries and afford to feed and clothe them.

C. [T]he tradition of Khufu's evil, which echoes down from more than one source, is an interesting one. To build his monument – a stone structure with something like two and a half million blocks of stone in it, each block an average weight of two and a half tons – Khufu mobilized one of the largest work forces in the world. Even if the laborers were not reduced to abject slavery, the king's ability to recruit such an enormous number of workers keenly illustrated his ability to oppress his people. The pyramids themselves stand as signposts to that power.

D. By Djoser's day, the pharaoh's rule as a buffer against change had solidified into ritual…Winning the *heb-sed* race reaffirmed the pharaoh's power to protect Egypt and to assure the continuing, regular rise and fall of the waters [of the Nile]…The fact that the Egyptians felt the need for a renewal festival at all suggests a certain fear that the pharaoh's power might fade if not ritually reinforced. The pharaoh was undoubtedly still credited with a kind of divinity, but the struggles of the first two dynasties had made his human side very obvious.

E. [The pyramids] stand as testaments, not to alien visits, but to the Egyptian reluctance to release power in the face of death. Gilgamesh had gone into the mountain and would not come again. But for the Egyptians, who could always see the house of the king's spirit looming in the distance, the might of the pharaoh was ever present.

F. Sekhemkhet's pyramid was planned to rise seven steps, not six as Djoser's had… The final pyramid of the Third Dynasty, the Meydum Pyramid, was also unfinished; it was built by the Third Dynasty's last king, Huni, and it would have had *eight* steps.

G. A pyramid and the complex underneath it "was a place where the pharaoh *still lived.*"

H. The fact that Snefru was able to complete one pyramid and build two more suggests that Egypt was now even richer, and more peaceful, and more subject to the authority of the pharaoh, than even before.

PART II:

Write two or three paragraphs, in your own words, describing the changes from the First to Fourth Dynasties in Egyptian thought and culture as related to the pharaoh and his power.

Section IV: Map Exercise: Ancient Egyptian Cities

1. Using a black pencil, trace the rectangular outline of the frame for Map 11.1: Pyramids of the Old Kingdom.

2. Using a black pencil, trace the Red Sea, the Nile River, and the Mediterranean Sea. Keep the orientation of the original map (with the south at the top). Repeat until the contours are familiar.

3. Trace the rectangular outline of the frame in black. Remove your tracing paper from the original. Using a regular pencil with an eraser, draw the Red Sea, the Nile River, and the Mediterranean Sea within the map frame while looking at Map 4.1. Erase and redraw as necessary.

4. When you are pleased with your map, lay it over the original. Erase and redraw any lines which are more than 1/4 inch off the original.

5. Remove your map. Study the locations of the Sinai Peninsula, the First Cataract, Hierakonpolis, Nubt, Abydos, Giza, and Heliopolis on the original. When you are familiar with them, close the book. Using your regular pencil, mark and label the First Cataract, Hierakonpolis, Nubt, Abydos, Giza, and Heliopolis. Label the Sinai Peninsula, the Red Sea, and the Mediterranean Sea. Then, check your map against the original. If the city or the labels are more than 1/8 inch off, erase and re-mark while looking at the original.

Chapter Twelve: The First Reformer

You MAY USE your text when answering the questions in sections I and II.

Section I: Who, What, Where

Write a one or two-sentence answer explaining the significance of each item listed below.

Amagi

Lugulannemundu

Sataran

Stele

Susa and Awan

Urukagina

Section II: Comprehension

Write a two/three sentence answer to each of the following questions.

1. Where were the cities of the ancient Elamite civilization located?

2. After Uruk was conquered by Ur, Ur was then "defeated in battle, and its kingship was carried off to Awan." What evidence do we have from the historical record that indicates an Elamite invasion of Ur?

3. How did Mesilim, the king of Kish, settle the dispute between Lagash and Umma concerning the proper boundary between the two cities?

4. What is the Stele of Vultures – who created it, what does it depict, and what does it tell us about Sumerian warfare?

5. What problems plagued Lagash during Urukagina's rule?

6. One of the actions Urukagina took to restore Lagash to a land of peace and justice was to take away authority from the priests by dividing religious and secular functions. How was this action partly responsible for the fall of Lagash to Lugalzaggesi's troops?

Section III: Critical Thinking

You may NOT use your text to answer this question.

Sumer's first epic hero was Gilgamesh. However, even though Gilgamesh was held to be a god, his godship was still limited by death. We learned, with relief, that "even the strongest king of Sumer dies." How did this time limit on the power of a king affect the way a Sumerian king ruled? In addition, how did the constant rivalry between Sumerian cities for dominance of the plain, as well as the constant threat of Elamite invasion, influence the way a king ruled over his Sumerian city? What connects the limited earthly power of a Sumerian king and the perpetual threat of invasion to Sumer's lack of an organized bureaucracy?

Section IV: Map Exercise: Sumerian Cities

1. Using a black pencil, trace the rectangular outline of the frame for Map 12.1: Battling Cities of Sumer and Elam.

2. Using a black pencil, trace the northern edge of the Persian Gulf, the Gulf of Oman, the southern and western coastlines of the Arabian peninsula and the Tigris and Euphrates Rivers (including the unlabelled right-hand branch of the Tigris). Also trace the Zagros Mountains. Repeat until the contours are familiar.

3. Trace the rectangular outline of the frame in black. Remove your tracing paper from the original. Using a regular pencil with an eraser, draw the Persian Gulf, the Euphrates, the Tigris, the unnamed right-hand branch of the Tigris, and the Zagros Mountains while looking at Map 12.1. Erase and redraw as necessary.

4. When you are pleased with your map, lay it over the original. Erase and redraw any lines which are more than 1/4 inch off the original.

5. Remove your map. Study carefully the locations of the Tigris, the Euphrates, the Zagros Mountains, and the cities of Mari, Kish, Nippur, Lagash, Uruk, and Ur. When you are familiar with them, close the book. Using your regular pencil, label the Tigris, the Euphrates, and the Zagros Mountains. Mark and label the cities of Mari, Kish, Nippur, Lagash, Uruk, and Ur. Check your map against the original. Correct any misplaced labels.

CHAPTER THIRTEEN: THE FIRST MILITARY DICTATOR

You MAY USE your text when answering the questions in sections I and II.

Section I: Who, What, Where

Write a one or two-sentence answer explaining the significance of each item listed below.

Agade
Nineveh
Rimush
Ur-Zababa

Section II: Comprehension

Write a two/three sentence answer to each of the following questions.

1. Part of the inscription that chronicles Sargon's birth reads:

   [My mother] cast me into the river, but it did not rise over me,
   The water carried me to Akki, the drawer of water,
   He lifted me out as he dipped his jar into the river,
   He took me as his son, he raised me,
   He made me his gardener.

   Why was Sargon's trip down the river important to his new identity? How did it help him take on Akki's heritage?

2. What most clearly distinguished the Sumerians of the south from the Semites of the north?

3. Describe the duties of an ancient cupbearer. What was the significance of carrying the king's seal? Why did the cupbearer have to taste the king's food?

4. As Lugalzaggesi approached Kish, Ur-Zababa sent the aggressor a message on a clay tablet asking him to kill Sargon. While this story may not be true, what evidence in the chapter suggests that Sargon was in fact not fully behind his king?

5. What type of secret weapon did Sargon's army have that helped them conquer the entire Mesopotamian plain? How might Sargon have gotten this weaponry?

6. How did the abuses of the elite leaders in Sumerian cities, coupled with Sargon's commoner background, help Sargon's conquest of Sumer?

7. Why did Sumerians find themselves living as foreigners in their own cities after Sargon created his new kingdom?

8. Why is Sargon's invasion of Purushkhanda questionable? Use a section of the surviving verses of Nur-daggal to explain why Sargon's attack on Purushkhanda seemed unlikely. What does the story of Sargon's invasion of the city tell us about Sargon's cultural importance?

9. How did Sargon keep control of the vast expanse of land he had claimed as his own?

Section III: Critical Thinking

You may NOT use your text to answer this question.

Sargon was the first man to successfully turn Sumer into an empire. Sargon was able to build a strong enough bureaucracy that his descendants kept the throne of Agade for over a hundred years. Yet, as soon as Sargon died, internal fighting threatened his legacy. Write two or three paragraphs, using the questions below to structure your answer, explaining how Sargon's policies both strengthened and threatened his kingdom.

- How did the standardization of weights and measures, and the implementation of a tax system run by state officials who managed the empire's finances, helSargon keep tabs on the cities under his control?

- How might Sargon's replacement of the Sumerian lugals with his own men help him build such a large empire so quickly? How did this policy cause unrest?

- Sargon kept representatives of old ruling families at his court in honor of their exalted lineage, however the chapter says "these representatives…were hostages for the good behavior of their cities" (102). How did this policy both help, and hurt, Sargon's kingdom?

Section IV: Map Exercise: Sumerian and Akkadian Cities

1. Using a black pencil, trace the rectangular outline of the frame for Map 13.1: Sargon's Empire.

2. Using a black pencil, trace the Persian Gulf, the Tigris and Euphrates Rivers (including the unlabelled right-hand branch of the Tigris), the Zagros Mountains, the Caspian Sea, and the mountains south and southwest of the Caspian. (You do not need to trace the Mediterranean or the Red Sea.) Repeat until the contours are familiar.

3. Trace the rectangular outline of the frame in black. Remove your tracing paper from the original. Using a regular pencil with an eraser, draw the Persian Gulf, the Euphrates, the Tigris, the unnamed right-hand branch of the Tigris, the Zagros Mountains, the Caspian Sea, and the remaining mountains while looking at Map 13.1. Erase and redraw as necessary.

4. When you are pleased with your map, lay it over the original. Erase and redraw any lines which are more than 1/4 inch off the original.

5. Remove your map. Study carefully the locations of the Tigris, the Euphrates, the Zagros Mountains, the Caspian Sea, and the cities of Mari, Kish, Nippur, Lagash, Uruk, Ur, Modern Baghdad, Assur, Nineveh, and Susa. When you are familiar with them, close the book. Using your regular pencil, label the Tigris, the Euphrates, the Persian Gulf, the Caspian Sea, and the Zagros Mountains. Mark and label the cities of Mari, Kish, Nippur, Lagash, Uruk, Ur, Modern Baghdad, Assur, Nineveh, and Susa. Check your map against the original. Correct any misplaced labels.

Chapter Fourteen: The First Planned Cities

You MAY USE your text when answering the questions in sections I and II.

Section I: Who, What, Where

Write a one or two-sentence answer explaining the significance of each item listed below.

Citadel
Harappa
Mohenjo-Daro
Sutkagen Dor

Section II: Comprehension

Write a two/three sentence answer to each of the following questions.

1. What artifact leads us to believe that the Harappan cities had kings? How does the architecture of Mohenjo-Daro support the idea that there was indeed a king of the city?

2. How do we know that Harappan merchants traded their goods with the people of Ur? How did Harappan merchants get to Ur?

3. Describe the general architecture of a Harappan city, and the layout of a Harappan house. What about the planning of Harappan cities, and houses, suggests that this civilization put a high value on washing?

4. Describe what archaeologists found as they excavated Kot Diji. What do these findings suggest about the history of the city?

5. There were three kinds of roads in a typical Harappan city. What were they used for, how big were they, and how were they organized?

6. What other relics from the Harappan excavations, beyond city planning and architecture, provide us with evidence that the Harappans were obsessed with uniformity?

Section III: Critical Thinking

You MAY USE your text to answer this question.

We know very little about the Harappan people. However, archaeological clues give us some insight into the Harappan culture. While the people remain voiceless, piecing together these clues allows us to extrapolate characteristics of the Harappan civilization.

- What evidence from the chapter suggests that the Harappan cities had thriving trade?

- What evidence from the chapter suggests that the Harappan cities had military might?

- Using what you know from your reading, how might you explain this paragraph from the chapter:

    "What were the Harappans so afraid of that they needed two sets of walls? Neither the Sumerians nor the Elamites ever sent an army quite so far to the east. Nor is there much evidence of savage nomadic tribes in the area. Yet the double walls are high and thick, with ramparts and watchtowers: built to keep out enemies" (107).

Section IV: Map Exercise: Northern India

1. Using a black pencil, trace the rectangular outline of the frame for Map 14.1: Harrapan Cities.

2. Using a black pencil, trace the coastline of India, the northern mountain ranges, the Indus, the un-named river on the right-hand side of the map (the Ganga), the Narmada river, and the mountains around the Narmada. Repeat until the contours are familiar. (Remember that you may draw simple peaks to represent the mountains; you do not need to shade them as the mapmaker does.)

3. Trace the rectangular outline of the frame in black. Remove your tracing paper from the original. Using a regular pencil with an eraser, draw the coastline of India, the three rivers, and all mountains while looking at Map 14.1. Erase and redraw as necessary.

4. When you are pleased with your map, lay it over the original. Erase and redraw any lines which are more than 1/4 inch off the original

5. Remove your map from the original. Looking back at Map 14.1, study carefully the location of the Indus River, the Punjab, the Kirthar Mountains, the Arabian Sea, the Narmada, and the Vindhya and Satpura mountain ranges, and the Khyber Pass. When you are familiar with them, close the book. Using your regular pencil, label the Indus River, the Punjab, the Kirthar Mountains, the Arabian Sea, the Narmada, and the Vindhya and Satpura. Check your map against the original. If your labels are misplaced, erase and re-mark while looking at the original.

CHAPTER FIFTEEN: THE FIRST COLLAPSE OF EMPIRE

You MAY USE your text when answering the questions in sections I and II.

Section I: Who, What, Where

Write a one or two-sentence answer explaining the significance of each item listed below.

Khafre
Menkaure
Obelisk
Ra
Seheteptawy
Sphinx

Section II: Comprehension

Write a two/three sentence answer to each of the following questions.

1. Why would Khafre want to guard the place where his soul would rest with the Sphinx? Also, why would Khafre put his face on the monument?

2. Menkaure reopened Egypt's temples and sanctuaries, raised the people from the misery which his predecessors had inflicted on them, and ruled them kindly. Yet, the gods were displeased with Menkaure's rule and sent him a message: he would die before his seventh year of rule. Why, if Menkaure was a benevolent ruler and a god-fearing man, did the gods want to punish him? What does Menkaure's fate tell us about the way a pharaoh was supposed to rule?

3. In what way did Shepseskaf's burial place mark the end of the Fourth Dynasty?

4. Who could an Egyptian pharaoh marry? Why was this a problem for the continuation of the royal line?

5. How does the Egyptian king list support the idea that intermarriage damaged the royal succession?

6. What are the distinct differences between the Fourth and Fifth Egyptian dynasties?

7. What is the significance of the demotion of Fifth dynasty kings from the earthly incarnation of god to the son of a god?

8. How do we know that in the Fifth Dynasty, the king was no longer thought to live forever on earth? Where did the Egyptians now believe the king went after his death?

9. Sixth Dynasty pharaoh Pepi II is credited with a ninety-four-year rule, yet he was placed on the throne when he was just six years old. How could Pepi II rule at such a young age, and then hold on to the throne for so long?

10. What were the four factors that brought an end to the Sixth Dynasty, and Old Kingdom, of Egypt?

Section III: Critical Thinking

You may NOT use your text to answer this question.

In this chapter we read about the first collapse of empire – the crumbling of the Old Kingdom of Egypt. The pyramids stand as proof of the exploitation of Egyptian lives and money, and the Pyramid Texts give us a glimpse into the changing relationship between the pharaoh, his people and the gods. We also know that the desert was creeping at the edge of Egypt's cultivable land, meaning a drought most surely occurred. But what about the theory that inbreeding was partly to blame for the downfall of Egypt's empire? While we don't have hard proof, we have some circumstantial evidence that supports this theory.

Explain how each passage below indicates that inbreeding was also part of the collapse of the first Egyptian empire.

*   Statues of Menkaure himself show a slightly odd-shaped head with weirdly prominent eyes.

*   Prince Khuenre lived just long enough to be proclaimed heir, and then succumbed to some unknown illness before his father's death.

*   Shepseskaf had an entirely undistinguished and very brief reign.

*   There is also the survival of a story that Menkaure fell in love with his own daughter and raped her, after which she hanged herself in grief. The story also says that the daughter was Menkaure's only child, which we know is not true. Herodotus remarks, "But this is all nonsense, in my opinion."

CHAPTER SIXTEEN: THE FIRST BARBARIAN INVASIONS

You MAY USE your text when answering the questions in sections I and II.

Section I: Who, What, Where

Write a one or two-sentence answer explaining the significance of each item listed below.

Barbarian
Manishtushu
Naram-Sin the Great
Third Dynasty of Ur
Ur-Nammu

Section II: Comprehension

Write a two/three sentence answer to each of the following questions.

1. How do we know Naram-Sin the Great was considered godlike? How is this relationship with godliness different from previous Mesopotamian kings?

2. Explain the reason for the bilingualism of the Akkadian empire.

3. On page 121, an excerpt from a historical text tells us how the Akkadians viewed the Gutians. Use the note reference to correctly fill in the blanks in the sentence below.

   In the book _____, *translated by* _____, *which was published in* _____, *we find out exactly how the Akkadians reacted to the invading Gutians.*

   Then, write a sentence or two about how the Akkadians felt about the Gutians, making sure to quote the excerpted passage

4. What happened to Naram-Sin's empire once the Gutians attacked? Use examples from the second excerpted passage on page 121.

5. What did Naram-Sin do to make the gods so angry that they would send barbarians upon his empire?

6. In what way is the damage of the Gutians linked to the destruction caused by the Great Flood?

7. Shar-kali-sharri battled what two forces that sought to destroy the Akkadian empire?

8. What historical evidence tells us the Gutians did not have a culture of their own?

9. What did Utuhegal do to claim the title "The King of the Four Quarters?"

10. How did Ur-Nammu use diplomacy to restore order and civilization to Sumer?

Section III: Critical Thinking

You may NOT use your text to answer this question.

"No one calls himself a barbarian, that's what your enemy calls you."

-historian David McCullough

While it is clear from our reading in this chapter that the Gutian invasions of Akkadian lands were terribly destructive, how did they benefit Akkadian culture? Though the Gutians overwhelmed the Akkadian civilization at one point, how did the Akkadians win in the eyes of history?

Section IV: Map Exercise: Naram-Sin's Empire

1. Using a black pencil, trace the rectangular outline of the frame for Map 16.1: The Mesopotamia of Naram-Sin.

2. Using a black pencil, trace the Persian Gulf, the Tigris and Euphrates Rivers (including the unlabelled right-hand branch of the Tigris), the Zagros Mountains, the Caspian Sea, the "Upper Sea" (that is the Black Sea) and the mountains southwest of the Caspian. Repeat until the contours are familiar.

3. Trace the rectangular outline of the frame in black. Remove your tracing paper from the original. Using a regular pencil with an eraser, draw the Persian Gulf, the Euphrates, the Tigris, the unnamed right-hand branch of the Tigris, the Zagros Mountains, the Caspian Sea, the Upper Sea, and the remaining mountains while looking at Map 16.1. Erase and redraw as necessary.

4. When you are pleased with your map, lay it over the original. Erase and redraw any lines which are more than 1/4 inch off the original.

5. Remove your map. Study carefully the locations of the Tigris, the Euphrates, the Zagros Mountains, the Caspian Sea, the Upper Sea, and the cities of Mari, Kish, Nippur, Lagash, Uruk, Ur, Susa, and Sippur. When you are familiar with them, close the book. Using your regular pencil, label the Tigris, the Euphrates, the Persian Gulf, the Caspian Sea, and the Zagros Mountains. Mark and label the cities of Mari, Kish, Nippur, Lagash, Uruk, Ur, Susa, and Sippur. Check your map against the original. Correct any misplaced labels.

6. While looking at Map 16.1, draw a light line with your regular pencil to show the borders of Naram-Sin's empire. Erase and correct as necessary. When you are satisfied, lay your map back over the original. Erase and redraw any lines which are more than 1/4 inch off the original.

Chapter Seventeen: The First Monotheist

You MAY USE your text when answering the questions in sections I and II.

Section I: Who, What, Where

Write a one or two-sentence answer explaining the significance of each item listed below.

Hagar
Ishmael
Jericho
Nuzi Tablets
Terah
YHWH

Section II: Comprehension

Write a two/three sentence answer to each of the following questions.

1. Why is it important for YHWH to rename Abram and Sarai, Abraham and Sarah?

2. Where was Shechem? Why was Abram uneasy about carrying out God's covenant in Shechem?

3. How did trade with Egypt help the economies of Byblos and Ebla?

4. In what way did the failure of cropland and the fall of the Old Kingdom cause problems for the Western Semites?

5. When Abram and Sarai moved to Egypt, why did Abram tell the nameless pharaoh that Sarai was his sister? How did this decision benefit Abram?

6. How does Abram's plan to father a child with Hagar as a substitute for the child Sarai had not yet conceived backfire?

7. What happened when a man other than Abram had a physical relationship with Sarai? Why is this important for the story of Abram and Sarai?

8. When God's promise to Abram and Sarai is finally fulfilled, how is their child, Isaac, differentiated from the people that came before him?

9. While Abram turned away from the worship of the moon-god, how did Shulgi trumpet his worship of the celestial divinity?

Section III: Critical Thinking

You may NOT use your text to answer this question.

- What is race? Consult your dictionary, and record the definition of race as related to humans.

- How is race different from identity? In your answer, use the example of different people in Sargon's empire.

- If Abram was of the same blood as the people that came before him, how could he be of a different race? How is Abram's monotheism inextricable from his race?

Section IV: Map Exercise: Egypt, Mesopotamia, and Canaan

1. Using a black pencil, trace the rectangular outline of the frame for Map 17.1: Abram's World.

2. Using a black pencil, trace the Persian Gulf, the Tigris and Euphrates Rivers, the Zagros Mountains, the bottom of the (unlabelled) Caspian Sea, the Red Sea, the Nile, and the Mediterranean. (You do not need to trace any islands or small bodies of water, including the Dead Sea and the Sea of Galilee--you will learn these in a later assignment.) Repeat until the contours are familiar.

3. Trace the rectangular outline of the frame in black. Remove your tracing paper from the original. Using a regular pencil with an eraser, draw the Persian Gulf, the Tigris and Euphrates Rivers, the Zagros Mountains, the bottom of the (unlabelled) Caspian Sea, the Red Sea, the Nile, and the Mediterranean while looking at Map 17.1. Erase and redraw as necessary.

4. When you are pleased with your map, lay it over the original. Erase and redraw any lines which are more than 1/4 inch off the original.

5. Remove your map. Study carefully the locations of the Tigris, the Euphrates, the Zagros Mountains, the Red Sea, the Nile, the Mediterranean Sea, and the cities of Ur, Assur, Nineveh, Catal Huyuk, Haran and Jericho. When you are familiar with them, close the book. Using your regular pencil, label the Tigris, the Euphrates, the Zagros Mountains, the Red Sea, the Nile, and the Mediterranean Sea. Mark and label the cities of Ur, Assur, Nineveh, Catal Huyuk, Haran, and Jericho. Check your map against the original. Correct any misplaced labels.

CHAPTER EIGHTEEN:
THE FIRST ENVIRONMENTAL DISASTER

You MAY USE your text when answering the questions in sections I and II.

Section I: Who, What, Where

Write a one or two-sentence answer explaining the significance of each item listed below.

Shu-Sin
The Martu/Amurru
Ibbi-Sin
Ishbi-Erra
Kindattu
Nanna

Section II: Comprehension

Write a two/three sentence answer to each of the following questions.

1. Describe the process of salinization. What happens when the ground is salinized?

2. Why did Sumerians switch from growing wheat to growing barley?

3. What is weed fallowing? What is the benefit of weed fallowing? What did practicing weed fallowing mean for the food supply of the Sumerian people?

4. Why was the fertile land in Mesopotamia so scarce?

5. How did the lack of grain in Sumer lead to the Ur III Dynasty's inability to defend itself?

6. The invading Amorites were not the only threat to Ibbi-Sin's empire. Chronicle the rebellion of the Sumerian people caused by famine and discontent during Ibbi-Sin's early reign.

7. In a last resort to feed his people, Ibbi-Sin sent Ishbi-Erra north to get grain and meat. How did Ibbi-Sin's plan backfire?

8. In what way was the fall of Ur symbolic of the fall of the Sumerian culture? Use the poem on page 143 to help answer this question.

9. What did the fall of Ur mean for the relationship of the Sumerians with the moon-god Nanna, and the other patron deities of Sumerian cities?

Section III: Critical Thinking

You may NOT use your text to answer this question.

This chapter is called "The First Environmental Disaster."   While you may have expected content that was similar to the flood stories we read about in Chapter Two, this environmental disaster was much more complicated. Write a paragraph, in your own words, explaining how the environment of Sumer during the Ur III dynasty was to blame for the fall of Sumer.

CHAPTER NINETEEN: THE BATTLE FOR REUNIFICATION

You MAY USE your text when answering the questions in sections I and II.

Section I: Who, What, Where

Write a one or two-sentence answer explaining the significance of each item listed below.

Achthoes/Akhtoy I
Amenemhet I
Itj-taway
Mentuhotep
Nomarch
Nome

Section II: Comprehension

Write a two/three sentence answer to each of the following questions.

1. Manetho says that Akhtoy's Ninth Dynasty was followed by a Tenth Dynasty and then neatly by an Eleventh Dynasty. However, in actuality, the Ninth, Tenth, and Eleventh Dynasties ruled simultaneously. How was this possible?

2. Why did Intef I call himself "King of Upper and Lower Egypt"?

3. What obstacles did Mentuhotep face as he fought his way into Lower Egypt? What evidence suggests Mentuhotep was a fierce warrior?

4. What clue do we have from Egyptian portraits of royal officials during Mentuhotep's rise to power that supports the idea that Mentuhotep was a powerful and dangerous man?

5. What was Mentuhotep's Horus-name, and why was it significant to Egyptian history?

6. Describe the "Prophecy of Nerferti" - how did it come into being, and where was it from? What did the prophecy predict about the new king and his relationship with the Asiatics? Use at least two lines from the actual prophecy in your answer.

7. Who was Sinuhe? Write a two/three sentence summary of the "Tale of Sinuhe."

8. What two practices in the Twelfth Dynasty reflect the continuing transition of the pharaoh from god to man?

9. Why was Senusret III's fortress at Buhen so large, and heavily fortified?

Section III: Critical Thinking

You may NOT use your text to answer this question.

Amenemhet I's rise to power, and what he did while on the throne, were very much in line with the actions of the great pharaohs of the Old Kingdom. However, unlike the pharaohs of the Fourth Dynasty, Amenemhet was not considered a god. Write a short paragraph describing what Amenemhet did while in power that mimicked the great pharaohs of Egypt's past. Then, write a short paragraph detailing how Amenemhet created a divine legacy for himself to make up for his humanity.

Section IV: Map Exercise: The Middle Kingdom

1. Using a black pencil, trace the rectangular outline of the frame for Map 19.1: The Middle Kingdom.

2. Using a black pencil, trace the Red Sea, the Nile River, the Mediterranean Sea, the Euphrates, and the Tigris. Keep the orientation of the original map (with the south at the top). Repeat until the contours are familiar.

3. Trace the rectangular outline of the frame in black. Remove your tracing paper from the original. Using a regular pencil with an eraser, draw the Red Sea, the Nile River, the Mediterranean Sea, the Euphrates, and the Tigris within the map frame while looking at Map 19.1. Erase and redraw as necessary.

4. When you are pleased with your map, lay it over the original. Erase and redraw any lines which are more than 1/4 inch off the original.

5. Remove your map. Study the locations of the First Cataract, the Second Cataract, Nubia, Libya, Upper Egypt, Lower Egypt, and the cities of Hierakonpolis, Thebes, Memphis, and Heliopolis on the original. When you are familiar with them, close the book. Using your regular pencil, mark and label the First Cataract and the Second Cataract. Label Nubia, Libya, Upper Egypt, and Lower Egypt. Mark and label the cities of Hierakonpolis, Thebes, Memphis, and Helipolis. Then, check your map against the original. If the markings or labels are more than 1/8 inch off, erase and re-mark while looking at the original.

CHAPTER TWENTY: THE MESOPOTAMIAN MIXING BOWL

You MAY USE your text when answering the questions in sections I and II.

Section I: Who, What, Where

Write a one or two-sentence answer explaining the significance of each item listed below.

1794 BC
Assyria
Gungunum
Hammurabi
Ishbi-Erra
Rim-Sin
Shamshi-Adad

Section II: Comprehension

Write a two/three sentence answer to each of the following questions.

1. In what ways did the Amorite presence in Mesopotamia hinder Ishbi-Erra from going after Eshnunna and Larsa?

2. Describe Ishbi-Erra's victory over the Elamites and his recapture of Ur. Use the poem on page 156 in your answer.

3. What cities made up Ishbi-Erra's kingdom?

4. While the Isin dynasty of Ishbi-Erra and the Amorite kings of Larsa fought it out against each other on the southern plain, what were the cities of Assur and Mari doing in the north of Mesopotamia?

5. How was Sumu-abum's rule in Babylon different from the leadership of the other cities of the Sumerian plain at the time of his rule?

6. Recount the embarrassing shift of power at Isin that followed the oracle's prediction that disaster was heading Erra-imitti's way.

7. What was happening in Assur when Rim-Sin took over Uruk?

8. In what way was Babylon's location on the Mesopotamian plain an advantage to Hammurabi and his expanding empire?

9. What were the terms of Hammurabi and Shamshi-Adad's official relationship?

10. What diplomatic moves did Hammurabi make after the death of Shamshi-Adad? How did Rim-Sin react to Hammurabi's actions?

Section III: Critical Thinking

You may NOT use your text to answer this question.

During the tumultuous time we read about in "The Mesopotamian Mixing Bowl," a king had to take drastic measures to keep his power. This was especially true in the case of Gungunum, the fifth king of Larsa. He declared himself the divine protector of the ancient city of Ur, and commissioned poems that promised the moon-god that he longed to restore the city's ancient ways. Write a paragraph explaining why this was an extreme move. What did Gungunum have to gain by making this declaration? In what way did Gungunum's capture of Ur and his promise to Nanna exemplify "The Mesopotamian Mixing Bowl?"

Section IV: Map Exercise: Ancient Mesopotamian Empires

1. Using a black pencil, trace the rectangular outline of the frame for Map 20.1: Mesopotamian Mixing Bowl.

2. Using a black pencil, trace the head of the Persian Gulf, the Tigris and Euphrates Rivers (including the unlabelled right-hand branch of the Tigris), the Lower Zab, the Zagros and Elburz Mountains, the Caspian Sea (unlabelled, in the upper right-hand corner of the map), and the Mediterranean (unlabelled, on the left side of the map). You do not need to trace other lakes and rivers. Repeat until the contours are familiar.

3. Trace the rectangular outline of the frame in black. Remove your tracing paper from the original. Using a regular pencil with an eraser, draw the Persian Gulf, the Euphrates, the Tigris, the unnamed right-hand branch of the Tigris, the Lower Zab, the Zagros and Elburz Mountains, the Caspian Sea and the Mediterranean while looking at Map 20.1. Erase and redraw as necessary.

4. When you are pleased with your map, lay it over the original. Erase and redraw any lines which are more than 1/4 inch off the original.

5. Remove your map. Study carefully the locations of the Persian Gulf, the Euphrates, the Tigris, the unnamed right-hand branch of the Tigris, the Lower Zab, the Zagros and Elburz Mountains, and the cities of Kish, Ur, Susa, Babylon, Assur, and Nineveh. When you are familiar with them, close the book. Using your regular pencil, label the Persian Gulf, the Euphrates, the Tigris, the Lower Zab, and the Zagros and Elburz Mountains. Mark and label the cities of Kish, Ur, Susa, Babylon, Assur, and Nineveh. Check your map against the original. Correct any misplaced labels.

6. While looking at Map 20.1, draw three sets of light lines with your regular pencil to show the borders of Rim-Sin's kingdom, Hammurabi's kingdom, and Shamshi-Adad's kingdom. Erase and correct as necessary. When you are satisfied, lay your map back over the original. Erase and redraw any lines which are more than 1/4 inch off the original.

7. Label the three kingdoms.

CHAPTER TWENTY-ONE: THE OVERTHROW OF THE XIA

You MAY USE your text when answering the questions in sections I and II.

Section I: Who, What, Where

Write a one or two-sentence answer explaining the significance of each item listed below.

Jie

Qi

Shao-Kang

Tang

Yi

Yü

Section II: Comprehension

Write a two/three sentence answer to each of the following questions.

1. What did Yü do to earn his place as a Sage King?

2. What was a patriarch in the context of the Longshan culture?

3. Where was Erlitou located? Why was it a good place for Yü's capital city?

4. Why did the Chinese move from choosing a worthy successor to be king to an era of blood succession?

5. What did Qi do to silence his dissenters in the village of Youhu?

6. Give a brief account of first years of Xia blood succession and the chaos that followed.

7. Explain Jie's last words: "I should have killed Tang when I had the chance."

Section III: Critical Thinking

You MAY USE your text to answer this question.

This chapter introduced two very important ideas about Chinese dynastic rule: 1) the greatest threat to a Chinese king's power came from his own nature, and 2) there was a particular cycle related to the Chinese throne. Explain what each of these important ideas means, and then write a few sentences explaining how these two major points are inextricable from one another. Make sure to include examples from the chapter as proof of your point.

Section IV: Map Exercise: Ancient Settlements of China

1. Using a black pencil, trace the rectangular outline of the frame for Map 21.1: Xia and Shang.

2. Using a black pencil, trace the coastline of China and the courses of the Yangtze and Yellow rivers, including the Lo branch of the Yellow. Repeat until the contours are familiar.

3. Trace the rectangular outline of the frame in black. Remove your tracing paper from the original. Using a regular pencil with an eraser, draw the coastline of China and the rivers while looking at Map 21.1. Erase and redraw as necessary.

4. When you are pleased with your map, lay it over the original. Erase and redraw any lines which are more than 1/4 inch off the original.

5. Remove your map from the original. Looking at Map 21.1, study carefully the locations of the Yangtze, the Yellow, the Lo, the East China Sea, the Yellow Sea, the Shandong Peninsula, and the city of Erlitou. When you are familiar with them, close the book. Using your regular pencil, label all six geographical features. Mark and label the city of Erlitou. Check your map against the original. If your labels are misplaced, erase and re-mark while looking at the original.

6. While looking at Map 21.1, draw two sets of light lines with your regular pencil to show the borders of the Shang and the Xia territories. Erase and correct as necessary. When you are satisfied, lay your map back over the original. Erase and redraw any lines which are more than 1/4 inch off the original.

7. Label the two territories.

Chapter Twenty-Two: Hammurabi's Empire

You MAY USE your text when answering the questions in sections I and II.

Section I: Who, What, Where

Write a one or two-sentence answer explaining the significance of each item listed below.

Ishme-Dagan
The Kassites
Kutir-Nahhunte
Samsuiluna
Yasmah-Adad
Zimri-Lim

Section II: Comprehension

Write a two/three sentence answer to each of the following questions.

1. How did Shamshi-Adad fuel the distance between his two sons Ishme-Dagan and Yasmah-Adad? Use the excerpt from the correspondence between father and son on page 170 in your answer.

2. Who was responsible for Yasmah-Adad's death? Use evidence from the text to support your answer.

3. Zimri-Lim had a hard time figuring out who to ally himself with, either Ishme-Dagan, Rim-Sin or Hammurabi. Who did he choose? How did his choice affect the shape of Hammurabi's kingdom?

4. Hammurabi, wanting to keep a close eye on Zimri-Lim, demanded the right to examine and control all of Zimri-Lim's correspondence with other powers. What happened when Zimri-Lim refused to allow Hammurabi access to his letters?

5. Give a short account of Rim-Sim's turbulent relationship with Hammurabi and his growing empire.

6. What two purposes did Hammurabi's code serve?

7. Below, fill in the specific penalty for breaking each of Hammurabi's laws.

    robbery   _____
    aiding in the escape of a slave   _____
    kidnapping   _____
    designing a faulty house   _____
    poor performance of an obligation to the king _____

8. Write a short sentence for each of the regulations associated with each act: marriage, injury, inheritance and firefighting.

9. How did control of all shipping routes allow Hammurabi to keep a tight grip on his empire?

Section III: Critical Thinking

You may NOT use your text to answer this question.

As evidenced by our reading in this chapter, Hammurabi was a fierce warrior and gifted leader. His kingdom extended far and wide, yet it did not last long after his reign ended. Write a short paragraph explaining why Hammurabi's kingdom crumbled almost as soon as the king retired.

Section IV: Map Exercise: Hammurabi's Empire

1. Using a black pencil, trace the rectangular outline of the frame for Map 22.1: Hammurabi's Empire.

2. Using a black pencil, trace the head of the Persian Gulf, the Tigris and Euphrates Rivers (including the unlabelled right-hand branch of the Tigris), the Lower Zab, the Zagros and Elburz Mountains, the Caspian Sea (unlabelled, in the upper right-hand corner of the map), and the Mediterranean (unlabelled, on the left side of the map). You do not need to trace other lakes and rivers. Repeat until the contours are familiar.

3. Trace the rectangular outline of the frame in black. Remove your tracing paper from the original. Using a regular pencil with an eraser, draw the Persian Gulf, the Euphrates, the Tigris, the unnamed right-hand branch of the Tigris, the Lower Zab, the Zagros and Elburz Mountains, the Caspian Sea and the Mediterranean while looking at Map 20.1. Erase and redraw as necessary.

4. When you are pleased with your map, lay it over the original. Erase and redraw any lines which are more than 1/4 inch off the original.

5. Remove your map. Study carefully the locations of the Persian Gulf, the Euphrates, the Tigris, the unnamed right-hand branch of the Tigris, the Lower Zab, the Zagros and Elburz Mountains, and the cities of Kish, Ur, Susa, Assur, Babylon, Aleppo, and Nineveh. When you are familiar with them, close the book. Using your regular pencil, label the Persian Gulf, the Euphrates, the Tigris, the Lower Zab, and the Zagros and Elburz Mountains. Mark and label the cities of Kish, Ur, Susa, Assur, Babylon, Aleppo, and Nineveh. Check your map against the original. Correct any misplaced labels.

6. While looking at Map 22.1, draw a light line to show the borders of Hammurabi's empire. Erase and correct as necessary. When you are satisfied, lay your map back over the original. Erase and redraw any lines which are more than 1/4 inch off the original.

7. Label the Kingdom of Hammurabi.

CHAPTER TWENTY-THREE: THE HYKSOS SEIZE EGYPT

You MAY USE your text when answering the questions in sections I and II.

Section I: Who, What, Where

Write a one or two-sentence answer explaining the significance of each item listed below.

Apepi I
Avaris
Hyksos/Hikau-khoswet
Queen Sobeknefru
Sequenere
Sheshi

Section II: Comprehension

Write a two/three sentence answer to each of the following questions.

1. What was the state of Egypt's Nubian holdings at the beginning of the Thirteenth Dynasty? What was it like in the north of Egypt, near the Delta, when the new dynasty began?

2. Why is the Thirteenth Dynasty considered by most historians to be the end of the Middle Kingdom?

3. Why did Manetho make such a violent account out of the Hyksos' takeover of Egypt? How do we know that most of the Hyksos had actually been in Egypt for awhile?

4. What were the Hyksos people like? How did they rule over the Egyptian people?

5. How was it that the Fifteenth, Sixteenth, and Seventeenth Dynasties of Egypt could exist simultaneously?

6. What happened to Sequenere when he went to fight against the Hyksos? What was the result of this battle?

Section III: Critical Thinking

You MAY USE your text to answer this question.

We have read about some gruesome fights in *The History of the Ancient World,* but Sequenere's severe mutilation might be the most grisly yet. While we can understand the tension between Avaris and Thebes, it seems Apepi I's letter to Sequenere did not foreshadow such a violent battle. In this critical thinking question, write out Apepi I's letter to Sequenere. Then, pull apart the language of the letter and explain how Apepi I's words fueled Sequenere's will to fight against the Hyksos.

Section IV: Map Exercise: Royal Cities of Egypt

1. Using a black pencil, trace the rectangular outline of the frame for Map 23.1: Three Simultaneous Dynasties.

2. Using a black pencil, trace the Red Sea, the Nile River, the Mediterranean Sea, the Euphrates, and the Tigris. Keep the orientation of the original map (with the south at the top). Repeat until the contours are familiar.

3. Trace the rectangular outline of the frame in black. Remove your tracing paper from the original. Using a regular pencil with an eraser, draw the Red Sea, the Nile River, the Mediterranean Sea, the Euphrates, and the Tigris within the map frame while looking at Map 23.1. Erase and redraw as necessary.

4. When you are pleased with your map, lay it over the original. Erase and redraw any lines which are more than 1/4 inch off the original.

5. Remove your map. Study the locations of the First Cataract, the Second Cataract, Nubia, Libya, and the cities of Hierakonpolis, Thebes, Memphis, Avaris, and Buto on the original. When you are familiar with them, close the book. Using your regular pencil, mark and label the First Cataract and the Second Cataract. Label Nubia, Libya, the Red Sea, the Nile, and the Mediterranean. Mark and label the cities of Hierakonpolis, Thebes, Memphis, Avaris, and Buto. Then, check your map against the original. If the markings or labels are more than 1/8 inch off, erase and re-mark while looking at the original.

CHAPTER TWENTY-FOUR: KING MINOS OF CRETE

You MAY USE your text when answering the questions in sections I and II.

Section I: Who, What, Where

Write a one or two-sentence answer explaining the significance of each item listed below.

Akrotiri
Daedalus
Fresco
Minotaur/Asterius
Knossos
The Labyrinth
Minos
Pasiphae
Poseidon
Thera

Section II: Comprehension

Write a two/three sentence answer to each of the following questions.

1. How do we know that the people of Crete traded with civilizations outside of the Greek islands?

2. Why was Poseidon displeased with Minos? How did Poseidon punish Minos? What was the result of Minos's punishment?

3. How does the story of the Minotaur, excerpted below, reflect the ongoing international sea trade carried on by the Minoan people?

   Minos fed [the Minotaur] on human flesh; after a battle with the inhabitants of the Greek mainland, he ordered them to send seven young men and seven young women each year to be eaten by the Minotaur.

4. Where do we see traces of the Minoan culture in the epic of Gilgamesh? How might this exchange of stories have happened?

5. Why was a mastery of the waterways around Knossos necessary for Minos to build and maintain his empire?

6. Explain this statement: As piracy decreased in the sea around Crete, the wealth of the Minoan people increased.

7. What is the Minoan bull-dance? In what way is the story of Minos and the Minotaur a reflection of the bull-dance?

8. Describe the possible environmental fallout after the volcano at Thera erupted. Why did the Minoans interpret this as an angry message from Poseidon?

Section III: Critical Thinking

You may NOT use your text to answer this question.

A myth often explains a phenomenon of nature, a cultural practice, or a cultural rite. In this chapter, we read the myth of Minos and the Minotaur. While this story was written hundreds of years after Minos occupied the Second Palace, we find telling details in the legend about life on the Ancient Greek Islands. First, write a short summary of the story of Minos and the Minotaur. Next, explain how this myth describes a phenomenon of nature that occurred during Minoan life. Finally, answer the question, "How does the story of Minos and the Minotaur tell us about a Minoan cultural practice/rite?"

Section IV: Map Exercise: The Greek Islands

1. Using a black pencil, trace the rectangular outline of the frame for Map 23.1: The Minoans.

2. Using a black pencil, trace the coastlines of Asia Minor and the Greek peninsula.

3. With the same pencil, carefully trace all of the islands. Because this map is so complex, you will only do this once.

Chapter Twenty-Five: The Harappan Disintegration

You MAY USE your text when answering the questions in sections I and II.

Section I: Who, What, Where

Write a one or two-sentence answer explaining the significance of each item listed below.

Jhukar culture

Arya

Section II: Comprehension

Write a two/three sentence answer to each of the following questions.

1. What archaeological evidence suggests an unexpected natural disaster struck Mohenjo-Daro between 1750 and 1700?

2. Explain hydrologist R. L. Raikes's theory that a silt dam could have been a cause for the destruction of the Harappan cities. What natural evidence does Raikes have to support his point?

3. What story do the archaeological findings from the Harappan ruins tell us about the agricultural plight of the Harappan people?

4. How do we know that the Harappans didn't reoccupy their cities?

5. Why did the nomads from the north call the first place they settled in India the "Land of the Seven Rivers?"

6. What skill did the nomadic invaders of India have that allowed them to survive and defeat their enemies?

7. While the term *arya* is sometimes translated as "pure," how do we know that the early Aryan civilization was anything but pure?

Section III: Critical Thinking

You may NOT use your text to answer this question.

In this chapter we see a sophisticated civilization pitted against nomadic adaptability. Prior to our reading in "The Harappan Disintegration," it seems the peoples of the ancient world championed settled living. Using examples from this chapter, play devil's advocate and argue for the advantages of a nomadic, uncivilized lifestyle.

Section IV: Map Exercise: Northern India

1. Using a black pencil, trace the rectangular outline of the frame for Map 25.1: Newcomers to India.

2. Using a black pencil, trace the coastline of India, the northern mountain ranges, the Indus, the unnamed river on the right-hand side of the map (the Ganga), the Narmada River (unlabelled), and the mountains around the Narmada. Repeat until the contours are familiar. (Remember that you may draw simple peaks to represent the mountains.)

3. Trace the rectangular outline of the frame in black. Remove your tracing paper from the original. Using a regular pencil with an eraser, draw the coastline of India, the three rivers, and all mountains while looking at Map 25.1. Erase and redraw as necessary.

4. When you are pleased with your map, lay it over the original. Erase and redraw any lines which are more than 1/4 inch off the original

5. Remove your map from the original. Looking back at Map 25.1, study carefully the location of the Indus River, the Punjab, the Hindu Kush, the Arabian Sea, and the cities of Mohenjo-Daro and Harappa. When you are familiar with them, close the book. Using your regular pencil, label the Indus River, the Punjab, the Hindu Kush, and the Arabian Sea. Mark and label the cities of Mohenjo-Daro and Harappa. Check your map against the original. If your labels are misplaced, erase and re-mark while looking at the original.

CHAPTER TWENTY-SIX: THE RISE OF THE HITTITES

You MAY USE your text when answering the questions in sections I and II.

Section I: Who, What, Where

Write a one or two-sentence answer explaining the significance of each item listed below.

Anittas
Ht & Hatti
Hattusilis I
Mursilis
Pimpira
Purushkhanda

Section II: Comprehension

Write a two/three sentence answer to each of the following questions.

1. How was the Mesopotamian plain divided in the years immediately following Samsuiluna's death?

2. In what way did trade with Assur help advance Hittite culture?

3. Describe the kingdom Anittas inherited from his father, and his war campaign against Hattusas and Purushkhanda.

4. Why did Hattusilis I risk moving the Hittite capital from Kussara to Hattusas?

5. What happened when Mursilis and his troops reached Babylon? Why didn't Mursilis add Babylon to his empire? Why did Mursilis sack Babylon?

Section III: Critical Thinking

You may NOT use your text to answer this question.

There was something rotten in the state of Hattusas around 1500 BC. We learn at the end of the chapter that "the dynastic succession of the Hittites had settled into a game of hunt-the-king."

- What happened on Hattusilis I's deathbed? In your answer, make sure to include all the people Hattusilis scorned, and list who ended up on the throne.

- How did the transfer of power from Hattusilis I to Mursilis foreshadow the coming turbulence of the Hittite throne?

- What does the phrase "hunt-the-king" mean? Give an example from the chapter to support your answer.

Section IV: Map Exercise: The Hittites

1. Using a black pencil, trace the rectangular outline of the frame for Map 26.1: The Hittite Homeland.

2. Using a black pencil, trace all seas and rivers. You do not need to trace the small lakes on the map. Repeat until the contours are familiar.

3. Trace the rectangular outline of the frame in black. Remove your tracing paper from the original. Using a regular pencil with an eraser, draw all rivers and seas while looking at Map 26.1. Erase and redraw as necessary.

4. When you are pleased with your map, lay it over the original. Erase and redraw any lines which are more than 1/4 inch off the original.

5. Remove your map. Study carefully the locations of the Euphrates, the Tigris, the Halys, Asia Minor, the Mediterranean, Black, and Caspian Seas, and the cities of Babylon, Assur, Mari, Aleppo and Hattusas. When you are familiar with them, close the book. Using your regular pencil, label the Euphrates, the Tigris, the Halys, Asia Minor, and the Mediterranean, Black, and Caspian Seas. Mark and label and the cities of Babylon, Assur, Mari, Aleppo and Hattusas. Check your map against the original. Correct any misplaced labels.

CHAPTER TWENTY-SEVEN: AHMOSE EXPELS THE HYKSOS

You MAY USE your text when answering the questions in sections I and II.

Section I: Who, What, Where

Write a one or two-sentence answer explaining the significance of each item listed below.

Ahmose

Kahmose

Queen Ahhotep

Sharuhen

Section II: Comprehension

Write a two/three sentence answer to each of the following questions.

1. Why did Kahmose see Nubia as an obstacle in the path of his campaign against the Hyksos?

2. How did Kahmose plan to intercept communication between the northern Hyksos and the southern Nubians? Did his plan work?

3. After marching on Thebes, why did Kahmose time his arrival back in Thebes with the Nile flood?

4. How did Queen Ahhotep help her son Ahmose reunify Egypt? How did Ahmose use the military head start given to him by his mother?

5. Why did Ahmose's general say that he "brought away a hand" from Avaris?

6. Describe the archaeological and historical evidence that supports the theory that the Hyksos people fled from Avaris en masse.

7. Why did Manetho name Ahmose the first king of the Eighteenth Dynasty?

8. What cultural changes marked the New Kingdom of Egypt?

Section III: Critical Thinking

You may NOT use your text to answer this question.

The major point of this chapter is clear: the Hyksos were kicked out of Egypt. The events leading up to the flight of the Hyksos remain somewhat unclear. Write a paragraph that explains how Manetho's account of Ahmose's attack of Avaris differs from the Egyptian version. In your answer, make sure to explain why each version of the story is possible.

Section IV: Map Exercise: The Nile River

1. Using a black pencil, trace the rectangular outline of the frame for Map 27.1: Ahmose Against the Hyksos.

2. Using a black pencil, trace the Red Sea, the Nile River, and the Mediterranean Sea, including the large island in the lower left-hand corner. Also trace the unnamed river and small sea on the left side of the map. Repeat until the contours are familiar.

3. Trace the rectangular outline of the frame in black. Remove your tracing paper from the original. Close the book. Using a regular pencil with an eraser, draw the Red Sea, the Nile River, the Mediterranean Sea, the large island in the Mediterranean, and the river and small sea on the left side of the map from memory. If you can't remember the placement of any of the elements, open the book, look again at the map, and then close it and draw.

4. When you are pleased with your map, lay it over the original. Erase and redraw any lines which are more than 1/4 inch off the original.

CHAPTER TWENTY-EIGHT: USURPATION AND REVENGE

You MAY USE your text when answering the questions in sections I and II.

Section I: Who, What, Where

Write a one or two-sentence answer explaining the significance of each item listed below.

Amenhotep I
Hatshepsut
Tuthmosis I
Tuthmosis II
Tuthmosis III
Senenmut

Section II: Comprehension

Write a two/three sentence answer to each of the following questions.

1. What circumstances made Tuthmosis I build a hidden tomb instead of a conspicuous pyramid for his burial place? Though it was underground, how was the tomb still like a pyramid? How was it different?

2. Why did Tuthmosis I appoint his son by his lesser wife heir to the Egyptian throne? What did Tuthmosis I do to strengthen his son's dynastic position?

3. What did Hatshepsut have carved on the mortuary temple she had built in honor of the sun-god Amun? What was the meaning of the carving?

4. To what lengths did Hatshepsut go, in addition to claiming she was Amun's daughter, in order to prove she was the true ruler of Egypt?

5. While Hatshepsut did not depose Tuthmosis III, she did keep him far away from her throne. What was Tuthmosis III doing while Hatshepsut reigned?

6. How did Tuthmosis III get rid of the obelisks Hatshepsut built in honor of Amun? Why did he deal with them in this way?

7. Why didn't the Egyptian army attack Kadesh? How did they eventually win the fight versus the city?

8. What made the Egyptian invasion of Joppa unique?

Section III: Critical Thinking

You may NOT use your text to answer this question.

Hatshepsut and Tuthmosis III had very different ruling styles. In fact, the chapter states that Tuthmosis III was the "anti-Hatshepsut." Write a paragraph contrasting the way Hatshepsut showed her strength as ruler of Egypt versus the way Tuthmosis III proved he was a great pharaoh. Explain why Hatshepsut and Tuthmosis III may have chosen these different styles of leadership.

Chapter Twenty-Nine: The Three-Way Contest

You MAY USE your text when answering the questions in sections I and II.

Section I: Who, What, Where

Write a one or two-sentence answer explaining the significance of each item listed below.

Hurrians
Maryannu
Mitanni
Parattarna
Saustatar
Telepinus
Washukkanni

Section II: Comprehension

Write a two/three sentence answer to each of the following questions.

1. Who ruled Assur before the Mitanni claimed the city? How did Assur fit into the Mitanni kingdom?

2. How did the political unrest of the Hittite people affect the nation's ability to protect itself?

3. What was the Edict of Telepinus?

4. Why was Tuthmosis III able to take Carchemish from the Hittites so easily?

5. Describe Saustatar's invasion of Hittite territory.

6. How did Saustatar help the Western Semitic cities revolt against the Egyptians after Tuthmosis III's death?

7. Why did Amenhotep II make a treaty with Saustatar? How did the alliance between Egypt and the Mitanni benefit both kingdoms?

Section III: Critical Thinking

You may NOT use your text to answer this question.

How do outside forces galvanize people or cities to become part of an empire? Write two paragraphs, one related to the Hurrians, and one about Assur, that describe how outside forces worked to put these people within the boundaries of the Mitanni kingdom.

CHAPTER THIRTY: THE SHIFTING CAPITALS OF THE SHANG

You MAY USE your text when answering the questions in sections I and II.

Section I: Who, What, Where

Write a one or two-sentence answer explaining the significance of each item listed below.

P'an Keng
Po
T'ai Jia
Yi Yin

Section II: Comprehension

Write a two/three sentence answer to each of the following questions.

1. Where was the capital city of the Shang dynasty between 1766 and 1400?

2. What makes Yi Yin's longevity in the house of Shang seem odd?

3. Why couldn't Yi Yin be considered for the Chinese throne?

4. How did Yi Yin use T'ai Jia's enthronement to his advantage?

5. What was the result of Yi Yin's declaration that T'ai Jia be sent to a detention center out of town?

6. Why might the capital have moved so many times during the Shang dynasty's rule?

Section III: Critical Thinking

You MAY USE your text to answer this question.

A strong king finds ways to strengthen his country, even in the worst of times. While the Hittites were tearing their kingdom apart, fighting over the seat of power, the rulers of the Shang dynasty used turmoil to their advantage. This is particularly true in the case of P'an Keng. Using the passage on page 222 that recounts P'an Keng's response to his suspicious courtiers, to support your response, write a paragraph that answers the following questions:

- Why did P'an Keng move the capital city to Yin?

- What did the oracle tell P'an Keng?

- How was P'an Keng able to use the history of Shang's moving capital to his advantage?

- What argument did P'an Keng make against having a fixed capital city?

Section IV: Map Exercise: The Yellow River

1. Using a black pencil, trace the rectangular outline of the frame for Map 30.1: The Shang Capitals.

2. Using a black pencil, trace the coastline of China and the course of the Yellow River, including the Lo branch of the Yellow (unlabelled). You do not need to trace the mouth of the Yangtze. Repeat until the contours are familiar.

3. Trace the rectangular outline of the frame in black. Remove your tracing paper from the original. Close the book. Using a regular pencil with an eraser, draw the coastline of China, the Yellow River, and the unlabelled Lo branch from memory. If you can't remember the placement of any of the elements, open the book, look again at the map, and then close it and draw.

4. When you are pleased with your map, lay it over the original. Erase and redraw any lines which are more than 1/4 inch off the original.

CHAPTER THIRTY-ONE: THE MYCENAEANS OF GREECE

You MAY USE your text when answering the questions in sections I and II.

Section I: Who, What, Where

Write a one or two-sentence answer explaining the significance of each item listed below.

Aegeus
Ariadne
Linear A/B
Theseus

Section II: Comprehension

Write a two/three sentence answer to each of the following questions.

1. What were the four major cities on the Greek peninsula around 1600? Why did each of these cities have its own royal palace?

2. Why do historians call the people of ancient Thebes, Pylos, and Athens "Mycenaeans?"

3. Why did Aegeus give his son both a black and white flag when he sailed to Knossos?

4. How did Theseus find his way out of the Labyrinth?

5. How did the body of water near Athens come to be called the "Aegean Sea?"

6. What is the importance of a Mycenaean cup found buried with an official of Tuthmosis III?

7. Why did trade with Egypt exacerbate the division between Cretans and the Greeks?

8. How did the eruption of Thera affect the cultural relationship between Crete and Greece?

Section III: Critical Thinking

You may NOT use your text to answer this question.

Exchange, both cultural and commercial, was rampant between the Minoans of Crete and the Mycenaeans of Greece. However, after the eruption of Thera, the cultural flow between the two kingdoms went primarily one way: the Mycenaeans had a stronger influence on the Minoans. How might the environment and location of Crete have influenced this cultural shift?

Section IV: Map Exercise: The Greek Peninsula

1. Using a black pencil, trace the rectangular outline of the frame for Map 31.1: The Mycenaeans.

2. Using a black pencil, trace the coastlines of the Greek peninsula and Asia Minor, all the way uto the Black Sea. Also trace Crete. You do not have to trace any other islands--the goal here is to become familiar with the coastline. Repeat until the contours are familiar.

3. Trace the rectangular outline of the frame in black. Remove your tracing paper from the original. Using a regular pencil with an eraser, draw the Greek peninsula, Crete, and Asia Minor while looking at Map 31.1. Erase and redraw as necessary.

4. When you are pleased with your map, lay it over the original. Erase and redraw any lines which are more than 1/4 inch off the original.

5. Remove your map. Study carefully the locations of the Aegean Sea, Crete, and the cities of Athens, Thebes, Mycenae, Knossos, and Troy. When you are familiar with them, close the book. Using your regular pencil, label the Aegean Sea and Crete. Mark and label Athens, Thebes, Mycenae, Knossos, and Troy. Check your map against the original. Correct any misplaced labels.

CHAPTER THIRTY-TWO: STRUGGLE OF THE GODS

You MAY USE your text when answering the questions in sections I and II.

Section I: Who, What, Where

Write a one or two-sentence answer explaining the significance of each item listed below.

Akhen-aten
Akhet-aten
Amenhotep III
Amenhotep IV
Aten
Suppululiuma

Section II: Comprehension

Write a two/three sentence answer to each of the following questions.

1. How was Amenhotep III's reign like Hatshepsut's? Use at least two examples from the chapter to support your answer.

2. List all the ways Tushratta of Mitanni and Amenhotep III of Egypt were related. How did these entanglements benefit Egypt?

3. Why wasn't Assur supposed to negotiate with foreign powers? How was Amenhotep's business with Assur a violation of his treaty with the Mitanni?

4. What were the arrangements of the Egyptian and Babylonian alliance?

5. Why was it politically advantageous for AmenhoteIII to align himself with the sun-god, Ra?

6. How did Amenhotep IV choose to outshine the power of his father? What made Amenhotep IV's worship of the sun different than the traditional worship of Ra?

7. Why did Abraham's descendants, the Hebrews, settle in Egypt?

8. How did the Egyptian pharaoh treat the Hebrew people, according to the book of Exodus?

9. Though Sargon lived 1,000 years before Moses, how did the ancient cupbearer help the Hebrew child?

10. What kind of plagues descended on Egypt during the Exodus of the Hebrews? How did these plagues affect the power of the Egyptian gods?

Section III: Critical Thinking

You may NOT use your text to answer this question.

Akhenaten's worship of Aten was like Moses's worship of YHWH in one way only: both religions were based on monotheism. While both Abraham and Moses felt the call of God, Akhenaten's move to follow Aten seems more political. Write a short paragraph arguing how we might understand Amenhotep IV's conversion to monotheism as a play for power rather than a true spiritual calling.

CHAPTER THIRTY-THREE: WARS AND MARRIAGES

You MAY USE your text when answering the questions in sections I and II.

Section I: Who, What, Where

Write a one or two-sentence answer explaining the significance of each item listed below.

Ankhesenamun
Assur-uballit
Ay
Burnaburiash I
Horemheb
Karaindash
Tushratta
Tutankhaten/Tutankh-Amun

Section II: Comprehension

Write a two/three sentence answer to each of the following questions.

1. What were the signs of Egypt's gradual backing away from the Mitanni alliance?

2. Why did Akhenaten choose to honor his alliance with the Hittites over his alliance with the Mitanni?

3. How did Assur-uballit take advantage of the Hittite attack on the Mitanni?

4. What happened to the Mitanni kingdom after the fall of Washukkanni? Where did the Hurrians go?

5. How did the plague affect the Egyptian royal family?

6. Why did the Egyptians dismiss Aten's power? What happened to Aten, the god, and Aten, the city, when Tutankhamun came into power?

7. Why did Ankhesenamun ask Suppiluliuma of the Hittites to send one of his sons down to Egypt?

8. How did Horemheb end up as the Egyptian pharaoh? How did he get past Ankhesenamun, the Hittite prince, and Ay on his way to the throne?

Section III: Critical Thinking

You may NOT use your text to answer this question.

While marriage was a typical way for a king to ally himself with a powerful nation, a marital bond between kingdoms did not grant absolute peace. Burnaburiash I was able to make a tenuous peace with Assur-uballit by marrying his daughter to a Babylonian prince. Explain how this alliance fell apart when Burnaburiash died, and how, if not for Assur-uballit, the Babylonian government may have fallen apart.

Section IV: Map Exercise: The Middle Kingdom of Assyria

1. Using a black pencil, trace the rectangular outline of the frame for Map 33.1: Assyria's Middle Kingdom.

2. Using a black pencil, trace all seas, rivers and mountains. You do not need to trace lakes or small islands, but do trace the large island of Cyprus (unlabelled, in the right hand corner of the Mediterranean Sea) and the eastern end of Crete (unlabelled, on the left margin of the map). Repeat until the contours are familiar.

3. Trace the rectangular outline of the frame in black. Remove your tracing paper from the original. Using a regular pencil with an eraser, draw the seas, rivers and mountains, as well as Cyprus and Crete, while looking at Map 33.1. Erase and redraw as necessary.

4. When you are pleased with your map, lay it over the original. Erase and redraw any lines which are more than 1/4 inch off the original.

5. Remove your map. Study carefully the locations of the Persian Gulf, the Euphrates, the Tigris, the Halys, the Caspian Sea, the Mediterranean, the Zagros Mountains, the Taurus Mountains, and the cities of Babylon, Assur, Nineveh, Aleppo, and Hattusas. When you are familiar with them, close the book. Using your regular pencil, label the Persian Gulf, the Euphrates, the Tigris, the Halys, the Caspian Sea, the Mediterranean, the Zagros Mountains, and the Taurus Mountains. Mark and label the cities of Babylon, Assur, Nineveh, Aleppo, and Hattusas. Check your map against the original. Correct any misplaced labels.

6. While looking at Map 33.1, draw a light line to show the borders of the Middle Kingdom of Assyria. Erase and correct as necessary. When you are satisfied, lay your map back over the original. Erase and redraw any lines which are more than 1/4 inch off the original.

7. Label the Middle Kingdom of Assyria.

CHAPTER THIRTY-FOUR:
THE GREATEST BATTLE IN VERY ANCIENT TIMES

You MAY USE your text when answering the questions in sections I and II.

Section I: Who, What, Where

Write a one or two-sentence answer explaining the significance of each item listed below.

Adad-nirari
Battle of Kadesh
Hattusilis III
Muwatalli
Rameses I
Rameses II
Seti
Shalmaneser I

Section II: Comprehension

Write a two/three sentence answer to each of the following questions.

1. Why did Rameses II want to fight the Hittites and win back Kadesh for the Egyptian kingdom?

2. How did Rameses II organize his army of twenty thousand men?

3. How did Muwatalli trick Rameses II into attacking Kadesh?

4. Describe Muwatalli's first attack on the invading Egyptian troops.

5. What strategic military move of Rameses II helped the Egyptian army recover after the attack on the men of Ra?

6. How did the Battle of Kadesh end? Who claimed victory?

7. Why can we assume, at the time of Muwatalli, that the Hittites had a treaty with Babylon?

8. How did Hattusilis III end up on the Hittite throne?

9. Why did Rameses II agree to a peaceful alliance with Hattusilis III, rather than taking over the Hittite empire?

Section III: Critical Thinking

You may NOT use your text to answer this question.

We've all heard the adage, "your reputation precedes you." In this chapter we learn that Egypt had become an empire that depended on reputation as much as actual strength to keep its position as a world leader. Similarly, Hattusilis III needed to fix his reputation in order to keep his position as King of the Hittites. Write two paragraphs below describing how Rameses II of Egypt and Hattusilis III of the Hittites manipulated their public perception in order to stay powerful.

CHAPTER THIRTY-FIVE: THE BATTLE FOR TROY

You MAY USE your text when answering the questions in sections I and II.

Section I: Who, What, Where

Write a one or two-sentence answer explaining the significance of each item listed below.

Achilles
Agamemnon
Helen
Menelaus
Nestor
Paris
Priam

Section II: Comprehension

Write a two/three sentence answer to each of the following questions.

1. What was the city of Troy like in its seventh incarnation?

2. What thwarted Agamemnon's attack on Troy? How long did the Greeks attack Troy without success?

3. Why is Homer's inclusion of historical detail in the Iliad, like the king of Pylos's use of the cup topped with two doves, important for our understanding of the real-life tensions that fueled the writing of the poem?

4. What were the Mycenaean cities of Mycenae, Thebes, Athens and Pylos like in 1260 BC?

5. How may a captive princess have actually sparked a battle between the Mycenaean cities and the Trojans?

6. How does historian Robert Graves explain the war between the Mycenaeans and the Greeks?

7. Why, according to Thucydides, did the siege against Troy by the Mycenaeans last for so many years?

8. Why is the Mycenaean victory over Troy tinged with sadness? Use pieces of the excerpt from

the Odyssey in your answer.

Section III: Critical Thinking

You MAY USE your text to answer this question.

The Trojan Horse is perhaps one of the most famous ruses in history. Using the excerpt from the poem the Aeneid, by Virgil, describe in detail how the Greeks used a wooden horse to finally break through Troy's walls and destroy the city.

Chapter Thirty-Six:
The First Historical King of China

You MAY USE your text when answering the questions in sections I and II.

Section I: Who, What, Where

Write a one or two-sentence answer explaining the significance of each item listed below.

I ching
Ideogram
Composite Ideogram
Fu Yueh
Shih ching
Shu ching
Wu Ting

Section II: Comprehension

Write a two/three sentence answer to each of the following questions.

1. In what way did the casting of bronze showcase the power of the Shang king?

2. Why are the bronze products of the Shang called "one of humankind's great artistic achievements"? Describe some of the great bronze works of ancient China.

3. What do the inscriptions, names and signs engraved on some of the Shang's bronze pieces tell us about Shang culture?

4. How was the development of Chinese writing different from the development of writing in other parts of the ancient world?

5. Describe the process of divination used by Shang priests to answer the questions of Chinese men and women.

6. What do the *I ching* and the *Shih ching* tell us about Wu Ting? How do these descriptions conflict with the representation of Wu Ting as spiritual leader?

7. What do the burial grounds of the Shang kings tell us about the rising power of Chinese rulers?

Section III: Critical Thinking

You may NOT use your text to answer this question.

During the Shang Dynasty, the king was known to be a spiritual leader, but the *Shih ching* suggests he was also a fierce warrior. Write two or three paragraphs explaining how the Chinese king could be both holy leader and strict overlord. In your answer, make sure to explain why Wu Ting needed Fu Yueh to rule. Also, make clear the connection between a king and his noblemen, and the large number of human sacrifices in the royal burial pits.

Chapter Thirty-Seven: The Rig Veda

You MAY USE your text when answering the questions in sections I and II.

Section I: Who, What, Where

Write a one or two-sentence answer explaining the significance of each item listed below.

Grama

Mandala

Rig Veda

Section II: Comprehension

Write a two/three sentence answer to each of the following questions.

1. How does the Sanskrit word "grama" reflect the changes in the culture of the arya people once they settled along the Indus River?

2. What place did the priests of the arya hold in society?

3. To what was the Rig Veda almost exclusively devoted?

4. What type of gods did the Indians worship?

5. What can we learn from the presence of Indra, Varuna, and Mitra as witnesses in a treaty between the Mitanni king and the Hittite empire-builder Suppiluliuma?

6. How does the Rig Veda help us to understand the military structure of the arya?

7. What does the Rig Veda tells us about internal struggles among the arya?

Section III: Critical Thinking

You MAY USE your text to answer this question.

The text tells us that the arya worshiped nature-gods, as was common to people who lived in harsh environments and along fierce rivers. The nature-gods reflect the anxieties the arya had about their natural environment. Below, list the name of each god mentioned in the text and the god's duty. Then, use the text to explain how Agni, Parjanya and Indra were manifestations of the arya's worries about their livelihood.

CHAPTER THIRTY-EIGHT: THE WHEEL TURNS AGAIN

You MAY USE your text when answering the questions in sections I and II.

Section I: Who, What, Where

Write a one or two-sentence answer explaining the significance of each item listed below.

Marduk

Merneptah

Tudhaliya

Tukulti-Ninurta

Section II: Comprehension

Write a two/three sentence answer to each of the following questions.

1. How did the drought rattle Hittite security?

2. Why was Tudhaliya worried about his position as king of the Hittites?

3. What did Tudhaliya do to prove his power as rightful king of the Hittites?

4. What was inherently wrong with Tudhaliya's massive building program?

5. How did Tukulti-Ninurta know that Tudhaliya was unsure that the Hittites could beat the Assyrians at Erbila?

6. What was the result of the Hittite-Assyrian battle at Erbila?

7. In what ways were Babylon and Assyria alike?

8. How did Tukulti-Ninurta react to Babylonian king Kashtiliash IV's attempted conquest of disputed land between the Assyrian and Babylonian borders?

9. Why might Tukulti-Ninurta have wanted to barricade himself in the little city he built, away from the people of Assur? Was the walled mini-city able to keep Tukulti-Ninurta safe?

Section III: Critical Thinking

You MAY USE your text to answer this question.

In this chapter, we see very drastic and important changes happening across the ancient world. How has the turning wheel of fortune treated these great empires? Using your text for reference, write a short paragraph for each empire, describing how the empire fared during this tumultuous time. Each paragraph should begin, "As the wheel of fortune turned…"

Section IV: Map Exercise: The Expansion of Assyria

1. Using a black pencil, trace the rectangular outline of the frame for Map 38.1: Tukulti-Ninurta's Assyria.

2. Using a black pencil, trace all seas, rivers and mountains. You do not need to trace lakes or small islands, but do trace the large island of Cyprus (unlabelled, in the right hand corner of the Mediterranean Sea) and the eastern end of Crete (unlabelled, on the left margin of the map). Repeat until the contours are familiar.

3. Trace the rectangular outline of the frame in black. Remove your tracing paper from the original. Using a regular pencil with an eraser, draw the seas, rivers and mountains, as well as Cyprus and Crete, while looking at Map 38.1. Erase and redraw as necessary.

4. When you are pleased with your map, lay it over the original. Erase and redraw any lines which are more than 1/4 inch off the original.

5. Remove your map. Study carefully the locations of the Persian Gulf, the Euphrates, the Tigris, the Halys, the Caspian Sea, the Mediterranean, the Sea of Galilee, the Zagros Mountains, the Taurus Mountains, and the cities of Babylon, Assur, Nineveh, Aleppo, Carchemish, and Hattusas. When you are familiar with them, close the book. Using your regular pencil, label the Persian Gulf, the Euphrates, the Tigris, the Halys, the Caspian Sea, the Mediterranean, the Sea of Galilee, the Zagros Mountains, and the Taurus Mountains. Mark and label the cities of Babylon, Assur, Nineveh, Aleppo, Carchemish, and Hattusas. Check your map against the original. Correct any misplaced labels.

6. While looking at Map 38.1, draw a light line to show the borders of Assyria. Erase and correct as necessary. When you are satisfied, lay your map back over the original. Erase and redraw any lines which are more than 1/4 inch off the original.

7. Label Assyria.

CHAPTER THIRTY-NINE: THE END OF THE NEW KINGDOM

You MAY USE your text when answering the questions in sections I and II.

Section I: Who, What, Where

Write a one or two-sentence answer explaining the significance of each item listed below.

Herihor
Rameses III
Setnakhte
Sea People
Wenamun

Section II: Comprehension

Write a two/three sentence answer to each of the following questions.

1. According to the papyrus from the reign of Setnakhte's grandson, how did Setnakhte right the mess of the Nineteenth Dynasty?

2. Why did Rameses III have the Libyan tribes that wandered into Egypt from the western desert slaughtered or enslaved?

3. Describe the "general seething mess" of the Western Semitic lands that threatened Rameses III's Egypt.

4. Why was Egypt a popular destination for wanderers during the time of Rameses III?

5. Who were the Weshesh, the Shekelesh and the Peleset? Why were these groups of people particularly threatening to Rameses III?

6. Why do historians think the Peleset were responsible for arming the force of allied tribes that invaded Egypt?

7. What is the meaning of the carvings of piles of hands in Rameses III's mortuary temple?

8. How did Rameses III configure his army to beat the Sea People?

9. Why did one of Rameses III's lesser wives want to assassinate the king and his appointed successor? What was the result of her assassination plot?

10. How were the priests of Amun able to prosper while the rest of Egypt slowly lost its territories and riches?

11. How did Horemheb's appointment of military officers to the priesthood – done in order to assure loyalty to the throne – eventually backfire?

12. What caused the civil war that started Egypt's Third Intermediate Period? Who claimed the north? Who claimed the south?

Section III: Critical Thinking

You may NOT use your text to answer this question.

This chapter covers the slow decline of the New Kingdom of Egypt. While Egypt's military power had been weakening for a long time, its reputation as a world power quickly plummeted after the death of Rameses III. Using the excerpted passage below, write a paragraph explaining how Wenamun's story reflects the fall of both Egypt's military power and reputation.

A court official named Wenamun, attempting to travel up the coast in order to negotiate a good price for cedar logs from Byblos, was set upon and robbed of his money; the thieves had no fear of Egyptian reprisals. Wenamun finally did reach Byblos, but his mission failed. The king of Byblos was not inclined to accept Egyptian credit, which was no longer any good up north. "I am not your servant," he remarked to Wenamun, "nor am I the servant of the one who sent you. The logs stay here on the shore." (279)

Chapter Forty: The Dark Age of Greece

You MAY USE your text when answering the questions in sections I and II.

Section I: Who, What, Where

Write a one or two-sentence answer explaining the significance of each item listed below.

Apollo Sminthian
Bubonic Plague
Dorians
Peloponnese

Section II: Comprehension

Write a two/three sentence answer to each of the following questions.

1. What was happening on the Greek peninsula around 1200 BC? How did Sparta, Mycenae and Pylos fare?

2. Explain how Codrus, king of Athens, sacrificed himself in order to save Athens from Dorian invasion.

3. What is the significance of the ninety year gap between the burning of Pylos and Mycenae?

4. How could a ship carrying only healthy people on board spread bubonic plague?

5. Why did the plague seem to follow famine?

6. Describe the circumstances that led the Egyptians to hire troops from the Aegean to fight *for* Egypt *against* the Libyans of the western desert.

7. While we don't know much about Dorian culture, what <u>do</u> we know about their life on the peninsula after the decay of the Mycenaean cities?

8. When is the term "dark age" generally used?

Section III: Critical Thinking

You may NOT use your text to answer this question.

After the war with Troy, the Mycenaean cities began to slowly decay. Though Thucydides and Herodotus blame the Dorian invasion, we know this is not accurate. If the Dorians didn't kick the Athenians out of their city, and Sparta was already empty when the invaders set fire to it, what is to blame for the decline of the Mycenaean cities?

In this critical thinking section, write three short paragraphs explaining how each of the conditions listed below played a part in the evacuation of the peninsula by the Mycenaean people.

- *WAR*

- *DROUGHT*

- *PLAGUE*

Section IV: Map Exercise: Greece

1. Using a black pencil, trace the rectangular outline of the frame for Map 40.1: Dorian Greece.

2. Using a black pencil, trace the coastline of the Greek peninsula, along with all islands. Repeat until the contours are familiar.

3. Trace the rectangular outline of the frame in black. Remove your tracing paper from the original. Using a regular pencil with an eraser, draw the Greek peninsula and the Greek islands while looking at Map 40.1. Erase and redraw as necessary.

4. When you are pleased with your map, lay it over the original. Erase and redraw any lines which are more than 1/4 inch off the original.

5. Remove your map. Study carefully the locations of the Aegean Sea, Crete, Attica, the Peloponnese, and the cities of Athens, Sparta, Thebes, and Mycenae. When you are familiar with them, close the book. Using your regular pencil, label the Aegean Sea, Crete, Attica, and the Peloponnese. Mark and label Athens, Sparta, Thebes, and Mycenae. Check your map against the original. Correct any misplaced labels.

CHAPTER FORTY-ONE: THE DARK AGE OF MESOPOTAMIA

You MAY USE your text when answering the questions in sections I and II.

Section I: Who, What, Where

Write a one or two-sentence answer explaining the significance of each item listed below.

Erra
Mushki
Nebuchadnezzar
Phrygians
Suppiluliuma II
Tiglath-Pileser

Section II: Comprehension

Write a two/three sentence answer to each of the following questions.

1. From where did the wandering people pressing into Asia Minor originate?

2. Describe the Phrygian attack that ended the Hittite kingdom.

3. What part of the Hittite culture survived the Phrygian attack?

4. What cities make the points of the upside-down triangle known as the Assyrian heartland? Why did the kings of Assyria want to keep the heartland safe?

5. When Nebuchadnezzar came to Babylon's throne, why was the statue of Marduk still in the hands of the Elamites of Susa?

6. What plan of attack did Nebuchadnezzar implement in order to attack Susa and, ultimately, retrieve the statue of Marduk?

7. How did Marduk become the chief god of the Babylonians?

8. Why did Tiglath-Pileser burn the king's palace at Babylon? In what way was this a symbolic act, rather than a true act of war?

9. Who were the Aramaeans? In what way did the Aramaeans threaten Tiglath-Pileser's kingdom?

10. What evidence do historians have that proves Assyria was not immune to the same famine and drought that plagued the rest of the known world?

11. What is the Erra Epic? What story does it tell?

12. How does the Erra Epic reflect the hardships Babylon faced at the end of Nebuchadnezzar's reign?

13. Why did Tiglath-Pileser's son make a treaty with the new king of Babylon? Was the treaty effective?

Section III: Critical Thinking

You may use your text to answer this question.

Tiglath-Pileser came from a long line of kings who, each in turn, ruled over the Assyrian heartland. Keeping this treasured upside-down triangle safe was not enough for Tiglath-Pileser, so he gathered his men and went out to conquer more land for Assyria. Write a paragraph, using quotes from the Assyrian king's inscriptions and annals, to describe how Tiglath-Pileser restored, even if for just a short time, Assyria's greatness.

CHAPTER FORTY-TWO: THE FALL OF THE SHANG

You MAY USE your text when answering the questions in sections I and II.

Section I: Who, What, Where

Write a one or two-sentence answer explaining the significance of each item listed below.

Chou
"Lord of the West"
Wen
Wu
Wu-yi

Section II: Comprehension

Write a two/three sentence answer to each of the following questions.

1. What threat did the Shang kings and their people face at the beginning of the 11th century BC?

2. If the Zhou tribe were "not exactly subjects of the Shang king," how were the Zhou connected to the Shang? To whom were the Zhou people most loyal?

3. Why was Wu-yi's production of idols a serious breach of his royal responsibilities?

4. In what way did Chou's love of wine and pleasure lead to the exploitation of the Shang people?

5. Give two examples of Chou's cruel methods of punishment in his court.

6. Why did Chou have Wen jailed?

7. What prompted Wen's release from jail?

8. What kind of deal did Wen make with Chou before returning home to the Wei River valley?

9. What caused the Zhou people to rebel against Chou? Describe the forces that gathered against Chou.

10. What happened at the Battle of Muye? What weapon did the Zhou have that gave them an advantage over the Shang? Why did the Shang forces retreat?

Section III: Critical Thinking

You may NOT use your text to answer this question.

Wisdom, not military might, was the force that held together ancient Chinese culture. Knowing this, explain why ancient Chinese historians did not celebrate Wu's overthrow of the Shang king, and why the Zhou dynasty starts with Wen, rather than Wu.

Use the prompts below to answer this question fully.

- Were the Zhou people subjects of the Shang kingdom?
- Was the aggression against the Shang king a rebellion?
- Why isn't Wen given credit for his military success against the Shang?
- How did ancient Chinese historians justify the Zhou defiance?
- Why does the Zhou Dynasty begin with Wen, rather than with Wu?

CHAPTER FORTY-THREE: THE MANDATE OF HEAVEN

You MAY USE your text when answering the questions in sections I and II.

Section I: Who, What, Where

Write a one or two-sentence answer explaining the significance of each item listed below.

Ch'eng

Feng & Hao

K'ang

Loyang

Lu-fu

Mu

The Nine Cauldrons

Tan

Zhao

Section II: Comprehension

Write a two/three sentence answer to each of the following questions.

1. Why did Wu put away his weapons and discharge his soldiers at the start of his reign?

2. Who were the "Lords of the Nine Rings?" Why was this a misnomer?

3. What did it mean if a Chinese nobleman was "enfeoffed" by the king of the Zhou? What kind of gifts was an "enfeoffed" lord given?

4. What did a gift of bronze stand for in ancient China?

5. What is the biggest difference between the feudalism practiced in later times and the Zhou system of power and authority?

6. How did Wu plan to keep the peace at newly pacified Yin? How did his plan backfire?

7. What was the result of the Shang loyalist uprising?

8. How did the Chinese people view Tan? Why were the Chinese people able to accept Ch'eng's authority after Tan turned over his authority to the young king?

9. What were the responsibilities of the Duke of Zhou? Why was it necessary for him to compile a book of ritual?

10. What are the five rings of the Zhou king's domain?

11. List the frequency of sacrifices each domain sent to the capital city. If a domain did not send sacrifices, how was loyalty displayed? How does this schedule reflect each domain's level of responsibility to maintain the Mandate of Heaven?

12. Why didn't Mu attack the northern Chuan-Jung tribe?

Section III: Critical Thinking

You MAY USE your text to answer this question.

While the Chinese people valued peace, at times war was necessary to protect the Chinese king, his divine powers, and his land. In a sort of circular reasoning we have seen before, the Mandate of Heaven gave the Chinese king the right to protect his empire through war, and the success of the Chinese in battle verified the Mandate of Heaven. Write a paragraph explaining how this circular reasoning worked. First define the Mandate of Heaven. Second, describe how King Zhao's death explains the limits of the Mandate of Heaven. Third, explain why a Chinese king could only go to war if he was certain he would win. Finally, explain how the Mandate of Heaven hurt the growing Chinese empire.

Section IV: Map Exercise: The Yellow and the Yangtze

1. Using a black pencil, trace the rectangular outline of the frame for Map 43.1: The Western Zhou.

2. Using a black pencil, trace the coastline of China, the course of the Yellow River, including all four minor branches, and the course of the Yangtze. Repeat until the contours are familiar.

3. Trace the rectangular outline of the frame in black. Remove your tracing paper from the original. Close the book. Using a regular pencil with an eraser, draw the coastline of China, the Yellow River, and the Yangtze from memory. You do not need to draw the minor branches of the Yellow. If you can't remember the placement of any of the elements, open the book, look again at the map, and then close it and draw.

4. When you are pleased with your map, lay it over the original. Erase and redraw any lines which are more than 1/4 inch off the original.

5. Remove your map from the original. While looking at Map 43.1, draw in the Lo, the Wei, the Fenghe, and the unlabelled fourth branch of the Yellow. Erase and redraw as necessary.

6. When you are pleased with your map, lay it over the original. Erase and redraw any lines which are more than 1/4 inch off the original.

7. Label the Yellow, the Yangtze, the Lo, the Wei, and the Fenghe.

CHAPTER FORTY-FOUR: THE BHARATA WAR

You MAY USE your text when answering the questions in sections I and II.

Section I: Who, What, Where

Write a one or two-sentence answer explaining the significance of each item listed below.

Bhisma
Doab
Draupadi
Hastinapura
Indo-Gangetic Plain
The "Kauravas"
Mahabharata
The "Pandavas"
Vyasa (Krishna)

Section II: Comprehension

Write a two/three sentence answer to each of the following questions.

1. Who are the *dasa* people? Why is it unlikely that "dasa" is another name for the Harappan people?

2. What evidence supports the notion that invading Aryans married *dasa* people? Why is this intermarriage culturally important?

3. What type of terrain did the settlers of the Ganga encounter when they arrived between 1000 and 6000 BC? Why were the forests thought to be populated with demons?

4. How did the Indian warrior clans clear the forests of the Ganga River valley?

5. What are the names of Vyasa's three sons? What are the distinct talents of each son?

6. How did Dhritarashtra come to have 100 sons? Who is the acknowledged oldest son?

7. Why was Yudhishtra able to lay claim to the Indian throne?

8. In what way was the marriage of the Pandavas to Draupadi a strategic alliance?

9. Describe the Pandavas' palace at Indraprastha. How was the Kaurava king Duryodhana embarrassed at the palace?

10. What did Yudhishtra lose to Duryodhana in a game of dice?

11. What hostility between the Kauravas and the Pandavas caused the Bharata War?

12. Who won the Bharata War? How is the conflict between the Pandavas and the Kauravas reconciled in heaven?

Section III: Critical Thinking

You may NOT use your text to answer this question.

The Bharata War was a battle fought between two clans who were not so far away from their old days as nomadic warriors. The transition from a network of warriors who watched over the good of the clan towards a more hierarchical idea of kingship was a bumpy one.

In order to make sense of this messy transition, <u>make a genealogical chart for the Kuru clan</u>.

These are the names that must be included in the chart:

Queen Mother	King of Kuru
Older Wife	Younger Wife
Maidservant of Older Wife	Bhisma
Vyasa (Krishna)	Vidura
Pandu	Dhritarashtra
Gandhari	Duryodhana
Yudhishtra	The Pandavas
The Kauravas	Draupadi
Pancala Clan	

Section IV: Map Exercise: The Ganga and the Indus

1. Using a black pencil, trace the rectangular outline of the frame for Map 44.1: Aryan Clans of India.

2. Using a black pencil, trace the coastline of India, the northern mountain ranges, the Indus and the Ganga (including all branches), the Narmada River (unlabelled), and the mountains around the Narmada. Repeat until the contours are familiar. (Remember that you may draw simple peaks to represent the mountains.)

3. Trace the rectangular outline of the frame in black. Remove your tracing paper from the original. Using a regular pencil with an eraser, draw the coastline of India, the three rivers with all branches, and all mountains while looking at Map 44.1. Erase and redraw as necessary.

4. When you are pleased with your map, lay it over the original. Erase and redraw any lines which are more than 1/4 inch off the original

5. Remove your map from the original. Looking back at Map 44.1, study carefully the location of the Indus River, the Ganga, the Punjab, the Doab, the Hindu Kush, the Himalaya mountain range, and the Indo-Gangetic Plain. When you are familiar with them, close the book. Using your regular pencil, label the Indus River, the Ganga, the Punjab, the Doab, the Hindu Kush, the Himalaya mountain range, and the Indo-Gangetic Plain. Check your map against the original. If your labels are misplaced, erase and re-mark while looking at the original.

Chapter Forty-Five: The Son of David

You MAY USE your text when answering the questions in sections I and II.

Section I: Who, What, Where

Write a one or two-sentence answer explaining the significance of each item listed below.

Dagon

David

Delilah

Goliath

Hiram

Israel

Joshua

Meshwesh

Pentapolis/Peleset/Philistines

Samson

Saul

Queen of Sheba

Sheshonq

Section II: Comprehension

Write a two/three sentence answer to each of the following questions.

1. From where did the Philistines borrow their culture? What archaeological evidence supports this theory?

2. Why were the 40 years the Hebrews wandered in the desert crucial to their culture?

3. How did Moses reorganize the Hebrews?

4. Why did Joshua order all adult Hebrew men circumcised?

5. Who succeeded Joshua as commander of the Israelites?

6. What happened when Saul led his men into Philistine territory? What kind of forces did the Israelites face?

7. How did David's defeat of Goliath affect the Israelite push against the Philistines? Why did Saul want to get rid of David after his success?

8. Describe how David expanded the Israelite kingdom when he first came to power.

9. Who were the Phoenicians? What united the Phoenicians? What type of trade did the Phoenicians control?

10. How did Solomon reorganize David's Israel? Why did he choose to restructure the kingdom?

11. How did Solomon's ruling style differ from David's?

12. How did Solomon fuel his massive building projects and court?

13. Why was Solomon in debt? How did Solomon propose to pay off his debts to Hiram?

14. How did Jeroboam come to be king of the northern part of Israel? What kingdom was Rehoboam left to rule over?

15. Why did Sheshonq invade the Western Semitic lands? In what way did Sheshonq's attack on the Western Semitic lands reinforce the division between Israel and Judah?

Section III: Critical Thinking

You may NOT use your text to answer this question.

Samuel, an old and weary Israelite, believed kingship to be an enormous mistake. He warned "[A king] will draft your sons to be soldiers in his army…. He will take them to plow his fields….He will take the best of your harvest…. You will cry out for relief from the king you have chosen." Considering the exploits of Solomon, and his son Rehoboam, Samuel was right. However, as we know, kingship is also tied with the success of a nation. Below you will find a description of two particular circumstances we read about in this chapter. Write a short paragraph for each explaining how kingship was necessary in order for the nations featured to progress.

#1 – Around 1050, Philistines raided Israelite villages, Israelites burned Philistine fields, both sides knocked off the odd hunting party caught out of bounds, and neither kingdom triumphed.

#2 – Around 950, Sheshonq headed up the armed forces of the north of Egypt, and also managed to create an alliance with the south by marrying one of the daughters of the pharaoh at Tanis. When the pharaoh died, Sheshonq had asserted his right, by marriage, to the throne of Egypt in Tanis.

Section IV: Map Exercise: Cities of Israel and the Surrounding Kingdoms

1. Using a black pencil, trace the rectangular outline of the frame for Map 45.2: Israel and Surrounding Kingdoms.

2. Using a black pencil, trace the coastline of the Mediterranean Sea, the outline of Cyprus, the Orontes, the Jordan, the Sea of Galilee, and the Dead Sea. Repeat until the contours are familiar.

3. Trace the rectangular outline of the frame in black. Remove your tracing paper from the original. Using a regular pencil with an eraser, draw the coastline of the Mediterranean Sea, the outline of Cyprus, the Orontes, the Jordan, the Sea of Galilee, and the Dead Sea while looking at Map 45.2. Erase and redraw as necessary.

4. When you are pleased with your map, lay it over the original. Erase and redraw any lines which are more than 1/4 inch off the original.

5. Remove your map from the original. Looking back at Map 45.2, study carefully the location of Cyprus, the Mediterrean Sea, the Orontes, the Sea of Galilee, the Jordan, the Dead Sea, and the cities of Tyre, Jericho, and Jerusalem. When you are familiar with them, close the book. Using your regular pencil, label Cyprus, the Mediterrean Sea, the Orontes, the Sea of Galilee, the Jordan, and the Dead Sea. Mark and label the cities of Tyre, Jericho, and Jerusalem. Check your map against the original. If your labels are misplaced, erase and re-mark while looking at the original.

CHAPTER FORTY-SIX: FROM WESTERN TO EASTERN ZHOU

You MAY USE your text when answering the questions in sections I and II.

Section I: Who, What, Where

Write a one or two-sentence answer explaining the significance of each item listed below.

Hsiao
Duke of Mi
P'ing
Duke of Qi
Quan Rong
Xianyun
King Yih

Section II: Comprehension

Write a two/three sentence answer to each of the following questions.

1. What archaeological evidence shows us that around 900 BC, the "Lords of the Nine Lands" were beginning to act with more and more independence?

2. In what way did the growing bureaucracy of the Zhou administration, which was meant to protect the king, actually reflect the king's weakening power?

3. How was Yi able to recapture the Zhou throne?

4. What was the purpose of Li's Grand Inquisitor? What were the consequences of speaking against King Li? How did the people in the capital react to the Grand Inquisitor?

5. In addition to Li's repressive politics, what environmental circumstance made the people of China more miserable than ever?

6. What did the Duke of Shao sacrifice in order to save Li's heir Hsuan? What were the circumstances of this sacrifice? Why the Duke of Shao make this sacrifice?

7. Describe the barbarians Hsuan faced.

8. What made the Xianyun particularly meddlesome invaders?

9. In what way was Yu's concubine responsible for the collapse of the royal family?

10. When King Yu ordered the beacon fires lit to signal the invasion of the Quan Rong, why did the feudal lords choose to ignore his cry for help?

11. When P'ing made Ch'in a duke as a show of gratitude for safe passage to the new capital, how was this action also an admission that the king no longer was protected under the Mandate of Heaven?

Section III: Critical Thinking

You may NOT use your text to answer this question.

Li's Grand Inquisitor may have stopped audible criticism of the king, but feelings of resentment against the royal house could not be quelled. The Duke of Shao warned Li that an explosion was coming: "To block people's mouths is worse than blocking a river…. When an obstructed river bursts its banks, it will surely hurt a great number of people." Write a paragraph explaining how this prophecy came true during Li's grandson Yu's reign. In your answer, make sure to include the consequences of the earthquake that shook the capital, and the results of Yu's decision to make his harem woman his queen.

CHAPTER FORTY-SEVEN: THE ASSYRIAN RENAISSANCE

You MAY USE your text when answering the questions in sections I and II.

Section I: Who, What, Where

Write a one or two-sentence answer explaining the significance of each item listed below.

Aram
Black Obelisk
Caleh
Damascus
Elijah
Jehu
Joram
Omri

Section II: Comprehension

Write a two/three sentence answer to each of the following questions.

1. What steps did Ashur-dan II take to help bring Assyria out of its dark age, into its new renaissance?

2. Why did Aramaic replace Akkadian as the common language spoken in Babylon?

3. Describe one instance of cruelty from Ashurnasirpal II's "reign of terror."

4. What was the political motive behind Ahab's marriage to Jezebel?

5. Why did Ahab choose to worship Baal, chief god of the Phoenicians?

6. What did Jezebel do to the prophets of the God of Abraham? What happened to those who escaped the queen's purge?

7. When Shalmaneser met Israelite forces at Qarqar in 853, who did he find allied with Ahab's army? How did Ahab manage to get all this support?

8. What is the Monolith Inscription? How did the Monolith Inscription differ from the account of the battle at Qarqar depicted in Assyrian reliefs?

9. After hearing Phoenician advisors predict certain victory for Ahab over the city of Ramoth-Gilead, why did Jehoshaphat suggest that Ahab consider asking a Hebrew prophet what Yahweh thought about the plan?

10. What were the details of Jezebel's death?

11. At what cost did Jehu purify the house of Israel?

Section III: Critical Thinking

You may NOT use your text to answer this question.

As we know from our textbook, alliances in the ancient world were both a blessing and a curse. While the longevity of some alliances was remarkable, even by today's standards, it was more common for an alliance to be broken prematurely. Write two or three paragraphs explaining how Ahab's opportunist tendencies showed when he decided to turn on the king of Damascus. In your answer, describe how Ahab and the king of Damascus came to make a treaty, why Ahab thought it would be opportune for him to break the treaty, and how the king of Judah probably had a secret alliance that protected his own neck in the advance on Ramoth-Gilead.

Section IV: Map Exercise: Assyria and Its Neighbors

1. Using a black pencil, trace the rectangular outline of the frame for Map 47.1: The New Assyrian Empire.

2. Using a black pencil, trace all seas, rivers and mountains. You do not need to trace lakes or small islands, but be sure to trace the large island of Cyprus (unlabelled, in the right hand corner of the Mediterranean Sea) and the Dead Sea and Sea of Galilee on either end of the Jordan. Repeat until the contours are familiar.

3. Trace the rectangular outline of the frame in black. Remove your tracing paper from the original. Using a regular pencil with an eraser, draw the seas, rivers and mountains, as well as Cyprus, while looking at Map 47.1. Erase and redraw as necessary.

4. When you are pleased with your map, lay it over the original. Erase and redraw any lines which are more than 1/4 inch off the original.

5. Remove your map. Study carefully the locations of the Euphrates, the Tigris, the Halys, the Orontes, the Mediterranean, the Sea of Galilee, the Taurus Mountains, and the cities of Babylon, Assur, Nineveh, Aleppo, Carchemish, Hattusas, Damascus, Tyre, and Jerusalem. When you are familiar with them, close the book. Using your regular pencil, label the Euphrates, the Tigris, the Halys, the Orontes, the Mediterranean, the Sea of Galilee, and the Taurus Mountains. Mark and label the cities of Babylon, Assur, Nineveh, Aleppo, Carchemish, Hattusas, Damascus, Tyre, and Jerusalem. Check your map against the original. Correct any misplaced labels.

6. While looking at Map 47.1, draw a light line to show the borders of Assyria. Erase and correct as necessary. When you are satisfied, lay your map back over the original. Erase and redraw any lines which are more than 1/4 inch off the original.

7. Label Assyria.

Chapter Forty-Eight: New Peoples

You MAY USE your text when answering the questions in sections I and II.

Section I: Who, What, Where

Write a one or two-sentence answer explaining the significance of each item listed below.

Adad-nirari III
Arcadia
Barbaro-phonoi
Gordium
Mada
Marduk-zakir-shumi
Marduk-balassu-iqbi
Parsua
Phrygians
Que
Ring Composition
Sammu-amat
Shamshi-Adad V

Section II: Comprehension

Write a two/three sentence answer to each of the following questions.

1. Why was Shalmaneser III unwilling to attack Babylon?

2. Where were each of the Semitic tribes at the head of the Persian Gulf, known collectively to the Assyrians as the Chaldeans, specifically located? Under whose control were the Chaldeans?

3. Why did Marduk-zakir-shumi make Shamshi-Adad V sign a treaty as a condition of getting Babylonian troops to fight against Assur-danin-apli? What were the terms of the treaty?

4. How was Shamshi-Adad V able to avenge the humiliation of Marduk-zakir-shumi's treaty? In your answer, be sure to explain the significance of the title "King of Sumer and Akkad."

5. How did Sammu-amat assert her right to the Assyrian throne?

6. Who were the Ionians? Where did they come from, and what peoples made up their culture?

7. Where did the Ionians go during the Dorian occupation?

8. Explain how the Ionians, Mycenaeans and the Dorians were, more or less, from the same race.

9. Who was Homer? Where did he come from?

10. How do the Iliad and the Odyssey reflect both a pre-800 BC world, and the world after the Dorian invasion?

Section III: Critical Thinking

You may NOT use your text to answer this question.

In the ancient world, the mingling of different peoples often occurred as a result of war and conquest. In ancient Greece, literature acted as another type of galvanizing force. Write a paragraph explaining how peace brought together the Ionians, Dorians and Arcadians. Then address how the blending of these cultures is reflected in Homer's writing. Finally, explain how the Iliad and Odyssey gave these three different peoples a shared past.

Section IV: Map Exercise: Greece and Asia Minor

1. Using a black pencil, trace the rectangular outline of the frame for Map 48.2: Mycenaeans, Dorians and Ionians.

2. Using a black pencil, trace the coastline of the Greek peninsula and Asia Minor, along with all islands. Repeat until the contours are familiar.

3. Trace the rectangular outline of the frame in black. Remove your tracing paper from the original. Using a regular pencil with an eraser, draw the Greek peninsula and the Greek islands while looking at Map 48.2. Erase and redraw as necessary.

4. When you are pleased with your map, lay it over the original. Erase and redraw any lines which are more than 1/4 inch off the original. Since this is a time-consuming map, you will not go on to label the locations.

CHAPTER FORTY-NINE: TRADING POSTS AND COLONIES

You MAY USE your text when answering the questions in sections I and II.

Section I: Who, What, Where

Write a one or two-sentence answer explaining the significance of each item listed below.

Alba Longa
Amphictyonys
Amulius
Apennine Culture
Lavinium
Numitor
Rhea Silvia
Titus Tatius

Section II: Comprehension

Write a two/three sentence answer to each of the following questions.

1. Where did Greek merchants sail in order to trade during Homer's time?

2. What clue do we have that the scattered settlements of people on the Italian peninsula were of the same descent?

3. How do archaeologists distinguish early Italian settlements from one another? List the different settlements and how they were grouped.

4. What did the Latial peoples do with their dead? How was the burial ritual a reflection of everyday Latial culture?

5. Why did the Latial peoples build their villages on the top of hills? What united these tiny villages?

6. What does "pan-Hellenic" mean? Give an example of pan-Hellenism from the chapter.

7. How did the Olympic festival come into existence? When would the games be held, and how did the Olympic truce work?

8. While the Olympics did not bring about sustained peace between Greek cities, how was the festival successful in galvanizing the ancient Greeks?

9. Who found Rhea Silvia's twin sons once they were dropped off on the banks of the Tiber? What were the boys named, and who paid for their education?

10. How did Romulus make up for Rome's shortage of women?

11. How did the formation of colonies help the growing cities of the ancient Greeks?

12. What happened to a Greek family's land when it was passed down to the next generation? Why was this problematic?

13. How did the limited amount of land on the Greek peninsula cause corruption in Greek land-owners and officials?

14. What Greek cities sent out colonists? What were the names of the new Greek colonies, and where were they located?

Section III: Critical Thinking

You may NOT use your text to answer this question.

In this chapter we find many instances of conflict associated with the formation of ancient Rome. Using the list of pairings below, write a short description of each and its association with Rome's origins. Then, write a paragraph describing how division was inextricable from ancient Rome's actual formation.

• Lavinium/Alba Longa

• Numitor/Amulius

• Romulus/Remus

• Romans/Sabines

Section IV: Map Exercise: Italy

1. Using a black pencil, trace the rectangular outline of the frame for Map 49.1: Italian Peoples and Greek Colonies.

2. Using a black pencil, trace the coastline of Italy and the Adriatic, along with the island of Sicily and the two unlabelled islands on the left side of the map. Only trace the eastern coast of the Adriatic as far down as Chalcis; do not go on to trace the Greek peninsula or the Aegean Sea. For this first assignment on Italy, you do not need to trace mountains. Repeat until the contours are familiar.

3. Trace the rectangular outline of the frame in black. Remove your tracing paper from the original. Using a regular pencil with an eraser, draw Italy, the Adriatic Sea, Sicily, and the two large islands while looking at Map 49.1. Erase and redraw as necessary.

4. When you are pleased with your map, lay it over the original. Erase and redraw any lines which are more than 1/4 inch off the original.

5. Remove your map. Study carefully the locations of the Adriatic, Sicily, and the city of Rome. When you are familiar with them, close the book. Using your regular pencil, label the Adriatic and Sicily. Mark and label Rome. Check your map against the original. Correct any misplaced labels.

CHAPTER FIFTY: OLD ENEMIES

You MAY USE your text when answering the questions in sections I and II.

Section I: Who, What, Where

Write a one or two-sentence answer explaining the significance of each item listed below.

Kar Assur
Nabonassar
Merodach-baladan
Pul
Sapea
Sarduri I
Syria
Urartu

Section II: Comprehension

Write a two/three sentence answer to each of the following questions.

1. How did Shalmaneser IV lose hold of Babylon?

2. How was the governor of Mari's decision to date events by the years of his own rule a sign of waning power at Caleh?

3. Why did the Greeks come to associate the term "astronomer" with "Chaldean"?

4. Why was the conquest of Arvad important to Tiglath-Pileser III's expanding empire? How did the fall of Arvad help Tiglath-Pileser III defeat the Urartu?

5. What happened to the Phrygians after Tiglath-Pileser III conquered the Urartu?

6. According to legend, how did Midas come to be king of Phrygia?

7. What historical evidence suggests that Midas did a great deal of trade with the Ionian cities on the Asia Minor coast?

8. Describe the submission of Judah and Israel to Tiglath-Pileser III.

9. Why did Tiglath-Pileser III choose to invade Babylon after the death of Nabonassar?

10. Why was it seemingly effortless for Tiglath-Pileser III to sway the citizens in the north of Babylonia to join the Assyrian empire?

11. Why was Tiglath-Pileser III's role as king of Babylon groundbreaking?

Section III: Critical Thinking

You may NOT use your text to answer this question.

The relationship between Assyria and Babylon was like a rollercoaster; up one minute, down the next. First, explain why Tiglath-Pileser III chose to make Babylon an ally when he first came to the throne, instead of trying to conquer his southern neighbor. Second, explain why Nabonassar did not challenge Assyria when Tiglath-Pileser III claimed to have conquered Babylon. In your answers, make sure to include how Babylon's prosperity and peace may have factored into both acts.

CHAPTER FIFTY-ONE: KINGS OF ASSYRIA AND BABYLON

You MAY USE your text when answering the questions in sections I and II.

Section I: Who, What, Where

Write a one or two-sentence answer explaining the significance of each item listed below.

Dur-Sharrukin
Hoshea
Kush
Napata
Nubia
Piankhe
Rusas
Samaritans
Sargon II
Shutruk-Nahhunte

Section II: Comprehension

Write a two/three sentence answer to each of the following questions.

1. What did Hoshea, king of Israel, do that made Shalmaneser V want to wipe out Israel?

2. How did Egypt come to have three separate capitals? In your answer, make sure to list the three capitals.

3. How did Manetho organize Egypt's ruling families in the century since the battle of Qarqar? Why was Manetho's categorization problematic?

4. What traditions did the Napatans have in common with the Egyptians?

5. Why didn't Piankhe help Israel fight against the Assyrians?

6. Why did Sargon II admire the Urartian king Rusas?

7. What was Sargon II's strategy for the invasion of Urartu?

8. What happened when Sargon II and his army met Urartian forces at Tabriz?

9. How did Merodach-baladan hope to persuade northern Babylonians to turn away from Assyria and support his rule?

10. In what ways did Sargon II's southern attack on Babylon trap Merodach-baladan?

11. What happened to Merodach-baladan after his surrender to the Assyrians?

Section III: Critical Thinking

You may NOT use your text to answer this question.

Ancient historical narratives tell us that the Israelites have always had a strong national identity based on Abraham's divine call from Yahweh. Though Israel had become part of Assyria's growing kingdom, the Israelites were still culturally separate from the Assyrians. Write a paragraph explaining why Sargon II, after hearing of Hoshea's attempt to revolt against him, chose to scatter the peoples of Israel in addition to physically destroying the nation. In your answer make sure to include why Israel became known as the "lost 10 tribes."

Section IV: Map Exercise: Egypt and the Middle East

1. Using a black pencil, trace the rectangular outline of the frame for Map 51.1: Egypt and Assyria.

2. Using a black pencil, trace all seas, rivers and mountains. You do not need to trace lakes or small islands, but as before, trace the large island of Cyprus (unlabelled, in the right hand corner of the Mediterranean Sea) and the Dead Sea and Sea of Galilee on either end of the Jordan. You do not need to trace the Upper or Lower Zab. Repeat until the contours are familiar.

3. Trace the rectangular outline of the frame in black. Remove your tracing paper from the original. Using a regular pencil with an eraser, draw the seas, rivers and mountains, as well as Cyprus, while looking at Map 51.1. Erase and redraw as necessary.

4. When you are pleased with your map, lay it over the original. Erase and redraw any lines which are more than 1/4 inch off the original.

5. Remove your map. Study carefully the locations of the Persian Gulf, the Euphrates, the Tigris, the Halys, the Red Sea, the Mediterranean, the Black Sea, the Caspian Sea, the Nile, the Zagros Mountains, the Taurus Mountains, and the cities of Babylon, Assur, Nineveh, Tyre, Tanis, and Thebes. When you are familiar with them, close the book. Using your regular pencil, label the Persian Gulf, the Euphrates, the Tigris, the Halys, the Red Sea, the Mediterranean, the Black Sea, the Caspian Sea, the Nile, the Zagros Mountains, and the Taurus Mountains. Mark and label the cities of Babylon, Assur, Nineveh, Tyre, Tanis, and Thebes. Check your map against the original. Correct any misplaced labels.

CHAPTER FIFTY-TWO: SPECTACULAR DEFEAT

You MAY USE your text when answering the questions in sections I and II.

Section I: Who, What, Where

Write a one or two-sentence answer explaining the significance of each item listed below.

Ashur-nadin-shumi
Bel-ibni
King Kahllushu
Marduk-apla-iddina II
Musezib-Marduk
Nineveh
Sennacherib

Section II: Comprehension

Write a two/three sentence answer to each of the following questions.

1. How did Sennacherib insult the Babylonian court? What was the result of this insult?

2. How did Merodach-baladan become king of Babylon once again?

3. What prompted Sennacherib to first send troops down to attack Babylon? What drove him to go down to Babylon himself?

4. Who was Tirhakah, and how did he come to be known as Egypt's pharaoh?

5. How did the imprisoned king of Ekron end up in Jerusalem?

6. What made Hezekiah bow out of the coalition against Assyria?

7. In what way did Merodach-baladan have the last word in his battle against Assyria?

8. Why did Sennacherib retreat from Babylon in the three way war between Assyria, Elam and Babylon? What shifted in the war that prompted Sennacherib to attack Babylon one more time?

9. What did Sennacherib do to Babylon once he finally broke down the city's gates?

10. What was the fate of Sennacherib's son, Ashur-nadin-shumi? What was the fate of Sennacherib himself?

Section III: Critical Thinking

You MAY USE your text to answer this question.

When Sennacherib came to Assyria's throne, he had the reputation of being "boneless and inadequate." Like his father, Sennacherib made prolific military strides, and secured Assyria's great empire. Yet, Sennacherib is most famously remembered for his inability to capture Jerusalem. Was Sennacherib's defeat caused by old-world disease, or was it God's will that protected Jerusalem? Using evidence from the chapter, explain how the plague could have been responsible for Sennacherib's retreat from Jerusalem. Then, using Lord Byron's words, explain how God's will may have been behind Jerusalem's triumph.

Section IV: Map Exercise: Sennacherib's Assyria

1. Using a black pencil, trace the rectangular outline of the frame for Map 52.1: Sennacherib's Campaigns.

2. Using a black pencil, trace all seas, rivers and mountains. You do not need to trace lakes or small islands, but as before, trace the large island of Cyprus and the Dead Sea and Sea of Galilee on either end of the Jordan. You do not need to trace the Upper or Lower Zab (unlabelled). Repeat until the contours are familiar.

3. Trace the rectangular outline of the frame in black. Remove your tracing paper from the original. Using a regular pencil with an eraser, draw the seas, rivers and mountains, as well as Cyprus, while looking at Map 52.1. Erase and redraw as necessary.

4. When you are pleased with your map, lay it over the original. Erase and redraw any lines which are more than 1/4 inch off the original.

5. Remove your map. Study carefully the locations of the Euphrates, the Tigris, the Halys, the Mediterranean, the Taurus Mountains, the Sea of Galilee, and the cities of Babylon, Assur, Nineveh, Aleppo, Tyre, Jerusalem, and Memphis. When you are familiar with them, close the book. Using your regular pencil, label the Euphrates, the Tigris, the Halys, the Mediterranean, the Taurus Mountains, and the Sea of Galilee. Mark and label the cities of Babylon, Assur, Nineveh, Aleppo, Tyre, Jerusalem, and Memphis. Check your map against the original. Correct any misplaced labels.

CHAPTER FIFTY-THREE: THE DECLINE OF THE KING

You MAY USE your text when answering the questions in sections I and II.

Section I: Who, What, Where

Write a one or two-sentence answer explaining the significance of each item listed below.

"Central States"
Chuang
Hegemon
Huan
"Square Wall"
Wen

Section II: Comprehension

Write a two/three sentence answer to each of the following questions.

1. Why was it advantageous for P'ing to hand over the old western Zhou territory to the Duke of Ch'in?

2. How did P'ing earn the name "P'ing the Peaceful?"

3. List the twelve major centers of power that were in existence during P'ing's reign.

4. Who were the Yi and Ti? Why were they a threat to China?

5. Why did the Duke of Qi declare himself Hegemon in 679 BC?

6. How did the Duke of Qi use his power as Hegemon to fight the Yi and the Ti?

7. Why did the Hegemon choose to ignore Shu Tai's treachery after King Hsiang ordered Shu Tai arrested and killed for plotting a revolt with the Ti and the Jung?

8. How did King Hsiang and Shu Tai come to marry the same Ti princess?

Section III: Critical Thinking

You MAY USE your text to answer this question.

The Mandate of Heaven was weak in 7th century BC China. While the king was still the nation's figurehead, he could no longer protect his kingdom. The new role of Hegemon, or military overlord, was created, making the king obsolete. Despite his lack of power, the king was still shown respect, and the formalities of the Chinese government were preserved. Write a short paragraph explaining why the role of king was not done away with, and how a "two-headed country with both a military and religious leader" worked.

Section IV: Map Exercise: The Yellow and the Yangtze (Review)

1. Using a black pencil, trace the rectangular outline of the frame for Map 53.1: States of the Eastern Zhou.

2. Using a black pencil, trace the coastline of China, the course of the Yellow River, and the course of the Yangtze. Repeat until the contours are familiar.

3. Trace the rectangular outline of the frame in black. Remove your tracing paper from the original. Close the book. Using a regular pencil with an eraser, draw the coastline of China, the Yellow River, and the Yangtze from memory. If you can't remember the placement of any of the elements, open the book, look again at the map, and then close it and draw.

4. When you are pleased with your map, lay it over the original. Erase and redraw any lines which are more than 1/4 inch off the original.

5. Remove your map from the original. Label the Yellow, the Yangtze, and the Yellow Sea.

CHAPTER FIFTY-FOUR: THE ASSYRIANS IN EGYPT

You MAY USE your text when answering the questions in sections I and II.

Section I: Who, What, Where

Write a one or two-sentence answer explaining the significance of each item listed below.

Bit-Dakkuri
Cimmerians/Gimirrai
Gyges
Façade monument
Nabu-zer-ketti-lisher
Prism
Psammetichus
Rusas II
Scythians
Shamash-shum-ukin
Tantamani
Teushpa
Tirhakah

Section II: Comprehension

Write a two/three sentence answer to each of the following questions.

1. Why was it somewhat problematic for Esarhaddon to claim he was rebuilding Babylon out of affection for Marduk?

2. On what did Esarhaddon blame the destruction of Babylon? Why did he start his account with the phrase "Before my time?"

3. Why did the statue of Marduk remain in Assyria after Esarhaddon rebuilt Babylon?

4. What made Esarhaddon cautious of the Cimmerians?

5. Who were the Lydians, and how did they come to have so much power after Phrygia's destruction?

6. Why did Esarhaddon retreat from the battle against the Egyptians at Ashkelon?

7. Who was the governor of Sais, and why did he remain loyal to Assyria after Esarhaddon left his newly conquered Egypt?

8. What did Ashurbanipal do with all of the Egyptian noblemen his father Esarhaddon had taken captive?

9. What was the impact of the destruction of Thebes on the ancient Near East?

10. Why was it a mistake for Ashurbanipal to appoint Psammetichus sole pharaoh of Egypt?

11. What happened to king Gyges after he helped Psammetichus regain control of Egypt?

Section III: Critical Thinking

You may NOT use your text to answer this question.

Chapter after chapter we read about the military conquests and subsequent losses of the kingdoms in the ancient Near East. The last few chapters, in particular, have focused on Assyria's constant war state. Write a paragraph explaining why king after Assyrian king comes to his throne with a voracious appetite for war. To substantiate your answer, consider what would have happened if Egypt had taken over Assyria, and what that would mean for Assyria's religious practice.

Chapter Fifty-Five: Medes and Persians

You MAY USE your text when answering the questions in sections I and II.

Section I: Who, What, Where

Write a one or two-sentence answer explaining the significance of each item listed below.

Ashur-etillu-ilani
Bastions
Cuthah
Cyarxes
Cyrus
Deioces
Ecbatana
Madius
Phraortes
Teispes

Section II: Comprehension

Write a two/three sentence answer to each of the following questions.

1. Why did the Elamite king Teumann expect a warm welcome at Babylon around 650 BC?

2. What happened to Teumann and his army as they marched toward Babylon?

3. Describe the layout of Ecbatana's walls, and the decoration of its bastions.

4. What did Ashurbanipal do to Babylon's inhabitants after his three-year siege on the city? What was Shamash-shum-ukin's fate?

5. In what way was civil war responsible for the obliteration of Elam?

6. What did Ashurbanipal do to the people of Elam in order to ensure that the nation would not rise again?

7. How did Teispes's move into the old Elamite territory of Anshan affect Persian culture and history?

8. What archaeological evidence found in ancient Urartian territory suggests aggressive Scythian attacks on Urartu?

9. Who was involved in the three-way battle over Babylon after the death of Ashurbanipal?

Section III: Critical Thinking

You MAY USE your text to answer this question.

In general, Assyrian kings were known for their brutality and unmerciful ruling tactics. Ashurbanipal, however, was not interested in constant warfare that yielded only a small increase in territory. The Assyrian king spent his energies on something else, building a library. Write a paragraph explaining the assembly of Ashurbanipal's library, and how this collection offered Ashurbanipal a legacy that would last longer than the constantly changing imperial borders of the ancient world.

Section IV: Map Exercise: The Tigris and Euphrates

1. Using a black pencil, trace the rectangular outline of the frame for Map 55.1: The Medes and the Persians.

2. Using a black pencil, trace all seas, rivers and mountains. You do not need to trace small lakes, but as before, trace Cyprus and the Dead Sea and Sea of Galilee on either end of the Jordan as well as the (unlabelled) Orontes. Repeat until the contours are familiar.

3. Trace the rectangular outline of the frame in black. Remove your tracing paper from the original. Using a regular pencil with an eraser, draw all seas, rivers (EXCEPT the Tigris and Euphrates) and mountains, as well as Cyprus, while looking at Map 55.1. Erase and redraw as necessary.

4. When you are pleased with your map, lay it over the original. Erase and redraw any lines which are more than 1/4 inch off the original.

5. Remove your map from the original and close the book. From memory, draw the Tigris and the Euphrates. If you can't remember the courses of these two rivers, open the book, look again at the map, and then close it and draw.

6. When you are pleased with your map, lay it over the original. Erase and redraw any lines which are more than 1/4 inch off the original.

CHAPTER FIFTY-SIX: CONQUEST AND TYRANNY

You MAY USE your text when answering the questions in sections I and II.

Section I: Who, What, Where

Write a one or two-sentence answer explaining the significance of each item listed below.

Acropolis
Archon
Chalcidice
Cylon
Cyrene
Draco
Ekklesia
Eusebius
Messene
Metropolis
Polemarch
Solon

Section II: Comprehension

Write a two/three sentence answer to each of the following questions.

1. How were Greek colonists able to maintain their Greek identity and culture in their new cities?

2. Once Messene was conquered by Sparta, how were the Messenians treated by the Spartans? What place did the Spartans hold in the new class system?

3. Why did the Spartan people prefer to be ruled by two kings at odds rather than a singular king with unchallenged power?

4. What were the three primary powers of any ancient kingdom? In what way did Israel fix this three-way power into law?

5. While the kings of Sparta held all three primary powers, how was their ability to use them limited?

6. How did one put a question to the Delphic oracle? Why was it difficult to get a straight answer from the oracle?

7. Define "tyrant" in terms of Greek politics.

8. What grave mistake did the archons make when they dealt with Cylon's conspirators after the rebels occupied the Acropolis?

9. What was a "Sixth-Part-Tenant?" In what way does a "sixth-part-tenant" exemplify the false nature of Athenian democracy?

10. Why did Draco assign the penalty of death to so many crimes in his newly written law?

11. How did Solon set about righting the inequalities of the wealth in Athens? Why were the debtors unhappy with Solon's redistribution plan?

12. What was Solon's reason for leaving Athens as soon as his laws were enacted? Why was leaving the city advantageous for Solon?

Section III: Critical Thinking

You may NOT use your text to answer this question.

Though Spartans wanted to avoid the tyranny often associated with Mesopotamian kings, they managed to create a society oppressed by an unwritten yet incredibly strict code of laws. Write a paragraph that first gives two examples of severe Spartan law. Next, explain the overall purpose of Spartan laws. In your answer, make sure to explain why Spartan laws were never written down. Finally, explain how the laws that were meant to free Spartans from sin actually trapped Spartans in a cage of fear.

Section IV: Map Exercise: Greece and North Africa

1. Using a black pencil, trace the rectangular outline of the frame for Map 56.1: The Spreading Greek World.

2. Using a black pencil, trace the coastlines of North Africa, Greece and Asia Minor. You do not need to include the smaller islands, but be sure to include Crete and the large island where Eretria is located. Repeat until the contours are familiar.

3. Trace the rectangular outline of the frame in black. Remove your tracing paper from the original. Using a regular pencil with an eraser, draw the coastlines of North Africa, Greece, and Asia Minor. Include Crete and the island where Eretria is located while looking at Map 56.1. Erase and redraw as necessary.

4. When you are pleased with your map, lay it over the original. Erase and redraw any lines which are more than 1/4 inch off the original.

5. Remove your map. Study carefully the locations of the Black Sea, the Bosphorus Strait, Asia Minor, Thrace, the Peloponnese, the Mediterranean Sea, and Libya. Check your map against the original. Correct any misplaced labels.

Chapter Fifty-Seven:
The Beginnings and End of Empire

You MAY USE your text when answering the questions in sections I and II.

Section I: Who, What, Where

Write a one or two-sentence answer explaining the significance of each item listed below.

Assur-uballit

Dionysius of Halicarnassus

Estruscans

Haran

Josiah of Judah

Lucumo (Lucius Tarquinius Priscus/Tarquin the Elder)

Nebuchadnezzar

Necho II

Numa Pompilius

Servius Tullius

Section II: Comprehension

Write a two/three sentence answer to each of the following questions.

1. What was the cause of King Romulus of Rome's death?

2. Why were the gates to the Temple of Janus, god of war, closed under Numa Pompilius?

3. In 650 BC, Rome seemed to be a city at peace; what division was still present within the city's walls?

4. How did Numa Pompilius's successors, Tullus Hostilius and Ancus Marcius, change the shape of Rome?

5. What was Sin-shum-ishkun's next move once the three-way fight at Babylon broke out?

6. Who helped Nabopolassar in his fight against Assyria? What agreement was made between the two allies?

7. Describe how Nabopolassar and Cyarxes worked together to take down Assur.

8. How was Necho and Cyarxes's army able to get through the wall surrounding Nineveh? Why was this act a particularly fitting way for the Babylonians to attack the city?

9. After the fall of Nineveh, how did the Medes and Babylon split the territory that was once Assyria?

10. Considering Egypt's tumultuous relationship with Assyria, why did Necho II want to help the dying empire?

11. After failing to take Babylon, how did Necho II avenge Josiah of Judah's surprise attack on his Egyptian troops?

12. Why didn't Nebuchadnezzar follow the fleeing Necho II all the way into Egypt after the battle at Carchemish?

Section III: Critical Thinking

You MAY USE your text to answer this question.

Rome was a city built on division. The racial division within Rome could cause tension, but it also allowed those of mixed race to find worth outside of their bloodline. Write a paragraph explaining how Rome's mix of races gave citizens the opportunity for success no matter their origins, and how the slow takeover of Roman life by Etruscans only added to Rome's strength.

Section IV: Map Exercise: Italy and Sicily

1. Using a black pencil, trace the rectangular outline of the frame for Map 57.1: Rome and Her Neighbors.

2. Using a black pencil, trace the coastline of Italy and the Adriatic, along with the island of Sicily. You do not need to trace the edges of the islands on the left side of the map or the coast of Africa in the lower left-hand corner. Also trace the Appeninnes, the Po, and the Tiber. Repeat until the contours are familiar.

3. Trace the rectangular outline of the frame in black. Remove your tracing paper from the original. Using a regular pencil with an eraser, draw Italy, the Adriatic Sea, Sicily, the Apennines, the Po and the Tiber while looking at Map 57.1. Erase and redraw as necessary.

4. When you are pleased with your map, lay it over the original. Erase and redraw any lines which are more than 1/4 inch off the original.

5. Remove your map. Study carefully the locations of the Adriatic, Sicily, the Po, the Tiber, the Apennines, and the city of Rome. When you are familiar with them, close the book. Using your regular pencil, label the Adriatic, Sicily, the Po, the Tiber, and the Apennines. Mark and label the city of Rome. Check your map against the original. Correct any misplaced labels.

Chapter Fifty-Eight: A Brief Empire

You MAY USE your text when answering the questions in sections I and II.

Section I: Who, What, Where

Write a one or two-sentence answer explaining the significance of each item listed below.

Alyattes
Apries
Carthage
Hanging Gardens
Ishtar Gate
Jehoiachin
Jehoiakim
Psammetichus II
Zedekiah

Section II: Comprehension

Write a two/three sentence answer to each of the following questions.

1. What caused Jehoiakim to drop his alliance to Necho II in order to become a vassal for Nebuchadnezzar II?

2. Describe the pet project Necho II worked on after drawing against Babylon twice, in 602 and 601.

3. Who did Necho II hire to help him train an Egyptian navy?

4. Following in the tradition of Mesopotamian kings, what did Nebuchadnezzar II build to establish his position as a great king?

5. What did Nebuchadnezzar II build in order to strengthen Babylon's walls? Against what threat was Nebuchadnezzar trying to protect the city?

6. What brought an end to the two-year Babylonian siege against Jerusalem, and to Zedekiah's reign?

7. What did Nebuchadnezzar II do to Jerusalem and its inhabitants in order to ensure the city would never again plot against Babylon?

8. What did Nebuchadnezzar II do to resolve the stalemate between the Lydians and the Medians? How was the peace between the two quarrelling nations sealed?

Section III: Critical Thinking

You may NOT use your text to answer this question.

If the epic "Hanging Gardens" of Babylon were symbolic of Nebuchadnezzar II's rule, then we could assume that he was a king who could wield great power, but who also valued peace and serenity. However, Nebuchadnezzar II's treatment of Zedekiah of Jerusalem, and stories of the king's madness, suggest that he was far more tyrannical that exemplified by the beautiful gardens. How did kingship change Nebuchadnezzar II? Write a passage that first describes Nebuchadnezzar II's transformation from man to animal, then use Nebuchadnezzar II's treatment of Zedekiah as an example of the king's turn, and finally explain what this transformation was meant to symbolize in terms of the way Nebuchadnezzar II ruled.

Section IV: Map Exercise: The World of the Babylonians

1. Using a black pencil, trace the rectangular outline of the frame for Map 58.1: The Medes and the Persians.

2. Using a black pencil, trace all seas, rivers, islands, lakes and mountains *very carefully.* You will only trace this map one time, so do a precise job. Do not trace any cities.

3. Remove your tracing paper from the original. Using a regular pencil with an eraser, and looking at Map 58.1, draw a light line to show the borders of the Babylonian Empire. Erase and correct as necessary. When you are satisfied, lay your map back over the original. Erase and redraw any lines which are more than 1/4 inch off the original.

4. Remove your map. Study carefully the locations of Arabia, the Persians, the Medes, Kush, Nubia, Phrygia, Lydia, and the Scythians. When you are familiar with them, close the book. Using your regular pencil, label all eight of these regions along with the Babylonian Empire. Check your map against the original. Correct any misplaced labels.

CHAPTER FIFTY-NINE: CYRUS THE GREAT

You MAY USE your text when answering the questions in sections I and II.

Section I: Who, What, Where

Write a one or two-sentence answer explaining the significance of each item listed below.

Astyages

Aryenis

Belshazzar

Cambyses

Croesus

Harpagus

Mandane

Nabonidus

Pasargadae

Section II: Comprehension

Write a two/three sentence answer to each of the following questions.

1. How did Astyages's wise men interpret the king's dream in which his daughter Mandane urinated so much that she not only filled his city, but even flooded the whole of Asia?

2. Why did Astyages choose Cambyses of Persia to be Mandane's husband?

3. What interpretation did Astyages's wise men give the king of his second dream concerning Mandane's child, where a vine grew out of his daughter and curled itself all around his territory?

4. Give a short chronicle of the men who wore the crown of Babylon between Nebuchadnezzar II and Nabonidus.

5. How was Cyrus II able to get both the Persians and most of the important Median officials on his side in an attack against Astyages, the high king of Media and Persia?

6. How did Cyrus II manage to lay siege to Sardis and take control of Lydia?

7. To which god was Nabonidus devoted? Why was Nabonidus's faith at odds with his kingship?

8. Why did Nabonidus choose to settle in Tema after he left Babylon?

9. How was Cyrus II able to take Babylon once Nabonidus and his people were barricaded inside?

10. Why was Nabonidus blamed for the fall of Babylon?

11. What was the political strategy behind Cyrus II's restoration of the temple of Yahweh at Jerusalem in Judah, and his returning of the valuables from the Temple of Solomon that were in the Babylonian treasury?

Section III: Critical Thinking

You MAY USE your text to answer this question.

In this chapter, we read that Xenophon, author of *The Education of Cyrus,* saw Cyrus II as a new kind of emperor, whose reasons for success were ultimately justice, benevolence and fairness. While there was some "newness" to Cyrus II's rule, it was not the "newness" to which Xenophon referred. Write a passage detailing both what was new about Cyrus II's rule and what about his rule seems to be pulled straight from China's ancient history.

Section IV: Map Exercise: The Persian Empire

1. Using a black pencil, trace the rectangular outline of the frame for Map 59.1: The Empire of Cyrus the Great.

2. Using a black pencil, trace all seas, rivers, islands, lakes and mountains *very carefully*. You will only trace this map one time, so do a precise job. Do not trace any cities.

3. Remove your tracing paper from the original. Using a regular pencil with an eraser, and looking at Map 59.1, draw a light line to show the borders of the empire of Cyrus the Great. Erase and correct as necessary. When you are satisfied, lay your map back over the original. Erase and redraw any lines which are more than 1/4 inch off the original.

4. Remove your map. Study carefully the locations of the Caspian Sea, the Black Sea, Thrace, the Tigris and Euphrates Rivers, the Persian Gulf, the Indus, the Nile, the Red Sea, and the cities of Memphis, Jerusalem, Babylon, Susa, and Athens. When you are familiar with them, close the book. Using your regular pencil, label the Caspian Sea, the Black Sea, Thrace, the Tigris and Euphrates Rivers, the Persian Gulf, the Indus, the Nile, and the Red Sea. Mark and label the cities of Memphis, Jerusalem, Babylon, Susa, and Athens. Check your map against the original. Correct any misplaced labels.

CHAPTER SIXTY: THE REPUBLIC OF ROME

You MAY USE your text when answering the questions in sections I and II.

Section I: Who, What, Where

Write a one or two-sentence answer explaining the significance of each item listed below.

Alalia
Celt/Gaul
Carthage
Hallstatt
Horatius
Janiculum
Lars Porsena
Massalia
Penteconter
Phocaea
Stonehenge
Tarquin the Younger/Tarquin the Proud

Section II: Comprehension

Write a two/three sentence answer to each of the following questions.

1. From where did the Celts originate? How are the Celts connected to the Hittites, Mycenaeans, and the Aryans?

2. What did the Hallstatt tribes include in the graves of their dead? What was the configuration of graves for dead Hallstatt chiefs and soldiers?

3. What was the Etruscan League, and why was it formed?

4. What prompted the Carthaginians to join the Etruscans in an alliance against the Phocaeans at Alalia?

5. What was the outcome of the sea battle at Alalia between the Etruscans, Carthaginians and the Phocaeans?

6. On what criteria did Servius Tullius base his division of the Roman people into different classes, and how did this division translate into defense of the city?

7. Describe the events that led up to the rebellion against the Roman monarchy.

8. Who took power in Rome after the collapse of the monarchy? How did the new system of government work? In your answer, make sure to define the term "consuls."

9. What did Tarquin the Proud's expulsion from Rome signify in terms of the relationship between the Etruscans and the Romans? How was this solidified by the treaty made with Lars Porsena?

10. Describe the details of Rome's treaty with Carthage.

11. Why did the Gauls move further and further into Etruscan land? To where did the Gaulish people spread?

12. How did internal strife cause the spread of the Celtic culture?

13. Who had the right to vote in Rome? For what reasons did the voting populace elect to have a dictator just eight years after the Republic began?

14. How did a Roman dictator come to power, and how long did his rule last? What powers were granted to the dictator? How did the presence of a dictator keep Rome's unruly population under control?

Section III: Critical Thinking

You MAY USE your text to answer this question.

Sometimes, ancient cultures can speak to us from the grave. For example, in the case of the Hallstatt civilization, archaeologists have learned much about these ancient peoples from the clues left behind in their graves. This is also true of the Celts. Write a paragraph first explaining what "Celt" means, and second, how the artifacts found in Celtic graves helps us to understand why the Celts were given this name by the Greeks and Romans. Finally, describe what we know about the Celtic takeover of the Hallstatt civilization, as evidenced by the stories their gravesites tell.

Section IV: Map Exercise: Italy and the Lands North and South

1. Using a black pencil, trace the rectangular outline of the frame for Map 60.1: The Empire of Cyrus the Great.

2. Using a black pencil, trace all coastlines, rivers, islands, and mountains *very carefully*. You will only trace this map one time, so do a precise job. Do not trace any cities.

3. Remove your tracing paper from the original. Study carefully the locations of the Rhine, the Danube, the Rhone, the Loire, the Tiber, the Po, the Alps, the Adriatic, Corsica, Sardinia and Sicily. When you are familiar with them, close the book. Using your regular pencil, label all eleven locations. Check your map against the original. Correct any misplaced labels.

4. Study carefully the location of the cities of Carthage, Rome, Mediolanium (Milan), Massalia (Marseilles), Verona, Hallstatt, and La Tene. When you are familiar with them, close the book. Using your regular pencil, mark and label all seven cities. (You may use either the Roman or modern names of Milan and Marseilles.) Check your map against the original. Correct any misplaced labels.

CHAPTER SIXTY-ONE: KINGDOMS AND REFORMERS

You MAY USE your text when answering the questions in sections I and II.

Section I: Who, What, Where

Write a one or two-sentence answer explaining the significance of each item listed below.

Bimbisara
Brahman
Gana-sangha
Jainism
Kshatriya
Mahajanapada
Nataputta Vardhamana/The Mahavira
Nirvana
Shudra
Siddhartha Gautama/Buddha
Vaishyas

Section II: Comprehension

Write a two/three sentence answer to each of the following questions.

1. List and define the roots of the word "mahajanapada."

2. Why did priests have so much power in sixth century BC India?

3. How could a man born into the vaishya class become a king? How could a common man become a priest?

4. With animal sacrifices out of favor in the growing urban populations of India, what services did priests perform in order to keep their central role in society?

5. What five principles did the Mahavira teach? In your answer, make sure to explain each principle.

6. What experiences caused Siddhartha Gautama to set out on a self-exposed exile?

7. Why did Bimbisara want to conquer Anga and make it part of Magadha?

Section III: Critical Thinking

You may NOT use your text to answer this question.

While it is common to associate the teachings of the Buddha with religion, it is less frequent that we think of Buddha as a political figure. Explain how the Buddha's religious beliefs were also a political position. In your answer, make sure to include the political ramifications of self-reliance.

CHAPTER SIXTY-TWO:
THE POWER OF DUTY AND THE ART OF WAR

You MAY USE your text when answering the questions in sections I and II.

Section I: Who, What, Where

Write a one or two-sentence answer explaining the significance of each item listed below.

King Ching
Duke of Chu/King of Chu
Prince Kai/King Ching II
Kong Fuzi/Confucius
Li ching
Lun yu
King Tao
Shi jin
Sun-Tzu
Ting

Section II: Comprehension

Write a two/three sentence answer to each of the following questions.

1. Name the Chinese states that were part of the Five Hegemonies. What four other states had major power at this time, and what were their locations in relation to the Five Hegemonies?

2. Who were the Jin fighting in the north? What was the result of this ongoing battle?

3. Describe the conquests of the southern state of Chu in the two and half centuries since the Zhou move.

4. What is the significance of the Duke of Chu calling himself "King of Chu?" How is this title connected to the Duke of Chu's retreat from Zhou?

5. Why did the Lu court first call on Confucius? What did Confucius do for the court after he was hired away from his record-keeping job?

6. While Confucius was not the inventor of the philosophy laid out in the Analects, how were his teachings innovative?

7. What happened to Confucius after he was forced to flee from Lu because the duke was driven out by a rival aristocratic family?

8. How did constant war against barbarians affect the Jin state, particularly by 505 BC?

9. Briefly describe the period of turmoil and war in China around 493/492 BC.

10. On what did Sun-Tzu believe war was based? Considering the warring Chinese states that surrounded Sun-Tzu, why did he think this way about war?

Section III: Critical Thinking

You may NOT use your text to answer this question.

The further away we move from the beginnings of ancient Chinese history, the looser the grasp of Zhou power on the Chinese states becomes. In this chapter, we read about the first visible crack in the Zhou's stronghold. Write a paragraph explaining why the King of Chu's demand to see the Nine Tripods was actually an assault on Zhou dominance. In your answer, make sure to first explain how the Duke of Chu came to be called the King of Chu, and the significance of this name change.

CHAPTER SIXTY-THREE: THE SPREADING PERSIAN EMPIRE

You MAY USE your text when answering the questions in sections I and II.

Section I: Who, What, Where

Write a one or two-sentence answer explaining the significance of each item listed below.

Ajatashatru
Amasis
Bardiya
Battus the Prosperous
Massagetae
Patizeithes
Psammetichus III
Smerdis
Tomyris
Wajet

Section II: Comprehension

Write a two/three sentence answer to each of the following questions.

1. In what kind of building was Cyrus laid to rest? How was he prepared for the afterlife? Who would watch over Cyrus's final resting place?

2. What was Cambyses II's first act as king? What was the motivation behind this act?

3. Why did the Egyptians rebel against Apries after the decimation of the Egyptian army by the Greeks in North Africa?

4. Who fought with Apries at Momemphis against the rebellious Egyptian army? What was the result of this battle?

5. What was the advantage of creating a Persian navy from the resources of the Ionians and Phoenicians?

6. Why did Cambyses II want to dismember the body of Amasis?

7. Describe Darius's professional Persian army. What did the foot soldiers in Darius's army call themselves?

8. Define satrapy and satrap. What was the risk of being a satrap?

9. How did Bimbisara's death cause a Kosal rebellion against Magadha?

10. What caused the twelve-year war between Ajatashatru and his brother, vice-regent of Anga? How was Ajatashatru able to take Kosal at the same time that he was fighting against his brother?

11. How did Ajatashatru handle the Buddha's death? What did he make sure to do in order to secure the Buddha's legacy?

12. What precious materials did Persia gain from Darius's expeditions and conquests in India?

13. What is the significance of the Babylonian inscription about a woman from India who kept an inn in the city of Kish?

Section III: Critical Thinking

You MAY USE your text to answer this question.

In this chapter, we found out that the successful and skilled warrior Cambyses II, king of expanding Persia, died suddenly, supposedly from a self-inflicted sword wound that turned gangrenous. Cambyses II's death and the events that followed were surrounded by mystery. Write a brief description of how Cambyses II came to fatally wound himself, followed by an explanation of what you think really happened to his brother, Bardiya. In your answer, argue for only one scenario related to Bardiya's disappearance.

Section IV: Map Exercise: The Spread of the Persian Empire

1. Using a black pencil, trace the rectangular outline of the frame for Map 63.1: Persia and Central Asia.

2. Using a black pencil, trace all seas, labelled rivers and mountains. You do not need to trace small lakes or unlabelled rivers, with the exception of the Dead Sea and Sea of Galilee on either end of the Jordan. Repeat until the contours are familiar.

3. Trace the rectangular outline of the frame in black. Remove your tracing paper from the original. Using a regular pencil with an eraser, draw all seas, labelled rivers and mountains, as well as the Dead Sea, Sea of Galilee, and Jordan River, while looking at Map 63.1. Erase and redraw as necessary.

4. When you are pleased with your map, lay it over the original. Erase and redraw any lines which are more than 1/4 inch off the original.

5. Remove your map from the original. Study carefully the locations of the Red Sea, Black Sea, Caspian Sea, Aral Sea, Persian Gulf, Tigris, Euphrates, Oxus, Indus, and Thar Desert. When you are familiar with them, close the book. Using your regular pencil, label all ten locations. Check your map against the original. Correct any misplaced labels.

Chapter Sixty-Four: The Persian Wars

You MAY USE your text when answering the questions in sections I and II.

Section I: Who, What, Where

Write a one or two-sentence answer explaining the significance of each item listed below.

Aeschylus
Amyntas I
Argead
Battle of Marathon
Battle of Thermopylae
Cleomenes
Helot
Hoplite
Hoplon
Leonidas
Mandrocles
Marathonomachoi
Mardonius
Megabazus
Miltiades
Pausanias
Peisistratus
Pheidippides
Royal Road
Skudra
Themistocles

Section II: Comprehension

Write a two/three sentence answer to each of the following questions.

1. Why was it hard to pinpoint a homeland for the ancient Scythians? Where was the Scythian homeland in 516 BC?

2. How did the Scythians avoid war with the invading Persians around 516 BC?

3. Who were the Illyrians and the Paeonians, and what made them give up attacking Macedonian borders?

4. How was the Athenian government organized under Solon's reforms? How could a man with no land eventually gain the right to vote?

5. List the three groups that squabbled over Solon's reforms, and the political beliefs of each group.

6. What were the circumstances of Hipparchus's death? How did Hippias react to his brother's death?

7. Why did Cleomenes help Athenians get rid of Hippias?

8. What motivated Athens to attempt an alliance with the Persians? What was the outcome of this negotiation?

9. Describe the Athenian custom of ostracism. How did ostracism help prevent tyranny?

10. How did Aristagorus manage to start war between the Greeks and the Persians?

11. What was Aristagorus's first coup against Darius in the Persian Wars? What was the "conflagration of Sardis?"

12. For what reason did Sparta refuse to help Athens fight the Persians at Marathon?

13. What was the purpose of the Hellenic League? Who was in the League?

14. How were the Greek forces able to defeat the Persians once they sailed into the narrows around Salamis?

15. What were the Persians relying on to defeat the Greeks at Mycale? Why did the Persians lose the battle?

16. In what way did the Persian Wars galvanize Greek culture?

Section III: Critical Thinking

You may NOT use your text to answer this question.

In this chapter, we read about battle after battle between Persia and Greece based on accounts culled from Greek histories. Where are the Persian accounts? Write a short explanation of why the Persian Wars register barely a blip in Persian history. In your answer, use the example of how the Persians treated the failed invasion of the Scythian homeland to explain how the Persians dealt with unfavorable histories.

Section IV: Map Exercise: The Coast of Asia Minor

1. Using a black pencil, trace the rectangular outline of the right-hand frame for Map 64.2: Greece at the Time of the Persian Wars. You will be working on the right-hand page *only*.

2. Using a black pencil, trace the coastline of Asia Minor (the "Ionian Coast"), including the inland sea to the north and the Black Sea. Also trace any islands which are large enough to be labelled (Karpathos, Rhodes, and Samos). Repeat until the contours are familiar.

3. Trace the rectangular outline of the frame in black. Remove your tracing paper from the original. Using a regular pencil with an eraser, draw the coast of Asia Minor, the inland sea to the north, the Black Sea, Samos, Rhodes, and Karpathos. Erase and redraw as necessary.

4. When you are pleased with your map, lay it over the original. Erase and redraw any lines which are more than 1/4 inch off the original.

5. Remove your map from the original. Study carefully the locations of Karpathos, Rhodes, Samos, the Hellespont, the Bosphorus Strait, the Black Sea, Thrace, and the cities of Byzantium, Troy, Sardis and Ephesus. When you are familiar with them, close the book. Using your regular pencil, label Karpathos, Rhodes, Samos, the Hellespont, the Bosphorus Strait, the Black Sea, and Thrace. Mark and label the cities of Byzantium, Troy, Sardis and Ephesus. Check your map against the original. Correct any misplaced labels.

Chapter Sixty-Five: The Peloponnesian Wars

You MAY USE your text when answering the questions in sections I and II.

Section I: Who, What, Where

Write a one or two-sentence answer explaining the significance of each item listed below.

Alcibiades
Chiliarch
Delian League
Inaros
Long Walls
Lysander
Nicias
Ochus/Darius II
Pericles
Plataea
The Thirty Years' Peace
Thurii
Tissaphernes
Xanthippus

Section II: Comprehension

Write a two/three sentence answer to each of the following questions.

1. Why did the Spartans agree to fight the Persians with the rest of the Hellenic League?

2. In what way did Athens get in the way of the Spartans claiming the overall lordship of Greece?

3. How did Themistocles ensure that Athens was rebuilt despite Spartan resistance?

4. What were the circumstances related to Pausanias's dismissal from command of Ionian Byzantium?

5. Why wouldn't Xanthippus give up control of Byzantium? How was this action the "death knell" for the old Hellenic League?

6. How did Themistocles's ostracism lead the Athenian to offer himself as an advisor to Xerxes?

7. Who killed Xerxes? Who killed Darius II? Who killed Artabanos? Who killed Hystaspes? Who ended up as king of Persia?

8. What caused the Delian League to turn into something like an Athenian empire?

9. What led the Athenians to propose a peace treaty with the Spartans in 446 BC?

10. How did fighting begin between Athens and Corinth in 433? What was the significance of the Battle at Sybota?

11. In what ways did the plague affect order and custom in Athens?

12. Describe the plan hatched by Alcibiades and Tissaphernes in which Sparta and Athens would destroy one another.

13. Who were the Thirty? How were the Athenians able to overthrow the Thirty?

Section III: Critical Thinking

You may NOT use your text to answer this question.

In this chapter, we are introduced to narratives related to Athenian patriotism. In Athens, citizens were not coerced to fight, but rather called on to defend their blooming culture. How was this rising sense of patriotism related to the harsh treatment of the great Athenian leader Thucydides? Write a brief description of Athenian culture just before the start of the Peloponnesian Wars, and Pericles's call for the ideological support of the war from the people of Athens. Then, write a sentence or two considering how Athenian pride might have led to Thucydides's exile.

Section IV: Map Exercise: The Cities of Greece

1. Using a black pencil, trace the rectangular outline of Map 65.1: Greece and the Peloponnesian Wars.

2. Using a black pencil, trace the coastline of the Greek peninsula. Also trace the islands which are large enough to be labelled (Corcyra, Aegina, and Euboea). Repeat until the contours are familiar.

3. Trace the rectangular outline of the frame in black. Remove your tracing paper from the original. Using a regular pencil with an eraser, draw the Greek peninsula along with the islands of Corcyra, Aegina, and Euboea while looking at Map 65.1. Erase and redraw as necessary.

4. When you are pleased with your map, lay it over the original. Erase and redraw any lines which are more than 1/4 inch off the original.

5. Remove your map from the original. Study carefully the locations of Corcyra, Aegina, Euboea, Macedonia, the Gulf of Corinth, the Isthmus of Corinth, and the cities of Sparta, Corinth, Athens, Marathon, Thebes, Delphi, and Thermopylae. When you are familiar with them, close the book. Using your regular pencil, label Corcyra, Aegina, Euboea, Macedonia, the Gulf of Corinth, and the Isthmus of Corinth. Mark and label the cities of Sparta, Corinth, Athens, Marathon, Thebes, Delphi, and Thermopylae. Check your map against the original. Correct any misplaced labels.

CHAPTER SIXTY-SIX: THE FIRST SACK OF ROME

You MAY USE your text when answering the questions in sections I and II.

Section I: Who, What, Where

Write a one or two-sentence answer explaining the significance of each item listed below.

Citizens
Decemvirs
Helots
Patricians
Plebians
Tribune
The Twelve Tables
Volscii

Section II: Comprehension

Write a two/three sentence answer to each of the following questions.

1. Why is it hard to define the Roman term "plebian?"

2. Though the plebians largely outnumbered the patricians, why did the patricians have so much power?

3. Under what circumstance might a plebian and his dependents become slaves? How did this increase the power of the patrician class?

4. What caused the 495 BC debt slave uprising in Rome?

5. Explain the terms of the hasty resolution made by the Roman Senate regarding debt slaves while the Volscii tribes advanced on Rome, and why the resolution was made.

6. Describe the world's first recorded strike, the Plebian Secession.

7. How did the Senate respond to the Plebian Secession?

8. When thousands of Celts showed up at Clusium's city gates waving weapons, why couldn't Rome send aid to its northern neighbor?

9. Why did the Gaulish army hold back when it first met the Roman defense at the Tiber?

10. How did the Massalians end the wretched standstill between Rome and the Celts who had invaded Rome?

11. In what way did the first sack of Rome leave a permanent mark on the city?

Section III: Critical Thinking

You may NOT use your text to answer this question.

In the 5th century BC, Rome was a city divided between patricians and plebians. Sanctions made on the behalf of the plebians after the debt slave uprising and the Plebian Secession were not enough to mend the ill feelings of the second class. In what way did the Twelve Tables attempt to combine the people with great power, and those with no power, into a harmonious whole? While the Twelve Tables gave more protection to the rights of the plebs, how did the newly written law continue to reinforce the differences between the high and low peoples of Rome?

CHAPTER SIXTY-SEVEN: THE RISE OF THE CH'IN

You MAY USE your text when answering the questions in sections I and II.

Section I: Who, What, Where

Write a one or two-sentence answer explaining the significance of each item listed below.

343 BC
403 BC
Chuang Tzu
Duke Hsiao
Huiwen
Mencius/Meng-tzu
Shang Yang

Section II: Comprehension

Write a two/three sentence answer to each of the following questions.

1. What happened in the twenty-fourth year of King Wei-lieh that caused the final destruction of the Jin?

2. Which state benefitted the most from the end of the Jin state, and why?

3. What were the strengths of each of the following states by 361 BC: Qi, Wei and Ch'in? Despite its size, why was Ch'in looked down upon by the Qi and Wei?

4. Where was Shang Yang from, and how did he end up in the Ch'in court?

5. How did Shang Yang feel about merchants? What happened to those who occupied themselves with trade under Shang Yang's reforms?

6. Why did the residents of Ch'in have to get official permission to move to a new home?

7. Why did Sima Qian call Ch'in, under the rule of Duke Hsiao and Shang Yang, a terrible place to live?

8. What were the circumstances of Shang Yang's death?

9. Why was Huiwen's proclamation of his kingly title anti-climactic?

10. For what reason was Mencius most likely turned down when he offered himself as an advisor to the dukes of several states?

11. What is the philosophy of the Tao-Teh-Ching? How was the Tao-Teh-Ching a practical philosophy to adopt during the Warring States period?

Section III: Critical Thinking

You MAY USE your text to answer this question.

Shang Yang was not a well-liked guy; his brutal death speaks to his unpopularity. Yet, he transformed the backwater and semibarbaric state of Ch'in into the home of the Hegemon. How was Shang Yang able to bring order to the previously lawless state of Ch'in? Write a paragraph describing Shang Yang's reforms: the network of squares, efficient agriculture, officially sanctioned land and meritocracy. Then, write a paragraph explaining how these reforms worked together to turn Ch'in into the most powerful of the Warring States.

CHAPTER SIXTY-EIGHT: THE MACEDONIAN CONQUERORS

You MAY USE your text when answering the questions in sections I and II.

Section I: Who, What, Where

Write a one or two-sentence answer explaining the significance of each item listed below.

Achoris
Alexander
Artaxerxes II
Artaxerxes III/Ochus
Attalus
Bagoas
Bucephalas
Corinthian League
Cyrus
Isocrates
Philip II

Section II: Comprehension

Write a two/three sentence answer to each of the following questions.

1. Describe the state of Athens and Sparta just before 400 BC.

2. Why was the March of the Ten Thousand an extraordinary feat?

3. How did Artaxerxes II lose his grip on Egypt?

4. What was the cause of the Corinthian War, and how was it resolved?

5. Why did Artaxerxes II need to declare a cease-fire between Sparta and Athens? What was the name of this peace treaty?

6. How did Nectanebo, founder of the Thirtieth Dynasty of Egypt, fight off the Persians and Athenians led by Artaxerxes II?

7. Why did Artaxerxes II have his oldest son, Darius, killed? Who succeeded Artaxerxes II as king of Persia?

8. Why did Alexander II of Macedonia send his ten-year-old brother, Philip, to live in Illyria?

9. How did Philip end up as a hostage in Thebes? How was Perdikkas able to rescue his younger brother?

10. Why did Isocrates write the speech, *To Philip*? What was the result of this speech?

11. What two things made the Battle of Chaeronea remarkable?

12. To what did Attalus toast at the wedding of his niece to Philip? Why was this toast so offensive to Alexander?

13. Who killed Philip, and why? What were the circumstance that led to Philip's murder?

Section III: Critical Thinking

You MAY USE your text to answer this question.

Often, disparate groups come together when faced with a common enemy. In the case of Phillip II and the Greeks, he forced the sparring nations to come together as one. Write a paragraph describing Philip II's Greek conquests. Then, write a second paragraph explaining how Philip II's strategy in subsuming the Greek nations under Macedonian rule was different from the strategies of other conquerors in the history of the ancient world.

Chapter Sixty-Nine: Rome Tightens Its Grasp

You MAY USE your text when answering the questions in sections I and II.

Section I: Who, What, Where

Write a one or two-sentence answer explaining the significance of each item listed below.

Agathocles
Appian Way
Latin League
Samnites

Section II: Comprehension

Write a two/three sentence answer to each of the following questions.

1. What decision was made in 367 BC that ended the plebian and patrician standoff in Rome?

2. Describe the terms of the Cassius treaty. In what way did the Cassius treaty legitimate Rome's power in the middle of the 4th century BC?

3. What were the terms of the renegotiated treaty between Carthage and Rome?

4. For what reason did Rome claim to go to war with the Samnites in 343? What was the real reason Rome decided to attack their neighbors?

5. Despite just having fought in the First Samnite War against the Romans, why did the Samnites fight on Rome's side in the Latin War?

6. What did Rome do to cut ties between the cities of the Latin League after victory in the Latin War?

7. What is the meaning of *civitas sine suffragio*? Who was given this label?

8. What caused the second Samnite War?

9. What archaeological evidence supports Diodorus's claim that Carthaginians sacrificed hundreds of children in order to assure victory over Syracuse?

10. How did Rome manage to reduce its opponents in the Third Samnite War from Etruscans, Umbrians, Samnites and Gauls to just Samnites and Gauls?

11. Why did the Roman cavalry scatter in terror when the Gauls charged at them during the battle in Sentinum? How did the battle at Sentinum end?

Section III: Critical Thinking

You MAY USE your text to answer this question.

Chapter Sixty-Nine begins with an account of Rome's refusal to join the Latin League, and ends with this phrase: "the Roman fist, closing over the countryside, was armored." Yet, as we read, Rome did not win every battle it started, and most of the time Rome had to sign a treaty in order to end a stalemate war. What, then, made Rome such a threat to its neighbors? Write a paragraph explaining how Rome could cause so much turmoil without the clout of numerous conquests and successes on its side.

Section IV: Map Exercise: Rome

1. Using a black pencil, trace the rectangular outline of Map 69.1: Roman Enemies and Allies.

2. Using a black pencil, trace the coastline of the Italian peninsula and the Adriatic as well as the coastlines of Sicily, Sardinia, Corsica, and the unlabelled coast of North Africa in the lower left corner of the map. Repeat until the contours are familiar.

3. Trace the rectangular outline of the frame in black. Remove your tracing paper from the original. Using a regular pencil with an eraser, draw Italy, the Adriatic, Sicily, Sardinia, Corsica, and the North African coast while looking at Map 69.1. Erase and redraw as necessary.

4. When you are pleased with your map, lay it over the original. Erase and redraw any lines which are more than 1/4 inch off the original.

5. Remove your map from the original. While looking at Map 69.1, draw in the Po, the Tiber, and the Appenines with your regular pencil. When you are pleased with your work, lay your map over the original. Erase and redraw any lines which are more than 1/4 inch off the original. Then label both rivers and the mountain range.

6. Study carefully the locations of Sardinia, Corsica, Gaul, Sicily, the Adriatic, and the cities of Syracuse, Capua, Rome, Carthage, and Tarentum. When you are familiar with them, close the book. Using your regular pencil, label Sardinia, Corsica, Gaul, Sicily, and the Adriatic. Mark and label the cities of Syracuse, Capua, Rome, Carthage, and Tarentum. Check your map against the original. Correct any misplaced labels.

CHAPTER SEVENTY:
ALEXANDER AND THE WARS OF THE SUCCESSORS

You MAY USE your text when answering the questions in sections I and II.

Section I: Who, What, Where

Write a one or two-sentence answer explaining the significance of each item listed below.

Arthashastra
Chandragupta
Cleitus the Black
Drypetis
Hephaestion
Kautilya
Kodomannos/Darius III
Mahapadma Nanda
Parmenio
Philip Arrhidaeus
Roxane
Stateira
King Taxiles
Wars of the Diadochi/Wars of the Successors

Section II: Comprehension

Write a two/three sentence answer to each of the following questions.

1. Why was Athens so quick to surrender to Alexander after their secession from the Corinthian League?

2. Where was Alexander when he charged his men to attack Persia? How did this influence the performance of Alexander's army?

3. Why, despite having a massive force behind him, was Darius III defeated at Babylon?

4. How did Darius III's actions after Alexander's success in Syria reinforce Bagoas's characterization of the puppet-king as mild-mannered?

5. Why did Alexander encourage his men to sack Persepolis? What command did Alexander give his men?

6. What stopped Alexander from killing the constantly-fleeing Darius III?

7. Why did Alexander's men turn against him after he was called "Great King?"

8. Why did the Macedonians turn around and head home after their victory against Porus, king of Hydaspes?

9. What happened to Alexander during his trek home from India?

10. Describe the two strategies Alexander employed to bring together the Macedonians and Persians, and their outcomes.

11. Who were the men that wanted a piece of Alexander's conquests after the king died?

12. What were the terms of the "Partition of Babylon?"

13. What became of Pyrrhus after he was driven out of Macedonia by Lysimachus?

Section III: Critical Thinking

You MAY USE your text to answer this question.

There is no question that Alexander was a great warrior and strategist. His headstrong nature, however, meant that Alexander would not stop until he had what he wanted, be it a horse, or a kingdom. Alexander's forceful ways may have created a larger-than-life empire, but that also meant the ties that bound the conquered territories together were weak. The "Partition of Babylon," created to keep all the parts of Alexander's kingdoms safe, was actually the quickest way to ensure the break-up of the empire. Write a brief summary of the seven scenes of the Wars of the Diadochi, showing each phase of the destruction of Alexander's kingdom.

Section IV: Map Exercise: The Empire of Alexander the Great

1. Using a black pencil, trace the rectangular outline of the frame for Map 70.1: Alexander's Empire.

2. Using a black pencil, trace all coastlines, rivers, islands, and mountains *very carefully.* You will only trace this map one time, so do a precise job. Do not trace any cities.

3. Remove your tracing paper from the original. Study carefully the locations of the Red Sea, the Nile, the Mediterranean Sea, the Bosphorus Strait, the Black Sea, the Tigris and Euphrates, the Persian Gulf, the Caspian Sea, the Aral Sea, the Oxus, the Indus, the Khyber Pass, the Makran Desert, and Arabia. When you are familiar with them, close the book. Using your regular pencil, label all fifteen locations. Check your map against the original. Correct any misplaced labels.

4. Study carefully the location of the cities of Alexandria, Tyre, Athens, Babylon, Susa, and Ecbatana. When you are familiar with them, close the book. Using your regular pencil, mark and label all six cities. Check your map against the original. Correct any misplaced labels.

5. Using a regular pencil with an eraser, and looking at Map 70.1, draw a light line to show the borders of the empire of Alexander the Great. Erase and correct as necessary. When you are satisfied, lay your map back over the original. Erase and redraw any lines which are more than 1/4 inch off the original.

CHAPTER SEVENTY-ONE: THE MAURYAN EPIPHANY

You MAY USE your text when answering the questions in sections I and II.

Section I: Who, What, Where

Write a one or two-sentence answer explaining the significance of each item listed below.

Aparigraha
Bindusara
Devi

Section II: Comprehension

Write a two/three sentence answer to each of the following questions.

1. What were the locations and names of the kingdoms of India during Bindusara's reign?

2. How might we explain the difference between the language spoken in the north and south of India?

3. Where did King Asoka carve inscriptions about his life? What names were given to the places where the inscriptions were carved?

4. What major events defined King Asoka's early life?

5. Describe King Asoka's 206 BC campaign against Kalinga.

6. What is dhamma?

7. What was Asoka's most lasting achievement?

Section III: Critical Thinking

You may NOT use your text to answer this question.

King Asoka attempted to build his empire the traditional ancient world way by conquering his enemies. Seeing the destruction caused by his military campaigns, Asoka shifted his perspective and tried to build his empire by other means. Write a paragraph explaining King Asoka's attempt to find a new unifying principle to build his empire. In your answer, explain whether or not this principle actually worked.

Section IV: Map Exercise: The Mauryan Empire

1. Using a black pencil, trace the rectangular outline of the frame for Map 71.1: Mauryan India.

2. Using a black pencil, trace the coastline of India, the northern mountain ranges, the Indus and the Ganga (including all branches), the Narmada River (unlabelled) and the mountains around the Narmada, the Oxus, and the island to the south (modern Ceylon). Repeat until the contours are familiar.

3. Trace the rectangular outline of the frame in black. Remove your tracing paper from the original. Using a regular pencil with an eraser, draw the coastline of India, the four rivers with all branches, modern Ceylon, and all mountains while looking at Map 71.1. Erase and redraw as necessary.

4. When you are pleased with your map, lay it over the original. Erase and redraw any lines which are more than 1/4 inch off the original.

5. Remove your map from the original. Looking back at Map 71.1, study carefully the location of the Indus, the Ganga, the Deccan, the Bay of Bengal, the Arabian Sea, and the Oxus. When you are familiar with them, close the book. Using your regular pencil, label all six locations. Check your map against the original. If your labels are misplaced, erase and re-mark while looking at the original.

6. Using a regular pencil with an eraser, and looking at Map 71.1, draw a light line to show the borders of the Mauryan empire. Erase and correct as necessary. When you are satisfied, lay your map back over the original. Erase and redraw any lines which are more than 1/4 inch off the original.

CHAPTER SEVENTY-TWO:
FIRST EMPEROR, SECOND DYNASTY

You MAY USE your text when answering the questions in sections I and II.

Section I: Who, What, Where

Write a one or two-sentence answer explaining the significance of each item listed below.

221 BC
Cheng/Shi Huang-ti
Han Dynasty
Hu-hai/Second Emperor
Hsiang Yu
Liu Pang/Gao Zu
Tzu-Ying/Third Emperor
Yen Lo

Section II: Comprehension

Write a two/three sentence answer to each of the following questions.

1. How did Ch'in handle the rising ambitions of the Chao kingdom?

2. What happened to the Nine Tripods after the end of Zhou rule?

3. Why did Cheng start recording the age of boys in Ch'in in 231 BC?

4. What were the circumstances around the crown prince of Yen's death?

5. How did Shi Huang-ti break down old lines of family influence, inherited wealth, and clan loyalties of the former Chinese states?

6. What other reforms, outside of breaking up old alliances, did Shi Huang-ti put in place to create an efficient society?

7. Why did Shi Huang-ti have all the records in the Scribes' offices which were not Ch'in's, as well as any books that were not books of medicine, divination, or gardening, destroyed?

8. Why was Shi Huang-ti buried with almost seven thousand life-size pottery soldiers and horses?

9. What prompted the Second Emperor to slaughter scores of people across China? What was the result of these deaths?

10. Why did Liu Pang claim a right to punish Hsiang Yu after the slaughter of the Ch'in court and redistribution of Chinese territories?

11. What was the course of events that led to Liu Pang's reunification of China?

Section III: Critical Thinking

You may NOT use your text to answer this question.

The Great Wall of China is a famous landmark that many believe Shi Huang-ti built during his time as First Emperor. This is not the case, however. Write a paragraph or two explaining how the Great Wall really came into existence. Then, draw a parallel between the building materials used to link together the pieces of the wall, and Shi Huang-ti's unification of China.

Section IV: Map Exercise: The Ch'in Empire

1. Using a black pencil, trace the rectangular outline of the frame for Map 72.1: Ch'in China.

2. Using a black pencil, trace the coastline of China, the course of the Yellow River, the course of the Yangtze, and the Great Wall. Repeat until the contours are familiar.

3. Trace the rectangular outline of the frame in black. Remove your tracing paper from the original. Using a regular pencil with an eraser, draw the coastline of China, the Yellow River, the Yangtze, and the Great Wall while looking at Map 72.1. Erase and redraw as necessary.

4. When you are pleased with your map, lay it over the original. Erase and redraw any lines which are more than 1/4 inch off the original.

5. Remove your map from the original. Label the Yellow, the Yangtze, the Yellow Sea, and the Great Wall.

6. Using a regular pencil with an eraser, and looking at Map 72.1, draw a light line to show the borders of the Ch'in empire. Erase and correct as necessary. When you are satisfied, lay your map back over the original. Erase and redraw any lines which are more than 1/4 inch off the original.

CHAPTER SEVENTY-THREE: THE WARS OF THE SONS

You MAY USE your text when answering the questions in sections I and II.

Section I: Who, What, Where

Write a one or two-sentence answer explaining the significance of each item listed below.

> Aetolian League
> Agathocles
> Antiochus I/Antiochus the Savior
> Antiochus III
> Antigonus II
> Arsinoe
> First Macedonian War
> First Punic War
> Gadir
> Galatians
> Hamilcar Barca
> Hasdrubal
> Peace of Phoenice
> Ptolemy II
> Ptolemy IV
> Ptolemy Ceraunus
> Scipio/Scipio Africanus
> Seleucia

Section II: Comprehension

Write a two/three sentence answer to each of the following questions.

1. In what way was Lysimachus's marriage to Arsinoe insurance against an attack from Seleucus?

2. How did Ptolemy Ceraunus get Lysimachus to turn against his son, Agathocles? Then, how did Ptolemy Ceraunus get Seleucus to turn against Lysimachus?

3. How did Ptolemy Ceraunus get hold of the Macedonian-Thracian throne? How did he lose it just two years later?

4. For what reason did Roman soldiers attack the Carthaginian troops that were occupying the Sicilian city of Messina?

5. What was the second "first" of the First Punic War? How did the Romans learn to build ships?

6. In what way was the marriage between Antiochus II and Ptolemy III's daughter meant to solve the problems of Antiochus II's disintegrating empire? Did the marriage solve Antiochus's problems?

7. What happened to Ptolemy IV's sister, her brother Agathocles, his young son Ptolemy V and Egypt's reputation, after Ptolemy IV's death?

8. Why did Hamilcar Barca want to plant a Carthaginian colony in Iberia?

9. For what reason did the Romans sail to the Greek island of Corcyra? Why did some Romans remain on the island?

10. What was Hannibal's first act as Carthage's new chief general? How did this act start the Second Punic War?

11. Why happened to Roman forces during the battles fought against Hannibal and his army at the Trebbia river and Lake Trasimene? Why were these battles so damaging to Roman morale?

12. How did Hannibal defeat the Roman army of over one hundred thousand soldiers at Cannae?

13. What were the terms of the peace treaty made between Carthage and Rome at the end of the Second Punic War?

Section III: Critical Thinking

You MAY USE your text to answer this question.

The oath Hannibal made to his father as a young boy to never become a friend to the Romans motivated his entire military career. It also tied him more closely to the Romans than it did to his home country of Carthage. Explain how Hannibal's vendetta against Rome stopped him from making a strong connection to his own country, and how this may have influenced his defeat at Zama.

Section IV: Map Exercise: Punic Wars

1. Using a black pencil, trace the rectangular outline of the frame for Map 73.2: The World of the Punic Wars.

2. Using a black pencil, trace all coastlines, rivers, seas, islands, and mountains *very carefully*. You will only trace this map one time, so do a precise job. Do not trace any cities.

3. Remove your tracing paper from the original. Study carefully the locations of Iberia, North Africa, Sardinia, Corsica, the Rhone, the Loire, the Rhine, the Danube, the Mediterranean, Macedonia, Greece, the Adriatic, the Tiber, the Black Sea, Galatia, and Cyprus. When you are familiar with them, close the book. Using your regular pencil, label all sixteen locations. Check your map against the original. Correct any misplaced labels.

4. Study carefully the location of the cities of Gadir, Carthage, Rome, Syracuse, and Sparta. When you are familiar with them, close the book. Using your regular pencil, mark and label all five cities. Check your map against the original. Correct any misplaced labels.

CHAPTER SEVENTY-FOUR:
ROMAN LIBERATORS AND SELEUCID CONQUERORS

You MAY USE your text when answering the questions in sections I and II.

Section I: Who, What, Where

Write a one or two-sentence answer explaining the significance of each item listed below.

Antiochus Epiphanes (Antiochus IV)
Antiochus the Great (Antiochus III)
Artaxias I
Asiaticus (Scipio)
Brhadratha
Coele Syria
Demetrius I (of Bactria)
Demetrius I (of Seleucid Empire)
Eumenes
Jonathan
Judas
Maccabean War
Perseus
Pusyamitra Sunga
Third Macedonian War
Treaty of Apamea

Section II: Comprehension

Write a two/three sentence answer to each of the following questions.

1. What caused the Second Macedonian War?

2. Describe the conditions of, and reasoning behind, the peace made between Rome and Macedonia at the end of the Second Macedonian War.

3. What kind of relationship did Rome have with Greece after the Second Macedonian War? What did the skeptics say about this relationship? What did the people say who were in favor of Roman and Greek relations?

4. Why was Antiochus III more inclined to go to war with Rome after the Second Macedonian War, despite Rome's new alliance with the cities of the Achaean League?

5. What did the Roman consul say to the troops from Rome and the Aegean League to inspire them to fight hard at the Pass of Thermopylae against the Seleucids and Aetolian League?

6. Explain why both Philip V and Seleucus IV had to send their sons to Rome as hostages?

7. What evidence is there that Pusyamitra Sunga failed to reestablish Hindu orthodoxy in India during his reign?

8. Why did Antiochus Epiphanes back away from his invasion of Egypt? Why did the Romans want to stop Antiochus Epiphanes from gaining more territory?

9. What was Antiochus Epiphanes's plan for keeping the Jews in Jerusalem loyal? Why did his plan backfire?

10. How did Judas earn the nickname "Judas Maccabeus," or "Judas the Hammer?"

Section III: Critical Thinking

You may NOT use your text to answer this question.

Over the course of the text, we've read about countless conquerors who took drastic measures to dismantle the cultures of the peoples in their newly acquired lands, and the struggles of these conquered peoples to keep their own cultural identities. Conversely, we've read about conquerors who left the cultures of their new conquests alone. In this chapter, we read about a conquered city that *asked* its overlord to make official changes in its home culture so it could be more like its conqueror. Write a paragraph explaining why, in 180 BC, the city of Cumae in Campania, asked Rome for permission to change its official language from its old dialect of Oscan to Latin.

CHAPTER SEVENTY-FIVE: BETWEEN EAST AND WEST

You MAY USE your text when answering the questions in sections I and II.

Section I: Who, What, Where

Write a one or two-sentence answer explaining the significance of each item listed below.

Chanyu
Ctesiphon
Demetrius II/Nicator
Heliocles
Hui-ti
Kao-hou
Lucius Cornelius Sulla
Mao-tun
Menander I
Mithridates I
Mithridates II, the Great
Wendi
Wudi
Xiongnu
Yuezhi
Zhang Qian

Section II: Comprehension

Write a two/three sentence answer to each of the following questions.

1. Describe Gao-Zu's ruling style, and explain how, by using this ruling style, Gao-Zu was able to hold his empire together.

2. How were the so-called barbaric Xiongnu like the "Chinese proper?"

3. What happened to Kao-hou's family after her death? Why was the Han Dynasty able to survive this crisis?

4. What policies did Wudi enforce in China to create a more established empire?

5. How did Zhang Qian described the land of Shen-tu? What was this land, and who lived there?

6. What historical evidence suggests Menander I of India did not become a Buddhist pilgrim? Why, if he was not a Buddhist pilgrim, is Menander remembered fondly by the Buddhist sacred texts?

7. According to Zhang Qian, what was the Parthian kingdom like? How did Zhang Qian describe T'iao-chih, or the Mesopotamian valley?

Section III: Critical Thinking

You may NOT use your text to answer this question.

As we move closer to the medieval world, we see the kingdoms of the ancient world growing more confident in their own identities, and more curious about the outside world. There is no better example of this than the trade between Parthia and China. Write a paragraph explaining how the walls around these two kingdoms actually opened up each empire to cultural exchange.

Section IV: Map Exercise: The Han Empire

1. Using a black pencil, trace the rectangular outline of the frame for Map 75.1: Han China.

2. Using a black pencil, trace the coastlines of China and India, the three large islands, the Yellow, Yangtze, and Ganga (unlabelled), and the Great Wall. Repeat until the contours are familiar.

3. Trace the rectangular outline of the frame in black. Remove your tracing paper from the original. Using a regular pencil with an eraser, draw the coastlines of China and India, the three large islands, all three rivers, and the Great Wall while looking at Map 75.1. Erase and redraw as necessary.

4. When you are pleased with your map, lay it over the original. Erase and redraw any lines which are more than 1/4 inch off the original.

5. Remove your map from the original. Study the locations of the Yellow, the Yangtze, the Great Wall, Outer Mongolia, the Yellow Sea, the Great Wall, and the city of Chang'an. When you are familiar with them, close the book. Using your regular pencil, label the Yellow, the Yangtze, the Great Wall, Outer Mongolia, the Yellow Sea, and the Great Wall. Mark and label the city of Chang'an. Check your map against the original. Correct any misplaced labels.

6. Using a regular pencil with an eraser, and looking at Map 75.1, draw a light line to show the borders of the Han empire. Erase and correct as necessary. When you are satisfied, lay your map back over the original. Erase and redraw any lines which are more than 1/4 inch off the original.

CHAPTER SEVENTY-SIX: BREAKING THE SYSTEM

You MAY USE your text when answering the questions in sections I and II.

Section I: Who, What, Where

Write a one or two-sentence answer explaining the significance of each item listed below.

Gaius Gracchus
First Servile War
Marcus Cato
Masinissa
Mummius
Publius Rupilius
Third Punic War
Tiberius Sempronius Gracchus

Section II: Comprehension

Write a two/three sentence answer to each of the following questions.

1. Why did Rome continue to trade with Carthage, despite their uneasy relationship?

2. Why did Scipio Aemilius sail on Carthage in 149 BC?

3. What was the cause of the dispute between Sparta and the Achaean League around 148 BC?

4. What was the last city Rome took before it finally swallowed Greece? What were the circumstances of this fight?

5. Why does historian M.I. Finley describe Roman slavery as a "very odd institution indeed"?

6. Who led the Sicilian slave revolt? What was the cause of the uprising?

7. Where were the conditions for life in Rome for free hired men? Why were they so bad?

8. How did Tiberius Sempronius Gracchus react to the veto of his reform bill?

9. Why did Romans - both those who did not support Tiberius Sempronius Gracchus and those who did - begin to worry when his bill was passed and Tiberius put himself in charge?

10. What started the Roman riot in 132 that ended in the death of Tiberius Sempronius Gracchus and three hundred other Romans?

Section III: Critical Thinking

You may NOT use your text to answer this question.

As the Roman general Scipio Aemilius watched the city of Carthage burn to the ground, he said, "[I]t is a grand thing, but I know not how, I feel a terror and dread, lest someone should one day give the same order about my own native city." In this chapter, we begin to see the destruction of Rome, not from arson, but from the manipulation of power within the seat of government. Write a paragraph explaining how Tiberius Sempronius Gracchus, thinking he was doing good, actually made a choice in his political actions that dealt a death blow to the Republic.

Section IV: Map Exercise: The Roman World

1. Using a black pencil, trace the rectangular outline of the frame for Map 76.1: Slave Revolts.

2. Using a black pencil, trace all coastlines. Do not trace rivers, tiny islands, or mountains. Do include seas. Repeat until the contours are familiar.

3. Trace the rectangular outline of the frame in black. Remove your tracing paper from the original. Using a regular pencil with an eraser, draw all coastlines while looking at Map 76.1. Erase and redraw as necessary.

4. When you are pleased with your map, lay it over the original. Erase and redraw any lines which are more than 1/4 inch off the original.

5. Using a blue pencil, trace the Rhone, the Loire, the Rhine, the Danube and the Nile.

6. Remove your map from the original. Study the locations of the Rhone, Loire, Rhine, Danube, Nile, North Africa, Iberia, Adriatic, Macedonia, Black Sea, Mediterranean Sea, and Asia Minor. When you are familiar with them, close the book. Using your regular pencil, label all twelve locations. Check your map against the original. Correct any misplaced labels.

Chapter Seventy-Seven: The Problem of Prosperity

You MAY USE your text when answering the questions in sections I and II.

Section I: Who, What, Where

Write a one or two-sentence answer explaining the significance of each item listed below.

Lucius Cinna
Crassus
Erh-shih
Eupator Dionysius
Jugurtha
Pomerium Pompey
The Social War
Sulpicius

Section II: Comprehension

Write a two/three sentence answer to each of the following questions.

1. What were the first signs of anti-Roman sentiment shown by Roman allies that were not granted voting rights in Rome?

2. How did Lucius Cornelius Sulla prove his worth in the Social War, compared to Gaius Marius?

3. Why did Marius Gaius want so badly to lead troops against Eupator Dionysus of Pontus?

4. How did Sulla take back control of the Senate after Gaius Marius bribed his way into the generalship? How did Sulla justify breaking the constitution and invading the pomerium?

5. How was Li Kuang treated by Emperor Wudi upon his return from his failed attempt at conquest of Ferghana?

6. What did Emperor Wudi believe was at stake in the conquest of Ferghana? How did Wudi attempt to help the problem?

7. Why was Li Kuang's first campaign against Ferghana unsuccessful? What did Li Kuang do differently in his second campaign against Ferghana?

8. Why was the conquest of Ferghana so important for the Han?

9. How did Marius and Cinna manage to get themselves back into the Roman senate after they were both ousted?

10. Describe the scene as Sulla addressed the Senate once he was back inside Rome after Marius and Cinna's departure. How did the Romans feel about their new leader?

Section III: Critical Thinking

You MAY USE your text to answer this question.

In this chapter, we continue to discover holes in the fabric of the Republic of Rome. Write a paragraph recounting the Jugurthine War. Then, write a paragraph explaining how the war, and its aftermath, were both examples of corruption inside of Rome.

Section IV: Map Exercise: Trade Routes

1. Using a black pencil, trace the rectangular outline of the frame for Map 77.3: The Silk Road.

2. Using a black pencil, trace the coastlines of China and India, the large island to the south, the Yellow, Yangtze, and Ganga, and the Great Wall. Repeat until the contours are familiar.

3. Trace the rectangular outline of the frame in black. Remove your tracing paper from the original. Using a regular pencil with an eraser, draw the coastlines of China and India, the large island to the south, all three rivers, and the Great Wall while looking at Map 77.3. Erase and redraw as necessary.

4. When you are pleased with your map, lay it over the original. Erase and redraw any lines which are more than 1/4 inch off the original.

5. Remove your map from the original. Study the locations of the Yellow, the Yangtze, the Ganga, the Great Wall, Outer Mongolia, the Yellow Sea, the Great Wall, and the city of Chang'an. When you are familiar with them, close the book. Using your regular pencil, label the Yellow, the Yangtze, the Ganga, the Great Wall, Outer Mongolia, the Yellow Sea, and the Great Wall. Mark and label the city of Chang'an. Check your map against the original. Correct any misplaced labels.

6. Using a regular pencil with an eraser, and looking at Map 77.3, draw light lines to show the Silk Road. Erase and correct as necessary. When you are satisfied, lay your map back over the original. Erase and redraw any lines which are more than 1/4 inch off the original.

7. Label the ends of the Silk Road "To the Caspian Sea" and "Across Central Asia."

CHAPTER SEVENTY-EIGHT: NEW MEN

You MAY USE your text when answering the questions in sections I and II.

Section I: Who, What, Where

Write a one or two-sentence answer explaining the significance of each item listed below.

44 BC
Brutus of Britain
Carrhae
Cassivelaunus
Cicero
Cleopatra VII
Gladiator War/Third Servile War
Historia Regum Britannia
Hyrcanus II (John Hyrcanus)
The Ides of March
Lud
Mandubracius
Marcus Brutus
Mark Antony
Novus homo (new man)
Octavian Orodes
Pompeia
Ptolemy XIII
Ptolemy XV Caesarion
Spartacus
Transalpine Gaul
Trinovantes

Section II: Comprehension

Write a two/three sentence answer to each of the following questions.

1. Why was much of the Roman army off of the Italian peninsula after the death of Sulla in 78 BC?

2. Who were the gladiators, and where did they come from? How were gladiators treated by Roman society?

3. What is the practice of "decimation?" What were the circumstances of Crassus's use of decimation?

4. Why is Pompey given the credit for ending the Gladiator War, and not Crassus?

5. What made Pompey and Crassus popular consuls, even though they constantly quarreled and got nothing done?

6. What were the terms of the arrangement made by Julius Caesar, Crassus and Pompey upon Caesar's return from Hispania? What were the terms of the second stage of the arrangement, made in 56 BC?

7. What were the circumstances that led to the Senate's decision to bar Caesar from entering Rome unless he surrendered his army upon his return from Gaul?

8. Despite Pompey and the Senate's ban, how did Caesar come to power in Rome after he returned from his years in Gaul? What were the events that led up to Caesar's appointment as consul?

9. Why did the Egyptian plan to present a dead Pompey to Caesar backfire? At the same time, how did the presentation of Pompey's head benefit Caesar?

10. Describe Caesar's homecoming in 46 BC, after his years of travel in Egypt, along the African border and the Iberian peninsula.

11. Though the public was indignant to having a king, what concession did the Senate make regarding Caesar and his crown? How was this also Caesar's kiss of death?

Section III: Critical Thinking

You may NOT use your text to answer this question.

As we continue to read about Rome, we see the growing division between the ideals of the Republic and the actions of its rulers. However, did these rulers see the widening gathemselves? Explain why, when Caesar was murdered, he cried out in surprise, "But this is force!"

Section IV: Map Exercise: Britain

1. Using a black pencil, trace the rectangular outline of the frame for Map 78.2: Britain.

2. Using a black pencil, trace all coastlines. Do not trace rivers, tiny islands, or mountains. *Do* include seas. Repeat until the contours are familiar.

3. Trace the rectangular outline of the frame in black. Remove your tracing paper from the original. Using a regular pencil with an eraser, draw all coastlines while looking at Map 78.2. Erase and redraw as necessary.

4. When you are pleased with your map, lay it over the original. Erase and redraw any lines which are more than 1/4 inch off the original.

5. Using a blue pencil, trace the Thames.

6. Remove your map from the original. Study the locations of the Thames, Kent, and the Channel. When you are familiar with them, close the book. Using your regular pencil, label all three locations. Check your map against the original. Correct any misplaced labels.

CHAPTER SEVENTY-NINE: EMPIRE

You MAY USE your text when answering the questions in sections I and II.

Section I: Who, What, Where

Write a one or two-sentence answer explaining the significance of each item listed below.

30 BC
Herod
Julia
Marcus Aemilius Lepidus
Modena
Phraates IV
Phraates V
Praetorian Guard
Tiberius
Vonones I

Section II: Comprehension

Write a two/three sentence answer to each of the following questions.

1. How did Brutus and Cassius treat Caesar's memory after his death? Why did they act this way?

2. Why did the public riot when they saw the mutilation of Caesar's body?

3. How did Brutus gain public support from his exile at Antium? With all of this work to improve his image, why didn't Brutus return to Rome?

4. How did Octavian and Cicero drive Mark Antony out of Italy?

5. Why did Octavian, after the defeat of Mark Antony at Modena, cease to regard Cicero? Who did Octavian ally himself with after his desertion of Cicero?

6. Why did Mark Antony stay in the east after the campaign against Brutus and Cassius was complete? Why did Mark Antony leave Syria for Alexandria in 41 BC?

7. Explain how Lepidus was forced to give up his title of Triumvir, and how he ended up under life-long house arrest.

8. What excuse did Octavian use to declare war on Antony? How was Octavian able to turn the Senate against Mark Antony, too?

9. What were the details of the compromise made between Octavian and the Senate in 27 BC?

10. What were the possible reasons that, in 23 BC, Augustus/Octavian declined to be elected for a tenth time as consul?

11. What were the powers given to Octavian when he was made proconsul by the Senate?

12. How did both Parthia and Rome benefit from Phraates IV sending all four of his sons to Rome as hostages?

13. In what ways did the Senate surreptitiously rebel against Octavian and his false republic? How did Octavian deal with these rebellious acts?

14. How was Palestine divided after Herod the Great's death?

Section III: Critical Thinking

You may NOT use your text to answer this question.

Augustus is the first Roman leader we have read about that could admit to the farce of the Republic. However, Octavian went to extreme lengths in order to preserve the façade of a Rome run by its people. Write a paragraph explaining what the title "Augustus" meant to Octavian, and why it was important for Octavian not to think of himself as a "prince" but as First Citizen.

Section IV: Map Exercise: Augustan Rome

1. Using a black pencil, trace the rectangular outline of the frame for Map 79.2: Rome Under Augustus.

2. Using a black pencil, trace all coastlines, seas, and islands *very carefully.* You will only trace this map one time, so do a precise job. Do not trace any cities, mountains, or rivers.

3. Using a blue pencil, trace the Loire, Rhone, Rhine, Danube, Tiber, Nile, Euphrates and Tigris Rivers.

4. Remove your tracing paper from the original. Study carefully the locations of North Africa, the Mediterranean Sea, Egypt, the Nile, the Red Sea, the Persian Gulf, Persia, the Tigris and Euphrates, the Caspian Sea, the Black Sea, Thrace, Macedonia, Greece, Sicily, Gaul, Britain, the Loire, Rhone, Rhine, and Danube. When you are familiar with them, close the book. Using your regular pencil, label all twenty-one locations. Check your map against the original. Correct any misplaced labels.

5. Using a regular pencil with an eraser, and looking at Map 79.2, draw a light line to show the borders of Augustan Rome. Erase and correct as necessary. When you are satisfied, lay your map back over the original. Erase and redraw any lines which are more than 1/4 inch off the original.

CHAPTER EIGHTY: ECLIPSE AND RESTORATION

You MAY USE your text when answering the questions in sections I and II.

Section I: Who, What, Where

Write a one or two-sentence answer explaining the significance of each item listed below.

Cheng-chun
Chengdi
Liu Xiu/Guang Wudi
Mingdi
The Red Eyebrows
Ruzi
Sutta in Forty-two Sections
Wang Mang
Xin Dynasty

Section II: Comprehension

Write a two/three sentence answer to each of the following questions.

1. List the succession of Han emperors that followed Chengdi.

2. Who protested Wang Mang acting as regent for Ruzi? How did Wang Mang manage to stay regent despite the opposition?

3. How was Wang Mang able to convince the people of the capital city to turn against the Han?

4. How did Wang Mang introduce the "New" Xin Dynasty to the Chinese people?

5. Describe the sweeping and sudden changes Wang Mang made once he was emperor. How did the people react to these changes?

6. Why did Guang Wudi move the capital city from Chang'an to Loyang? What was this part of the Han empire called as a result of the move?

7. What changes did Guang Wudi make in order to stop the nepotism of previous Han rulers?

8. Why were the new counties of Guang Wudi's China filled with fewer people than the previous Han dynasty?

9. Why, and how, did Mingdi have to make peace with the north of China upon his enthronement?

Section III: Critical Thinking

You may NOT use your text to answer this question.

The Eastern Han brought many changes to China, including a new religion: Buddhism. Explain how Buddhism made its way into Chinese culture, both Mingdi's account and the more probable version. Then, explain how Buddhism reinforced the new Eastern Han power structure.

CHAPTER EIGHTY-ONE: THE PROBLEM OF SUCCESSION

You MAY USE your text when answering the questions in sections I and II.

Section I: Who, What, Where

Write a one or two-sentence answer explaining the significance of each item listed below.

Agrippina
Artabanus III
Boudiccea
Caligula
Caratacus
Claudius
Galba
Germanicus
Germany
Gondophernes
Jesus
Kujula Kadphises
Lucius Aelius Sejanus
Lucius Domitius/Nero
Otho
Pontius Pilate
Vespasian
Vitellius

Section II: Comprehension

Write a two/three sentence answer to each of the following questions.

1. Why did Tiberius leave Rome for Campania? What did Tiberius do once he settled in Capri?

2. Describe the special circumstances around Caligula's appointment as leader of Rome.

3. How did Caligula maintain loyal followers during his reign of terror?

4. How did Artabanus III keep tight control over Parthia?

5. What did it mean for a kingdom to be "Roman protected?"

6. What was the result of Parthia's Armenian attack?

7. Who were the Kushan people? Describe the coins used by the Kushan, and explain what the details of the coins tell us about the Kushan culture.

8. What did the Senate want to do with the office of princeps after Caligula's death? In what way was the Praetorian Guard responsible for Claudius's installment as princeps?

9. How did Nero begin his reign? Give an example of how the course of Nero's actions changed after he turned 20 years old.

10. Why did Nero give up Armenia to Parthia?

11. Where did the real power of princeps lie? How did the princeps ensure his power in this area, and in what way did this fundamentally differ from the way the Republic of Rome was meant to be ruled?

12. Once he was nominated as a rival for the power of princeps, why didn't Vespasian go immediately to Rome? What were the circumstances of the battle Vespasian had to clean up?

13. What happened in the fighting between the Roman troops that supported Vespasian and the troops that were loyal to Vitellius when they met at Cremona, and then in Rome?

14. What does *damnatio memoria* mean? Why were the names of the five princeps who ruled prior to Vespasian erased from the record?

Section III: Critical Thinking

You may NOT use your text to answer this question.

As the Roman empire spread, it subsumed provinces that contained people who were torn between the identities of their birth and their new identities as Romans. While the struggle between these two ends was difficult for some, Christians were able to be both Roman and Christian because of the very nature of Christianity. Write a paragraph that explains the dualism inherent in the origins of Christianity, and that describes why Christianity would endure through Rome's unstable times.

Section IV: Map Exercise: North of India

1. Using a black pencil, trace the rectangular outline of the frame for Map 81.2: Kushan.

2. Using a black pencil, trace the coastline of India, the northern mountain ranges, the Indus, the Ganga and Narmada rivers (unlabelled), the mountains around the Narmada, the Oxus, and the island to the south (modern Ceylon). Repeat until the contours are familiar.

3. Trace the rectangular outline of the frame in black. Remove your tracing paper from the original. Using a regular pencil with an eraser, draw the coastline of India, the four rivers with all branches, modern Ceylon, and all mountains while looking at Map 81.2. Erase and redraw as necessary.

4. When you are pleased with your map, lay it over the original. Erase and redraw any lines which are more than 1/4 inch off the original

5. Remove your map from the original. Looking back at Map 81.2, study carefully the location of the Indus, the Deccan, the Punjab, the Arabian Sea, the Khyber Pass, and the cities of Pataliputra and Kabul. When you are familiar with them, close the book. Using your regular pencil, label all the Indus, the Deccan, the Punjab, the Arabian Sea, and the Khyber Pass. Mark and label the cities of Pataliputra and Kabul. Check your map against the original. If your labels are misplaced, erase and re-mark while looking at the original.

6. Using a regular pencil with an eraser, and looking at Map 81.2, draw a light line to show the Silk Road. Erase and correct as necessary. When you are satisfied, lay your map back over the original. Erase and redraw any lines which are more than 1/4 inch off the original.

CHAPTER EIGHTY-TWO:
THE EDGES OF THE ROMAN WORLD

You MAY USE your text when answering the questions in sections I and II.

Section I: Who, What, Where

Write a one or two-sentence answer explaining the significance of each item listed below.

Domitian
Hadrian
Mount Vesuvius
Nerva
Pliny the Younger
Simon Bar Kochba
Titus
Trajan

Section II: Comprehension

Write a two/three sentence answer to each of the following questions.

1. When Vespasian finally arrived in Rome, how did he make sure the army would not destroy his power?

2. What events led to Syria's absorption of Palestine?

3. Though Domitian ruled with general disregard for Rome and the Senate, why was Domitian's severity not necessarily a bad thing? Give one example of how Domitian's harsh policies were actually good for Rome.

4. Why did Roman historians bestow praise upon Trajan?

5. Define the Roman philosophy of stoicism. How did Epictetus apply stoic principles to the problem of emperor?

6. What was different about the threat posed to Rome by Christians as opposed to the threat that was posed by the Jews?

7. In what way did Trajan choose to deal with the growing number of Christians in Rome?

8. How far did the Roman Empire reach under Trajan's rule? How did Trajan himself help the growth of the empire?

9. How did the Jews take advantage of Roman fighting in Parthia? What did Trajan do to stop the Jewish rebellions?

10. What caused the huge Jewish uprising, led by Simon Bar Kochba, against Rome? How did Hadrian put down the revolt?

11. What was the practical reason for Hadrian to build a wall across Roman Britain? What was the ideological reason behind the creation of the wall?

Section III: Critical Thinking

You may NOT use your text to answer this question.

As we've read about the growth of the kingdom of Rome, we've read about the continued struggle to keep up the façade that Rome was a republic of the people. For years imperators laid down their powers to the Senate in a play-act, and the names of rulers who had claimed the power of princeps but acted as tyrants were stricken from the record, their existence denied by the Senate. How is it, then, that with one simple phrase Domitian turned the Roman Republic into an empire? In your answer, define the meaning of the title *dominus et deus,* and explain how, with the adoption of this title, Domitian changed the very fabric of Roman government.

Section IV: Map Exercise: Roman Provinces

1. Using a black pencil, trace the rectangular outline of the frame for Map 82.1: The Roman Empire.

2. Using a black pencil, trace all coastlines, seas, and islands *very carefully.* You will only trace this map one time, so do a precise job. Do not trace any cities, mountains, or rivers.

3. Using a different color of pencil, trace the borders of the Roman empire and the dotted lines that separate the provinces from each other.

4. Remove your tracing paper from the original. Study carefully the locations of the following provinces: Mauretania, Numidia, Libya, Egypt, Arabia, Syria, Mesopotamia, Armenia, Cappadocia, Pamphylia, Lycia, Galatia, Bithynia/Pontus, Asia, Macedonia, Thrace, Moesia, Dalmatia, Pannonia, Noricum, Belgium, Gaul, Britain, and Hispania. When you are familiar with them, close the book. Using your regular pencil, label all twenty-four provinces. If you forget, label all provinces that you are sure of. Then, open the book and restudy. Close the book and attempt to mark the rest. When you are finished, check your map against the original. Correct any misplaced labels.

Chapter Eighty-Three: Children on the Throne

You MAY USE your text when answering the questions in sections I and II.

Section I: Who, What, Where

Write a one or two-sentence answer explaining the significance of each item listed below.

Andi

Chang Chueh

Empress Dowager Dou

Hedi

Huandi Liang Ji

Lingdi

Ten Regular Attendants

Yellow Turbans

Zhang Rang

Section II: Comprehension

Write a two/three sentence answer to each of the following questions.

1. Why did Hedi order the palace eunuchs to kill off his mother's relatives?

2. What role did the palace eunuchs serve, and why weren't they considered a threat to the royal family?

3. List the succession of rulers that followed Andi until AD 146 – make sure to list the age of each ruler at the time he came to power.

4. Who ran Han China during the succession of child-kings? Who made the decisions for Huandi when he was a child, and how did this affect Huandi's behavior?

5. What two important rulings were made in favor of the eunuchs that allowed eunuchs to create their own ruling clan?

6. What happened when Chen Fan, an advisor to the Empress Dowager Dou, suggested that all the palace eunuchs be wiped out?

7. Describe the disasters that hit China between the years of 172 and 179 AD.

8. What did Chang Chueh claim his magical powers could do for the people of China? Why did so many Chinese people believe in Chang Chueh?

Section III: Critical Thinking

You may NOT use your text to answer this question.

How did ambition drive the shape of China between 88 and 182 AD? Great leaders are often driven by ambition, but their success always comes at a price. In this chapter, we read about the ambitious and able men of China making a place for themselves in a Han Dynasty ruled by children and extended family. Write a paragraph describing how the men who governed China's provinces made a successful life for themselves while simultaneously creating a new kind of feudal system in Han China. Then, write a paragraph explaining how ambitious merchants were able to change their position in society from parasitic middlemen to traders that made a vast fortune at the cost of China's poor laboring class.

Chapter Eighty-Four:
The Mistake of Inherited Power

You MAY USE your text when answering the questions in sections I and II.

Section I: Who, What, Where

Write a one or two-sentence answer explaining the significance of each item listed below.

Antonius Pius
Caracalla
Commodus
Elagabalus
Geta
Jian Shi
Jiao (Jue), Bao and Liang
Macrinus
Marcus Aurelius
Meditations of Marcus Aurelius
Lucius Verus
Septimus Severus
Shaodi
Sima Guang
Tung Cho
Ts'ao Ts'ao
Vologases IV
Xiandi

Section II: Comprehension

Write a two/three sentence answer to each of the following questions.

1. Why did Roman emperors adopt heirs instead of leaving the throne to their actual sons?

2. Describe the plague that Roman troops brought back with them from Syria. Why did Marcus Aurelius outlaw the building of new tombs after the plague hit?

3. How did Marcus Aurelius stay popular with his people, even though he chose to spend most of his reign stationed along the Danube rather than in the capital city?

4. Why did the Roman system of adopted-heirs work so well? Why did Marcus Aurelius break the system?

5. How did the Romans justify the murder of Commodus?

6. How did Septimus Severus ensure the Praetorian Guard's loyalty?

7. What happened when the chief general of the Han army found out that Jian Shi was plotting to have him murdered?

8. Why, when Xiandi was finally returned to Loyang and placed on the throne by Ts'ao Ts'ao, was he considered powerless and unimportant?

9. Who made up the Three Kingdoms that replaced the Han Dynasty, and where were these new kingdoms located?

10. How did Caracalla manage to win back the loyalty Praetorian Guard after Geta's murder? What did he do to anyone whose loyalty he still questioned?

11. What was going on in Parthia in 212 that led Caracalla to believe he could reduce the Parthians to vassals? How did Caracalla's plan backfire?

Section III: Critical Thinking

You may NOT use your text to answer this question.

When Rome was a republic, citizenship was a privilege that gave a man the ability to vote. In 212 AD, Rome was no longer a republic. Since the vote no longer mattered, what advantages were there to being a Roman citizen? Write a paragraph explaining what a free man had to gain from Caracalla's declaration that all free men in his empire were now Roman citizens, and explain what the government had to gain by accepting all of these new citizens.

Section IV: Map Exercise: Three Kingdoms of China

1. Using a black pencil, trace the rectangular outline of the frame for Map 84.2: The Three Kingdoms.

2. Using a black pencil, trace the coastlines of China and India, the three large islands, the Yellow, Yangtze, and the (unlabelled) Ganga (you do not need to trace the Min), and the Great Wall. Repeat until the contours are familiar.

3. Trace the rectangular outline of the frame in black. Remove your tracing paper from the original. Using a regular pencil with an eraser, draw the coastlines of China and India, the three large islands, all three rivers, and the Great Wall while looking at Map 84.2. Erase and redraw as necessary.

4. When you are pleased with your map, lay it over the original. Erase and redraw any lines which are more than 1/4 inch off the original.

5. Remove your map from the original. Study the locations of the Yellow, the Yangtze, the Great Wall, Outer Mongolia, the Yellow Sea, the Great Wall, and the cities of Chang'an and Loyang. When you are familiar with them, close the book. Using your regular pencil, label the Yellow, the Yangtze, the Great Wall, Outer Mongolia, the Yellow Sea, and the Great Wall. Mark and label the cities of Chang'an and Loyang. Check your map against the original. Correct any misplaced labels.

6. Using a regular pencil with an eraser, and looking at Map 84.2, draw light lines to show the borders of the three kingdoms (the shaded area shows the outside border, the dotted lines are the borders between the kingdoms). Erase and correct as necessary. When you are satisfied, lay your map back over the original. Erase and redraw any lines which are more than 1/4 inch off the original.

7. Label the Wu, the Shu Han, and the Old Han kingdoms.

CHAPTER EIGHTY-FIVE: THE SAVIOR OF THE EMPIRE

You MAY USE your text when answering the questions in sections I and II.

Section I: Who, What, Where

Write a one or two-sentence answer explaining the significance of each item listed below.

Ardashir I
Aurelian
Constantine
Constantius
Daevas
Decius
Galerius
Gallienus
Goths
Maxentius
Maximian
Ostrogoths
Philip
Sassanian
Severus
Shah
Shapur
Valerian
Visigoths
Zoroastrianism

Section II: Comprehension

Write a two/three sentence answer to each of the following questions.

1. What happened when Ardashir met Artabanus V at the plain of Hormizdagan?

2. How do we know Ardashir I made Shapur co-ruler before his own death? Why would Ardashir crown his son before he died?

3. In what way did Zoroastrianism bring the new Persian empire together?

4. How did church historians from after Valerian's time characterize Valerian's capture by the Persians?

5. What happened to the Roman empire while Valerian was in Shapur I's captivity?

6. Why did Aurelian have a wall built around the city of Rome? What did the construction of the wall say about the nature of Rome's army?

7. Though Carus seems to have escaped the fate of the five other emperors who were murdered in the nine years following Aurelian's death, why might we believe his bodyguard Diocletian was involved in Carus's death? In what way does the death of Numerian, and Carus's other son, suggest that Diocletian was behind all three deaths?

8. What happened to Diocletian's system of managing the Roman empire's succession when Constantius died?

9. Why did Constantine engrave the first two Greek letters in the name of Christ, the chi and rho, onto his helmet and standard?

10. Why did Constantine believe Christianity would help to reunite the Roman empire?

Section III: Critical Thinking

You may NOT use your text to answer this question.

Histories of Rome written by church fathers depict Diocletian in a negative light because he persecuted Christians. They accuse him of almost ruining Rome because of his idea to divide up the rule of the empire. However, Diocletian's idea of breaking up Roman rule actually saved the empire. Explain how, under Diocletian, Rome went from recognizing one emperor to recognizing four men in power. Why did Diocletian think this division would save Rome? In your answer, explain what Diocletian hoped to achieve by abdicating his throne to his junior.

Section IV: Map Exercise: The Divided Empire

1. Using a black pencil, trace the rectangular outline of the frame for Map 85.3: The Roman Empire, Divided.

2. Using a black pencil, trace all coastlines, seas, and islands *very carefully*. You will only trace this map one time, so do a precise job. Do not trace any cities, mountains, or rivers.

3. Remove your tracing paper from the original. Using a regular pencil with an eraser, and looking at Map 85.3, draw light lines to show the borders of the undivided Roman Empire and the borders fo the Persian Empire. When you are satisfied, lay your map back over the original. Erase and redraw any lines which are more than 1/4 inch off the original.

4. Using a regular pencil with an eraser, and looking at Map 85.3, draw a line to divide the Eastern and Western Empires. Lay your map back over the original. Erase and redraw the line if it is more than 1/4 inch off the original.

5. Remove your tracing paper from the original. Study carefully the locations of the Western Empire, the Eastern Empire, the Persian Empire, Germany, and Syria. When you are familiar with them, close the book. Using your regular pencil, label all five locations. Check your map against the original. Correct any misplaced labels.